The Origins and Ancient History of Wine

Food and Nutrition in History and Anthropology
A series edited by Solomon H. Katz, University of Pennsylvania

The Origins and Ancient History of Wine

Edited by

Patrick E. McGovern

Stuart J. Fleming

and

Solomon H. Katz

*The University of Pennsylvania Museum
of Archaeology and Anthropology
Philadelphia*

Gordon and Breach Publishers

Australia • Canada • China • France • Germany • India • Japan
Luxembourg • Malaysia • The Netherlands • Russia • Singapore
Switzerland • Thailand • United Kingdom

Amsteldijk 166
1st Floor
1079 LH Amsterdam
The Netherlands

Cover photo: Godin Tepe jar (Godin Tepe Project, no. Gd. 73-113, Royal Ontario Museum, West Asian Dept.), from room 20. Deep sounding, Late Period V. (Photograph by W. Pratt, courtesy of the Royal Ontario Museum, Toronto, Canada.)

British Library Cataloguing in Publication Data

Origins and Ancient History of Wine.–
(Food & Nutrition in History &
Anthropology Series, ISSN 0275-5769;
Vol. 11)
 I. McGovern, Patrick E. II. Series
 641.2209

ISBN 90-5699-522-9

Contents

Series Editor's Preface

The study of the origin, development and diversity of the human diet is emerging as a coherent field that offers a much-needed integrative framework for our contemporary knowledge of the ecology of food and nutrition. This authoritative series of monographs and symposia volumes on the history and anthropology of food and nutrition is designed to address this need by providing integrative approaches to the study of various problems within the human food chain. Since the series is both methodologically and conceptually integrative, the focus of the individual volumes spans such topics as nutrition and health, culinary practices, prehistoric analyses of diet, and food scarcity and subsistence practices among various societies of the world. As a series, it offers many unique opportunities for a wide range of scientists, scholars and other professionals representing anthropology, archaeology, food history, economics, agriculture, folklore, nutrition, medicine, pharmacology, public health and public policy to exchange important new knowledge, discoveries and methods involved in the study of all aspects of human foodways.

Solomon H. Katz

Introduction

Patrick E. McGovern

The Making of a Unique Conference,
Its Accomplishments,
and an Agenda for the Future

The international symposium on "The Origins and Ancient History of Wine" was held at the Robert Mondavi Winery during the week of April 30 through May 3, 1991. The Napa Valley of California was the ideal setting for such a meeting. Although Old World vines and wines were the focus of our discussions, Napa Valley wines vie with the best that the Old World has to offer, and Robert Mondavi has recently joined forces with Baron Philippe de Rothschild of Médoc to produce a first-class Cabernet Sauvignon wine, Opus One. At the time of the conference, this grape variety and others such as Pinot Noir, Chardonnay, and Merlot, all of European descent (*Vitis vinifera*), were setting their fruits on the Napa vines. Our deliberations, in the spirit of a Greek *symposion*, liberally interspersed conversation with fine wines and cuisine.

The circumstance that led to this unique symposium was the discovery in the summer of 1990 of the earliest wine vessel as yet attested by chemical analysis. The ancient pottery jars from Godin Tepe, Iran, which are discussed in detail and illustrated in chapters 4 and 5, date between ca. 3500 and 2900 B.C. Here was a finding that pushed back 3000 years the earliest chemical evidence for wine, from the Roman period (see chapter 7) to before the Bronze Age, and that showed that wine was already an important commodity before the rise of the great civilizations of Mesopotamia and Egypt. Once the deposits in this jar were identified as "well-aged" wine lees, the cultural and biocultural "fallout"—the implications of the findings—have been enormous. Wine, as a valuable trade commodity and as an important beverage in everyday life and the cultic ceremonies, evidently played a role in the earliest development of literate complex societies—civilized life as we know it—in the ancient Near East.

The Godin jars were excavated at a site high up in the Zagros Mountains of western Iran by a team of archaeologists under the direction of Dr. T. Cuyler Young Jr. of the Royal Ontario Museum in Toronto, Canada, in the late 1960s and early 1970s. The vessels came from what is believed to be a proto-Sumerian colony, which serviced traders, administrators, and the military from lowland Mesopotamia. These groups were involved in procuring valuable raw materials, including lapis lazuli and other semi-precious stones, metals such as copper, silver and gold, and even such mundane goods as wood, which were unavailable in the Tigris–Euphrates valley. One of the goods that might have led to their establishing an outpost in the Zagros Mountains could have been wine, since grapevines are grown with difficulty in the lowlands but flourish in upland regions such as the Zagros Mountains.

The proto-Sumerians at this time, the so-called Late Uruk Period, were already well on their way toward developing a thriving urban economy (see chapter 8). The city-states in the Tigris–

Euphrates valley were based on the irrigation agriculture of cereals, dates, figs, and other plants. Barley cultivation was very intensive, which explains the fact that beer was the common beverage of the lowlanders. The first writing with pictographic signs appears in which characters represent the thing or idea that is conveyed.

If one were to go looking for a site that might yield early evidence for winemaking, Godin Tepe would be an excellent candidate. It is located along the Great Khorasan Road, which later becomes the famous Silk Road, going from China to the Mediterranean. Consequently, Godin was in touch with developments occurring elsewhere. Quite likely, the Eurasian wild grape—*Vitis sylvestris*—grew there in antiquity, or was brought there at an early date from the Transcaucasia, a short distance to the north where the wild vine grows today. A burgeoning population in the lowlands, with an appetite for exotic goods, would assure a ready market for wine produced in bulk. The large investment of time and energy in the growing of vines, which eventually led to the domestication of the grape, would have been amply rewarded. In this scenario, it is assumed that horticulture (including grapes, as well as dates, pomegranates, and figs) was already well established in Mesopotamia, and that Godin Tepe during the Uruk period was a society of sufficient complexity to engage in viticulture and viniculture. But one might also argue the reverse—that wine production and trade, which first developed as a household industry using wild grapes, actually spurred the development of more complex societies throughout Mesopotamia.

The Godin discovery raised many more questions than it answered. Were the wine jars, which are of a type that is not known elsewhere, imported from a region that has not been explored archaeologically or at least that has not been reported on in the literature? Or were the unique jars, in which wine apparently was stored in stoppered vessels laid on their sides (greatly anticipating our modern wine rack!), rather evidence of local wine production, which might have been shipped out in containers made of an organic material, such as leather or wood, long since disintegrated?

Much broader questions can be posed. Since cereal agriculture is known to have started as much as 5000 years earlier in the Near East, what is the archaeological and archaeobotanical evidence for grapes and wine preceding 3500 B.C.? Presumably, many centuries of experimentation in plant domestication and crossbreeding, winemaking itself, and in pottery technology (to produce relatively airtight, stoppered vessels of dense fabrics) would have been required to reach the level of expertise revealed at Godin Tepe at the "dawn of human civilization."

At an even more basic level, where, when, and why was wine first made? One might imagine a Palaeolithic caveman or woman spotting the colorful, sugar-rich wild grapes, and picking and eating them. Some grapes might have been accidentally squashed in a rock crevice or primitive container, where the exuded juice would begin to ferment naturally in several days' time. Someone happening along might dabble a finger in the concoction, lick it, and be pleasantly surprised by the result. More intentional squeezing of larger quantities of grapes would follow. The likelihood, however, of finding preserved organic residues to confirm this hypothesis is obviously very small.

The genetic "history" encoded in the genomic and mitochondrial DNA of modern wild and domesticated grapes, together with that of any available ancient samples, suggests another approach for delimiting the specific region(s) of the world and the approximate time period(s) when the wild grape was domesticated. Like the Eve hypothesis which claims to trace all of humanity to an original mother in East Africa on the basis of mitochondrial DNA lineage trees, the progenitor of modern domesticated grape varieties, which overwhelmingly belong to a single Eurasian species (*Vitis viniferis*), might be sought. A "Noah hypothesis"—so named for the biblical patriarch and "first vintner" who is said to have planted a vineyard on Mount Ararat after the flood, with dire consequences when he drank the fermented beverage (Genesis 9)—implies that the grape was domesticated in a single place at a single time. Multiple origins for the domesticated grape are perhaps more likely, given the relative ease of making wine from grape must and the wide geographic extent of the wild grape today.

A Noah hypothesis, however, may apply to a relatively late stage of human biological and cultural development. How much time passed before wine produced from wild grapes, presumably on a very limited scale, was displaced by that using domesticated varieties? Once domesticated, were grape seeds or vine cuttings (canes) transplanted by human or animal agents to other regions, including those where the wild vine did not grow? Where and when did winemaking become an important commercial endeavor? Why is wine, more so than other fermented beverages, so often regarded as a luxury good associated with high status? Why were wines not produced, at least to any documentable extent, in East Asia and North America, although more species of the wild grape grow in these regions than anywhere else in the world?

These are some of the questions that we asked ourselves prior to the conference. The Godin discovery was only the first step in a much larger investigation, and a conference to explore in depth the contemporary evidence for the origins and earliest history of wine was a logical place to begin.

The idea of such a conference had already been entertained several years earlier by Solomon Katz and Robert Mondavi and his sons and successors in the business, Michael and Tim. Robert Mondavi has had a long-standing interest and commitment to wine and its important role in civilization. The research of Sol Katz, a bioanthropologist, has focused on how human food preparation, especially fermentation, can enhance the nutritional content and preservation of foods (also see chapter 1). In addition to anti-microbial properties, fermented beverages also have profound mind-altering effects that led to their incorporation into social and religious rites and customs of peoples around the world from antiquity up to the present. Better nourished societies, which were less prone to sickness, would have had a selective advantage in human biological and cultural development, and both the benefits and drawbacks of fermented beverages, especially when used in excess, were passed along to succeeding generations.

The Godin discovery prompted renewed discussion between this writer and Sol about an international conference on the origins and ancient history of wine. When Robert Mondavi agreed to host the conference, it became a reality. Specialists in a wide range of fields—archaeology, archaeobotany, food science, genetics, history, linguistics, art, and enology—were called upon, since the story of viticulture and viniculture is not the province of a single discipline but intertwines itself with the rich fabric of human culture and environment. Besides laying out and debating the available evidence from different perspectives, an equally important goal of the conference was to set future research priorities.

Participants were encouraged to bring ancient artifacts, materials, and samples that related to ancient viticulture and winemaking, so that they could be examined firsthand by the participants. Methods of culling the most scientific data from them were discussed. Excavation and conservation strategies, as other crucial means of retrieving information about vineyards, winemaking installations, and the functions of wine in ancient society, were also assessed. By the end of the conference, everyone was sent off with the admonition to "re-excavate" wine-related artifacts and samples in their museums, storerooms, and laboratories.

A special public media day was set aside to present the artifacts and other objects which the conferees brought. The wine jar from Godin Tepe was the star of the show. Virginia Badler made a special trip to The Royal Ontario Museum in Toronto, Canada, to pick up the vessel and accompany it by plane to California and back again to Toronto. Her adventures are amusingly retold in "Travels with Jarley," in the *Archaeological Newsletter* of the museum (series II, no. 44,

May/July 1991). The wine jar was later displayed at the entrance to the museum. Other notable objects presented that day in May were Early Bronze Age sherds with grape leaf impressions from Greece (Jane Renfrew), the dregs of Roman amphorae found in the hull of a ship sunk off the coast of France (Françoise Formenti), a fermentation stop and fragments of an Egyptian wine amphora from New Kingdom Egypt (Leonard Lesko), and a Rhodian stamped amphora handle (Carolyn Koehler).

The chapters of this volume were not presented as oral papers as such at the conference. Rather, the essential points of a preliminary version of each paper were briefly summarized by its author. Then followed a lively discussion of debatable and unresolved issues, the interdisciplinary implications, essential data that had gone unmentioned, and of future research objectives. Such exchanges continued over meals and well into the night. The final written version of each chapter is the end result of a kind of ageing process, which has hopefully brought out the best and removed or at least disguised the worst elements.

Despite its multidisciplinary pretensions, this volume does not provide all the answers about the origins and ancient history of wine. As a case in point, no authority on Transcaucasia was able to attend the conference. Many modern interpreters of wine history suggest that Georgia has yielded the earliest evidence of winemaking in the world, based on the excavation of domesticated grape seeds, silver-encased vine cuttings, and Neolithic pottery vessels decorated with grape cluster appliqués. Unfortunately, it proved impossible to arrange the travel of a leading Russian archaeologist, who had agreed to discuss these and other findings at our conference; an exchange of letters between the United States and Russia took half a year, faxes were lost, and telephone calls rarely got through. The opportunity was thus lost to appraise critically the dating and interpretation of this Transcaucasian data and other unpublished finds. Several of the chapters do touch on Transcaucasia, again tentatively suggesting that the earliest grape domestication and winemaking might have occurred here, but we simply have no way of critically assessing the evidence.

A Noah hypothesis for the domesticated vine, if such should ever be developed, would certainly need to be bolstered by modern and ancient evidence from the Transcaucasus region, as well as other areas of the Near East (e.g., the Taurus mountains of southeastern Anatolia) that are poorly known viniculturally and viticulturally. Even with the gaps in our knowledge, the plant breeders, geneticists, and archaeobotanists at the conference were still able to take us on an exciting and plausible hypothetical journey from the sexually dioecious wild vine to the domesticated hermaphroditic, more fruitful varieties (see chapters 2, 3, and 16). The relationships of many modern hybrids and reversions of the domesticated vine back to the wild remain to be explained, and, regrettably, most of areas where the wild grape still grows in Eurasia today will probably have disappeared within a generation.

The analytical study of wine and winemaking in antiquity is also very much a nascent discipline (see chapters 5–7). Yet, the ease and precision of testing for a variety of organics, which might be present in only microgram amounts, is continually improving. Many hypotheses about ancient wine are based on archaeological data, which stand or fall on whether organic substances derived from grapes can be identified, and, if so, whether a grape juice had been intentionally fermented to wine. If wine had already established itself as a unique beverage with special dietary benefits and psychotropic effects much earlier, with its economic, social, and religious importance continuing to expand in later periods, then much more evidence of it must be available and potentially extractable from the archaeological record. As always, there will be the problem that organic materials will have deteriorated, so that if wine were processed, stored, and/or transported in leather skins or wooden containers, most of the evidence will have disappeared or be difficult to detect.

Pottery vessels (or containers made of other inorganic materials, e.g., glass, faience, and stone) provide an excellent resource for further study. For example, chapter 15 of this book highlights how wine was stored and transported in "Canaanite Jars" in the ancient Mediterranean world during the Bronze Age, and in wine amphoras of related types during later periods (chapter 20). Some of the Canaanite Jars that were made in various parts of New Kingdom Egypt have inscriptions on their sidewalls that record their contents (see chapter 14). These hieratic (cursive hieroglyphic) graffiti record not only that a vessel contained wine, but also where the vineyard was located, sometimes the vintner's name, the production date according to the year of the pharoah's reign, and often some mention of the kind or quality of wine ("very good," "sweet," "wine for a happy return," and so on). Here, we have essentially the ancient equivalent of a modern wine label. It is the archaeologist's and scientist's dream come true—an ancient vessel whose date of manufacture, place of origin, and contents are known.

Collections of such ostraca from the Palace of Amenhotep III (Malkata, Thebes), in The Metropolitan Museum of Art (New York) and The University of Pennsylvania Museum (Philadel-phia), are presently being analyzed by this writer and co-workers. Inscriptions are almost as explicit as the labels on a modern bottle of Bordeaux or Napa Valley wine, reading, for instance, "Very good wine, Year 30 of the reign of Amenophis III, from the Western River [i.e., the western Nile Delta]." Particularly promising sherds, said to come from several regions of Egypt—the western and eastern Nile Delta, the Kharga oasis in the western desert, and so on—with visible deposits on their interiors were chosen for analysis. Neutron activation analysis of the jars' pottery wares is also being carried out in conjunction with the residue analysis, to determine whether both the jars and wine come from the same regions of Egypt.

By tailoring our analytical techniques to specific questions, we hope to go beyond merely confirming that these vessels once contained wine. Although we may never know the particular grape varieties that went into producing these ancient Egyptian wines, it may be possible to distinguish between "sweet" and "dry" wines or reds and whites by analyzing for a range of constituents that are still relatively intact. Ancient yeasts or bacteria involved in fermentation might also be identified by standard microscopic or more modern molecular biological techniques. With persistence and ever-improving instrumentation, researchers one day may even be able to say whether the ancient winemaker had an appreciation for malo-lactic fermentation or preserved the finished product by sulfite treatment!

This chemical approach can be extended to other regions and periods, particularly those for which the archaeological, literary, and pictorial evidence is less definitive. Various physical criteria, for example, narrow mouths and high necks that can be stoppered, spouts, or rims and shapes that facilitate drinking, may suggest that a vessel was used for processing, storing, transporting, serving, or drinking a liquid. As crops up again and again throughout this book, such vessels should be targeted for analysis.

Winemaking installations, including presses, settling basins, and storage facilities, are another area of fruitful research, which might benefit from closer collaboration between archaeologists and other scientists. Relatively few such installations, however, have been excavated, most likely because they were located away from human settlements. Systematic surveying in areas where domesticated vines might once have been grown (on the basis of textual and pictorial evidence, tradition, the location of modern vineyards, and so on), followed by careful excavation and a program of analyses, might well elucidate the stages, tools, and techniques in the gathering and pressing of the grapes, and the processing of the wine.

Once an organic material from an ancient vessel or from a winemaking installation has been identified to be most likely wine, then the interdisciplinary task of appraising its biocultural significance begins. In prehistoric periods, the associated artifacts, ecofacts, skeletal material, and the archaeological context are our only guides, and they represent a very small, highly selective fraction of what was originally present. Interpretation is correspondingly precarious. Where contemporaneous written or pictorial evidence exists, as is well exemplified here by the discussions of Egyptian (chapters 13 and 14), Mesopotamian (chapters 8–10, and 12), Anatolian (chapter 11), Phoenician/Punic (chapter 19), and Greek (chapters 17, 18, and 20) wines and winemaking, we are on somewhat firmer ground. But again, texts and art have their own canons of analysis, and meaning is not always what it seems; writers, editors, and scribes sometimes over-exaggerate or omit details, and artists or copyists can create idealized or inaccurate pictures.

Simple economic records—receipts, orders for delivery, lists of goods—are least likely to be tendentious. They reveal in unadulterated prose that wines were being produced on a relatively large scale throughout the ancient Near East by the mid-2nd millennium B.C. Wines were transported in pottery jars by ship, as well as overland by donkey. Wine played a central role in the religious, ceremonial, social, and economic life of many different societies of this period, despite differences of language, customs, and sociopolitical organization. For Egypt, this situation can be extended back as far as the late 4th millennium B.C., when hieroglyphic writing begins. If similarly early materials were available from Greece, Anatolia, and Upper Mesopotamia, wine would probably already be seen to be well-established there.

In the light of the enological, archaeobotanical, and scientific findings reported on in this volume, a much more intensive reexamination of the available archaeological, textual, and artistic data in historic periods is called for. For example, much more can probably be learned about how wine was produced and transported, whether it was a household or mass-production industry, wine's relative economic value through time and space, its functions in society, and so forth. Important texts and artwork bearing on the ancient history of wine very likely remain to be discovered in old publications and museum storerooms.

Why did wine become an essential part of civilized life or of "the gracious way of life" as Robert Mondavi refers to it on his wine label? Its dietary and anti-microbial benefits, with the accruing selective reproductive advantages, have already been mentioned. Wine's mind-altering effects, of course, partly explain its popularity in social gatherings and cultic activities. A more debatable theory to account for wine's importance, which was proposed by Sol Katz at the conference, is that its pharmacologic properties provided a socially acceptable way to ease tensions between individuals in increasingly larger, more complex urban communities. Like having a drink after a hard day, the ancient farm laborer or the temple functionary might have had a cup or two of wine to sublimate his aggressive hunting proclivities. But wine is unlikely to have been the drug of choice, at least in ancient lowland Mesopotamia, where beer in particular could be produced from barley at any time of the year and was drunk in quantity by all strata of society (see chapter 9, and another first from Godin Tepe—Michel et al. 1992).

Prestige exchange of wine and special wine-drinking ceremonies among elite individuals have also been suggested as models for understanding the role of wine in increasingly more complex social and political contexts (see chapter 18). This hypothesis has been articulated for the Mycenaean and Classical Greek, Etruscan, and Celtic worlds, and is supported by an array of evidence from other regions of the Near East and Egypt. A conference held just prior to ours in Rome was entitled "*In Vino Veritas*," now a hackneyed phrase but for the ancient Greek male, a succinct expression that quite literally described the upper-class *symposion*. Contributing to wine's value wherever and whenever it has been drunk are limited production, and a range and subtlety of tastes and bouquets which improve with age. According to this model, wine eventually passed from the realm of the rich to the general populace by way of cultic rites, ceremony, celebration, and simple social gatherings. In modern western culture, wine is still viewed as a high-end status symbol, yet enters into our daily life, whether a wine-and-cheese party or the mystery of the Eucharist or Passover. As the reader will quickly discover by dipping into the text almost at any point, this volume contains a wealth of detail and intriguing, provocative perspectives about ancient wine. A book devoted solely to the origins and ancient history of wine is a first, like the Godin Tepe discoveries, but hopefully it will inspire and foster many more firsts in the years to come, and contribute in some small way to the appreciation and better understanding of the ancient "culture of the vine."

Acknowledgments

Many individuals, not least the conference participants, have brought this volume to fruition. At the Robert Mondavi Winery, we are especially grateful to Harvey Possert and Regina Lutz for coordinating the myriad details of the *symposion*—travel from around the world to Napa, local tours, special events, and a memorable week of meetings. Robert Mondavi and his wife, Margrit Biever, were our hosts *extraordinaires*. On the first evening, Margrit and Nina Wemyss welcomed the conferees to the winery with the illustrated Mission presentation on wine in art and history, followed by a tour of the winery. Our proceedings (and the wine!) had an excellent finish—a farewell dinner at Robert and Margrit's home, looking out across the vineyards of the valley.

The conference was jointly sponsored by The University of Pennsylvania Museum of Archaeology and Anthropology. The University Museum and the Royal Ontario Museum in Toronto kindly provided ancient artifacts from their collections to be displayed at the winery on the public media day. Institutional sponsors from the Napa Valley included Swanson Vineyards and Winery in Rutherford and the Clos Pegase Winery in Calistoga, whose owner, Jan Schrem, treated us to a luncheon in the wine grottoes, with Roman satyrs laughing down on us.

The task of readying this manuscript for publication has been shared by many students and personnel at The University Museum, including Desiree Martinez, Paul Zimmerman, Irini Haralambopoulou, Michael Danti, and Susan Bing. Other credits to publishers, artists, photographers, mentors, reviewers, and so on, too numerous to list here, will be found in the captions to the figures and in the acknowledgments to individual chapters.

Contributors

GUILLERMO ALGAZE is an associate professor of anthropology at the University of California, San Diego. He received his Ph.D. in 1986 from the Department of Near Eastern Languages and Civilization at the University of Chicago, where he concentrated in Mesopotamian studies. He received an Andrew Mellon Fellowship for postdoctoral research at The University of Pennsylvania and research grants from the National Endowment for the Humanities, the National Geographic Society and the American Research Institute in Turkey. His books include *The Uruk Expansion: A World System of the Late Fourth Millennium B.C.* and *Town and Country in Early Southeastern Anatolia.* He is currently working in Titris Höyük in southeastern Turkey.

VIRGINIA R. BADLER received her B.A. *cum laude* from the University of California, Santa Barbara, in 1970 and her M.A. from the University of Toronto in 1972, both in art history. She is currently a doctoral candidate in Near Eastern studies, West Asian archaeology at the University of Toronto. Her dissertation, "Godin V and the Chronology of the Late Uruk Period," includes chronological and functional analyses of pottery types and their regional distribution. Her research interests include pottery manufacturing techniques; topological, functional and chemical analysis of pottery; and computer reconstruction of both old and new excavations. She is also a practicing potter. She is co-author of "Chemical Evidence for Ancient Beer" (*Nature*), "Drink and Be Merry!: Infrared Spectroscopy and Ancient Near Eastern Wine" (*Organic Contents of Ancient Vessels*), and "Interaction with a Color Computer Graphics Display System for Archaeological Sites" (*Computer Graphics*).

J. M. DUTHEL is affiliated with the Laboratory of Biochemistry, Toxicology, and Trace Analysis at the Edouard Herriot Hospital in Lyons.

STUART J. FLEMING received his B.A. and D.Phil. from Oxford University, specializing in radiation damage processes in minerals and their role in the thermoluminescence properties of ancient pottery. In 1978 he took up his current position as Scientific Director of the Museum Applied Science Center for Archaeology (MASCA) at The University Museum of The University of Pennsylvania. He is the author of four books—*Authenticity in Art*; *Dating in Archaeology: A Guide to Scientific Techniques*; *Thermoluminescence Dating in Archaeology*; and *The Egyptian Mummy: Secrets and Science*—and of numerous scholarly papers on topics as diverse as X-ray spectrometry of Nigerian bronzes and Roman glass, neutron activation analysis of Near Eastern pottery, X-ray studies of Peruvian mummies, the medical aspects of the image on the Turin Shroud, the authenticity of Renaissance terra-cotta sculptures, and the glazing on early Chinese pottery tomb goods. While in England he was archaeometry correspondent to the *New Scientist* magazine, and after his move to the United States he became science columnist for *Archaeology* magazine and co-editor of *The MASCA Research Papers* at The University Museum. Over the period 1982–85, he served as consultant to the United States A-Bomb Reassessment Program for Hiroshima and Nagasaki. During the period 1989–91, he was co-planner of two of The University Museum's traveling exhibits—*River of Gold* and *Symbols of the Ancestors*—and he is currently preparing an exhibit of its Hellenistic and Roman glass collections.

FRANÇOISE FORMENTI is a professor of atomic spectroscopy in the Department of Analytical Chemistry at the Université Claude Bernard in Lyons. She received her doctorate (thèse de 3ème cycle) in analytical chemistry there in 1969. She has worked in archaeometry for more than twenty years. Her current research interest is analysis of organic compounds in archaeological materials (e.g., residues of foods, cosmetics, and paints). She has developed many of the analytical methods used in this field.

RONALD L. GORNY received his Ph.D. in Anatolian archaeology from the Oriental Institute of the University of Chicago. His main interests are Hittite Anatolia, the role of environment in shaping Anatolia's history, and the eastern Mediterranean in the Late Bronze Age. He has researched at Tel Dan and Askelon in Israel, Kurban Höyük and Titris Höyük in Turkey, and Horom in the Republic of Armenia. His recent publications include "Environment, Archaeology, and Hittite History" and "The Biconvex Seals of Alişar Höyük." He also compiled and edited "Reflections of a Late Bronze Age Empire: The Hittites." He is currently an academic advisor in the dean of students' office at the University of Chicago and is preparing his dissertation, *Alişar Höyük in the Second Millennium B.C.*, for publication.

JOSEPH A. GREENE studied Near Eastern archaeology at the Oriental Institute of the University of Chicago. He has conducted field research in Tunisia, Cyprus and Jordan. From 1979 to 1980, he directed the Carthage Survey, which gathered data on ancient settlement and land use in the hinterland of Carthage. The results of this survey are now published as *Ager and 'Arōsōt: Rural Settlement and Agrarian History in the Carthaginian Countryside*. He is currently the curator of publications at the Semitic Museum of Harvard University.

LOUIS E. GRIVETTI is a professor of geography and nutrition at the University of California, Davis. His work focuses upon the nutritional consequences of human food behavior and dietary change, whether from historical or contemporary perspectives. His recent publications include "Threads of Cultural Nutrition" (*Progress in Food and Nutrition Science*); "Prescientific Origins of Nutrition and Dietetics," parts one ("Legacy of India"), two ("Legacy of the Mediterranean"), and four ("Aztec Patterns and Spanish Legacy") (*Nutrition Today*).

T. G. H. JAMES spent his whole academic career in the Egyptian Department of the British Museum (1951–88). He was Keeper of Egyptian Antiquities for the final fourteen years of his service. His Egyptological interests include hieroglyphic and hieratic texts as well as the history of Egypt. He has recently published *Egypt: The Living Past* and *Howard Carter: The Path to Tutankhamun*. His interest in wine is general, his knowledge practical (modern) and theoretical (ancient).

CAROLYN G. KOEHLER is an associate professor of ancient studies at the University of Maryland, Baltimore County. She co-directs AMPHORAS, a research project that traces ancient Greek trade by studying its shipping containers. These large clay jars, or transport amphoras, are our main evidence for trade in commodities such as wine, oil, and preserved fish; they also furnish archaeologists with much-needed context dates for the sixth through first centuries B.C. Having worked for years with Virginia R. Grace, whose archives at the Agora Excavations of the American School of Classical Studies at Athens are the primary such collection in the world, Koehler currently focuses on creating an electronic database of these ten thousands of fragments and on publishing amphoras exported from Greek cities such as Knidos and Corinth.

ALBERT LEONARD JR. is a professor of classics at the University of Arizona. He received his Ph.D. from the Department of Near Eastern Languages and Civilizations at the University of Chicago in 1976. Since then, he has directed and co-directed archaeological exploration in Portugal, Italy, Greece, Cyprus, Egypt and Jordan, and has written extensively on the subject of ancient Mediterranean commerce. He currently serves as a co-editor of the *Bulletin of the American Schools of Oriental Research.*

LEONARD H. LESKO received his Ph.D. from the University of Chicago in 1969. He is the Wilbour Professor and chairman of the Department of Egyptology at Brown University. Author of *The Ancient Egyptian Book of the Two Ways: A Dictionary of Late Egyptian* and *King Tut's Wine Cellar*, Professor Lesko has also co-authored and edited several other books and written numerous articles for professional journals, as well as encyclopedias. A wine maker for thirty-five years, he continues to get the California Cabernet Sauvignon grapes for the wine he produces from Rhode Island.

PATRICK E. McGOVERN is a research scientist in archaeological ceramics and chemistry at the Museum Applied Science Center for Archaeology (MASCA) of The University of Pennsylvania Museum of Archaeology and Anthropology. Most recently, his research has focused on the organic analysis of vessel contents, which has led to the chemical confirmation of the earliest instances of three organics—Royal Purple dye dating to ca. 1300–1200 B.C., and wine and beer dating to ca. 3500–3100 B.C. Together with over sixty scholarly articles, his publications include *Organic Contents of Ancient Vessels*; *Cross-Craft and Cross-Cultural Interactions in Ceramics*; *The Late Bronze and Early Iron Ages of Central Transjordan*; *Late Bronze Palestinian Pendants*; and *The Late Bronze Egyptian Garrison at Beth Shan.* As a Fulbright Scholar at the University of Stockholm and a Visiting Research Scholar at the University of Copenhagen in 1994–95, he has become involved in analyzing Scandinavian "drinking vessels," including horns, cups, and cauldrons.

RUDOLPH H. MICHEL, born in 1925, received his Ph.D. in physical organic chemistry from the University of Notre Dame. In 1984, after thirty-two years in polymer research with the Dupont Company, he retired as a research fellow. During the next seven years, he was a volunteer research associate at the Museum Applied Science Center for Archaeology at The University of Pennsylvania Museum and used his chemical expertise in archaeological research on organic residues. Among his publications are "Royal Purple Dye: Tracing Chemical Origins of the Industry" (*Analytical Chemistry*) and "Chemical Evidence for Ancient Beer" (*Nature*).

NAOMI F. MILLER is a research specialist at the Museum Applied Science Center for Archaeology (MASCA), The University of Pennsylvania Museum. Her research focuses on environment, agriculture, and plant use in the ancient Near East. She has worked on plant materials from sites in Turkey, Iran, Tunisia, Turkmenistan, and elsewhere. Her recent publications include "The Near East" (*Progress in Old World Palaeoethnobotany*) and "The Origins of Plant Cultivation in the Near East."

HAROLD P. OLMO received his Ph.D. in genetics from the University of California, Berkeley, and is a professor of viticulture emeritus at the University of California, Davis. His principal field of interest is the study and improvement of grape varieties. He has conducted basic research on evolution and cytogenetics of grapevines and introduced some thirty-five new varieties, many now commercially important. His present research has emphasized the complexity of the origin and domestication of the *vinifera* grape. His publications include "The Potential Role of (*vinifera x rotundifolia*) Hybrids in Grape Variety Improvement" (*Experientia*), "Grapes" (*Encyclopedia of Food Science, Food Technology and Nutrition*) and "Grapes" (*Evolution of Crop Plants*).

RUTH PALMER received her M.A. from Cornell University and her Ph.D. from the University of Cincinnati. She was a fellow of the American School of Classical Studies in Athens from 1983 to 1985. She specializes in aspects of Minoan and Mycenaean economy as seen through administrative texts, and at present is focusing upon the use and relative importance of specific crops to the Mycenaean and Minoan palace administrations.

MARVIN A. POWELL is the Presidential Research Professor in ancient history at Northern Illinois University. A specialist in the history and culture of ancient Sumer, he has for the past decade been studying Sumerian agriculture. One of the founders of the Sumerian Agriculture Group, he is also co-editor with Nicholas Postgate (Trinity College, Cambridge) of the *Bulletin on Sumerian Agriculture*.

JANE M. RENFREW (Lady Renfrew of Kaimsthorn), M.A. Ph.D. F.S.A., F.S.A. (Scot), F.L.S., has been the vice-president of Lucy Cavendish College, Cambridge, since 1992 and a trustee of the Royal Botanic Gardens Kew and Wakehurst Place since 1991. She is an affiliated lecturer in the Department of Archaeology at Cambridge University. As a palaeoethnobotanist, she has worked in southeastern Europe, the Near East and Egypt. Her publications include *Palaeoethnobotany, First Aid for Seeds*, and *New Light on Early Farming*, as well as numerous articles and site reports.

VERNON L. SINGLETON is a professor emeritus in the Department of Viticulture and Enology of the University of California, Davis. He joined that department in 1958, following positions in antibiotic research and fruit quality research with a Ph.D. in agricultural biochemistry from Purdue University in 1951. He has authored or co-authored over 180 books, research papers, patents, and so forth, including *Wine: An Introduction* and *Phenolic Substances of Grapes and Wine, and Their Significance*.

DAVID STRONACH read archaeology and anthropology at Cambridge University before holding fellowships at the British Institute of Archaeology at Ankara and the British School of Archaeology in Iraq. He was a member of the Nimrud excavation team from 1957 to 1960, and in 1961 he was asked to direct the newly founded British Institute of Persian Studies. While in Iran, he conducted excavations at both Pasargadae and Tepe Nush-i Jan. More recently, he excavated at Nineveh, the last capital of Assyria, and at Horom in northwest Armenia. He was made an O.B.E. in 1975 and has been a professor of Near Eastern archaeology at the University of California, Berkeley, since 1981. His publications include *Pasargadae*, and he has recently been engaged in research on early textiles and ancient gardens.

JAMES C. WRIGHT is a professor in the Department of Classical and Near Eastern Archaeology at Bryn Mawr College. He has excavated in England, Italy, and Greece, most recently directing the Nemes Valley Archaeological Project in Greece. His research interests are on reconstructing the formation of complex societies in the Aegean, particularly Minoan Crete and Mycenaean Greece. Aside from publication of excavation material from Kommos in Crete and Nemea in the Peloponnesos, he has published extensively on Mycenaean architecture and society.

RICHARD L. ZETTLER received his B.A. (1972) from the University of Notre Dame and his M.A. (1975) and Ph.D. (1984) from the University of Chicago. He was the assistant to the curator of the Department of Ancient Near Eastern Art at The Metropolitan Museum of Art, New York (1983), a research associate at the Oriental Institute of the University of Chicago (1984–86) and a visiting lecturer at the Department of Near Eastern Studies of the University of California at Berkeley (1985–86). He is currently an associate professor at The University of Pennsylvania in the Department of Anthropology and associate curator-in-charge of the Near Eastern Section at The University Museum. He has excavated in Iraq and Syria and currently directs excavations at Tell es-Sweyhat (a large, late third millennium B.C. site on the Euphrates in northern Syria). His publications include *The Ur III Temple of Inanna at Nippur—The Operation and Organization of Urban Religious Institutions in Mesopotamia in the Late Third Millennium B.C.*; *Excavation at Nippur: Kassite Buildings in Area WC-1*; *Velles Paraules: Studies in Honor of Miguel Civil*; and numerous journal articles and reviews. His special areas of interest include urbanism and early, complex urban society in the Near East.

DANIEL ZOHARY is a professor of genetics at the Hebrew University, Jerusalem. In the last twenty-five years, his main field of interest has been variation and evolution in plants, with particular emphasis on the origin of cultivated plants and on plant genetic resources.

I

Ancient Sayings
About Wine

During Spring, one should eat meat of *sarabha* [wapiti], *sasa* [rabbit], *ena* [antelope], *lava* [common quail] and *kapinjala* [grey partridge] and drink harmless vinegars and wines. Thereafter, he should enjoy the blossoming beauty of women and forests.

Caraka-Samhita: Sutrasthana 6.22-26

When you sit with a glutton, eat when his greed has passed; when you drink with a drunkard, take when his heart is content.

The Instruction Addressed to Kagemni, from Papyrus Prisse, fol. 1., 18–21

Infants should be bathed for long periods in warm water and given their wine diluted and not at all cold. The wine should be of a kind which is least likely to cause distension of the stomach and wind. This should be done to prevent the occurrence of convulsions and to make the children grow and get good complexions.

Hippocrates of Cos, *Regimen for Health*

The main points in favor of ... white strong wine ... it passes more easily to the bladder than the other kind and is diuretic and purgative, it is always beneficial in acute diseases.... These are good points to note about the beneficial and harmful properties of wine; they are unknown to my predecessors.

Hippocrates of Cos, *Regimen in Acute Disease*, pt. 51

His jaws are fixed, and he is unable to open his mouth.... Grind wormwood [*Artemisia absinthium*], bay leaves, or henbane seed with frankincense; soak this in white wine, and pour it into a new pot; add an amount of oil equal to the wine, warm and anoint the patient's body copiously with the warm fluid, and also his head ... also give him a very sweet white wine to drink in large quantities.

on tetanus, Hippocrates of Cos, *Internal Affections*, pt. 52

Bowels are confined by: wine resinated or harsh, and that undiluted, vinegar, mead which has been heated, also must boiled down, raisin wine.

Celsus of Verona, *On Medicine* 2.30.3

Some are dissolved in vinegar, or in wine, water, *oxymel* [vinegar-and-honey], sour wine and water, and honey-mixture. [Such] Lemnian earth dissolved in any of the above makes a suitable application to promote the closure of recent wounds, and to cure [patients who] are chronic, slow to [heal], or [are] malignant.

on *terra sigillata* pottery as medication, Galen of Pergamum, *On Simple Drugs* 9.2

Boys under eighteen shall not taste wine at all; for one should not conduct fire to fire; wine in moderation may be tasted until one is thirty years old, but the young man should abstain entirely from drunkenness and excessive drinking; but when a man is entering upon his fortieth year he, after a feast at the public mess, may summon the other gods and particularly call upon Dionysus to join the old men's holy rite, and their mirth as well, which the god has given to men to lighten their burden—wine, that is, the cure for the crabbedness of old age, whereby we may renew our youth and enjoy forgetfulness of despair.

Plato of Athens, *Laws* 2.666.A-B

[While] the drunkard is insolent and rude ... on the other hand, the complete teetotaler is disagreeable and more fit for tending children than for presiding over a drinking-party.

Plutarchus of Chaeronea, *Table Talk* 1.620.C

When [old men] drink, it is likely that the wine is soaked up, for their bodies because of dryness are like sponges; and then the wine lies there and afflicts them with its heaviness. For just as the flood-waters run off from compact soils and do not make mud, but are soaked up in greater degree by soils of loose texture, so in the bodies of old men wine lingers on, attracted by the dryness there.

Plutarchus of Chaeronea, *Table Talk* 3.650.D

One may hide all else ... but not these two things ... that he is drinking wine, and that he has fallen in love. Both betray him through his eyes and through his words, so that the more he denies, the more they make it plain.

Athenaeus of Naucratis, *The Deipnosophists* 2.38.B-C

Milo of Croton used to eat twenty pounds of meat and as many of bread, and he drank three pitchers of wine.... At Olympia he put a four-year old bull on his shoulders and carried it around the stadium; after which he cut it up and ate it all alone in a single day.

Athenaeus of Naucratis, *The Deipnosophists* 10.412.E-F

If it so happened that people who get drunk every day had a headache before they drink the unmixed wine, not one of us would ever drink. But as it is, we take our pleasure too early, before the pain, and so arrive too late to get the good.

Athenaeus of Naucratis, *The Deipnosophists* 14.613.B

Among the Western Locrians, if anyone drank unmixed wine without a physician's prescription to effect a cure, the penalty was death under the code instituted by Zaleucus.

Athenaeus of Naucratis, *The Deipnosophists* 10.429.A

Thin white wines ought to be used [to reduce obesity]; dry rubbing with thick towels [also] is calculated to reduce the fat.

Paulus Aegineta, *Epitome* 1.57

Wine taken in moderation induces appetite and is beneficial to health.... Wine is the greatest of medicines. Where wine is lacking, drugs are necessary.

Talmud: Tractate Berachoth 35b and 58b

Late morning sleep, wine at midday, chatting with children, and sitting in the meeting houses of the ignorant drive a man from this world.... Eight things are beneficial in small amounts but harmful in excess: bloodletting, business, cohabitation, sleep, warm water, wealth, wine, and work.

Talmud: Aboth de Rabbi Nathan 37.5

Wine is a nutrient.... It is a very good nutrient.... It generates praiseworthy blood.... [It] will generate flatus, and possibly tremor ... nevertheless if mixed and left for twelve hours or more and then drunk, it is very good ... and the temperament improves.

Musa Ibn Maymum of Cordova [Maimonides],
On the Causes of Symptoms 134r.5-15 and 134v.1-6

[Mad dog] ... [if done before onset of hydrophobia, otherwise patients always die] ... flour of vetch kneaded in wine and applied as a poultice.

Musa Ibn Maymum of Cordova [Maimonides],
Treatise on Poisons 1:5

For hardening of the heart: give him the dung of rats in drink, or the dung of horses in wine, or the milk of a bitch in wine.

from *Sefer Mif‘alot* Elokim [The Book of God's Deeds]

The most detrimental of the effects of wine is that upon the brain.... If called to [treat] a person who has drunk wine to excess, emesis [vomiting] should be procured as speedily as possible. Failing that he may drink a considerable quantity of water, with or without honey. When emesis has been procured, he should bathe in a full length bath. Then he should be thoroughly rubbed with oil, and left to go to sleep.

Ibn Sina of Afshena [Avicenna], *Canon 809*

To give wine to youths is like adding fire to a fire already prepared with matchwood. Young adults should take it in moderation. But elderly persons may take as much as they can tolerate. Wine is borne better in a cold country than in a hot one.

Ibn Sina of Afshena [Avicenna], *Canon 810*

If it is desirable to get a person unconscious quickly, without being harmed, add sweet-smelling moss to wine.

Ibn Sina of Afshena [Avicenna], *Canon 814*

[To preserve the body during times of pestilence] Take one part of the following: rose water, sour quince juice, sour apple juice, sour citron juice, sweet and sour pomegranate juice; and white wine or sweet basil juice that is not very old like the rest. Boil all of it until it becomes the proper consistency for drinking.

Ibn Ridwan of Al-Giza, *On the Preventions of Bodily Ills in Egypt* 48a

Then to the Lip of this poor earthen Urn
I lean'd, the secret Well of Life to learn:
And Lip to Lip it murmur'd "While you live,
Drink! for, once dead, you never shall return."

Omar Khayyam, *Rubaiyat* 38

Foure speciall vertues hath a sop in wine,
It maketh the teeth white, it cleares the eyne,
It addes unto an emptie stomack fulnesse,
And from a stomack fill'd, it takes the dullnesse.

Regimen Santitatis,
Salerno version

II

Grapes and Wine

Hypotheses and Scientific Evidence

CHAPTER 1

Wine: The Food with Two Faces

Louis E. Grivetti

1. Introduction

Throughout recorded history, the wines produced from *Vitis vinifera* have been glorified and praised. Writers, as early as the 3rd millennium B.C., have commented upon wine's positive attributes and uses. Characteristics of generic and varietal wines have been examined and their dietary, medical, and social roles have been discussed extensively in all kinds of ancient literature. Wine has been called, among other things, "a chemical symphony," "bottled poetry," and "captured sunshine" (Becker 1979; De Luca 1979). But throughout that recorded history, those same wines have been denounced and vilified; and there is also a vast body of literature which comments upon wine's negative attributes. Oenophobes have likened it to "the destroyer of homes," "the opener of graves," and "the quencher of hopes" (Turnball 1950).

Wine contains energy and nutrients and so by any definition is a food—assuredly, however, a food with two faces. Perhaps no other food can claim wine's unique dichotomy: praised when consumed in moderation, condemned when consumed in excess. That dichotomy has been expressed in so many ways in the past. In Caravaggio's late 16th century depiction of Bacchus in the Uffizi Museum, the god's eyes tantalize the viewer, his outstretched cup draws one nearer and forecasts the joys to follow when the good wine is drunk. But the eyes of Silenus in the Capitoline Museum are wine-maddened and cast down, while the body's slouch foretells the loss of reason and stupor which will follow when wine is consumed to excess. Assuredly here we have one food, two faces.

2. Early Attitudes

In examining the positive and negative attitudes that have pervaded towards the use of wine in diet, nutrition and medicine, I have followed the culture-historical approach commonly taken by nutritional geographers (Grivetti 1981). The goal of such research is to identify, then compare ancient views with modern socio-scientific and chemical literature of recent decades. What emerges from such studies most immediately is a remarkable degree of consistency, whatever the ancient culture involved. Wine had a practical role to play in almost all aspects of human endeavor, a role that placed the dichotomy about its alcoholic effects in a secondary position, the grist for philosophers rather than farmers.

For example, the *Caraka-Samhita: Sutrasthana*, which was written ca. 1500 B.C. and was the earliest Indian text to describe appropriate diet and its role in the everyday human experience (Sharma 1981; Grivetti 1991a), addresses the hardships of Winter thus: "one should use ... meat of burrow-dwelling and *prasaha* [who eat by snatching] types of animals. Thereafter, the person should drink wine, vinegar, and honey" (6.9-18). On the positive side, one part of this text notes that "wine is exhilarating, nourishing, removes fear, grief and fatigue, provides boldness, energy, imagination, satisfaction, corpulence, and strength" (27.193-195). Yet, elsewhere we find a counterview:

> One who saturates himself excessively with ... fresh wine ... and at the same time abstains from physical movements including day-sleep, suffers from diseases ... such as diabetic boils, urticarial patches, itching, anemia, fever, leprosy, anorexia, drowsiness, impotency, over-obesity, disorders of consciousness, sleepiness, swelling, and other disorders. (23.3-7)

That caution aside, the Ayurvedic physicians responsible for this text's ideas generally wrote favorably of wine's medicinal values, prescribing it, for example, to counter muscle-wasting and limited appetite (27.319-324). And modern practitioners of Indian Ayurvedic medicine seem to maintain that stance (Dash and Kashyap 1987). More negative views only prevail after the *Dharma-Sutra* texts of the 6th century B.C. onwards began to regulate Hindu dietary codes. One such text (*Apastamba* 1.5.17.21) forbade consumption not only of wine but also of all intoxicating beverages (Buhler 1896).

The early Indian allopathic practices in medicine were adopted and expanded by the Chinese during the 1st millennium B.C. It is, therefore, not surprising that one of the earliest Chinese medical texts, *Nei Ching* (Han Dynasty, ca. 2nd century B.C), besides classifying foods with male–female, hot–cold, dry–wet, light–dark aspects (Anderson 1980; Grivetti 1991b,c), would include observations on the use of alcoholic beverages. Here the view is critical and moralizing in tone:

> In ancient times people who understood Tao patterned themselves upon the Yin and the Yang and they lived in harmony with the arts of divination.... There was temperance in eating and drinking.... Nowadays people are not like this; they use wine as beverage and they adopt recklessness as usual behavior. They enter the chamber of love in an intoxicated condition; their passions exhaust their vital forces; their cravings dissipate their true essence. (*Nei Ching*)

At that time, grape wine was something quite novel in China (Hulsewe 1979), but was surely viewed with the same concern as the traditional cereal wines of centuries-long standing. From such ideas, however, there emerged a typically Chinese view of wine's two faces, a view expressed in some fine axioms for moral behavior (Simoons 1991), among them: "The first glass, the man drinks the wine; the second glass, the wine drinks the wine; the third glass, the wine drinks the man" (Hahn 1976: 143).

Chinese poets who drank to excess were called "Drunken Dragons." The 8th century A.D. poet, Li Po, who was considered the "Dragon of Dragons" by his contemporaries, saw only merit in his view that "the rapture of drinking and wine's dizzy joy, no man who is sober deserves." But tradition has it that a much intoxicated Li Po went sailing one night, and as he attempted to embrace the moon's reflection, fell overboard and was drowned.

Other contributors to this volume address in detail the interest of the ancient Egyptians in wine (see James and Lesko, this volume), so I will comment only on how they also saw fit to draw

Figure 1.1. Woman vomiting at banquet, New Kingdom, Egypt. (Photograph courtesy of the Musées Royaux d'Art et d'Histoire, Brussels, Belgium.)

attention to wine's two faces. Thus, in the *Admonition to Schoolboys* (ca. 1400 B.C.), the consequences of drunkenness are provided apt metaphor:

> Thou art like a broken steering-oar in a ship, that is obedient to neither side. Thou art like a shrine without its god; and like a house without bread.... men run away from before thee, for thou inflictest wounds upon them. Would that thou knewest that wine is an abomination. (Blackman 1966: 190–91)

Even among ancient Egyptian tomb paintings which, first and foremost, were intended to depict an idealized afterworld, the negative effects of wine provide a jarring note. While in most banquet scenes, the wine is a seemly complement to an abundance of good food, and often playing an important social role, in some there are clear depictions of inebriation and vomiting (Fig. 1.1). And in the tomb of Paheri (ca. 1500 B.C.), a servant is presented an empty cup by an elegantly dressed lady who says: "Give me eighteen measures of wine, behold I should love to drink to drunkenness, my inside is as dry as straw." The servant offers only encouragement: "Drink; do not refuse; behold, I am not going to leave you. Drink, do not spoil the entertainment; and let the cup come to me" (Darby et al. 1977: 2:584).

And so the story continued throughout the subsequent two millennia. Early in the 4th century B.C., Hippocrates of Cos integrated into a comprehensive healing system almost all the early Greek views on the physiological constructs of the natural elements, the humors of health, and the temperature–moisture attributes of specific diseases and their appropriate cures. Such ideas spread quickly throughout the Mediterranean cultures. They gained greatly in sophistication from the experience of other physicians such as Ctesias, who traveled in India and Persia and learned of many new treatments.

The ideas of Hippocrates and his followers were fully embraced by the Roman medical profession. They were particularly well articulated by Celsus of Verona (27 B.C.–A.D. 37), who focused upon nutrition and the role of diet in medical therapeutics (Spencer 1935–38), and by Galen of Pergamum (A.D. 131–201) whose methods for the treatment of wounds and description of the efficacy of drugs was accepted well into the Middle Ages (Brock 1928; 1929a,b).

Wine found a comfortable niche in such concepts. Thus, Hippocrates wrote how, in the maintenance of good health, wine's consumption had an important aspect of seasonality (Chadwick et al. 1978a):

> In Autumn the quantity [of wine] taken should be decreased and taken less diluted so that he will have a good winter. He takes the smallest quantity of the least diluted drink and the largest quantity of cereals of the driest kind. (*Regimen for Health* 1)

Meanwhile, his *Regimen in Acute Disease* goes so far as to prescribe specific types of wine for certain disorders (Chadwick et al. 1978b); and his *Regimen for Health, Diseases*, and *Internal Affections* all place emphasis on the place of wine in the treatment of specific diseases (Potter 1980). We learn that jaundice comes on in Winter from drunkenness and chills, so:

> after seven days have passed have the patient drink hellebore.... Give blister-beetles, too, with their wings and heads removed; grind flour, dissolve in a half-*cotyle* [cup] of white wine, immediately add a little honey, and give thus to drink.... Let the patient eat whatever he will accept, and drink dry white wine. (*Internal Affections* 36)

Hippocrates seems to have a high regard for wine's role in medicine (Chadwick et al. 1978c), even going so far as to state: "It is better to be full of wine than full of food" (*Aphorisms* 2.11). Here, though, he is probably criticizing gluttony rather than drinking to excess, since elsewhere the doses of wine prescribed always seem to have been small. He actively discouraged giving wine, "if there is any suspicion of a violent headache or derangement of the mind in these diseases" (*Regimen in Acute Disease* 63).

It is unlikely that Hippocrates would have gone so far as the Alexandrian physician, Herophilus of Chalcedon (335–280 B.C.), who is said to have kept some patients with cardiac diseases at the point of intoxication day and night while using bloodletting and all sorts of poultices to achieve a cure (von Staden 1989).

Non-physicians of the classical era seem to have been fascinated by wine's two faces, especially in the way that wine's two faces revealed themselves in social conduct. Pliny the Elder (A.D. 23–79) loved wine, and so remarked succinctly: "There are two liquids that are specially agreeable to the body, wine inside and oil outside" (*Naturalis Historia* 19.29.150). But he, like many of his contemporaries, found the intoxication of women inexcusable. Thus, he notes several upsetting incidents in Roman society:

we find that the wife of Egnatius Maetennus was clubbed to death by her husband for drinking wine from the vat, and [he was] acquitted.... A matron was starved to death by her relatives for having broken open the casket containing the keys of the wine cellar; and Cato says the reason why women are kissed by their male relations is to know whether they smell of "tipple." (*Naturalis Historia* 14.14.89)

Meanwhile, Plutarchus of Chaeronea (A.D. 46–127) was to echo the words of many more ancient texts when he observed (Clement and Hoffleit 1969): "Song, laughter, and dancing are characteristic of men who drink wine in moderation; but babbling and talking about what is better left in silence is at once the work of actual intoxication and drunkenness" (*Table Talk* 3.644.F).

Special mention should be made here of Athenaeus (A.D. 170–230), a Greek from the village of Naucratis, in the Nile Delta (Gulick 1927–41). In his *Deipnosophists* ("Philosophers at Dinner"), he discussed the geographical distribution and regional dietetics of the entire Mediterranean. (As importantly, from an academic standpoint today, he credited as his sources more than a thousand ancient authors who wrote on food-related topics.) Within this vast compilation, more than anywhere else, are to be found past views on wine's two faces.

Using the literary mechanism of a banquet discourse, Athenaeus had his dinner guests review the true joy and essence of drinking wine. They took pleasure in recalling the famous phrase of the 6th century B.C. playwright, Aeschylus of Eleusis: "Bronze is the mirror of the outward form; wine is the mirror of the mind" (*Deipnosophists* 10.427.E). And they agreed with the poet Panyasis who had said: "[Wine] drives all sorrows from men's hearts when drunk in due measure, but when taken immoderately it is a bane" (*Deipnosophists* 2.37.A-B). They advocated wine to artists and writers as a means of improving creativity, and decried water as a beverage for poets if they wanted to "produce anything good" (*Deipnosophists* 2.39.C); and they spoke highly of how it gave energy to old men for dancing. Yet on the debit side, the banqueters could cite Alexis of Thurii (ca. 336 B.C.): "And so, is not drunkenness the greatest bane in the world to mankind, and the most harmful … [and] … much wine causes the commission of many crimes" (*Deipnosophists* 10.443.E-F). The host himself observed that "false opinions occur to drunken men" (10.445.E-F).

It is not hard to imagine how at this kind of banquet, as it wore on and wine-clouded minds became maudlin, sadder thoughts emerged—of how Dionysus the Younger, tyrant of Sicily ruined his eyesight with wine; and how, in 491 B.C., Cleomenes of Lacedaemon, a drinker of unmixed wine, "slashed himself to death with a knife in a fit of intoxication" (*Deipnosophists* 10.436.E-F).

3. Wine's Place in Mediterranean Religious Attitudes

The period after Athenaeus is just as rich in references to the medical and social roles of wine as it was in the classical era, but there are some changes in emphasis. Jewish, Christian, and Muslim physicians alike continued to have quite positive views towards wine. Thus, the Muslim physician, Ibn Sina of Afshena (A.D. 937–1037), known in the West as Avicenna, wrote (Gruner 1930): "The advantage of wine is that it excites the secretion of urine, thus removing the bilious humor with it, and that it moistens the joints" (*Canon* 735). And the Jewish physician, Musa Ibn Maymum of Cordova (A.D. 1135–1208), known in the West as Maimonides, wrote (Rosner and Muntner 1970–71): "We possess nothing more appropriate than wine for strengthening one who is weak and enfeebled. The same applies for one whose body is completely cooled, or whose appearance is abnormal" (*Aphorisms* 20.26). But their theological counterparts, while not denying that there were some medico-social merits to wine, tended to focus more than anyone had done before upon the evils of intoxication and the role of wine in producing unseemly behavior (Gallagher and Gallagher 1966; Fig. 1.2). Thus, St. Augustine (A.D. 345–407) argued:

> It is clear to me why we ought to abstain from meat and wine. Their purpose is threefold: to check the sensual delight ordinarily roused by this sort of food and drink, and which all too frequently leads to drunkenness; to protect the weak from those things which are sacrificed and offered in libation; and what is most praiseworthy of all, to refrain for the sake of charity. (*The Way of Life of the Manichaeans* 14.35)

So it is that, in the Talmudic literature of the 6th century A.D. (Rosner 1978), alongside comments such as "when wine flows like water, the house is prosperous" (*Erubin* 65a), we have many pithy criticisms, such as "nothing brings lamentation to man other than wine" (*Sanhedrin* 70b) and the view that "red wine is especially dangerous to women" (*Kathuboth* 65).

It is in Islamic literature, however, where we find the strongest condemnations of wine, since it is the only one of these three faiths that expressly prohibit its devout from consuming it. In this respect, the key sentence in the *Koran* is: "O believers, wine and arrow-shuffling, idols and diving-arrows are an abomination, some of Satan's work" (*The Table* 5.90), where the translated word for "wine" is the Arabic term *khmr* (Kassis 1983).

Islamic prohibition nowadays tends to extend to include all alcoholic beverages. However, the fact that many devout Muslims will drink beer, brandy, and other spirits—but not wine—indicates that such a strict attitude was not universally accepted (Grivetti 1978). Some modern scholars even question the usual translation of *khmr*, adding to their linguistic evidence the fact that there are ancient illustrations of Muslims drinking wine, indeed of them being intoxicated by it.

4. Wine in Perspective

The additional, more recent citations that could be offered here for past views of wine's nature, both social and medical, positive and negative, are nearly endless. It is sufficient perhaps to note just two major medieval sources on such matters—the 13th century *Regimen Sanitatis*, and the late 14th century *Tacuinum Sanitatis*—both of which are medical texts that address the way in which wine presents two faces just as clearly as those abstracted above (Arano 1976). The review of these texts in Darby 1981 is exemplary.

What is clear from all the quotations above, and the numerous other comments in the texts from which those quotations are drawn, is that the ancients knew full well that wine held the potential for joy and pleasure as well as the potential for danger and disaster. Some of the ways in which the past understandings are expressed may read quite strangely when set alongside the chemistry- and psychology-specific data of modern scientific literature. There are, however, large areas of commonality between the ancient and modern sources. For example, one may note the generality in ancient texts that recognize how moderate consumption of wine increases blood flow, which matches today's ideas of how wine acts as a vasodilator (Baus 1973; Klatsky 1979) and how it has a specific therapeutic role in some diseases of the peripheral circulatory system (Kane 1981; Seigneur et al. 1990). And ancient notions of how wine might improve one's appetite and digestion match many modern studies of wine's impact upon the stimulation of salivory excretion, and gastric secretion and motility (McDonald 1981).

At the same time, the sometimes florid admonitions by ancient writers against excessive consumption, in the way that they highlight the resulting physical failings, conjure up the same social and medical images that we now parcel under the terms "abuse" and "alcoholism" (Tarter and van Thiel 1985; Kottek 1989; Mongrain and Standing 1989; Benjamin et al. 1990; Werch 1990). The stories recounted by ancient writers as to potentially extreme consequences of immoderation—perhaps most notably how Alexander of Macedon, in a drunken rage, murdered

Figure 1.2. Drunkenness of Noah by Giovanni Bellini (1430–1516 A.D.). (Photography courtesy of the Musée de Besançon, France.)

Cleitus, one of his best friends—find parallels today in the reports on drink-related incidents of child abuse, and in professional assessments of elevated crime statistics (Watkin 1979; Denton and Krebs 1990; Wieczorek et al. 1990). We can claim only as of our own era the central role played by intoxication in automobile accidents (Soderstrom et al. 1990; Vingilis et al. 1990).

If we are to find fault in ancient textual references to wine's two faces, it would be in some minor specifics—for example, notions that too much wine led to premature baldness, premature gray hair in men, and hemorrhoids in both genders—and in their ongoing support for the idea that wine in moderation could sharpen the intellect, even strengthen the brain. But it is true today that popular attitudes towards drinking blur the *perception* of its real impact just as easily as they did in the past.

In drawing together the materials for this contribution, I embarked upon not only a journey through the dusty stacks of a major research library, but also an enjoyable trip through time. In the process, I discovered in the text of Dali's *The Wines of Gaia* (see Bernier 1978), a passage that captured the essence of why this literary search was so enjoyable:

> To make a great wine, one needs:—a madman to grow the vine;—a wise man to watch over it;—a lucid poet to make the wine; [and]—a lover to drink it. If you call, the local wine grower will see you. He is the St. Peter of this mini-paradise, but he will never ask you if you have sinned before allowing you into his heaven! [His] is the cry of a nation of wine growers. If you have heard it, you will no longer drink wine: you will taste a mystery.

Appendix: Some Modern Perspectives on Wine

The ancients knew that wine held a potential for joy and disaster. From ancient Egypt, India, and China came both praise and admonishment to drinkers of wine. Ancient Greek and Roman texts extolled the vine's virtues, but cautioned moderation. Medieval Jews, Christians, and Moslems expressed the duality of wine in religious and medical texts that have survived the centuries. The present chapter attempted to draw together these ancient views of wine in a way that underscored their similarities, yet pointed up some of the culture-based differences. Such a review leads naturally to the question of whether the positive and negative attributes of wine that were mentioned in the ancient literature were actually correct.

Our most immediate yardsticks for making a judgment on this issue are modern scientific assessments of wine's medicinal and nutritional capabilities. Given the current biological approach to medicine and nutrition, what positive attributes ascribed to wine in the past can also be identified in the contemporary scientific literature? Conversely, what negative effects of immoderate wine consumption can be identified and confirmed among those same contemporary sources?

Standard literature retrieval methods used in cultural geography and cultural nutrition reveal a vast resource of data on wine that cover not only the subthemes of this book (e.g., Lutz 1922; Ricci 1924; Lucas 1962; Darby et al. 1977; and CILOP 1983), but also its geographic dispersals and social uses through time (e.g., Christoffel 1957; Allen 1961; Lucia 1963; Younger 1966; Stanislawski 1970; and Todhunter 1979). Similarly, the literature on the medical and dietary attributes of wine is abundant and widespread. Medical-nutritional *praise* for wine can be found in many places and many languages (e.g., Leal 1944; Eylaud 1960; Lucia 1971; Maury 1976; Köhnlechner 1978; Kliewe 1981; Fiorani and Fedecostante 1981; Cornelssen and Albath 1984; and Held 1984). Praise for the use of wine as a component or essential ingredient in cooking is also extensive (e.g., Chase 1960; McDouall 1968; Sarvis 1973; California Wine Advisory Board 1978; Ballard 1981; McConnell and McConnell 1987). And there are also several symposium volumes on wine and fermented beverages that present medical-dietary ideas about wine alongside various other historical and social aspects (e.g., Lucia 1969; California Wine Advisory Board 1975; Gastineau et al. 1979; Darby 1981).

As for wine's *critics*, they are numerous as well. Temperance organizations, so many of which were very active at the end of the 19th century, have been especially vociferous in their condemnation of wine and the "social evils" that accompany its use, even in moderation (e.g., Kerr 1881; Ellis 1882; Eddy 1887; Bechtel 1893; Turnball 1950; Lees 1970; and Christian Economic and Social Research Foundation 1976).

How valid anyone finds either side of the argument about wine's "two faces" must be largely a subjective response. What I have done in this Appendix is to draw together in one place, in as objective a manner as possible, the scientific data available on wine's nutritional content. I have done this via a set of Tables (1.1–1.3) of data that indicate wine's relative energy, mineral, and vitamin composition.

Table 1.1 gives the nutritional composition of 3.5 fluid ounces of generic red and white wines (Pennington 1989). These data are compared to the U.S. Recommended Dietary Allowances (STE 1989) for men and women aged 25–50, then set against similar data for 12 fluid ounces of beer of various kinds (generic, generic light, Budweiser®, and Stroh's Lager®); and of milk, coffee, and tea (also STE 1989).

Table 1.2 presents the percentage of the U.S. Recommended Dietary Allowances for men and women aged 25–50 that would be obtained from 1 glass, three glasses and 1 bottle (= ca. 10 glasses) of each wine type (STE 1989). Notable here are the significant amounts available in wine of the vitamins B_2 and B_6, and of the essential elements manganese and iron.

Table 1.3 presents data on the energy and nutritional composition of of a typical southern Mediterranean meal, with and without the inclusion in it of three glasses of red wine. Notable here is the fact that such a wine-linked meal allows women to meet their RDA for iron, yet has little or no impact on the requirements of either sex for protein, vitamins A, C, B_1 (thiamine), and B_{12}, or folic acid, niacin, calcium, and zinc.

Table 1.1

Nutritional Content of Selected Beverages[1,2]

Energy: Protein, Fat, Carbohydrate (CHO), and Cholesterol (CHOL)

Unit of measure	Energy (kcal)	Protein (g)	Fat (g)	CHO (g)	CHOL (mg)
RDA (Age 25–50):[3]					
Male	2900	63	RNE[4]	RNE	RNE
Female	2200	50	RNE	RNE	RNE
Beverage					
Table wine: red	74	0.2	0.0	1.4	0.0
Table wine: white	70	0.1	0.0	0.8	0.0
Beer (generic)	146	0.9	0.0	13.2	0.0
Beer (generic light)	100	0.7	0.0	4.8	0.0
Beer (Budweiser)	153	1.5	0.0	13.2	0.0
Beer (Stroh's Lager)	145	9.9	0.0	13.4	0.0
Milk (whole, 3.5% fat)	150	8.0	8.0	11.0	34.0
Coffee (brewed)	4	0.1	0.0	0.8	0.0
Tea (black, brewed)	2	0.0	0.0	0.4	0.0

cont'd

Table 1.1, cont'd

Selected Vitamins

Unit of measure	A (µgRE)	C (mg)	B₂ (mg)	B₆ (mg)	Folate (µg)	B₁ (mg)	Niacin (mg)	B₁₂ (µg)	Panto-thenate (mg)
RDA (Age 25–50):									
Male	1000	60	1.7	2.0	200	1.5	19	2.0	RNE
Female	800	60	1.3	1.6	180	1.1	15	2.0	RNE
Beverage									
Table wine: red	0.0	0.0	0.03	0.04	2.0	0.01	0.1	0.01	0.04
Table wine: white	0.0	0.0	0.01	0.01	0.0	0.00	0.1	0.0	0.02
Beer (generic)	0.0	0.0	0.09	0.18	21.0	0.02	1.6	0.06	0.21
Beer (generic light)	0.0	0.0	0.11	0.12	15.0	0.03	1.4	0.02	0.13
Beer (Budweiser)	–	0.0	0.14	0.16	–	0.01	1.4	–	0.41
Beer (Stroh's Lager)	0.0	0.0	0.07	0.18	–	0.01	1.8	–	0.17
Milk (whole, 3.5% fat)	80.0	5.0	0.42	0.02	37.0	0.1	0.2	1.34	0.85
Coffee (brewed)	–	0.0	0.0	0.0	0.0	0.0	0.4	0.0	–
Tea (black, brewed)	0.0	0.0	0.03	0.0	9.0	0.0	0.0	0.0	–

Selected Minerals

Unit of measure	Na (mg)	Ca (mg)	Mg (mg)	Zn (mg)	Mn (mg)	K (mg)	P (mg)	Fe (mg)	Cu –
RDA (Age 25–50):									
Male	–	800	350	15	–	–	800	10	–
Female	–	800	280	12	–	–	800	15	–
Beverage									
Table wine: red	6	8	13	0.10	0.615	115	14	0.44	0.021
Table wine: white	5	9	11	0.07	0.473	82	14	0.33	0.022
Beer (generic)	19	18	23	0.06	0.043	89	44	0.11	0.032
Beer (generic light)	10	18	17	0.11	0.057	64	43	0.12	0.085
Beer (Budweiser)	9	16	22	0.01	0.040	142	57	0.01	0.014
Beer (Stroh's Lager)	25	22	25	0.03	–	64	48	0.0	0.0
Milk (whole, 3.5% fat)	122	288	24	1.0	–	351	227	0.12	–
Coffee (brewed)	4	3	10	0.03	0.048	96	2	0.72	0.012
Tea (black, brewed)	5	0	5	0.04	–	66	1	0.04	0.018

[1]Source: Pennington 1989. [2]Beer (12 fl. oz.); Coffee (6 fl. oz.); Milk (8 fl. oz.); Tea (6 fl. oz.); Wine (3.5 fl. oz.). [3]Source for recommended dietary allowance (RDA): STE 1989. [4]RNE: RDA requirement not established.

Table 1.2

Percentage U.S. Recommended Dietary Allowances[1] Provided by Three Quantities of Generic Red and White Table Wine

Nutrient	1 glass		3 glasses		Bottle[2]	
	Red	White	Red	White	Red	White
Energy						
Male[3]	2.5	2.4	7.7	7.2	25.5	24.1
Female[3]	3.4	3.2	10.1	9.5	33.6	31.8
Protein						
Male	0.3	0.2	1.0	0.5	3.2	1.2
Female	0.4	0.2	1.2	0.6	4.0	2.0
Vitamin A						
Male	0.0	0.0	0.0	0.0	0.0	0.0
Female	0.0	0.0	0.0	0.0	0.0	0.0
Vitamin B$_1$						
Male	0.7	0.0	2.0	0.0	6.7	0.0
Female	0.9	0.0	2.7	0.0	9.1	0.0
Vitamin B$_2$						
Male	1.8	0.6	5.3	1.8	17.6	5.9
Female	2.3	0.8	6.9	2.3	23.1	7.7
Vitamin B$_6$						
Male	2.0	0.5	6.0	1.5	20.0	5.0
Female	2.5	0.6	7.5	1.9	25.0	6.3
Vitamin B$_{12}$						
Male	0.5	0.0	1.5	0.0	5.0	0.0
Female	0.5	0.0	1.5	0.0	5.0	0.0
Folate						
Male	1.0	0.0	3.0	0.0	10.0	0.0
Female	1.1	0.0	3.3	0.0	11.1	0.0
Niacin						
Male	0.5	0.5	1.6	1.6	5.3	5.3
Female	0.7	0.7	2.0	2.0	6.7	6.7
Vitamin C						
Male	0.0	0.0	0.0	0.0	0.0	0.0
Female	0.0	0.0	0.0	0.0	0.0	0.0
Calcium						
Male	1.0	1.1	3.0	3.4	10.0	11.3
Female	1.0	1.1	3.0	3.4	10.0	11.3
Iron						
Male	4.4	3.4	13.2	9.9	44.0	33.3
Female	2.9	2.2	8.8	6.6	29.3	22.0
Manganese						
Male	3.7	3.1	11.1	9.4	37.1	31.4
Female	4.6	3.9	13.9	11.8	46.4	39.3
Phophorus						
Male	1.8	1.8	5.3	5.3	17.5	17.5
Female	1.8	1.8	5.3	5.3	17.5	17.5
Zinc						
Male	0.7	0.5	2.0	1.4	6.7	4.7
Female	0.8	0.6	2.5	1.8	8.3	5.8

[1]STE 1989. [2]Calculated at 1 bottle = ca. 10 glasses. [3]Male and female aged 25–50.

Table 1.3

Energy and Nutrient Contribution of Wine to a Representative Meal (three glasses of generic red table wine)[1,2]

Energy, Protein, Fat, Carbohydrate

Unit of measure	Energy (kcal)	Protein (g)	Fat (g)	Carbohydrate (g)
RDA (Age 25–50):				
Male	2900	63	RNE[3]	RNE
Female	2200	50	RNE	RNE
Antipasta				
Ham, 1 slice	65	6.2	3.0	3.0
Melon, 1 cup	55	1.5	0.4	13.7
Pasta				
Spaghetti, 1 cup	216	7.3	0.7	44.0
Mariana sauce, 1/2 cup	79	1.3	3.8	10.0
Parmasan cheese, 1 tbsp.	33	2.1	1.5	0.2
Salad				
Spinach, 1/2 cup	19	2.2	0.4	2.9
Lemon juice, 1 tsp.	4	0.1	0.0	1.3
Olive oil, 1 tsp.	119	0.0	13.5	0.0
Croutons, 1/2 oz.	70	3.0	0.0	14.0
Bread				
French bread, 1 slice	70	2.4	1.0	12.6
Garlic powder, 1 tsp.	9	0.5	trace	2.0
Butter, 1 tsp.	36	0.0	4.1	trace
Dessert				
Ice cream, 1 cup	269	4.8	14.3	31.7
Beverage				
Coffee, 1 cup brewed	4	0.1	0.0	0.8
Sugar, 1 tsp.	16	0.0	0.0	4.0
Light cream, 1 tbsp.	29	0.4	2.9	0.6
Total without wine	1093	31.9	45.6	140.8
Red wine: 3 glasses	222	0.6	0.0	4.2
Total with wine:	1315	32.5	45.6	145.0
% RDA without wine				
Male	38	51	–	–
Female	50	64	–	–
% RDA with wine				
Male	45	52	–	–
Female	60	65	–	–

cont'd

Table 1.3, cont'd

Selected Vitamins

Unit of measure	A (μgRE)	C (mg)	B$_2$ (mg)	B$_6$ (mg)	Folate (μg)	B$_1$ (mg)	Niacin (mg)	B$_{12}$ (μg)	Panto-thenate (mg)
RDA (Age 25–50):									
Male	1000	60	1.7	2.0	200	1.5	19	2.0	RNE
Female	800	60	1.3	1.6	180	1.1	15	2.0	RNE
Antipasta									
Ham, 1 slice	0.0	0.17	0.03	0.02	–	0.17	0.9	–	–
Melon, 1 cup	307	11.0	0.04	0.18	45.0	0.29	1.1	0.0	0.28
Pasta									
Spaghetti, 1 cup	0.0	0.0	0.15	–	–	0.26	2.0	–	–
Mariana sauce, 1/2 cup	–	4.00	0.04	–	–	0.08	0.9	–	–
Parmasan cheese, 1 tbsp.	–	0.0	0.02	0.01	trace	trace	trace	–	0.03
Salad									
Spinach, 1/2 cup	–	13	0.12	0.07	58	0.02	0.03	00	0.07
Lemon juice, 1 tsp.	0.0	7	trace	0.01	2	0.01	trace	0.12	0.02
Olive oil, 1 tsp.	0.0	0.0	0.0	0.0	0.0	0.0	0.0	0.0	0.0
Croutons, 1/2 oz.	trace	–	0.14	trace	trace	0.09	1.2	–	–
Bread									
French bread, 1 slice	trace	trace	0.09	0.01	9	0.12	1.0	0.0	0.09
Garlic powder, 1 tsp.	.	–	–	trace	–	–	0.01	trace	0.00.0
Butter, 1 tsp.	38	0.0	0.0	trace	trace	trace	0.0	–	–
Dessert									
Ice cream, 1 cup	133	1	0.33	0.06	3	0.05	0.1	0.63	0.65
Beverage									
Coffee, 1 cup brewed	–	0.0	0.0	0.0	0.0	0.0	1.2	0.0	–
Sugar, 1 tsp.	0.0	0.0	0.0	0.0	0.0	0.0	0.0	0.0	0.0
Light cream, 1 tbsp.	27	trace	0.02	0.01	trace	0.01	trace	0.03	0.04
Total without wine	540	36.2	0.98	0.37	117.0	1.11	7.63	0.78	1.18
Red wine, 3 glasses	0.0	0.0	0.09	0.12	6.0	0.03	0.3	0.03	0.12
Total with wine	540	36.2	1.07	0.49	123.0	1.14	7.93	0.81	1.30
% RDA without wine									
Male	54	60	58	19	59	74	40	39	–
Female	68	60	75	23	65	101	51	39	–
% RDA With wine									
Male	54	60	63	25	62	76	42	41	–
Female	68	60	82	31	68	104	53	41	–

cont'd

Louis E. Grivetti

Table 1.3, cont'd

Selected Minerals

Unit of measure	Na (mg)	Ca (mg)	Mg (mg)	Zn (mg)	Mn (mg)	K (mg)	P (mg)	Fe (mg)	Cu (mg)
RDA (Age 25–50):									
Male	RNE	800	350	15	RNE	RNE	800	10	RNE
Female	RNE	800	280	12	RNE	RNE	800	15	RNE
Antipasta									
Ham, 1 slice	71	1.0	2.0	0.18	–	114	39	1.0	0.18
Melon, 1 cup	484	22	0.5	0.104	00	5	1	6.0	0.09
Pasta									
Spaghetti, 1 cup	1	16	29	–	–	115	95	1.6	–
Mariana sauce, 1/2 cup	925	18	–	–	–	413	–	0.88	–
Parmasan cheese, 1 tblsp	93	69	3	0.16	–	5	40	0.05	–
Salad									
Spinach, 1/2 cup	356	122	46	0.55	–	317	34	1.39	0.15
Lemon juice, 1 tsp.	0.0	1	1	0.01	0.001	19	1	0.0	0.004
Olive oil, 1 tsp.	0.0	trace	0.0	0.01	–	–	trace	0.05	–
Croutons, 1/2 oz.	260	20	8	0.21	–	27	20	1.08	0.04
Bread									
French bread, 1 slice	138	28	5	0.16	–	22	20	0.77	0.04
Garlic powder, 1 tsp.	1	2	2	0.07	–	31	12	0.08	–
Butter, 1 tsp.	41	1	trace	trace	trace	1	1	0.01	–
Dessert									
Ice cream, 1 cup	116	176	18	1.14	–	257	134	0.12	–
Beverage									
Coffee, 1 cup brewed	4	3	10	0.03	0.048	96	2	0.72	0.012
Sugar, 1 tsp.	0.0	trace	0.0	0.0	0.0	0.0	0.0	0.0	0.0
Light cream, 1 tbsp.	14	14	1	0.04	–	18	12	0.01	–
Total without wine	2504	493	126	2.66	0.05	1440	411	13.76	0.52
Red wine, 3 glasses	18	24	39	0.3	1.945	345	42	1.32	0.063
Total with wine	2522	517	165	2.96	1.99	1785	453	15.08	0.58
% RDA without wine									
Male	–	62	36	18	–	–	51	138	–
Female	–	62	45	22	–	–	51	92	–
% RDA with wine									
Male	–	65	47	20	–	–	57	151	–
Female	–	65	59	25	–	–	57	101	–

[1]Pennington 1989. [2]STE 1989. [3]RNE: RDA requirement not established.

CHAPTER 2

The Domestication of the Grapevine *Vitis Vinifera* L. in the Near East

Daniel Zohary

1. Introduction

This chapter aims at a survey of the domestication of the grapevine *Vitis vinifera* L. in the Old World, by attempting to answer the following questions:

1. From what wild stock did the cultivated grapevine evolve?

2. Where and when was this plant taken into cultivation?

3. What were the main developments in this fruit-crop, once it came under domestication?

As with many other Old World cultivated plants (Zohary and Hopf 1993: 1), the evidence for answering these questions for the grapevine comes mainly from two sources:

1. Survey of the living wild relatives of the fruit-crop and identification of its wild ancestor. Such a survey also includes an assessment of the traits that distinguish the cultivated varieties from their wild progenitor and the determination of the genetic basis for these changes.

2. Analysis of culturally associated and well-dated grapevine remains retrieved from archaeological excavations. These archaeological studies also include the evaluation of artifacts associated with grapevine cultivation, wine production, and wine storage.

In addition, from the second part of the 3rd millennium bc (non-calibrated radiocarbon ^{14}C date) onwards, grapevine cultivation and wine production are also documented by early inscriptions—first in Mesopotamia, and soon thereafter, in Egypt (see both Powell, and James, this volume). Finally, linguistic comparisons also help in tracing the place of origin for the cultivated grapevine and the spread of viticulture and wine use (Stager 1985).

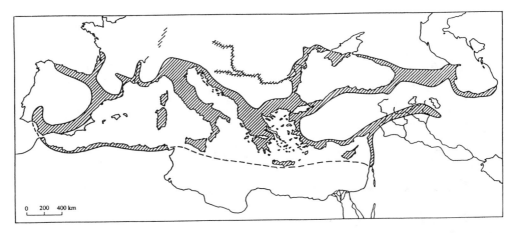

Map 2.1. The distribution range of wild grapevine *Vitis vinifera* subsp. *sylvestris*. Note that toward east the wild grapevine extends beyond the boundaries of this map and reappears in a few places in Turkmenistan and Tadzhikistan.

2. The Wild Progenitor

Identification of the wild progenitor of a crop is a prerequisite for reconstruction of its evolution under domestication. Only when the wild ancestor is satisfactorily known can one proceed to compare and contrast the wild-type with the domesticated derivatives, in order to determine what happened under domestication. Delimitation of the distribution range of the wild ancestor is also critical, since it orients the crop plant evolutionist as to the geographic area where domestication could have taken place.

In the case of the grapevine, both comparative morphological studies and tests of genetic affinities have identified its wild progenitor with certainty (for reviews, see Zohary and Spiegel-Roy 1975; and Olmo, this volume). The crop is closely related to an aggregate of European and West Asiatic wild grape forms (Fig. 2.1). These forms were originally regarded as a separate species of *Vitis sylvestris* C.C. Gmelin; now, however *sylvestris* grapes are considered as the wild race (subspecies) of the cultivated fruit-crop, and are botanically named *Vitis vinifera* L. subsp. *sylvestris* (C. C. Gmelin) Berger.

Sylvestris grapes are widely distributed over southern Europe and Western Asia (Map 2.1)—from the Atlantic coast of Spain and France to Tadzhikistan (de Lattin 1939, Levadoux 1956, Zohary and Spiegel-Roy 1975, Rivera Núñez and Walker 1989). They abound in the relatively mesic, northern fringes of the evergreen "maquis" vegetation belt in the Mediterranean basin; and they thrive as climbers in the broad-leaved forest belt along the mild and wet southern coasts of the Black Sea and of the Caspian Sea (the Euxinian and Hyrcanian vegetation regions). *Sylvestris* grapes also occur in some more xeric woodland areas in the Near East arc and (in some localities) in Central Asia. Here, however, the vines are usually confined to gorges and to the vicinity of streams. Scattered populations of sylvestris grapes also penetrate deeply into temperate Europe along the Rhine and the Danube. Paleobotanical finds indicate that during warmer phases in the Pleistocene and Holocene periods they extended even farther north.

In areas where *sylvestris* vines grow in close proximity to viticulture, the boundary between wild-types and cultivated varieties is frequently blurred by the occurrence of wild-looking escapees and by products of spontaneous hybridization between tame and wild. Such elements

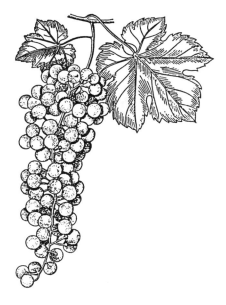

Figure 2.1. Wild gravevine *Vitis vinifera* subsp. *sylvestris*. (After Zapriagaeva 1964.)

usually occupy edges of cultivation, abandoned groves, roadsides, and similar manmade secondary habitats. As a consequence, *Vitis vinifera* comprises a variable complex of genuinely wild forms growing in primary habitats; seed propagated escapees and hybrid derivatives which thrive mainly in disturbed surroundings; and vegetatively propagated cultivated clones, planted in vineyards. Often it is difficult (even impossible) to distinguish morphologically between true wild forms and secondary "weedy" forms. Moreover, it is very probable that the pre-agriculture distribution of wild *sylvestris* vines has been extended by feral or naturalized forms. However, there can be little doubt that *sylvestris* vines are indigenous to southern Europe, to the Near East, and to the Euxinian–Hyrcanian belt. This notion is supported by paleobotanical and pre-horticulture archaeological finds.

Vitis vinifera is the sole Mediterranean and West Asiatic representative of the genus *Vitis*. This is a rather large genus comprising several dozen species (de Lattin 1939; Levadoux 1956; Olmo 1976 and chapter 3 herein). More than half of them are centered in North America; the rest, excluding *V. vinifera*, are distributed through East and Central Asia. All species of *Vitis* are perennial woody climbers with coiled tendrils; all have $2n = 38$ chromosomes and can be easily cross-fertilized with one another. In nature, *Vitis* species are reproductively isolated from one another not by cross-incompatibility or hybrid sterility, but by geographical and ecological barriers. In some parts of northern America and East Asia, this reproductive isolation is not complete and the boundaries between different wild species are blurred by hybridization. This makes the delimitation of *Vitis* species a difficult task.

Before the European colonization of North America, viticulture in the Old World was based solely on the gene pool present in *V. vinifera*. Thereafter, however, several additional wild grape species native to North America have been used in grape breeding programs, either as genetic resources for developing hardier varieties or for acquiring phylloxera-resistant stocks. The latter saved European viticulture from the ravages of this root aphid a century ago.

3. The Impact of Cultivation

Comparison between the wild forms and the cultivated varieties of *Vitis vinifera* show that domestication resulted in drastic changes in the reproductive biology of the plant. Critical was the shift from sexual reproduction (in the wild) to vegetative propagation (under domestication). Under domestication, the grapevine was also changed from a dioecious plant (separate male and female individuals) into a hermaphroditic crop, which is able to pollinate itself and thus set fruit without the need for outside pollination.

Wild *sylvestris* grapes reproduce from seed. Because they are dioecious, they are also allogamous (cross-pollinated). Under such a reproductive system, wild grapevine populations maintain considerable genetic polymorphism and manifest wide variability. Consequently, seedlings raised from most mother plants segregate widely in numerous traits, including size, shape, color, juiciness, sweetness, and palatability of the berries.

In contrast, cultivated varieties of grapevine are maintained vegetatively, either by rooting of twigs (the earlier, more primitive device), or by grafting (the more advanced technique). In the hand of the grower, the invention of vegetative propagation has been a powerful device to prevent genetic segregation and to maintain or "fix" desired types. By avoiding seed-planting and inventing clonal propagation, the cultivator was able to select, in a single act, exceptional individuals with superior fruit traits from among a large number of variable, less attractive individuals; and to maintain, and multiply, the few chosen types as clones. In other words, vegetative propagation made possible the planting of groves consisting of genetically identical superior plants. This is no small achievement. Because *Vitis* plants in nature are cross-pollinated and strongly heterozygous, most progeny obtained from seed (even those derived from superior individuals) are economically worthless and produce inferior berries. For most fruit crops, the change from seed planting to vegetative propagation has been a practical solution to avoid wide genetic segregation and maintain a steady supply of the desired types. In the grapevine, this invention made cultivation possible!

As already mentioned, the second conspicuous change in the reproductive biology of *Vitis* was the shift from dioecy to hermaphrodism. Wild populations of grapes usually contain equal numbers of male individuals (in which the flowers contain only anthers) and female individuals (in which the flowers bear only pistils). In contrast to the wild-types, flowers of nearly all cultivated varieties have both anthers and pistils. Such hermaphroditic flowers facilitate self-pollination and make possible fruit-setting without the need for male pollinators. In other words, the breakdown of wild-type bisexuality and the shift to hermaphroditic flowers freed the cultivator from the need to supply the plantation with male plants and/or to resort to artificial pollination (as is the practice for the date palm and the fig). This is a major advantage under cultivation.

Bisexuality in wild *sylvestris* plants is governed by a single gene (Olmo 1976 and chapter 3 herein). Female individuals are homogametic, i.e., they carry a homozygous recessive genotype Su^mSu^m which suppresses the development of anthers. Male plants are heterozygous for a dominant, pistil-suppressing Su^F allele and have a Su^FSu^m genotype. The shift, under domestication, to hermaphrodism was attained by a single mutation to Su^+, which is dominant over Su^m, and brings about the development of both pistil and anthers in each flower. Many cultivated hermaphroditic clones are still heterozygous and show a Su^+Su^m constitution; others have a Su^+Su^+ genotype.

Occasionally one encounters also female Su^mSu^m cultivated grapevine clones. Such female cultivars can set numerous berries provided they are interplanted with hermaphroditic cultivars and receive their pollen. Female cultivated clones are not necessary old relics. Many of them seem to be secondary derivatives picked up by growers from among segregating progenies of heterozygous Su^+Su^m hermaphroditic cultivars.

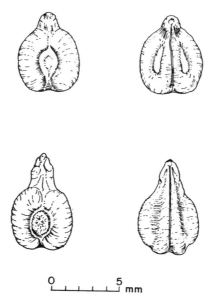

0 ⌊_____⌋ 5 mm

Figure 2.2. Representative pips of wild *sylvestris* grape (upper row) and of cultivated *vinifera* grape (lower row), dorsal view on left, ventral view on right. (Renfrew 1973; figs. 79–80.)

Finally, *sylvestris* grapes differ from the cultivated varieties by their relatively smaller and frequently less juicy and/or more acid berries. Most wild grapes also have rounder pips with relatively short beaks, while the seeds in cultivated varieties tend to be more elongated and with longer beaks (Fig. 2.2). Since pips are the main element retrieved in archaeological excavations, the appearance of relatively elongated, long-beaked pips was considered by several archaeobotanists as a sure sign for grapevine cultivation. However, since both the wild forms and the cultivated varieties manifest wide variation and much overlapping in the shape of their seeds, pip morphology cannot be considered as a fully dependable diagnostic feature. Reliability depends on the size of the samples and on how well developed is this "domestication trait" in the material examined (see also discussion in chapter 16 herein by Renfrew). In some cases, particularly when numerous pips can be measured), the breadth/length ratio suggests domestication. But in numerous other instances (when only few seeds are available), the morphological differences encountered are statistically not significant and do not give reliable distinctions. Recently, Smith and Jones (1990) pointed out another complicating factor. They charred seeds of cultivated grapevine artificially and found that under certain heating conditions the breadth/length ratios of those seeds were deformed to resemble those of the more rounded pips of wild grapes.

4. Archaeological Finds

Carbonized grape pips have been uncovered in numerous prehistoric Neolithic sites in Europe and the Near East (for the enumeration of sites, consult Rivera Núñez and Walker 1989, and the various regional surveys in van Zeist et al. 1991). Almost all Neolithic remains, however come from sites situated within the present range of distribution of wild *sylvestris* grapes; and the morphology of these pips conforms fully with that of the wild forms. As already argued by Zohary

(1993: 145), these finds do not provide definite evidence for grapevine cultivation. Until more definite evidence is forthcoming, these early remains should be regarded as representing berries collected from the wild.

The earliest convincing indications for *Vitis vinifera* cultivation come from Chalcolithic (ca. 3700–3200 bc non-calibrated radiocarbon time) and Early Bronze Age (ca. 3200–1900 bc) sites in the Levant. Charred pips were recovered (together with olive stones) in Chalcolithic (mid-4th millennium bc) Tell esh-Shuna (North) in the Jordan Valley (R. Neef, personal communication); and parched berries, containing 2–3 pips, were discovered in Early Bronze (ca. 3200 bc) Jericho (Hopf 1983). These finds are complemented by grapevine remains in Early Bronze Arad (Hopf 1978) and Lachish (Helbaek 1958) in Israel and from Numeira (McCreery 1979) in Jordan. Jericho yielded not only pips, but also two samples of charred wood. At Numeira, numerous pips and hundreds of whole berries were discovered. The fruits are quite small and the pips roundish and short-beaked. These five sites in Isreal and Jordan, however, are situated geographically in relatively dry regions—far outside the present-day natural range of *sylvestris* grapes. It is also unlikely that such xeric districts (south Judea, the lower Jordan Valley, and the Dead Sea basin) supported wild grapes in the 4th or 3rd millennia bc As stressed by Zohary and Hopf (1993: 148), this is strong circumstantial evidence indicating that by second half of the 4th millennium bc *V. vinifera* was already under cultivation in the southern Levant. Furthermore, the ability to maintain grapevines in environments very different from those in which *sylvestris* plants grow in nature should be taken as an indication for a well-established horticultural tradition.

Additional evidence for early cultivation of *V. vinifera* comes from the northern Levant, viz., from Kurban Höyük in Urfa province of southern Turkey. Here, pips of grapes were recorded (Miller 1991) from 5% of the samples collected from Late Chalcolithic levels. They increased to 10% of the samples in the Early Early Bronze Age levels. They appeared in 66% of the samples from mid– to late–Early Bronze Age levels. One mid– to late–Early Bronze Age deposit was filled with charred grape seeds, peduncles, and fruits. Very probably these data reflect a rapid growth of viticulture in the northern Levant from the end of the 4th millennium bc through the middle of the 3rd millennium bc.

Archaeobotanical finds become increasingly more common in later stages of Bronze Age in the Near East. These are complemented by an increasing number of presses, vessels for storing wine, and the artistic depiction of grapes and viniculture (Stager 1985). Fresh grapes, raisins, and wine are also recorded in the early Mesopotamian cuneiform sources, from the second half of the 3rd millennium bc onwards (Postgate 1987; see also Powell, Gorny, and Zettler and Miller, this volume).

Abundant evidence for early cultivation of grapevine comes from ancient Egypt. Remains of raisins and other evidence for wine production and importation appear in the Nile Valley by the start of the Old Kingdom (Stager 1985; see James, this volume). Grape pips were discovered in 1st Dynasty (ca. 2900 bc) tombs in Abydos and Nagada; and a rich find of fragments of raisins is available from the 3rd Dynasty (ca. 2600 bc) Djoser pyramid at Saqqara (Lauer et al. 1950; Germer 1985). Also, several hieroglyphic representations of the winepress are available from Old Kingdom tombs, whose furnishings include numerous purported wine jars (Stager 1985). Scenes of winemaking were found in tombs from the 5th Dynasty onwards (chapter by James, this volume). Since wild *Vitis* is totally absent in the Nile Valley, these finds demonstrate that the expansion of viticulture and/or the importation of raisins and wine from the Levant into Egypt were already an ongoing tradition by Early Bronze Age times.

In the Aegean area, definite signs of grapevine cultivation appear somewhat later (Hansen 1988; Zohary and Hopf 1993: 149; and Renfrew, chapter 16, this volume). In Thessaly and Macedonia, pips become so common at several Late Neolithic (ca. 4300–2800 bc) sites that Kroll (1991) remarks that their sheer numbers could suggest cultivation. The earliest convincing evidence, however, comes only from Early Helladic IV (ca. 2200–2000 bc). Lerna in southern Greece, where numerous pips approaching cultivated *vinifera* in their breadth/length ratio were recovered (Hopf 1961). Another clue comes from Sitagroi in northern Greece. Here, Renfrew (1973: 30) recovered pips in a series of levels dating about 4500 and 2000 bc, and observed a definite shift from *sylvestris*-like short-beaked material in Middle Neolithic levels to *vinifera*-like pips in Middle Bronze Age levels, suggesting the emergence of viticulture in Macedonia well before 2000 bc. But, as noted by Hansen (1988), the finds comprised only 32 seeds, and this is too small a sample for drawing safe conclusions.

Additional remains conforming in their shape to the cultivated grapevine were recovered from Middle and from Late Bronze Age Aegean sites (Hansen 1988; see chapter 16 herein by Renfrew). They include a rich find of several hundred elongated *vinifera*-type pips from Late Helladic Kastanas (ca. 1600–1000 bc; Kroll 1983). Parallel to the situation in the Levant, the development of grapevine cultivation in the Mycenaean and Minoan cultures is indicated by textural evidence of probable presses, and forms for storing and drinking wine (see Leonard, Wright, and Palmer, this volume).

Archaeobotanical documentation of Bronze Age *Vitis vinifera* is also available from Transcaucasia (Wasylikowa et al. 1991: 235). Pips showing the morphology of cultivated forms start to appear in Georgia in the Early Bronze Age (3rd millennium bc). They became common in the Middle and Late Bronze Ages (2nd and 1st millennia bc). In Armenia, *vinifera*-type pips were also frequently retrieved from 2nd millennium bc onwards.

Farther east, numerous grapevine seeds were recovered from Shahr-i Sokhta in eastern Iran (Costantini and Costantini-Biasini 1985; Miller 1991: 150). The mid–3rd millennium bc specimens have an average breadth/length ratio of over 0.60, whereas those from the late 3rd millennium bc are under 0.60, indicating cultivation.

Viticulture was apparently introduced to the western Mediterranean basin by Greek and Phoenician colonists (Stager 1985; see Greene, this volume). It was not until the expansion of the Roman Empire that this crop was brought to the Rhine Valley and to temperate Europe generally (Loeschcke 1933; König 1989).

5. Discussion of the Evidence

Attempts to reconstruct the domestication of the grapevine in the Old World are hindered by the following obstacles:

1. In contrast with many other Old World crops, the wild ancestor of the grapevine is distributed over vast areas (Map 2.1). Consequently, the distribution range of *sylvestris* grapes provide just a very general orientation as to where this progenitor could have been taken into cultivation.

2. The archaeobotanical documentation is still very uneven; the Levant and Greece, for example, have been intensively studied, as compared with Anatolia that lies in between them. In Caucausia, Transcaucasia and Iran, the available archaeobotanical evidence is far from sufficient.

3. Grape remains uncovered during excavations do not show fully dependable morphological features that could safely mark them as cultivated varieties and set them apart from material collected from the wild.

Thus, our knowledge of the start of grapevine cultivation and of the early spread of viticulture is still fragmentary, and the material evidence available is largely circumstantial. It is clear, however, that by the second half of the 4th millennium bc (non-calibrated radiocarbon time) viticulture had emerged as an integral part of food production in the Levant. Furthermore, as stressed by Zohary and Spiegel-Roy (1975), Stager (1985), and van Zeist (1991), the grapevine was not domesticated alone. It was a member of the "first fruits" of the Old World. Together with the olive, fig, and date-palm, fruit-growing became an established part of the Near Eastern economy. Exactly when clonal propagation-based horticulture was initiated is hard to say. Yet, the available evidence strongly suggests (Zohary and Hopf 1993: 235) that all four "first fruits" were already under cultivation in Chalcolithic times (ca. 3700–3200 bc). The fact that, already at this early period, remains of grapes and olives appear in sites far away from the distribution ranges of the wild progenitors indicates that this new technology was already well established. Very possibly, all these "first fruits" were taken into cultivation somewhat earlier. In other words, grapevine growing could have started in the Near East by the Late Neolithic (5th millennium bc).

The evidence from the living plants complements the archaeological finds. Since wild *sylvestris* grapes are widely spread over the Mediterranean basin and southwestern Asia, the distribution range of the wild ancestor does not permit a precise delimitation of the place of origin of the cultivated fruit crop. Yet, it may well be significant that wild forms—from which the cultivated clones could have been derived—thrive in wild niches in the Levant and southern Anatolia, i.e., in the same geographic region that archaeobotanical evidence suggests as the most plausable place for grapevine domestication.

CHAPTER 3

The Origin and Domestication of the *Vinifera* Grape

H. P. Olmo

1. Introduction

The *Vitis vinifera* grape is certainly one of the oldest of cultivated plants for which living progenitors still exist. The wide geographic range of the wild *sylvestris* and a bewildering number of different forms stretching from the western end of the Mediterranean basin to east of the Caspian Sea (see Maps 2.1 and 16.1, this volume) have intrigued historians and naturalists alike. The crucial question that has been posed is what is the relationship between these widely scattered populations to the origin and domestication of this grapevine? In addressing this question, one observation can easily be verified and needs to be stressed: the wild vines are disappearing at an alarming rate, and their study and preservation therefore should be given high priority. Within these wild populations and their derivatives are all the genes which have been juggled to produce the most civilized and enjoyable of all beverages—fine wine. Hopefully some of the ideas presented here may stimulate much-needed study of these gene resources, which can tell much more of the past and enlighten the future.

2. The Genus *Vitis*

The grape genus *Vitis* comprises three natural groups based on geographical location: North American, Eurasian, and Asiatic. Botanists list some 25 to 30 species of American origin, about the same number for Asia, but only a single species for Eurasia, the *vinifera*, which has contributed the most to the advancement of grape culture throughout the world. Most of these species occupy the temperate zone of the northern hemisphere, and are typically most abundant in forested areas of relatively high rainfall. Unfortunately, the enumeration of species is far from complete. According to Zhang et al. (1990: 50), "nearly half of the 80 or so species of *Vitis* in the world are native to China (and ten more new species yet to be published) some of which have been directly used in winemaking industry or used for breeding, or as rootstock." These species are described as distinctly different than *vinifera*.

In contrast to the American and Asian vines, the wild populations of *vinifera* in Europe are now almost extinct, occurring in widely separated clumps, often reduced to a few vines in protected localities. In the presumed eastern boundary of the Transcaucasian region, they are more plentiful. The present distribution of wild (spontaneous) *vinifera* is thought to be the remnants of a much wider distribution, which survived in refuges during the glacial periods. In more recent times, the expansion of vast deserts in North America, North Africa, and Central Asia restricted the natural *Vitis* even more and created a barrier to its southern migration. Remaining populations in North Africa are not far inland from the Mediterranean coast or in mountainous areas of Morocco.

Within the last century, the loss of many wild *vinifera* vines has accelerated. This has been attributed to the introduction of pests from North America, to which the *vinifera* is very susceptible (Levadoux 1956: 63). In many cases, however, the natural habitat formerly suited to the vine has been destroyed by removal of forests and by grazing, as well as the natural phenomena associated with climatic change (colder and drier periods have restricted growth). The establishment of new seedlings is also becoming a rarity. The number of wild vines in the Upper Rhine has greatly diminished, and the former variability described by Bronner (1857) no longer exists (Schumann 1974). For example, in a population classified at Ketsch by Schumann, 15 vines were male; of 15 fruit-bearing plants, three were female and one was a hermaphrodite.

Levadoux (1954, 1956) classifies populations of *vinifera* vines that apparently grow in the wild but may derive from domesticated populations as "lambrusque" (literally, "wild vine"). He distinguishes three types:

1. Post-cultural, in which cultivated vines were previously cultivated and have been abandoned.

2. Subspontaneous, in which vines become established in non-cultivated areas from the seeds of cultivated ones.

3. Spontaneous, in which the vines are present as part of the natural flora.

In turn, the last of these types is subdivided into (a) Colonials: vines that have reached a favorable natural environment and reverted to the natural state; (b) Autochtones: indigenous vines descended from ancestors that have never been cultivated; and (c) Métisses: vines resulting from hybridization of autochtones with one or other of the groups listed.

Levadoux was principally interested in establishing the fact that all wild populations represented forms of the single *vinifera* species, to counteract the trend started by Gmelin in 1805 of naming wild vines of the Middle Rhine Valley as a separate species, *sylvestris*.

3. The Comparative Morphology of Wild and Cultivated *Vitis vinifera* L.

Comparisons of wild vines with associated varieties cultivated in the same area have been undertaken frequently, especially in Southern Europe. Although the high variability of many characters has been noted, the number of individual vines available for comparison is limited and sometimes inaccessible. Nonetheless, in reviewing the fragmented reports and also visiting and noting the behavior of seedling populations, a general consensus of the most striking differences emerges (Table 3.1).

Since reproduction is most closely related to fruit production, and hence early domestication, the inflorescence and its behavior is of prime importance. Levadoux (1956: 63) lists the dioecious character of the wild vine as the most important characteristic that distinguishes it from the cultivated forms which are hermaphroditic. The more primitive genera of the *Vitaceae* are

Table 3.1

Comparative Morphology of Wild and Cultivated *Vitis vinifera* L

	Wild (*sylvestris typica*)	Cultivated (*sativa*)
Trunk	Often branches, slender, bark separates in very long thin strips, less deciduous.	Thick bark separates in wider and more coherent strips.
Canes	Slender, long internodes, flexible hard wood, round in cross-section, tendrils very wiry and very strongly coiled, dormant buds, small pointed apex, scales tightly sealed.	Large diameter, shorter internodes, elliptical cross-section; tendrils larger and more extended, coiling more at terminal ends; dormant buds large and more prominent, apex flattened, scales loosely sealed.
Leaves	Small, usually deeply three-lobed, to entire; petioles short and slender, dull aspects; petiolar sinus wide and open.	Large, many entire or with shallow sinuses; petiole thick, glabrous to downy, many with shiny aspect, petiolar sinus partly closed.
Inflorescence	Vines dioecious, rarely polygamodioecious. Males (♂) have fertile pollen, but are not fruitful; females (♀) are pollen sterile, and require cross-pollination for fruiting. Reversion males (♂→♀̂) in exceptional cases in which males develop ovaries and function as hermaphrodites.	Vines usually hermaphroditic, very few are females (♀). Self-pollination is the rule in hermaphrodites.
Fruit clusters	Small, globular to conical, loose, irregular set, berry maturity variable in cluster, berries dehiscent, peduncle very long and slender.	Large, elongated, compact to well-fitted, berries uniform in maturity, firmly attached, peduncle thick and rigid.
Berries	Small, round or oblate, few elongate, black, rarely white; skin resistant, highly pigmented, astringent; high seed content; juice watery, high in acid, low in sugar.	Large, oval to ellipsoidal, wide range of color, with decrease in pigment; few seeds, number variable; moderate acidity and sugar content.
Seeds	Small, rounded body, high width/length ratio (>0.70), highly viable, beak short.	Large, pyriform body, lower width/length ratio (<0.60), low viability, beak long, very variable in size and shape.

hermaphroditic, i.e., both pistil and stamens are fully developed in the same small flower, and are so arranged that self-pollination is the rule. We assume therefore that primitive *Vitis* was likewise hermaphroditic at some early point.

In contrast, wild *Vitis* is is dioecious. Some vines bear only female flowers with fully developed pistils, their anther filaments are short or reflexed and have sterile pollen. These plants must receive pollen from a male vine to be fruitful. The male vine has functional pollen in abundance, but the pistil is much reduced in size and abortive, and therefore unfruitful. The degree of abortion is variable; only in exceptional cases is fruit produced. Both female and male flowers, however,

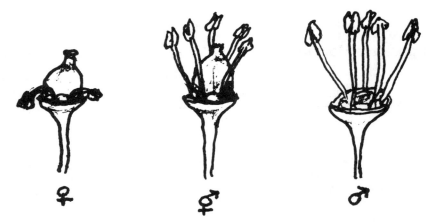

Figure 3.1. Flower types in *Vitis*: a) functional female (anthers with refined or coiled filaments); b) hermaphrodite (perfect flower); c) functional male (pistil rudimentary).

retain the organs of the more primitive hermaphrodites, although in a more rudimentary stage of development. Levadoux (1946) has classified the types of males (androids) according to the development of the pistil, and notes that normal development occasionally can occur due to extrinsic factors, in which the plants bear fruit (fertile android). The genetic determination of sexual flower type is dependent on three genes or alleles at the same locus of the chromosome. The effect of the genes is to suppress the development of the male or female organs. Suppression of male development is a recessive mutation, Su^m. Suppression of female development is a dominant mutation. Su^F. Su^+Su^+ is the hermaphrodite, primitive type. Dominance relationships are Su^F (♂) > Su^+ (⚥) > Su^m (♀). The flower types are illustrated in Figure 3.1.

Secondary sexual characteristics are often observed in endemic populations of *Vitis* that are seldom observed in the cultivated forms. Male vines produce inflorescences which are much larger and more numerous than those on female vines. A collection of *vinifera* vines, used in the study of sex conversion of male vines, showed these characteristics (Negi and Olmo 1971a). Male vines also blossom in advance, and continue to produce pollen over a longer period of time than female vines.

One of the most significant changes brought about by grapevine isolation and selection is the shift from a cross-pollinating and dioecious species to flowers which are self-pollinated and fruitful. This circumstance is also reflected in the poor development and loss of function of the nectaries in cultivated forms, so that they are no longer attractive to pollinating insects. The few female varieties in culture depend largely on wind pollination, which is only effective when blossoming occurs in warm and dry weather and the pollen moves over relatively short distances. Wild male vines propagated as clones for long periods of time attract pollen-gathering insects, usually honeybees.

4. The Classification of *Vinifera* Cultivars and Varieties

In studying the geography of the grapevine, ampelographers, noticing resemblances between certain widely dispersed cultivated varieties, began to speak of families or groups of varieties. The most provocative effort has been that of M. A. Negrul, a disciple of N. I. Vavilov (1926, 1931), the latter renowned as the protagonist of the world centers of origin of cultivated plants. The basic concept is that the primary center for a given plant is its region of greatest genetic diversity.

Negrul (1946) had the opportunity to collect and describe a large number of *vinifera* varieties in both Europe and Central Asia. He subdivided the varieties according to geographic area, morphological characters, and physiological reactions, denoting them "proles" (best translated as ecotypes). The following summary of the varieties is based on Levadoux (1956: 96–97), as he interpreted Negrul's work.

1. *Occidentalis* — France, Germany, Spain, and Portugal. Varieties typical of many of the wine grapes of Western Europe, with small compact clusters; leaves with arachnoid hairiness; small berries, white or black, medium sugar content and high acidity; vine very productive and cold tolerant. Example: Pinot noir.

2. *Orientalis* — Central Asia, Iran, Afghanistan, Armenia, and Azerbaijan. Low cluster number; glabrous or setose shoot tips; glabrous leaves, mostly entire; berry large and elongate, meaty flesh, mostly white, but many red, low acidity; seed medium to large, with long beak, some seedless; vine with low resistance to cold; long growing season. Example: Thompson Seedless (Sultanina).

3. *Pontica* — Asia Minor, Greece, Hungary, Romania, Georgia, and Bessarabia: Cluster medium, compact; leaves with mixed hairiness, or arachnoid and felted type on lower surface; berry usually round, medium size, juicy; white, red, and black about equally represented; seeds small to very large, many partially seedless. Vine very fruitful, many clusters per shoot; mostly wine grape types, with medium sugar content and high acidity. Seed from self-pollination often produces bizarre leaf types and dwarfism in the progeny. Example: Saperavi.

Several subclasses of these varieties were defined by Negrul ccording to the field studies of natural populations of *vinifera*. Wild populations in the northern and western part of the range have mostly a three-lobed leaf, with very shallow sinuses and cobwebby hairs, and are referred to as *occidentalis* var. *typica* Negrul. To the south and east, in Azerbaijan and Turkmenistan, the leaves are glabrous or felted, and are classified as *orientalis* var. *aberrans* Negrul. *Occidentalis* var. *balkanica* Negrul occurs in Bulgaria, along the Black Sea basin; its vines have cuneiform leaves, with a very dense short tomentum mixed with cobwebby hairs.

Negrul concluded that the *V. sylvestris* Gmel. is taxonomically equivalent to the cultivated forms of *vinifera*, and that a continuous series of variations between them prove their identity. In exploring the grape populations of Central Asia to the southeast of Tajikistan, in the regions of Koulab, Garm and Darvaz, Negrul (1960) described primitive types that were supported on native fruit trees, as well as wild and semi-cultivated forms in the mountain valleys up to elevations of 1500 m. above sea level. He concluded that the cultivated forms were of aboriginal origin peculiar to each locality, and were propagated by seed; vegetative propagation was rarely practiced. After studying specimens and reviewing the historical and archaeological data, he repudiated the earlier conclusions of I. T. Vassilchenko (1955) of the existence of relict species in Tajikistan and western Tian-Shan, such as *V. hissarica* Vass. and *V. schischukinii* Vass. Negrul questioned whether these and other authors had actually examined vines in the flowering season, to verify that male vines were not present in the spontaneous populations.

In 1963, an expedition to Bulgaria was organized by Negrul et al. (1965) to study the wild vines of the littoral of the Black Sea and in the Strandge Mountains. During the flowering period, 146 vines were examined, of which 67 were male and 71 female; eight had no flowers. No hermaphrodites were found. Examinations which were made in the autumn on 518 vines from seven different habitats along the Black Sea, eight habitats in the Strandge range, five habitats in the valleys of the Balkans, and three neighboring the Danube showed that the wild vines had lax clusters of small black berries and leaves with arachnoid hairiness (var. *typica* Negrul), with glabrous or setose hairiness (var. *aberrans* Negrul), or, most commonly, a mixed type of pubescence (var. *balkanica* Negrul). On the whole, the populations approached local cultivated varieties in both leaf and fruit characters. The wild vines appear to represent an ancient, primitive species from which the hermaphroditic cultivars arose.

Seeds were large and beaked in the wild populations of Bulgaria, which is also more typical of cultivated varieties. The wild grape populations of Nuristan, in the northeast mountainous country of Afghanistan, need further study, since the dioecy expected in the wild vine has not been verified. I have made several trips to the northwestern province of India (now part of West Pakistan) and did not find wild *vinifera*, although other very different wild *Vitis* are present, such as *Vitis lanata* and *Vitis jacquemontii*. These are distinctly different from *vinifera*. A joint expedition (Thompson et al. 1989) to collect fruit and nut germ plasm in northern West Pakistan, mostly following the Indus River canyon and the southern flanks of the Himalaya chain, found *vinifera* cultivated in many villages, but did not locate wild plants, although other wild *Vitis* were present.

Based on the distribution of wild and domesticated varieties of *vinifera*, the sequence in the domestication of the *vinifera* grape can be summarized, according to Levadoux (1956: 10), as follows:

1. *Vitis vinifera* was already in existence during the final stages of the Tertiary period or at the beginning of the Quaternary as attested by fossils in many locations of western Europe and the Mediterranean Basin.

2. During the Pleistocene period, fossil evidence suggests that *vinifera* survived in the forests circling the Mediterranean and along the southern shores of the Caspian Sea. Populations became isolated during many hundreds of millennia, evolving in different directions.

3. In the Neolithic period, *vinifera* occupied almost the same distribution although more restricted by climatic fluctuations, as at present. The primitive polymorphism and dioecious liana of the forests remained intact because of heterozygosity.

4. Cereal agriculture was first developed in the Near East between the 9th and 6th millennia B.C., eventually spreading to other parts of the Mediterranean Basin and Europe.

5. The domesticated culture of *vinifera* appeared ca. 8000–6000 B.C. in Transcaucasia.

6. Towards the end of the 5th millennium B.C., grape culture spread to the Aegean, Mesopotamia, Syria, and Egypt.

7. In the course of the 1st millennium B.C., the culture of *vinifera* began in central and northern Italy, France (Provence), North Africa, and Spain.

8. One variety of *vinifera sylvestris aberrans* Negrul, at the extremity of the range, appeared to dominate in the sub-Caspian region. Elsewhere in Europe, Anatolia and North Africa, and to the west of the Caucasus, only *sylvestris typica* Negrul was found. These varieties were not homogeneous, and developed different ecotypes, as verified in the Danube and Rhine River valleys, and elsewhere. Hybridization between neighboring ecotypes cannot be excluded. The genesis of ecotypes in the more temperate zones of Portugal, France, and the Rhineland can be envisaged.

In the evolution of the domesticated culture, man interceded to improve the vines. The goal in selection was to increase fruit production and improve palatability. Crosses between cultivated and wild vines modified the primitive aspects of the populations.

The classification of Negrul established three general groups of *vinifera* vines. According to his basic assumptions, certain geographical areas could be defined broadly, although not precisely. Much to the chagrin of the Italians, their numerous varieties were not even mentioned nor included within the classifications and North African varieties are likewise omitted. The principal difficulty was that mostly cultivated varieties were being compared on the basis of morphological and physiological characteristics. The fact that many cultivars had resulted from hybridization in one area and were then transported to another, even evolving further in the interim, could not be ascertained. The edicts of rulers and religious bodies, in particular following the Islamic conquest, drastically altered the variety composition in many areas. For example, the preponderance of table grape types in the *orientalis* group possibly may be explained by the Koran's prohibition of wine production and the use of alcohol.

The difficulty in classifying varieties prompted Negrul to study populations of the wild vines in their natural habitat and compare them with indigenous varieties that were being cultivated nearby. This was a more logical approach and resulted in further subdivisions, particularly in the *pontica* and *orientalis* categories. For example, it has become evident, as more populations of wild *vinifera* have been studied, that the *pontica* group is an intermediate or transitional between *occidentalis* and *orientalis* in most of its characteristics. This would be expected by the introgression of the *orientalis* forms as they migrated westward, with their gene exchange diminishing over distance. Here again, Islamic regimes favored the introduction of the larger berried table grapes, which were adapted to desert climates.

5. The Hypothetical Stages of Domestication

The first exploitation of *vinifera* would most likely occur in areas where the wild vine was part of the native flora. Two requirements were uppermost for grapevine domestication: a dependable source of water (if not naturally provided, then suitable for irrigation), and protection of the vine from grazing animals, principally goats and sheep. The first requirement was best met at fairly high elevations in mountain valleys where perpetual streams were fed by melting snows from very high mountain ranges during the summer. The southern slopes of east–west ranges were also preferable because they are protected from damaging arctic air masses. Vines especially required protection if the supporting forest canopy were destroyed by fire or lumbering.

The selection and sparing of individual vines in their natural forest or riparian habitat was based largely on the fruitfulness of the vine and its regularity of production. Regularity of production would have been especially important to early hunters and gatherers, who followed routes that brought them back to the same areas year after year. Possibly, the tree or other support for the vine was slashed or otherwise marked. If wild fruit were very abundant in one vicinity, then the quality of fruit, principally its sweetness, might have assumed greater importance.

One may envision the following developmental sequence. When permanent habitation began in an area, some wild fruit trees and vines were probably retained, assuming that the forest had not been thinned out to supply fuel and open pasture land. An area close to a residence might then be enclosed by mud walls, stone boundaries, or thorny brush to exclude trespassers, both animal and human. Trees might have been left on the boundary lines, especially along small streams of water used for irrigation. Such an enclosure eventually became a more diversified garden where seeds and plants could be propagated. Yet, the idea of a natural symbiosis of the forest tree and the grapevine might also have continued, so that deciduous fruit and other trees were used to support the vines, and propagated by transplanting a naturally rooted layer from an older vine or by partially burying dormant canes in a trench alongside the tree. In fact, in some viticultural areas, the traditional culture of vines supported on living trees continues, e.g., the Vinho Verde district of northern Portugal and in numerous mountain villages of Central Asia. Such a garden might soon take on the aspect of a thicket-like jungle. Cultivation and considerable pruning was necessary to allow passage between plants. In order to contain the vines within a restricted area, it was likely discovered that the vine responded to a heavy reduction of the dormant growth, thereby yielding more and better fruit. Moreover, the fruit could then be harvested without climbing the tree, which certainly offset the disadvantage of pruning.

As viticulture spread from the forest edges to the dry and hot desert areas of the interior, the vine prospered and was grown without support, often simply spreading over the surface of the ground from a very short trunk. Without sufficient rainfall, irrigation would have been necessary in some areas. This was more efficiently accomplished on gently sloping land, which also afforded larger expanses of vineyard. Production in excess of local needs was then possible, and commercial viticulture expanded as a monoculture, with a small number of specialized varieties, each adapted for specific products and markets.

One fact of considerable importance is that the *vinifera* grapevine in its feral state supplied an abundance of palatable and nutritious fruit, especially in the eastern part of its range. Most of the other common fruits in their wild state were hardly so appetizing, such as the very small, hard-fleshed, acidic and astringent figs, apples and pears, or the bitter almonds and the rock-hard walnuts with minute morsels of edible matter. The extensive fossil record of seeds of the *vinifera* type (below), point to a widespread distribution of the plant well before permanent human settlements were established, and it would be unreasonable to expect that early humans did not avail themselves of this resource, even as happens to this day. Indeed, the domestication of the *vinifera* type vine could well have antedated that of cereals, which require a longer seasonal presence to cultivate, sow, harvest, and process the grain.

6. The Paleontological Evidence for *Vinifera*

The fossil seeds of the vine which were incorporated into sedimentary or other geological deposits furnish the best evidence of the presence and early evolution of the *vinifera* grapevine. The unique morphology of the seed survives to a remarkable degree, and the bony structure can often survive desiccation and carbonization, yet still retain its form (see Zohary and Renfrew, this volume). Leaf imprints, however, are less informative, since they can resemble other plants and result in uncertain identification. Leaf morphology is very variable, especially the degree of lobing, and uniform methods of sampling cannot be utilized by the palaeobotanist.

Seed size and the width/length ratio have been used frequently by paleontologists to distinguish the wild *vinifera* from domesticated forms. The idea stems from Stummer (1961), who measured 200 seeds from wild vines near Klosterneuberg, in Austria, and compared them to the seven cultivated varieties in local culture. Although there was considerable overlap in the distribution, the range of the width-to-length ratio was 0.44 to 0.53 for cultivated populations and 0.76 to 0.83 for the wild ones. Levadoux (1956: 63) considered this difference in seed dimensions to be one of the "absolute" characters for separating spontaneous *vinifera* from cultivated forms. He notes (1956: 69) "Si dans la pratique son utilization peut conduire à de nombreuses erreurs, en particulier, ce qui est parfois le cas en phytopaléontologie, lorsqu'on ne possède qu'un échantillon, il n'en reste pas moins vrai que nous semblons nous trouver en présence d'un caractère spécifique remarquable."

The use of the index has recently been reviewed by Rivera Núñez et al. (1989), in order to justify a theory of prehistoric exploitation of spontaneous *vinifera* in Spain and the western Mediterranean, which also challenges the assumption that the domesticated grape originated in Transcaucasia.

The morphology and cellular structure of the seed coats are unique within each species, and can be used as a means of identification. Unfortunately, only the grosser outlines have received attention and more detailed studies on the tissue anatomy and cell structure, including biochemical assays, have not been carried out .

The report of Miki (1956), on the fossil seeds of the *Vitaceae* family in Japan, are of great interest, since they are compared with their living counterparts, according to morphological patterns that are often neglected in identification. Even then, Miki confesses to misidentifications made in a previous study. No *vinifera* type seeds have been reported from Eastern Asia.

Other attempts to identify fossil grape seeds by comparing them with existing species have yielded promising results (Tiffney and Barghoorn 1976). The Brandon Lignite has been the focus of continuous investigation by Barghoorn and collaborators since 1947. This restricted deposit is of particular interest since it represents the only known Tertiary bed containing plant megafossils north of New Jersey in eastern North America, approximately 230 km northwest of Boston in the state of Vermont. Fossil seeds (106 specimens), closely resembling *Vitis rotundifolia*, were collected from lignite. Only slight differences were noted between modern and fossil specimens. The grooves radiating from the chalaza were less pronounced in fossil material, whereas the chalaza itself was thinner and more parenchymatous in the cross-section of modern specimens. The fossil form was comparable to that described by Berry in 1910 from the Pleistocene in New Jersey as *V. pseudo-rotundifolia*.

In addition to *rotundifolia*, the fossil species *Vitis eolabrusca* compared to modern *labrusca*. A new species of fossil, *Vitis brandoniana*, was based on only two seeds. The authors state, "the rarity, poor preservation and generalized morphology of these specimens cause hesitation in comparing them to a modern species.... Seed shape alone cannot be used as a definitive characteristic, and the effect of shape on other morphological characters occasionally renders taxonomic interpretations difficult." Paleobotanists must remain aware that fossil remains of *Vitis* in the same distribution range as existing wild *vinifera* may well represent other species that are now extinct.

The principal means of natural seed dispersal, at least of the small-berried wine grapes, are migratory birds (Martin et al. 1961). Losses of crop in commercial vineyards are often reported, especially if roosting areas are provided by adjacent trees or forested areas. The seeds remain viable after passing through the alimentary tract, and are voided when the birds alight in the trees. Occasional seedling vines may become established under a tree where partial shade and enough moisture permits germination, eventual growth, and then attachment to the lower branches. However, lack of sufficient moisture in the springtime due to competition of annual plants reduces successful establishment to a rarity. The exceptional opportunity for seedling survival exists on newly washed silty deposits on the edges of stream banks or pools not yet colonized by other plants, yet partly shaded by overhanging shrubbery.

7. The Reproduction of Wild versus Cultivated Vines

Cultivated vines are easily reproduced asexually by cuttings, layering, or grafting, and can retain many lethal and detrimental genes. In general, the longer the time a given clone is propagated, the greater is the load of recessive deleterious mutations which become apparent on self-pollination. Inbreeding depression is often observed, especially negative effects on gametes, seed development, germination, and later reduced plant vigor and fruitfulness.

Progenies of feral species on the other hand are derived from cross-breeding, and are more uniform and homozygous than cultivated types. Seedling vines derived from crossing different American species are usually much alike in the first generation. Some early breeders of rootstock vines in Europe lumped vines of similar appearance under the same identification number, and later workers testing their performance found them to be mixtures of clones, rather than a single genotype.

Heterozygosity has been alluded to by Levadoux (1956) as a factor in explaining the polymorphism found in spontaneous populations of *vinifera*, presumably because of the enforced cross-pollination of these vines. Based on our experience in growing seedling vines from some of these populations, progeny of great uniformity can be produced. This seems to indicate that, even though cross-fertilization is mandatory, it is confined to short distances and essentially an inbred population can result. Wind-pollination is not too effective. Female varieties, when grown in solid blocks and interplanted with pollinators, do not produce reliable fruit crops, and hand-pollination must be resorted to. Almeria in southern Spain is an example of a female variety requiring such hand-pollination.

There is a paucity of information concerning the role of insect pollinators in both wild and cultivated forms of *Vitis*. Honey bees and syrphid flies are very active on male vines in California. They feed on and collect pollen. On the other hand, they rarely visit female varieties; apparently nectaries are abortive and offer no incentive. I do not know of any study on the pollination mechanism in wild *vinifera*. In forested areas, both male and female vines may grow in close proximity, and male vines often are more vigorous and produce canopies in the higher trees and shed pollen in considerable quantity on other plants below. Fruiting lateral canes of female vines are often pendant because of the weight of fruit, and thus hang below the canopy of male vines above.

The discovery by Negi and Olmo (1966, 1971a,b) that some wild male vines from Azerbaijan can revert and function as self-pollination hermaphrodites. The seed matures and germinates well. The progeny are very uniform, and no deleterious recessives have been noted. Classification of the progeny verifies the fact that the genetic constitution of the male is Su^FSu^m, since the following ratio of three males to one female has been obtained: $1Su^FSu^F$ (♂) : $2Su^FSu^m$ (♂) : $1 Su^mSu^m$ (♀). The occurrence of some flowers undergoing sex conversion in some wild vines would explain the puzzling observations that the ratio of males to females generally exceeds the expected theoretical ratio of 1 : 1. Thus, in one most recent Italian count of wild vines, 70 males and 30 females were reported (Scienza et al. 1986). This condition exists in other *Vitis* species as well.

8. The Evolution of Cultivars

The great genetic diversity between *vinifera* cultivars, of which as many as 10,000 have been estimated in the world collection, is still further complicated by the rather unique complexity that exists within the cultivar itself. French workers prefer to use the term "cepage," which essentially is a population of clones, each being genetically different from the other. Pinot noir, for example, is considered to be a population of several hundred clones. The breeding technique for selecting the most useful variants and comparing their performance has been called clonal selection.

Although the nature of these mutations and their inheritance has received scant attention, they are mostly confined to somatic tissue, thus bypassing the segregation of many genes via sexual reproduction that would lead to very different results and much larger deviations from the parental types. Since gene mutation is time-related, they would tend to accumulate in old cultivars. Their recognition would presumably become more frequent with the increase in the number of vines propagated, as well as being a function of human curiosity and understanding. A factor of considerable importance is the relative ease of propagation of dormant cuttings, and the repeated and excessive segmentation of the vine tissue by pruning, thus enabling new outgrowths and releasing mutant genes to express themselves by somatic segregation. The chimeral nature of the grapevine growing tip (Thompson and Olmo 1963), consisting of a core and an outer epidermal layer, each derived from different anlagen, results in the perpetuation of two genetic systems side by side. But a shift in tissue development may result in rearrangements that expose genetic types previously trapped within the core.

The grapevine is also very different from deciduous fruit trees in the growth pattern of the shoot. The shoot tip dies back when growth conditions become unfavorable, and new growth is then resumed from lateral buds, thus activating many new growing points from older tissue. Bud meristems may become buried in older tissues of the trunk (latent buds) for many years and are capable of regeneration after pruning.

A study of the origin and course of evolution of wine grapes, even the most noble varieties, is beset with difficulty. Ancient naturalists and historians may have sometimes used names, but interpretation is difficult and adequate descriptions are unfortunately lacking. Similar morphological features or phenotypes do not always reflect a similar genotype.

If one were to choose a well-known variety that best illustrates a close resemblance to the wild type, it would be the Cabernet-Sauvignon, not the Cabernet franc or Carmenet, which long preceded the former in culture in southwestern France. It is intriguing that the French "sauvignon" vine might have derived from a wild vine, but this may only mean the vine shows characteristics that recall a rampant and unkempt truant. Only tedious and persistent study of the genotypes via DNA analysis may provide the critical evidence in determining variety descent (Striem et al. 1990).

9. Hybridization and Introgression

All of the species of *Vitis*, with the exception of the *rotundifolia* group, which is more correctly placed in the genus *Muscadinia*, can be easily hybridized with one another. Numerous hybrids have been produced between many species of the three geographical groups and no incompatibility has been noted. From this standpoint, *Vitis* shows no limitation of gene exchange or introgression, which is often not characteristic of a "good species."

All *Vitis* species are characterized by having 38 very small chromosomes, which pair regularly to form 19 bivalents in meiosis (Lavie 1970). Deviations in chromosome number have never been established in the long evolution of *Vitis*, which is obviously a very stable system. Thus taxonomists have difficulty in separating or defining *Vitis* species, and must appeal to morphological and physiological differences that appear important and practical, even though they are not based on phylogenetic evidence. Vines of interspecific hybrids frequently show hybrid vigor, and are fertile and fruitful if not limited by sexual dimorphism (Olmo 1978).

Although breeders have experienced no difficulty in producing hybrids, there are different opinions on whether hybridization can modify natural populations, even though they are sympatric. Olmo and Koyama (1980) have found that natural hybrids of two native species have been introgressed by the introduction of cultivated *vinifera*.

Two well-defined *Vitis* species are native to California—*V. californica* in the northern part, *V. girdiana* in the south. The *vinifera* grape was first introduced from Mexico in 1779, and the first vineyards established near San Diego and Los Angeles. The largest planting developed at the San Gabriel Mission, reaching 200 acres by 1834. Only the *vinifera* cultivar called "Mission" had been introduced by the Spanish padres at this time. In 1858, a grape grower and an astute observer (Keller 1859) published a review of the grapes and wines of Los Angeles, noting a million and a half bearing vines and 875,000 coming into production. He noted that the wild grape (*girdiana*) abounded in all parts of the country. He described three types of wild vine, from which descriptions it is easy to deduce that there were male vines, female vines with small berries and heavy coloring matter, and a third type which is a very fruitful vine with larger clusters and berries. The latter was a natural hybrid between *girdiana* and the Mission cultivar. Many very vigorous vines of this combination were erroneously called Mission, and produced famous vines of enormous size and productivity. Despite the fact that such species hybrids can survive and reproduce in California, the cultivated *vinifera* has shown no tendency to become naturalized. This is rather surprising in view of the fact that the cultivars of many wine varieties are grown extensively in many foothill areas adjacent to natural habitats that support a native species, and migrating birds must certainly distribute the seeds. The progeny vines probably lack the vigor to survive under natural conditions, whereas the hybrids have multiplied. The importance of hybridization between unlike populations for increasing heterozygosity is thus evident.

10. Biochemical Differences

There are many biochemical differences between the *vinifera* complex and other species of the genus, which are of complex inheritance and involve multigenic reactions. One contrasting character with simple inheritance relates to the anthocyanidins. In the wild *vinifera* grape of Azerbaijan, the pigments are all monoglucosides, whereas in American and Asiatic *Vitis*, both monoglucosides and diglucosides are present (Ribéreau-Gayon 1959). The inheritance of diglucosides is determined by a dominant gene, so that American spp. × *vinifera* have diglucosides in the F1 generation (Boubals et al. 1962). The F1, however, has both mono- and di-forms. Since the *rotundifolia* group are characterized by diglucosides as the most prominent form (Goldy et al. 1986; Lamikanra 1989), the genetic types may be more accurately represented by the following scheme:

> D = principally diglucosides, dominant
> Dm = both monoglucosides and diglucosides
> d = recessive, only monoglucosides

The dominance relationship is D > Dm > d. Cultivars of the *vinifera* are dd. In many *vinifera* cultivars, there is evidence that recessive mutations affecting particular anthocyanidins have reduced the intensity and frequency of pigmentation.

Scienza et al. (1986) have compared anthocyanin profiles of wild populations in Italy, as well as their acid and sugar content with some of the cultivated Tuscan varieties. They concluded that two cultivars, "Colorino" and "Canaiolo," were similar and likely descended from the wild vines.

11. Secondary Centers of Origin?

The general group of cultivars commonly referred to as "Muscats" are most commonly found in the Eastern Mediterranean. The best known example is the "Muscat of Alexandria," which is used for table, raisin, and wine production. Perhaps because of the large berry size, this variety has been assigned by Negrul (1946) and others to the *orientalis* group, along with the small-berried Muscat blanc widely used in table wine production as a flavor additive or for sweet dessert wines. Muscat varieties, however, were unknown in Central Asia, including Iran, Afghanistan, and Asia.

A mild Muscat-type aroma or bouquet has also been identified in some varieties assigned to the *occidentalis* group, including Chardonnay, White Riesling, Traminer, and Chasselas doré. The characteristic aroma can arise by somatic mutation, and clones with more intense aroma are known, although the mutant is otherwise indistinguishable from the parent, e.g., Chasselas doré and Chasselas musqué; Chardonnay and Chardonnay musqué; Traminer and Gewürztraminer. Since such mutations are not known to have occurred in the table grapes typical of the oriental group, this may well indicate a difference in genetic background between the two groups.

Similarly, a group of Cabernet varieties have a characteristic flavor and aroma: the Carmenere, Cabernet franc, Fer Servadoux, Petit Verdot, Merlot, and Cabernet-Sauvignon, which are typical of the Bordeaux region and the Adour basin. The history of many French varieties has been recounted by Bouquet (1982), but their origins are difficult to trace before the Middle Ages.

12. Summary

According to the hypothetical scenario outlined above, the first stage in developing a domesticated grape culture was to select particularly fruitful vines in their native forest habitats. These vines were propagated by detaching already rooted layers and moving them to adjacent cleared areas. As they became more isolated, male vines were included to insure fruit set.

Male vines which were sporadically hermaphroditic ($\sigma \rightarrow \female$) would also have been planted, and these were crossed with females. Some seedlings eventually produced the hermaphroditic type, which is characterized by greatly increased fruit production, and a much greater number and much larger size of clusters. Female vines were progressively abandoned. These changes originated in the wild populations of the southern Caspian area, in vines already characterized by large and only slightly lobed leaves which were lightly pubescent or glabrous. These very fruitful hermaphrodites eliminated the need of saving male vines, so only females and hermaphrodites remained eventually.

The "new" hermaphroditic forms were widely disseminated, mostly westward, later to the east beyond the natural range of *vinifera*. Since no wild *vinifera* was present, the vines were largely hermaphrodites.

Fruitful male vines also arose from a gene mutation or mutations closely linked to the dominant suppressor gene Su^F. This resulted in an increase in cytokinin production and the restoration of the suppressed ovary and fruit production, negating the action of the dominant suppressor. A similar theory to that of Negi and Olmo (1973) has been proposed by Carbonneau (1983a,b), to explain the segregation of occasional male types in some hermaphroditic varieties. This development occurred in ecotypes in the Caspian area that were already noted for large cluster size, and resulted in forms that were extremely fruitful. They were moderated, however, by the selection of types with partial sterility due to lower cytokinin levels, resulting in lower fruit set and lax clusters typical of many table grapes.

The derived hermaphrodites were rapidly disseminated because of the restoration of self-fertility and the favorable genes which are sex-linked, such as those for large and abundant clusters. As the derived hermaphrodites moved westward into areas where the wild *occidentalis* was more abundant, the introgression of genes was less pronounced because of dilution, due to time lapse and distance traversed.

CHAPTER 4

The Archaeological Evidence for Winemaking, Distribution and Consumption at Proto-Historic Godin Tepe, Iran

Virginia R. Badler

The bones of the last meal had been discarded in the corner of the room. Fragments of wheat littered the floor. The wine had been completely consumed—remnants of the residue left a stale perfume which hung in the air. The embers of the hearth were dying down as they prepared to leave. But where was the necklace? The necklace, of precious stone beads, remained lost in the black darkness of the room as its inhabitants passed through its doorway for the last time.

Such is the stuff of novels, but archaeologists must deal with drier details: the factual basis for this reconstructed scene in the last moments of the occupation of Godin Tepe room 20 during Period V at the end of the 4th millennium B.C.

1. Introduction

The ancient site of Godin Tepe in central western Iran lies between the modern cities of Bakhtaran (Kermanshah) and Hamadan in the Kangavar plain of the Zagros mountains, overlooking the Khorram river (Map 4.1). Here, the earliest evidence for winemaking and wine use has been found which dates to the later part of the 4th millennium B.C.

Lowland Greater Mesopotamia, comprising the wide alluvial plains of the lower Tigris and Euphrates Rivers in southern Iraq and of Khuzistan in southwestern Iran, was home to the oldest literate civilizations in the world—that of the Sumerian and Elamite city-states, dating back to the 4th millennium B.C. This period was one of the most dynamic in the ancient Near East. Many trade routes were actively being used, implying widespread cultural stability. There is a remarkable degree of interaction between distant regions which is indicated by the profusion of imported artifacts, styles, and even economic systems. Objects and pottery belonging to the southern Mesopotamian and southwestern Iranian lowland repertoire (denoted as "Late Uruk," after the

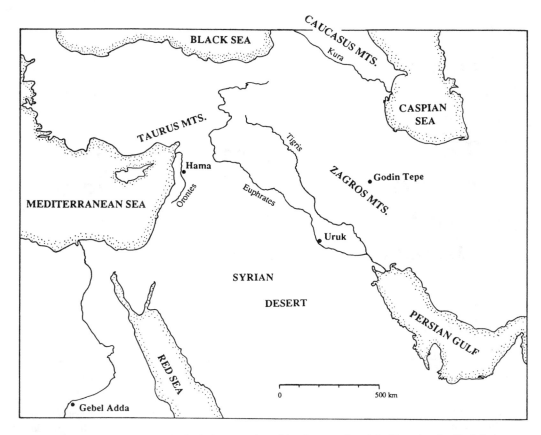

Map 4.1. The Near East: principal sites mentioned in chapters 4 and 5. (Drawing by R. Schulz, University of Pennsylvania.)

important ancient site in southern Iraq) are found in Egypt, Syria, Turkey, Transcaucasia, northern Iraq, and Iran (see Algaze, this volume; also Algaze 1989; Kohl 1989). The bureaucratic system of lowland Greater Mesopotamia began to be used outside this region, as reflected in early pictographic tablets and cylinder seals and sealings. New architecture of both local and southern Mesopotamian style was built to contain the foreign material culture at sites in northern Syria and Iran, including Godin Tepe. At some sites, this architecture is physically separated from the native occupation by an enclosure wall.

Many explanations have been proposed for these developments (see chapter 8 by Algaze, this volume; Algaze 1989; *Current Anthropology* 30 [1989]: 591–601 and 31 [1990]: 66–69; *Science News* 137 [1990]: 136–39]). Although the precise mechanisms behind these events are difficult to ascertain, the major impetus was probably more than the economic forays of independent, private traders. Considerable resources and political influence would have been needed to undertake building projects in distant lands, requiring both the procurement of land and the probable recruitment of local labor. These circumstances, together with the presence of imported artifacts, the local manufacture of foreign types, and the wholesale importation of an entire bureaucratic system suggest that the driving force came from lowland Greater Mesopotamia governments.

It is not surprising that Godin Tepe took part in these social and economic developments, since it was the largest site (approximately 14–15 hectares) in the area during this period (Young 1986:

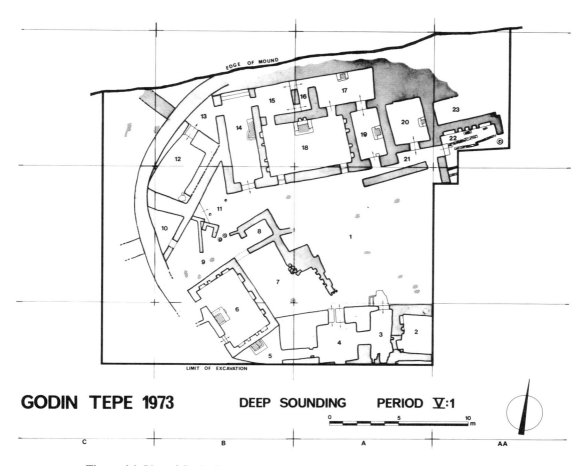

Figure 4.1. Plan of Godin Tepe, deep sounding of the upper citadel mound, Period V.

218–19), and it has a strategic location (Young 1969: 1; Young 1986: 212) along a major east–west trade route, called the High Road or Great Khorasan Road. This route was later known as the "Silk Road," which linked the Mediterranean and China.

2. Godin Tepe During Period V

The archaeological evidence for winemaking and wine use comes exclusively from Period V within the Deep Sounding oval, which occupies the summit of the Citadel Mound and which was the broadest horizontal exposure of this period (approximately 550 m^2) (Fig. 4.1). Within the oval enclosure wall, there is a large complex of buildings and rooms surrounding a courtyard. Gateway "room 4" is the only apparent entrance, implying controlled access. In all the rooms within the oval there is a sequence of at least two floors. The pottery deposit resting on the earliest floor associated with the buildings is called "Early Period V," and that from the latest floor, "Late Period V." There is evidence for wine from both Early and Late Period V. Period V is dated by corrected radiocarbon determinations to ca. 3500–3100 B.C. for the early phase, and ca. 3100–2900 B.C. for the late and final phase of the period (Dyson 1987: 666–67, 677).

Figure 4.2. Godin Tepe wine jar no. Gd. 73-113 (see Fig. 4.3a) with hole near base. (Photograph courtesy of B. Boyle, Royal Ontario Museum, Toronto, Canada.)

3. The "Wine" Jars (Fig. 4.2)

Jars containing a residue which has been chemically identified as a grape product (see chapter 5 by McGovern and Michel, this volume) were found at Godin Tepe exclusively within the Deep Sounding oval, viz., room 18 in Early Period V (Godin Tepe Project, lot no. A01 44, Royal Ontario Museum [ROM]), and room 20 in Late Period V (Gd. [Godin] 73-113, ROM). Several other examples of the same type of jar, but lacking any residue (and testing negative for a grape product), were found in room 18 in Early Period V and in room 2 in Late Period V. The basis for identifying the grape residue as wine derives from the specific features of the jars and their archaeological contexts.

The handleless jars (Figs. 4.2 and 4.3a) have elongated, inverted piriform shapes with tall necks. The rim is present only in the examples from room 2 in Late Period V: the edge is rolled to the exterior to form a thickened bead, effectively reinforcing an area prone to damage. Although the Early Period V examples of this jar type are larger (70 l) than the later examples (31 l and 38 l), all have the same shape and relative proportions. The relatively narrow mouths of the smaller

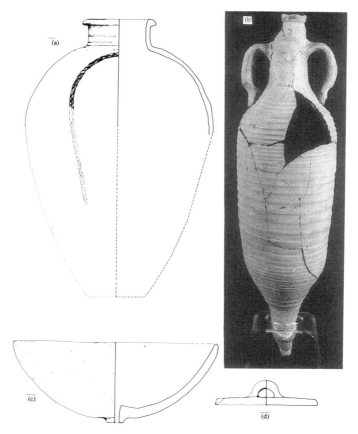

Figure 4.3. Godin Tepe wine jar (a), funnel (c) and "lid" (d) from room 2, deep sounding, Late Period V (Godin Tepe Project, lot no. A2 1176, Royal Ontario Museum, West Asian Dept.); Nubian wine amphora (b) Royal Ontario Museum, Egyptian Dept., no. 65:3:63). The lower part of (a) is reconstructed from Gd. 73-112 and Gd. 73-113. The funnel and lid are circular in top view. (Drawings courtesy of K. Ciuk, Royal Ontario Museum.)

examples of the type (average interior diameters of ca. 12 cm) compared with other jar types of the period (average diameters of ca. 16 cm), as well as their tall necks (average of ca. 6 cm) compared with other types (average ca. 2.3 cm of other jar types) highlights their suitability for storing and pouring out liquids.

This unique jar, which first appears at Godin Tepe in Early Period V, develops out of earlier types. Everted rim jars begin to appear in Early Period VI (Operation B, stratum 34), and jars with tall necks first occur in Middle Period VI (Operation B, stratum 23), together with the earliest beveled rim bowls, a lowland Mesopotamian type. Most jars are represented only by rim and other sherds, but a nearly complete jar with an everted rim and elongated body from Period VI (Brick Kiln Cut, Gd. 73-301, ROM) stands 63 cm tall. Its shape, however, is uniformly oval rather than inverted piriform.

The interior of one of the Early Period V jar sherds appears to be lined with a slip (a compact, fine clay layer that was fired), which would have made the vessel more impervious to leakage if it contained a liquid. The exteriors of both Late Period jars were also slipped. Another significant feature, possibly relating to liquid contents, is a hole, ca. 7 mm in diameter, which had been drilled through the side of the vessel after firing, about 9.5 cm above the base of one of the Late V jars (Gd. 73-113) (Fig. 4.2; see below).

Certain decorative features of these Period V jars also indicate that they may have served a specialized function for liquids. An exterior rope decoration (an applied band with regularly spaced oblique incisions) forms a unique pattern on each jar. The rope appliqué forms an elongated upside-down "U" on two opposite sides of each vessel. This pattern of decoration is unusual. Earlier and contemporaneous rope decoration on jars is located exclusively around their necks, indicating where a real rope would have been tied around the neck of the jar to secure a lid.

Rope decoration on Late Uruk type four-lugged jars provide an excellent parallel for the appliqué on the piriform jars of lowland Greater Mesopotamian inspiration. Found only in the Deep Sounding oval, the rope decoration on the four-lugged jars connects four evenly spaced, pierced nose-like lugs. This jar form is perhaps represented by a Late Uruk sign, *dug + geštu*, literally "jar with ears," as suggested by M. W. Green (personal communication, 1985; also see Green and Nissen 1987: 191, sign #98). The position of the rope appliqué makes sense in real terms: a rope which is run through the nose-like lugs will sit on the shoulder of the vessel where it is easier to impress a cylinder seal over clay attached to the rope. At Godin, the evidence for the use of such seals to make clay sealings is also exclusive to the Deep Sounding.

During both Periods VI and V at Godin Tepe, rope decoration consistently shows where actual rope would have been placed to serve a specific function. Yet, the inverted "U" appliqués of the inverted piriform jars are puzzling. Since this arrangement obviously does not indicate where a lid should be fastened, perhaps rope was being used in an innovative way that was associated with the special contents of the jar. One possible explanation for this decorative arrangement might have been to indicate where real rope was placed beneath the elongated jar, to stabilize it when it was laid on its side. One reason to place a jar on its side would be to keep a clay stopper moist, assuming that the vessel held a liquid. If the clay were prevented from drying out and shrinking, very likely even expanding by absorption of liquid, the opening would be protected against air intrusion which could cause spoilage of the contents.

In keeping with the hypothesis that these vessels were placed on their sides to keep their liquid contents tightly sealed, the red deposit on the interior of the most complete jar—Gd. 73-113 (Figs. 4.2 and 4.3a)—extended from the base to the shoulder only along one side of the vessel. Materials settling out of a liquid inside a vessel placed on its side might be expected to form such a deposit. Other explanations for the red deposit—for example, an originally upright vessel which was turned to pour out its contents, with any accumulation of material on the bottom sliding down one side—cannot be ruled out. The uniform thickness and the area of distribution of the deposit along the side, however, points to a longer-term storage of the vessel on its side.

As mentioned above, jar Gd. 73-113 has a small hole just above its base. Perhaps significantly, this hole, which had been drilled after the jar had been fired, is located too far down toward the base of the vessel on the side opposite the residue to have been used to release any build-up of gas pressure. Another possibility is that the hole, to facilitate pouring a liquid, provided a counter-pressure in a steady flow from the neck of the vessel. Vernon Singleton (personal communication, 1991) has suggested that the hole was used to drain a liquid from inside the vessel, without disturbing any accumulated materials on the bottom of the vessel. There is a noticeably thicker accumulation of residue below the hole. If the vessel had been stored on its side, first one would set it upright, any accumulated solids sliding partly to the bottom, then a hole would be drilled on the opposite side, and the liquid drained out. Third millennium B.C. Minoan jars have similar holes near their bases (see chapter 15 herein by Leonard). A Transcaucasian everted rim jar from the site of Norsuntepe in east-central Anatolia has a hole with a trough-spout beneath it that could have guided the flow of a liquid (Sagona 1984: fig. 89.2).

Seven clay stoppers (or fragments thereof) were recovered from Period V contexts (Weiss and Young 1975: fig. 5.4). These stoppers, which had been used to close jars and bottles of various sizes, were not found *in situ*. Occasionally, the imprint of the interior of the jar which they sealed is still preserved. Some are marked on the top with one or two cylinder seals. They were found exclusively within the rooms of the oval (below 2, 3, between 3 and 4, 11, 12 [two examples], and 18), and belong mostly to Early Period V. The best preserved stoppers have diameters of 5.3, 8.4, 8.5, greater than 9.1, and 11 cm. Although the larger examples are somewhat smaller than the interior diameters of the small inverted piriform jar necks (i.e., ca. 12 cm), possibly the stoppers expanded when wetted by liquid in a vessel laid on its side. The necks of the two vessels from room 20 (see below) appear to have been carefully chipped away in antiquity, as if special care had been taken in opening the vessel to remove a tight stopper (cf. ancient Egyptian practice—see Hope 1977:8).

The above evidence—the characteristic shape of the jars with their relatively tall and narrow necks, the slip used on the exteriors or interiors, and the hole located near the base of the jar—all point to the jars originally containing a liquid. The unique rope decoration may indicate that these jars were meant to lay on their sides to keep any clay stoppers moist. Such features, along with the chemical evidence (see chapter 5 by McGovern and Michel, this volume) indicate that the liquid inside the jars was most likely wine.

4. The Evidence for Winemaking

Some of the unique jars, which were hypothetically used to store wine, came from archaeological contexts where winemaking may have taken place within the Godin Tepe Period V oval. The principal evidence is a nearly complete, exceptionally large funnel (Fig. 4.3c) that was found together with a unique architectural feature and other finds in room 2 (Late Period V). It should also be mentioned that a fragment of a possible Early Period V funnel (a 6 cm diameter spout) was also found in room 10 on the west side of the courtyard (lot B1 479, sherd #173). Since the artifacts from this room are clearly from fills, the original location and function of the funnel spout is unclear.

Large funnels could have been used with the aid of a textile "filter," to press the juice from grapes (originally suggested by M. Gibson, personal communication, 1988). Such funnels, which have argued to have been used in winemaking, have been found at later sites, such as Iron II Gibeon in Jordan (Pritchard 1964: fig. 33.16). Large funnels of similar type, which date to the Late Uruk Period, have been found at sites in the region where the wild grape grows today: Kurban Höyük (Algaze 1990: 255, pl. 35H) and Arslantepe-Malatya (Palmieri 1973: fig. 66.12) in eastern Anatolia, and Tell Brak in Syria (Oates 1985: 181, fig. 1.8; G. Algaze, personal communication, 1991).

Room 2, where an almost complete funnel was recovered, is located on the southeastern side of the courtyard, and was only partly excavated. Whole or nearly complete vessels on a poorly preserved floor indicate that it is an *in situ* deposit. The finds include the funnel, several of the unique jars, a large, heavy "lid" (Fig. 4.3c), and part of a "bin," all which may have been used in winemaking.

The sherds from two (or possibly three) jars had no visible red deposits on their interiors. The lack of interior residues could indicate they were empty jars waiting to be filled with grape juice, but other scenarios are possible, e.g., the organic contents had been consumed by animals or the dregs even given out as rations (Kinnier Wilson 1972:113). Alternatively, the jars could have contained something else such as white or rosé wine which left little visible evidence, or the organic contents were not preserved in this part of the excavation.

The "lid," which has a simple loop handle, weighed about a kilogram. It could have been used to put pressure on the grapes within the funnel. Although of simple type, this "lid" first occurs at Godin Tepe in Late Period V, and is similar to Transcaucasian-type lids found both at Godin Tepe in later Period IV (unpublished, Gd. 73-190, ROM) and in Transcaucasia itself (Sagona 1984: fig. 101.1, 101.3: forms 220 and 221 [type B]). The "bin," presumably of mudbrick, has walls 6–8 cm thick and 6 cm in height. Its exposed area measured approximately 50 by 50 cm, but was not completely excavated to the east. From parallels to installations elsewhere (see chapters 11 by Gorny, 15 by Leonard, 9 by Palmer, 13 by James, and 14 by Lesko, this volume) it might have functioned as a grape-crushing or settling basin.

If wine was indeed being made in this room, it was not the only activity taking place there. Other finds, including three large worked flint cores, an unfinished incompletely pierced small stone disk (which has been interpreted as a spindle whorl), and a metal chisel, suggest that this room functioned as a multi-use workshop. The making of wine would only have been one of several activities.

One difficulty in the way of interpreting this room as a winemaking installation is that no paleobotanical remains of grapes were recovered. Future excavation of the remainder of the room should make this a priority. Samples from the "bin" walls should also be tested for tartaric acid. Even without the paleobotanical and chemical evidence, the assemblage of finds strongly supports this room's use as a winemaking installation.

5. The Early Period V Evidence for Wine Distribution and/or Trade

Several of the unique jars, belonging to the large type (with a volume of about 70 l) came from room 18 in Early Period V, on the northern side of the oval. Several unique architectural features and the special character and location of the Early Period V material remains suggest that the room had a specialized function as a distribution or trade center. The notable architecture of room 18 is described by its excavator, T. C. Young, Jr. (Weiss and Young 1975: 3):

> Room 18 was clearly the focal point of the structure. Its walls had been laid out with great care and with architectural forethought. Note particularly the balance of the several elements: the two doors equidistant on either side of the central hearth of the north wall, the twin windows in the south wall looking out into the courtyard with their sills at waist height, the opposed niches in the east and west walls with two larger niches flanking two smaller ones. The hearth was built with equal care, its flues having been constructed with the wall. It is a fireplace, not a cooking hearth.

It was also the largest room within the oval (6 m wide to almost 4 m deep), and both its windows and fireplace features are not found in any of the other rooms. Its two doors, both located in the back of the room, provided a unusually circuitous route of access through the other rooms of the complex; most other rooms within the oval could be entered directly from the courtyard. The location of room 18 is significant. It was placed at the northern edge of the oval, directly opposite gateway room 4, and clearly visible from room 18's two windows. The function served by these windows is suggested by the Early Period V artifacts within the room. Nearly 2000 sling balls were found piled up in the corner next to the east window. This assemblage suggests that these windows were used to distribute objects (in this instance, slingballs) possibly to the enclave's foreign residents or local workmen.

Food may have been another item distributed through these windows. The floor of this room was littered with large amounts of carbonized lentils and smaller amounts of other grains, most notably barley, but it could not be determined whether these grains were raw or cooked (Miller

1990). Some rodent activity is indicated by the number of mouse bones found. The grain may have been kept in the numerous, large jars represented on the floor of the room. Several of the smaller jars were likely imports from the south. A beer residue has recently been chemically confirmed inside a large open-mouthed jar from this room (Michel et al. 1992, 1993).

Wine would have been another food item that was possibly distributed from this room. The earliest "wine" jars, of the same type and decoration as Late Period V examples but of larger size, were found in this room. Several sherds had a heavy, red deposit on their interiors, but other sherds did not (for possible explanations, see above). The large jars when filled with liquid could have been moved only with great difficulty. There is no evidence, however, that winemaking was carried out in this room, although the presence of a worked tooth and flint cores and debitage indicate that some craft activity occurred here. Another explanation for "wine" jars in this room is that it was a luxury item which was possibly traded. Various other "luxury" goods are among the small finds from the Early Period V deposits of this room, including four copper or bronze items (2 pins, 1 needle, and 1 bird-shaped object), and 8 stone beads. This miscellaneous assortment of items suggests an exchange of goods; wine, and other foodstuffs may also have been traded to local inhabitants of the region from here.

The mechanism for the distribution or trade of goods is unknown. The food could have been rations to local or foreign workers and soldiers (as suggested by the slingballs). Luxury items, on the other hand, may have been paid for in kind, according to a fixed exchange rate (see chapter 9 herein by Powell) by individuals of higher status coming from the wider region of Godin Tepe. Administrative records were being kept of at least some of those transactions (however they are understood), since three tablets were found on the floor of the room. By contrast, the finds from the subsequent Late Period V floor show a dramatically different function for this room; there are no "wine" jars, luxury goods, craft related items, nor slingballs—only an ordinary domestic assemblage of local pottery. Evidently, the specialized function of this room is limited to Early Period V.

6. The Late Period V Evidence for Wine Consumption

Two nearly intact "wine" jars (Gd. 73-112 and Gd. 73-113; Figs. 4.2 and 4.3a) were recovered from room 20, Late Period V, located to the east of room 18 on the northern side of the oval. Both the architecture and finds from this room point to it being a private upper class residence. Moreover, the way that the jars were handled suggest that wine was consumed in this room. The private nature of room 20 is indicated by its small size (approx. 2.5 m wide by 3 m deep) and limited means of access (through a single doorway located in the middle of its south wall). Additional privacy was provided by the placement of a curtain wall in front of the doorway, shielding it from the courtyard. There was a hearth in the middle of its east wall, which probably was used for both cooking and heating. In Late Period V, this room had a fine plastered floor.

Of all the rooms around the courtyard with certain Late Period V deposits, room 20 produced the most luxury items. These items include a fragment of a marble bowl and a necklace composed of 208 black and 2 white stone beads (the only complete necklace from Period V at Godin Tepe). Wine can also be in this list. A whetstone and flint blades, as well as whole pottery vessels, numerous sherds, and wheat (Miller 1990), probably spilled out from one of the pottery vessels, were found scattered on the floor.

Wine consumption may be inferred, because the inverted piriform jars had their necks chipped off in antiquity—perhaps to avoid the contamination of the beverage from the stopper, which most likely was of clay (see above). As mentioned, one jar (Gd. 73-113, the only one available for examination) had a hole punctured near its base, which could have been used to decant wine from the vessel. The interior of the jar had a red deposit, suggesting the vessel had once been filled with a grape product. The jars were of the small type, which is the standard size for ancient transport of liquids, including wine (see chapters 9 by Powell and 15 by Leonard, this volume).

7. The Implications of Wine Use and Winemaking at Godin Tepe During Period V

The probable production, storage, and consumption of wine at Godin Tepe Period V has important implications for the site's foreign relations, trade, socio-economic organization, and horticulture. Foreign relations with the south—southern Mesopotamia and southwestern Iran—predominate at Godin Tepe, even in levels preceding the Period V oval construction, as attested by a conical clay token (see Schmandt-Besserat 1992 for the significance of tokens), beveled rim bowls, and an imported spouted jar (Badler 1989). These items, however, are relatively rare, and most of the material assemblage is of local style and origin (Badler n.d.).

In contrast, the majority of the material from within the Early Period V oval is stylistically identical with that of the Late Uruk Period of lowland Greater Mesopotamia, viz., red slipped ware, four-lugged and bottle-necked jars, crudely made trays, crude conical cups with string cut bases, and large numbers of beveled rim bowls (Weiss and Young 1975; Young 1986). Even though of foreign type, most of the jars may have been made of local clay by local potters. Both the ware and fabrication techniques are similar to that of Period VI, and clearly different from that of lowland Mesopotamia and Iran. Certain vessels combine local and imported features, and show the influence of one pottery tradition upon another (Badler n.d.). The hypothesis of local pottery production, reflecting lowland Mesopotamian stylistic and technological features, needs to be tested by scientific analysis.

Southern influence is particularly evident in the paraphernalia of a Late Uruk bureaucratic system found only within the Period V oval—43 tablet and tablet fragments (including one with a pictographic sign, *dug*), cylinder seals, and sealings. The seal impressions occur on tablets, bullae, and jar stoppers. The presence of not only imported artifacts but the import of a foreign bureaucratic system implies that lowlanders were actually living and working at Godin Tepe in Period V. Why these foreigners built an outpost at the site can be explained in various ways (Weiss and Young 1975; Young 1986; Badler 1989). Whatever model is followed, however, involves Godin's strategic location on a major east–west trade route. The lowland foreigners were also responsible for building the oval complex of rooms and central courtyard. Local labor may have been used as suggested by the preponderance of local pottery types in buildings in areas surrounding the oval. The architectural features of these buildings are also partly reflected in the oval's structures.

Although southern lowland influence is especially strong in Early Period V at Godin, it is unlikely that the winemaking or predilection for wine at Godin came from this direction. Lowland Greater Mesopotamia is a beer-drinking culture (see chapter 9 by Powell, this volume), and is well removed from the modern regions where the wild grape grows. The domesticated grape and wine thus had to be introduced into the lowlands from farther north. The Sumerian sign for grapes, *geštin*, does not appear until the following Jemdet Nasr Period (Green and Nissen 1987). However, another sign, *tin*, interpreted by Green (1989: 44) as also meaning wine, occurs in the earlier Late Uruk Period.

Contacts with Transcaucasia, as attested by possible pottery imports at Godin Tepe as early as the beginning of Period V, are important because the wild grape does grow there today and winemaking possibly has a longer history there. Furthermore, pottery of Uruk type has been found in Transcaucasia (Kohl 1989: 593–94), and these contacts may eventually have led to the grape being introduced into lowland sites. By Late Period V at Godin Tepe, distinct Transcaucasian wares account for up to one third of the total pottery assemblage (Badler n.d.).

Transcaucasian influence appears to have increased in Late Period V, at the same time that contact between Godin and the south decreases. Room 18 in Late Period V was no longer functioning as a distribution or trading center. There is also a marked decrease in the number of tablets, cylinder seals, and sealings, perhaps reflecting a contraction of the southern bureaucratic system and its influence in the region. In the latest building phase of Period V, architectural changes within the oval also suggest a change in use, as the integrity of the large courtyard was broken up by walls, doorways to rooms were blocked, etc. There is an interesting parallel in modern Iran where rooms are remodelled solely for the purpose of changing a room's function (Horne 1988: 190).

The archaeological evidence for winemaking and its use also reflects major changes in the sociopolitical system between Early and Late Period V. In Late Period V, wine is no longer found in room 18 with Late Uruk administrative items, but in a small private room where it was probably consumed. The individuals who drank the wine had access to other luxury objects, as well. During this later time, resources were apparently being controlled by a small group of elite individuals, rather than by a Uruk bureaucracy. In both Early and Late Period V, Godin Tepe society must have been at a significant level of complexity. The long-term investment required in the horticulture of established vineyards is possible under such circumstances. Stager (1985: 177) has written: "Permanent fields, residential stability, and general tranquility are prerequisites for the production of horticultural crops." In contrast to agricultural crops, horticultural crops such as grapevines have lower yields per acre, a more limited harvest time, and relatively more perishable products (Charles 1987: 14–19). For horticulture to develop, a society must have progressed beyond a subsistence economy to surplus agricultural production. An agricultural surplus at Godin is suggested by the large deposit of grains on the floors in room 18 of Early Period V and in room 20 of Late Period V. But the question of whether the presence of wine at Godin demands the presence of local vineyards is difficult to answer without the corresponding botanical remains of grapes. Small scale, household production of wine, using locally available wild grapes, might account for the 5 to 10 vessels recovered from Period V over a few hundred years. It should be noted that wild grapes grow in the Godin region today (personal communication, T. C. Young, 1988), and the climate and other environmental conditions could have supported it in the past (see Miller 1990: 3, for the presence of later grape pips from Iron Age Godin Tepe Period II).

Godin Tepe's location along a major trade route was ideally positioned for long distance exchange. If there were any trade in wine, it is likely that it occurred during Early Period V, perhaps even through the windows of room 18. Wine could have been transported from Godin in skins which have left no trace. Possibly because the inverted piriform jars were too heavy to have been easily transported, thus far this jar type has only been recovered from Godin Tepe. Unless the vessels are recovered intact or can be reconstructed, however, the characteristic U shape of the rope decoration would not be readily apparent.

8. Conclusions

The earliest evidence of a grape product (on the basis of chemically identified tartaric acid) has been found at 4th millennium Godin Tepe in Period V. The archaeological context of this grape product suggests that it is most likely ancient wine. Local morphological and decorative pottery traditions were adapted to produce a unique jar type, especially suited for storing wine. Some of these jars, which contained the grape residue, were found in an Early Period V (c. 3500–3100 B.C.) distribution room and a Late Period V (c. 3100–2900 B.C.) residence where the beverage was consumed. Additional jars, which had no interior residues and were possibly empty jars, were found in a room which may have been used for a variety of craft-related activities, including very likely winemaking.

Although none of the unique jars have been found at other sites, closer examination of sherds and reconstruction of larger forms with rope decoration could reveal similar vessels elsewhere. More importantly, the analysis of residues from other sites (e.g., in Transcaucasia) could extend the history of domesticated grape-growing and winemaking further back in time.

During Period V at Godin, goods and technologies evidently traveled over a wide area of the ancient Near East. The cross-cultural transference of wine and winemaking could have been just one example during this exceptional period of history. Wine, with its powerful, mood-altering, alcoholic potential, which is still considered a "luxury," appears linked, even at this earliest occurrence, with social and economic control of mankind's first complex society.

> The despised beveled rim bowls, symbols of
> foreign oppression, were smashed.
> The courtyard, where long lines of humanity
> had waited for food and weapons, was divided up
> by walls. The precious wine was still being made,
> but now consumed by the new order without moderation,
> so that even treasured things lay broken and lost.

Acknowledgments

The author wishes to thank Drs. T. Cuyler Young, E. J. Keall, and Nicholas B. Millett of the Royal Ontario Museum, Toronto, Canada. The advice and help of Drs. Åke Sjöberg, Vernon Singleton, Hermann Behrens, Guillermo Algaze, Bonnie S. Magness-Gardiner, Naomi Miller, and Wolfgang Röllig are much appreciated.

CHAPTER 5

The Analytical and Archaeological Challenge of Detecting Ancient Wine: Two Case Studies from the Ancient Near East

Patrick E. McGovern and Rudolph H. Michel

1. Introduction

An archaeological excavation will often yield a set of seemingly interconnected data that appear to be linked together by a specific human activity, though convincing evidence for that activity may or may not be present. When organic materials are directly involved—as they often are, since human beings and much of what they surround themselves with are largely constituted of organics—a satisfactory solution to an archaeological puzzle will be all the more elusive, because of the ease with which most organic compounds degrade, dissolve, and disappear. On the other hand, if an organic compound that is highly specific to a given plant or animal were preserved and identified, this evidence could well prove to be the "missing link" in a chain of reasoning. Apropos of how chemistry can provide the missing link in resolving an archaeological problem, see Evans 1990.

The field of organic microanalysis applied to archaeological remains, especially the contents of pottery vessels, has rapidly developed over the past two decades (see Biers and McGovern 1990, for an overview). Lipids, resins, dyes, perfume ingredients, and other organic compounds have been found to be well enough preserved in certain archaeological contexts—usually either in a dry climate or, alternatively, a waterlogged environment where microbial activity and autoxidation is reduced—that they can be extracted and analyzed by a variety of techniques (gas and high performance liquid chromatography, mass spectrometry, infrared and UV-visible spectroscopy, nuclear magnetic resonance spectrometry, etc.; for applications, see chapters by Röttlander, Beck and Borromeo, McGovern and Michel, and Gerhardt et al. in Biers and McGovern 1990).

Even if organics are well preserved and can be analyzed in a relatively straightforward fashion, it does not follow that chemistry can provide quick, easy solutions for archaeological problems. Interdisciplinary collaboration of chemists, archaeologists, palaeobotanists and zoologists, and other specialists, is essential to assess the significance of a given organic compound in an ancient context. Is a compound, or the relative amounts of several compounds, specific to a given plant or animal? For example, Royal Purple (6,6′-dibromoindigotin), the famed ancient dye of the Phoenicians, ancient Japanese, and Peruvians, is found naturally only in certain marine mollusks that occur throughout the oceans of the earth (McGovern and Michel 1990b). If the source of the organic is known, has it been processed by man, does the ancient context suggest anything about what the source or product was used for, and can broader implications of biocultural significance be drawn? Such questions obviously take the chemist into the uncharted waters of ancient technology, economic exchange systems, and cultural dynamics.

2. Wine Analysis

Wine, as a processed beverage made from grape must, would appear to be especially amenable to such an interdisciplinary approach. It is an unusually complex mixture of quite different organic compounds—alcohols, aldehydes, acids, carbohydrates, esters, polyhydroxyphenols including tannins and anthocyanins, proteins, vitamins, etc.—so there is a likelihood that some organics, or their degradation products, might be preserved in ancient contexts. Some of these compounds—in particular, tartaric acid—are known to be specific to grapes, occurring in much smaller quantities in only a few other plants (see Singleton, chapter 6 this volume). Degradation products of the anthocyanins and tannins also serve to distinguish wine from other liquids popular in antiquity, including beer and olive oil. A variety of analytical procedures and techniques have been developed to test ancient materials for these compounds (Condamin and Formenti 1976; Formenti et al. 1978; Para and Riviere 1982; see also Formenti and Duthel, chapter 7, this volume).

The prospects of identifying ancient wine using modern techniques far exceeds that which was possible by wet chemical methods (Haevernick 1963, 1967). Although some excellent work on wine was done along the latter lines (for example, by the well-known 19th century chemist, M. Berthelot), many analyzed samples, whether because of the insensitivity of the tests or for other reasons, were identified as water (e.g., "Ergebnis: Der 'Wein von Nis' ist Wasser"—Haevernick 1963: 120). Other sizable liquid samples were lost during "taste tests."

We have primarily employed infrared spectroscopy to test for tartaric acid. As shown in the case studies below, tartaric acid can be identified according to several characteristic absorption bands and by a process of elimination that rules out other compounds. Infrared spectroscopy also has the advantage that other compounds or classes of compounds which are associated with tartaric acid can be identified or inferred to be present in a single analysis. The disadvantage of analyzing a mixture of compounds, however, is that the interpretation of the spectrum is made more difficult due to overlapping absorpion bands. By separating and isolating the tartaric acid and other distinctive compounds by chromatographic techniques, unequivocal identifications can be made.

3. A Case Study from 4th Millennium B.C. Iran: Chemical Confirmation of Wine in Early Civilization

In the preceding chapter, Badler described the puzzle that emerged from the excavations at Godin Tepe, Iran, a site in the Zagros Mountains which dates to the late 4th millennium B.C. and so is

Figure 5.1. Godin Tepe jar (Godin Tepe Project, no. Gd. 73-113, Royal Ontario Museum, West Asian Dept.), from room 20. Deep sounding, Late Period V. (Photograph courtesy of W. Pratt, Royal Ontario Museum, Toronto, Canada.)

contemporary with the Late Uruk Period in lowland Greater Mesopotamia (now southern Iraq and Iran). She details a set of archaeological data from Period V which appear to be interrelated—the unique jars with applied rope designs on their sides (Figs. 4.2, 4.3a, and 5.1), the red deposits found on the base and only one side of their interiors (directly opposite the rope designs on their exteriors—Fig. 5.2), the finding of a large funnel and "lid" (Fig. 4.3a,c,d) with these jars in what appears to be workroom, the unbaked clay stoppers that fit the mouths of the jars, the carefully chipped-away necks of jars in another room that was most likely occupied by "upper-class" individuals, etc. She goes on to posit that the jars in the workroom were either "empties" waiting to be filled with wine or vessels that had already been filled with wine. The must possibly was obtained by pressing and sieving grapes in the large funnel which was covered with a coarsely woven cloth. After heaping grapes into the funnel, pressure might have been applied with the "lid." The jars recovered from the habitation context, on the other hand, are proposed to be bottles of wine that had been opened, their necks chipped away to remove the stoppers, and the beverage then consumed.

That the unique jars once contained a liquid was further supported by their relatively narrow mouths and tall necks, which would be better suited for storing and pouring out liquids than other jar types from the site. A compact clay layer or slip on the interior of at least one of the vessels would also have made this vessel more impervious to leakage. It also seemed likely that the jars

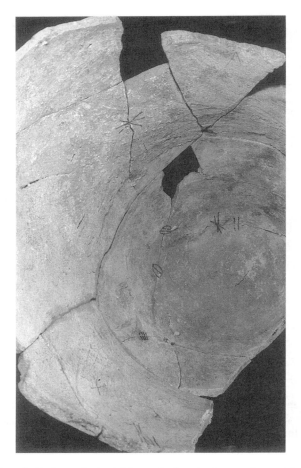

Figure 5.2. Red deposit (dark patches) visible on the interior base and one side of Godin Tepe jar Gd. 73-113 (Fig. 5.1). (Photograph courtesy of W. Pratt, Royal Ontario Museum.)

had once been stoppered, since two unfired stoppers, slightly smaller than the neck diameters of the jars, were found nearby.

If one grants that the unique rope-appliqué jars once contained grape juice, which had evidently been stored in a relatively airtight fashion, it is but a short step to propose that the red deposits inside the jars represent wine dregs. After all, although we may prefer cork to raw clay, today wine is also stored in sealed bottles placed on their sides. Moreover, the red deposits on the interiors of the jars are precisely in the areas that might have been predicted for precipitates to have settled out from a liquid in a vessel which was stored on its side sometime during its history.

Although the vessels might have contained other non-fermented or fermented fruit juices, vineyards are very prevalent today throughout the Zagros mountains, especially in Godin region (see Badler, chapter 4 this volume). No unequivocal archaeobotanical evidence of grape remains, however, was recovered from the Late Uruk period, although grape pips were found in later contexts at the site.

4. Chemical Identification of Tartaric Acid and Other Organic Compounds

Clearly, the hypotheses of wine production and consumption at Godin Tepe, which interrelate the archaeological data, stand or fall on whether the jars indeed contained organic substances derived from grapes, and, if so, whether a grape juice had been intentionally fermented to wine.

Transmission and diffuse-reflectance Fourier transform infrared spectrometry (FTIR) are versatile techniques that are particularly useful in an archaeological chemical investigation when one must first determine whether a sample is an organic or inorganic residue. Diffuse-reflectance FTIR spectrometry has the advantage that the archaeological sample need not be damaged, while eliminating the need for preparing an optically transparent KBr (potassium bromide) wafer. The spectra from either technique will show the same absorption bands at the same wavelengths.

The FTIR spectrum of the surface scrapings of the interior red deposit of one of the Godin Tepe jars revealed the presence of organics, but was dominated by silicates. More definitive results were obtained by extracting several sherds with boiling acetone. Evaporation to dryness of the extract gave 6–7 mg of resinous solid for both a 17 g sample with a visibly thicker deposit and a 73 g sample with a thinner deposit. Because whole sherds were extracted, it is not known whether this relatively small amount of solid derives from the reddish deposit, from the interior ware of the vessel, or from both areas. A control sample from a deposit-free area of one jar, however, showed no organics.

The FTIR spectra of the Godin Tepe jar extracts (Fig. 5.3a and 5.3b) and an ancient reference sample of wine (Fig. 5.3c), our second case study below, have many similarities. These include an intense C—H peak around 2900 cm^{-1}, a

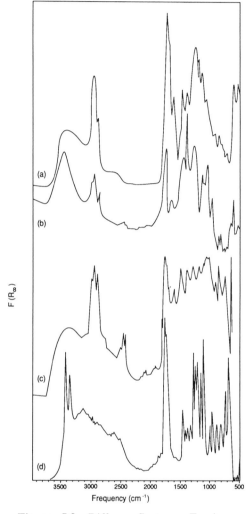

Figure 5.3. Diffuse-reflectance Fourier transform infrared spectra of Godin Tepe jar extractions (a,b) and Nubian amphora deposit (c), with infrared transmission spectrum of L-(+)-tartaric acid (d) for comparison.

sharp, intense carbonyl peak, with a shoulder, at 1720–1740 cm^{-1}, and carboxylic acid-related bands between 1385–1470 and 1240–1250 cm^{-1}. Of particular interest is the 1720–1740 cm^{-1} carbonyl band, which is at the upper end of the range for carboxylic acids (1680–1740 cm^{-1}) and is characteristic of those carboxylic acid groups located near strong electron-withdrawing groups, such as halogens and carbonyls. Additionally, the bands at 1600–1650 cm^{-1} suggest the presence of carboxylic acid salt(s). The hydroxyl bands at 3400–3500 cm^{-1} are broad and result from the presence of several types of hydroxyls. The strong band at 2900 cm^{-1} and the numerous absorption

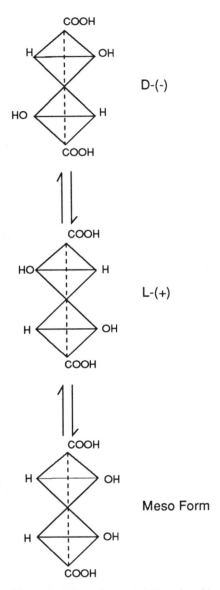

COOH

D-(-)

COOH

COOH

L-(+)

COOH

COOH

Meso Form

COOH

Figure 5.4. Stereoisomers of tartaric acid.

bands from 1550 to 800 cm^{-1} indicate a variety of organics, possibly some of those listed above as wine or grape components.

The FTIR results strongly suggest that the carboxylic acid in the extracts is tartaric acid. For comparison, we examined the spectrum of the naturally occurring isomer of tartaric acid—the L-(+)-form (Fig. 5.3d). Because the three stereoisomers (Fig. 5.4) have very similar FTIR spectra, racemization of the unknown would not affect the results. Most significant for comparison are the bands at 1445 cm^{-1} and 1250 cm^{-1}, as well as the doublet peaks at 1740/1720 cm^{-1}, all of which are due to carboxylic acid groups in the molecule. These values are very close to those of the unknown deposit and extracts.

Although the FTIR analysis provides strong evidence for tartaric acid, it does not unambiguously identify the compound. Separation and characterization of tartaric acid by chromatography, followed by spectroscopic analysis, is one way to gain greater certainty. A simpler approach is to test the unknown mixture with a highly specific Feigl spot test for tartaric acid.

In the Feigl test, the tartaric acid in the mixture is converted with β,β'-dinaphthol and concentrated sulfuric acid to an unknown compound that exhibits green fluorescence under ultraviolet light. Samples (surface scrapings) from the Godin Tepe jars and the Nubian amphora (see below), as well as synthetic L-(+)-tartaric acid, all gave the same, characteristic green fluorescence.

Another unanswered question is why tartaric acid is present primarily as the free acid and not, to any considerable extent, as its salt. The free acid is more water soluble than the monopotassium salt (the form in which it crystallizes from wine) and would be expected to dissolve and disappear through groundwater percolation. One might conjecture that this dihydroxy dicarboxylic acid was strongly adsorbed on silicates by hydrogen bonding. Thus, it could be removed from the hydrolysate of the bitartrate and preserved in the pottery matrix. The equilibrium between the acid and salt would be shifted to the acid side, as more and more acid was bound up in the ceramic.

5. Winemaking Implications of the Godin Tepe Jars

The chemical authentication of tartaric acid in the Godin Tepe jars agrees with the archaeological scenario that they originally contained a grape product. Although the presence of tartaric acid is the crucial link in the chain of argumentation, it is insufficient to establish whether the grape product was a liquid and, if so, whether it was fermented to wine. For these inferences, we must rely on the archaeological evidence. The available data (e.g., the narrow mouths, elongated necks and clay linings of the jars, and the red deposits that had been formed from materials settling out) point to the jars having been filled with liquids. Under normal conditions and at room temperature, grape juice easily and quickly ferments to wine.

Grape must fermentation proceeds rapidly, because a variety of wild yeasts, primarily the genera *Saccharomyces* and *Candida*, are present in the "bloom" of the grape skins (Farkaš 1988: I:171–237). The ability of yeasts to ferment grape sugars (e.g., glucose, maltose, and sucrose) depends upon the presence of specific enzymes (such as oxidoreductases, hydrolases, and ligases). Oxygen respiration is required for the growth and multiplication of the yeast cells, and consequently for the course and degree of fermentation. The continued availability of oxygen after fermentation has ceased leads to the multiplication of the bacteria (*Acetobacter*) that are responsible for the conversion of ethanol to acetic acid (i.e., vinegar) (Farkaš 1988: I:208–14, 255).

The apparent precautions that were taken in storing the liquid contained by the Godin jars—stoppering the vessels and laying them on their sides—makes most sense if this liquid were wine. Air was thus prevented from entering and nourishing the bacteria that will convert wine to vinegar. Other reasons for placing or turning vessels on their sides cannot be ruled out—whether to allow residues to settle out more quickly, as a convenient, space-saving measure, or for pouring or scooping out the vessels' contents—but have less evidence in their favor. The interior clay lining of at least one jar, besides preventing liquid from leaking out, might also have been intended to prevent oxygen from penetrating the vessel through pores in the pottery fabric.

The fact that some of the special Godin vessels did not have red deposits on their interiors can be variously explained. Since they were found in a context where grapes were apparently being processed into wine, rather than where the beverage was being consumed, perhaps they were "empties," which were to be used when the next grape harvest came in. Alternatively, it is possible that these vessels did originally contain wine, but it had been cleaned out by animals or the dregs even given out as rations (Kinnier Wilson 1972: 113). Other possibilities are that the vessels originally contained a white or rosé wine that left little visible evidence, or that the organic constituents of wine had been differentially preserved in various areas of the excavation. Over thousands of years, different environmental conditions—groundwater percolation, temperature, attack by microorganisms, and so on—might well have resulted in the vessels in one area of the excavation retaining organics better compared to those in other areas. For instance, the relatively greater amount of tartaric acid as compared to its salt, according to the FTIR spectrum, suggests that the wine jars were preserved in an acidic environment and/or that coordination of tartaric acid with silicates in the soil shifted the acid–base equilibrium towards the acid.

6. A Case Study from Byzantine Egypt: Chemical Corroboration of Wine in Later Historic Times

From the opposite end of the Fertile Crescent, the site of Gebel Adda in southern Egypt or ancient Nubia (see Map 4.1) provides a contrasting archaeological situation to that of Godin Tepe. From the late 4th through the early 6th century A.D., the so-called Ballana period, there is no question that wine-drinking was widespread and wine was a very popular commodity: "Taverns and/or

Figure 5.5. Nubian wine amphora (Royal Ontario Museum, Egyptian Dept. no. 65:3:63). (Photograph courtesty of W. Pratt, Royal Ontario Museum.)

wine cellars were prominent features...and the quantities of broken amphorae and goblets which accumulated within and around these buildings are astonishing" (Adams 1977: 418).

One complete amphora (Fig. 5.5) of this period, from cemetery 4, tomb 217 at Gebel Adda, was investigated. It was probably imported from Upper Egypt, where this pottery type is believed to have been used exclusively for wine storage and transport (N. B. Millet, personal communication, 1989). The vessel was lined with a dark-colored, resinous deposit. As it was found unsealed, it might have been placed in the tomb with only the dregs remaining in it.

In the case of the Gebel Adda amphora, the chemical evidence serves to corroborate what is highly probable from the archaeological data. If a wine deposit is identified in the Egyptian vessel, it has the additional advantages of providing a "reference standard" for chemical study of ancient wine sediments from less well-controlled archaeological contexts, such as that of Godin Tepe (above), and possibly documenting wine varieties and ageing processes through time.

The deposit from the Nubian amphora was mixed directly with KBr powder, and analyzed similarly to that of the Godin Tepe extracts by FTIR spectroscopy. The deposit's spectrum (Fig. 5.3c) attests to the presence of tartaric acid and its salts, together with other nonspecific organic constituents.

As detailed by James (chapter 13 herein), grapes and winemaking had already been introduced into Egypt, presumably from the Levant, by the earliest period for which written evidence is available—Dynasty 1. How much earlier wine was being made in, or imported into Egypt, has not been ascertained. Over the next several thousand years, however, wine continued to be the preferred beverage of the upper class and the gods. As often happened in ancient Egypt, what had previously been solely the province of the elite spread to the general populace, so that by Byzantine times wine had become a popular beverage in everyday life, which accompanied the deceased into the "hereafter."

7. Conclusions

The presence of tartaric acid and its salts inside unique vessels at Godin Tepe, which are dated to a very early period—the mid- to late 4th millennium B.C.—is quite remarkable because of its early date near the beginnings of complex societies in the Near East. The archaeological context had already suggested wine production and consumption. Even at this earliest stage in human history, it was evidently appreciated that stoppering of the vessels and storing them on their sides was a necessary means to preserve wine, so as to prevent it from converting to vinegar. This scenario has now been confirmed by physicochemical data.

Acknowledgments

The authors are grateful to Drs. T. Cuyler Young, Jr. and E. J. Keall of the West Asian Dept., and Nicholas B. Millett of the Egyptian Dept. of the Royal Ontario Museum, Toronto, Canada, for providing samples from the Godin Tepe jars and the Nubian amphora. Dr. Bruce Chase and his staff, in particular N. Rapposelli, at the Experimental Station of The Du Pont Company in Wilmington, Delaware ran the infrared spectra. Helpful advice was also provided by Dr. Curt W. Beck, Dr. Stuart J. Fleming, Dr. Michael A. Hoffman, and Dr. Vernon Singleton. Jeremy Badler assisted in the laboratory work in MASCA.

CHAPTER 6

An Enologist's Commentary on Ancient Wines

Vernon L. Singleton

A wine chemist's approach to the origins and ancient history of wines can be helpful in two areas: (1) suggestions for the study of wine-related artifacts, and (2) some additional perspectives on grapes and wines in antiquity. The ideas presented here, however, must be correlated with textual and archaeological studies of which this writer admits limited direct knowledge, despite considerable reading on the subject.

1. Evidence for Wine Use Based Upon Residues in Containers

Liquid-retaining containers were necessary before wine could be made, kept or moved. Ancient containers are unlikely to be found intact, and even less likely to have their original liquid contents. Containers made of organic materials (such as wood or skin) rarely survive in any form as compared to pottery, glass, or stone vessels. Even the latter do not remain sealed and volatiles inside are eventually lost. If the container is open or broken and comes in contact with water, soluble substances and those readily attacked by microorganisms will be lost.

In the most archaeologically favorable case, such as desiccation in a protected arid spot, what chemical constituents are stable enough and distinctive enough to survive as indicators of wine having been present? The two most likely candidates appear to be tartaric acid salts and syringic acid derived from red wine's pigmented tannins. For example, tartrate crystals are reported from a Cypriote amphora of 800 B.C. (Psaras and Zambartas 1981; see also chapter 5 by McGovern and Michel and chapter 7 by Formenti and Duthel, this volume).

a. Tartaric acid

Even very ripe, low-acid grapes and wines from them contain L(+)-tartaric acid at about 4 g/l; underripe grapes contain up to three times that amount. No other fruit of the familiar kinds has significant amounts of tartaric acid; rather they contain other predominant acids especially citric and malic (Ulrich 1970; Lee 1951). For this reason, the presence of tartaric acid is considered evidence of mislabeling or illegal adulteration of other juices by mixing in grape juice (Nagy et al. 1988). Since tartaric acid is associated with the metabolism of ascorbic acid, which is widespread in plants, tartaric acid may be found in small amounts in other plant material (<100 mg/l). Nevertheless, the presence of tartaric acid or its salts as an appreciable component of the residue from a fruit juice or wine is generally good evidence that grapes were a major source. Tamarind fruit and pulp from the baobab tree trunk are exceptions. They have high tartaric acid and are conceivable sources of confusion for archaeological interpretation in regions where they might co-occur with grapes. Other exceptional plants can be eliminated for historical, geographical, or practical reasons; some of these plants also produce different isomers of tartaric acid.

A potentially rewarding aspect of tartrate studies might be to date an archaeological find by racemization with time. The natural form of tartaric acid and tartrate in grapes is the dextrorotatory [L(+)] isomer. Heating in alkali converts it to a mixture of the D(−), L(+) and *meso* forms. Tartrate racemization probably would occur slowly in wine residues depending on temperature and it might be possible to derive a useful dating technique analogous to amino acid racemization used for other biological and organic materials. Owing to relatively constant temperatures, wine residues from caves or underwater would be particularly appropriate for such application.

Tartaric acid is quite water-soluble—about 1400 g/l at 20°C. Its potassium half-salt, potassium bitartrate, also occurs in grapes and wine, and is less soluble, about 4 g/l in cold water. Unless the wine had been treated with limestone, or the residue picked up calcium from its container or ground water, calcium tartrate contents would be low. Such pickup, however, might be common in archaeological contexts. Calcium tartrate, magnesium tartrate, etc., are only soluble at about 0.3 g/l in cold water. If there is appreciable leaching, this solubility is much too high for long-term retention. Thus, the presence and salt forms of tartaric acid can be highly variable. Tartrate absence does not mean a container was *not* used for wine.

Tartaric acid or its salts can be detected and identified by various methods. Simple "spot tests" (see below) may be useful in the field and as a preliminary step in the laboratory. Just as an archaeologist should supervise any excavation, direct involvement of a chemist before samples are processed or analyzed is recommended. In view of the specialized nature of the sample preparation and analyses, and their variability depending upon the kind, amount, and uniqueness of the residue being examined, only general guidelines are given for collection and analysis. Samples containing a milligram or so of tartrates may be sufficient, depending upon the contaminants.

NMR (nuclear magnetic resonance) and IR (infrared) spectrometry are desirable techniques, because they do not destroy the sample. With sufficient experimentation, NMR can not only identify and probably quantify any tartrates, but also may be able to determine the isomers present. Use of NMR in wine analysis, or archaeological chemistry generally, has barely begun to reach its potential (Rapp and Markowetz 1990; Beck et al. 1974). IR has recently been applied in identifying tartaric acid inside pre–Bronze Age jars from Godin Tepe (Iran) and inside a Byzantine amphora from Gebel Adda (Egypt) (see chapter 4 by Badler and chapter 5 by McGovern and Michel, this volume).

Modern high-performance liquid chromatography (HPLC), or gas chromatography after preparation of volatile derivatives, can be specific, quantitative, and sensitive (0.1 mg or less per injection). HPLC is widely used and is capable of determining, at the same time, other organic acids present in the sample (e.g., Bissel et al. 1989; Marcé et al. 1990). The usual procedures should differentiate *meso*-tartaric acid from the L(+) form, but not the L(+) isomer from the D(−) isomer.

For more precise studies, it may be necessary to concentrate and partially purify the acids present. If the artifact (or a residue scraped from it) can be treated with dilute hydrochloric acid (HCl), tartrate salts will be converted to the free tartaric acid and dissolved. The hydrochloric acid solution volume should be kept small and if complete recovery of tartrates is desired, a few repeated washes with a low combined volume is preferable. Remaining HCl on the artifact can be rinsed off and discarded. The acid wash containing putative tartaric acid may be carefully concentrated and the collected dry residue may be warmed for about two hours at 120°C to volatilize excess hydrochloric acid. If tartaric acid is heated above about 165°C, it chars and emits a diagnostic burnt sugar odor. Other organic acids do not behave the same, although if this simple test is used, direct comparisons should be made among known samples of citric, malic, succinic, lactic, and other organic acids.

To purify the acids as a group from other substances, a few milliliters of the acid solution is treated by ion exchange. The acidic solution is made alkaline with ammonium hydroxide and passed onto a small column packed with a commercial, strong anion-exchange resin in an appropriate initial form (usually chloride loaded). Such a resin will retain tartrate and most other anions, while passing through non-acid (non-anionic) contaminants. After suitable washing, the organic acids are eluted as a group with a suitable mineral acid, such as dilute sulfuric acid. If the eluting acid is run slowly and collection stopped as soon as the organic acid front has passed, a more concentrated acid fraction can be obtained. HPLC and other techniques can now be more effectively applied to the recovered acids to identify any tartaric acid in the fraction and, if all procedures have been properly done, quantify it.

It is important to assess as quantitatively as possible the amount of tartaric acid in the residue being examined. A higher total amount or relative percentage of tartaric acid vis-à-vis contaminants makes much more certain the identification of a grape wine source. An estimate of the total volume of the original container and particularly the volume of "wine" that would have evaporated to give the residue is helpful, as is the weight of the residue itself. From stains on the inside of the vessel a liquid level may be inferred, a volume before evaporation estimated, and the expected amount of tartaric acid and/or tartrate calculated. For example, a vessel holding 650 ml should have about 3.9 g of tartaric acid (assuming an initial percentage of 0.6%), if its full content of wine were evaporated; or a 50 ml volume will yield about 300 mg.

Qualitative identification of tartaric acid may be convincing and there are a few specific "spot tests" that may be useful (Feigl et al. 1966). In one test, a small amount of the solid to be tested is heated to 120–150°C in 1 ml of 0.01% gallic acid in concentrated sulfuric acid. With increasing amounts of tartaric acid or its salts, in the range of 2–100 μg, yellowish green to blue colors result. The color depends on the formation of glycolaldehyde; carbohydrates, formaldehyde, and a few rare acids do interfere, but other common acids (oxalic, citric, lactic, malic, succinic, salicylic, cinnamic, and various fatty acids) do not. Another test which can detect 10 μg of tartaric acid by producing a green fluorescence (in ultraviolet) produces no or different colors with most of the potentially interfering acids; a possible exception is malic acid, giving green color, but is a tenth as sensitive as tartaric acid (Eegriwe 1933). For this test, heat a small amount of the dry sample 20–30 minutes at 85°C with 1–2 ml of 0.05% β,β'-dinaphthol in concentrated sulfuric acid.

b. Syringic acid

Grape wine differs from beer, date wine, olive oil, honey, and other liquids likely to have been stored in ancient containers in its phenolic content, especially the anthocyanin pigments and tannins of red wine. These compounds are initially reactive and are likely to oxidize and polymerize in ways that prevent direct identification. However, the resulting polymers are somewhat like humic acid in the soil, i.e., they are long-lasting and not readily attacked by microbes or insects. Becoming water insoluble, these polymers are also more likely to persist than tartaric acid in moist circumstances.

A promising approach is alkaline fusion of the test residue (see chapter 7 by Formenti and Duthel, this volume), and identification of syringic acid from it. Malvidin-3-glucoside is the predominant anthocyanin of *Vitis vinifera* (Eurasian) grapes. Whether polymerized or not, it is partially converted upon alkaline fusion to syringic acid (3,5-dimethoxy-4-hydroxybenzoic acid). A young red wine usually has about 200 mg/l of malvidin, but may have as much as five times that amount. It also contains other flavonoids and tannins that yield 3,4-dihydroxybenzoic (proto-catechuic) acid, vanillic acid, and gallic acid upon alkaline fusion. The presence of syringic acid is most definitive for grapes since no other juice or liquid likely to be present in the ancient wine areas of the Near East and Mediterranean regions is high in malvidin. The other acids and their ratios to one another and to syringic acid could also be informative. For example, if lignin (such as might arise from fig skins, stems, and seeds as well as grapes, etc.) was the main constituent of the residue, vanillic acid content would be high relative to that of syringic acid, and grape origin uncertain.

Alkaline fusion to identify phenolic fragments is an old procedure now used only rarely (Zugla and Kiss 1987). We successfully applied it as shown in Figure 6.1 to the residue from 3 ml of typical red wine. Syringic acid was identified along with other expected acids after potassium hydroxide (KOH) fushion and extraction by ethyl acetate of the resultant acids. Mix about 100 mg of the scrapings to be examined (especially reddish deposits inside the ancient container) with about 500 mg of powdered solid KOH. The mixture is carefully heated, so as to avoid charring, until the KOH has melted and continue heating the melt for about five minutes. The cooled melt is dissolved with care in a minimum of water. This solution is acidified carefully to avoid spattering, then analyzed by gas, HPLC, thin-layer, or paper chromatography using known syringic, protocatechuic, and vanillic acids as standards. HPLC, with monitoring absorbance at about 280 nm, is preferable and may be easily quantified. A few micrograms of syringic acid should give a recognizable peak. It may be necessary to use more sample, if the residue being tested is high in extraneous material. An organic acid purifying step, as described before, an ethyl acetate extraction, or solid phase adsorption-elution on reversed phase material may be useful to concentrate syringic and other acids from the acidified melt before measurement is attempted.

c. Other possible analytes

Other constituents or adjuncts from wine may be worthy of study in specific instances. The positive identification of abietic and dehydroabietic acid inside amphorae covered by ash from Vesuvius in A.D. 79 is a good example (Addeo et al. 1979). These amphorae were found neck down, probably after draining and prior to reuse. The identified triterpenoids are characteristic of conifer resin and still exuded a resinous odor. Resin was found on the inside of the neck. (Well-known modern Greek wine [retsina] is still made by dissolving a fairly large dose [perhaps 1%] of pine resin in wine.) Because of its solubility, resin is not very suitable for coating the inside of an unglazed pottery container, to impede wine's evaporation through the vessel wall. Pitch—resin that has been modified by heating—is less soluble. Stoppering by a wad of fibrous material saturated with pine resin or pitch is known to have been used in ancient Greece and Rome (see chapter 20 by Koehler, this volume), and appears likely for the Vesuvius amphorae.

In Egypt, where pine resin had to be imported, clay was also used to seal vessel mouths (see chapter 13 by James and chapter 14 by Lesko, this volume). An early application of chemistry in archaeology was to show that most of the so-called "bitumen" associated with ancient Egyptian artifacts was plant resin and not petroleum-derived (Lucas 1924).

A common method of closure for amphorae, however, was stoppering with clay. In order to fit reasonably tightly, the stopper itself could not be fired before use and certainly not when it was in

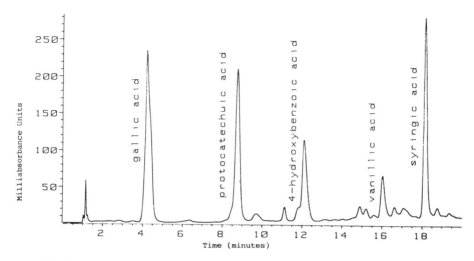

Figure 6.1. High-performance liquid chromatgram (milliabsorbance units at 280 nm) of the residue from 3 ml of red table wine fused in potassium hydroxide, acidified, and extracted with ethyl acetate. The syringic acid is the most significant constituent in identifying grape wine, because it comes from malvidin, the predominant anthocyanidin of red grapes.

place; rather, clay was molded tightly around the mouth of the vessel. Such clay stoppers were rather large and elaborate (see chapter 14 by Lesko, this volume). Sealing a clay stopper with resin would have consolidated it and prevented it from disintegrating in wine.

Such stoppering is of particular importance to enologists, since stored wine needs to be protected from air or it will soon become vinegar by bacterial action, as well as being drastically changed in flavor and color by direct reaction with oxygen. Although an amphora from ancient Athens (500 B.C.) is reported to have been found cork-stoppered (Trescases 1980; later Hellenistic examples are cited by Koehler, chapter 20, this volume), this does not appear to have been the usual ancient method of closure. Cork oak is native to the Mediterranean region, and cork was probably known and used for various purposes (e.g., fishing floats) from an early period. But, while cork easily makes a complete, tight seal on a small, smooth glass neck, it does not on a large, uneven, rough pottery neck. Large ancient corks were also more irregularly shaped, since they were cut as circles from the bark face; modern wine corks are cut as cylinders on the vertical axis of the tree bark. A resin residue on the inside of the ancient Athenian amphora neck suggests both that the stopper was covered with resin and by itself did not fit tightly.

Why were amphorae almost invariably pointed on the bottom? It has been suggested, probably by modern wine students who know that corks in glass bottles need to be kept wet, that the point was to prevent standing them up. Based upon the difficulty and fragility of their stoppering, this is clearly wrong. Nearly all drawings, including some on ships, show the amphorae upright. The ancient paintings of bearers carrying amphorae show them *upright* on the shoulder and not horizontal in two hands or over their shoulder, as would be easier. For such reasons, we know that keeping ancient wines sealed was a problem minimized by keeping the container neck up. A narrow neck and a good seal would be more important for wine, owing to its propensity to convert to vinegar, than for honey or olive oil, two other contemporary liquids. Wines were apparently not hermetically sealed in those times and ancients did not know "bottle bouquet" as we do. The very old wines occasionally noted in ancient writings are noted as evaporated to the point of being syrupy and requiring dilution before drinking.

2. Some Topics Likely to Benefit from Collaboration Between Wine Scientists and Archaeologists

A number of more general publications discuss wine as an important ancient food that contributed to the development of early civilization (e.g., Brothwell and Brothwell 1969; Pariser 1975; Clark and Goldblith 1975; Peterson 1975; Darby et al. 1976; Root 1980; Parry 1969; Tannahill 1988; Soyer 1977). Other books and articles specifically treat the history of wine (Lesko 1977; Enjalbert and Enjalbert 1987; Barry 1775; Allen 1961; Seltman 1957; Hyams 1965; Aragon 1916; Johnson 1989). Since most of these studies have not drawn on modern enology, let us propose some observations and interpretations from the latter viewpoint.

a. Winemaking was very early

There seems to be little doubt that in the transition from hunting and gathering to deliberate agriculture, domesticated cereal grains came before cultivated grapes or before horticulture generally. In the development of more advanced civilization, however, the grape, along with olives, dates and a few other early perennials, deserve special consideration.

Contrary to much speculation in the literature, wine should have preceded beer as the earliest fermented beverage. To convert starch into fermentable sugar, starchy cereal grain must first be sprouted, and used to make beer before appreciable growth has occurred. The only alternative for the first brewer was to chew the grain and spit it into a vessel, so that salivary amylase could convert the starch to sugar. Yeasts must then be added to ferment the sugar to alcohol. Grapes, on the other hand, only need to have their skins broken open to release the juice. Yeasts naturally resident on their skins then act on the high content of directly fermentable sugar in the juice. Furthermore, the higher sugar content of grapes, compared to that of malted grain which was diluted by leaching water, resulted in a higher level of alcohol in wine. Wine's elevated alcohol content, combined with much greater acidity (lower pH), enabled wines to be preserved easier and longer compared to beer. Both easier production and more dependable temporary storage would have made wine probably earlier and preferable to beer in early human societies. The effect of drinking wine is, of course, also more quickly astounding.

As early as 3000 B.C., beer is depicted as more widespread and a larger production activity than winemaking (see chapter 9 by Powell, this volume). This has been used as an argument that beermaking precedes winemaking, but that does not necessarily follow. Wine was more valued than beer and tended to be in shorter supply, reserved for priests, rulers, and special occasions (Allen 1961; Hyams 1965; Seltman 1957; also see chapter 13 by James, this volume). Beer could be made from grain, once the complicated technique was learned, any week that was not too cold. Since the grain was storable and more portable, beer had these advantages over grape wine. Nevertheless, wine, at least that made from wild grapes, was probably the first important alcoholic beverage, since its production was much easier to understand and repeat than that of beer or even mead. For mead, honey must be diluted, yeast added, and for best results, acid added as well. That wine was later less common, although usually more highly esteemed, does not invalidate these considerations.

The grape was naturally wild in much of the area where agriculture and western civilization began (see chapter 3 by Olmo, chapter 16 by Renfrew, and chapter 2 by Zohary, this volume). Some argue that the sugar content of wild grapes was not sufficient to make wine as we know it, but even at considerably lower sugar content, wine would result as easily. Wild grapes presently found in the areas of probable wine grape origin reach 18% sugar or more and with shriveling in dry climates, can reach much higher levels.

Beyond about 30% sugar in shriveled grapes, yeasts cannot ferment all the sugar to alcohol and the wines will remain sweet. Very early records from Mesopotamia, Egypt, Greece, and Rome indicate that sweet wines were made and highly esteemed. Highly ripe (shriveled) grapes must have been used. Raisins occur naturally on wild or tended vines in warm, dry climates. They were known and used as stable, high-calorie food in early historical times (see chapter 9 by Powell, this volume).

The perennial nature of the grapevine, requiring at least three years for appreciable bearing by a new vine, the short and somewhat variable harvesting season, competition from birds and animals, and the early discovery of wine must have been powerful incentives encouraging sedentism. It is necessary to protect the growing vines and the ripening grapes the year-round. Thus, an enologist argues that wine was an important impetus to civilization, not just an early consequence of it.

Another factor that seems pertinent is a special desirability of wine for the ancients (and up to quite recent times). Wine is reminiscent of fruit juice, and tided humans over the long annual periods when fresh fruit was unavailable. With all manner of fresh and well-preserved produce constantly available today, we tend to forget how important a storable fruit juice such as wine would have been. Wine lifts the spirits and ameliorates harsh living conditions not only because of its alcoholic content, but also because of its preserved, flavorful attractiveness. Wine and raisins made grapes a much more useful year-round food source than other early fruits, with the possible exception of dates.

b. The grapevine was greatly modified prehistorically

The earliest depictions of grapevines (see chapter 13 by James, this volume) indicate that modifications from the wild to the domesticated grape were so great, but already so ancient, that no note was taken (or remembered) of these modifications. Consider these major facts: (1) wild grapes are dioecious (i.e., have separate pollen-bearing but fruitless male vines and fruit-bearing female vines), whereas domesticated vines are hermaphroditic, and (2) vines grown from seed are unlikely to resemble the parent vine (Olmo 1976, and chapter 3, this volume; Spiegel-Roy, 1986; Zohary and Hopf 1988; Zohary and Spiegel-Roy 1975; also chapter 2 by Zohary, this volume).

The normal incidence of male vines from wild seed is thought to be about 50%, and a single gene has been indicated. However, wild vines also range between fully male and fully female. In none of the pictures or writings from the earliest times does there appear to be any indication of a random, high percentage of non-bearing vines. Evidently, the transition had already been completed to the modern condition of fruitful and mostly pollen-bearing vines. Female varieties requiring external pollen survive, but are of low commercial importance; one is Almeria (Ohanez)—a relatively rare table grape variety.

This complete transition from the wild to the domesticated grape surely occurred somewhat as follows. A high percentage of wild vines or vines planted from seed were fruitless. Unfruitful ones were rogued out, and the remaining fruiting vines were thus deprived of pollen and ceased to bear. There are stories of this still happening in old vineyards in Europe when modern monovarietal culture is attempted. A few hermaphroditic vines among seedlings from the wild plant bore both a little fruit and pollen. Under ordinary circumstances, their fruit yield was less than a female vine, but without male vines, they would obviously be preferable. Selection by man subsequently improved the fruit yield. Seedling vines from a self-pollinated hermaphroditic parent are very weak due to the expression of deleterious recessive genes. The highly heterozygous grape is thought to result from dioecy enforcing outcrossing. Natural selection would tend to eliminate hermaphrodism from such a population unless man intervened. Reversion to the primitive dioecious condition by backcrossing is easily accomplished in relatively few generations (see chapter 3 by Olmo, this volume).

The changeover from the wild dioecious to the farmed and fruitful hermaphrodite would certainly have required considerable time, especially since male vines were "eradicated" and forgotten. Furthermore, although grape vines now raised from seed are heterogeneous, they are rarely dioecious. Moreover, domesticated grapes have been exclusively vegetatively propagated for a long time. The selection must therefore have occurred very early and for many *seedling* generations, to lower the percentage of male vines and improve the fruitfulness in self-fertile vines, as is vividly portrayed in the earliest pictorial evidence from Egypt (see chapter 13 by James, this volume).

A desirable grape must be propagated vegetatively (a cutting from the mother vine is a clone of itself), because, if grown from its seeds, the special characteristics are diminished or lost. This is true of other perennial horticultural crops as well, but again the grape appears to have been especially easy for the early development of vegetative propagation. Being vines, grapes grow along the ground, unless supported. The canes often root themselves where they lie on the ground. The early grower must have soon realized that, once rooted, this new plant can be cut loose from the mother vine and transplanted with all of the mother vine's characteristics intact. Pliny the Elder described about ninety varieties of grapes in use for wine, table fruit and raisins, and these necessarily represented separate vegetative clones. Vegetative propagation is crucial for maintaining specific characteristics such as berry color, cluster size, desirable flavor, or early ripening.

Today, there are thousands of varieties of Eurasian grapes. A few of them can be traced back with reasonable surety and apparently have undergone minimal genetic change for 1500 years or more. In spite of differences within a clone that can slowly arise with time, varieties like Cabernet Sauvignon are believed to derive from the Roman era. For major differences, selection of new clones from among seedling populations would be necessary. Using modern DNA methods in conjunction with indicated rates of mutation, it should be possible to calculate reasonably reliable estimates of clonal time and seedling generations that would have been necessary to produce our older varieties. I predict that the earliest varieties originated as early as 8000 B.C. Other studies (e.g., Rivera Núñez and Walker 1989) also suggest cultivation of grapes over a wider area and earlier than previously thought.

Descriptions of wine in early Egypt (e.g., Lesko 1977, and chapter 14, this volume) show that many types of wine were available from very early times. These were sometimes designated by vineyard (which also must have varied by mixes of cultivars) and included sweet, dry, white, and different red wines. Given the winemaking technology of the period, white grapes would be necessary to make white wines. Wild grapes are all naturally red (the red color being genetically dominant) until an "albino" mutant arises. A selected white variety must be maintained by planting cuttings. Very probably, the present genetic makeup of grapes of European origin is similar to that of Egyptian, Greek and/or Roman varieties, again attesting to long-term human intervention. The necessity of combining hermaphrodism with all horticulturally practical varieties, maintaining this and other special characteristics in any one variety by vegetative (clonal) propagation, and yet producing highly diverse cultivars by selection among seedlings was a major achievement. Even if coupled at every step with astute observation, it could only have occurred over an extended time period.

c. Wine more healthful than water

Were there other incentives for wine to be valued in antiquity, in addition to its flavor and alcoholic content? It is well documented from Roman and earlier sources that wine was usually diluted before consumption. The dilution was often equal volumes of water to wine; sometimes more water was added, but seldom less than one-third water. The person who drank undiluted wine was considered unsophisticated at best. One obvious reason for this custom, which was likely more than simple fashion, is that the weather where grapes thrive is hot, at least in the summer, and thirst may not be quenched without drunkenness with undiluted wine.

On the other hand, ancient wines were often sweet. Of course, a sweet wine is not particularly thirst-quenching. Since sweet wines usually have higher alcoholic content, why did the ancients appear to want high alcohol and then dilute the wine? The only way that the earliest vintners could have produced sweet wine was to use very ripe and partially dried grapes. Adding honey to a dry wine would work, but that was likely too expensive and would cause refermentation. Boiled down must and raisins also appear to have been used as additives, at least by Roman times. Various reasons could be proposed for diluting alcoholic, sweet wines ranging from "taste" to more economical transport of the more concentrated beverage. The one compelling reason is that much of the drinking water would make a person ill, but mixed with wine the water would be sanitized.

It has been shown experimentally that living typhoid and other dangerous microbes rapidly die when mixed with wine. It is axiomatic that food-poisoning organisms, much less human pathogens, cannot survive and certainly not multiply in the acidic pH, the tannic, and alcoholic medium of wine. Wine was and is so healthful, because it cannot be a source of microbial health problems. Thus, wine could have been used to make contaminated water safe, as well as more palatable.

As one example of antimicrobial use of wine, an ancient army can be thought of as carrying its own human and animal contamination with it. Perhaps contributing to the success of the Roman legions was that they carried wine and mixed it with the local water. Wine seems to have been an expected ration of legionnaires. Successful sieges were sometimes noted as partly the result of the plentiful wine that was supplied to the troops, since contamination of water would be particularly likely under siege conditions. This practice, of course, was not based on scientific knowledge, but was empirically discovered. If an army is to "travel on its stomach" while foraging for most of its food and water, the health value of wine in the water was likely recognized by the leaders, as well as appreciated by the soldiers. Reexamining ancient accounts, provisioning practices, and medical attitudes in the light of such ideas, which are based on modern enology, is valuable for both the historian and the natural scientist. In a similar way, Peterson (1975) attributes the success of the Mongols in 13th century Europe to the consumption of blood and milk from "portable" herds, including the soldier's own steed, thereby avoiding water contamination problems.

3. Other Topics in Need of Better Historical and Scientific Information

Enologists would like to have further information about, and could possibly shed light on, a number of other topics which are presently poorly documented historically. Although only three examples can be discussed here, other areas (e.g., distillation) could also be usefully restudied.

a. Sulfur dioxide use

When was sulfur dioxide (SO_2) first used in preserving wine? We will probably never know for sure, but further investigation would be useful for a number of reasons. It is known that sulfur was burnt to fumigate mines, dwellings and ships from at least classical times. Possibly, the venting of volcanic SO_2 through mines or roasting of pyrite ores for metal recovery was recognized as a source of this potent gas, which eliminated vermin. Even in modern times, since World War I, sulfur was commonly burned for "deratization" of ships and in "sulfur houses" for bleaching and preserving fruit being dried. Ulysses, upon returning from Troy, called for disinfecting sulfur and a fire so that he could fumigate his home (Hammond and Carr 1976).

The bleaching and preservative properties of SO_2 probably were discovered when flowers, fruits, or other foods were accidentally left exposed during such room fumigation. A gradual development of applications and control of SO_2 use might then have developed. Archaeological evidence from burning sites, analysis of any remaining sulfur or pyrite, and ancient descriptions or drawings should elucidate the scale, timing, and exact procedures of particular uses.

It is stated that wine vessels were cleansed with the fumes of burning sulfur first by the Egyptians and later by the Romans (Hammond and Carr 1976). Powdered or sputtered sulfur left in the vessel during wine's fermentation produces hydrogen sulfide, the gas with the smell of "rotten eggs." To avoid this problem, the SO_2 gas is conducted into the container without leaving unburned sulfur behind. The initial method of getting SO_2 into the beverage itself, rather than just treating the container, very likely was to add the must, wine, other fruit juice, or beer to the container while it was still full of "smoke" from burning sulfur. This method was first clearly described in 1670 (Hammond and Carr 1976). However, if a sulfur-containing candle or any other source of sulfur is burned in a wet container, the moisture can dissolve a very high content of SO_2 and, as many amateurs continue to relearn, when the wine or must is then introduced into the vessel, this moisture will contribute high SO_2 content to the wine.

Today, the SO_2 gas itself or its sulfite salts are dissolved directly in the must or wine in minimal and closely controlled amounts. With modern understanding and special care, SO_2 might not be added at all, but the discovery of its antioxidant, antimicrobial and general preservative action must have been a great boon to the early winemaker.

b. The wooden barrel

The precursor to the wooden barrel and its cousins was probably a section of a hollow tree, its ends covered perhaps by skins to make either a drum or a liquid container. To make it stronger and resist leakage by splitting, wooden hoops might have been wound around the barrel. The key to making a strong barrel of several staves is the double arch, i.e., a circular arch around the vessel and an end-to-end bulge or bilge arch in the middle. A drum with these features is known from perhaps 1500 B.C. in Egypt (Hankerson 1947). Herodotus about 500 B.C. described coracles floated from Armenia down the Euphrates or Tigris rivers to Babylon with the principal cargo of wine in palm wood casks (see also chapter 9 by Powell, this volume). Palm is difficult to bend and make a tight, double-arched barrel. Probably these casks were not true barrels. Hooped barrels of "modern" type were common by Roman times; they are depicted on Trajan's Column, and found as well lining from Roman Britain. Pliny the Elder credits their invention to residents of the Alpine valleys. Such barrels are claimed to have been introduced into China about 1150 B.C. (Pan 1965).

More information concerning the stages of barrel improvement and the spread of their use would be helpful in understanding storage, ageing, and transport of wines and other liquids. Barrel-making, of course, has much in common with making wooden ships watertight. Barrels also have other advantages for wine, which have been understood only recently. Not only do oaken barrels give special attractive flavors to wine, they well protect the wine within from air oxidation as long as it is full, or nearly so, and well bunged (stoppered). Further study of the origins and use of barrels would also be relevant to the history of provisioning and military supply.

c. Tools for winemaking and grapegrowing

The tools associated with grapegrowing and winemaking can have special significance, which can be elucidated by a wine specialist. The "Swiss Army Knife" of the time, the Greco-Roman vineyardist's tool called the *falx vinitoria*, had a handle, a knife edge for cutting away from the body, a sharpened hook for cutting toward the body, a sharpened back as a hatchet for chopping, and a point presumably for splitting or separating canes (de St. Denis 1943; White 1967). This highly evolved tool is directly related to the early development of pruning and trellising.

Darby et al. (1977) show four different depictions of so-called wine presses from ancient Egypt (see also chapter 13 by James and chapter 14 by Lesko, this volume). One press appears quite workable and well-illustrated, another is of questionable function, while the remaining two presses are nonfunctional as shown. The workable press involves putting the grape pomace in a bag before, or especially after, fermentation and squeezing out the juice or wine by stretching and twisting. If artists then (as now) did not always depict things in a factually correct fashion, out of ignorance or because of artistic license, then collaboration among enologists, archaeologists, text specialists, and art historians may begin to remedy these deficiencies.

Acknowledgments

M. Andrew Walker (Grape Geneticist), Department of Viticulture and Enology, University of California at Davis, and James T. Lapsley (Historian), University Extension, University of California at Davis, are thanked for helpful discussions. They share no blame for my speculations.

CHAPTER 7

The Analysis of Wine and Other Organics Inside Amphoras of the Roman Period

Françoise Formenti and J. M. Duthel

1. Introduction

Evidence for commercial traffic in wine exists as early as the mid-3rd millennium B.C. in the Ebla corpus (also see chapter 9 by Powell and chapter 10 by Zettler and Miller, this volume). "Canaanite" jars or amphoras constitute the earliest material evidence for such commerce (see chapter 15 by Leonard, chapter 14 by Lesko, and chapter 5 by McGovern and Michel). These pottery containers were used to transport foodstuffs including wine, as attested by shipwrecks along the Turkish coast dating as early as 1700 B.C. (Sheytan Deresi), and are frequently shown in Egyptian reliefs and frescoes. The Canaanite jar was the precursor of later Greek amphoras, which were employed in an extensive Mediterranean wine trade (see chapter 20 by Koehler, this volume).

2. Amphoras of the Greek and Roman Periods in Southern France

Amphoras, as the ancient wine containers par excellence throughout the Mediterranean, have been recovered from late 7th century B.C. sites in western Languedoc, together with Greek, Etruscan, and Punic pottery. Marseille, a Phocaean (Ionian) colony, was founded at about this time, and led to an intensification and diversification of the Mediterranean wine trade. Specific pottery amphoras called "Massaliettes" (Fig. 7.1) were produced locally. At first, Massaliettes were no more common than Greek and Etruscan imports, but later their numbers increased, indicating greater local production of wine (Laubenheimer 1990). A virtual monopoly of the French wine trade was achieved by Marseilles during the 5th and 4th century B.C.

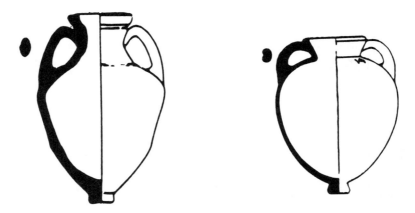

Figure 7.1. Massaliettes amphoras, with storage capacities of 32–34 l.

The economic domination of Marseille was eclipsed by the Roman Empire at the beginning of the 1st century B.C. As early as the 2nd century B.C., however, the Roman wine trade was well organized in southern Gaul. Greco-Italic amphoras (Fig. 7.2) from Sicily and Greece, with their unglazed pottery fabrics, pointed bottoms and narrow necks, occur throughout the Mediterranean Basin.

Greco-Italic amphoras are found as far north as Toulouse and Limoges in Gaul. A good deal of wine in Gaul was evidently coming from Italy before the Romans conquered the province, and this continued to be the case in the succeeding centuries. At the beginning of the 1st century B.C., pottery vessels denoted Dressel 1a–c amphoras (according to Heinrich Dressel's classification— see Fig. 7.3) begin to appear. Lamboglia 2 and Dressel 6 type amphoras were also used to a lesser extent at this time. At the end of the 1st century B.C., Dressel 2–4 amphoras gradually displace Dressel 1 vessels.

Because of a greater volume to weight ratio, Dressel 2–4 amphoras can carry 30% more wine than type 1 vessels (Hesnard 1977). Nevertheless, Dressel 2–4 vessels were produced on a much smaller scale than Dressel 1 amphoras. This may be explained by the introduction of the *dolia*, a large container for transporting wine in bulk, groups of which are frequently associated with Dressel 2–4 amphoras in shipwrecks (Fig. 7.4). The wine in these large vessels was transferred at the dock to barrels, wineskins, and new and reused amphoras (Tchernia 1986). Gallic containers ("Gauloise" types 1 and 2) were probably also being used at the beginning of the 1st century B.C. (Laubenheimer 1990: 118–19).

The importation of Mediterranean wines into Gaul continued, as attested by chemical analyses of amphoras coming from Rhodes and Cos (Picon 1986). The chemical "signatures" of Dressel 2–4 amphoras, on the other hand, showed them to have been manufactured in Lugdunum (Lyon). The increasing popularity of Dressel 2–4 vessels, which imitate imported Roman A type amphoras, imply a return to intensive local wine production.

During the 1st century A.D., the local production of Gauloise amphoras began to predominate (see Map 7.1), after the official lifting of the Roman prohibition against the culture of the vine in Gaul. The Gallic amphoras are made of a thinner, more brittle pottery fabric. To prevent breakage, they were wrapped in straw like glass bottles today.

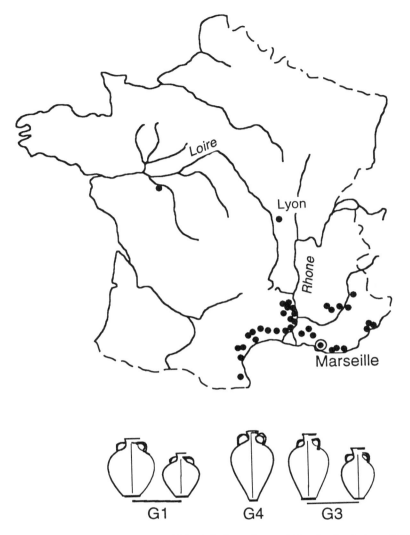

Map 7.1. Principal production centers of "Gauloise" amphoras. (After Laubenheimer 1989.)

3. Chemical Analysis of Residues and Liquids in Dressel Type Amphoras

Amphoras are known to have been used to transport other goods besides wine (especially, olive oil and fish products, such as *garum*, a liquid made from decomposed fish), and the question may be raised whether scientific criteria and methods exist by which these organics can be identified with certainty? This question led to our initial investigations of oils (Condamin et al. 1976), following which we studied resinous and other compounds in wine residues (Condamin and Formenti 1978). We assumed that a given amphora had originally contained only one organic material, since they were generally considered as nonreturnable containers in antiquity (much like plastic bottles today). Because of its porous structure, the pottery ware of the amphoras might retain some organics. In our papers, we show that very small quantities of fatty acid salts were

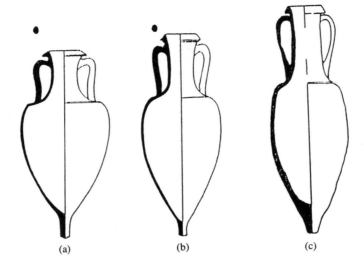

(a)   (b)   (c)

Figure 7.2. Greco-Italic amphoras from Mediterranean shipwrecks off the coast of southern France (Gaul): a) vessel from shipwreck *Secca di Capistello*, near Lipari; b) vessel from shipwreck *Grand Congloué*, near Marseille; c) vessel from shipwreck *Chrétienne C*, from Anthéor near St. Raphaël.

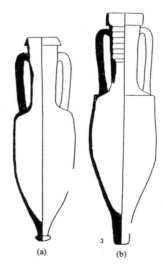

(a)   (b)

Figure 7.3. Dressel types 1 and 2–4 amphoras: a) type 1 vessel from shipwreck *Epave de l'îlot Barthélémy*, near St. Raphaël; b) type 2–4 vessel from shipwrieck *Chrétienne A*.

derived from oils. Phenolic acid derivatives, principally from tannins and anthocyanins, and calcium tartrate, were characteristic of wine (see chapter 6 by Singleton and chapter 5 by McGovern and Michel, this volume).

    The amphoras that were tested for wine were Dressel type 1 vessels from the shipwrecks of *la Madrague in Giens* (Condamin et al. 1976) and *Lamboglia 2* (Formenti 1978), and Dressel type

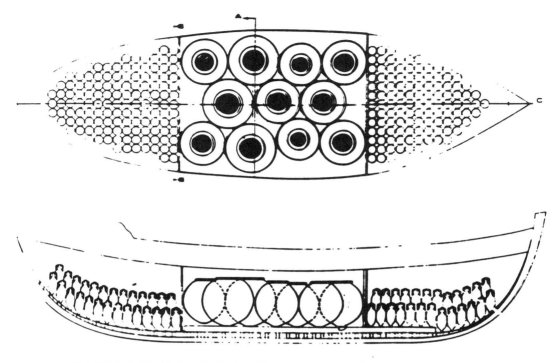

Figure 7.4. Ship's hold with hypothetical packing arrangement of Dressel type 2–4 amphoras and *dolia*.

2–4 vessels, which were dredged up in Port-la-Nautique. The amphoras had a red residue on their interior bottoms, and those which were still sealed with corks contained a relatively transparent liquid. The same compounds—phenolic acid derivatives and tartrate acid and its salts, the latter found only in grapes in large amounts—were identified in the residues and liquids. Tannins and anthocyanins precipitate out of the liquid due to the high sodium chloride content of sea water, as has been demonstrated in the Bordeaux laboratories' analyses of modern wine. Tannins and anthocyanins are natural condensed polymers, which are highly stable and degrade very slowly over time.

a. Solid residue analytical procedures

In order to find phenolic acid derivatives, the solid residue was degraded by alkaline attack for 12 hours at 250°C. Phloroglucinol, pyrogallic acid, parahydroxybenzoic acid, and 3,4-dihydroxybenzoic acid, which are degradation products of tannins and anthocyanins, were then identified by thin layer and gas chromatography. The chromatograms of these compounds in Dressel type 1 amphoras from Giens were comparable to decomposition products in modern St. Emilion-Calvet wine from the Bordeaux region (Fig. 7.5).

b. Liquid analytical procedures

Tartaric acid and its salts were separated from the liquid by ionic exchange resin (Amberlite IRA 401). Following acidification and extraction by ether, the compounds were detected by gas chromatography (note that infrared spectrometry was used to identify the same compounds in the

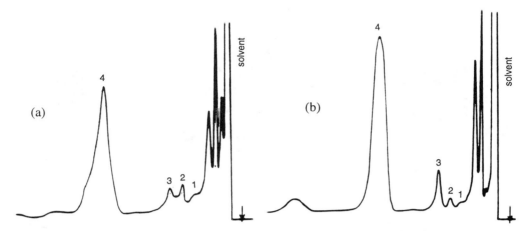

Figure 7.5. Gas chromatograms comparing tannin and anthocyanin decomposition products from a Dressel type 1 amphora from Giens (a) and modern St. Emilion-Calvet wine (b). Individual peaks mark pyrogallic acid (1), tartaric acid (2), parahydroxybenzoic acid (3), and 3-4-dihydroxybenzoic acid (4). An Intersmat IGC 120L instrument with a flame ionization detector was employed. The separation column was packed with OV 17 (10%) on chromosorb G (3 m × 1/8 in). Temperatures were as follows: oven (180°C), injector (200°C), and detector (200°C).

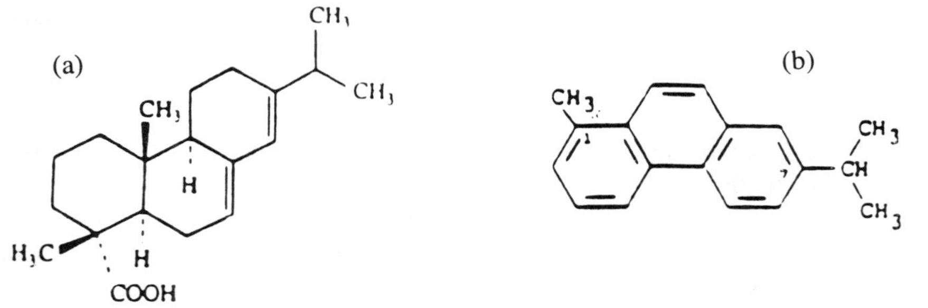

Figure 7.6. Dehydroabietic acid (a) and reten (b), degradation products of pine resin.

pre–Bronze Age Godin Tepe jars—see chapter 4 by Badler and chapter 5 by McGovern and Michel, this volume).

c. The analysis of resins

The organic residues of wine from the vessels that we have analyzed are always accompanied by resinous acids, because the interiors of amphoras dating to the Greek and Roman periods were coated with resin (see chapter 20 by Koehler, this volume). Since the amphoras were porous and unglazed, resinous linings served to seal the interiors. Containers for oil did not require such a coating, because oil itself acted as a sealant. Resins are generally better preserved in underwater contexts as compared with land sites where resin degradation is accelerated by soil bacteria.

Gas chromatography coupled with mass spectrometry was used to identify dehydroabietic acid and reten (Fig. 7.6). These compounds are degradation products of pine resin over time (Laubenheimer 1991).

4. Conclusion

Our analyses have demonstrated that even after thousands of years, traces of wine and resinous linings, as well as other organic products, inside Greek and Roman amphoras can be chemically identified and clearly distinguished.

III

_____

The History and Archaeology of Wine

The Near East and Egypt

CHAPTER 8

Fourth Millennium B.C. Trade in Greater Mesopotamia: Did It Include Wine?

Guillermo Algaze

1. Introduction

The second half of the 4th millennium B.C. was a pivotal time in the development of complex societies in the Near East. Nowhere is this clearer than in the alluvial lowlands of southern Iraq, where Mesopotamian civilization had its origins. The process whereby this occurred is only beginning to be fathomed, but it is clear that communities in the southern Mesopotamian alluvium were expanding rapidly. Internally, this is discernible in the explosive growth of cities and their dependencies, as documented in surveys by Adams (1981). The city of Warka (ancient Uruk), for example, grew to an estimated 200 hectares by the Late Uruk period (Finkbeiner 1987), largely by incorporating rural populations from the surrounding countryside. Rapidly developing social and political differentiation is also observable within alluvial polities at this time. This may be inferred from architectural complexes at Warka and Eridu, where earlier prehistoric temples give way without interruption to ever more massive and complex Uruk administrative structures (Heinrich 1982; Safar et al. 1981). Other innovations include new forms of economic arrangements and record keeping, possibly for the first time in human history (Nissen 1985, 1986). Pertinent archaeological, representational, and textual evidence (such as Warka's Archaic Texts) suggest that by the Uruk period the state held control of a portion of the means of production (encumbered labor) and of its surplus (Zagarell 1986), and that craft and occupational specialization on an industrial scale had been developed (Nissen 1970, 1976). These changes were accompanied by the creation of new forms of symbolic representation that were presumably needed to validate the transformations taking place in the realm of social and political relationships. In turn, this led to the creation of an artistic tradition and iconographical repertoire that was to set the framework for pictorial representation in Mesopotamia for millennia to follow.

The internal processes just described, however, could not and did not occur in isolation. Save for the products of irrigated agriculture and animal husbandry, the alluvial lowlands of southern

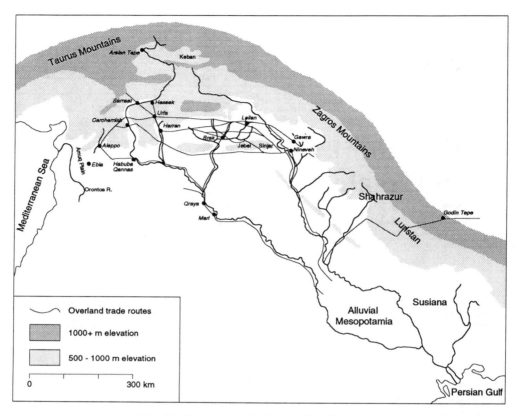

Map 8.1. Trade routes in the late 4th millennium.

Iraq are devoid of almost all the material requirements needed to sustain complex civilizations. Thus, while many endogenous factors may have contributed to the increasing complexity of societies in the Mesopotamian alluvium prior to and in the early stages of the Uruk period, the emergence of Sumerian city-states in the later part of the period was unintelligible outside of a framework of interaction with communities in the resource-rich areas at the periphery of the alluvium, principally in the Zagros highlands of Iran and the Taurus highlands of Anatolia. These regions supplied alluvial societies with the key commodities they required (principally metals and wood) and furnished alluvial elites with the prestige goods they demanded. Some evidence exists to suggest that wine may have been traded as part of this procurement effort, but more research is needed to clarify whether or not this was indeed the case.

2. Trading Settlements

The mechanisms whereby the needed resources were procured at the onset of Mesopotamian civilization have become clear only recently, largely as a result of an array of archaeological salvage programs necessitated by the construction of a number of dams alongside the most important waterways crisscrossing the fertile plains of northern Mesopotamia (Demirji 1987), northern Syria (van Loon 1967), and southeastern Anatolia (Özdogan 1977; Algaze et al. 1991). This evidence has contributed to a more precise understanding of the nature, intensity, variety, and direction of contacts between communities in the southern Mesopotamian alluvium and surround-ing areas in the Uruk period. As a result, it now appears certain that in the late 4th millennium B.C. Mesopotamian societies acquired the resources they needed by means of outposts placed at key junctions in the surrounding periphery. As I have argued at greater length elsewhere (Algaze 1989, 1993), these settlements served to mediate contacts between core and peripheral groups; no doubt to the long term benefit of the former, since commerce between the two groups was unequal by its very nature, involving as it did the exchange of core manufactured products for raw peripheral resources. Such outposts are often encountered in situations of initial contact between societies at markedly different levels of sociopolitical evolution, and allow well-organized core polities maximum access at minimal expense to less developed peripheries (Smith 1976).

Analysis of the locational circumstances of late 4th millennium Uruk Mesopotamian settle-ments in peripheral areas suggests that they occur only at selected nodes in connection with well established trade routes (Map 8.1). Three distinct types may be recognized, each characterized by material culture that is largely of southern Mesopotamian/southwestern Iranian Uruk affiliation: outposts, stations, and enclaves. Outposts are small isolated Uruk installations within indigenous sites in intermontane valleys that traverse the surrounding highlands. Attested examples include Godin Tepe (V) in the Kangavar valley of the Zagros, where a small Uruk fort dominating a larger local site was uncovered (Weiss and Young 1975; see chapter 4 by Badler, this volume), and Tepe Sialk (IV.1) near Kashan in the Iranian Plateau (Amiet 1985), each alongside the principal routes across the Iranian plateau.

Stations are also relatively small but are only found within the Mesopotamian plains, com-monly along the principal routes in and out of the Mesopotamian alluvium, which followed the Tigris and the Euphrates northwards. Excavated examples include Hassek Höyük in southeastern Turkey (Behm Blancke et al. 1984) and Tell Qraya (Simpson 1988) in northeastern Syria, both along the Euphrates.

The enclaves are much larger than either of the preceding. Examples recognized thus far are urban in size, and appear to have been considerably larger and more complex than indigenous societies in the midst of which they were implanted. Enclaves are found principally at the intersection of the most important east/west overland routes across northern Mesopotamia and the main north/south waterways. Until now, none is attested away from the waterways. The best known, but by no means only examples, are Habuba Kabira-süd (Strommenger 1980) and the associated site of Jebel Aruda on the Euphrates in Syria (van Driel and van Driel-Murray 1979, 1983), Tell Brak on the Upper Khabur (Oates 1986), also in Syria, and Nineveh (Algaze 1986) on the Upper Tigris in northern Iraq. Best understood is Habuba Kabira-süd, where extensive horizontal exposures of Uruk levels were practicable. These exposures revealed that an earlier, apparently small and short-lived occupation was replaced by a well-planned fortified city, which was minimally 18 hectares in extent. Excavations at this site have exposed carefully laid-out streets and well differentiated residential, industrial, and administrative quarters—all apparently constructed as part of a single master plan. The material culture recovered at the site and at nearby related settlements such as Aruda and Arslan Tepe is wholly southern Mesopotamian in type, and leaves no doubt that their inhabitants were colonists from the southern lowlands (Strommenger 1980; Sürenhagen 1986) (Fig. 8.1).

Because of their carefully selected positions at locations of considerable transportational significance, it must be inferred that the network of Uruk enclaves, stations and outposts must have exercised considerable control over the flow of goods in and out of the alluvium, the highlands, and across the northern plains. Because of their isolated positions in the midst of an alien hinterland, however, it must be presumed that, initially at least, the less developed societies in the midst of which they were located were amenable to trade.

Guillermo Algaze

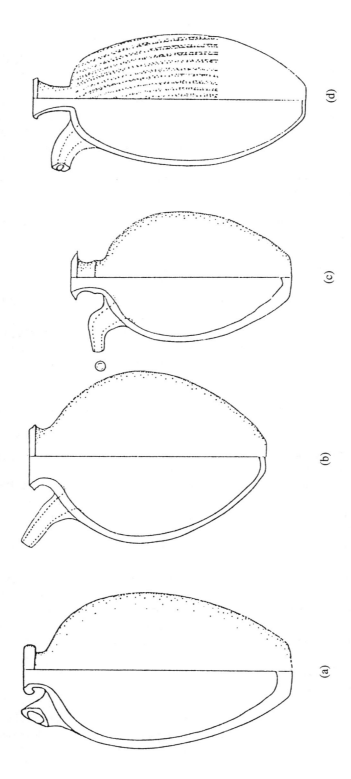

Figure 8.1. Uruk spouted jars and bottles from Period VIA levels at Arslan Tepe. Scale approximately 1:5 (after Palmieri 1989: fig. 3, 4-7.)

3. The Nature of the Trade: Imports

If the primary rationale of Uruk outposts in the periphery was indeed trade, then what exactly were the commodities being traded? The answer may be inferred from two complementary data sets: (1) the range of imported peripheral resources in Uruk sites, and (2) traces of Uruk material culture in peripheral sites attesting to contacts with the Uruk world, contacts that were no doubt mediated through the outposts and enclaves described above. While some of the commodities imported into the Uruk core in the late 4th millennium had been imported before, their variety—and presumably quantity—in Uruk times appear to represent a sharp increase over previous conditions, although, admittedly, fully representative and quantifiable samples are not yet generally available. The imported commodities may be divided into two types: (1) essential, unprocessed resources that are necessary for the day-to-day operation of complex social organizations in the resource-poor alluvial regions, and (2) non-utilitarian, prestige commodities that are necessary for the consolidation and maintenance of social and political relationships within elite groups.

Of all the essential resources brought in by Uruk societies, the most difficult to discern in the archaeological record is wood. There can be no doubt, however, that timber must have been imported in substantial quantities to satisfy the architectural requirements of rapidly growing Uruk urban centers (Margueron 1992). It is likely that the eastern Taurus region of the Anatolian highlands was the primary source. Trunks cut in the Malatya and Keban areas could have been easily and cheaply floated downstream on the Euphrates (Rowton 1967), and this may well have been a factor influencing the location of Uruk enclaves along its banks. A second import that is difficult to detect, but of potentially considerable economic impact, was dependent labor: slaves acquired in exchange for other goods or as prisoners of war. The signs for slaves that are specifically stated to be of foreign origin (i.e., from the mountains) can be recognized already in the Archaic Texts from the Eanna Precinct at Warka (Eanna IV/III), which are partly contemporaneous with the Uruk outposts (Vaiman 1976).

More easily traced in the archaeological record are other essential imports, such as bitumen, common stones, and base metals—particularly copper, which figures prominently in the Archaic Texts (Nissen 1985). Copper objects, vessels, and tools are amply documented in Uruk contexts both in the Mesopotamian alluvium and in Khuzestan (Heinrich 1938, Lenzen 1958; Le Brun 1971, 1978), and numerous unworked copper lumps and metallurgical installations were recognized at Warka (Nissen 1970). Copper was obtainable either from sources in central Iran (Caldwell 1967) or in the Ergani Maden area of the eastern Taurus (de Jesus 1980). The importance of copper in the exchange networks of the late 4th millennium is additionally borne out by small amounts of Uruk pottery found at various indigenous sites which exploited known copper mines in Iran and Turkey, such as Tal-i-Iblis in Kerman (Caldwell 1967), Tepe Ghabrestan in Qasvin (Majidzadeh 1979), and Tepecik in the Keban/Altinova area (Esin 1982). This pottery attests to contacts between known native copper-processing sites and nearby Uruk outposts.

Another import was bitumen, which could be procured from natural seepages at various locations in southwestern Iran, in the Middle Euphrates region, or in the Upper Tigris area near Mosul (Marschner and Wright 1978). It was used as mortar and for general waterproofing in Uruk period architecture (Heinrich 1937; Lloyd and Safar 1943). A common stone import was flint, available as nodules in the western desert, the Zagros piedmont, and the northern plains. It must have been imported from a variety of sources as raw material for the local production of tools and implements in Uruk sites (Eichmann 1986), but Canaanean-type blades of northern Syrian manufacture are also documented (Sürenhagen 1986). Other stone imports include (1) basalt, of northern Mesopotamian or northern Syrian origin and (2) variously veined marbles and limestones, common in the Zagros range and the Central Plateau of Iran (Beale 1973).

No less important than the above in their social impact (Schneider 1977), but acquired in smaller quantities during the Uruk period, were various non-utilitarian commodities, such as rare metals and semiprecious and precious stones. Such exotic imports have been recovered at a number of Uruk sites in the alluvium and Khuzestan, but most strikingly in the Eanna Precinct area at Warka (Heinrich 1936; Lenzen 1958). Rare metals and alloys, in fact, are frequently mentioned in the Archaic Texts found in that city (Nissen 1985). Silver, lead, and gold were obtainable from sources in highland Iran (Caldwell 1967), and silver was mined in the Keban region of highland Anatolia at the time of the Uruk expansion (Yener 1983). Obsidian tools (Lenzen 1959) and vessels (Heinrich 1937) commonly found in Uruk contexts are surely of eastern Anatolian origin and both finished products (compare Tobler 1950) and raw materials may have been imported. The lapis lazuli from which numerous fragments of jewelry and inlays were made (Lenzen 1958) could only have originated in Badakhshan in northern Afghanistan (Hermann 1968). Steatite/chlorite and alabaster (calcite), used for the manufacture of a variety of high prestige artifacts (Asher-Greve and Stern 1983), must have come from sources in southeastern Iran (Beale 1973), while the carnelian and agate used in jewelry would have been obtained from sources in India and south-central Afghanistan (Lamberg-Karlovsky and Tosi 1973).

4. The Nature of the Trade: Exports

We do not know much about the nature of the commodities exported in exchange for the imports enumerated above, but, if later 3rd millennium B.C. documentation may be used as a guide, the majority of the goods exported from the alluvium would have been perishables that leave few or no traces in the archaeological record (Crawford 1973). Paramount among these would have been carefully crafted, finished textiles produced in state-administered industrial establishments staffed largely by encumbered labor, principally dependent women. Although we do not yet have unequivocal evidence for the manufacture of textiles specifically for export in the Uruk period, such as we can document clearly later in the 3rd millennium (Waetzoldt 1972), what evidence is available reveals that all the necessary preconditions for such an activity were already in place by the floruit of the Uruk outposts. The existence of the required technology is demonstrated by a cylinder seal impression from Susa clearly depicting a horizontal loom and weavers (Amiet 1972: no. 673). State control over necessary raw materials (wool) seems assured in light of a group of Archaic Texts dealing with animal husbandry, which attests to the existence of state-managed flocks (Green 1980). Similarly, control over required labor is implicit in the specific term used for female slaves in the Archaic Texts (Sumerian SAL + KUR), which means not only slave of foreign origin in the strict sense, but also dependent woman or serf (Gelb 1982: 91–93)—and it is these who figure prominently in the later documentation as the principal source of labor involved in the production of textiles for export. Significantly, the already noted sealing from Susa showing a weaving scene depicts the attendant personnel as wearing long pigtails, an indication that the labor was performed by women. A final precondition for long-distance exchange is a state role in the storage and redistribution of raw materials and finished products. This too is substantiated by the Archaic Texts, even the earliest of which appear to represent the work of central administrators recording inflows or outflows of specific commodities. According to Nissen (1986: 330), a substantial number of the tablets appear to deal with the distribution and storage of textiles.

Whether or not the various types of Uruk pottery occasionally recovered in indigenous settlements across the northern plains and the surrounding highlands were acquired for their contents is unclear. The answer is likely to depend on the function of each type involved, and this remains largely undetermined. Other than beveled rim bowls, the most common Uruk forms found in peripheral sites include four-lugged jars and spouted jars, although not all sites have each of these types and not every example identified need be an actual import. Intuitively, it is difficult to see how the coarse but ubiquitous beveled rim bowls that constitute our most frequent evidence of cross-cultural contacts could have been traded. This inference now appears substantiated by the results of neutron activation analyses of beveled rim bowls from the environs of Samsat in the Atatürk Dam region of southeastern Anatolia, where the characteristic bowls were made from site-specific local clays (Evins 1989).

5. A Hypothesis About Wine

More likely to have been prized for their contents are the diverse Uruk spouted bottles that have occasionally been found in various local sites across the Mesopotamian periphery, as for example in the Rania and Shahrizur valleys of Iraqi Kurdistan (Abu al-Soof 1985). Best documented are several examples found in storerooms, near the discarded clay stoppers that once sealed them, at the site of Arslan Tepe (Period VIA), an important indigenous Late Chalcolithic regional center in the Malatya region of the southeastern Anatolian highlands (Palmieri 1989: fig. 3.4-7) (Fig. 8.1). These jars are almost certainly of Uruk manufacture and unequivocally indicate Mesopotamian involvement in long-distance movement of valuable liquids. In the absence of chemical characterization analyses, it is not known what exactly was transported in these jars. While beer was certainly made at the time by Mesopotamian societies (Katz and Voigt 1986; also see chapter 9 by Powell, this volume), it can be dismissed as a possible content of the jars, since it would not have kept for any extended period of time without pasteurization and thus could not have been transported over any great distances. Two more likely possibilities are wine and oils. Traditionally, however, neither were commonly exported from southern Mesopotamia (Pettinato 1972), and thus it must be presumed that the jars could not have originated in the south. If wine or oils were indeed the commodities in the Uruk Jars at Arslan Tepe, then the jars could have been exported from one or more of the Uruk enclaves across the northern plains, which were situated in areas known to have produced both wine and olive oil in antiquity. The best candidates for this role are the various Uruk enclaves along the Upper Euphrates in northern Syria and southeastern Anatolia, which are located in wine and olive oil producing areas. These enclaves fall well within the area of natural geographic distribution of *Vitis vinifera* (see chapter 2 by Zohary, this volume), and must have had access to grain from the inland plains of Syria to ensure their survival. Wine and oils from the Gaziantep-Aleppo region, a traditional producer, could well have formed part of the commodities being brought in. These prized liquids could then have been shipped downstream to the alluvium, and could also have been repackaged for re-export across the north—as indicated by the Arslan Tepe evidence. Later textual documentation from Mari provides a close parallel: in the early 2nd millennium B.C., Mari served as an indigenous riverine entrepôt and had a role as a collection, repackaging, and transshipment point for agricultural products (including wine) from the Aleppo area to the west (Finet 1969: 44; see also chapter 9 by Powell and chapter 10 by Zettler and Miller, this volume). The hypothesis that wine may have been a component of Uruk period exchange across greater Mesopotamia is buttressed by evidence discussed by Badler (chapter 4) and McGovern and Michel (chapter 5, this volume) for the making, storage, and consumption of wine at Godin Tepe, one of the already noted Uruk trade outposts in the Zagros highlands.

Whether or not wine was being distributed as part of the Uruk exchange network, the fact that valuable liquids were being moved about in Uruk containers means that the Uruk outposts succeeded in interposing themselves as participants in intraregional trade within the areas of the periphery in which they were located. We can only guess at how this came to pass, but I would argue that their control of the structures of long-distance exchange across the northern Mesopotamian plains and the immediately surrounding highlands gave Mesopotamian merchants an organizational "headstart" with which local entrepreneurs could not easily compete. A close parallel for the sort of situation just described is provided by the Old Assyrian trade network of early second millennium date. Available historical documentation shows that, in addition to being involved in long-distance exchange between Mesopotamia and Central Anatolia, Old Assyrian merchants based at Kaneş (Kültepe, near modern Kayseri) used capital and contacts derived from their long-distance trade activities and the transportational infrastructure inherent to those activities to successfully participate in local trade within Anatolia, trade that involved the exchange of wholly indigenous products (Larsen 1987).

6. Epilogue

For reasons not yet fully understood, the network of Uruk outposts across the Mesopotamian periphery collapsed with apparent suddenness shortly before the end of the Uruk period. Some portions of the periphery reverted to conditions that obtained prior to the establishment of outposts, as, for example, northern Syria and northern Mesopotamia in the Ninevite V period. Other portions of the periphery, however, developed further on their own right, spurred by the earlier Uruk intrusion.

In southwestern Iran, for instance, the Uruk retrenchment was closely followed by the rise of a strong local state at the very end of the 4th millennium B.C. and the transition to the 3rd millennium B.C. This was the Proto-Elamite kingdom centered at both Susa and Anshan (modern Tal-i Malyan). Within a century or so after its emergence, this successor state expanded the trans-Iranian routes towards the east, as compared with the preceding period (Alden 1982), and took control of trade routes in and out of the Mesopotamian alluvium via the Diyala basin, which had previously been held by Uruk city states (Collon 1987).

The rise of these various local powers astride portions of the international trade routes explains why, in spite of the collapse of the network of Mesopotamian enclaves and outposts of the Uruk period, contacts between southern Mesopotamia and its surrounding periphery continued unabated (Zagarell 1986). Later 3rd millennium B.C. documentation shows that wine was one of the commodities being traded at the time (see chapter 9 by Powell, this volume). Though cross-cultural trade continued in the 3rd millennium, it is to be presumed that the terms of the trade would not have been as favorable to the alluvium as they had been in the Uruk period when alluvial outposts had actually served to organize regional production and resources and to ensure indigenous participation in the long-distance exchange structure controlled by the emerging southern Mesopotamian city-states.

CHAPTER 9

Wine and the Vine in Ancient Mesopotamia: The Cuneiform Evidence

Marvin A. Powell

1. Introduction

Some seventy years ago the Orientalist H.F. Lutz tried, in his work *Viticulture and Brewing in the Ancient Orient* (1922), to give an overview of viticulture in the whole of the ancient Orient including Egypt "from the beginning of historic times down to the wine-prohibition of Muhammed." The most important point of Lutz's work, which still holds true today, was that, once upon a time, the Near East was the home of remarkable wine and beer cultures, the traces of which—like the great civilizations in which they flourished—have been so thoroughly obliterated or transformed by the passage of time and humankind that one could never imagine their former existence without turning to the ancient records. Mention of "the wine-prohibition of Muhammed" is no accident, for Lutz clearly had in mind another Prohibition, under whose gathering cloud and dismal reality his work came into existence.

Lutz's work was good for its time, and it can still be read with profit and pleasure by the scholar, but the discoveries of this century, as well as progress in understanding the ancient languages and cultures, have long since made revisions necessary. Though a few attempts to treat the more abundant evidence for beer have been made, no one since Lutz has tried to provide a systematic account of wine. This is not because of lack of new evidence but rather the opposite. A wealth of additional information has been discovered, but it requires tedious labor and presupposes the work of many specialists to answer when, where, and what the ancient texts are really talking about. No scholar would blame Lutz for his attempt to deal with Egyptian, Babylonian, Hebrew, and Arabic sources for the whole of the ancient Orient, but the nonspecialist reader should be aware that—in spite of the fact that no one has attempted a similar work—the treatment is uneven, sometimes superficial, and frequently erroneous.

This is not to deny the desirability of a sound general treatment of the history of ancient Near Eastern viticulture and viniculture, and perhaps this is a topic whose time has at last come or is about to come. This goal presupposes, however, serious attempts by specialists to evaluate and put together the evidence for wine in the various areas and eras of the ancient Near East. The present paper attempts an overview, based primarily on cuneiform sources, of one segment of that lost world of grape and wine culture: ancient Mesopotamia.

Still, this chapter does not treat every aspect of the topic actually attested in the sources. For example, there is no discussion of the viticultural and vinicultural terms contained in the ancient bilingual glossaries. These terms occur in contexts that make them difficult to identify precisely, and even the Akkadian dictionaries, have recognized, for example, that *ini alpi*, "eye of ox," means more likely the individual grape berry, and that *saḫtu*, "what is drawn off/racked off," is probably the general term for must. Since these terms occur in a specially marked off section in the sequence "grape berry," "must," "raisin," their identities seem certain. Whether the "mother of the grape," also called the "rack," however, is the trunk of the grapevine, a trellis, a tree on which the vine was trained, or some combination of these translations remains uncertain. To solve such problems may not be feasible at the present time, and discussion of them would merely bewilder most readers and leave them not much wiser about the history of viticulture and wine in ancient Mesopotamia.

Consideration of wine in religious and medicinal use has also been excluded, though this evidence has been examined for its possible significance. I would not debate for a moment the food or medicinal value of wine, but wine apologists who proudly cite the ancient use of wine for medicinal purposes should take a look at what else was mixed in by the ancient physicians. Wine, like beer, was in most cases merely the medium for drugs. In any case, libations of wine to the gods and medicinal use is so widespread that it tells us nothing distinctive about viticulture or wine culture.

By limiting the topic to Mesopotamia—which is quite enough in any case—I have not felt obliged to treat material outside of this geographical area. The cuneiform evidence for wine which turns up in the Late Bronze Age in the royal correspondence from Amarna (Egypt) and in texts from Ras Shamra/Ugarit (Syria) belong properly to the history of Syria–Palestine, just as the evidence for wine in ration documents from Persepolis in the period of the Achaemenid Empire belong to the history of wine in Iran. They do not contradict the picture drawn for the overall development of viticulture and viniculture in Mesopotamia and therefore do not concern us here.

With the reader who is not a cuneiformist in mind, translations have generally been cited in preference to editions of cuneiform texts, which are worthless to the nonspecialist and can be easily tracked down by the specialist. Citation of a translation, however, does not imply that it is all correct; part of it may be well-based, another part dubious or entirely wrong. Translations can only serve the purpose of general orientation. Unfortunately, the only way for a nonspecialist confidently to use this material is to solicit the aid of an Assyriologist or Sumerologist. E. Hyams' popular account of the history of viticulture (1965) is a good example of what a muddle can result when a well intentioned but unsuspecting historian tries to interpret the cuneiform evidence based on outdated translations (see, especially, Hyams 1965: ch. 2). This muddle is raised to the level of sublime nonsense in general works like the introductory section on the "History of Wine" in the fourth edition of Alexis Lichine's *New Encyclopedia of Wines and Spirits* (1985).

Still, when one looks at how little progress cuneiformists have made in sorting out the evidence for viticulture and wine, one can hardly blame the would be historian of wine. There are very few studies of wine in ancient Mesopotamia. While an attempt has been made here to utilize and cite every serious study of wine or viticulture in Mesopotamia and even some that are only peripherally related, this still does not add up to very much. The serious historian of viticulture will have to turn to the Akkadian dictionaries, cited under von Soden (1959–81), Oppenheim et al. (1956, 1956a, 1959, 1960, 1961, 1973) and Reiner et al. (1980, 1982), which translate many passages and will help even the nonspecialist to form an independent opinion. For this reason, as well as to avoid having to cite cuneiform texts already entered in the dictionaries, key Akkadian words are cited, such as those for wine, which one can find by looking them up alphabetically.

In general, where I disagree with one or both of the dictionaries, I simply state what I believe to be correct without citing contrary or supporting opinion or evidence. Only in a few instances, such as the postulated idea that the Mesopotamians mixed water with wine, in which both dictionaries have clearly gone astray, has an attempt been made to give the grounds for the disagreement. In assessing the general development and spread of viticulture and wine, no one can possess adequate knowledge for a topic with so many ramifications and so lacking in previous systematic work. The present study claims neither exhaustive comprehensiveness nor infallible interpretation. Rather it attempts to lay out what is perceived as the basic outlines, keeping always in mind that viticulture and wine did not lead independent existences apart from ecological, agricultural, economic, social, and political factors. My primary aim has been to use the evidence to construct a picture of the development of viticulture in ancient Mesopotamia that will give the general reader an idea of where we stand now and that will provide the specialist with a paradigm for further study.

a. Languages, time span, and geography

Cuneiform is a system of writing that was invented by the Sumerians around 3000 B.C., give or take a few centuries. It had a long history, lasting about three thousand years, during which it was used to write about a dozen languages, and perhaps more that are yet to be discovered. The manuscripts survive mostly in the form of clay tablets and a much smaller number of inscriptions on stone and other materials. Manuscripts already in museums number in the hundreds of thousands, and more are discovered almost annually by archaeological excavation. Many remain unstudied beyond cataloging, but sufficient numbers, also numbering many thousands, have been published, enabling us to chart out the basic outlines of many aspects of the ancient cultures which they reflect, including viticulture and viniculture.

The geographical areas represented by cuneiform sources are, above all, the Tigris–Euphrates basin, followed by Syria, and Anatolia, corresponding to modern Iraq, Syria, and central Turkey (see Maps 8.1 and 11.1 for these regions and specific sites mentioned below). Other, less abundant, sources extend the geographical horizons to include the area lying roughly between the 29th and 41st parallels north latitude and between western Iran and the Aegean Sea.

Of primary concern here are Sumerian, the language of the inventors of the script, and Akkadian, a Semitic language closely related to Arabic and Hebrew, which carried on Sumerian cultural traditions when Sumerian itself died out some time after 2000 B.C. Sumerian and Akkadian were spoken in Mesopotamia for thousands of years and represent the extremes in time covered by the sources, with Sumerian at the beginning and Akkadian continuing on until the cuneiform script dies out in the 1st century A.D. Sources in Sumerian pertain primarily to southern Iraq, ancient Babylonia. The Akkadian sources, beginning in the late 3rd millennium B.C. inform us about Babylonia, as well as about the upper parts of the Mesopotamian basin and even beyond.

b. Nature of the cuneiform evidence for viticulture

Cuneiform sources rarely provide us with descriptions of plants or of their cultivation. Successful identification of species depends upon analysis of the written evidence in the light of the history and geography of botany and agriculture and in the light of plant remains (e.g., seeds) and of other evidence discovered by archaeological excavation (e.g., visual depictions of grapevines on ancient monuments; see chapters 10 by Zettler and Miller, 11 by Gorny, and 12 by Stronach, this volume). This allows us to identify, with varying degrees of certainty, ancient names for plants with the modern botanical names. However, for the Mesopotamian area, although a corpus of dated plant materials is gradually being built up, it is still extremely fragmentary, and for southern Iraq it is completely inadequate. Finds of fruit plants from Iraq have been recently reviewed by J. Renfrew (1987), and those of general plant remains by Zohary and Hopf (1988: 183–84; also see chapter 2 by Zohary, this volume). Like all historical inferences, the modern identities that we assign to the ancient names are only a matter of probability. However, the generally assumed identity of Sumerian *geštin* and Akkadian *karanu* with the wine grape *Vitis vinifera* is sufficiently high to omit detailed justification for this identification.

If the identification of species is a laborious process, then a picture of horticulture is still more difficult, for this must be pieced together mainly from economic records whose primary function was to record the income and outgo of commodities. Non-economic texts occasionally contain valuable remarks about horticulture, though these are more like hints than direct information. Nevertheless, the overall picture of viticulture which emerges from the cuneiform sources is consistent with other lines of evidence for the history of ancient agriculture and economics.

2. Viticulture in the Lower Tigris–Euphrates Valley

a. The horticultural context

Fruit cultivation in alluvial southern Iraq seems to have been a sort of "horticultural package" that from the early 3rd millennium B.C. onward included the date-palm (*Phoenix dactylifera*), apple (*Malus pumila* Mill., synonym *Pyrus malus* L.), fig (*Ficus carica*), and grape. The prototype sign for the vine (*geštin*) as well as the prototype signs for date (*gišimmar*), apple (*ḫašḫur*), and fig (*peš*) all turn up in early Sumerian texts from Uruk (Green et al. 1987: nos. 202, 230, 252, 336), around 3000 B.C. This "basic four"—which is joined by the pomegranate before 2000 B.C.—perseveres in cuneiform sources from Babylonia into the period of the Persian empire when the cuneiform evidence begins to dwindle away (Oppenheim et al. 1956: 139–40, 1956: 102–4, 1971: 202–6; Postgate 1987; Powell 1987, 1987a).

The written evidence therefore confirms what we expect from the archaeobotanical record (admirably reviewed in Zohary and Hopf 1988: 128–66): domestication of all these fruit crops preceded writing. Only the date-palm can have been native to southern Iraq. Apple, fig, and grape must all have been first domesticated in their natural habitats and then acclimatized to conditions in southern Iraq.

How much earlier than writing must we place domestication of the vine? As already indicated, the archaeobotanical record from southern Iraq tells us nothing useful about the time period at which a specific plant began to be cultivated there. This is because systematic searches for this kind of evidence have been recent and exceptional rather than the rule. If we took the archaeobotanical record as a representation of reality, one would have to conclude that agriculture was hardly practiced at all in ancient Babylonia.

Outside of Mesopotamia, the archaeobotanical evidence for the earliest period of domestication is somewhat better. Even there, however, arguments from plant remains are of necessity somewhat ambiguous, because the distinctions drawn between wild *Vitis vinifera* L. subsp. *sylvestris* and the domesticated *Vitis vinifera* rest primarily upon the breadth to length ratio of the pips or seeds (see chapters 2 by Zohary, 3 by Olmo, and 16 Renfrew, this volume). Thus, whether the four grape pips reported from ca. 7000 B.C. from Tell Aswad in the Damascus area of Syria (van Zeist and Bakker-Heeres 1979) are from wild or cultivated grapes remains more a matter of belief than of science; four seeds simply do not constitute a large enough group for drawing reliable statiscal inferences. Even taking into account the inadequate samples of available archaeobotanical materials, however, the general paucity of evidence for grapes, whether wild or cultivated, prior to the Bronze Age suggests that widespread cultivation of the vine first occurred in the 4th millennium B.C. Given the far reaching cultural connections evidenced by archaeological assemblages in the Uruk period during the second half of the 4th millennium B.C. (see chapter 8 by Algaze, this volume), stretching through Mesopotamia in a great arc extending from southwestern Iran to the Mediterranean, it would hardly be surprising to find widespread viticulture in this era.

b. Nature and aims of viticulture

Before discussing the nature and aims of viticulture and viniculture in ancient Babylonia, it should first be noted that all ancient sources—and this is perhaps doubly true of cuneiform sources—can be incredibly noncommittal about what is intended: "grape" in both Sumerian and Akkadian seems to denote grapevine and grapes, as well as the juice of the grape. Whether this juice always means "wine" seems by no means as certain as is generally assumed.

c. Wine as an expensive import

Unlike beer, one searches in vain in texts from Babylonia for evidence for making wine; moreover, when it does turn up, it is very expensive. This does not necessarily mean that wine was never made, but its almost total absence from economic records until the 1st millennium B.C. suggests that it was a rare commodity indeed. This fits the overall pattern of the evidence: wine drinking cultures began outside of Babylonia beyond the edges of the alluvium. The points of equilibrium where barley–beer and grape–wine culture met were probably, on the Euphrates, around the Syrian–Iraqi border and, on the Tigris, around modern Tikrit. True wine cultures seem to have begun still farther up the river valleys and at slightly higher altitudes, in other words, within the perimeter of natural rainfall agriculture.

This general picture of wine as a rare commodity perseveres from the 3rd through the 1st millennium B.C. As we have seen, the Sumerian sign for grapevine turns up early in the 3rd millennium. Nevertheless, even as late as around 2000 B.C., when the Ur Empire controlled much of the Tigris–Euphrates basin, there is no unequivocal evidence for wine in Babylonia itself, whether in the form of native production, of tribute, or of imports. The overall picture which emerges from the cuneiform texts from Babylonia is that wine consumption increased gradually over the centuries, but it remained to the end primarily the prerogative of the gods and the rich.

That wine never became the drink of ordinary people can be gathered from a boast made by Nabonidus (555–539 B.C.), the last Semitic ruler of Babylonia until the Islamic period. Nabonidus tells us that "wine, the excellent 'beer' of the mountain (regions), of which my country has none," became so abundant that about 18 l sold for one shekel of silver (Röllig 1964: 248). This describes the "wine culture" of ancient Babylonia in a nutshell: wine was available as an expensive import or as booty or taxes delivered from outside Babylonia.

Comparative prices (literature and discussion in Powell 1990) reveal that, in spite of Nabonidus' boast, wine was affordable only for the rich. Even in the age of Nabonidus, one shekel of silver per month was still treated like a "minimum wage," which means that one liter (sila) of wine at the rock bottom prices about which Nabonidus was so proud would have cost about one and two-thirds day's labor. Equating prices of one age with those of another is fraught with numerous uncertainties, but we can arrive at an approximate idea of relative cost in 1991 dollars by assuming that a shekel represents a monthly wage of $600, which translates into $33.33 per liter.

Other evidence substantiates this picture of wine as a foreign import in Babylonia. The famous Nebuchadrezzar (605–562 B.C.), who preceded Nabonidus by a few years, offered to the gods "mountain 'beer', (that is to say) 'bright' (or 'pure') wine like the uncountable waters of a river." Nebuchadrezzar's wine came from eight foreign countries, which seem to lie in northern Iraq, Turkey, and Syria (Langdon 1912: 90–91, 154–55). Thus, even in the era when Babylon ruled over an area that included modern Iraq, Syria, Jordan, Israel, and even parts of Iran, Turkey, and Saudi Arabia, wine was a rare and expensive commodity in Babylonia itself. It can hardly have been greatly different in earlier times when the total volume of wine produced in the Near East seems to have been much lower.

The same picture of a land essentially without wine is painted by the Greek historian Herodotus (1.193-194—Godley 1920), who visited Babylonia about a century after the time of Nabonidus. Herodotus gives us an impressionistic, but highly informative, traveler's account of a land where oil came from sesame rather than from the olive and where fruit, "wine," and "honey" were furnished by the date-palm rather than by figs, grapes, and bees. Moreover, Herodotus adds that wine came into Babylonia from upriver, being floated down river via round skin boats in date-palm containers. Some editors have been inclined to emend the Greek text to read "jars full of date-palm wine," but this is not likely, because Babylonia abounded in dates and, as Herodotus rightly observes, used dates to make a kind of fermented drink, whereas it was grapes—not the date-palm—that flourished farther north. Thus, Herodotus's comment about date-palm containers seems indeed to be the oldest mention of wine cooperage, as others have claimed (Hyams 1965: 49).

Herodotus says that this wine traffic originated "among the Armenians, who live higher up than the Assyrians," but, of course, he is only repeating what he was told, because he never claims firsthand knowledge of Assyria, much less of Armenia. It is even unclear from Herodotus' narrative whether the river down which the wine was shipped was the Euphrates or the Tigris, and, because of the complex canal system in northern Babylonia to which he himself bears witness, it is highly probable that he had no clear idea of the actual river routes. However, if his informants were correct that the wine originated among the Armenians, it is much more likely to have come down the Tigris. Transport along the Tigris fits better with his additional note that the wine boatmen, after disposing of their cargo, dismantled their boat, sold the wood of which the ribs were made, loaded the skins on a donkey brought along for that purpose, and then trekked back upstream. In earlier times, as we shall presently see, wine probably came primarily down the Euphrates, when a different set of economic and political factors prevailed.

A generation or so after Herodotus, in describing the retreat of the Greeks after the failed expedition of Cyrus the Younger in 401 B.C., Xenophon gives a similar description of northern Babylonia: date-palms and grain abounded, and for drink there was lots of date wine, another sourish drink (*oxos*), and yet another sweetish drink that caused headaches, but no grapes or grape wine. Unqualified wine, by which Xenophon surely means grape wine, begins to turn up in his story only far to the north in the land of ancient Assyria, first being mentioned about three days south of where the Upper Zab flows into the Tigris and again about eight or nine days up the Tigris above the Zab crossing. Just to the north of Assyria, among the Kardoukhoi in the mountains of Kurdistan, Xenophon reports much wine, stored in containers that resembled cisterns. Then, crossing into what Xenophon calls Western Armenia, after a march of about ten days, somewhere west of Lake Van they come upon villages with fragrant old wines and raisins. This brings them to the upper Tigris tributaries, from which the Greeks crossed over the mountains into the Euphrates watershed, and here in the heart of Armenia four days' march beyond crossing the Euphrates near its source, the Greeks found not grape wine but "barley wine," which was drunk through a straw as shown on early representations from Mesopotamia (*Anabasis* 2.3.14-16, 2.4.28, 3.4.31, 4.2.22, 4.4.9, 4.5.26).

We have, therefore, statements by eyewitnesses that wine in Babylonia was an imported and rare commodity in the Chaldean and Persian periods. This is clearly the case for ages past. In the Old Babylonian period (roughly 2000–1600 B.C.), the north Babylonian town of Sippar was apparently the main entrepôt for wine entering Babylonia. Though, in theory, wine could have come down the Tigris and via canal to Sippar, the evidence from northern Mesopotamia suggests that there was very little wine along the Tigris in this era, and most probably came down the Euphrates. The merchants' organization of Sippar maintained deputations in important towns on the Middle Euphrates like Mari and in Mišlan a bit farther upriver in the neighboring territory of Terqa. As we shall presently see, Mari imported wine, which came to it down the Euphrates from still farther upriver. Moreover, there were connections between Sippar and the northwest that went beyond business, as evidenced, among other things, by the fact that Zimri-Lim, the last independent king of Mari before its destruction by Hammurabi of Babylon, maintained a religious presence in Sippar by sending one of his daughters there to be a living votary in the cloister of the Sun God.

It is therefore not surprising to find letters from a merchant in Babylon to his agent in Sippar notifying him of the arrival of the "wine boat" and instructing him to purchase wine and bring it to Babylon (Leemans 1960: 103–4, Frankena 1974: no. 52). What is remarkable is that this is the extent of the evidence for wine in Babylonia in the Old Babylonian period. The *Assyrian Dictionary* (Oppenheim et al. 1971: 203) cites another instance for wine in a list of provisions, but this turns out to be a haunch of meat (Frankena 1974: no. 62). No doubt, more evidence for wine will turn up, but that it will fundamentally change this picture is beyond the bounds of probability.

d. Viticulture without wine

All of this points to one conclusion: though wine may have occasionally been produced in Babylonia, it cannot have been the primary purpose of viticulture. Nevertheless, viticulture occupied an important, if small, niche in the economy.

The symbolic importance of the vine is reflected in the frequent pairing of *lal* (grape syrup) and *geštin* (grapes or some form of must, including wine) as the mark of good times and abundance in Sumerian literary texts. These texts reflect the world of the late 3rd millennium, because, even though most of the manuscripts are later than 2000 B.C., the original compositions or the inspirations for those compositions have roots in the era before 2000 B.C.

This pair of Sumerian words, corresponding to *dišpu* and *karanu* in Akkadian, has often been interpreted as "honey and wine"; however, like the familiar biblical image "flowing with milk and honey," it probably means something else. As Lutz (1922: 25) long ago pointed out, the biblical expression probably refers to something like yogurt and grape syrup. The Sumerian phrase is to be interpreted along similar lines, and as most likely referring to concentrated syrups of grapes, dates, and/or figs. We have already seen that wine is a rarity in Babylonia even in the era when Babylon ruled much of the Near East west of the Zagros Mountains. Thus, interpretation of "grape" (*geštin*) as "wine" is *a priori* unlikely in Sumerian texts. As far as "honey" (*lal*) is concerned, there is no evidence for beekeeping in Babylonia. Beeswax first turns up in Sumerian texts of the Third Dynasty of Ur (shortly before 2000 B.C.), and, although the name for it (*eškurum*) comes into Sumerian from Akkadian, it seems to be a foreign loanword in both languages (Oppenheim et al. 1960: 251–52; von Soden 1959–81: 396). Thus, although "honey" was also produced from dates and figs, it seems likely that it was often derived from grapes by reducing the must to a syrupy form by slow heating. It is a technique with which the Sumerians were long familiar, being similar to that used to make ghee from butter, and the result in both cases is concentration and preservation of the product. Moreover, the Akkadian word *dišpu* (von Soden 1959–81: 173; Oppenheim et al. 1959: 161–63) has an Arabic cognate *dibs* that even today still denotes grape syrup.

In Babylonia, viticulture seems to have been directed, above all, toward production of raisins. A lot of what is called "white wine" in older works is really raisins, based on misinterpretation of the ideogram "grape + sun," which stands for *geštin ḫea* in Sumerian, literally, "dried grape." The Akkadian word for raisin is *muziqu* (Oppenheim et al. 1977: 322–23; von Soden 1959–81: 692), which probably means "the little sucked-out one." Moreover, a good deal of what still is interpreted as "wine" is likely to have been raisins (cf. Postgate 1987: 117). The grapes that were not dried were probably, for the most part, turned into grape syrup. Explicit mention of fresh grapes is very rare, and how much of the vintage was made into wine remains an open question. In view of the extreme rarity with which wine occurs in cuneiform sources from Babylonia, part of what we interpret as wine may be fresh must or must that had been treated to prolong its life like the Latin *semper mustum*.

One naturally asks: but why no wine? Is it possible that we have somehow overlooked it? This is not likely if we recall the "no wine" testimony of Nabonidus, Herodotus, and Xenophon, and its almost exclusive attestation as drink for the gods. There is, in fact, a cluster of interlocking reasons that would have inhibited wine production.

In the first place, cheap sugar is a relatively recent phenomenon, which is one of the reasons why "sweet" and "good" are so often synonymous in ancient times. Grape sugar, which ranges from about 20 percent in the juice to 80 percent in the raisin, was a tasty and versatile sweetener. For example, the "sweet" beer called *kurunnu* in Akkadian, which has often been interpreted in the past as some type of wine, was made from barley malt with a sizable additive of emmer wheat and probably owes its name to grape syrup used to sweeten and strengthen it (discussed in Powell forthcoming). Raisins could also be used in a variety of ways, but the cuneiform sources, conformable to the principle that the obvious is not mentioned, tell us very little about the specifics of raisin use. Lutz (1922: 37) long ago called attention to a beverage with a sourish taste called "raisin water" in Arabic sources from the Islamic period, and this may have been one of the things comprised under the Sumerian expression *a geština*, which seems literally to mean "water of the grape" and which is a synonym of the Akkadian word *ṭabatu* that includes sourish beverages as well as vinegar. The composition of such beverages is usually obscure. We should recall that the Greek word *oxos* used by Xenophon to describe the sourish drink in northern Babylonia also means vinegar and is the same Greek word used to describe the drink offered to Jesus during his crucifixion. The ancient sources are obstinately taciturn about what precisely these things are.

Other economic and ecological factors would have inhibited large scale viticulture in Babylonia. Barley was ideally suited to produce sufficient food as well as a surplus that could transformed into a tasty and nourishing beer. Grapes were more costly to produce and, moreover, they do not like "wet feet" and do not tolerate salinity well. Southern Iraq tends to be very flat, is not very much above sea level, and in most areas the water table is rather near the surface. How did the Babylonians overcome this problem?

We know from Sumerian sources (before 2000 B.C.) that grapes were grown in "gardens," along with apples, figs, date-palms, other trees, and a number of other crops. The earliest coherent records (Deimel 1925: 45–52) date to around the late 24th century B.C. and come from Girsu (modern Telloh), capital of the state of Lagash, which lay in southeastern Iraq. By the end of the millennium, viticulture was widely practiced in the state of Lagash, because we have records from the era of the Ur Empire (British Museum nos. 14309 and 14334; unpublished paper by P. Steinkeller) showing that grapes were also being grown around the middle of the state at

Lagash-City (modern al-Hiba) and farther to the southeast at the city of Nina (modern Zurghul). Contemporary records from Ur, capital of the empire, likewise attest to viticulture. There was, for example, a farm named after the "Garden of Vines" (Legrain 1937: nos. 1364, 1371), which must have been either part of the farm or on its periphery. This farm had an area of at least 140 hectares (ca. 350 acres) devoted to grain cultivation. The area covered by the "Garden of Vines," could have been as much as a ten acre strip along the levee slope of a canal from which the field was irrigated. The text does not provide any concrete figures, but it does gives an idea of the possible parameters.

We have no useful information about how these gardens were laid out. As a rule, they were probably located on the levee slopes, where drainage was better, salinity lower, and access easier to water for summer irrigation. Akkadian texts specifically mention gardens (*kirû*) being enclosed within walls (*igaru, limitu*; cf. Oppenheim et al. 1971: 411–15; 1960: 38; 1973: 192), and Sumerian texts which record storing a variety of things in gardens suggest that this was already standard practice in the 3rd millennium. These enclosures not only put tasty fruit beyond reach of human cupidity but also provided a secure place for temporary or even more permanent storage of a variety of things including agricultural implements.

Whether grapes were "wedded" to trees, as described in the Roman sources, we do not know, though this procedure was certainly known in Upper Mesopotamia in the 1st millennium B.C., being depicted in Assyrian relief sculpture (Albenda 1974; Bleibtreu 1980). It is barely possible that, within these gardens, grapes were planted on artificial mounds. Lutz (1922: 37) long ago suggested that a passage in a temple hymn of Gudea (ca. late 22nd century B.C.) implied that vineyards were planted on "artificially raised plots." Unfortunately, the Gudea passages in question (Thureau-Dangin 1925, Cyl. A 28: 10–11, 23–24) are rather difficult to interpret and do not mean quite what Lutz thought they meant, but they could possibly mean "its orchard is a mountain dripping grape" and "its garden (called?) '(some kind of) Shade(?),' which is heaped up toward(?) the temple, is a mountain dripping grape."

There is also a structure, loosely associated with irrigation, called in Sumerian *pu* or *pu sang*, in Akkadian *šitpu* (Powell 1988: 170), which may denote a reservoir together with the earth that is thrown out of it. The term *pu* is, in turn, treated as a synonym of an Akkadian word *šppatu*, which is perhaps derived from a verb denoting a special type of irrigation. This word *šippatu* describes a place where fruit trees were grown and is equated with yet another Sumerian synonym called *ki šara*, "*šara* earth/ground." Both the Sumerian and Akkadian terms are described by a verb which seems to mean, in this case, "heap up." The *pu* of a garden is also said to be "heaped up" with baked brick, and, occasionally, it is said to produce *lal* and *geštin*, i.e., grape syrup and either grapes, raisins, must, wine, or perhaps all of these (literature in Powell 1972: 191). This suggests the possibility that we may have here some type of special horticultural layout, but its precise character remains obscure.

Even if viticulture in Babylonia did not require raised plots, it still cost a great deal more to produce grapes than barley or dates. The price of a liter of raisins in the Ur III period shortly before 2000 B.C. ranged from about five to ten times the price of barley or dates (Snell 1982: 134). The "cheap" prices about which Nabonidus boasted some 1500 years later are not very different: wine by volume was thirteen times as expensive as barley, fifteen times as expensive as dates (Röllig 1964: 248).

Although there are great gaps in our evidence for viticulture (as is also true of everything else), there seems no reason to doubt that grapes were grown in Babylonia from the 4th millennium B.C. through the whole history of ancient Babylonia. Thus, even when Nabonidus says "there is no *wine* in my country," that is not synomous with "no *grapes*." Documents from the reign of Nabonidus and his Persian successors prove the contrary (good examples of which are cited in

Oppenheim et al. 1956a: 44–45; 1971: 206; 1973: 255–56; Reiner et al. 1982: 164). Indeed, in the Chaldean and Persian periods (7th–4th centuries B.C.), in addition to the ubiquitous date-palm, to which the cuneiform sources as well as Herodotus and Xenophon all bear witness, the vine also turns up, along with apple, fig, and pomegranate. Our Greek visitors would not generally have seen the latter trees, because, as we know, they were safely sealed away behind high mud walls. A few texts even give us an idea of productivity, for example, about 50 to 100 pomegranates per tree or 3 to 12 liters of grapes per vine, which doubtless includes a whole range of ages and fruitfulness.

Production of grapes was therefore not *prohibitively expensive*, but it was *significantly more expensive* to produce grapes than barley or dates, which tended to cost about the same throughout the history of Babylonia. Rather, the decisive economic factors against large scale viticulture are likely to have been these: lack of a ready market and competition with good quality beer at much lower cost.

e. Summary

The ancient inhabitants of southern Iraq obviously had no prejudice against the gift of Dionysos. And they probably would have imbibed it with pleasure on occasion. However, their barley beer was better suited to quench thirst and may well have tasted noticeably better than most wines readily available. Moreover, even the best Babylonian beers must have been significantly cheaper than the cheapest wines. In short, Babylonia like Bavaria was essentially a beer drinking culture. No one with their wits about them would have gone there to drink wine any more than a sensible person would go to the Mediterranean today to drink beer. It was not always so: as we have seen, Xenophon found beer in the heart of Western Armenia, and even as late as the 1st century A.D. that remarkable Roman encyclopediast Pliny the Elder (*Natural History* 14.29.149—Rackham 1945: 284–85) regarded France and Spain as being essentially beer provinces. This fits well with the evidence from Babylonia, which, though arising from a beer culture, attests to a knowledge of viticulture that extends back into the prehistoric period and, moreover, suggests a growing level of viticulture and wine production in neighboring areas to the north, to which we now turn.

3. Viticulture in Upper Mesopotamia and Anatolia

The most informative cuneiform evidence for viticulture in Upper Mesopotamia comes from the era contemporary with Hammurabi of Babylon (ca. 1792–1750 B.C.) and from the heyday of the Assyrian Empire (9th–7th centuries B.C.).

In examining the account given by Xenophon of the march up the Tigris in 401 B.C. to the headwaters of the Tigris and Euphrates, we have already seen that once the Greeks left the alluvial lower part of the Mesopotamian valley and reached the region of ancient Assyria they began to encounter cultures where wine was readily available. Wine was not only available there, but it must have been available in considerable quantities, because the surviving Greeks represented a force of around 10,000 soldiers. Only on the first occasion where wine is mentioned is a city involved, and here the inhabitants bring wine across the river to the east bank of the Tigris. On the three other occasions, villages are involved, and wine is either explicitly or implicitly said to have been plentiful. A similar picture emerges from Xenophon's account of the earlier march down the Euphrates into Babylonia: wine is still plentiful around the confluence of the Khabur River with the Euphrates, but this is the last time it is mentioned, and when the subject of drink comes up again it is date-palm wine coupled with a millet-like grain (*Anabasis* 1.4.19, 1.5.10). Xenophon's valuable eyewitness testimony to conditions along the Euphrates corresponds remarkably well with the picture deducible from cuneiform sources almost fifteen centuries earlier, except for one detail: the "numerous villages with grain and wine" which he mentions around the Khabur–Euphrates confluence suggests considerable expansion of viticulture in this region in the interim.

a. Mari: Wine in the north and west in the Middle Bronze Age

In the era of Hammurabi of Babylon, Mari briefly controlled the territory along the Euphrates downstream from the confluence of the Balikh River with the Euphrates. Exactly how far south of the city of Mari, which lies south of the Khabur confluence, this control extended is not really clear. In the mid-18th century B.C., Hammurabi destroyed Mari, the capital of his former ally Zimri-Lim, and thus "froze" in time—somewhat like the disaster that overtook Pompeii and Herculaneum in A.D. 79—a record of life on the Middle Euphrates. The excavations at Mari have revealed a kaleidoscopic picture of a world that would otherwise be difficult for us to imagine. Above all, the thousands of letters and palace records provide a unique glimpse into this world that extends over a period of some three decades in the early 18th century B.C.

The evidence for wine in the Mari records is, like most information to be gleaned from cuneiform records, oblique and elusive in meaning. Nevertheless, it is more abundant than one finds elsewhere in this era, and Mari specialists have assembled enough documentation to give us an idea of the development of viticulture and viniculture in northwestern Mesopotamia and its periphery (Bottéro 1957; Birot 1960; Burke 1964; Finet 1974–77; Durand 1983: 104–19; Talon 1985; Lafont 1988).

We have seen that grapes were being grown in Babylonia at least as early as the 3rd millennium B.C., and a recently published text from Mari mentioning several hundred jars of wine in association with specific vineyards has at last made it clear that wine was indeed being produced in the early 18th century in the same general region where Xenophon found it 401 B.C. The extent of viticulture cannot be estimated, but its elusive character alone suggests that it was not large. Moreover, most wine whose origins are specifically named does not come from the Middle Euphrates but from farther north and west.

Emar or Imar (later called Meskene) on the Euphrates was terminus of the east–west road running through north Syria, past Aleppo to the Mediterranean, of which the western anchor point was Alalakh on the northern bend of the Orontes River, not far from where the great city of Antioch later grew up. Alalakh also lay astride the road that went northward into Anatolia and south up the Orontes Valley into Syria. We know from texts found at Alalakh belonging to the Late Bronze Age that by that time (15th century B.C.) vineyards had come to be an important part of the agricultural economy (Dietrich and Loretz 1969). The evidence is insufficient to determine whether this was already true in the 18th century, but, being near the sea, Alalakh could well have imported wine from places at much greater distance and passed it on to Aleppo. Some of the wine that made its way to the Euphrates could therefore have come to Alalakh via the Mediterranean or via the north–south road and thence to Aleppo. The ruler of Aleppo was related by marriage to the king of Mari, and sent wine, occasionally in rather large amounts (e.g., 100 "jars"), along with other valuable commodities to the palace at Mari.

These overland shipments do not represent the ordinary wine trade, for reasons which we shall consider presently, but are to be understood as luxury goods and as the royal "presents" that typify the political life of the Bronze Age. Overland transportation into Mesopotamia of luxury wines from Syria probably continued, and, in the 1st millennium B.C., after domestication of the camel toward the end of the Bronze Age, the volume of these imports probably increased. Mention has already been made of Nebuchadrezzar, who after defeating the Assyrians and their Egyptian allies at Carchemish in 605 B.C. went on to conquer most up the Near East from the Taurus Mountains southward to the borders of Egypt. Nebuchadrezzar prided himself on offering imported wine to the gods of Babylon, and the wine of Hilbunu probably came via the caravan route which ran from Damascus northeast to Palmyra, ancient Tadmer or Tadmor, and across the desert to the Euphrates. Hilbunu seems certainly identical with biblical Helbon, which is assumed to be Arabic Hilbun, the name for a valley and village in the Anti-Lebanon Mountains northwest of Damascus.

In the 1st millennium, the wines of the Damascus region had become famous indeed, for not only are they mentioned by Nebuchadrezzar but they also turn up in the "Lamentation over Tyre," in Chapter 27 of the book of Ezekiel. There the prophet describes the far flung commerce of Tyre, mentioning trade with Damascus and the wine of Helbon in the same context. This wine from the Damascus region probably came down the Biqá Valley and thence via the Litani River Valley to Tyre. It is uncertain whether wine from this region reached Mesopotamia in the second millennium, though, in theory, it would have been possible via the Palmyrene desert route or via the north–south road that ran along the Orontes Valley. Mari had connections with both Tadmer-Palmyra and with the important city of Qatna in the upper Orontes Valley, which was the western terminus of the Palmyrene caravan road. Moreover, as we know from recently discovered evidence, the Syrians possessed the key to overland transport of wine: the wineskin (see below).

b. Overall character and age of the Euphrates wine trade

As already indicated, the real wine trade operated along the Euphrates. Being heavy and somewhat awkward to transport by land, wine production for markets beyond a local area demanded access to water transportation in order to be economically viable. This was universally true until the 19th century A.D., so it is not surprising to find the wine trade concentrated in the Euphrates Valley. How old this trade was is impossible to determine; however, this segment of the economy appears to be already well developed in the early 18th century B.C. This is indicated by the large amounts of wine mentioned, by the existence of local industries that provided jars and transportation, and by the already noted interest in the Euphrates wine trade on the part of merchants in northern Babylonia.

c. The center of production

The major entrepôt for the wine trade on the Euphrates was Carchemish, an ancient town that continued to flourish until 605 B.C., when it was destroyed by Nebuchadrezzar of Babylon. Carchemish lies on the Euphrates just south of where it debouches from the mountains that ring the Anatolian plateau. We have no documents from Carchemish itself that would allow demonstration that wine was actually grown in this region, but the price, which is low compared to wine prices elsewhere, as well as references to "filling" empty jars suggest that the wine purchasable in Carchemish came from the territory under its control and not from further up the Euphrates in the direction of what later became Armenia.

d. Cost factors in the wine trade

As we have said, wine at Carchemish may have been *comparatively* inexpensive, but the cost of transportation was relatively high in proportion to the cost of wine. This emerges from three letters written by an individual named Ṣidqum-Lanasi (Lafont 1988: nos. 537–39), a highly placed citizen of Carchemish who represented commercial and other interests for the king of Mari. In these letters, money has been sent to him from Mari to buy wine and send it back to Mari. The ratio between the money allocated for wine and the money for the "price of boat" is 3:1. This rule of thumb calculation suggests a more or less stable price for wine, because—unless taxation is involved—the "price of "boat" will have varied according to the amount, not the value, of wine being transported. The "going rate" for wine in Carchemish seems to have been six "jars" per shekel of silver, which is equivalent to 30 barleycorns (1/6 shekel) of silver per "jar." The numbers in these texts need to be checked with the original tablets, but provisionally we can translate the cost of a jar of wine in Carchemish into 1991 dollars as about $100 (see above).

A higher rate has been deduced from a legal document (Boyer 1958: no. 78, with Durand 1983: 110–12) drawn up in Carchemish, although this text is susceptible to other interpretations. It specifies payment of 30 shekels in a town on the northern border of Mari, either in silver or, if not in silver, at the rate of five "jars" of wine per shekel, according to the "market rate of Carchemish." Taken at face value this would seem to imply that the "market rate of Carchemish" was five "jars" per shekel. It must be borne in mind, however, that the obvious is not mentioned: the "five jar rate" may assume the "six jar rate" already noted, with the cost of one jar out of six allocated for transportation, just as the other texts, already mentioned, allocate one-third of the wine price as the transportation cost for the longer distance to Mari.

The "six jar rate" is also implied by yet another legal document involving the aforementioned Ṣidqum-Lanasi (Boyer 1958: no. 80, with Durand 1983: 111), where a lump sum for wine and empty jars works out to 30 barleycorns per jar of wine and 3 barleycorns (1/60 shekel) each for the empties. Wine, however, was not always such a good buy. The same Sidqum-Lanasi, writing to one of his friends in Mari, requests more money to buy wine, because "wine has become expensive this year" (Lafont 1988: no. 545).

These texts give us an insight into the financial aspects of the wine trade, but, perhaps more important, they indirectly tell us something about its socioeconomic features. As usual, the writers of letters and makers of documents omit mentioning circumstances that were obvious to them, so we are forced to read between the lines. The trade was downstream, but this does not mean that transporting large quantities of wine was easy. Moreover, the skills and labor involved in actual transport must have been provided by professional boatmen who knew the river and specialized in navigating cargoes downstream using only the current. It is likely that the boatmen themselves constructed the boat which they piloted. However, they would not have hauled their boats back upstream any more than did the wine transporters described by Herodotus but would rather have made their way back overland to begin over again.

This explains why the cost of transport is high, why the "boat" became the property of the person contracting for transportation, and why the "value" of the boat at the end of its downstream run seems to be only one-tenth of its value at its point of origin upstream. In the first place, the cost of a large number of days of skilled boatmen is included in the price, because no additional amount is allocated for wages. Second, in such a system, a boat at the end of the downstream run would be nothing but a financial liability to the boatmen, who would be forced to sell it quickly at a low price in order make their return journey. Thus, the boat became the property of the wine shipper, who in turn had to dispense with it for what he could get.

Indeed, the whole business of selling wine and providing jars and transport seems to have been a closely linked operation at Carchemish, as one might expect. A glimpse behind the scenes is provided in a letter of the already mentioned Ṣidqum-Lanasi (Lafont 1988: no. 538), writing to a highly placed official, perhaps the steward of the palace, at Mari:

Say to Asqudum (the words of) your friend Ṣidqum-Lanasi (namely): Your servant Abi-andulli arrived safely with what I needed, and I was very happy. He brought half a mina of silver [30 shekels] for wine and ten shekels of silver for the price of one boat. And then I asked myself: am I going to buy a boat for ten shekels of silver when it won't bring one shekel of silver in Mari? So I made a deal for the wine and the boat together (literally: got the price of wine and boat together), and (it cost) one half mina eight shekels of that which Abi-andulli brought me. I bought ... jars of wine for one half mina eight shekels.

As is often the case, the numbers are broken at crucial places, but the point of the letter seems to be that the buyer got a better deal by contracting for wine, jars, and boat together. Given the hidden labor costs of the "price of boat," it is easy to understand why the actual "boat" for which ten shekels were paid in Carchemish would fetch less than one shekel in Mari.

e. Size of the Mesopotamian wine amphoras

Our knowledge of the nature of this Euphrates wine trade would be greatly enhanced if we could pin down the size of the "jars." Unfortunately, the texts are absolutely ambiguous about this, and the only way to decisively answer this question would be to investigate the sizes of containers that could have been used for wine (see chapter 10 by Zettler and Miller, this volume). Since inscribed containers from Mesopotamia are extremely rare, such an investigation is not easy and has never been undertaken, except to a very limited degree.

A size in the range of 10 l (i.e., ten *sila* per "jar") has been suggested. This is not impossible, but there are both economic and metrological problems with this theory. It is known, for instance, that the price of barley was reckoned at one shekel for two Mari *gur* (containing 120 *sila* per *gur*; compare Kupper 1982: 115), i.e., 240 *sila* are putatively 240 l. If the wine "jar" were only 10 l, then one shekel would buy 60 l at the 6 "jar" Carchemish rate. This would mean that in Carchemish one liter of wine cost 4 l of barley at Mari rates; in Mari by contrast, it required 12 l of barley to buy one liter of wine. By the rule of thumb that one shekel approximates $600, this would be $10 (a sixtieth of a shekel) per liter of wine in Carchemish, as compared to $30 (a twentieth of a shekel) per liter in Mari, which seems a bit high.

Another solution that agrees somewhat better with the history of prices and metrology is that the volume of the "wine jar" at Mari was the same as that of the amphora and that, like the Babylonian jar, it was 30 *sila*, i.e., ca. 30 l (Powell 1989–90: 499–500, 1990). This would mean that, by the rule of thumb that a shekel equals $600, a liter of wine in Carchemish cost $3.33, and was $10 in Mari. Also, one would expect merchants from Babylonia (see above) to be interested in wine at $10 per liter, but hardly at $30. Of course, the assumption here—for the sake of price comparison—is that the basic volume measures of Babylonia and Mari were identical. The actual size of the "jar" in Babylonia was about 30 l; in Mari, it may have been no more than the later Palestinian *bath*, i.e., about 24 l In spite of the difficulties in establishing the absolute values of the ancient capacity units, a 30 *sila* norm (i.e., somewhere in the 24 to 30 l range) for the Mari wine jar is also suggested by the valuation of wine at two jars per shekel (Durand 1983: 110; Kupper 1982: 115), i.e., a valuation of one shekel per 60 *sila* of wine. Sexagesimal unities (1 = 60) and the cuneiform system of writing always turn up together, even in decimal counting milieux, because sexagesimal arithmetic was an integral part of learning cuneiform.

f. Wine cargoes and tolls

A group of letters, apparently representing the records of a tollmaster from the year that Mari was destroyed, provides a vivid testimony to the wine trade along the Euphrates (Burke 1964). Thirty-nine of these letters are notices by an associate tollmaster of tolls paid farther upstream or notices that the toll is still to be paid, and about two-thirds of these seem to concern wine cargoes. The amount of toll assessed seems to have been ten percent of the valuation of the cargo in silver or ten percent of the actual cargo. As usual in letters, we have to read between the lines. "Boats" are mentioned, but it is virtually certain that all of them were some type of raft. Some are called "cargo boats," and, in Babylonia, these "cargo boats" (Reiner et al. 1980: 69–70) were built of wood and reeds.

Some of these "boats" transported wine in the standard sized amphoras discussed above; up to 600 such jars are mentioned. Others seem to have carried large pithoi. These are called in Akkadian "*našpakum* jars," which means something like "storage jars." These large "storage jars" also appear to have been of standard size, because each *našpakum* unit is assessed one shekel of silver. At a ten percent assessment rate, this would mean that each unit was appraised at ten shekels and contained 600 *sila*. A single container holding roughly 600 l seems rather large, so there may be something more complex concealed under the term "storage jar." In Babylonia, a *našpakum* seems to be some kind of container that held ten *gur* or roughly 3000 l.

g. Bulk storage and its implications

Use of large storage jars brings up another feature of the Euphrates wine trade that is worthy of noting, viz., that the transfer of wine from container to container in the course of conveying it to the consumer must have been rather common practice. In the texts involving purchase of wine in Carchemish, the evidence points in the same direction: "empty" jars are purchased and "filled," which, in turn, suggests that "wholesale" vintners in Carchemish likewise stored wine in large containers, as explicitly described by Roman writers on agriculture. This circumstance, as well as the already mentioned letter remarking on the high price of this year's wine, suggests that the wine shipped on the Euphrates, including that destined for the king of Mari, was new wine. Most of it was probably consumed within the year in which it was produced. Hesiod's picture of carefully rationing one's wine so that it does not run out too much before the next vintage is probably closer to the realities of the Ancient Orient than our idea of fine aged reds.

h. Extent of the Euphrates wine trade

Aside from the wine that was purchased specifically for use of the palace, part of the wine that came down the Euphrates from Carchemish probably stayed in the kingdom of Mari. Unfortunately, the interest of the palace in the movement of goods seems not to have extended much beyond taxation, and thus its records are silent about other aspects of the wine trade, even in Mari itself. However, one record from the tollmaster's archive (Burke 1964: no. 83) makes it clear that merchants from further down the Euphrates in the region around Anah (ancient Hanat) were involved in this trade. And it has already been seen that some of this wine was certainly purchased by Babylonians and shipped on down the Euphrates to Sippar.

Babylonia, however, seems to have been the end of its journey. Goods were shipped out of Babylonia to points south and east, but, although there is no reason to believe that we have a complete record of these exports, the absence of wine from Ur III and Old Babylonian merchant records suggests that it was neither a normal object of commerce nor did it enter into the international trade that went out of southern Mesopotamia via the Persian Gulf. This is a point of some interest for the history of the wine trade, because good evidence exists for Mesopotamia trade contacts with India—at least via middlemen—in the centuries clustering around 2000 B.C., but unlike the Roman period when wine was one of the luxury commodities shipped out of the Mediterranean via the Red Sea to India (Casson 1989), cuneiform records from Mesopotamia have no trace of a luxury wine trade. It is barely possible that a more representative sample of documents would reveal transshipment of wine, but this seems unlikely.

Firstly, the kind of wine technology which made possible the shipping of aged, luxury wines, such as one finds in the 1st millennium B.C., either had not yet been developed or simply was rare in the Middle Bronze Age. Moreover, even though there seems to be quite a lot of wine available around Carchemish on the Upper Euphrates, we are still a long way from mass production, and it is far from cheap. Indeed, the wine imported into Babylonia is likely to have been destined for persons among the ruling Amorite elite who had not lost their Syrian taste for wine. Here again, in mentioning the *elite*, we must keep the price in mind: using the rule of thumb that one shekel approximates $600 in 1991 and assuming that a "jar" is approximately 30 l, good wine at Mari cost $10 per liter. Since this is three times the price in Carchemish, a similar rise in price between Mari and Babylonia is likely. In other words, wine could have sold for $20 or $30 dollars per liter in Babylonia, and, given the fact that Nabonidus in the 6th century B.C. was proud of the fact that it cost only $33.33 per liter, such high prices in the Old Babylonian period are not only thinkable but likely.

In short, wine was still a very expensive beverage. And this, in turn, tells us something about the overall development of viticulture and viniculture in northern Mesopotamia in the Middle Bronze Age. In the first place, the relative proportion of agricultural labor devoted to viticulture must still have been rather limited. Second, the taste for wine and the economic ability to purchase it were not yet sufficiently widespread to encourage large scale viticulture and viniculture, which would have led to lower prices. Third, the technology for conserving and ageing wines that could have catered to these luxury tastes does not yet seem to have been in existence.

i. Drinking customs and types of wine

Aside from the glimpses into what was clearly a developing section of the agricultural economy of the north and west, the Mari records also provide some insight into the culture of wine drinking in the 18th century B.C. Among the upper social strata, wine already seems to be a regular part of the diet in this part of the world. We have already noted that wine turns up in royal presents exchanged between kings. It also seems to be a standard component in diplomacy, because it turns up when the king is receiving foreign visitors or ambassadors, and the same custom is attested at contemporary Karana'a about two hundred kilometers northeast of Mari (see below).

One can hardly speak of a science of enology at Mari, which lay, after all, outside of the primary area of wine production. Still the persons who supervised storage and serving of the king's wine must have had a rudimentary knowledge of those aspects of enology which pertain to conservation of wine and the like. However, as is usual with cuneiform sources, both letters and economic records are interested in the technical side of enology only insofar as it pertains to "how much" and "how good." And, even on this elementary level, such technical terms are very difficult to interpret precisely. In the discussion below, both the difficulties and the kinds of terms that can be interpreted with some certainty are indicated.

Did the ancient Mespotamians dilute their wine with water? This question can be answered with almost one hundred percent certainty in the negative. Nevertheless, both Akkadian dictionaries have interpreted the north Mesopotamian term *samiḫu* as "wine mixer" (von Soden 1959–81: 1018; Reiner et al. 1984: 116), and the same idea is now percolating into works intended for a broader public (e.g., Dalley 1984: 90), which means that it is going to be around for a long time to come. It is, nevertheless, without foundation.

First, both dictionaries have ignored or rejected the well founded opinions of Mari specialists. Birot (1960: 333) thought that *samiḫu*, the word now being translated as "wine mixer," meant someone added to a contingent to bring it up to strength. Finet (1974–77: 126), whom the Assyrian Dictionary cites in support of its interpretation, evinced grave doubts about "wine mixer." The key passage, in a letter from Mari (Finet 1964 no. 142), has been translated by the Assyrian Dictionary as "they should assign to him three *s.*-s [i.e., wine mixers] so that this wine will not be too weak," and, as justification, the analogy of the Greek symposium is adduced. However, precisely the evidence from Greek practice makes clear that mixing water with wine did not require a professional.

Second, the dictionaries have supplied the "wine" in "wine mixer" without justification. This "mixer" is never associated with wine, and, moreover, this is a dubious solution because it is dubious grammar. The word *samiḫu* is a participle, and it should, like the verb from which it is derived, have an intransitive sense. They are intransitive "mixers" and are, therefore, just as Birot thought, "joiners" or "auxiliaries."

Third, in the key passage already quoted in the translation of the *Assyrian Dictionary*—the only passage in which these so-called "mixers" are even remotely associated with wine—it is improbable that the word translated "wine" really means wine. It is written, not syllabically, but with the Sumerogram *giš.geštin.ḫi-a.* Interpreted literally this means "woody plant: grape + collective plural." In texts from Mari, however, wine is usually written without the "woody plant" class marker. Thus, Dalley (1984: 90) has translated the passage as follows:

> And about the vines of the men of Nagabbini—there are no (suitable) men at Mashum's disposal, so may my lord have a letter sent to Samum, that they may give him three mixers, so that the vines be not ruined and lest Mashum complain.

This is surely closer to the truth, but I think it more likely that the passage means this:

> And concerning the "grape" of the Nagabbinians, there are not (enough) men at the disposal of Mashum. My lord should send a tablet to Samum, so that three auxiliaries will be given to him, and so that the "grape" does not deteriorate (or become inferior/less), and so that Mashum does not get cause for complaint.

What does this mean? A clue to what is going on is that the bulk of this letter is concerned about a dispute over irrigation water to plant sesame, which places the time of year in late spring or early summer. This means that it is too early for the vintage, so it is highly probable that these "auxiliaries" are being requested to do irrigation work. There is nothing whatever suggesting that these "auxiliaries" have any kind of expertise in wine technology. Of course, the innocent reader who turns to volumes of the Chicago Assyrian Dictionary published since 1971 or to Dalley's recent book (1984: 86) will discover the idea that *šamaššammu* means linseed rather than sesame. I have recently reviewed this hypothesis in detail (Powell 1991), and it has all the probability of snow in July.

Consequently, there is no evidence for mixing wine with water, but there is good evidence for "blending" wines. The Akkadian verb is *ḫiaqu*, and the Mari material became available too late to help the dictionaries with this word. It also occurs with beer, and there too it is "blending" that is is described rather than diluting beer with water as the dictionaries thought. Blending was a technique for salvaging "old" wine, as well as for improving the quality of other unspecified types of wine. Other, more obscure, processes involved "filling out," "purifying," and "testing" wine, in the latter case to see whether it was "sweet," i.e., good (Durand 1983: 105–9). As in Babylonian literary texts, "honey" and wine turn up together in economic records from Mari, making it likely that this "honey" is none other than grape syrup. After all, a thousand years later, in the heyday of the Assyrian empire, a local ruler, named Šamaš-reš-uṣur, prided himself on having introduced the previously unknown science of apiculture to the Middle Euphrates area (Oppenheim et al. 1959: 163). Thus, it is rather probable that grape syrup is part of what is being blended into the Mari wines.

As to type, "red" is the only color type specifically mentioned. In general, wine is simply wine without any qualification at all. There was a "second quality" wine, which was also used in the palace, so this cannot have been "poor." At Mari, it seems to have been rated at 75 barleycorns of silver per jar (Durand 1983: 110 n. 9), in other words, the wine which was appraised at 90 barleycorns (a half shekel) per jar (see above) cost 20 percent more and must represent the better grade. Occasionally, this "second" wine is contrasted with "red wine" (e.g., Durand 1983: no. 97; Talon 1985: nos. 78–79), which naturally makes one think of white wine, but as yet there is no secure basis for identifying it as such. And, as already indicated, "sweet" denotes good, but "old" does not.

j. Conclusions

Unlike Babylonia, where grape growing was very ancient, but which never developed a real wine culture, here on the Middle Euphrates in the early 18th century B.C., we find evidence for both viticulture and viniculture. Evidence for actual production is still sparse, and does not resemble Xenophon's picture of easily accessible wine some 1400 years later. The major wine producing areas seem to lie along the southern slopes of the mountains that separate the Anatolian upland from the Mesopotamian basin. But, luxury wines come in as royal presents from the west, revealing that the region around Aleppo and farther south is already wine country.

Evidence for this wine culture is limited to the ruling stratum of the "Amorites"; however, this evidence is significant for the history of wine in the ancient Near East in general. These "Amorites" were of Syrian origin, and they brought with them into Mesopotamia a variety of cultural baggage as diverse as the principle of "eye for eye and tooth for tooth," the assload (homer) as a measure of capacity, and a taste for wine. These "Westerners"—as the Babylonians thought of them—begin to turn up in significant numbers shortly before 2000 B.C. in Babylonian documents from the Ur Empire, often in military positions. By the 18th century, they have become the ruling elite all across Mesopotamia, and along with their typical "Amorite" names, they seem to have retained their taste for wine. Zimri-Lim of Mari sends wine to Babylon at the request of Hammurabi, who, even after six generations in a beer paradise like Babylonia, seems not to have lost the taste for the grape of his Syrian forefathers. The evidence from Mari suggests that these Syrians—like the Greeks who likely spread a taste for the gift of Dionysos to southern Italy—were a major factor in diffusion of wine culture. Also, though the Egyptians, like the Babylonians, delight in depicting the Syrians as a bunch of barbarians, it seems highly probable that, along with the horse and chariot, another of their legacies to Egypt was a heightened interest in wine, and this is perhaps reflected in what appears to be significantly higher levels of production, especially in the Delta, in the Late Bronze Age (see chapter 14 by Lesko, this volume).

4. Wine in Assyria and the North before the Assyrian Empire

The heartland of ancient Assyria was not large, stretching along the Tigris from the confluence of the Lower Zab River to north of present day Mosul, but, in the era of its greatest political power (9th–7th centuries B.C.), Assyria dominated the Near East west of the Zagros Moutains. Our written evidence for Assyria stretches over a period of about a millennium and a half from the time of Naram-Sin of Akkad (perhaps to be dated around 2200 B.C.) to the fall of Nineveh in 612 B.C., but it is sparse for most periods and of a different type from that which has previously been discussed. Economic records like those from Mari and Babylonia are somewhat less well represented, but government records, "official" publications, such as the annals of kings and the like are better represented. The evidence is not suited to tell us much about the details of viticulture or viniculture, but it does provide supplementary information that helps us piece together a picture of the major developments in the history of ancient wine.

a. Eastern Assyria ca. 2200–1350 B.C.

The earliest group of documents that might be expected to say something about wine date to around 2200 B.C. and are from Gasur, later called Nuzi, in the Kirkuk region, about a hundred kilometers east of the Tigris River. However, instead of wine, we find beer (Meek 1935: nos. 56–57, 160). This, of course, does not mean a great deal, because this small group of documents (about two hundred tablets and fragments) is neither a random sample nor, since it probably reflects the needs of the garrison from Babylonia, does it necessarily reflect the taste and character of the surrounding countryside. Nevertheless, beer is what we find, and no wine.

Wine is also absent from the extensive family archives of Nuzi in the Late Bronze Age (15th–14th centuries B.C.). This too may be only happenstance, but these records are sufficiently numerous and reflect the lifestyles of an elite which might be supposed to have drunk wine had it been available. Not only does no wine turn up, but even the records of gardens and orchards fail to mention anything suggesting viticulture (Zaccagnini 1979: 119–53). This area later became part of eastern Assyria, and, by the 9th century B.C., the land of Zamua, which lies in the modern Sulaymanyah district some 60 kms. farther east, had become famous for its wines. If viticulture were already well established here in the Late Bronze Age, it seems likely that we would find at least some reflection of this in the Nuzi records.

b. Between the Khabur and the Tigris in the 18th century B.C.

In the 18th century B.C., contemporary with the records from Mari, wine was clearly being produced in other areas of the upper Tigris–Euphrates basin. This emerges from a group of tablets found at Tell al Rimah (ancient Karana'a) recording issues of wine for the king and for visiting royalty and their ambassadors, as well as delivery of wine from various places in the region (Walker 1976). Tell al Rimah is about 60 kms. due west of the Tigris, around 40 kms. southwest of ancient Nineveh and 120 kms. northwest of Ashur. It lies in a region southeast of the low mountain range known as the Jebel Sinjar in the watershed of the seasonal river called the Wadi Tharthar. Today it is said to be "not a wine-growing district" (Dalley 1984: 29), but modern conditions are not always reliable paradigms for conditions in antiquity.

The ancient name of Tell al Rimah was Karana'a. This name is similar to Akkadian *karanu*, "grapevine/wine," and a goddess with a name meaning "Grapevine/Wine of Heaven" also turns up along with the Storm God in salutations (God bless you!). The evidence connecting the town Karana'a with the goddess Geštinana is strictly circumstantial, not enough to convict in court but enough to raise suspicion. As Finet (1974–77: 122) has suggested, probability lies on the side of a connection between Karana'a and Geštinana, in other words Wine-Land and Wine-Goddess. For the perceptive historian, whether Karana'a is really derived from *karanu* or whether Geštinana is really the tutelary goddess of Karana'a must necessarily be of secondary importance to explaining why the two turn up together along with documentary evidence for wine. On the whole, it suggests a fairly important role for viticulture in the agricultural life of this area in the 18th century B.C.

Another interesting point of these "wine records" from Tell al Rimah is the first appearance of the wineskin (*ziqqu*). This was previously known from only as early as the 9th century B.C. and thought to be an Aramean loanword, but its occurence at Tell al Rimah nine centuries earlier, long before Arameans turn up in Mesopotamia, makes this unlikely (Walker 1976: 183). The word is probably of Syrian origin. Both the Arameans and the earlier Amorites are from Syria, and both must have brought the word for wineskin with them into Mesopotamia.

It is true that one text from Babylonia in era of the Ur Empire (21st century B.C.) seems to mention 128 wineskins (Stol 1980–83), but the meaning of the text is obscure, and one would like to have a look at the original tablet to see whether the sign which seems to be "wine" is in fact correctly copied. If these Ur III skins were really wineskins, it is remarkable that no word for wineskin is attested in standard Mesopotamian Akkadian and especially that no explicit "skin for wine" turns up in the lexical lists of leather bags, which do attest the use of skins for many purposes, including waterskins. Of course, the wineskin may be hidden under the Sumerian name for "Amorite bag." This is the Sumerian name for Akkadian *maškaru*, which is probably derived *šakaru*, "to become inebriated," and which is used for floating. Thus, the "Amorite bag" may be the same type of airtight, floating bags depicted on Assyrian reliefs of the 1st millennium. The evidence points to a Syrian origin for invention of the wineskin (see below).

c. Anatolia ca. 2000–1200 B.C.

By 1800 B.C., some of the more northerly regions of Mesopotamia were producing sufficient wine for the consumption of the Amorite elite. To what extent this was true of the heartland of Assyria remains in doubt, because we have hardly any sources from this region. Some Assyrians were probably already drinking wine, though not necessarily those who lived in Assyria itself. Assyrian merchants were actively involved in trade with Cappadocia, with major activity centering in the town of Kanesh (modern Kültepe) near the modern Turkish town of Kayseri. Assyrians who went to Cappadocia were into a life of profitable adventure, exciting and envigorating but also grueling and dangerous. Via pack asses, they brought from Assyria primarily textiles and tin. These items were suitable for ass caravan and seem to have had a ready market in Anatolia, allowing quick recovery of capital at good profit, which in turn permitted other trading. Within central Anatolia, these merchants seem to have traded anything that would bring sufficient profit. Wine also turns up in the business records of these Assyrian merchants (Oppenheim et al. 1971: 203), but there is no clear indication of where it was produced or who drank it. References to the vintage (literally "picking of grape"; Reiner et al. 1982: 282) as a term for a specific time of year probably reflect Anatolian, not Assyrian, agricultural realities (see chapter 11 by Gorny, this volume).

Although Anatolia lies beyond Mesopotamia proper, we should pause for a glance into that world across the Taurus Mountains, because it affords us the opportunity of taking stock of the development of viticulture on the northwestern periphery of Mesopotamia. Hittite sources from the Late Bronze Age (*grosso modo* 1600–1200 B.C.) reveal a culture well acquainted with wine, but even here it is not an everyday drink (Steiner 1966; for details, see chapter 11 by Gorny, this volume).

The most informative source is the Hittite Laws compiled in the Late Bronze Age. For the English reader, the English translation of Goetze (1969) is cited here, but the basic text edition is that of Friedrich (1959). These laws reflect, in part, conditions of the earlier Middle Bronze Age (ca. 2000–1600 B.C.) and bear witness to a long tradition of viticulture and viniculture, corroborating the rather sparse evidence in the records of Assyrian merchants from the 19th–18th centuries (Hoffner 1974: 39–141, 113). The Hittite Laws contain many definitions of relative values of goods and services, which were designed to help judges in translating a money fine into the goods in which the fine would have, in most cases, actually been paid. All ancient Near Eastern "law codes" have these definitions, but, since Hittite justice relied heavily upon the concept of compensation, nowhere do we find such an elaborate system of definitions of the values of goods and services as in the Hittite Laws. Since definitions like this had to be normative, i.e., generally recognized as correct and just, they constitute some of the best data that we have for relative prices in the ancient Near East, and they are especially helpful in bringing the relative value of wine—for which we have really very little evidence—into better focus.

Table 9.1 brings together a small selection of these definitions, redefined in terms of one shekel of silver. A number of these are stated in the Hittite Laws themselves, not in silver, but in barley

Table 9.1

Sample Values of One Shekel of Silver in the Hittite Laws

Assumed approximations

   1 Hittite shekel = ca. 1.5 Babylonian shekel = ca. 12.5 g

   Hittite *iku* = ca. 1 Babylonian *iku* = ca. 0.36 ha

   Hittite *parīsu* = ca. 1 Babylonian "jar"(?) = ca. 30 l(?)

Purchasing power of one Hittite shekel of silver

   2 *parīsu* wine

   3 *parīsu* emmer wheat (bulgur)

   6 *parīsu* barley

   160 shekels of copper

   1/3 *iku* of nearby(?) agricultural land

   2/3 *iku* of mid-distant(?) agricultural land

   1 *iku* of border(?) agricultural land

   1/40 *iku* of vineyard

   1/10 of the vintage of one *iku* of vineyard

   12 days' hire: team of oxen

   18 days' hire: harvest, man with 90 day contract

   30 days' hire: harvest, woman with 60 day contract

   30 days' hire: one plowing ox

or emmer wheat (probably already removed from the husks). Moreover, the actual sizes of such basic Hittite measures as area and capacity remain in a state of limbo (summarized in van den Hout 1990). Nevertheless, the history of metrology and prices in the ancient Near East (Powell 1989–90, 1990) allows us to arrive at some rough guidelines.

The crucial term is *parīsu*, which is an Akkadian word, probably of Syrian origin, that should mean something like "half-measure." The "whole," of which it forms the "half," remains uncertain. Two solutions seem possible: (1) that it is half of the 60-*sila* Babylonian measure *panu*; or (2) that it is half of the western "assload," the "homer" of the Bible. Recently published evidence suggests that at Mari the *parīsu*, was reckoned at 50 *sila* (see Lafont 1991: nn. 19 and 23). Since the homer was normally 100 *sila*, this would seem to favor the second solution. Nevertheless, the actual size of the measure remains somewhat uncertain, because we do not know how close the basic unit resembled the Babylonian *sila*, on which all inferences depend.

A size for the *parīsu*, somewhere in the range of the "amphora," i.e., ca. 30 l, is suggested by paragraph 158 of the Hittite Laws, which defined the wages of a male harvester for the whole three months of the harvest as 30 *parīsi*. If the *parīsu* was roughly 30 l, this would make the Hittite rates of compensation equal to standard Babylonian rates of the Middle Bronze Age (2000–1600 B.C.), namely ten liters of barley per day. Since barley was more abundant in Babylonia than elsewhere, Hittite wages in barley are not likely to have been much higher than those in Babylonia itself.

This hypothesis, in turn, enables us to offer a plausible interpretation for several clauses in the Hittite Laws dealing with viticulture. Paragraph 185A defines the value of one *iku* of vineyard as one mina, which is 40 Hittite shekels. Paragraph 107 defines the compensation to be paid for sheep ruining a vineyard bearing fruit as 10 shekels per *iku*. In other words, compensation is one-fourth of the value of the vineyard itself; therefore, ten shekels compensation probably represents the valuation of one year's crop in wine per *iku*. Since paragraph 183 defines the value of one *parīsu* of wine at one-half shekel, we can infer that the expected vintage from one *iku* was 20 amphoras of wine or somewhere in the range of 600 l for ca. 0.36 hectares or *grosso modo* 160 gallons per acre.

By comparison, Columella, writing in the 1st century A.D. and presumably speaking about conditions in Campania (Italy), expected a minimum yield of 20 amphora (ca. 524 l) per *iugerum* (roughly 0.25 ha). This works out to about 220 gallons per acre, in other words, 30 to 40 percent more than the "standard" yield that I have posited for Hittite Anatolia. Columella expected top quality vineyards to produce five times the minimum rate, or ca. 1100 gallons per acre, but it is clear from his own words that there were people who were not able to average the minimum, even in such an age of highly developed viticulture (*Res rustica* 3.3—Ash 1941). Therefore, the figure of 20 "Hittite amphoras" per *iku* provides us with some idea of the expected productivity of Near Eastern viticulture. Land planted in vines was valued at 13⅓, 20, and 40 times the value of other agricultural land, as paragraphs 183 and 185A of the Hittite Laws explicitly demonstrate.

d. Summary of the era before the Assyrian Empire

Viticulture and a wine culture seem well established from the Middle Bronze Age onward in Anatolia and in the regions just south of the mountain chains that separate modern Syria and Iraq from Turkey. By contrast, none of the documents found in the area along the Tigris and eastward to the Zagros Mountains evidence viticulture and viniculture in either the Middle or Late Bronze Age (ca. 2000–1200 B.C.). It is difficult to know what to make of this, but it seems possible that this silence reflects a very minor role for viticulture there prior to the 1st millennium B.C. Things look very different in this area by the 9th century B.C. (below). The causes underlying this change are obscure, but one cannot help suspecting Syrian influence again, associated with the influx of Arameans into Upper Mesopotamia beginning around the end of the Bronze Age.

e. Wine and viticulture during the Assyrian Empire

1. The world of wine in the 9th century B.C.

With the reigns of Ashurnasirpal II (883–859 B.C.) and his son Shalmaneser III (858–824 B.C.), wine begins to be mentioned as a desirable object of tribute, along with such items as horses, mules, cattle, sheep, gold, silver, bronze vessels, dyed wools, and, on occasion, more expensive and exotic items (Luckenbill 1926: 142, 144, 146, 148, 151, 153–56, 164, 178, 179, 214–16, 220; see chapter 12 by Stronach, this volume). This evidence is interesting for the history of viticulture in the ancient Near East, because, in the first place, it documents the existence of a well-established wine culture in a broad arc running from the region around modern Sulaymaniyah in the Iraqi–Iranian borderlands northward to Lake Van, turning west along the Euphrates and then south to the region of the Orontes Valley. Second, none of the areas which supply wine as tribute lies outside of the limit of rainfall agriculture, and most of them seem to be either in the mountains or in the foothills of mountains. Third, its appearance with other expensive and exotic items tells us that wine too is still an expensive and relatively rare item. Of course, one might object that sheep, cattle, and horses are not exotic. True, but they are valuable—and they carry themselves.

The era represented by the reigns of Ashurnasirpal and Shalmaneser is a turning point in the political history of the ancient Near East and perhaps also in the history of viticulture and viniculture as well. During their reigns the foundations of an Assyrian Empire stretching from western Iran to the Mediterranean are laid. Both kings are particularly concerned with Syria, which by this time had a predominantly Aramean ethnic character, and there are reasons to suspect that Arameans have repeated the feat of the Syrian Amorites of a thousand years earlier, moving easily into positions of power without fundamentally disturbing the lower levels of society. The Syrian connection is evidenced also by the 10,000 wineskins that turn up in the extravagant banquet given by Ashurnasirpal to celebrate the inauguration of his new royal residence at Kalah (Wiseman 1952). The oldest visual representations of wineskins appear on the Bronze Gates of Shalmaneser from Balawat, now in the British Museum (Barnett n.d.: pl. 138f, 148a, 151b, 152a), and these can be correlated with tribute of wine from Gilzani (somewhere in Turkey south of Lake Van) and Unki (in the Orontes valley area of Syria, near Alalakh) mentioned in the annals of Shalmaneser for his accession year and for the first full year of his reign (859–858 B.C.). Thus, the wineskin is intimately linked with this Syrian agricultural product, which is valuable but difficult to transport overland.

2. Wine and viticulture in the 8th and 7th centuries

When we look, for comparison, at the world of wine mirrored in royal inscriptions from the last century of the Assyrian Empire (722–612 B.C.), we see differences almost as remarkable as those which separate the 9th century of Ashurnasirpal and Shalmaneser from the Bronze Age. Wine has disappeared from the enumerations of tribute, obviously because it has ceased to be both expensive and exotic. Instead we find a world like that mirrored in Xenophon's *Anabasis*, where soldiers drink wine whenever they can get it and where wine is enumerated with basic military supplies rather than with exotic objects of tribute.

A well-developed viticulture stretching from the area around Lake Urmia in northwestern Iran to the area around Lake Van in southeastern Turkey is suggested by an account, in the form of a letter to god, of the eighth campaign of Sargon II, king of Assyria from 722 to 705 B.C. (Luckenbill 1927: 76, 78, 86–90). During this campaign, directed against the kingdom of Urartu, Sargon passed through the modern Iranian–Iraqi–Turkish border region in the watershed of the Upper Zab River, which is described as an almost impassable terrain with high mountain ranges, thunderous waterfalls, and all kinds of fruit trees and grape vines, thus confirming for antiquity what modern botanists have long known: the grapevine grew wild in this region. We should note, however, that although Sargon's army was able to swill down lots of wine stored in the royal strongholds of the king of Urartu and also indulge in that favorite pastime of 1st millennium armies—cutting down the vineyards—none of this supports the widespread opinion that Armenia was the original "home" of viticulture. The Assyrian evidence merely establishes the fact that kings of this region had access to reasonably large supplies of wine in the late 8th century B.C. It tells us nothing about the extent or antiquity of viticulture and wine production in this area, which remains to be established.

Other Assyrian sources create the impression that wine is becoming increasingly plentiful over the course of the 7th century B.C. Sargon's son and grandson, Sennacherib (705–689 B.C.) and Esarhaddon (689–668 B.C.), both speak of "irrigating the insides" of the populace as part of the festivities associated with taking up residence in their new palaces (Luckenbill 1924: 116, 125; Borger 1956: 63). Sennacherib's account mentions *karanu duššupu*, which is probably wine sweetened with the addition of grape syrup, while Esarhaddon's account mentions "wine and *kurunnu*," which, as has already been discussed above, was probably beer made of barley malt with additives of emmer wheat and grape syrup. In addition to making its appearance at great festivals, wine has become a regular part of religious ceremony, as in Babylonia at a slightly later period of time.

Of course, wine continued to come in as tribute. Sennacherib even mentions it specifically (Luckenbill 1924: 55). Likewise, a letter from a certain Bel-iqiša and another official addressed to the king (possibly Esarhaddon) notes that the "official gift" (*namurtu*)—obviously wine in this case—for the month of Kanunu (ca. December 15–January 15) is behind schedule, that the king has a lot of wine, that they are worried about finding a place to store it, and asks for directions (Postgate 1974: 249).

What did the king do with all this wine? In the first place, the royal household itself required lots of wine. This emerges very clearly from a remarkable archive of the 8th century B.C. discovered at Kalah, modern Nimrud, dealing with wine rations (Kinnier Wilson 1972; Dalley and Postgate 1984: 22–25 and nos. 119–49; also see chapter 12 by Stronach, this volume). This archive does not tell us much about viticulture, but it does makes clear that the amounts issued increased with rank. Alas, the inscribed storage jars discovered at Nimrud were not adequately evaluated and have since disappeared, leaving in a state of limbo the actual sizes of the Assyrian capacity measures recorded in the texts (Powell 1989–90: 502).

It has already been observed from the annals of Sargon that, by the end of the 8th century, soldiers were expected to drink wine whenever they could get it. An official writes to the king (probably Sargon) that he has set aside 200 homers of wine for the military guard as per the king's directive (Waterman 1930–36: no. 387). This is probably something on the order of 20,000 l. Certainly not all of these soldiers drank in moderation. A letter, perhaps from the same Bel-iqiša mentioned above, informs the king (probably Esarhaddon or Ashurbanipal) that three men who have just been promoted to important positions in the army and royal bodyguard are drunkards (*šakranutu*) and that "when they are drunk not a man of them will turn the iron dagger aside from his fellow," adding that "I am sending word to the king of what I know; the king my lord should do as he wishes" (Waterman 1930–36: no. 85). A parallel, but somewhat different, situation seems implied in a letter written to one of the Assyrian kings by the mayor and a high temple official at Ashur, who complain that two named commanders of the Ituaians are "eating and drinking wine" and causing problems outside the main gate of Ashur (Waterman 1930–36: no. 419). Since these Ituaians turn up as fearsome crack troops from one end of the Assyrian Empire to the other, one cannot escape the suspicion that the king, as well as the military officers on whose recommendation the aforementioned promotions must have taken place, turned a blind eye to such things, so long as men like this proved themselves intrepid, fearless soldiers, and obeyed orders.

For soldiers and for the upper stratum of Assyrian society, it seems that, by the 7th century B.C., wine has come to occupy the inseparable linkage with food that it still occupies in some Mediterranean societies. Thus, we find members of the educated group of scribes who ministered to the manifold administrative, psychological, and physical needs of King Esarhaddon, writing him and urging him not to fast but to eat bread and drink wine (Parpola 1970: nos. 51 and 143). Still, the evidence of the palace wine rations from Nimrud in the 8th century (Kinnier Wilson 1972) suggests that per capita consumption was probably rather low, even in the palace household.

This picture of relatively low per capita consumption of wine even in the upper strata of society is borne out by a letter written to the king (probably Ashurbanipal) on behalf of another "servant of the king my lord" requesting the king to assign him in the district of Nineveh "a fifty-estate and a garden that draws off two homers of wine" (Waterman 1930–36: no. 456). A "fifty-estate" is probably what the Babylonians called "fifty *sila* [i.e., liters] in the big cubit," a system of measuring land by its minimum standard seed requirement. This means that a "fifty-estate" would be about 1.35 hectares, and the "two homers of wine" would be around 200 l (or possibly no more than 160), which could be produced, according to our norm of 600 l per *iku* deduced above on no more than 0.12 hectares. All of the metrological data fit together rather neatly, suggesting that, since the 200 l of wine is intended as the annual consumption of a whole family of the upper stratum, most people still did not drink a lot of wine in the Assyrian area, even in the 7th century.

Indirect though they be, these indicators of the levels of wine consumption among the upper stratum of the Assyrian Empire help us put in perspective what is by far the most striking evidence for viticulture in this era. This is the so-called "Assyrian Doomsday Book" (Johns 1901), a group of rather fragmentary tablets which seem to record the results of a census made in the 7th century B.C. in the Harran District in the upper watershed of the Balikh River. In these records we find—along with grain land, threshing floors, wells, and personnel—tens of thousands of vines (Johns 1901: 21). Since this is the general area where viticulture is attested for the 18th century B.C. in the records from Mari, one might be inclined to picture the whole region covered with vines. This may indeed have been the case, but caution is advisable. As Postgate (1974: 28–39) has pointed out, the "Doomsday" records probably concern royal estates and lands which were exempt from taxation. Moreover, the people on the land are not independent farmers but persons of dependent social status, roughly the equivalent of "serfs." This plausible theory, which also explains why these unique census records wound up in the central archives, cautions us that the rest of the district may not have looked quite like these properties of the crown and royal bureaucrats. Nevertheless, they do evidence an extensive viticulture that agrees with the overall developments that we have sketched out above.

3. Summary of the evidence from the Assyrian Empire

Unlike the official records of Assyrian kings in the Bronze Age, which never mention wine, by the 9th century B.C. wine has become a prized object of tribute considered worth mentioning along with other valuable and exotic items. The evidence points to an expanding viticulture for wine production, especially in the mountains and foothills stretching from western Iran, through southern Turkey, to Syria and the Mediterranean. Still, wine consumption per capita probably continued to be relatively low, and the evidence as a whole suggests that it continued to be considerably more expensive than beer throughout most of Mesopotamia, and thus was probably consumed on a regular basis only by the upper economic strata and by professional soldiers.

5. Conclusions

Early Sumerian tablets confirm the archaeological evidence, which indicates that domestication of the vine is at least as old as the 4th millennium B.C. However, viticulture is not synonymous with wine culture, because the Sumerians and all their successors in southern Mesopotamia continued to raise grapes, but they drank beer, and wine continued to be both rare and expensive there. Our first solid evidence for a developed wine culture appears around 1800 B.C. in northwestern Mesopotamia in connection with the Amorites, making it likely that Syria was the major center for difusion of wine culture into Mesopotamia, and it is virtually certain that it was the Syrians who introduced the wineskin to Mesopotamia. Sparse but unequivocal evidence from across the Taurus Mountains to the northwest makes clear that a wine culture is already well established in Anatolia by this same period of time. Up to now, we have no cuneiform evidence for viticulture of any kind in the area east of the Tigris until the 1st millennium B.C.

The 1st millennium seems a whole new world as far as wine culture is concerned. In the period of the Assyrian Empire, we find a well developed wine culture not only in Syria but all along the borderlands between Turkey in the north and Syria and Iraq to the south. And, for the first time, Assyrian sources mention wine in connection with Urartu, making it clear that Armenia has at last become the wine producing country that gave it a famous name in later antiquity. Wine also appears in the mountainous country represented by the Iraqi–Iranian borderlands, and some areas, such as the land of Zamua near modern Sulaymaniyah, became famous for wine. In the era of the Chaldean Empire, even in Babylonia wine begins to turn up regularly in royal inscriptions and in offerings to the gods. And wine as a desirable import, but affordable only by the wealthy, begins to come into Babylonia from as far away as the Damascus area of Syria. It is probably not due to accident that this increased evidence for movement of wine over long distances coincides with the creation of large empires. Although we know very little about tolls within these large states, they can hardly have been as numerous as those exacted by the many small states of the Bronze Age. Thus, the increased evidence for long distance shipment of wine may be, in part, a function of the emergence of large empires in the Near East. The story told by Herodotus of the shipment of wine from Armenia into Babylonian in the 5th century B.C. fits this general pattern.

CHAPTER 10

Searching for Wine in the Archaeological Record of Ancient Mesopotamia of the Third and Second Millennia B.C.

Richard L. Zettler and Naomi F. Miller

Southern Mesopotamia, an area variously dubbed the "cradle of civilization" and the "heartland of cities," was home to a beer-drinking culture, and the archaeological record reflects that fact. A wide array of evidence exists for beermaking and consumption by the peoples of ancient Sumer, Akkad, and Babylonia (Map 10.1, Table 10.1). A sherd from a pottery jar found at the site of Jemdet Nasr and dating to the late 4th or early 3rd millennium B.C., for example, has the signs for jar and beer inscribed on the neck. The jar would have had a capacity of 25–30 l (Englund and Grégoire 1991: 9). At Lagash, D. P. Hansen (1980–83) uncovered a brewery of the mid-3rd millennium B.C. The brewery included tanks for the making of beer-bread (Sumerian *bappir*), a mixture of dough and aromatic herbs, and a large oven in which, according to the hymn to the beer goddess, Ninkasi, the beer-bread would have been baked (Civil 1964: 72). A silver jar and a gold drinking-tube, probably used for drinking beer, were found in the tomb of the lady Pu-abi in the Royal Cemetery of Ur (Katz and Voigt 1986: fig. 11). Depictions of beer-drinking, for example, at banquets and during sexual intercourse, are common on cylinder seals (Woolley 1934: pls. 193: 17, 20; 194: 22–26, 29, 33), as well as on clay plaques (Parrot 1959b: 75; Saggs 1962: pl. 51C).

No unequivocal archaeological evidence exists from southern Mesopotamian sites that is relevant to grape cultivation or wine production, shipment, storage, and drinking. At least until recent years, archaeologists working in southern Mesopotamia did not routinely try to recover archaeobotanical remains and, in any case, preservation is poor in the area's salty soils. Production and distribution sites have not been identified, either. Even the written documentation is scarce (see chapter 9 by Powell, this volume). In the nearly three thousand documents of the late 3rd

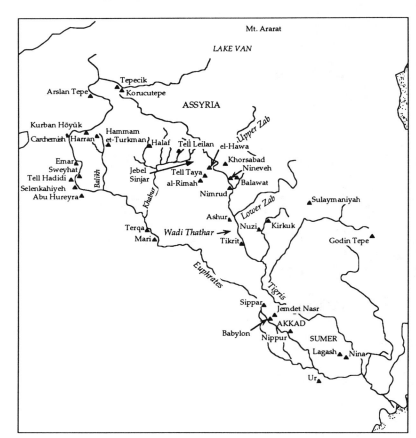

Map 10.1. The Near East: principal sites.

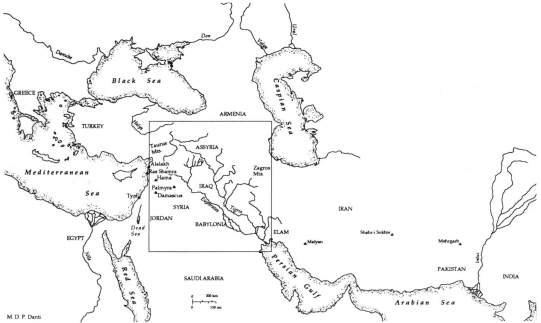

M. D. P. Danti

Table 10.1

Evidence of Grapes and Wine-Making[1]

Site	Period[2]	Evidence	Source
Abu Hureyra*	Neo	Seed (wild)	Hillman 1975
Hama*	Chal, EI	Impressions	Thuesen 1988: 90
Korucutepe*	Chal, EBA	Seed	van Zeist and Bakker-Heeres 1975
Kurban Höyük	Chal, M-L EBA	Seed, charcoal	Miller 1986
Arslan Tepe*	EBA	Seed	Follieri and Coccolini 1983
Tell Hadidi*	LBA	Seed	van Zeist and Bakker-Heeres 1985
Tell Selenkahiyeh*	EBA	Seed	van Zeist and Bakker-Heeres 1985
Hammam et-Turkman*	EBA	Seed	van Zeist, Waterbolk-van Rooijen, and Bottema 1988
Tell Leilan*	Late 3MB	Seed	Weiss 1990: 205
Tell Taya	Akkadian	seed	Waines 1973
Mari	2MB	Text	Finet 1974–77
Godin Tepe	4MB	Organic trace	Badler et al. 1990
Malyan	Ban, Kaf	seed, charcoal	Miller 1982: 183–86, 219, 222–25 and 241–44
Shahr-i Sokhte	3MB	Seed, charcoal	Costantini 1977
Mehrgarh	Mid-3MB	Seed, charcoal	Thiebault 1989

[1]Sites within the natural habitat zone of wild grape are asterisked. [2]Time periods are abbreviated as follows: Neolithic (Neo) = 6th millennium B.C. and earlier; Chalcolithic (Chal) = 4th millennium B.C.; Early Bronze Age (EBA) = 3rd millennium B.C.; Akkadian = ca. 2350–2150 B.C., Mesopotamia; Banesh (Ban) = ca. 3400–2600 B.C., southern Iran; Kaftari (Kaf) = ca. 2200–1650 B.C., southern Iran; Middle Bronze Age (MBA); M-L = Middle-Late Bronze Age; Late Bronze Age (LBA); Early Iron Age (EI); 2MB = second millennium B.C.; 3MB = 3rd millennium B.C.; 4MB = fourth millennium B.C.

millennium B.C. that are available from the large urban center of Nippur, in the center of the southern Mesopotamian floodplain, there are fewer than ten references to grapes, and nearly all of these refer to dried grapes or raisins (*geštin hàd*).[1] As Powell (in the preceding chapter) so colorfully expresses it, "Babylonia like Bavaria was essentially a beer-drinking culture. No one with their wits about them would have gone there to drink wine any more than a sensible person would go to the Mediterranean today to drink beer."

1. Archaeobotanical Evidence in Greater Mesopotamia

In contrast to southern Mesopotamia, archaeobotanical remains and archaeological evidence for grapes exist for the surrounding area (Miller 1991). Although we do not know when and why the vine was domesticated in the Near East, its cultivation seems to have been established sometime before 3000 B.C. in the natural habitat zone of the wild grape, whence it spread to other parts of the Near East (see chapters 2 by Zohary and 3 by Olmo, this volume).

The morphological distinction between seeds of European "wild" and "domestic" types of *Vitis vinifera* is not that useful for determining Near Eastern archaeobotanical remains (see chapters 2 by Zohary, 3 by Olmo, and 16 by Renfrew, this volume). Wood charcoal is another source of information. Although one cannot tell whether *Vitis* wood comes from the wild or domesticated type, it is unlikely to be collected from the wild for fuel; grape-bearing vines would not grow in dense stands, and the vine stem would not break easily. If, on the other hand, people were growing grapes, yearly pruning of the vines would provide occasional fuel for the fire. Given the ambiguities of the seed evidence, one can even argue that the best evidence for grape cultivation is occurrence of its charcoal in an archaeobotanical assemblage, especially if the site lies outside the area where the wild type grows (cf. Thiebault 1989). Archaeobotanical remains allow the growing importance of grape in the 3rd millennium to be assessed.

There are a few scattered early finds of grape. Some seeds from Neolithic Abu Hureyra presumably came from wild vines growing along the upper Euphrates (Hillman 1975). Unexpected organic traces of wine were found inside late 4th millennium B.C. jars from Godin Tepe in western Iran (Badler et al. 1990), though flotation samples from the same level contained no charred grape seeds (Miller 1990). It is not until the Early Bronze Age (3rd millennium B.C.) that grape seeds are consistently encountered, sometimes in concentrations, in the archaeological record. By the mid-3rd millennium B.C., grape cultivation had reached far beyond the natural range of wild grape, as far as Shahr-i Sokhte in eastern Iran (Costantini 1977) and Mehrgarh in Pakistan (Thiebault 1989).

Carbonized pips have been found at sites on the upper Euphrates in southeastern Turkey and northern Syria, an area that is within the natural range of wild grape: Korucutepe and Tepecik (van Zeist and Bakker-Heeres 1975), Arslan Tepe (Follieri and Coccolini 1983), Kurban Höyük (Miller 1986: 88), Tell es-Sweyhat (Hide 1990: 16), Tell Hadidi, and Tell Selenkahiyeh (van Zeist and Bakker-Heeres 1985). Impressions of *Vitis vinifera* were identified in pottery from Hama in central Syria (Thuesen 1988: 90). A few carbonized grape pips were recovered from Hammam et-Turkman on the Balikh in Syria (van Zeist et al. 1988), from Tell Leilan in the upper Khabur drainage (Weiss 1990: 205), and from Tell Taya in northern Iraq (Waines 1973).

To the southeast of Mesopotamia, carbonized and mineralized pips and charcoal were identified from 3rd millennium B.C. deposits at Malyan, ancient Anshan, in Iran (Miller 1982: 183–86, 219, 222–25, 241–44). Malyan lies well outside the modern distribution zone of wild grape, so grape at Malyan was probably cultivated (Miller 1983: 184–85).

Inasmuch as they provide plausible evidence for the growing, pressing, and consumption of grapes, the archaeobotanical data from Kurban Höyük, in southeastern Turkey, and Malyan, in southern Iran, merit detailed description. Both sites have small quantities of grape charcoal from 3rd millennium B.C. levels. At Kurban Höyük, the amount of grape remains increased from the late Chalcolithic to the Mid-Late Early Bronze Age (Miller 1991: 150). A sample from a Mid-Late Early Bronze Age pit in Area A yielded unusually high densities of both charred nutshell and grape pips and fragments. In addition, the sample contained the peduncle (stem) and pressed fragments of the fruit itself. The sample, though charred, contained virtually no charcoal and very few of the weed seeds that might be expected in dung, so it was unlikely to have been the remains of fuel. It might , therefore, represent the burned debris of two production processes, grape-pressing for juice, wine or vinegar, and nut grinding for oil or meal (Miller 1986: 88–89).

At Malyan, grape apparently increased in importance between the Banesh (ca. 3400–2600 B.C.) and Kaftari (ca. 2200–1650 B.C.) periods. A few grape seeds and no charcoal of the vine were extracted from Banesh period deposits. Over 100 carbonized grape pips and some *Vitis* charcoal fragments were recovered from Kaftari period deposits. The more than 1200 uncarbonized grape pips from a Kaftari period latrine confirms the conclusion that people consumed grapes (Miller 1982: 241–44). It is therefore not surprising that grapes and grape vines are a feature of one particular group of Kaftari period cylinder seals. The seals (Fig. 10.1) feature a male seated on a stool and a female seated under a grapevine (Amiet 1986: figs. 113–14; Porada 1990: 174–75).

Figure 10.1. Kaftari cylinder seal. (Amiet 1986: fig. 113.5.)

2. Mari

The more than 20,000 clay tablets from the early 2nd millennium B.C. royal palace at Mari (modern Tell Hariri) contain information about grape cultivation, winemaking, transport and transshipment, and consumption (see chapter 9 by Powell, this volume). Consequently, it is worth examining the archaeological remains of the palace for information bearing on the handling of wine. Is it possible, for example, to determine where and how wine was stored in the palace, or to identify vessels or vessel types that might have held wine?

The Mari palace (Fig. 10.2) covered ca. 2.5 hectares, and contained at least three hundred courtyards, rooms, and corridors (Parrot 1959a: 5). The ground floor of the Mari palace, the only part of the building preserved, contained several storerooms or complexes of storerooms. For example, storeroom 116 off courtyard 106 contained large storage jars (a typical jar measures 1.05 m. in height, with a rim diameter of 50 cm. and a maximum diameter of 1.28 m.) set into a low mudbrick socle (Parrot 1959a: 94–97). The room has tentatively been identified, based on information drawn from tablets, as a storeroom for oils (al-Khalesi 1978: 12).

Complexes of storerooms (121–23 and 215–18) opened off a corridor (120) in the south-central part of the palace. The storeroom numbered 122 (Fig. 10.3) contained three rows of low, rectangular blocks made of mudbrick. The blocks served as supports for jars, a few of which were found *in situ* (Parrot 1959a: 286–87). The storerooms numbered 216–18 (Fig. 10.4) were not well-preserved, but each contained low mudbrick socles against the walls into which storage jars would have been set. Room 216 could have held 33 jars; room 217 could have held 20 jars. The floors of both 216 and 217 consisted of tamped earth over a bed of pebbles. Although room 218 was the largest of the three rooms, it had enough space for only 15 jars (Parrot 1959a: 289–92).

For the most part, the jars that existed in the storerooms were not preserved, but the bases of some were found *in situ* (Parrot 1959a: 289; Margueron 1982: 338). The jars would have had a maximum dimension of 70 cm. (Margueron 1982: 338). Several pottery lids were found on the floors in the three rooms; the two published examples from room 216 had diameters of 30 and 32 cm. (Parrot 1959b: 140).

Carbonized wood was found in some of the depressions left by the jars on the tops of the socles, as well as on the floor of the rooms (Parrot 1959a: 289–92). Margueron (1982: 338) has suggested that it represented the remains of racks or frameworks built around the jars that would have served to stabilize them.

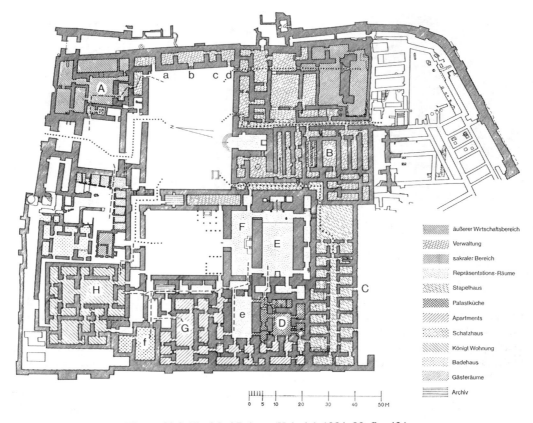

Figure 10.2. The Mari Palace. (Heinrich 1984: 80, fig. 42.)

Is it possible that the storerooms numbered 216, 217, and 218 might have been "wine cellars"? In his study of wine in the Mari documents, A. Finet (1974–77: 125–26) noted that depending on need, wine purchased or received by the king of Mari was kept in the palace either in storerooms (Akkadian *nakkamtum* or *rugbum*) or sent to the "cellars" (Akkadian *kannum*). He also observed that in the storerooms wine was held in the jars in which it was shipped. The wine jars were emptied, and the wine was treated in various ways in the cellar. The term *kannum* might have designated a socle that would support containers with rounded or pointed bases such as wine jars. The term *bīt kannim* would then have designated the room or building where such installations existed. The *bīt kannim* doubtless had large-capacity vats where wine could be stored, racked, decanted, tasted, or put into jars that could then be sealed (Finet 1974–77: 126).

Finet described *kannum* as a fixed installation, but *kannum* might also designate a more portable construction, perhaps made of wood. C. Walker has suggested that *kannum*, translated as "wine rack," might have been part of the furniture of the dining area (Dalley et al. 1976: 184). He based his suggestion on his reading of documents from Tell al-Rimah (ancient Karana) in northern Iraq that imply that wine designated as for the wine racks (*ana kannim*) was wine intended for immediate consumption. Thus, the Akkadian term *kannum* might plausibly have designated either the fixed or portable installations.

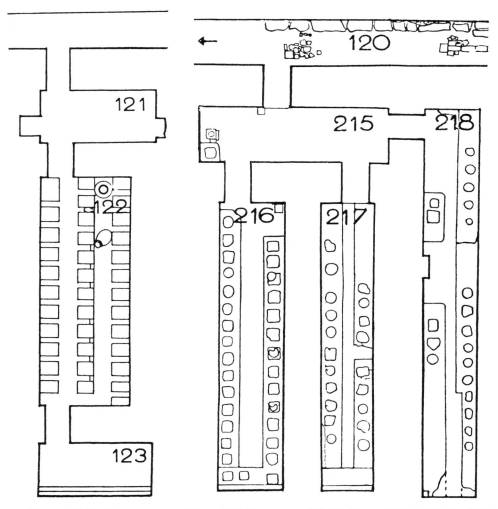

Figure 10.3. Store-
room 122. (Parrot
1958; 2:287, fig. 348.)

Figure 10.4. Storerooms 216–18. (Parrot 1958: 2:288, fig. 350.)

Could the terms *nakkamtum* or *rugbum* refer to the storerooms numbered 122 or 216–18? The terms *nakkamtum* and *rugbum* are commonly used in the Mari documents with a form of the Akkadian verb *elûm* (*šulûm*) that means to move objects to a higher location (Talon 1985 41; Oppenheim et al. 1958: 128–29; see also Finet 1974–77: 125–26; Durand 1983: 104–5), and the term *rugbum*, in fact, means roof (von Soden 1959–81: 993). M. Powell (chapter 9, this volume) has suggested that wine sent to storerooms with those designations would have been sent to storerooms on the second floor of the Mari palace. Concentrations of artifacts high in the fill of certain rooms of the palace, e.g., molds in room 77, indicate that either the roof was functional space or that part of the palace had a second floor. The current director of excavations at Mari has discussed the evidence and proposed reconstructions of the palace's second story (Margueron

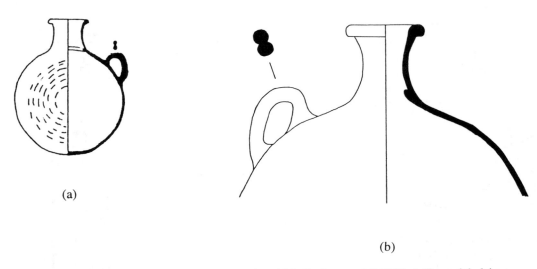

(a)

(b)

Figure 10.5. Shipping containers from sites on the middle Euphrates: a) (left) Mari, "jarre globulaire à anse bifide," M. 857m, scale 1:8.3 (Parrot 1959: fig. 84); b) (right) Kurban Höyük, similar type as in a, scale 1:4 (Algaze 1990: 2: pl. 116a.)

1982: 288–309; Margueron et al. 1990). The range of activities, however, that took place in second story rooms or on the roof is not well known.

If Finet's understanding of *kannum* as "cellar" is correct, at least in its essentials, I would suggest that the term might well have designated storerooms such as 216, 217, and 218. Such an identification, however, could only be confirmed if the bases of one or more of the jars found there could be located and tested for traces of organic remains of wine (see chapters 5 by McGovern and Michel, 6 by Singleton, and 7 by Formenti and Duthel, this volume). Parenthetically, a storeroom (139 off courtyard XVI) at Khorsabad, ancient Dur-Šarrukin (Place 1867: 102–3), with identical features (i.e., socles against the walls and inset jars), functioned as a storeroom for wine in the palace of Sargon II (721–705 B.C.). The term that designated that particular storeroom remains unknown.

3. Artifactual Evidence

Do artifacts, such as pottery or clay sealings, from the Mari palace shed any light on the handling and use of wine? André Parrot published very little of the pottery found in the Mari palace, and without a knowledge of the full ceramic repertoire, identifying wine jars would be difficult. The size of a standard wine jar is not even certain. Finet (1974–77: 129) suggested 10 l; Powell (chapter 9, this volume) has indicated that 30 l would be a better guess.

M.-H. Gates (1988: 69–73) has identified a particular type of flask found at Euphrates sites as shipping containers for wine sent from the Levant, since sites in that part of the Near East contain the closest parallels for the shape. The flasks (Fig. 10.5) have a high, narrow neck and a double-stranded handle on the shoulder. An example from the Mari palace would have held 10 l, while an example from Tell Atchara (ancient Terqa), just up river from Mari, would have held 30 l. In addition to the sites noted by Gates, such flasks have also been found at Kurban Höyük in southeastern Turkey (Algaze 1990: 376). On the one hand, the flasks do stand out as imports and their sizes are roughly what might be expected. On the other hand, Gates' identification of their specific function is little more than guesswork. Perhaps, the jars ought to be examined for traces of their contents.

As a letter from Zimri-lim, king of Mari, to Siptu, his queen, demonstrates, both palace storerooms containing wine and wine jars were sealed. In one letter, for example, Zimri-lim writes, "Fill ten jars with red wine and seal them with this seal; and give them to Bahdi-lim. However, send the seal on the chain back to me" (Dossin 1978: 192–93). The sealing of wine is not surprising. A study of the sealings and their distribution in the Mari palace might have provided some indication of the rooms that would have held wine, and at the same time provided the rim and/or neck and shoulder profiles of sealed jars. D. Beyer (1985) reexamined the sealings from the Mari palace. Few of them proved to have secure archaeological contexts, although one door sealing was from room 217. Beyer determined that of the sealings from the palace, the majority had been broken off doors. Only one sealing had apparently closed a small jar. As was the case with regard to wine cellars and jars, the evidence of sealings from the Mari palace is inconclusive.

4. Summary

In contrast to Sumerian and Akkadian texts, the ancient Mesopotamian archaeological record for the 3rd and 2nd millennia B.C., with the possible exception of archaeobotanical remains from Kurban Höyük, contains no conclusive evidence for the production and consumption of wine. Evidence is lacking even at sites where written documentation indicates that wine was stored and consumed, as for example, in the Mari palace. Perhaps more rigorous excavation and analysis of the palace and its artifacts might have turned up some trace of wine. The search for wine in the archaeological record of Mesopotamia, however, has not proven to be a "fruitless" task. It has at least provided a particularly forceful reminder of the limitations of archaeological and textual evidence studied in isolation and should encourage cooperation between archaeologists, cuneiformists and other scientists in the reconstruction of all facets of ancient Mesopotamian culture, including gastronomy.

Notes

1. See, for example, Nippur cuneiform tablets 4 NT 191, 4 NT 197, 4 NT 212, 4 NT 218, 6 NT 176, 6 NT 226, 6 NT 805, NATN 375 (though perhaps from Umma, not Nippur), and NATN 563.

CHAPTER 11

Viticulture and Ancient Anatolia

Ronald L. Gorny

(Behold) the raisin. Just as it holds its wine in (its) heart; just as the olive holds its oil in (its) heart, so you (also) Stormgod, hold wealth, life, vigor, long years (and) joy of the King, the Queen (and) their children in (your) heart.

KUB[1] 33.68 obv. ii 13–16[2]

Anatolia has long been linked with the origins of viticulture and wine-making, especially in its eastern region to which the ancient authors commonly ascribe its origins.[3] Noah, for instance, is credited in the Bible with planting vineyards on the slopes of Mount Ararat in eastern Turkey (Fig. 11.1 and Map 11.1), and then over-indulging in the wine produced (Genesis 8–9). Herodotus (1.193–194), in similar fashion, suggests Armenia as the source of wine-making. Opinions such as these, however, are as much legend as truth and may or may not have any real basis in fact.

The earliest native references to the wines of Anatolia are found in Old Assyrian documents from Kültepe and date to the early second millennium B.C. These citations, however, are few and somewhat limited in scope. It is not until the ensuing Hittite era (ca. 1600–1200 B.C.) that written documents from Boğazköy-Ḫattuša finally begin to inform us about the role of viticulture during the second millennium. The first millennium witnessed further dissemination of viticulture in the Near East (cf. Stronach in this volume), and wine seems to have become more commonplace, as is attested by the introduction of new vessel shapes which become commonplace across the region and are linked with wine and its consumption (Boardman 1974: 196–233).

By classical times, wine had become an integral part of the Anatolian diet and almost as many varieties existed as there were settled communities. The wines of Anatolia were fondly referred to by authors such as Pliny (*Natural History*, Books 14 and 23), Strabo (*Geography*, Book 12), and Athenaeus (*Deipnosophists*, Books 1–10). Among other places, well-known wines were produced along the west coast at Clazomenae (Pliny *NH* 14.235), Cnidos, and Telmessos (Magie 1988: 518; see chapter 20 by Koehler, this volume) and on islands like Chios, Cos, and Lesbos which lie just off the coast (Pliny, *NH* 14.235, 251; Magie 1988: 45, 51, 255, 492). Pramnian wine, which is mentioned in Homer (*Iliad* 11.639; *Odyssey* 10.235), was still being produced at Smyrna in

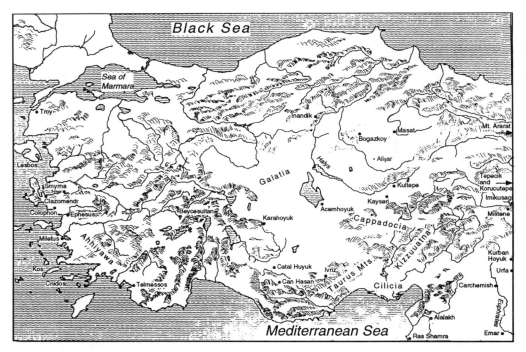

Map 11.1. Anatolia: principal sites.

Roman times (Pliny, *NH* 14.223). Further inland a sweet wine called *Scybelites* was manufactured in the central Anatolian region of Galatia and was said to have the taste of mulsen or honeyed wine (Pliny, *NH* 14.239) and the town of Amblada, situated between Lake Beyşehir and Lake Suğla in Pisidia was famous for a wine with medicinal qualities (Strabo, *Geography* 12.7.2:570). To the east, the wines of Melitine (Modern Malatya) were considered equal to those of Greece (Strabo, *Geography* 12.2.1: 351, Magie 1988: 494). In addition, Herodotus (15.1.58) lauds the wines of Armenia, and Pliny (*NH* 14.241; cf. Magie 1988: 715) commends the wines of Cilicia along the southeastern Mediterranean coast, especially its raisin-wine. Although the fertile volcanic soils around the central Anatolian city of Nevşehir in Cappadocia constitute a grape-producing area today, there is little textual evidence of grape-growing there during antiquity. In general, however, the wines of Anatolia were well known during the classical period and considered the equal of most Mediterranean wines, and in certain instances, the Anatolian products were actually thought to be superior to their western counterparts.

Wine continued to be an important product of the Anatolian peninsula during Byzantine times (Khazdan 1991: 2199), and as late as the period of early Turkish expansion, Chinese sources record various types of Anatolian and Turkish wines.[4] In fact, prior to their conversion to Islam, the Turks believed that wine was blessed by the sky-god and that no evil spirit could penetrate a vineyard or any place where wine was stored. When a young man was born, a goblet was buried in the earth from which he would drink wine on the day of his wedding.[5]

Wine-drinking was later proscribed by Islam, but in truth, many Turks regularly partook of the beverage. Emerson (1908: 376–94) describes the preparation and effects of several varieties in his narration on Turkish beverages. This was especially true in areas where there was close contact

Figure 11.1. Vineyards at foot of Mt. Ararat with the Iron Age site of Artashot (Armenia) in the background. (Photograph by R. Gorny.)

with foreigners. In Istanbul, for instance, a government wine inspector occupied an office by the Iron Gate at Galata, where many taverns were located. These drinking establishments were frequented by not only Christian and Jewish customers, but also Turkish Muslims (Lewis 1971: 140). Nevertheless, the emergence of Islam sent Anatolian wine production into a decline that has only begun to be reversed in recent years.

1. Environment and Viticulture in Anatolia

The natural habitat of the modern wild grape (*Vitis silvestris*) partly parallels that of the olive, although thriving in a cooler and more humid climate than the former (Zohary 1975: 321). According to its modern distribution, the wild ancestor of the domesticated grape (*Vitis vinifera*) had apparently established itself along an extended east–west axis running from the Caucasus through northern Anatolia and deep into Europe. The southernmost point of this Eurasian axis was along the southern slopes of the Taurus mountains in southeastern Turkey. These areas hold out the greatest promise in locating the ancient antecedents of Anatolian viticulture. Different climatic conditions, human innovation and persistence, however, may be responsible for modern patterns of cultivation that are somewhat different from those found in antiquity (Hoffner 1974: 41).

Grapes were surely collected as food for an extended period of time prior to the vine's domestication, and the fruit was probably utilized for wine-making long before the process of domestication was finally accomplished. During the early phase of viticultural experimentation, grapes would have been collected from wild vines, the fruit remaining small and somewhat bitter. As early as the Neolithic period, botanical examples of wild grapes appear in archaeological deposits alongside other uncultivated fruits such as bittersweet nightshade, elderberry, cornelian cherry, blackberry, and raspberry (Helbaek 1960: 116). The presence of *Vitis vinifera* in Çayönü deposits dating to the ninth millennium (Stewart 1976: 221) illustrates once again that grape gathering must have commenced in Anatolia as early as the Neolithic period and raises the possibility that the beginnings of viticultural experimentation in Anatolia could have occurred much earlier than is commonly assumed.

The natural habitat from which this early vintage was collected remains obscure. In some areas, local inhabitants may have protected and exploited wild vines as natural resources.[6] This would have surely facilitated the process of domestication in that it would have encouraged the selection of grapevines with larger more succulent fruit. Other vines may have already been transplanted from their natural habitat during this period of horticultural experimentation, but since there are no clear examples of grape pips from this period that display the diagnostic changes commonly associated with domestication, it is difficult to make any definitive observations regarding the process of domestication. Production, however, would have been local and on a limited scale.

In due time, the grape crossed the threshold of domestication, the completion of a process which had been preceded by several millennia of human observation and experimentation. Exactly when and where that point was reached is still unclear, and it may be that it occurred at different times in different places. The most reliable evidence, however, points to the Early Bronze Age (third millennium) as the period which witnessed the real expansion of grape cultivation. The appearance of pips from Early Bronze deposits that are transitional in character between the early wild vines and the later domesticates indicates that some sort of cultivation had begun to take place by that time,[7] and although it is hazardous to speculate on origins, Logothetis links these transitional types with East Mediterranean and Black Sea varieties used for wine-making in later periods, and this suggest the possibility that the expansion of viticulture in the Early Bronze Age can be linked to the development of a grape that was better suited to wine-making than its predecessors, a description that seems to suggest a larger and sweeter fruit.[8]

Another indicator that points to the Early Bronze Age as the period of viticultural expansion is the change noted in the ceramic assemblages of that period. In general, there are more chalices, flasks, and narrow-neck vessels in evidence, forms which suggest an association with specialty drinks, most likely, alcoholic in nature. In particular, we note the appearance of chalices in the Ninevite 5 assemblage of northern Mesopotamia (Roaf and Killick 1987) and "metallic ware" pedestalled vessels in north Syria (Kühne 1976). The Aegean and western Anatolia also saw additions to their repertoires which included vessels such as the Early Helladic sauceboat and the *depas amphikypellon* (Renfrew 1972: 282–84, 487; Mellink 1986; Sherratt 1987). In Cyprus there are many examples of elaborate ceramic vessels from this period that were, most likely, associated with alcoholic consumption (Karageorgis 1991). Finally, elements of the third millennium Bell Beaker repertoire which are alleged to be copies of Aegean and Anatolian prototypes are cited as evidence for the spread of alcoholic consumption to Europe (Sherratt 1987).

While the introduction of these new forms is not always linked securely to wine consumption, the coincidental introduction of these vessels at the very time and in the same places where archeological evidence confirms the spread of viticulture is reason enough to suggest a link between form and function. Such changes, however, not only point to an agricultural transformation at this time, but clearly suggest a link between production and craft specialization. Even more telling is the link between wine and emerging states where drinking and its associated accouterments have been shown to be connected with the position of the elite, political integration and cultic belief (Joffe n.d.). In this respect, it is not surprising to see the development of elaborate chalices, rhyta, and relief vessels in association with the rise of the early Hittite state around 2000 B.C. (N. Özgüç 1950).

The original home of Anatolian viticulture remains unknown, but the modern widespread habitat of the wild grape provides several alternatives. One possibility is Transcaucasia where the presence of domesticated grape pips in the archaeological record are said to predate their appearance in central Anatolia by a millennium or more (Lisitsina 1984: 291, table 2; Badler, McGovern, and Michel 1990: 33; also see chapters 4 by Badler and 5 by McGovern and Michel, this volume). If this is, indeed, the case, viticulture might well have been introduced into Anatolia by elements of the Early Transcaucasian culture that dominated the eastern reaches of Anatolia in the 4th millennium B.C.[9]

There are, however, reasons for questioning a Transcaucasian origin. In the first place, archeobotany is a poorly developed science in this area of the world and the dating criteria is poor. In addition, there is a strong political agenda in the area for the "earliest cultivation." Furthermore, the grape's wild progenitor is known from the Taurus mountains, the gentle slopes that ring coastal areas of Turkey, and along the river valleys of northern, western, and southeastern Turkey (Zohary and Spiegel-Roy 1975: 322, pl. 1). Such considerations have not only fueled doubts about a Transcaucasian origin for viticulture (Rivera Núñez and Walker 1989: 220), but have clearly demonstrated that many areas in Anatolia had the potential for horticultural development, and the possibility exists, therefore, that the introduction of a grape culture into Anatolia could have come from one or several of these sources.

The extent to which viticulture spread throughout Anatolia was determined, in part, by the makeup of its physical environment. The seemingly monotonous terrain of the plateau gives way, on closer examination, to a landscape composed of numerous micro-environments, each with its own peculiar set of ecological features. Within the context of this ecological framework, Harvey Oakes (1954) identified 18 major soil types, and although his study is only a "reconnaissance," it has proved to be invaluable, yielding fundamental information on the character of the Anatolian soils and providing considerable information on the areas where viticulture might be expected to succeed.

As Oakes found, Anatolia's central plateau is dominated by rough mountainous terrain composed primarily of limestone (Oakes 1954: 130). In general, the soil is shallow and somewhat unproductive. The area is characterized by insufficient rainfall and the natural poverty of the soil is increased by centuries of human misuse (Dewdney 1971: 112) Within this larger complex, however, are found isolated pockets of more fertile alluvial soils that have developed in the intermontane valleys. Among these are chestnut, brown, and brown forest soils (Oakes 1954: 130). Although much of the central plateau is unsuited for agriculture, Oakes found that about 6% of the land was used to support vineyards, orchards, or croplands (1954: 130). This figure has risen dramatically in recent years due to the intensification of agriculture which took place in Turkey after 1950 (Dewdney 1971: 99–100). The more fertile volcanic soils in the region of Cappadocia produce grapes and wine today but do not appear to have attained the level of wine production in antiquity that made other areas of the country known throughout the Mediterranean world.

The actual potential for a widespread extension of viticulture into the region of the plateau does not seem to have been very high in antiquity. The limited prospects for viticultural development in the interior may have been moderated, however, by the expansion of the grape culture around the periphery of the plateau. This was due, in general, to the favorable conditions found there, and in particular, to the fact that the mountains, coastal areas, and river valleys which surround the Anatolian plateau were composed of soils much better suited to the development of viticulture than are those of the interior (Temir 1974: 783).

Although the two most prominent soil types associated with such areas are the red podzolic soils and reddish chestnut soils, the coastal areas of Anatolia vary greatly in soil types. The humid northern mountains, for instance, are characterized by brown forest (Oakes 1954: 120–21, 146) and red to reddish-brown podzolic soils (Oakes 1954: 43, 142–43), while gently sloping areas of terra rosa are found along the major river valleys of the west (Oakes 1954: 80–82, 131–32). Other productive soils in the area include the reddish-brown (Oakes 1954: 69), reddish chestnut (Oakes 1954: 76–77), and gray calcareous regosol soils (Oakes 1954: 118), most of which are found further inland and at lower elevations than the podzolic soils (Oakes 1954: 146). These soils formed the natural habitat of the wild grapevine, and provided favorable conditions for the further development of viticulture.

While grapes seem to prefer heavy soils with good moisture retention (Logothetis 1962: 34), the world's best wines are traditionally produced from grapes grown in soils with a high percentage of stones or gravel, a necessary component of good drainage (White 1970b: 229). Several such areas with stony soil are noted among the grape-producing areas of modern-day Turkey, particularly along the major river valleys of western Anatolia (Oakes 1954: 117–18, 132). In the Hittite heartland, however, the dominant soils are of the alkaline reddish-brown and brown steppe varieties, land that is heavily utilized for cereal crops (Oakes 1954: 9, 83; Dewdney 1971: 47). Saline and desertic gray soils of low productivity also cover large areas of the interior plateau (Dewdney 1971: 47; Temir 1974: 783). They are associated with areas of low grape production such as Konya and are generally arable only after irrigation (see Table 11.3). In general, these soils display a shallow and calcareous nature (Dewdney 1971: 47; Oakes 1954: 160). Unlike the richer red soils which retain moisture well, this product of the plateau's broken limestone marl is extremely porous and heavily dependent on annual rainfalls (Mitchell 1993: 144). This fact makes them especially vulnerable to the effects of climatic variability and provides a risky backdrop against which to frame the development of agriculture on the Anatolian plateau (for soils also see Wenzel 1937: 617–18).[10]

In addition to the favorable character of its soil, the coastal areas of Anatolia are subject to a much higher degree of rainfall than the interior (Dewdney 1971: 39, 112). This condition is the result of both topography and a high pressure system that develops over Anatolia between the months of November and April, a pattern that diverts rainfall around the interior and deposits it along the north and south coasts of the peninsula (Fisher 1978: 335), where rainfall amounts generally reach or exceed 500 mm. The result is a very productive horticultural zone replete with all the ingredients necessary for the sustenance of the vine. The success of the vine in these areas ultimately may have encouraged the exportation of the vine into adjacent, but climatically less favorable, environment of Anatolia's interior plateau.

The vulnerability of the horticulture on the central plateau is underscored by two additional climatic factors that regularly afflict the Anatolian highlands, viz. the very low precipitation (Fisher 1958: 335) and/or the irregular rain patterns (Fisher 1958: 338; Erinç 1950: 231; Dewdney 1971: 112). Because the Anatolian plateau is ringed by mountains, most precipitation will fall before it can reach the interior. Regions along the periphery of the mountains generally expect about 300 mm of rain, but much of the interior is a semi-arid region where between 200 and 250 mm of precipitation fall annually (Dewdney 1971: 112; Mitchell 1993: 144; cf. Erinç 1950). As 200 mm is the minimum amount of precipitation necessary for cereal harvests, one begins to sense the urgency of the situation in these areas.

When one adds to this situation the fact that the gray soils of the interior do not retain moisture well, it is easy to see that any delay in the expected rains can have a disastrous effect on crops. Not only will germinating seedlings shrivel and die, but the soil becomes hard-baked, and when the rains do arrive, the hardened soils inhibit further absorption of moisture. Instead of facilitating the absorption of moisture and enhancing the productivity of the land, the soil becomes a runway that channels water away from the thirsting fields and, in the process, becomes an agent of erosion as each flow carries away a little more of the vulnerable soil. This combination of unsuitable soil and deficient moisture, especially when combined with the excessive heat of the Anatolian summer, frequently has led to prolonged droughts (Erinç 1950, 1978; Ünal 1977) that have had deleterious affects on all crops grown in the region, including the grape.[11]

Another factor that must be taken into account when considering the practicality of vineyards and wine production in central Anatolia is the susceptibility of the vine to frost. Although the grape itself is fairly resistent to frost (Dewdney 1971: 106), the vine must have freedom from late Spring frosts during which time the plant is flowering, as well as a dormant winter season in which frosts are seldom serious (Nyrop 1973: 65). Records from Medieval England and Northern Europe suggest that frost was a limiting factor in grape production and in some cases, viticulture ceased in these areas after prolonged periods of frost and extreme winters (Lamb 1977: 296–99). Between 1150 and 1300, temperatures in these regions were higher than today and frosts were evidently rarer in May. The cooling of the temperature in subsequent centuries, however, resulted in earlier frosts and colder winters which decimated large tracts of cultivated vineyards. Similarly, on the Anatolian plateau, where frosts can occur for more than 100 days (Nyrop 1973: 65), the prospect of debilitating frosts adds another element of risk to the spread of viticulture on the plateau.

Conditions on the Anatolian plateau (Taeschner 1960: 464–65) were such that Hittite horticulturalists may have faced a similar threat. Rising to an average altitude of around 1000 m above sea level, the plateau formed a rather improbable place to launch a wine industry. Although the optimal altitude for the wild grapevine seems to be about 400 m, the plant does well up to a height of 800 m (Savulesai 1958: 300; Renfrew 1973: 125) and can be found in modern Turkey growing as high as 1600 m (Davis 1967: 521). Temperatures in these elevated areas, however, drop very low in the winter (Wenzel 1937: 10–16) and frosts can occur frequently (Nyrop 1973: 65), thus adding another element of risk to the spread of viticulture on the plateau. In fact, not only do modern environmental studies show that such periods of cold periodically affected Anatolia and the Middle East during the second millennium (Brentjes 1982: 470; Ergenzinger et al. 1988) and afterwards (Brentjes 1982: 19–20), but written records dating to the Hittite period vividly describe some of the difficulties caused by frost and cold (Ünal 1977: 455–56). Bearing this in mind, it is not unreasonable to suggest that the climatic shifts attested for these periods could affect, not only agriculture in general, but viticulture in particular.

In sum, the evidence suggests that environmental factors on the central Anatolian plateau can cause major differences in the volume of crops harvested annually (Dewdney 1971: 112). Good years produce a surplus that can be exported, but the norm is for a crop that is sufficient only for local and national use. This fact was not lost on the Romans, as Mark Antony cautioned during a speech delivered in 43 B.C. that by asking for specific proportions of the agricultural produce to meet local tax liabilities instead of a set total, the Romans were sharing the risks inherent in the region's variable harvests with the growers.[12] Klengel likewise observed (1986: 24) that during Hittite times, the interplay of these environmental factors resulted in "a dispersed and small-scale agriculture of a fluctuating effectiveness" in Anatolia, a condition that would have certainly affected grape-growing. In any case, the Anatolian horticulturalist found himself in a risky situation that was directly related to the unpredictability of rainfall and the calcareous soils that predominated on the plateau. As Mitchell astutely notes, "there is almost no margin for error" in an environment such as this (1993: 144).

The importance of the environmental setting to viticulture on the central Anatolian plateau is further borne out by the agricultural records of grape production in modern Turkey.[13] By examining an eighteen-year period between 1933 and 1950, it is possible to make some interesting comparisons (Tables 11.1–4).[14] During this period, the yield for Turkey is 2.628 tons per hectare with a low yield of 1.360 tph (1947) and a high of 4.499 (1945). In Yozgat province (Table 11.1), an area typical of the central plateau ecological scheme, the average yield is 2.036 tph. The high yield is 4.249 (1943) and the low is 0.500 tph (1940). While the average yield for Turkey remains fairly consistent during this period, the yield for Yozgat fluctuates greatly from year to year. A similar pattern in Çorum province (Table 11.1; where Boğazköy is located) suggests that this scheme is fairly typical of the central Turkish provinces as a whole.

By comparison, we can also check the Yozgat statistics against those of the traditional wine producing province of Manisa (Table 11.2) where the high yield is 9.488 (1946) while the low is 2.360 (1940). The average yield for Yozgat during this period is 2.036 tph. and the average for Manisa is 4.725 tph. This is interesting in that it provides an indication of what the production yields in a pre-fertilization and pre-mechanization situation would have been and this gives us some idea of what expectations in the Hittite period might have been. The results of the technological advances in viticulture are also enlightening. Whereas the average yield in Yozgat rose to a modest 3.8 tph in 1991, the yield in Manisa during the same period shot up to a staggering 14 tph. This appears to be evidence of a widespread manipulation of the surroundings through fertilization, intensive irrigation, and modern mechanization.

The pattern of low yields on the central Anatolian plateau is repeated at other highland provinces such as Çorum where the Hittite capital of Ḫattuša-Boğazköy was located (Table 11.2) and Malatya (Table 11.4). On the other hand, high returns can be documented for areas such as Çanakkale and Manisa (Table 11.2) which border the plateau and where rainfall is not diverted by protruding mountain ranges. Upon reaching lowland areas around Diyarbakır and Urfa in the southeast we again find higher yields (Table 11.4), and although rainfall is also limited in this region, the higher yields are probably attributable to more productive soils, a lesser threat from frost, and the ability of the cultivators to irrigate.

The one exception to this rule of thumb appears to be areas in the provinces of Niğde and Kayseri which are situated along the productive land of the Kızıl Irmak. While rainfall does not seem to differ significantly here, the red volcanic soils of the region boast very high fertility and the waters of the Kızıl Irmak are accessible for irrigation. It is not surprising, therefore, to see that the statistics for this area (Table 11.3) show a significantly higher yield than the rest of the central Anatolian plateau. Even here, however, the effects of environment can be seen clearly in the 1942, 1947, and 1950 statistics when particularly bad years seem to have affected crops across the whole plateau.

In light of the agricultural statistics from 1933 to 1950, a further word about the general suitability of central Anatolia as a wine-producing area is warranted. While it can be suggested that the record of wine-production in central Anatolia today is to be viewed as an indication of the role viticulture played in the region during antiquity, there are several things to consider. In the first place, although present-day yields indicate that there are no permanent environmental barriers to wine production in the area, it seems clear that the central plateau, outside of the Cappadocian region around Nevşehir and Ürgüp, is not as productive as areas that can count on more reliable precipitation. It should also be recalled that much of the Cappadocian production seems to come

Table 11.1

Annual Grape Production in Turkey Plus Yozgat and Çorum Provinces, 1933–50

Year	Ha/Turkey	Production figures for Turkey		Production figures for Yozgat Province			Production figures for Çorum Province		
		Production (tons)	Yield (tons/ha)	Ha	Production (tons)	Yield (tons/ha)	Ha	Production (tons)	Yield (tons/ha)
1933	346,633	755,499	2.237	9,960	20,000	2.008	4,500	15,700	3.488
1934	346,633	879,924	2.538	9,960	14,000	1.140	4,500	12,000	2.666
1935	346,633	1,057,272	3.050	9,960	19,900	1.997	4,500	9,350	2.077
1936	344,998	937,810	2.718	9,960	14,450	1.450	4,500	5,140	1.143
1937	383,582	740,270	1.929	9,960	13,450	1.350	4,615	8,300	1.798
1938	374,588	977,373	2.609	1,590	3,180	2.000	4,670	10,300	2.205
1939	391,029	1,195,372	3.056	1,795	3,590	2.011	4,675	7,805	1.669
1940	387,209	941,961	2.432	1,805	903	0.500	4,675	3,053	0.653
1941	405,266	868,793	2.143	2,627	2,884	1.097	4,675	3,137	0.671
1942	427,748	945,636	2.210	2,627	2,540	0.966	4,775	3,655	0.765
1943	448,805	1,142,837	2.546	3,130	13,300	4.249	4,775	3,766	0.788
1944	472,269	1,355,928	2.871	3,410	13,590	3.985	5,250	9,899	1.885
1945	324,777	1,461,227	4.499	5,790	23,160	4.000	5,250	11,463	2.183
1946	534,102	1,592,227	2.981	5,522	10,719	1.941	5,319	10,411	1.957
1947	539,735	734,592	1.360	7,870	5,700	0.724	5,365	600	0.111
1948	535,669	1,331,488	2.485	12,310	22,240	1.806	5,365	7,500	1.397
1949	555,847	1,750,545	3.149	12,650	36,436	2.880	5,365	20,000	3.727
1950	561,119	1,399,337	2.493	13,950	35,577	2.550	5,365	37,000	6.896
Avg.			2.628			2.036			2.004
1991	586,000	3,600,000	6.143	5,231	19,952	3.814	62,629	890,245	14.214

Ronald L. Gorny

Table 11.2

Annual Grape Production in Çanakkale, Manisa, and Izmir Provinces, 1933–50

| Year | Ha/Turkey | Production figures for Çanakkale Province | | Production figures for Manisa Province | | | Production figures for Izmir Province | | |
		Production (tons)	Yield (tons/ha)	Ha	Production (tons)	Yield (tons/ha)	Ha	Production (tons)	Yield (tons/ha)
1933	3,333	16,486	4.946	26,776	123,297	4.604	20,939	62,708	2.994
1934	3,333	20,105	6.032	26,776	91,160	3.404	20,939	80,288	3.834
1935	3,333	24,325	7.298	26,776	158,306	5.912	20,939	120,348	5.747
1936	3,333	1,769	0.532	26,776	176,476	6.590	20,939	80,585	3.848
1937	5,861	11,061	1.887	28,693	86,984	3.031	18,746	89,257	4.761
1938	5,892	32,859	5.576	29,187	178,581	6.118	18,937	101,524	5.761
1939	10,324	18,454	1.787	29,453	185,158	6.286	20,000	86,764	4.338
1940	3,893	17,196	4.417	31,631	74,671	2.360	20,067	42,201	2.103
1941	3,893	14,225	3.653	32,550	112,465	3.455	20,608	46,499	2.256
1942	3,896	15,323	3.933	41,550	118,525	2.852	19,366	73,855	3.813
1943	3,896	20,380	5.231	42,025	131,743	3.134	17,743	37,819	2.131
1944	3,896	20,382	5.231	40,550	142,260	3.508	19,058	7,972	1.992
1945	3,895	21,445	5.505	40,875	262,751	6.428	21,323	131,556	6.169
1946	3,813	13,718	3.597	41,981	398,341	9.488	22,009	109,825	4.990
1947	4,491	12,624	2.810	42,404	70,437	1.661	22,233	54,398	2.446
1948	5,406	15,423	2.852	40,263	256,805	6.378	29,818	121,935	4.204
1949	5,104	31,590	6.892	43,903	276,203	6.241	26,203	85,008	3.244
1950	5,247	20,310	3.870	53,139	191,895	3.611	29,201	74,940	2.566
Avg.			4.224			4.725			3.733
1991	7,392	54,899	7.426	10,599	31,394	2.961	28,268	236,932	8.381

Table 11.3

Annual Grape Production in Niğde, Kayseri, and Konya Provinces, 1933–50

Year	Ha/Turkey	Production figures for Niğde Province		Production figures for Kayseri Province			Production figures for Konya Province		
		Production (tons)	Yield (tons/ha)	Ha	Production (tons)	Yield (tons/ha)	Ha	Production (tons)	Yield (tons/ha)
1933	13,228	26,300	1.988	43,701	93,862	2.147	15,114	20,742	1.372
1934	13,228	24,500	1.852	43,701	103,894	2.377	15,114	20,757	1.373
1935	13,228	30,738	2.323	43,701	77,959	1.783	15,114	67,525	4.467
1936	13,228	53,650	4.055	43,701	49,653	1.136	15,114	49,269	3.259
1937	19,869	9,845	0.495	22,639	45,540	2.011	44,887	37,535	0.836
1938	13,575	100,127	7.374	20,564	40,520	1.970	45,225	39,254	0.867
1939	29,425	133,665	4.542	21,360	64,062	2.999	46,731	41,710	0.892
1940	29,522	94,555	3.202	21,332	66,286	3.107	35,165	37,278	1.060
1941	28,830	119,750	4.153	21,400	70,000	3.271	35,207	37,738	1.071
1942	28,830	34,520	1.197	21,500	77,930	3.624	54,074	35,780	0.661
1943	30,350	120,180	3.959	21,167	86,246	4.074	74,452	44,203	0.593
1944	33,400	147,750	4.423	21,167	99,500	4.700	78,126	42,422	0.542
1945	37,000	120,720	3.262	29,322	96,700	3.297	78,196	34,782	0.444
1946	34,100	99,640	2.921	29,462	99,900	3.390	79,210	34,764	0.438
1947	33,775	30,380	0.899	29,452	10,000	0.338	81,089	16,180	0.199
1948	33,800	110,800	3.278	29,542	58,624	1.984	43,139	33,509	0.776
1949	33,300	122,127	3.459	30,452	73,630	2.417	43,250	104,326	2.412
1950	35,500	45,545	1.301	25,075	29,945	1.194	45,317	120,466	2.658
Avg.			3.037			2.545			1.328
1991	5,552	16,910	3.045	2,704	12,978	4.799	38,162	110,039	2.883

Table 11.4

Annual Grape Production in Malatya, Diyarbakır, and Urfa Provinces, 1933–50

Year	Ha/Turkey	Production figures for Malatya Province		Production figures for Diyarbakır Province			Production figures for Urfa Province		
		Production (tons)	Yield (tons/ha)	Ha	Production (tons)	Yield (tons/ha)	Ha	Production (tons)	Yield (tons/ha)
1933	9,926	12,835	1.333	11,743	15,950	1.358	4,163	1,474	0.354
1934	9,926	19,313	2.006	11,743	86,500	7.366	4,163	2,562	0.615
1935	9,926	55,681	5.784	11,743	80,382	6.840	4,163	17,207	4.133
1936	9,926	23,790	2.471	11,743	84,001	7.153	4,163	12,117	2.910
1937	9,910	20,750	2.093	11,645	77,050	6.616	32,765	12,117	0.369
1938	9,814	11,664	1.188	11,650	84,896	7.287	32,957	1,458	0.044
1939	12,411	80,512	6.487	13,422	115,180	8.582	15,225	47,404	3.113
1940	23,132	70,620	3.052	13,488	120,872	8.961	16,752	48,950	2.922
1941	28,920	18,198	0.629	13,518	28,998	2.145	16,758	14,890	0.888
1942	24,830	10,835	0.436	13,863	148,340	11.421	14,981	87,860	5.864
1943	24,830	41,095	1.655	14,463	158,340	10.947	16,310	82,224	5.041
1944	25,830	45,133	1.747	14,440	118,500	8.206	17,350	139,000	8.011
1945	25,880	46,353	1.791	15,358	145,701	9.486	17,610	140,950	8.003
1946	26,730	57,350	2.141	24,810	128,540	5.180	17,830	76,650	4.298
1947	30,330	62,378	2.056	25,210	65,000	2.578	17,140	39,660	2.313
1948	45,100	56,483	1.252	24,865	80,000	3.217	17,030	44,110	2.590
1949	23,321	15,385	0.659	16,645	100,000	6.007	65,182	77,215	1.187
1950	20,870	26,280	1.259	16,000	68,917	4.307	42,577	23,760	0.545
Avg.			2.113			6.536			2.955
1991	10,038	31,334	3.121	24,959	95,716	3.834	20,240	49,025	4.422

after the advent of fertilizers and mechanization. Comparisons of the pre-1950 statistics with those of 1991 generally show a rise (sometimes dramatic) in the production of grapes in central Anatolia. This is attributable, I believe to the increased use of water from the Kızıl Irmak that was made available for vineyard irrigation by electric pumps and other mechanical devices.

Although environment was a critical element in the spread of the wine culture in Anatolia, human agents played a vital role in promoting wine as an alternative beverage. While the earliest producers of wine remain clouded in the mist of history, it may have been the Hittites who actually nudged Anatolia into the spreading wine culture of the Near East. By the beginning of the second millennium, the Hittites had become entrenched on the Anatolian plateau, and because of its growing association with the palace and the cult, wine had begun to play a pivotal role in many of their most important societal functions. As we will explore below, this association between wine and the elite almost certainly reflects the early differentiation of classes within Anatolian society and the onset of a more complex social fabric. The fact that wine came to play any role in Hittite society is of interest, not only because it attests to the fact that the inhabitants of the plateau succeeded in their attempts to overcome the detrimental effects of an environment that was not especially conducive to grape-raising, but that in the process they were able to give grape production a socioeconomic underpinning that played a major role in defining the prerogatives of the ruling class.

Because of its vulnerability to men and nature, the success of viticulture demands environmental regularity and political stability. The absence of either can quickly reduce the horticulturist to a state of ruin. In the case of Anatolia, the many dangers which loomed as potential threats to the grape culture meant that special efforts had to be made to ensure a successful crop.

The fact that grapes also grow well on soil best-suited for wheat and olive orchards presented Hittite agriculturalists with an added dilemma. Would it be better to make a long-term investment in vineyards, which are more profitable but also more labor-intensive and more susceptible to the ravages of nature, or to plant less profitable, but more stable crops such as wheat or olives? Since grapes are often grown on hillside vineyards, the two crops are not mutually exclusive, but the decision to grow grapes on more fertile soil meant that the horticulturalist was consciously allocating land to grape-growing that might otherwise be used to produce the more stable crops, a strategy that would effectively reduce the amount of arable land available for staples. In making this decision, the land owner had to take into account the relative values of wheat and olives, and by comparison, try and visualize the long-term potential of a vineyard. Because grapes are more sensitive to climatic adversity and more labor-intensive than either olives or wheat, the decision to raise grapes meant that the horticulturalist had elected to forego the relative security of the latter in favor of the more profitable but less predictable fruit of the vine.

The relative success of early viticultural experimentation in marginal agricultural areas must have confirmed the adaptability of the grapevine and showed that, with proper tendance, the grapevine could become a profitable venture, even in the less suitable environment of the plateau. Arable land, of course, was an important factor in grape production, but while soil fertility played a crucial role in determining the character of Hittite viticulture, it was moisture, or the lack of it, that proved to be the chief nemesis of Hittite horticulturalists, and because of the unreliable nature of precipitation on the plateau, the Hittites may have been forced, in some instances, to rely on irrigation as a means of relieving the region's moisture deficiency.

Although grapevines could be cultivated within a dry-farming regimen such as that of the central Anatolian plateau, the advantages of irrigation would not have been lost on Hittite horticulturalists. Water management provided a means of producing a crop that was less susceptible to the unpredictable nature of the plateau. Irrigation, however, was complicated on the plateau by the fact that central Anatolia's river systems are often deeply engraved into the surrounding terrain, making the practice difficult and expensive. Reliance was generally placed on local water sources such as springs and rivulets, the likes of which could be just as susceptible to droughts as the crops they were intended to secure. Nonetheless, just as in present-day Turkey, irrigation presented Hittite horticulturalists with a plausible means of alleviating the plateau's critical lack of moisture, and while the practice was costly and labor intensive, water management may well have decreased the vulnerability of some vineyards while increasing their productivity. For those reasons, it is not surprising to find the Hittites making use of the innovation.

The true extent of irrigation in second millennium Anatolia remains unknown, but Hittite narratives make it clear that irrigation served as an aid in the exploitation of central Anatolia's arable lands during the second millennium B.C. (Hittite law §162), especially in the case of fruit orchards (Hittite law §109). The existence of festivals dedicated to the deities associated with rivers, springs, and canals points out the fundamental importance of such resources to the Hittite state (McMahon 1991: 189–209). However, while vineyards are associated with irrigation (KIRI$_6$.GEŠTIN.ḪI.A, KUB 31.100 ii 14 ff.),[15] a regular and widespread practice of irrigating vineyards can not be substantiated from the texts (Hoffner 1974: 24).[16] As is generally the case, one would expect to find the better vineyards situated on well drained slopes (Columella, *On Agriculture* III.2.7–32; Hoffner 1974: 22–24). As noted above, however, the specific climatic peculiarities that made dry-farming a precarious occupation in central Anatolia may have led the Hittites to invest more heavily in the irrigation of some vineyards as insurance against their vulnerability in difficult times. These watered vineyards, because of the relatively heavy expenditures necessary for their operation, probably had a special place in the Hittite horticultural scheme and it would not be surprising to find them associated with the palace economy.

As we have seen, grapes need proper conditions in which to prosper. There is the need for fertile moisture retaining soil along with the freedom from spring frosts. A good balance between heat and moisture is necessary, for while grapes require water and heat for successful maturation, excessive amounts of either at the wrong time can lead to disaster (Renfrew 1973: 130). In addition, viticulture requires an investment in manpower and capital in order to make it productive. A final element necessary for successful viticulture, however, is a stable sociopolitical climate.

Stager (1985: 177), following Ampolo (1980: 31–32) and Perevolotsky (1981: 341–44), has noted that a secure economy and a predictable environment is necessary for the development of horticulture in general, and grapevines in particular. Not only does it take between five and seven years of careful preparation before the vine produces its first fruit, but a great deal of time, labor, and other resources have to be invested in the plants with no assurance of success. Routine tasks such as trenching, fertilizing, pruning, and weeding were constantly required if the vineyard was to remain productive.[17] White (1970: 229) noted, grapevines "require a greater degree of tendance and control than any other Mediterranean crop" and may actually take generations before producing their best quality vintage (Stager 1985: 177).

In light of this, we can conclude that the risk associated with viticulture stems, not only from the prospect of poor harvests in bad years, but from the lengthy amount of time it takes to replace and nurture a vineyard that has been lost. This contrasts with grains which, even if killed off one year, may prosper the next if climatic conditions improve. As a hedge against such losses, the small-scale farmer may have willingly ceded the prerogative of production to a central administration or the large landowners. Because of their resources, they would be better able to assimilate any potential losses. Such risk-abatement may well have been one of the major factors in the elevation of wine to an elite status in early stratified societies and may well have resulted in more restrictive controls as the role of the elite was further defined over time.

Such considerations point up just how tenuous an enterprise grape-growing could be. Ancient texts inform us that vineyards frequently faced threats, not only from natural agents, but human ones as well. In the ancient world, the groves and agricultural produce of a land were generally the first things invading armies exploited or despoiled (cf. Lichtheim 1973: 20). Given the instability and internecine fighting that characterized the emergent Old Hittite period,[18] it is not hard to imagine the difficulties and challenges facing Hittite horticulturalists.

By overcoming these challenges, the Hittites proved that viticulture could be practiced in the heartland of Anatolia, but because of the restricted nature of the texts, our knowledge is limited to what we can learn from the perspective of a small producer–consumer elite. Thus, it appears that while the Hittite elite had developed a taste for wine, there is uncertainty as to how widespread the predilection for wine was among the general populace. While it seems clear that viticulture and wine-making had came into its own as early as the third millennium B.C., texts suggest that consumption remained primarily a drink of the elite during the second millennium and that only later did the "commodification" of the beverage (below) lead to a broad-based demand and the adaptation of wine as an alternative beverage for those beyond the halls of the elite.

The impetus for the expanding wine culture seems to have come from a series of interrelated developments. The increased availability of the grapevine and the relative ease with which wine could be produced may have engendered a broader appeal among the masses and a separation of the drink from its earlier associations with the palace and the cult (see below). In addition, the increasingly sophisticated oenological technology was probably manifested, not only in larger and more numerous vineyards, but in more sophisticated vessels for transport and trade, an element vital to the wine industry's long-term development. Moreover, the development of varietal wines may have led to a diversification of the drink that augmented its popularity.

In the final analysis, the farmer–consumer relationship is the key to determining the "suitability" of a crop. A market-economy of the type the Hittites were engaged in would encourage farmers to grow what people paid them to grow. If they were paid enough to make a crop worthwhile, they would grow it. Such decisions, however, must have been tempered by individual farmers concerns over subsistence and the means by which the Hittite elite procured their grapes. As I indicate below, this is by no means certain as the texts do not make it clear whether the grapes come from private vineyards or as taxes on rural farmers. It is not even clear that grapes (or the wine produced from them) came from central Anatolia. Current records showing superior yields along the west coast and in the southeast suggest the possibility of the beverage being imported from more productive wine producing areas. In any case, the rising popularity of the beverage soon reached beyond the producer–consumer elite of the Late Bronze Age and became a mainstay at the table of later generations, a fact that must have further expedited the commercialization and exploitation of the beverage.

2. Ancient Sources for Viticulture and Viniculture in Central Anatolia

According to the botanical evidence, grapes had clearly become an important part of the Anatolian diet by the Early Bronze Age. Unfortunately, the details of viticulture during this early period are unknown. Only with the introduction of writing during the Middle Bronze Age can we begin to document the development of both viticulture and viniculture in Anatolia.

The Old Assyrian Colony Age (ca. 2000–1750 B.C.) furnishes our first literary evidence for grape-growing in central Anatolia where it is noted under the Assyrian name *karānu* (*kirānu* in Old Assyrian). References to the grape-harvest, which was known as *qitip karānim* (literally, "the picking of the grape" Reiner 1982: 202; also cf. Varro's description of the vintage in White 1977: 70), suggest that organized viticulture was well established by this time. The exact role of the

Assyrian colonists within this nascent Anatolian viticulture, however, is unclear. The lack of texts referring to Mesopotamian grape-growing leaves one with the impression that the Assyrian colonists might not have been well acquainted with viticulture at this early date (Powell, chapter 9, this volume). References to the use of wine as an item of trade, however, appear in several Old Assyrian documents (Oppenheim et al. 1971: 203), and even though the origin and destination of the beverages mentioned in the Old Assyrian texts are elusive, apparently the colonists were beginning to realize the inherent potential of the beverage. The mention of wine in Old Assyrian documents may reflect an Anatolian agricultural regimen in which wine production had already become deeply entrenched in central Anatolia by the beginning of the second millennium. In other words, the Assyrian's usage may well have been the direct result of their immersion in the native Anatolian culture.

The decline of the Old Assyrian trade network in Anatolia resulted in a new political reality in which native Anatolian inhabitants coalesced under the Hittite leaders of Ḫattuša (Gorny 1989). Cuneiform texts written in the newly fashioned Hittite script reveal the earliest efforts to unify the land during a period known as the Hittite Old Kingdom (ca. 1600–1400 B.C.). The mention of wine in a variety of texts from this period provides us with our first really informative pool of written evidence relating to the grape harvest and wine production in Bronze Age Anatolia.

Hittite texts provide various details about the grapevine. The actual grape or grapevine is usually denoted in Hittite with the Sumerogram (GIŠ)GEŠTIN (= Hittite *wiyana-*). This term can denote the whole plant, a young and still transplantable "Reifling," as well as a mature "Wein-stock." In addition the texts have preserved the names of various parts of the grape-vine including the vine branch (GIŠ*maḫla-*), the grape cluster (*muri-*) and the roots (*šurki-*).[19] The texts show that the harvest season for grapes and other fruits was in the autumn when the festival of the cutting of the grapes (EZEN GIŠGEŠTIN tuḫ-šu-u-wa-aš, KUB 38.12; cf. Güterbock 1967: 142–45; Hoffner 1974: 39) took place. Although there are no extant texts describing the festival in detail, the event probably had its origins in the practices of an earlier period, and in all likelihood, the festivities surrounding the Hittite festival probably differed little from the activities which presumably took place after the *qitip karānim* of the Old Assyrian period.

The fruit of the grape harvest could be used in various ways. While one portion of the vintage may have been eaten as fresh fruit, the problems of storage would have necessitated the drying of a large portion, so that, in the form of the raisin, it could be used for long-term food storage and rationing. Whether the vine leaves were used, as they are today, for *yaprak dolmas* (i.e., grape leaves stuffed with other foods) is not known. A significant portion of the produce was very likely directed towards the production of wine. The frequent mention of wine use in the Hittite texts indicates that the beverage was an important product. While it served a multitude of needs within the circles of the Hittite elite, the records give no hint of everyday consumption among the masses (Steiner 1966: 308). The narratives indicate that water, milk, and beer were the preferred beverages of the lower classes, with wine apparently reserved for royal consumption and libations to the gods (Steiner 1966: 307).

Care must be taken, however, when considering Hittite viticultural designations because the Hittites did not always clearly differentiate between terms. The GIŠGEŠTIN, for instance, that is libated in KBo 6.26 i 30 (GIŠGEŠTIN ši-pa-an-du-zi) probably refers to wine instead of the grapes. The same may be true of KUB 33.68 ii 15, where wine is said to be found in the heart of the raisin (GIŠGEŠTIN.ḪÁD.DU.A) instead of the grape (GIŠGEŠTIN).

Among the written documents of the Hittites, the laws constitute the single most important source for our understanding of viticulture and viniculture in Anatolia at this early period.[20] As we now know, the laws are among the earliest written documents of the Hittites and were revised during the reign of either Ḫattišili I or Muršili I. The revision of the Hittite statutes resulted in a compensatory system of justice, based on a predetermined system of measures (summarized by van den Hout 1990: 517–30). The laws are particularly valuable because they provide us with some of the earliest details of life in Hittite Anatolia, and occasionally take note of circumstances surrounding Anatolia's viticultural practices. In the case of law §101, for instance, the earlier version of the law states that the penalty for the theft of a vine or a tendril involved some form of corporal punishment along with the fine of a shekel of silver, whereas the penalty in the second version excluded corporal punishment and raised the fine to six shekels of silver for a free man and 3 shekels of silver for a slave. Other laws relating to viticulture discuss the fines for burning down a vineyard (§105), for turning one's sheep into a productive vineyard (§107), for the theft of tendrils from a fenced-in vineyard (§108), and for cutting down a vine (§113).

Perhaps the most significant information regarding Hittite viticulture and viniculture is found in laws §183 and §185A which provide us with the price of wine (1/2 shekel of silver for 1 *parīsu* of wine) and the cost of a vineyard (1 mina of silver for 1 IKU of vineyard) respectively. Comparison of these prices with those from other parts of the ancient Near East provide an idea of wine's value (see chapter 9 by Powell, this volume). The critical measure in the Hittite system is the *parīsu* (PA), which Powell postulates to be a 30 liter measure, and from which he calculates a vintage, based on Babylonian evidence, of about 20 amphora per IKU (0.036 hectares), a measure which translates into approximately 600 liters per IKU or 160 gallons per acre (Powell, chapter 9, this volume; also see Hawkins 1986: 94–95, 99). He also maintains that Hittite vineyards were valued at 13, 20, and 40 times the value of other agricultural land on the plateau (table 9.1, this volume), and that compensation for damages done to a vineyard was generally set at one quarter the value of the whole field (Powell, chapter 9, this volume).

Such calculations suggest that the initial price of a vineyard would have been high. An enterprise of this sort would have also demanded long-term investments in time and labor, especially if large-scale irrigation was employed. Ventures of this sort were probably not practical for peasants who, aware of their own vulnerability, have traditionally invested their resources in subsistence farming and less labor intensive means of survival. Brunt (1971: 709) went so far as to state:

> Only a grower with some capital could bear the loss of a poor season, or even the unprofitability of a bumper vintage. Only he could afford to wait for the best prices. Moreover, the peasant could hardly begin to plant without capital, since the young vines yield nothing for five or six years.

Following this line of reasoning, only the elite would have been in a position to make the commitments necessary for successful wine-making.

Although wine apparently became a regular part of the elite's table fare, its popularity with the court does not seem to have stimulated the growth of a large-scale wine industry in second millennium Anatolia. In addition to dependable harvests, sufficient quantities of the fruit, and adequate financial resources, a successful self-supporting wine industry requires a broad-based demand that can offset the cost of starting a vineyard, while at the same time, lowering the cost of wine for the consumer. This combination of events probably never occurred in Bronze Age Anatolia, and instead of conspicuous wine consumption, the texts seem to suggest that the native population preferred other drinks. In short, the cost of maintaining a vineyard, the appeal of wine to a limited constituency, the difficulties of transport, and the need for remuneration seem to suggest that wine was an expensive luxury good that was enjoyed by a relatively small segment of the population during the Middle and Late Bronze Ages.

The characterization of wine as a luxury good, however, may not be in total conformity with the texts and such a generalization, may apply only to the development of a large-scale wine industry. The fact that most Hittite households had vines (Klengel 1986) suggests that the planting of grapevines was neither technically difficult nor prohibitively expensive, and that limited amounts of grape-growing probably took place in most villages. Wine production is not a particularly complicated process and could well have become a "cottage industry" by the early second millennium. Since there were apparently no laws restricting the use of grapes, much of the local produce might have remained at the disposal of village peasants and it would have been a rather simple matter for villagers to make limited amounts of wine or wine-related drinks.

In Mycenaean Greece, for instance, the Linear B texts indicate that wine was produced in local vineyards during this same period and came to the palace through an assessment placed on the local land owners.[21] If, by analogy, the grapes grown in central Anatolia came from local land holdings with a portion of the harvest being exacted by the Hittite palace, the villagers might still have been able to utilize their portion in whatever way they saw fit. The absence of such information in the Hittite records could simply reflect the Palace's concern with luxury consumption and its relative indifference to the distribution of whatever portion of the crop remained in the hands of the village. Then again, the demands of the palace may have been so great that there was no local surplus and any reimbursals may have been sunk into other non-Mediterranean crops.

a. Wine in the Hittite texts

The Hittite texts provide scholars with a wealth of information about life in the second millennium. It must be remembered, however, that these texts are from a major cosmopolitan center and are, therefore, heavily weighted in favor of diplomatic, political, and religious matters. While other concerns of a local nature are noted, these are generally noted in respect to things that may affect the palace (e.g., the instructions for local officials in the *BEL.MADGALTI* texts). The documents themselves are fragmented and incomplete, barely scratch the surface of things related to village administration, local customs, and agricultural economy. For that reason they are often a good source for the important sociopolitical developments of the period, but generally have next to nothing to say about the grassroots level of state organization. This is especially true of grape production and must be kept in mind when discussing the spread of viticulture in central Anatolia.

A common root word for wine is shared throughout much of the eastern Mediterranean basin (*yn* in Ugaritic, *yayin* in Hebrew, *[w]oinos* in Greek, *wo-i-no* in Cypro-Syllabic, and *wiyanas* in Hittite (Brown 1969 and Stager 1985: 173). The origin of the word is unclear, but given the difficulties in isolating a valid Northwest Semitic etymology (van Selms 1974), an early Hittite form has been postulated as the most likely possibility (Brown 1969: 148).

In Hittite texts *wiyana* was normally replaced by the Sumerogram GEŠTIN, and in this general usage it was often coupled with other descriptive terms that denote specific types or qualities of wines. The various kinds of wine include "red wine" (SA₅ GEŠTIN, KUB 31.57 obv. i 23′),[22] "good wine" (DÙG.GA / SIG₅-an-ta-an GEŠTIN, VBoT i 35), "pure wine"[23] (parkui- GEŠTIN, KUB 36.110:35), "honeyed wine" (LÀL GEŠTIN, KUB 12.5 i 17–21), "sweet wine" (GEŠTIN.KU₇, KBo 25.178 rev. 27′),[24] and "sour wine" (GEŠTIN *EMṢA*, ABoT 7 i 11′). In addition, "new wine" (GEŠTIN GIBIL) is also mentioned on occasion (KUB 9.16:17–26; KUB 25.14 rev. iii 2, 4, 9 and 11; also KUB 10.48 i 4),[25] as is what seems to be a generic "wine for drinking" (GEŠTIN.NAG = Hittite *wiyanaš akuwanna*).[26]

Steiner (1966: 308) has postulated that the king may have been responsible in a general way for the manner in which the distribution of wine was carried out. In the Old Hittite *Palace Chronicles* (KBo 3.34 ii 1–7; Beal 1983: 123–24), we find that:

Zidi was the [LÚ]ZABAR.DAB official. The King, my father, assigned a *ḫarḫara*—vessel of wine—to (the woman) Ḫištayara and (the man) Maratti. (Zidi) provided the King with good wine, but to them they (Zidi's men?) gave another (inferior) wine. (Ḫišayara) came and told the King, "They did not give (us) the wine which the king saw." The other (Maratti) came and reported the same thing. So, they led him (Zidi) away and "worked him over (?)," so that he died.

While the text may be more of a report on an event that took place at the king's table, the underlying significance of the incident, as defined below, may have run much deeper.

In one sense, the king, as the divine representative, would have been looked on as the titular head of agriculture and horticulture in general, and of viniculture and viticulture in particular. Since this may have been more of a symbolic role, the actual details of the process would have probably been administered by other officials including a royal wine supplier ([LÚ]ZABAR.DIB, see Singer 1983: 104) and a staff of wine stewards ([LÚ.MEŠ]ZABAR.DIB). The wine supplier apparently could be a local official as indicated by a [LÚ]ZABAR.DIB from the town of Madilla (KBo 10.31). The official and his staff were responsible for the dispensing of good wine (SIG$_5$-an-ta-an) to specified royal personages. Steiner (1966: 308), in fact, goes so far as to speak of a wine monopoly administered by one of the high court officials, who was generally known during the Hittite Empire period as the GAL GEŠTIN (also GAL ŠA GEŠTIN, KBo 3.35:14/Old Script; GAL LÚ.GEŠTIN, KUB 10.11 iv 29; but cf. Beal 1986: 409–22).[27]

Whether a monopoly on wine production actually existed is debatable, especially in the absence of texts relating to the common people. On the one hand, the author of *The Blessings of Labarna* notes that "the king's bread we eat, and his wine we drink; from a gold goblet pure wine we keep drinking" (KUB 36.110 rev. 5–7), almost as if wine was part of the exclusive domain of the king. Although this text should almost certainly be understood as an acknowledgement of the king's symbolic role as leader of the land, the personage in whom the health and prosperity of the kingdom rests, it leaves one with the impression that some portion of the wine was considered the property of the king. Other texts suggest that the Hittite king may have been involved in certain aspects of trade, with merchants (*TAMKARU*) operating as agents of the court and involved in the procurement of luxury goods (Klengel 1979: 77; Heltzer 1985: 14). Grapes (GEŠTIN[ḪI.A]-aš, Hoffner 1968: 36) are listed among the merchandise being stored and transported by these merchants. It seems more likely, however, that operations such as these were concerned, not strictly with trade itself, but with the transfer of royal tribute (see Götze, *Detailed Annals of Muršili II*, year 25, KUB 19.37 rev. iii 47–48; also Klengel 1979: 78). If this was the case, the texts would not speak so much of a monopoly as it would a royal prerogative to be exercised at the expense of subject lands.

b. The uses of wine in Hittite society

One might assume that the primary use of wine in Hittite culture was for drinking. Thus, it is surprising to discover that, even though texts note "wine for drinking" (GEŠTIN *akuwannaš*; KUB 43. 58 i 21), it is infrequently mentioned as a beverage. Steiner (1966: 307) comments that when used as a refreshment, wine was probably the prerogative of the court. The previously cited anecdote from the *Palace Chronicles* (KBo 3.34) illustrates how an important couple from the Hittite court was cheated out of a preferred wine. Although the text does not explicitly state that the couple was going to drink the wine, this seems to be a case when wine was intended for consumption.

Examples of wine-drinking can be found in Hittite mythology. Ullikummi, for instance, is noted as drinking "sweet wine" (GEŠTIN.KU$_7$ a-ku-wa-an-na u-te-er; They took (him) sweet wine to drink; KUB 33.98 + obv. ii 18–30, Hoffner 1990: 53) and Illuyanka, the serpent, becomes inebriated after drinking several beverages including wine (Hoffner 1990: 12). In the *Ašertu Myth*, on the other hand, Anat-Astarte, sensing danger and aware of the intoxicating influence of wine, seems to discourage Baal from going to the residence of Ašertu and specifically warns the god not to drink wine with her (^{d}U *ŠA* ^{d}A-še-er-ti-wa [par-na-aš-ša le-e i-ya-te-ni / pa-i-te-ni (?)] GEŠTIN-ya-wa le-e e-ku-ut-te-ni; Baal, [do not go to the house (?)] of Ašertu and do not drink the wine; cf. Hoffner 1990: 70).

The consumption of wine also had a place in other aspects of Hittite life, among which were rituals and festivals. Medical rituals, for instance, provide several cases where wine was consumed (x [o o o] x *NAM-MA-AN-TAM* GEŠTIN-ya a-ku-wa-an-na 3 *NAM-MA-TUM* kat-ta-an-ta iš-ḫu-wa-i nu kat-ta wa-ar-nu-zi; [o o o] measures of wine for drinking, 3 measures he pours out, (and) he boils it down (?), KUB 44.63 obv. ii 17′–30′, Burde 1974, 30–31; also KUB 44.61 obv. 1–16 and KUB 44.64 obv. i 26). If later classical belief is any indicator, this usage was rather common (cf. Pliny *NH* 23.21–33). Wine-drinking also appears in the *Ištanuwa Ritual* (GEŠTIN a-ku-wa-an-zi-ya-an; and they drink wine, KUB 55.65 = KBo 8.101+107; also cf. KUB 55.54 i 11′–23′). Similarly, wine-drinking is also reported in Hittite festivals. In the *Karaḫna Festival*, for example, the participants "fill three rhyta with wine and place them back on the stele (for) the Sungod," and then "they drink three times" (Bo 3298 + KUB 25.32 + KUB 27.70 + 1628/u, McMahon 1991: 67). Parallel activities must have been common to other festivals as well.

In the religious sphere, wine was used primarily for libations and supplications, activities performed in hopes of propitiating the diverse divinities of the Hittite pantheon. Within this broad distribution of references several discrete categories can be defined. Wine played a role in Hittite royal prayers, as attested by the *Prayer to Tešub of Kummani* (A.ŠA A.GÀR-ma-kán <^{GIŠ}KIRI$_{6}$> GEŠTIN mi-ya-tar ne-ya-ri, growth will result (?) (in?) fields, fallow (and) vineyards, KBo 11.1 obv. 25); *Prayer to the Sungoddess of the Underworld* (*A-NA* DINGER^{MEŠ} NINDA.GUR$_{4}$.RA$^{ḪI.A}$ GEŠTIN iš-pa-an-du-uz-zi, He offers thick breads (and) wine to the gods, KBo 7.29 i 1–21); *Prayer of Muwatalli to the Stormgod Piḫaššašši* (1 ^{DUG}KU-KU-UB GEŠTIN BAL-ti, He libates 1 jar of wine, KUB 6.45 rev. iv 27, 32). Libations also played a role in Hittite festivals, including the *Festival of the Month* (GEŠTIN-an-na ta-pí-ša-ni-it GIR^{4} ke-e-da-aš DINGER^{MEŠ}-aš ši-pa-an-ti, He libates wine with a clay pitcher for these gods, KUB 2.13 i 43–44), the *KI.LAM Festival* (a-ku-wa-an-na-ya-aš-ma-aš GEŠTIN, wine for their drinking, KBo 25.176 rev. 11′), and the *Spring Festival of Zippalanta* (GAL $^{LÚ.MEŠ}$ME-ŠE-DI *A-NA* $^{LÚ.MEŠ}$ALAM.ZU$_{9}$ ^{DUG}ḫu-u-up-par GEŠTIN tar-ku-mi-ya-zi, The chief palace guard announces one ḫuppar vessel of wine for the performers, KUB 25.6 + 2 rev. 11′–12′, see Güterbock 1989: 309).

Wine is also used for libations in rituals and analogic magical ceremonies. A ritual performed at the *Kizzuwatna Festival* (KUB 43.58 ii 45–50, Middle Hittite/Middle Script, with dupl. KUB 15.42 ii 34–36; Güterbock and Hoffner 1990f: 445) states:[28]

And as this swe[et] wine [is ...], and further whe[n] a man [drinks(?)] it (variant omits "it"), and becomes inebriated(?), from him all [ill vanishes], from you gods in the same way may [the evil word, the oath], the curse, the blo[od (and) tears] van[ish].

One might also point out a related quote from a ritual for the founding of a new palace (KUB 29.1 iv 13–16, see Hoffner 1974: 41, now Hoffner and Güterbock 1990b: 112):[29]

They place a branch of a grapevine and speak as follows: just as the grapevine sends down roots and sends up branches, let the king and queen also send down roots and send up (text erroneously reads: send down) branches!

In similar fashion, the mixture of wine and water mentioned in the soldier's oath (KUB 43.38 rev. 13–20, StBoT 22: 20) was part of a ritual meant to guarantee the soldier's loyalty:[30]

Then he pours out wine and speaks the following:
This is not wine, it is your blood, and as the earth has sipped it,
even so also let the earth sip your blood and [ ].

> Then he pours forth the water into the wine and says the following:
> As this water and wine were mixed together
> hereafter let this oath and disease of your bodies be likewise mixed.

Wine was also employed in the performance of other activities which can be loosely described as religious in nature. Among these are Hittite texts that reveal a strong belief in wine's cleansing and purifying quality. Included in this same category are a ritual for the purification of a town (NINDA.GUR$_4$.RA GEŠTIN iš-pa-an-du-z[i], he/she offers wine and thick bread, KUB 30.34 iii 15); a purification ritual against sex offenses (1 DUG GEŠTIN i-wa-ar-wa-an-ni, we give 1 vessel of wine, KUB 41.11 rev. 18′), and the funeral ritual for deceased Hittite kings (nam-ma ^{DUG}ḪAB.ḪAB GEŠTIN ú-da-an-zi na-an a-pí-e-el ZI-ni ši-pa-an-ta-an-zi, then they bring the ḪAB.ḪAB vessel of wine and offer it (wine) to his soul, KUB 30.16 + KUB 39.1 obv. 13–14 (Otten 1958: 18–19). In treaties such as that of Arnuwanda I (?) with the Kaškeans (GEŠTIN ši-i-e-eš-šar [o o o šipandanzi?], Wine (and) beer [...they offer?], KBo 16.27 ii 11 (= 1373/c), von Schuler, 136) wine has religious overtones in that it acts as a means of appeasement meant to ensure the continued support of the gods for the agreement in question.

In retrospect, most of the wine-drinking recorded in Hittite texts appears to have been associated with the cult and served a religiosocial function which, while not denying the more pleasurable aspects of wine consumption, extended the role of wine beyond that of a common table beverage. If wine was consumed as a form of "social" drinking, such a use was not mentioned explicitly in the texts, and wine-drinking, when alluded to at all, is seen primarily in association with royalty. One should be cautioned, however, that such conclusions can only be tentative, at best, because the texts in question deal with wine in terms of its specific relationship to the palace and the cult. By definition this artificial situation excludes many details regarding the use of wine in the everyday life of those who lived beyond the pale of the urban bureaucratic setting. While texts dealing with subjects outside of these parameters may eventually paint a completely different picture, our current knowledge suggests that wine-drinking was an activity somewhat outside the realm of the everyday laborer.

As a counterpoint to the argument for exclusivity, however, the Hittite *ARZANA-* house should be mentioned. As Hoffner (1974b) observed, this interesting establishment probably functioned in much the same way as inns in other parts of the ancient Near East, a place where patrons could find food, drink, merriment, women, and lodging. Wine was among the drinks served to a group of visitors in the *ARZANA-* house (KUB 53.14 and KUB 53.17, Hoffner 1974b: 118). Since the visitors noted in these texts were official personnel, however, perhaps the recipients of refreshment did not include the general public. Nevertheless, the association of GEŠTIN with this establishment leaves open the possibility that wine may have had a wider clientele than is generally assumed.

c. Hittite wine production

What was the composition of Hittite wine? Later classical writers indicate that a variety of additives were mixed with wine to improve its flavor and other qualities (see note 23; Brothwell and Brothwell 1969: 170–71; Homer, *Iliad* 11.637–9). The Roman wines of western Anatolia, for example, often were diluted with sea water (Magie 1988: 51, n. 111). The Hittites also adulterated their wines. Both water and honey could be added (KAŠ.GEŠTIN LÀL-it wa-a-tar an-da GEŠTIN-aš su-uḫ-ḫa-an-za nu ši-pa-an-ti, The wine is poured into the beer-wine, honey, (and) water, (and) she libates, KUB 9.28 ii 10″ f.). Another text mentions some sort of tree-oil (EGIR-an-da-ma ^{SAL}ŠU.GI GEŠTIN LÀL Ì.GIŠ-ya an-da tak-ša-an im-mi-ya-az-zi, And after-

wards, the old woman mixed together wine, honey, and tree-oil, KUB 9.6 + KUB 35.39 i 6–8).
Some texts suggest that a fine oil (Ì.DÙG.GA) was also sometimes mixed with the wine
(ar-ḫa-ya-an-na 1 ᴰᵁᴳKU-KU-UB GEŠTIN 1 ᴰᵁᴳNAM-MA-AN-TUM IŠ-TU GEŠTIN LÀL
Ì.DÙG.GA an-da i-mi-ya-an-ti-it, Separate from these are kept one wine jug and one pitcher filled
with wine, honey (and) fine oil mixed together, KUB 15.34; nam-ma GEŠTIN Ì.DÙG.GA-ya
an-da i-mi-an kat-ta-an la-a-ḫu-u-wa-an-zi, then the wine is mixed into the fine oil, and they pour
(it) out, KBo 21.34 ii 55–56; and ke-e-ez-ma-aš-ši ŠA GEŠTIN Ì an-da i-im-mi-ya-an-zi, And here
they mix oil together with the wine, KUB 15 34 iii 30). Such practices appear to parallel closely
the later classical procedures for adding spices and fragrants to wine in order to enhance its taste
and scent.

The frequent association between wine and fine oil in the Hittite sources suggests that another
possible use for wine may have been in perfume-making. The classical sources for perfume
making are Theophrastus, *De Odoribus*, Dioscorides, *Materia Medica* (Book 1), and Pliny, *NH*
(Book 13).[31] They note that, as part of the perfume-making process, a mixture of wine, honey, and
oil was heated in order to evaporate the alcoholic content of the wine and to incorporate its
fragrants into the olive oil. Mycenaean sources of the 13th century also speak of this process,[32] so
it may well have been known to the Anatolian populace, even though it can not be precisely
documented at this time.

Powell (see chapter 9, this volume) suggests that the word LÀL ('honey') very likely refers to
a sweetener manufactured from grape juice (cf. LÀL GEŠTIN, a grape honey known from
Mesopotamia, Oppenheim et al. 1959: 163). Since the grape has a high degree of sugar in both its
juice (18–20%) and in its dried fruit, the raisin (80%), it could have been used to sweeten some
drinks and to restore older or drier wines to a more palatable state.

A grape-syrup sweetener may have some merit within a Mesopotamian context, but it is not
without problems in ancient Anatolia. Although beeswax is certainly known as early as the Ur III
period (Oppenheim et al. 1960: 251–52), Mesopotamian peoples do not appear to have begun
keeping bees until the first millennium (Herodotus, 1.193–94; see chapter 9 by Powell, this
volume), while the practice is well attested in Anatolia from a very early date (see Hittite laws
§91–92, Ehelolf 1933: 1–7, Hoffner 1974a: 123–24).[33] As Hoffner (1968: 41) pointed out, Hittite
documents mention the use of fresh honey (LÀL.GIBIL, KUB 10.48 obv. i 4 and KUB 9.16 obv.
i 20), and indicate that undiluted honey was used as a libation to the gods along with beer and
wine. LÀL commonly appears in Hittite texts as LÀL-it where the Sumerogram is clearly
replacing the underlying Hittite word for honey, *milit* (Güterbock and Hoffner 1990c). In this form
honey is mentioned in association with bees (ŠÀ-it LÀL-it ḫarši, (The mother goddess addressing
a bee:), You have honey in (your) belly, KUB 33.13 ii 21; also KUB 33.10 ii 3; Güterbock and
Hoffner 1990d: 251). LÀL thus signifies honey in the Hittite texts, and not a grape-syrup
sweetener. Yet, the use of grape-syrup as a sweetener cannot be ruled out entirely, for the word
milit also conveys the idea of sweetness (ᵈTe-ši-me-eš-wa-ta GEŠTIN-aš mu-re-eš mi-li-it ma-a-
an kan-kan-za, Tešimi is hanging upon you like a sweet grape cluster, KUB 36.89 rev. 58–59;
Güterbock and Hoffner 1990c: 333). The contemporary Turkish usage of a similarly manufactured
grape-based sweetener called *pekmez* gives additional credence to this possibility (Emerson 1908:
384–85; Köymen 1982: 43).

Another text, however, may shed some light on the question of wine sweeteners. An additional
ingredient was also mixed in with the wine, honey, and fine oil, something called BA.BA.ZA (ŠA
BA.BA.ZA-ya ŠA LÀL Ì GEŠTIN an-da [im-mi-y]a-an-ti[(-it)], And he/she mixed (a portion) of
the fruit puree, (a portion of) honey (and) oil, into the wine, KUB 15.34 iv 17'). The word is
translated in the Sumerian Dictionary (Sjöberg 1984) as "a kind of porridge." Friedrich (1952:
266), however, translates the word as *Brei* or *Mus* (i.e., a puree, pulp, or stewed fruit), a definition

that fits with the modern notion of grape must which refers to either the mass of crushed grapes or the unfermented grape juice, with or without the skins (Amerine 1974: 878). Grape must was then prepared in several ways according to the classical sources, often being reduced by boiling off a portion of the liquid, and then used as an additive to enhance the taste of some wines, to fortify old or weak wines or as a supplement to medicinal treatments (Pliny *NH* 23.18). The above passage mentioning a medicinal wine as being "boiled down" (kat-ta wa-ar-nu-zi, KUB 44.63 obv. ii 17'–30', Burde 1974, 30–31), may indicate just such a procedure. In this case, the BA.BA.ZA may be referring to the must or a reduced version of it. Perhaps this preparation served the same function as the grape-syrup sweetener proposed by Powell.

The advanced techniques for improving the quality of wine mentioned in the Mari texts (Durand 1983: 105–9) suggest various processes for wine-blending which would have been available to Hittite wine-makers as early as the 18th century B.C., and certainly after their conquest of the north Syrian region in the fifteenth century B.C. By the thirteenth century B.C. advanced wine-making techniques are also documented in Mycenaean Greece,[34] making it probable that similar techniques would have been known and used by contemporary Hittite viticulturalists. If so, Hittite wine production might have been somewhat more complex than previously assumed.

Do any of the Hittite texts refer to grape juice rather than its intoxicating derivative? Although no actual texts exist describing the process of Hittite wine-making, the sources make it clear that most if not all of the beverages that come under the designation of GEŠTIN were of the fermented variety. In the Myth of the Serpent Illuyanka (Hoffner 1990: 12), for instance, Illuyanka is lured from his den by a feast replete with large quantities of GEŠTIN, *marnuwa*, and *walḫi*.[35] As a result, the serpent became inebriated, was unable to descend back into his hole and fell asleep, after which he was slain. Similarly, the implication of the *Ašertu Myth* passage (above) and the *Kizzuwatna Festival* is that wine is a powerful drink that can be the source of much trouble. The implication of such passages is that GEŠTIN was potent and could be inebriating. The premise that Hittite wine was, in most instances, considered to be an intoxicating drink logically follows.

All products of the grapevine in Hittite Anatolia were not necessarily intoxicating. In modern Turkey, several beverages derived from grapes such as *basduk* and *kessme* are non alcoholic and produced by boiling down the grape juice into a molasses-like substance which is then dried until it takes on the appearance of leather. This substance is valuable in that it resists deterioration, can be eaten as a solid, and can be dissolved in water to make a refreshing drink (Emerson 1908: 390–91). Another beverage produced from the reduced juice of the grape is called *bazaq*. The resulting product is mixed with herbs and is ready for consumption in a short time; it can also be stored for several years becoming quite potent. Modern drinks made from other fruits can also be mentioned here. *Baqa*, for example, is made from figs and dates fermented together in water (Emerson 1908: 377). Thus, we can entertain the possibility that some of the drinks known from Hittite texts are similar in character to these modern beverages. While it seems likely that the designation GEŠTIN normally refers to fermented grape wine, it may also serves as an umbrella-term for a group of grape-derived beverages. It is more likely, however, that unfermented drinks were distinguished from their intoxicating relative by separate names which have yet to be determined.

As we noted above, Hittite wines were generally known by qualitative terms. Color designations, however, are apparently not a normal part of that repertoire. Since the Hittites generally did not differentiate their wines by color, it is not certain whether they made both red and white varieties. Most, if not all, of the wines were probably of the red type (*GEŠTIN* ŠA$_5$) as the incidences of white wines are few and uncertain. One possibility involves the use of the term *karši*-, a word generally translated as "clear" (nam-ma-kán ta-wa-al wa-al-ḫi KAŠ.GEŠTIN.KU$_7$ GEŠTIN kar-ši ḫa-pu-uš-ti-ya-an LÀL Ì.DÙG.GA Ì.NUN GA.KU$_7$ an-da la-ḫu-wa-a-an-zi, And they pour in the *tawal*, *walḫi*, sweet beer-wine, wine, clear stuff, *haputiya-*, honey, fine oil, butter, and sweet milk, 1897/u 1'–12': also KUB 15.34 iii 26; KUB 12.16 i 3', Bo 3648, 14'; KUB 457/b + 465/b iii [?] 6': and KUB 44.64 obv. i 26). If *karši* were to be taken as an adjective modifying GEŠTIN, it would be a neuter and not agree with GEŠTIN, which would be unusual. Although the use of *karši* in this passage is not clear, it seems to be employed, not as an adjective referring to GEŠTIN, but as a substantive that is to be translated as "the clear stuff," and in this case, its connection with clarity could be a reference to some sort of clear beverage, perhaps something like the anise-based liquor known in modern Turkey as *rakı*. A more likely possibility for denoting white wines, however, is found in several references to KÙ.BABBAR GEŠTIN, EGIR-šu za-an-za-pu-uš-ši-in KÙ.BABBAR GEŠTIN šu-un-na-an-zi, Afterwards they fill a pitcher with white wine (?), KUB 10.91, rev. iii 11'–19'; also see KÙ.BABBAR GEŠTIN-it šu-u-an-da-an *BE-EL É-TIM*, the lord of the palace poured white wine, KBo 29.211 rev. iv 20'; and ᴸᵁMUḪALDIM DINGER*ᴸᴵᴹ*-ma-za 2 ta-pí-eš-nu-uš KÙ.BABBAR GEŠTIN [o o o] xx-an *A-NA* DUMU.LUGAL pi-ra-an ḫu-u[-], And the cook took 2 pitchers [that are filled with?] white wine to the princes, KUB 25.36 ii 27'–37'). The fact that GEŠTIN BABBAR DÙG.GA (Oppenheim et al. 1971: 205) is used to describe a sweet wine in Akkadian lends some credence to the possibility that KÙ.BABBAR GEŠTIN is used in Hittite texts as a qualitative term for white wine. In any case, the designation of wines by color is extremely rare in Hittite Anatolia.

Another form of wine-related drink goes under the designation KAŠ.GEŠTIN, a drink which has often been taken to be a mixture of beer and wine in some form (Steiner 1966: 307). In Hittite texts KAŠ.GEŠTIN is distributed solely by the ᴸᵁZABAR.DIB or wine supplier, an official who apparently had no role in beer provisioning (Singer 1983: 157). This suggests that the drink is more wine than beer, perhaps on a par with the barley-wine mentioned by Xenophon (*Anabasis* 2.3.14–16, 2.4.28, 3.4.31, 4.2.22, 4.4.9, and 4.5.26) or the millet wine noted by Pliny (*NH* 14.101). The drink also seems to have been known in Mesopotamia where it nearly always went by its Akkadian name *kurunnu* (cf. Reiner 1982: 579 f.), though on at least one occasion (*OECT* 4.152 viii 38) *kurunnu* is equated with KAŠ.GEŠTIN. In Mesopotamia beer was drunk through straws, but since Xenophon's account indicates that the drink he found in Armenia was also drawn through a straw, it may be that several of the iconographic representations in Hittite art which depict beverages being consumed through straws are meant as illustrations of KAŠ.GEŠTIN being consumed (Figs. 11.2–11.3).

In Xenophon's description (*Anabasis* 4.5.26) of barley-wine, his soldiers found it to be harsh, unless diluted with water. Perhaps the Hittite penchant for mixing KAŠ.GEŠTIN with additional ingredients (KAŠ.GEŠTIN LÀL-it wa-a-tar an-da GEŠTIN-aš šu-uḫ-ḫa-an-za nu ši-pa-an-ti, The wine is poured into the beer-wine, honey (and) water. Then they libate. KUB 9.28 ii 10″ f.) can be traced to conditions similar to those observed by Xenophon. In both cases, it is very likely that honey was being used along with other ingredients to dilute the harshness of a barley-wine type drink.

The question of where the Hittites acquired their wine from has been largely ignored. It has been assumed, with some justification, that the grapes used for Hittite wine came from areas around the capital, Ḫattuša. Hittite texts mention vineyards (ᴳᴵˢKIRI₆.GEŠTIN) which are evidently in close proximity to the capital. Since each city of the empire seems to have had its own wine supplier (ᴸᵁZABAR.DIB), presumably each city also produced its own wine. A portion of that wine might then have been exacted by the central government at Ḫattuša, unless wine intended for the palace came exclusively from royally owned vineyards.

Little is known about how Hittite vineyards were organized and cared for. As noted in a Hittite law (§108) and the *BEL.MADGALTI* text (CTH 261, §§27 and 43), some vineyards were walled in. The walls probably served to keep various animals out and might have been located in or near

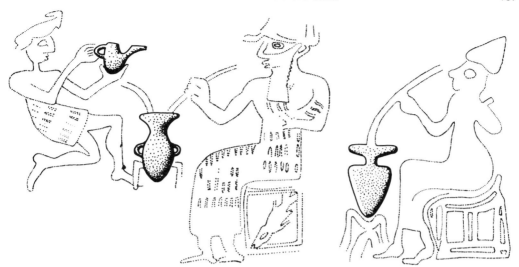

Figure 11.2. Possible representation of KAŠ.GEŠTIN drinking on Seal Impression from Kültepe. (After Müller-Karpe 1988.)

Figure 11.3. Possible representation of KAŠ.GEŠTIN drinking on Seal Impression from Kültepe. (After Müller-Karpe 1988.)

towns and villages, areas where animals were more likely to trample the plants. As is frequently noted in rural areas of Turkey today, however, this precaution would not always be necessary, especially in the case of vineyards situated in outlying areas. As we noted above, some vineyards might have been irrigated, but the majority were probably situated on gentle well-drained slopes some distance from villages, towns, and cities. As in contemporaneous Near Eastern cultures (Postgate 1987: 119; Palmer 1990: 57–58), Hittite vineyards could be interplanted with other fruits (KBo 5.7 rev. 28 ff. and 34 ff.; Klengel 1986: 27). Hittite law §105 appears to discuss compensation in a case where vines and interplanted fruits are burned down together. This could indicate that Hittite vines were still not free-standing and orchard trees were used as a means of support for the vines. Another text, however, seems to suggest the opposite, that vines were already well-trained and grown on supports ([…š]a-li-ik ^{GIŠ}ma-aḫ-li na-pa iš-ki-ši-it-ti a-ap-pa la-a-ak, Approach the branch (of the grapevine) and train (it) on your back, KBo 21.22 rev. 46, Güterbock and Hoffner 1990b: 112). In any case, the vineyard was probably tended by a gardener (^{LÚ}NU.^{GIŠ}KIRI$_6$), though the extent of this individual's responsibilities is unknown, as is the manner in which the vines were planted, trained, or pruned (for methods of laying out vineyards in the Roman period see White 1970b: 231–41).

Alternatives to the local vineyards may also have been available to the Hittites. Over the course of time, several important localities which later came to be known as important wine producing regions, were brought under Hittite rule and these areas very likely contributed wine as part of their tribute. As evidence for this we have the previously mentioned text concerning a wine tribute from Ḫurna (KUB 19.27:47–48). In addition. an oracle text mentions wine from Naḫita and Ḫiliqqa (IBoT 2.129:12), towns that are thought to have been located in southern Turkey, perhaps in the area of Cilicia (cf. del Monte and Tischler 1978: 279). Elsewhere, wine gardens are known from 15th century Alalakh (Dietrich and Loretz 1969). Ugarit is also said to have produced its own wine (Campbell 1966: 29), and because of the special relationship between Ḫatti and Ugarit, it is reasonable to assume that some of that wine made its way to the Hittite capital. In addition, recently published texts from Mari (Lion 1992) inform us that the Upper Euphrates region was well on its way towards becoming an important viticultural center by the 18th century, and it is clear that Carchemish and Emar (later Meškene) played especially prominent roles in the expansion of the wine industry in this area (Finet 1974–77, Durand 1983, Talon 1985, Finet 1985, Lafont 1988, and Bunnens 1989). Nearby Cilicia (ancient Kizzuwatna, along the southeastern coast of Turkey) provides another example of a viticultural area under Hittite domination from which wine might have been procured (Goetze 1940: 60–71). Alternatively, wine could have also come in exchange with viticultural centers to the west. Wine seems to be mentioned as an item of trade in a fragment mentioning Aḫḫiyawa and Mira (GEŠTIN pe-ḫu-te-ni, you have brought wine, KUB 21.34 rev. 6(?), Sommer 1932, 251–52), and since it is also known that wine was being produced in the Mycenaean world (Palmer 1990), one might postulate trade with that region. Simply put, not all Hittite wine need be of the domestic variety. Wine very likely made its way to the Hittite capital at Ḫattuša from various regions under its control. More than likely, this wine would have been wine of a better sort and not the customary table wine. In this case, the "good wine" (DÙG.GA / SIG$_5$-an-ta-an GEŠTIN) referred to in the Hittite texts could refer to better quality imported wines. Unfortunately, the Hittites generally did not specify the point of origin for their wines, perhaps an indication that the vineyards of the homeland produced enough wine to meet the Hittites' limited needs.

d. Raisins and wine production

The raisin (^{GIŠ}GEŠTIN.ḪAD.DU.A) was an important component of Hittite viticulture. Dried and stored, the dried fruit could be used for a variety of purposes, most notably for food and drink. The raisin often formed part of the dried ration for military campaigns (KUB 31.71 rev. iv 1–15). It also played a role in activities such as magic rituals (KUB 33.68) and funerals (KUB 39.34). Raisins were also placed in foundation deposits for a temple (KUB 29.2 ii) and a new palace (KUB 29.1 ii 1–17), and entered into the *ḫišuwa* Festival (KUB 55.51 rev. left col. 1'–15') and the enthronement of a king Tudḫaliya (KBo 10.34 i 1–21). In fact, the raisin was represented in nearly all important events recorded in ancient Hittite manuscripts. A more specialized use of particular importance, however, was the production of a distinctive type of "raisin wine."

There is a long tradition of raisin wines in Anatolia. Pliny (*NH* 14) describes several types and the process of making these sweet wines. A variety known as *Scybelites* from Galatia has already been noted. *Siræum*, which is described in more detail, was produced by boiling down the must to one-third of its original volume. These wines, especially when adulterated with honey (Pliny *NH* 14.11: 248–49), were highly regarded. Before boiling down the must, the grapes were dried on the vine until they had lost about half their weight. They were then crushed and the juice extracted. A second quality wine was made by adding an equal portion of well water. Careful wine-makers, however, added an intermediate step to produce a preferred type of "raisin wine." Good wine was added to the pulp which was then allowed to swell before being pressed. As before the resulting wine was diluted with water. As Emerson notes (1908: 376), this tradition continued into later Turkish times, most notably in the form of the intoxicating liquor *tayf*.

Because it was assumed that the juice used in wine-making came from the crushed or pressed grape, our epithet at the beginning of the chapter about wine being in the heart of the raisin was not understood. If the Hittites, however, produced a sweet "raisin wine" using the pulp of the raisin, then this phrase is understandable. In light of Hesiod's description of wine made from dried grapes in *Works and Days* (611–14) and the continuation of the tradition in later classical authors, it is reasonable to assume that Hittite wine-makers had already begun to produce raisin wines in Anatolia a thousand years or more before the procedures described in Pliny.

e. The symbolic nature of wine

A theme common to nearly all ancient Near East cultures is the association of agricultural productivity with divine favor and prosperity. Although the metaphor is not as vivid in Anatolia, viticulture and wine production are symbolic of prosperity and well-being there too. The author of *The Blessings of Labarna* (above) maintained that "the king's bread we eat, and his wine we drink; from a gold goblet pure wine we keep drinking" (KUB 36.110 rev. 5–7). The text, which is a statement on the ideology of kingship in Hittite Anatolia, presents a philosophic outlook that ties the prosperity of the fields (bread and wine) to the position of the king and the favor of the gods. Conversely, as *The Edict of Telipinu* shows, the lack of viticultural productivity, often in association with other unproductive commodities, was used as a symbol of adversity and divine displeasure (KBo 3.1 i 69–71 = BoTU 23A, Kammenhuber 1958: 144, n. 41; Hoffner 1974: 39).

> And Ammuna became king. And then the gods avenged the blood of his father, Zidanta; they did not prosper (?) him (or) in his hands the grain, [the orchards (?)], the grapes, the cattle, and the sheep.

Wine seems also to have been a symbol of high status. Historical documents indicate that by the Old Hittite Kingdom, the wine culture had developed into an important enterprise, with sociopolitical overtones. Besides the fact that wine was offered as tribute on various occasions, there were other instances which indicate the special place of wine in the Anatolian mentality. In the *Palace Chronicles* (above), the punitive way in which Maratti and Ḫištayara's deceiver was punished, suggests that the distribution of wine was as much political as it was culinary, having considerable symbolic significance. That an individual could be executed for carrying out this deception suggests that the use of wine was not only the prerogative of the royal house, but that attempts to bypass the established order were tantamount to treason. In the case of Maratti and Ḫištayara, we have two important personages, who may well have been the parents of a king (Beal 1983: 122–24). The ^{LÚ}ZABAR.DIB's men (probably the ^{LÚ.MEŠ}ZABAR.DIB) attempted to deceive them into believing that they had received "good wine." The deception was quickly discovered and the guilty party punished. The exact intent of the deception, however, is unclear. It might well have been a matter of simple economics in which a little extra cash could be made by passing on cheaper wine where he thought he would not get caught, and selling the better wine elsewhere for more money. It could also indicate, however, a split in the court over the loyalty due not only to Maratti and Ḫištayara but, if they were indeed the king's parents, to the king himself. Assuming that the king was Muršili I, the text could provide evidence of the divisiveness that eventually led to his assassination after a triumphant return from the conquest of Babylon. Thus, it may be that wine had become a symbol of status, and the abuse of this symbol could lead to disastrous results.

The honorific place accorded to wine is also suggested in two otherwise unrelated texts in which the beverage has some association with value. In one case, wine appears to have been presented as a prize (ma-an LUGAL-wa-aš pi-ra-an ši-e-kán-zi ku-iš ḫa-az-zi-iz-zi nu-uš-eš GEŠTIN-an a-ku-wa-an-na pí-an-zi, when they hold a shooting match before the king, whoever scores a hit, to him they give wine to drink, KBo 3.34 ii 33 [Old Hittite], Puhvel 1984a, 264–65). Similarly, in the *Ḫedammu Myth*, the text speaks of giving, *KU-KU-BI* ^{ḪI.A} GEŠTIN-ma-aš-ma-aš ^{NA₄}ZA.GÌN-aš pa-a-i, And he gives to them wine vessels of lapis lazuli [...], KBo 26.82 (= 985/v rev. 8), Siegelová 1971: 70). The only link between these texts is the associated sense of value. So, while not specifically saying that wine was somewhat more esteemed than other products of the field, the texts leave us with the impression that wine was understood to possess some kind of high intrinsic value. It is never portrayed as a staple of the Hittite table but is always presented as a high-status food.

Hittite descriptions of wine's symbolic importance coincides with evidence from other complex social structures and affirm what has been described as a diacritical role for alcoholic beverages in general, and wine in particular. Such beverages, along with their containers and attendant social customs, became a way to further distinguish the position of the elite and separate them from the rest of society. Dietler (1990) observes that alcohol (in this case wine) "is a medium that allows surplus agriculture to be converted into labor, prestige, 'social credit,' political power, bride-wealth, or durable valuables." As Joffe (Forthcoming) notes, the "creation, control, and capture of alcoholic beverage consumption and distribution are especially important for understanding early state institutions." Wine, as much as any alcoholic beverage, symbolized the high status of the elite and provided a means whereby they might redefine and add to their lofty position.

The separation of the elite created a group which was empowered to continually redefine its own role. By controlling production, consumption, and distribution, the elite was able to create a demand for beverages such as wine and to foster an image of status that further solidified their prerogatives. Such developments affected not only wine itself, but the attendant crafts, as well as interregional exchange. Foreign or imported wines that made their way to the court of the elite as a result of such interaction only added a greater aura to this sense of privilege. Once Again, Dietler (1990) appears to be correct when he states that,

> in hierarchal systems imported drinks and/or drinking practices would be valued mainly for their diacritical function, and imported drinking gear could be extremely useful in differentiating elite drinking even when the supply of the exotic drink was meagre or irregular.

Thus, the restrictive tendencies of the elite, along with the notion of risk abatement through the auspices of an integrated central administrative apparatus, came to be viewed as an economic legitimization of the Anatolian elite.

Similarly, the association of wine with Hittite ritual practices is in keeping with the role of alcohol in other early stratified societies in that it tends to forge a link between nascent sociopolitical structures, the religious belief system, and the agricultural producers by legitimizing the elite through divine favor as the guarantors of agricultural productivity and prosperity, an apologetic that finds its ultimate formulation in the concept of "divine kingship" noted above. As Joffe (Forthcoming) explains, the ability to control the redistribution of these diacritical beverages not only "secured allegiance but also fused subsistence, labor, and belief."

As with other symbols of the elite, however, there appears to be a "commodification" of the wine in ancient Anatolia. What began as a prerogative of the Hittite elite eventually "spilled over" and "trickled down" to other areas of society (Joffe Forthcoming). Evidence for the diffusion of high-status prerogatives may be reflected in the downward mobility of elite styles and ideology as suggested by the ceramic imitation of metallic prototypes (Vickers 1986). In Anatolia this vertical movement may be illustrated in the imitative ceramic rhyta found in many Hittite sites which appear to be modest reflections of metallic vessels such as the well-known Schimmel Rhyta (Fig. 11.4; Muscarella 1974). If such "down-market" activity is to be associated with paraphernalia linked to drinking, it may well be true of the beverage itself. Such a diffusion may have been connected with the collapse of the Late Bronze Age Palace economy and the disbursal of its prerogatives to later inhabitants.

In Anatolia, the so-called Dark Age that followed the fall of the Hittites has left us without much information about wine production in the area. A Neo-Hittite relief sculpture on the side of a cliff at İvriz in southeastern Turkey illustrates, however, that there was some continuity in vinicultural traditions during the succeeding period with that of their Hittite predecessors. The sculpture

Figure 11.4. Silver stag rhyton (BIBRU) from Schimmel Collection. (Photograph courtesy of The New York Metropolitan Museum of Art; gift of the Norbert Schimmel Foundation, 1989 [1989.281.10].)

Figure 11.5. Neo-Hittite representation of Tarḫunta from İvriz. (Photograph by R. Gorny.)

portrays king Warpalawa and the Stormgod Tarḫunta (Fig. 11.5), who was often propitiated with wine during the Hittite period (above). Moreover, a hieroglyphic Luwian inscription on a statue from nearby Sultanhan reads "Tarḫunta of the Wine-gardens" (Meriggi 1967: 117; Hawkins 1974: 50; Haas 1988: 142), further indication that oenocological skills had survived the fall of the Hittites.

During the early first millennium, the traditions of these Neo-Hittite states were merging with those of the Neo-Assyrian world where the wine industry had also become widespread (see chapters 12 by Stronach and 9 by Powell, this volume). By this time, viticulture was also gaining prominence in other areas of the Mediterranean, and Anatolia had progressed a long way towards fulfilling Šuppiluliumma's admonition to Ḫuqqana of Ḫayasa to "eat, drink, (and) make merry!" (*nuza ezattin ekuttin duškiškittin*, KBo 5. 3 iii 37).

3. The Archaeological Evidence for Anatolian Viticulture

The earliest botanical evidence of grape-growing in Anatolia seems to come from the eastern part of the country where wild grape pips dating to the Neolithic period (ca. 7200–6500 B.C.) were found at Can Hasan III (French 1972: 187) and Çayönü (Stewart 1976: 221). Chalcolithic finds (ca. 4500–3500 B.C.) include wild grape specimens at Korucutepe (van Zeist 1988: 228) and a possibly domesticated variety of *Vitis* from Tepecik (van Zeist 1988: 230). Grape remains dating to the Late Chalcolithic (ca. 3500–3200 B.C.) were also found at Kurban Höyük, but whether they were wild or domesticated is uncertain (Miller 1986: 88–89; Wilkinson 1990: 94). Recent discoveries at nearby Titriş Höyük, however, make it clear that viticulture had become a well-established fact in this region by the Early Bronze Age (Algaze 1995). Taken as a whole, the evidence suggests that true cultivation of domesticated grapes did not get under way in Anatolia until nearly the beginning of the third millennium. In the west, however, archaeological evidence of grape domestication is less certain than in the east. While *vinifera* was allegedly found at Troy and Beycesultan (Zohary and Spiegel-Roy 1975, p. 322), this report is somewhat problematic.[36] Nonetheless, within a short period of time, viticulture was to become a well-established fact in Anatolia with evidence coming from many sites (Fig. 11.6).

Evidence for viticulture in the Hittite heartland is quite scant. The site most likely to produce evidence of grape-growing and wine-making is Ḫattuša-Boğazköy. It was the capital, the center from which Hittite culture radiated. Here was located both the court and the cult, the two entities which were most dependent on wine. The absence of viticultural and vinicultural remains is, therefore, somewhat puzzling. The fact that Ḫattuša was probably a temple city (Neve 1987) might explain the lack of physical remains. It is also possible that the decision to throw all plant remains on the spoil heap for the last 70 years has something to do with this lack of evidence (Hopf 1990).

Production areas are unknown at Boğazköy, but it may be that the production of wine was restricted to areas outside of the capital city or to special work areas within its walls. While one would welcome the discovery of a Hittite wine "processing plant," not a single grape treading facility or wine-press, to my knowledge, has yet been uncovered in Anatolia.[37] The closest examples are the unpublished presses recently found at Tel es-Sweyhat (Syria) which appear to belong to the Roman period.[38]

Pottery associated with wine production, storage, trade and consumption in the texts, together with excavated examples of the pottery that are styles thought to be referred to, provide an additional dimension to the question of wine use in ancient Anatolia. Because of the various stages in the whole process, one might expect to find a range of vessel types.[39] Some vessel types that may have been involved can also be gleaned from an examination of the viticultural equipment noted in the writings of classical authors (White 1975: 112). Once the grapes have been crushed and pressed, the range of vessels for storage, transport, consumption, and other purposes dramatically increases. Unfortunately, although the large number of texts relating to the wine industry from Hittite Anatolia is an excellent resource, the names of vessels known from the texts have not been unequivocally tied to excavated pottery types, and a great deal of confusion has accompanied attempts to link textual names with the actual vessels found in central Anatolian excavations.

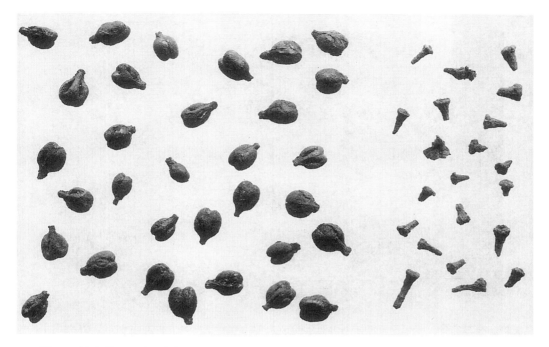

Figure 11.6. Grape pips (left) and stalks (right) from Iron Age levels at Tille Höyük, southeastern Turkey. These date to about 600 B.C. and have been preserved by charring. The pips show the characteristic slender shape and long stalks of domesticated grapes. (Photograph courtesy of M. Nesbitt.)

Coşkun (1979) has shown in his short monograph that a variety of vessels were also associated with the storage and dispensing of wine in the Hittite texts, including ^{DUG}*huppar-*, ^{DUG}*harši-*, ^{DUG}*huprušhi-*, ^{DUG}*haniišša-*, and ^{DUG}HAB.HAB.GÚ GÍD.DA, and no single vessel seems to be denoted as the typical "wine bottle." In fact, the vessels associated with wine in the texts were also utilized for other liquids, including beer, and foodstuffs. While the texts mention a ^{DUG}GEŠTIN (30 ^{DUG}GEŠTIN ^{LÚ.MEŠ}ZABAR.DIB pí[-an-zi?], the men of the wine-steward give 30 wine vessels, KUB 38.19 + IBoT 102 obv. 1'–4'; also KUB 30.15 + KUB 39.19 obv. 1-18; KUB 36.89 obv. 5–11), it is unclear whether this term refers to a particular type of wine vessel or was a generic term for a variety of vessels containing wine. Since it is mentioned as part of a metal inventory, the vessel was presumably made of metal (KBo 18.161 rev. 2'). On the other hand, since it could be smashed (*arha duwarnanzi*, KUB 30.24a + 30.16 65 obv. i 20–26 and obv. ii 1–11) some examples also might have been ceramic. Its size and shape are not given, frustrating any attempt to determine the vessel's function and correlation to excavated examples.

The wine-making process began with the picking of the grapes, which might have been collected in reed baskets, according to the later practice (White 1975: pls. 3–4). Simple vats (Hittite *luli*?, Güterbock and Hoffner 1990: 81–82) might have been employed for crushing the grapes, although none have been recovered from Hittite sites, perhaps because they were constructed of wood and have not survived (for a description of the treading process in classical times see *Geoponics* 6.11 in White 1977: 70–71, 132). Some of the ceramic "bathtubs" (Fig. 11.7) which have been recovered from Old Assyrian and Hittite sites may also be good candidates for

Figure 11.7. So-called "bathtub" *in situ* near oven at Kültepe. (Photograph courtesy of T. Özgüç.)

Figure 11.8. Repre-
sentation of beak-
spouted vessel on re-
lief shard from Kara-
höyük. (After Müller-
Karpe 1988: 26, fig.
1.2.)

grape-crushing vats. (Similar tubs have been reported from Minoan
sites; see chapters 18 by Wright and 15 by Leonard, this volume.) At
Kültepe, these "bathtubs" are not associated with water systems, but
rather are situated mostly in corners of rooms, especially with
hearths, and alternatively in kitchens or courtyards, i.e., areas that are
more appropriate for wine production (Özgüç 1949: 176). Corroborating evidence may come from plastered basins recently found in
late EBA levels at Titriş Höyük, which produced traces of tartaric
acid residue on their surfaces (Algaze 1995). Similarly described
receptacles (Latin *alveae*) are described in later Roman texts in
connection with various activities, including viticulture (White
1975: 119–22). Another vessel which seems to be a closer parallel to
the "bathtubs" is a stone quadrangular basin which is artistically
depicted being used in wine-making scenes. Its use in the wine
process (Lat. *forus*, cf. White 1975: 132, pl. 7) is very similar. These
vessels, though made of stone, are remarkably similar in style to the
Hittite "bathtubs." It should be stated, however, that even if the
association of these "bathtubs" with the hearths and courtyards at
Kültepe provides some evidence of viticultural practices, the uses of
the piece were probably not limited to wine, for the vessel very likely
had multiple functions. If, however, such vessels are ultimately shown to have been utilized in the
production of wine, they would have been most appropriate for small-scale production, and this
could be taken as an indication that each household made its own wine. However, while I suggest
wine production as one function of these vessels, further studies of this particular vessel are
needed before any definitive statements can be made.

Figure 11.9. Hittite supplication scene depicting libation of wine from beak-spouted vessel on silver rhyton in Schimmel Collection. (After Boehmer 1983.)

Figure 11.10. Libation arm fragments from Alişar: a) (left) Gorny 1990: pl. 47; b) (middle) von der Osten 1937: fig. 207,c1276; c) (right) von der Osten 1937: fig. 207,c1277. (Photograph courtesy of the Oriental Institute.)

Beak-spouted pitchers are pictured frequently in Hittite iconography (Figs. 11.8–11.9), and based on such depictions, this vessel type must have received its name ([DUG]*išpantuzzi/išpantuzz-ieššar*, i.e., "libation vessel," Müller-Karpe 1988: 25) from its association with libation offerings (Hittite *šipand-*). The vessels was common in the Old Assyrian Colony period as attested by the finds from Kültepe and reaches its artistic peak in the Old Hittite Period before its style becomes somewhat degraded by the end of the Hittite Empire Period (Fischer 1963: 38).

Libation arms (Fig. 11.10) are yet another instrument of libation and may also have been called a "libation vessel" ([DUG]*išpantuzzi*, Coşkun, 83–84; Müller-Karpe 1988: 145), but if Alp (1967: 531) is right in understanding the vessel as a representation of the lower portion of the arm, it might more properly be called a [DUG]*kattakurant* (Müller-Karpe 1988: 145). Libation arms occur frequently in the temples of the Upper City at Boğazköy, where they must have been used for libations related to the cult activities of the temples.

Figure 11.11. Orthostat relief from Alaca Höyük showing royal personage with drinking bowl. (After Müller-Karpe 1988: 26, fig. 1.8.)

Small shallow bowls (^{DUG}ḫuppar, Müller-Karpe 1988: 93) are commonly found in excavations and appear to have been a common vessel used for both drinking or libating, a fact once again illustrated in Hittite iconography (Fig. 11.11). Shallow drinking bowls also occur as a recurrent theme in the Near East linking royalty and wine (cf. Stronach in this volume). Since such representations can be traced back to the third millennium B.C. (Haran 1958: 21–22), it should come as no surprise that it is also present in Anatolian iconography. In this particular case, the bowl in question provides a welcomed example of how the royal drinking bowl could also be used in Anatolia as a canonical symbol of successful royal stewardship.

Another vessel often associated with wine in Hittite texts was the rhyton (BIBRU), a cup fashioned in the form of an animal head (Figs. 11.12) and popular during both the Old Assyrian and Hittite periods (ca. 2000–1200 B.C.; cf. chapters 18 by Wright and 15 by Leonard, this volume). Many examples have been found in central Anatolian excavations, some of pottery (N. Özgüç

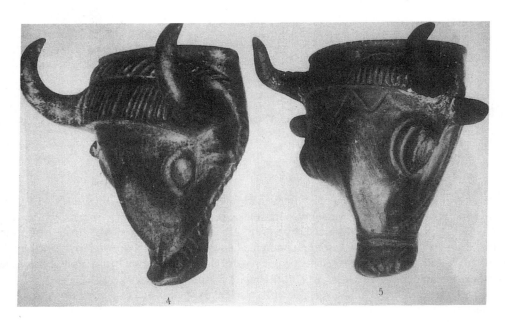

Figure 11.12. Steer rhyta (BIBRU) from Kültepe. (Photograph courtesy of T. Özgüç.)

Figure 11.13. Large storage jars found at Boğazköy. (Photograph by R. Gorny.)

1950) and others of metal (Muscarella 1974; Çınaroğlu 1990–91: 53–59).

Liquids are thought to have been stored in large storage jars (^{DUG}*ḫarši-/*^{DUG}*ḫaršiyalli*) such as those found in the magazines of Temple I (Fig. 11.13; Coşkun 1979: 1–7, 9–16; Müller-Karpe 1988: 61, 93, see fig. 11). These vessels could hold from 900–1750 liters (Coşkun 1979: 7, 16), and because of the apparent agreement between tablets mentioning wine storage in the capital and the numerous pithoi found lining the magazines of Temple I, it is not unreasonable to expect that some of these containers were filled with grapes or wine. Although the pithoi are known from texts to have held various contents, the most frequent mention is of wine. The absence of grape pips from these vessels could indicate that they contained a liquid (wine?) rather than solid stores (grapes/raisins).

Smaller versions of the pithos (^{DUG}*ḫaršiyallani-*) were evidently used for lesser unspecified quantities (Coşkun 1979: 16; Müller-Karpe 1988: 62). Perhaps these smaller vessels are to be equated with the flared-rim storage vessels that are well-attested at Old Assyrian sites including Kültepe, Maşat, and Alişar (Fig. 11.14). Another vessel name associated with wine was the two-handled pot with an everted neck (^{DUG}*-ḫaneḫišša-*). It had a capacity of about 1.5 liters (Coşkun 1979: 49–56; Müller-Karpe 1988: 83). Generally known as an "amphora" (Fig. 11.15), excavated examples are known from several central Anatolian sites. Another vessel with a long narrow neck (^{DUG}ḪAB.ḪAB.GÚ.GÍD.DA) would have been particularly well suited for storing and pouring liquids (cf. Badler, McGovern, and Michel 1990: 27, Coşkun 1979: 59–62). Vessels that might fit this general description are known from a variety of Hittite sites and are cited in relation to wine production (Fig. 11.16; Müller-Karpe 1988: 31–33, Type K 2). Comprising 19.3% of the finds from the Upper City at Ḫattuša (Müller-Karpe 1988: pl. 50) this vessel might have been most frequently utilized by the Hittites for the storage and transportation of wine. As yet, none of these vessels have been tested for tartaric acid or other organic wine or grape residues.

An Old Assyrian period vessel whose shape suggests its use as a wine container is the so-called grape-cluster vessels (Fig. 11.17) found at several sites in central Anatolia, including Acemhöyük (T. Özgüç 1950: 186, pl. 44, 1a–b, fig. 447), Boğazköy (Bittel 1950: 579: Orthmann 1984: 57, fig.

Figure 11.14. Flared-rim storage jar from Alişar. (After von der Osten 1937: 156, fig. 197, c2377, pl. 7, c2377; photograph courtesy of the Oriental Institute.)

Figure 11.15. Amphora from Alişar. (Photograph courtesy of the Oriental Institute.)

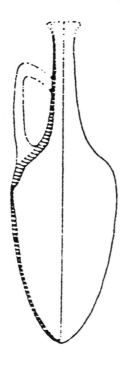

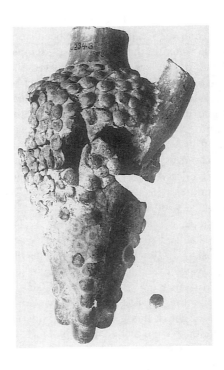

Figure 11.16. Long-necked bottle from Imıkušağı. (After Yakar 1986.)

Figure 11.17. Grape-cluster vessel from Alişar. (After von der Osten 1937; photograph courtesy of the Oriental Institute.)

Figure 11.18. Pilgrim-flask from Boğazköy. (Photograph courtesy of P. Neve.)

24, nos. 212 and 213), Karahöyük-Konya (Alp 1968: 289. pl. 6, no. 12), and Alişar (von der Osten 1937, fig. 194, d2343 and d2344; Gorny 1990: 103–4). These vessels were molded in the shape of a grape cluster and were probably used for libations during the cult festivities. Curiously, the use of the grape-cluster vessel is not attested after the Old Assyrian Colony Period.

Wine may also have been associated with several other vessels known from central Anatolian excavations, but whose Hittite names remain uncertain. One such vessel is the so-called pilgrim-flask (Fig. 11.18), a specialty piece which may have been used in the transportation of wine. Another is the well-known relief vase (Fig. 11.19), the best example of which comes from Inandık (Özgüç 1988a: 83–106, fig. 27, pls. D 4 and F–M). Based on the interior spouts common to this type of vessel (Özgüç 1988a, pls. D 4 and H 3–4), one may suggest that these vases were used as blending vessels for various Hittite rituals and perhaps can be associated with the [DUG]GÌR.KIŠ vessel known from the Hittite texts to have been used for just such purposes (cf. KUB 53.13 rev. iv 1′–19′).

Although it is clear that the Hittites used a variety of vessels to accommodate the numerous uses they had contrived for wine, it is very difficult to tie a particular style of excavated container to the vessels mentioned in the Hittite texts. The contents of the pottery vessels found at Hittite sites can only be speculated upon at this time, Thus, while it seems likely that some if not all of the vessels mentioned were used in wine production and/or consumption, there is no clear way of confirming any such usage from the archaeological materials. Since, as far as I know, none of these vessels have been examined for the presence of tartaric acid, it is impossible to make anything more than speculative statements regarding their contents. In light of this, an Infrared

Figure 11.19. Inandık vase. (After T. Özgüç 1988: 163, fig. 27.)

Spectroscopy Analysis of these vessels would be welcomed and could provide some interesting insights into the production, trade, and storage of early Anatolian wines.

The mention of a thriving wine trade along the Euphrates River points to the long distance movement of wine in the Old Assyrian and Hittite periods and begs another question. If Hittite wine was included in movements of this sort, were special transport containers employed? Theoretically, wine could have been conveyed in any type of closed vessel with flat, round, or pointed bases. The contemporaneous Canaanite jar had a rounded, sometimes pointed base that relieved interior pressure from a liquid at the most vulnerable points (Parr 1973: 176–77: also see chapter 15 by Leonard, this volume). Such pressure could crack the vessel walls and cause the container to split open, thereby losing the valuable contents. It is probably not a coincidence that large number of storage jars with rounded or pointed bases have been excavated at central Anatolian sites (e.g., Košay and Akok 1966: pls. 9–10; 1973: pls. 24–25; cf. Gorny 1990: 271–72).

4. Conclusions

Although the evidence is limited, we may say that viticulture and viniculture were well established in Anatolia from at least the beginning of the third millennium B.C. What may be described as a wine culture emerged under the Hittites during the second millennium, when wine, perhaps more than any other foodstuff, became central to the Hittite way of life. It served at that time not only as a dietary supplement for the elite, but as a symbol for all that was thought to be good and pure. Wine had a special significance in the privileged sanctum of the Hittite palace, as well as in the cult, where it was a principle means of communicating and supplicating the divine. Because it was a precious highly valued commodity with a purifying quality, wine came to symbolize life itself. In one sense, wine symbolized the relationship between god and man, for just as wine could be squeezed from the heart of the grape, so could life and prosperity be coaxed from the heart of divinity. As suggested in the epithet to this chapter, wine played an important role in the life of the Hittite elite being especially prominent in Hittite royal and religious life, and while it appears from the extant literature that the common folk of Hittite society did not actively participate in this wine culture, further excavation in non-royal, non-cultic contexts may well show that this conclusion to be premature.

Acknowledgments

I would like to thank Dr. Harry Hoffner of the Oriental Institute who graciously allowed me to make use of the Chicago Hittite Dictionary files for work on this article. I also wish to thank Mark Nesbitt, Patrick McGovern, Richard Beal, Joseph Baruffi, and Gregory McMahon for reading various drafts of this article and making very valuable comments and suggestions. Needless to say, the conclusions I have drawn are mine alone and do not necessarily reflect the opinions of those who made comments on the ideas contained in this paper.

Notes

1. This paper relies heavily on materials drawn from editions and publications of Hittite sources which because of their long names are here abbreviated. The primary documents and their abbreviations are as follows: Ankara Arkeoloji Müzesinde bulunan Boğazköy Tabletleri (ABoT); Istanbul Arkeoloji Müzelerinde Bulunan Boğazköy Tabletleri(nden) Seçme Metinler (IBoT); Keilschrifturkunden aus Boğazköi (KUB), Keilschrifttexte aus Boğazköy (KBo); Verstreute Boğazköi-Texte (VBoT). Other abbreviations as noted in the Chicago Hittite Dictionary.

2. The cuneiform text reads:

    GIŠGEŠTIN.HÁD.DU.A ma-aḫ-ḫa-an GEŠTIN-*ŠU* ŠÀ-it ḫar-zi GIŠ*ZE-ER-TUM*
    ma-aḫ-ḫa-an Ì-*ŠU* ŠÀ-it ḫar-zi DIM-ša *ŠA* LUGAL SAL.LUGAL
    ŠA DUMUMEŠ-*ŠU-NU* a-aš-šu TI-tar in-na-ra-u-wa-tar MUḪI.A GÍD.DA
    tu-uš-ga-ra-at-ša-an *QA-TAM-MA* ŠÀ-it ḫar-ak.

3. For discussion of the term Anatolia, see Taeschner 1960: 461 and 480.

4. For information on Turkish wine production, see R. Bleichsteiner 1951–52: 181–208; Lauer 1967: 220–45; Vámbéry 1913; and Köymen 1982: 41–43.

5. See "Turkish Wines Gain Recognition," in *Magazin*, Istanbul: Türk Hava Yolları (1989): 9.

6. Logothetis 1970: 51.

7. Logothetis 1970: 52; Hansen 1988: 48.

8. Logothetis 1970: 53, 74. Note, however, that, as Mark Nesbitt shared with me (personal communication), "in charred grape pips it would be a brave archaeobotanist who tried to deduce their area of origin."

9. For Early Transcaucasian culture, see Kelly-Buccelati 1974; Lisitsina 1984; and Sagona 1984.

10. H. Wenzel, *Die Steppe als Lebensraum: Forschungen in Inneranatolien*, vol. 2 (Kiel, 1937) is a valuable resource for central Anatolia that has been largely neglected because of associations in its title to Nazi Germany. Stephen Mitchell (*Anatolia: Land, Men and Gods of Asia Minor*, 1993, pp. 141–47) relies heavily on Wenzel in his own analysis of Anatolia's physical setting.

11. A particularly disastrous example occurred in 1873, as documented in several sources. See E. J. Davis, *Anatolica* (1874), appendix K, pp. 364–69; Capt. F. Burnaby, *On Horseback through Asia Minor*, vol. 1 (1877), p. 133; see also the letter by W. A. Farnsworth, chaplain in Caesareia (Kayseri) printed in *Levant Herald*, 29 July 1874, and quoted by Davis (1874) and Mitchell (1993: 145).

12. Appian, *Bellorum civilium* 5.4; Greek text cited in Mitchell (1993: 248, n. 40).

13. This data is collected from the records of the Turkish Department of Statistics and includes materials from the following volumes: *Meyva Istatistiği* 1937–39, no. 172, Ankara, 1942; *Meyva Istatistiği* 1938–42, Ankara 1944; *Meyva Istatistiği* 1941–45, no 277, Ankara, 1947; and Tarimsal yapi ve Üretim (Agricultural Structure and Production), no. 1633 Ankara: Devlet Istatistik Enstitütüsü Maatbası, 1991.

14. Supplemental climatic data can be found in S. Erinç, "Climatic Types and the Variation of Moisture Regions in Turkey," *Geographical Review* (1950: 224–35). This data covers the 19-year period from 1928 to 1946.

15. For vineyards (^{GIŠ}KIRI$_6$), see Powell 1977.

16. For relevant information on irrigation in contemporary Mesopotamian societies, see Stol 1976–80.

17. Forbes 1982: 259–61.

18. See, for instance, Houwink ten Cate 1983: 91–109.

19. Güterbock and Hoffner 1990b: 113

20. For Hittite laws, see Friedrich 1959; for complete English translations, see Hoffner 1963 and Goetze 1969.

21. Palmer 1990: 180–82, 189–90; see also chapters 17 by Palmer and 18 by Wright, this volume.

22. The designation GEŠTIN ŠA$_5$ is noted by Rüster and Neu (1989), but in looking through the files of the Oriental Institute only one questionable reference was located. While others may be available to Rüster and Neu, it seems clear that the designation is rather rare, perhaps an indication that it was taken for granted that the wine was normally red wine.

23. The question of what constituted "good wine" is not resolved, but there are several possibilities. It may be that this was a "first quality" wine variety or a wine made from the must of the initial crushing instead of from a later pressing. This phrase could also refer to an undiluted wine as opposed to a diluted one. By classical times, it had become a common practice to add other materials (pepper, capers, wormwood, etc.) to the wine, to improve its color, bouquet, and flavor. During the Roman era, only the finest wines went without some sort of treatment (Columella, *On Agriculture* 12.2:222). Such adulteration was already practiced in Hittite times (see discussion under "Hittite Wine Production," below) and it may be that wine described in their texts as either "good wine" (DÙG.GA / SIG$_5$-an-ta-an GEŠTIN) or "pure wine" (parkui-GEŠTIN) was simply a wine that had not been enhanced with additives.

24. The process of fermentation lies at the heart of wine-making, but it was not always controllable in ancient times. Both Greeks and Romans had difficulty arresting the fermentation process and wines generally had to be drunk within a space of three to four years or they would turn to vinegar. The Hittites probably faced the same constraints, and it is, therefore, not surprising to find Hittite wines

denoted in qualitative terms. The fact that there are so few references to "new wine" (GEŠTIN GIBIL) among the Hittite texts may indicate that the "new wine" was synonymous with the "sweet wine." Both wines would be anticipated to contain a high percentage of sugar. On the other hand, wine mixed with honey is called sweet wine in KUB 12.5 obv. i 21, and it may be that other instances of "sweet wine" in Hittite texts are to be understood as honeyed wines.

25. Hoffner (1967: 17–18) has shown that GIBIL (new) is often contrasted with LIBIR.RA (old). The combination GEŠTIN LIBIR.RA, however, does not occur (also see note 24).

26. The Sumerogram NAG appears frequently with GEŠTIN in a variety of forms where it stands for the Hittite word *AKUWANNAŠ*. Common examples are NAG-na and GEŠTIN NAG-aš (for NAG-na, see GEŠTIN NAG-na, wine to drink, KUB 55.54 i 21′–23′, also KUB 17. 24 iii 22; for NAG-aš, see GEŠTIN NAG-na-aš, wine for drinking, KUB 33.120 i 10).

27. The title GAL GEŠTIN (chief wine steward) provides an interesting point of departure for this discussion. The role of the GAL GEŠTIN (also GAL *ŠA* GEŠTIN, KBo 3.35.14 (Old Script); GAL LÚ.GEŠTIN, KUB 10.11 iv 29; cf. Hoffner 1974: 39–40; Pecchioli Daddi 1982: 535–37; and Beal 1986: 409–22) is of some interest because of the association with wine that the title immediately implies. Any role that he might have had in this network can only be speculated on, however, because his later history is much different. As we have already noted, the GAL GEŠTIN was an individual of some importance in the Hittite court. He already appears as an influential personage during the reigns of the first Hittite kings, and, by the time of the Hittite New Kingdom, had become one of the most powerful court officials at Ḫattuša. Although there is no textual evidence upon which to base a strong argument, the use of the symbol GEŠTIN in the title GAL GEŠTIN may provide some clues to the original character of this powerful functionary. We can speculate that from a lowly beginning, the office evolved into that of a high ranking general who, though serving under the authority of the king, could mount independent military actions (Hoffner 1974: 39–40; Beal 1986: 409–22). Exactly how such a transformation took place is unclear. Perhaps a more menial role in wine procurement preceded his rise in the palace hierarchy. In the *Festival for All the Tutelary Deities* we find a text connecting the GAL GEŠTIN with the king and wine. The text (KUB 11.21 8′–20′, McMahon 1991: 93) gives us a perspective on the relationship between the King and the GAL GEŠTIN, and may provide us with a clue as to his original position.

> [The king] comes down from the x [The chief of the wine stewards (?) holds out(??)] a storage container. [x] goes. The chief royal bodyguard is (there). [The overseer of the cooks (?)] and the chief of the wine stewards [walk] behind the king. [The overseer of the wait]ers [ho]lds out one thick bread to the king. The king takes it in his hand. [The overseer of the wait]ers breaks it open. He places it in [the storage container]. The chief of the wine stewards breaks [the storage contain]er. The chief of the wine stew]ards (!) gives a silver cup to the king. [The king] draws up the wine three times. Then he pours it out three times.

While the GAL GEŠTIN has a ceremonial function in this text, his role may hearken back to a position he enjoyed during the period prior to the introduction of written records in the Old Kingdom period. One can speculate that the GAL GEŠTIN originally had something to do with the procurement of wine or service to the king, and by serving wine to the king, the GAL GEŠTIN could have gained special access to the sovereign, perhaps eventually becoming a *confidant* in palace affairs. From this base, his position could have developed into that of a royal guardian, safeguarding the king against such things as assassination by poisoning, and from there into his semi-independent role in the military. A biblical analogy may be found in the rise of Nehemiah (Nehemiah 2). A position evolving along lines such as these is not unreasonable and would explain the continual advancement in the GAL GEŠTIN's status and the ultimate position of power and prestige that he came to enjoy.

28. The cuneiform text reads as follows:

> ki-i-ya-aš-ša-an ma-aḫ-ḫ[a-an ⌜GEŠTIN?⌝ K)U₇ ...]
> nam-ma-at (variant omits -at) an-tu-aḫ-ḫa-aš [(ku-wa-p)í e-ku-zi?]
> na-aš-za ni-in <-ik> (or: <ga>)-zi

nu-[(⸢uš-ši-kán ḫu-u-ma-an⸣) i-da-a-lu? ar-ḫa me-er-zi?]
šu-ma-ša-kán DINGIR.MEŠ-aš [i-da-a-lu ut-tar li-in-ga-iš]
ḫu-u-ur-ta-iš ⸢e-eš⸣[-ḫar iš-ḫa-aḫ-ru]
ar-ḫa *QA-TAM-MA* m[e-er-du]

29. The cuneiform text reads:

nu ^{GIŠ}GEŠTIN-aš ^{GIŠ}ma-aḫ-la-an ti-an-zi KI.MIN ^{GIŠ}GEŠTIN-wa
ma-aḫ-ḫa-an kat-ta šu-u-ur-ku-uš ša-ra-a-ma-wa
^{GIŠ}ma-aḫ-lu-uš ši-i-ya-iz-zi LUGAL-ša SAL.LUGAL-ša kat-ta
šur-ku-uš kat-ta-ma ^{GIŠ}ma-aḫ-lu-uš ši-i-ya-an-du.

30. The cuneiform text reads:

[EGIR-a]n-da-ma-kán GEŠTIN ar-ḫa la-a-ḫu-i nu-kán an-da k[i-iš-an me-ma-i]
[ki-i-w]a *Ú-UL* GEŠTIN šu-me-en-za-an-wa e-eš-ḫar nu-wa ki-i [ma-aḫ-ḫa an]
[ta-g]a-an-zi-pa-a-aš kat-[ta] pa-aš-ta [šu-me-en]-za-an-n[a e-eš-ḫar]
[ ]x-ya ta-ga-an-zi-pa-aš kat-t[a *QA-TAM*]-*MA* [(~)(~)(~)] pa-[a-šu]

[EGIR-an-d]a-ma A-NA GEŠTIN wa-a-tar me-na-ah-ha-an-da la-a-ḫu-i nu-[kán an-da]
[ki-iš-ša-a]n me-ma-i ki-i-wa wa-a-tar GEŠTIN-ya ma-aḫ-ḫa-an[im-me-at-ta-ti]

[EGIR-an-d]a-wa ki-i *NI-IŠ* DINGER^{LIM} i-na-[an-na] *<I-NA> RA-MA-NI* ^{MEŠ} [*KU*]-*NU*
[*QA-TAM-M*]*A* im-me-at-ta-ru

31. Forbes 1965: 31–32.

32. Palmer 1990: 83–87.

33. An interesting sidelight to the use of honey as an additive to wine is its possible detrimental side-effects. Although there is no mention of this danger in the Hittite texts, it has been discussed by several commentators on classical viticulture (Xenophon, *Anabasis* 4.8.22: 87; Pliny *NH* 23.44–45: 215–217; cf. Emerson 1908: 391–94).

34. See Palmer 1990 and chapter 17, this volume.

35. Beverages such as *marnuwa* (Güterbock and Hoffner 1990b: 193–95), *limma* (Güterbock and Hoffner 1990a: 62), *walḫi*, and *tawalit* are frequently noted alongside wine (GEŠTIN) in Hittite texts, especially as part of the troop rations (KBo 3.34 i 6–9). Though *marnuwa* and *walḫi* are generally felt to be different varieties of beer, the exact character of the other beverages is unclear.

36. Zohary and Spiegel-Roy cite Hopf (1961: 239) for evidence of *vinifera* at these two sites, but neither Troy nor Beycesultan is mentioned in her article as having produced any evidence for grape-growing. The only mention of grape pips in Hopf is from Middle Helladic Lerna (Level 4). There is mention of grape pips at Troy, however, in Schiemann (1953): 320, where it appears in Table 11.1 as entries no. 28 and 39.

37. For a description of classical presses, see Pliny, *NH* 18.317; cf. White 1975: 113 and 225–33.

38. Personal communication from Tony Wilkinson.

39. Descriptions and distribution of various Hittite vessels can be found in Gorny 1990, chapters 2 and 4.

CHAPTER 12

The Imagery of the Wine Bowl: Wine in Assyria in the Early First Millennium B.C.

David Stronach

1. Introduction

In an inscription which celebrates the inauguration of his new capital at Nimrud—ancient Kalhu—Assurnasirpal II (883–859 B.C.) provides a detailed account of the food and drink that was prepared for the almost 70,000 persons that were present on that occasion. In terms of liquid refreshment alone, we read of 10,000 skins of wine, 10,000 (measures of) beer, and 100 (measures of) fine mixed beer. Grapes also figured among the many fruits that were supplied (Wiseman 1952: 32).

Another passage in the same inscription refers to a new royal garden that was evidently constructed beside the mound of Nimrud, in a vicinity where canals and waterfalls could be introduced (Wiseman 1983: 142). Here, Assurnasirpal chose to plant the seeds, cuttings, and trees that had been collected on his far-flung campaigns. In one sense, therefore, this was a garden which demonstrated the fruits of imperial conquest (Stronach 1991: 171). In another sense, it was intended as a beguiling image of plenty: it was a garden in which, in one telling phrase, the pomegranate trees were "clothed with clusters of fruit like vines" (Wiseman 1983: 142).

It is possible to presume, in short, that both the bounty of the king's table and the fecundity of the royal garden were stressed with the same intent. That is to say that each of these images in the banquet inscription was designed to reinforce the same concept: the concept of the king as the provider of the fertility of the land.

The opportunity was also taken, in the course of the construction of Assurnasirpal's palace, to spell out a similar message in permanent visual terms. At two key points, the relief-clad walls of the throne room of the new palace show the same carved scene (Fig. 12.1a), which is at once a

Figure 12.1. Nimrud reliefs: a) (above) complementary images of the king and a winged genius stand on each side of a sacred tree, from the east end of Assurnasirpal II's throne room; b) (below) Assurnasirpal II seated in state. (Photographs courtesy of The British Museum.)

powerful icon for the legitimacy of the king and the fruitfulness of his realm. In this composition, confronted images of the king stand on each side of a highly stylized, sacred palm tree while a god in a winged disc—probably either Assur or Shamash—hovers directly above the vertical trunk of the symbolic tree. In an immediate reference to the circumstance that the domesticated palm tree always needs to be fertilized—and in a still wider reference to the place of the king in assuring the fertility and continuity of the land as a whole—two winged geniuses, each bearing the necessary implements for the pollination of the palm, stand at the outside limits of this singular design.[1]

In the long list of plants that were brought to the royal garden of Assurnasirpal for local cultivation, special note deserves to be taken of the grapevine. Even though the vine is known to have been under cultivation in northern Mesopotamia since at least the 3rd millennium B.C. (Renfrew 1987: 158; see also chapters 2 by Zohary, 9 by Powell, 10 by Zettler, and 11 by Gorny, this volume), and even though an early 2nd millennium text from Tell al Rimah mentions a wine producing locality that may have been located to the north of Nineveh (Dalley 1984: 90), there is remarkably little evidence on the whole for the production of grapes in the immediate vicinity of Assyria before the 9th century B.C.[2]

From the prestigious place that was given to the consumption of wine in Assurnasirpal's celebrated banquet, it is only reasonable to infer that the early 1st millennium B.C. rulers of Assyria were interested in more than a convenient, local source of grapes and raisins. Confirmation comes, moreover, from a number of separate clues which show that, within 9th to 7th century B.C. Assyria, wine was not only a popular drink but a commodity that could be used to denote rank and status. Indeed, as the present chapter will attempt to demonstrate, there are many reasons to think that the possession of wine, and the disbursement of wine, each came to be counted as telling elements in the expression of royal authority, not only in Assyria but in other adjacent and especially upland areas of the rest of the Near East.[3]

With reference to one of several canonical ways in which the Assyrian king could be represented, such 9th century monarchs as Assurnasirpal and Shalmaneser III can be seen to have turned with enthusiasm to the potent symbol of a drinking bowl—a recurrent attribute of gods and kings going back to at least the 3rd millennium B.C. (compare M. Haran 1958: 21–22). This telling emblem of successful stewardship—of prosperity and abundance—consists, in the Late Assyrian context, of one or another type of small, presumably gold, drinking bowl (see below), which is almost always shown elegantly balanced on the fingers of the right hand, in front of the body and at the level of the face.[4]

One of the prime monuments which underscores the extent to which the imagery of the drinking bowl was now being called upon is a relief of Assurnasirpal which depicts the king, seated in state on a backless throne, with a shallow, rounded bowl prominently displayed on the fingertips of his upturned hand (Fig. 12.1b). Those who wait upon the monarch include one attendant who holds a fly-whisk in the customary position for such an article above and behind the king's head, and a second attendant who, as the king's cupbearer, holds both a wine-server and a second fly-whisk (the principal purpose of which may have been to prevent flies from alighting in the royal wine).[5] The metal wine dispenser can be described as an open container with flaring sides, a nipple base, and a short handle. The handle is distinctively shaped in that its proximal end curves sharply downwards before terminating in a minuscule serpent's head. While other explanations for a handle of this shape may exist, it is not impossible that such a design allowed the dispenser to be hung, whenever it was not in use, on the lip of a larger vessel.[6]

A fragmentary strip of ivory (Fig. 12.2a), which is carved in the local Assyrian style of the 9th century B.C. (Mallowan and Davies 1970: 8), provides an equally instructive scene. The design shows a banquet scene in which, among other motifs, we see an attendant with a fly-whisk standing over a group of uncovered wine jars that are held in position by a table-shaped pottery

Figure 12.2. Banquet scenes from Nimrud, 9th century B.C.; a) (above) on an incised, fragmentary ivory strip (Mallowan and Davies 1970: pl. 5.7); and b) (below) on a glazed tile. Note the bunches of grapes suspended from the forward edge of the parasol which shelters the standing, drinking king. (Photograph courtesy of The British Museum.)

stand; a monarch who is seated before the first of a number of tables, a drinking bowl in his raised right hand; two standing body guards and the standing cupbearer of the king; and a series of further banqueteers, each apparently seated four to a table, who appear to include, in the position nearest to the king, a prince or a high official. Of particular interest in the present context is the equipment of the cupbearer. He again holds a fly-whisk in his more elevated hand and, even if the handle of his wine-server appears slightly longer than the dispenser of Fig. 12.1b, there is probably no reason to suppose that it represents a substantially different kind of object. The way that this latter vessel is held would suggest, moreover, that it was also meant to be tilted by a controlled movement of the wrist, in which case the wine itself was probably poured by means of a slightly pinched lip set at right angles to the position of the handle.

For the one incontrovertible representation of Shalmaneser III in a drinking pose, we have turn to that ruler's celebrated Black Obelisk, which dates to about 825 B.C. There, one of the upper panels documents the receipt of the tribute of Jehu, the king of Israel. In this scene Shalmaneser stands beneath the shade of a parasol with a wine bowl balanced on the fingers of his right hand and with his left hand resting comfortably on the hilt of his sword (Roaf 1990: 175). It is a relaxed and confident pose that was no doubt intended to underscore the extent of the difference between the Assyrian monarch and other rulers.[7]

2. The Nimrud Wine Lists

The next chapter in the history of wine in Mesopotamia owes much to the recovery of some 60 tablets, or fragments of tablets, that were excavated at Nimrud in the 1950s and the early 1960s. These 8th century B.C. records represent no more than a minuscule part of the once extensive archives that were originally maintained at this Assyrian capital in connection with the administration of wine rations. While the wine lists from the early part of the century were compiled for the most part between 791 and 779 B.C., that is to say during the last nine years of the reign of Adad-nirari III and the first four years of Shalmaneser IV (Kinnier Wilson 1972: 2), the remaining records stem from the reigns of Tiglath-Pileser III (744–727 B.C.) and Sargon II (721–705 B.C.) (Dalley and Postgate 1983: 22–24).

Few in number as these tablets are, they nonetheless suggest that rations of wine were made available to as many as 6,000 persons who counted, in one sense or another, as members of the king's household (Mallowan 1972: vii). Since the monarch's own allocation of wine is not alluded to, the first entry on most lists consists of that of the queen and her household. In this respect, the consorts of Adad-nirari III and Shalmaneser IV are each represented, if not named, and it is apparent that each received an identical, substantial allocation (Kinnier Wilson 1972: 44).[8] Other entitled individuals appear to range from officials of the highest rank to such menial figures as "shepherd boys and assistant cooks" (Mallowan 1972: vii).

According to information derived from these records, ten men were entitled to receive 1 *qa* of wine on a given day (or, perhaps more accurately, on a given festive occasion). The same measure, on the other hand, could also be given to only six skilled workers, and it is assumed that still more generous rates may have been available on the basis of one or another "special privilege" (Kinnier Wilson 1972: 117). With reference to other Assyrian units of capacity, one tablet records a ration issue of 1 *sappu* jar of wine for the harem of the "women of Arpad" (Kinnier Wilson 1972: 117), and reference is made elsewhere to a unit known as the *kasu* or "cup measure" (Kinnier Wilson 1972: 115).

It has to be said, however, that the exact quantity of all such rations remains a matter for debate. In particular, it has been pointed out that the results of certain experiments that were conducted some years ago on jars which were marked after firing with such Assyrian measures of capacity as the *qa*, *sutu*, and the *homer* cannot be used for "metrological investigation." (Powell 1984: 57; also compare, Powell 1990: 547–48, and chapter 9, this volume). Even if it seems clear, in short, that there were ten *qa* to the *sutu* and ten *sutu* to the *homer* (Kinnier Wilson 1972: 114), the *qa* itself can probably still only be defined in approximate terms as a measure of about one liter.

While one group of wine lists from Nimrud was recovered from the North West Palace and another was found more than 2 km away in Fort Shalmaneser, each group was still encountered in or near the location of a presumed wine cellar. Thus, one collection was found in ZT 30, a magazine of the North West Palace which formerly held two rows of huge storage jars, and the other was found in the vicinity of SW 6, a large magazine in the southwestern quadrant of Fort Shalmaneser, where narrow gangways were found to divide "serried ranks" of large jars that were "set in mud-brick benches" (Mallowan 1966: 407). Furthermore, both these presumed centers for the distribution of wine can be seen to have been conveniently placed with respect to those official quarters where many of the indicated rations were presumably required (Mallowan 1972: viii).

The sources of the wine that came to be stored at Nimrud in such great quantities—the vessels in SW 6 were capable of housing 4,000 gallons (Mallowan 1966: 408)—have already invited conjecture. A good part of the wine is likely, of course, to have been supplied by local Assyrian vineyards. In this respect, one of the traditional sources of wine, going back to the time of Shalmaneser III, was a locality known as Yaluna (Mallowan 1966: 384). Speculation on the location of Yaluna tends to place it to the east of Nineveh, in the direction of Aqra (Kinnier Wilson 1972: 111, n. 33), perhaps in the vicinity of the long renowned vineyards of the small hillside town of Ba'shiqa (Mallowan 1972: x). Still other wine came from farther afield. Mention is made in particular of Zamua, a highland district that was situated well to the southeast of the Assyrian homeland. In this last case, wineskins were certainly not the only kind of container in which wine for the royal household was transported, since one text makes specific reference to "a jar of Zamuan wine" (Kinnier Wilson 1972: 107).[9]

The source of a given wine was also not the only matter that called for notice in early 1st millennium B.C. Mesopotamia. Thus, while a reference to "sweet/good white wine" (Ebeling 1927: 290.1) supports other evidence to the effect that red and white wines were distinguished in this period (for the 2nd millennium B.C., cf. chapter 9 by Powell, this volume), additional references can be found to such categories as "bitter wine" and "strong wine" (Landsberger and Gurney 1958: lines 182–83). Still other texts speak of "sour wine" (=vinegar?) and of "early wine" (Landsberger and Gurney 1958: line 187). And while it has been suggested, no doubt correctly, that much of the wine that was drunk at this time would have been "immature" (Mallowan 1972: xiv), there are explicit references, from both early 2nd millennium B.C. Mari (Finet 1974–77: 127) and Late Babylonia (King and Thompson 1966: line 37.15), to "aged wine."[10]

3. Zoomorphic Drinking Vessels

A somewhat different class of evidence emerges from the second half of the 8th century B.C., especially from the time of Sargon II when Assyria was fast approaching a second pinnacle of power. In a series of reliefs from his palace at Khorsabad—ancient Dur Sharrukin—Sargon goes out of his way, for example, to record not only the drama of the sack of the Urartian city of Musasir at the close of his eighth campaign in 714 B.C., but also something of the nature of the subsequent festivities.

One of Sargon's reliefs that can be cited in this regard shows a number of attendants in the process of drawing wine from an elevated cauldron before proceeding to the site of a banquet (Fig. 12.3a). Three of these attendants hold an apparently bucket-handled, lion-headed situla in each hand, and the last of them is depicted in the act of still filling one of his two vessels. At the scene of the banquet itself, an elegant table divides two pairs of courtiers, each of whom lifts a lion-headed vessel in his right hand (Fig. 12.3b). These same banqueteers are seated on backless Assyrian chairs and, as befits their less than regal station, their feet are shown dangling in the air rather than resting on a footstool.[11]

One question which very naturally arises is whether the zoomorphic vessels that are shown in Sargon's reliefs should be connected with indigenous, late 8th century B.C. Assyrian metalwork or with plunder of this same date from the city of Musasir (cf. Young 1958: 152, n. 27). In one series

Figure 12.3. Reliefs from Khorsabad showing a) (above) several beardless attendants employ lion-headed situlae to draw wine from a cauldron before proceeding to the site of a banquet; and b) (below) a banquet scene showing a standing attendant and a number of seated nobles holding lion-headed vessels. (Botta and Flandin 1894: pls. 64 and 78, respectively.)

of reliefs where numerous precious items, including two lion-headed situlae, are being carried in procession towards the king by various Assyrian attendants (cf. Botta and Flandin 1849: pl. 16), there is every reason to suppose that samples of booty are represented. It is one thing, however, to allow that vessels of this kind could have existed outside Assyria and quite another to assume (as some scholars would seem to have) that this same form would not have been in production in contemporary Assyria.

If one should in fact choose to marshal all possible support for an "Urartian only" solution, such an argument would have to take much of its force from the fact that no lion-headed vessels are depicted in any Assyrian relief before the time of Sargon. Also, because Sargon's reliefs appear to give so much prominence to the lion-headed shields which served to decorate the walls of the temple of Haldi (Fig. 12.4a) before they were carried off to Assyria (Fig. 12.4b), it could be argued that each of the many lion-headed drinking vessels in the Khorsabad reliefs should themselves constitute items of plunder.

The problem with this last line of reasoning is that it fails to take all aspects of the available evidence into account. It is clear, for example, that Urartu neither invented the zoomorphic beaker nor exercised any kind of monopoly over the early use of the form. Animal-headed beakers of fine pottery are already present in some quantity at Kültepe at the beginning of the 2nd millennium B.C. (Özgüç 1986: pls. 115–17; see also Gorny, chapter 11, this volume), and there is abundant textual evidence from 18th century B.C. Mari to show that similar zoomorphic beakers were being regularly produced in precious metal, either for local use or as diplomatic gifts (Dunham 1989: 213).[12] Furthermore, Late Assyria did not lag behind its neighbors as a center of fine metalwork; rather, it was home to a large and active industry that was not only notable for its own characteristic products, but also for its evident ability to absorb exotic forms and then to transmit such forms elsewhere (Curtis 1988: 92).

It is of course true that no lion-headed vessels have yet been found *in natura* in Assyria itself. But this is by no means the whole story. Not only is it clear that the evidence of the bas-reliefs cannot always be taken as a reliable guide to the first moment at which a given class of object began to be used in Assyria (Curtis 1988: 87), but an ample number of textual references can be cited to show that lion-headed situlae or beakers were employed in Assyrian court and religious circles from at least the 8th century B.C. onwards (Parpola 1979: pl. 1.2; Deller 1985). Indeed, it is now known that such vessels even find a place in the Nimrud wine lists (Dalley and Postgate 1983: nos. 135 and 144).

The presence of animal-headed drinking vessels in Assyria in the 8th and 7th centuries B.C. is affirmed by the recovery of a single bronze ram's head beaker that can be dated to ca. 800 B.C. (Kepinsky and Lebeau 1985: 55), and by the parallel excavation of a good number of somewhat later either whole or fragmentary ram's head beakers of fine pottery.[13] The list of pottery ram-headed beakers from Assyria includes one example from an early 7th century house at Nimrud (Mallowan 1966: 191–93, no. 124), a second specimen from a terminal Neo-Assyrian occupation at the small site of Khirbet Khatuniyeh to the north of Mosul (Curtis and Green 1986: 76 and pl. 4), two examples from Assur (Haller 1954: pl. 26d; Klengel-Brandt 1992: pl. 125), the head of a fifth beaker from Tell al-Hawa (Ball 1990: 83 and pl. 28.4), and part of the head of yet another such vessel from a probable 7th century B.C. context in the lower town of Nineveh.[14]

This brief review of the place of zoomorphic drinking vessels in early first millennium B.C. Assyria cannot close without some reference to the drinking equipment that was found at Gordion, in the capacious tomb chamber of Tumulus MM. Amidst the splendor of what has been called the "most comprehensive" of all Iron Age drinking sets (Moorey 1980: 195), the University of Pennsylvania expedition of 1957 found two animal-headed bronze situlae. Although these two vessels, one of which is lion-headed (Young et al. 1981: 121, pl. 3) and one of which is ram-headed

Figure 12.4. Reliefs from Khorsabad showing a) (above) the sack of the temple of Haldi at Musasir; and b) (below) the victorious Assyrians chopping up a metal statute, weighing booty, and carrying off a plain situla, a lion-headed shield, and a cauldron with a slim splay-footed stand. (Botta and Flandin 1849; pls. 140 and 141, respectively.)

(Young et al. 1981: 122, pl. 4), are noticeably "finer and more elaborate" than the rest of the bronze vessels from the tomb (Young et al. 1981: 122) and, although vessels of this particular design are otherwise unparalleled in any Phrygian context, it has nonetheless been argued that they could represent articles of indigenous Phrygian workmanship (Knudsen 1961: 260–72).

A suggestion that the lion-headed vessels in the Khorsabad reliefs were neither pieces of booty from Urartu, nor articles of local Assyrian manufacture, but examples of tribute that Sargon could have received from King Midas of Phrygia in 718 B.C. (Young et al. 1981: 123) is clearly in line with this latter interpretation. This argument is one that does not allow, however, for the statement made by Sargon in his annals for 709 B.C. (Luckenbill 1927: para. 43) that the Phrygians had not submitted to him before that time. In addition, as the text of the Gordion monograph in the end indicates (Young et al. 1981: 123, 265–66), the situlae from Tumulus MM could owe at least part of their inspiration to a more southerly source.[15] Indeed, if any Syro-Mesopotamian place of manufacture should be posited for the two Gordion situlae, a workshop in North Syria would not be an improbable point of origin.[16]

To return to the evidence from Khorsabad, if any single item in either Fig. 12.3a or 12.3b might be connected with the representation of booty from Musasir, the most likely object would appear to be the distinctive metal cauldron that is shown in Fig. 12.3a. The principal supporting evidence comes from another Khorsabad relief (Fig. 12.4b) which shows a group of Assyrian shoulders carrying off a variety of Urartian objects, including a bronze cauldron. Yet, the available data is not without its ambiguities. It is obvious, for example, that the creators of the Khorsabad reliefs, who seem to have tried to be precise in so many particulars, did not make the two depicted cauldrons in Figs. 12.3a and 12.4b look exactly alike. Thus, while both cauldrons exhibit a relatively shallow bowl and a tall stand with a splayed foot, the vessel in Fig. 12.4b appears to have both a more slender stand and a more widely everted rim. Also, while just enough can be seen of the top of the stand of the cauldron in Fig. 12.4b to suggest that it was without any distinctive molding just below the bowl, one of the more striking features of the other splay-footed cauldron (Fig. 12.3a) is a large ribbed moulding which occupied a point very close to the top of the stand.[17]

It may also be noted that, while bronze mouldings with drooping leaves or sepals were common to both Urartu and Assyria, the precise form of the moulding on the cauldron in Fig. 12.3a is remarkably similar to that which is found on an item of furniture from Nimrud (Mallowan 1966: 396, pl. 322) and that a further prominent (if different) "collar" was also located near the top of the splayed stand of a cauldron of the time of Assurbanipal (see, conveniently, Albenda 1976: fig. on p. 60). But whether or not the tall footed vessel in Sargon's celebratory banquet scene would have struck a contemporary audience as an exotic product (and it seems to me that this can hardly be known for certain at the present time), it should be underlined that many of the vessels that have usually been called "cauldrons" may never have been intended for the heating of liquids but rather, as Moorey (1980: 192) has indicated, for the serving of drinking water, wine, or even, as in a Greek symposium, a mixture of wine and water.[18]

That large "blending bowls" of this kind should have been just as much at home in Urartu as anywhere else is, perhaps, only to be expected. In descriptions of his northern campaigns, Sargon appears to place an unusual emphasis, directly or indirectly, on the presence of grapes and wine when in the territory of Urartu. Thus, in one case he refers to the Urartian city of Ulhu where "the trees were loaded with fruits like bunches of grapes" (Thureau-Dangin 1912: line 223; Wiseman 1983: 137), and in another passage he compares certain of the fortified cities of the region to wild grapevines growing on the mountainside (Luckenbill 1926: 33, 84). In addition, Sargon's detailed account of the events that took place in and near Musasir not only describes the way in which the Assyrians cut down the local orchards and grapevines, but it also asserts, in a pointed reference to the customary privileges of the Urartian king, that this action was one which "(thus) made drink unavailable to him" (compare Thureau-Dangin 1912: line 265).

Before taking final leave of Khorsabad and proceeding to consider the nature of other late 8th to late 7th century B.C. evidence, it may not be out of place to recall that the members of one of the early expeditions to this site came remarkably close to the experience of seeing and smelling (but not reportedly tasting) the still recognizable traces of a wine of Assyrian date. In the course of his pioneer excavations in the palace of Sargon at Khorsabad, Victor Place found one magazine (Room 139) to be of unusual interest (Place 1867: 102–3). Although the huge jars in the magazine were for the greater part shattered, some were preserved to a certain height. These examples were carefully cleaned in such a way as to expose "une sort de pâté ou de mastic noirâtre." Not long after this intriguing discovery the work was interrupted by a torrential downpour of rain. Then, when Place returned to resume the excavations, he noticed that, where the rainwater had gathered in the jars, the black paste had become diluted to a violet tint which he found to be close to the color of wine dregs. At the same moment, he was struck by "une odeur singulière, rappelant celle d'une cave abandonnée," which further reinforced his impression that he could have exposed the last remnants of a wine that was 2500 years old. This finding was so unexpected, however, that he decided to summon two of his colleagues in order to explore their reactions. They too were unanimous that what could be seen consisted of the dregs of wine diluted by water; and a like verdict was returned by three of the local foremen.

It is a matter for regret that this memorable moment in the annals of Mesopotamian excavation took place at a time when the residues in question could not be subjected to a closer analysis than that provided by sight, smell and, one may presume, taste. All the same, however, the episode deserves fresh notice; and for Place himself there was reward enough. From all that had transpired, he felt able to assert that Room 139 had been nothing less than "le cellier du Palais" (Place 1967: 123).

4. Side-Spouted Strainer-Jugs

Moorey has already demonstrated that metal wine sets make their first appearance in the Western Asia in Syro-Palestine, probably as a consequence of Egyptian influences, from whence such sets "travelled westwards, some perhaps from Cyprus, in the eighth and seventh centuries B.C., to Greece and Italy" (Moorey 1980: 197). At the same time, there appears to have been a contemporary, more easterly counterpart to such a movement of ideas and designs, which was closely connected to the ceremonial consumption of wine—if not also the consumption of beer (compare Sams 1977: 108–15)—and which can be said to find its expression in certain exchanges that took place between the metalshops of at least Assyria, Phrygia, and North Syria. The sudden, relatively brief popularity of side-spouted strainer-jugs can illustrate something of these last exchanges, not least because a case can be made for the association of these unusual vessels with the ever greater prestige that was beginning to be attached to the possession of metal drinking sets.

The evidence in question is represented in part by a gold side-spouted jug with a high vertical handle and a rounded base, which was found at Nimrud in July 1989 during the excavations of Muzahim Mahmud Hussein of the Iraqi Department of Antiquities and Heritage. It was discovered in the third of the rich vaulted tomb chambers which are now known to have been constructed under the private quarters of the North West Palace. The short trough-spout of this unusual vessel has a built-in sieve, and it can be assumed that this same form became one of several separate types of utensil that were eventually available for the purpose of filtering wine at the royal table.

Since the best parallels in metal to this side-spouted jug from Nimrud are currently represented by a single side-spouted bronze jug dating to ca. 750 B.C. from Tumulus W at Gordion (Fig. 12.5a),

Figure 12.5. a) (top) side-spouted bronze jug with a built-in sieve, from Gordion, ca. 750 B.C. (Young, et al. 1981; pl. 88d); b) (middle) Assyrian bronze filter bowl with an original base sieve and a secondary trough-spout and strainer (Moorey 1980: pl. 3b); c) (bottom) Gold bowl from Nimrud with a slightly flaring rim and a relatively shallow, vertically ribbed wall. (Photograph courtesy of *The Los Angeles Times*, November 13, 1989.)

and by two other bronze examples dating to ca. 700 B.C. from Tumulus MM (Young et al. 1981: pl. 59), it is tolerably certain that sieve-spouted vessels of this unusual design were originally a Phrygian, or at least a central Anatolian, invention.[19] It is apparent, moreover, that the Nimrud jug has different proportions, viz., a rounded base rather than a ring base, and three bands of repoussé decoration, one of which shows a battle scene rendered in an Assyrian style. For all of these reasons, it is possible to infer that Assyrian goldsmiths chose to borrow (and to then transform) the original Phrygian model.

That metalsmiths from other regions were also engaged in producing their own versions of this special form is indicated by a number of clues from North Syria. Thus, while one bronze vessel with a side spout (Fig. 12.6a) is known from Tell Halaf (Akurgal 1968: Fig. 12.91), other vessels of this same general kind are shown being carried in to a feast in a late 8th century B.C. bas-relief from Carchemish. It is notable in fact that one figure in this latter relief (Akurgal 1968: pl. 32) appears to hold a side-spouted wine server in one hand and a drinking bowl in the other hand. This association might indeed be used to refute an earlier contention that side-spouted jugs were intended to allow a drinker to pour a liquid "directly from the spout into his mouth" (Young 1960: 230), and it would seem to strengthen an alternative view that such jugs "were for transferring liquid from the large, deep blending bowls to the drinking bowls" with the aim of "extracting alien matter in the filter as this was done" (Moorey 1980: 196).[20]

In contrast to the situation in Anatolia, however, side-spouted strainer-jugs were never imitated in pottery in Assyria. Indeed, it is more than probable that filter funnels (Fig. 12.6c) or filter bowls (Fig. 12.5b) each continued to act as a complement to side-spouted servers (Fig. 12.6b) during the last century or so of Assyrian rule. In terms of the legacy of these last Assyrian vessels, it is also worth noting that a number of them came to be supplied with a tall, strongly bent handle (such as was to become a still more tightly curled element in many ladles and strainers of Achaemenid date) and that handles of this

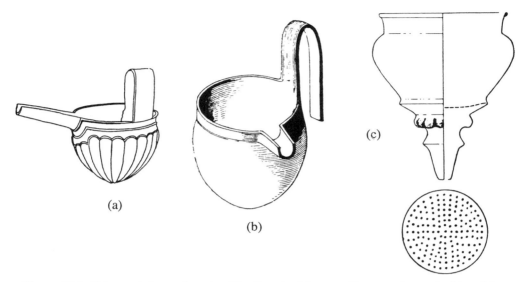

Figure 12.6. Side-spouted vessels and a filter-funnel: a) bronze side-spouted vessel of late 8th century B.C. date from Tell Halaf (Akurgal 1968: fig. 91); b) bronze example of design closely similar to 12.6a, from Nimrud, late 7th century B.C. (Layard 1853; fig. on p. 181); c) bronze filter-funnel from Nimrud, late 7th century B.C. (Moorey 1980: fig. 5).

kind could already be given the kind of elegant zoomorphic terminal (Fig. 12.5b) which was to become such a ubiquitous trait in the course of the Achaemenid period.[21]

5. Royal Drinking Bowls from Assyria

More than half a dozen bowls from two of Nimrud's most important new tombs (Tombs 2 and 3) now complement a range of otherwise only indirect evidence for the changes in design and decoration that almost certainly overtook the gold drinking bowls of Assyria between the accession of Assurnasirpal and the fall of the empire in 612 B.C. In particular, four of the bowls from Tomb 2 are inscribed and these each carry, as an indication of ownership, the name of one of three queens. In chronological order, the queens who are named are Yaba, the wife of Tiglath-Pileser III; Baniti, the wife of Shalmaneser V (726–722 B.C.); and Atalia, "queen of Sargon, king of Assyria" (George 1990: 29). It is true that none of the bowls from Tomb 3 (or indeed any of the other objects that can be associated with the secondary use of this apparently 9th century B.C. vaulted chamber) are similarly inscribed; but nonetheless much of the remarkable metalwork from this tomb looks as if it should also date from during or near the reign of Sargon II (721–705 B.C.).[22]

It is evident, for example, that none of the newly discovered bowls from Nimrud conform to the design of the shallow, plain type of metal bowl (Fig. 12.7a), which was so popular with the 9th century B.C. rulers of Assyria. Most of the gold bowls from the new tombs instead belong to a single basic design in which a slightly flaring rim was combined with a pronounced shoulder and a relatively shallow lower body (Fig. 12.5c). Apart from a representation of a possibly related metal bowl type (Fig. 12.7b), which was originally to be seen on a relief of the time of Tiglath-Pileser III (Barnett and Falkner 1962: pl. 47a), the closest parallel (particularly if we discount the compression of the lower body and the height of the flaring rim) would appear to be represented by a bronze bowl from Nimrud (Fig. 12.7c) that was found in a grave beneath the floor of room 13 in the North West Palace, probably of the latter part of the 8th century B.C. (Mallowan 1966: 116; compare also Hamilton 1966: pl. 2). But whereas the latter vessel has a plain lower body, the lower bodies of the new gold bowls tend to be highly decorated, either by slim vertical ribs (Fig. 12.5c), by horizontal fluting on the shoulder, or by some still more eye-catching device, such as an overall, studded surface. Yet, the Nimrud bronze bowl (Fig. 12.7c) joins a number of the new gold bowls, including that in Fig. 12.5c, in showing several bands of finely engraved lines on the neck and in possessing a handsome centerpiece in the form of a repoussé rosette.

Each of the various shouldered gold bowls from Nimrud is representative, in fact, of the generic carinated bowl of Assyria. It is an indigenous form, which had its origins in the Middle Assyrian period and which was particularly at home in both metal and pottery during the 8th and 7th centuries B.C. (Curtis 1988: 89; Oates 1959: 132, pl. 37,59). A strong indentation at the top of the shoulder is of course a recurrent feature in bowl design that can be traced all the way back to Halaf bowls of the late 6th millennium B.C. But while this feature is likely to have provided certain structural and functional advantages from the outset, it was suggested some years ago that the sharp indentation in the side walls of Late Assyrian bowls (Fig. 12.7c) could have answered one highly specific purpose. According to this thesis (Hamilton 1966: 2), a bowl of this design (such as would have been ideal for drinking "a liquor" that was consumed "in relatively small quantities") would also have been able to catch any "unpleasant sediment" in its sharp shoulder at the moment that it was drained. Such a line of reasoning may or may not carry conviction (and, if anything, it could be viewed as pertaining with still more force to bowls with deep gadroons), but at the very least it does draw attention to the need for a more rigorous search for the organic remains of wine—and other liquids—in such containers.

Shoulderless, sub-hemispherical drinking bowls were more rarely encountered in the new tombs. While one sumptuous example consists of a gold "Phoenician" bowl, a second gold bowl, with an omphalos base and a striking petal design, could prove to be a local product. It is true that the latter vessel bears a certain resemblance to the petal-decorated omphalos bowls of Tumulus MM at Gordion (Young et al. 1981: pl. 70) but at the same time it could well represent a Mesopotamian version of the same type[23]—and hence a forerunner of a later type of silver bowl that came to be attested in Achaemenid Susa, not to mention other parts of the far-flung Achaemenid world (compare Hamilton 1966: fig. 6a; Stern 1982: figs. 240–41).

Finally, it is worth stressing that the precise kind of bowl that is held by Assurbanipal's consort in that monarch's "banquet relief" of ca. 645 B.C. is not represented among the newly recovered bowl shapes from Nimrud. In other words, this type of almost flat-based bowl with large, more or less circular gadroons on the body (Fig. 12.6b) is only likely to have emerged as one of the more preferred Assyrian bowl shapes during the course of the 7th century B.C.[24]

6. On the Representation of Grapes and Vines in Neo-Assyria

Grapevines are depicted in Assyrian reliefs on only one occasion in a 9th century B.C. context. On the now lost relief, a vineyard is shown beyond a walled city which is under attack (Barnett and Falkner 1962: pl. 118). Unfortunately, the location of the city is uncertain, and all that can be concluded is that it lay in a region that was already conspicuous for its viticulture.

From the second half of the 8th century B.C. onwards, however, grapes can be shown to be illustrated in a number of striking ways. Thus, the ivories from Nimrud include a fragmentary, Assyrianizing piece in which two confronted, beardless males each reach up with one hand to clasp one of the many clusters of grapes which hang above them, either suspended from slim tendrils or from the palmette-like appendage of a winged sun (Strommenger 1964: pl. 266).

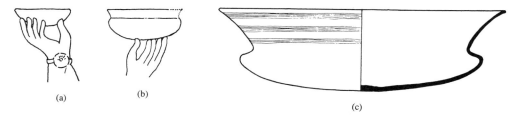

Figure 12.7. a) Drinking bowl in a relief of Assurnasirpal II at Nimrud (compare Fig. 12.1); b) drinking bowl as depicted in a relief of Tiglath-Pileser III; c) a bronze example of late 8th century B.C. date, from Nimrud. (Hamilton 1966: figs. 5b, 5c, and 1b, respectively.)

Whatever is to be made of the relationship between the winged disc and the "grapevine" in this composition, a more explicit reference to the grapevine as a symbol of divine plenty comes from an imposing relief that was carved into a rock face at Ivriz in northwestern Cilicia. In this relief we see a local ruler, Warpalawas of Tuwana, who paid tribute to Tiglath-Pileser III in the year 738 B.C., and who continued to rule until at least 710 B.C., standing before the anthropomorphic form of the storm and vegetation god, Tarkhunzas (Hawkins 1982: 421, 439). The latter figure not only suspends a bunch of grapes from his right hand, but he is also distinguished by two massive bunches of grapes which in part cover his belt and which can be seen to hang from a live vine that twists obliquely round his body (Roaf 1990: figure on p. 181). In keeping with the increasingly vital role of viticulture in the Near East, this appears to be the first occasion in which the vine is associated in visual terms with a deity of fertility.

Amidst the discovery of so much else from the Nimrud tombs which has documented the remarkable wealth and craftsmanship that was available to the Assyrians towards the end of the 8th century B.C., particular note should be taken of the unique crown of a queen that was found in Tomb 3. A complex construction, it consists of a thick canopy of gold vine branches that stands connected to a richly decorated gold headband by eight-winged, apotropaic, female figures. Furthermore, numerous small bunches of grapes, either carved from lapis lazuli or from silicate material of the same color, can be seen to dangle from either the circumference of the elevated canopy or from the lower edge of the rosette-decorated headband. For now, no comparable object is known from ancient Assyria.

Only a little less remarkable in some ways is the manner in which vines emerge as an almost commonplace feature of the landscape in the reliefs of Sennacherib (704–689 B.C.) (Bleibtreu 1980: 131–39). To mention only two instances, they are shown in the hills adjacent to the Judean city of Lachish (Frankfort 1970: pl. 101), where they were apparently trained to grow both with and without props (Albenda 1974: 6); and they are prominently portrayed in the rolling country-side to the north of Nineveh, where Sennacherib took a direct interest in the work of his quarry masters (Reade 1983: pl. 50).

Nonetheless, it is the reliefs of Sennacherib's grandson, Assurbanipal (668–627 B.C.), which seem to place an almost mystical stress on the presence of the vine, at least as it represented in the parks and gardens of Nineveh. This is apparent, not least, in a peaceful, almost paradisiacal scene which is known from several fragmentary reliefs. In these reliefs, the artist has drawn musicians with their instruments, servants leading hunting dogs on the leash, standing and striding lions, and a resting lioness. The tranquil quality of the scene is completed by flowers of different kinds that alternate with date-palms and coniferous trees, and a series of vines, heavy with fruit, which twine round the trunks of the conifers and which stretch out to end in long forked tendrils (Reade 1983: pl. 76).

It is this last motif that forms a link with the celebrated relief which depicts Assurbanipal and his consort, Queen Assur-shurrat, at ease in a garden setting (Fig. 12.8a). As one commentator has pointed out, the royal couple appear to be taking refreshment under the shade of an arbustum, an elaborate covering of grape-laden vines (Albenda 1974: 6). In order to construct such a natural canopy, separate vines were presumably planted on each side of the intended arbor, and these vines were then "wedded" or twisted round the trunks of paired conifers before being trained to meet across the intervening space (Albenda 1974: 6).

The extent to which it is possible to retrieve the full significance that was attached to this grape-laden bower of vines is far from clear. In keeping with what we know of the ancient world, there may well have been many separate levels of interpretation. To some degree, the imagery in question was undoubtedly attached to the traditional role of the king as the maintainer of the prosperity of the kingdom. In particular, the productive associations of the palm tree would now appear to have been increasingly challenged by those of the trained and luxuriant vine; and, as can be surmised from the somewhat earlier relief of Warpalawas, the abundance that could be derived from (a) the favor of the gods and (b) the piety of the monarch was beginning to be most readily expressed through an unequivocal association of the ruler with the vine and its fruits.

On another plane, one should not forget that Assurbanipal's "banquet scene" was at the center of a victory celebration. In terms of prior Assyrian reliefs, it served as a complement, in other words, to both the ceremonies which extolled Sargon's victory at Musasir and to the representation of Sennacherib, enthroned on a hill near Lachish, at the time of the submission of that city. Thus, while the tumult of battle was reserved for other carved slabs, this small gem of a relief (Fig. 12.8a) would still have been viewed as containing a number of explicit references to the recent defeat of Elam. At the very least, these included the decapitated head of the Elamite ruler, Teumman, which had been brought from the field of battle to hang from a metal ring near the top of a tree, and the forced attendance of a number of Elamite dignitaries (whose only apparent part in the occasion was to play the role of servants) (Reade 1983: pl. 101).

With reference to other outdoor scenes in which a motif of overarching vines can be seen to have played a symbolic role, earlier parallels can be cited from both Elam and Egypt. In the case of Elam, Amiet (1986: 159, figs. 113–14) has already drawn attention to the striking similarities that exist between the composition of Assurbanipal's vine-shaded banquet scene and the composition of a number of seal designs of early 2nd millennium B.C. date from Anshan—the upland, viticultural region of ancient Elam. In these seals, it is possible to discern, in several instances, a divine couple feasting beneath the shade of a grape-laden vine. Both the god and the goddess hold a drinking bowl in one hand and, in the presence of the grapes which dangle above them, there can be little doubt that such miniature vessels were understood to be filled with wine. It is apparent, moreover, that while the god always sits on a throne with a table beside him, the goddess occupies an unusual kind of platform (Amiet 1986: fig. 113.5). From such a range of parallels, it is not beyond the bounds of possibility (even if these correspondences are assuredly distant in chronological terms), that Assurbanipal chose—in the specific circumstances of this triumphal scene—to appropriate a still extant, traditional Elamite formula for prosperity and well being.

With reference to Egypt, it is possible to point to the parallel popularity, in at least the second half of the 2nd millennium B.C., of a design in which either one or two figures sit inside a throne kiosk, sometimes beneath the shade of an overarching vine. Such kiosks are also frequently decorated with bunches of grapes which hang from the flat ceiling (compare Davies 1930: pl. 11a)—a motif which probably did not take long to spread elsewhere (Fig. 12.2b). Furthermore, the notion that Assurbanipal had somehow settled the disputes of his time, and could therefore rest

Figure 12.8. Relief from Nineveh: a) (above) to the accompaniment of music, Assurbanipal and his queen take refreshment in a vine-shaded garden setting; and b) (below) part of Fig. 12.8a showing Assur-shurrat, the consort of Assurbanipal, and a portion of the feasting-couch on which the king reclines. (Photographs courtesy of The British Museum.)

from his labors, would clearly not have been complete without certain specific allusions to Egypt and the western territories of the Empire. In this connection, a manifestly non-Assyrian type of necklace that is suspended from one end of Assurbanipal's feasting-couch (Fig. 12.8b) has been plausibly interpreted as either a gift or a trophy of Egyptian origin (Albenda 1977: 35)—and even the distinctive royal couch itself could well represent an Assyrian version of a prestigious item of furniture which was first made fashionable well to the west of the Euphrates.[25]

7. Conclusions

The very varied kinds of evidence which can now be seen to document the importance of wine-drinking equipment both inside and outside the limits of the Late Assyrian homeland, the records that survive for the wide disbursement of wine within the king's household in the 8th and 7th centuries B.C., and the indications that can be found, at least from the latter half of the 8th century onwards, for an increased reliance on the grapevine as a new emblem of power and prosperity, can all be said to underline the extraordinary place that wine came to occupy in Assyria during the first half of the 1st millennium B.C. In the starkest terms, if you possessed wine at this time, you were not slow to flaunt it; and, if you normally lacked this same commodity, you could do little more than deplore the high cost of its acquisition. As a Babylonian, that unusual and highly interesting monarch, Nabonidus (555–539 B.C.), was keenly aware that the vine would not grow in a substantial part of his dominions. Thus it is that we have his terse—and rueful—definition of wine as that drink "of the mountains, which is unavailable in my country" (Röllig 1964: 248).

Acknowledgments

It is a pleasure to acknowledge that I profited significantly, while I was gathering material for this paper, from discussions with many colleagues including, in particular, John Curtis, Stephanie Dalley, Crawford Greenewalt, Jr., Kent Hillard, Roger Moorey, Oscar Muscarella, Marvin Powell, Michael Roaf, Irene Winter, and Richard Zettler.

Notes

1. In this instance, Assyrian royal iconography still adheres (albeit in an extremely stylized manner) to a long-standing Mesopotamian emblem of plenty and prosperity: the palm tree. For further commentary on the motifs in this relief, see especially Mallowan (1966: 97–98) and, more recently, Winter (1983: 16).

2. While the relatively small number of texts that have been published from the Middle Assyrian period could offer one explanation for this unexpected circumstance, it is also worth noting that the mid–2nd millennium B.C. tablets from Nuzi appear to take little note of either grapes or wine (see chapter 9 by Powell, this volume).

3. This is not to say that wine lacked prestigious connotations in the Near East before this date. In the 18th century B.C. kingdom of Mari, for example, wine was not only abundant at the royal table but was also used by the monarch as an instrument through which he could reward his subjects (Finet 1974–77: 122–31; see also chapter 10 by Zettler and Miller and chapter 9 by Powell, this volume). The way in which the possession of wine comes to be so repeatedly stressed in the iconography of Late Assyria is, however, particularly striking.

4. This motif bears an especially striking resemblance to a device that is known from cylinder seals of Akkadian to Ur III date (compare Winter 1986: 260–61, pl. 62.4; Collon 1987: 35–36, nos. 107, 118, 121, 122). In this late 3rd millennium convention one of the distinguishing marks of elite rank consists of a small cup that is held in front of the body and displayed on the fingertips of one hand.

5. The post of chief cupbearer was one of considerable consequence. Occupants of the post not only had charge of the king's wine, but probably also had to test it for poison. In keeping with privileges enjoyed by members of the royal family and other notables of the realm, the chief cupbearer was also permitted to present offerings of suitable merit in the temple of Assur, in the city of Assur (Fales and Postgate 1992: xxxv–xxxvi).

6. For the manner in which the handles of certain late Assyrian specialized metal vessels certainly came to be shaped for more secure suspension, see Fig. 12.5b and especially Fig. 12.6b.

7. Note, among still other representations which show either Assurnasirpal or a later 9th century B.C. Assyrian king in the act of holding a drinking bowl, both the standing royal figure on a fragment of ivory from Nimrud (Mallowan and Davies 1970: pls. 112) and that depicted on a glazed tile from the same site (Fig. 12.2b). In this last representation, moreover, the bunches of grapes on the underside of the royal parasol would seem to provide a clear indication as to the nature of the drink that was being consumed.

8. It may be assumed, following Finet's review of the evidence for an earlier period, that wine for the king's personal use was drawn from a separate "cru supérieur" (Finet 1974–77: 127). At the same time, however, the generous allotments of wine that were extended to the households of two successive Late Assyrian queens do much to recall a further parallel with 18th century B.C. Mari, where, according to Finet's calculations, the allowances of wine that were placed at the disposal of Zimri-Lim's queen would have permitted that politically and administratively active personage to assume an additional role as a "dégustatrice privilégiée" (Finet 1974–77: 130).

9. A tablet from Nineveh of probable 7th century date also refers, most interestingly, to a jar of wine brought from as far afield as Helbon in Lebanon as well as to another from Izalla in Turkey. Each comprised part of an offering that was presented in the temple of Assur, in the city of Assur, by the Queen of Assyria (Fales and Postgate 1992: 182, no. 184).

10. Separate reference is also made to "libation wine" (Kinnier Wilson 1972: 112), and one may presume that precisely such a liquid is depicted in the well-known relief of Assurbanipal (Strommenger 1964: pl. 260), which shows that monarch using a carinated bowl to pour a libation over four lions that he had just killed.

11. While the lofted vessels in Fig. 12.3b appear to be handleless—a circumstance that would make them beakers, not situlae—it is legitimate to wonder if these vessels were originally intended to be understood as such. Any situla that was already held in the hand for drinking purposes would necessarily have had its handle folded downwards (and hence, arguably, out of sight), and the "cinematic" or sequential nature of a good number of Assyrian reliefs could well—if the slightly smaller size of the lofted vessels is not crucial—indicate that the courtiers were represented in the act of drinking from the very same vessels that had just been charged with wine. (After all, the designer of this complex set of scenes can already be shown to have ignored, in Fig. 12.3a for example, the ring attachments that must have once secured the handles of the vessels depicted there.) With reference to yet another subject, the sequence of events in the two reliefs does not show the moment—if there was such a moment—at which the individual draughts of wine were sieved, in order to remove any remaining alien matter. If this indeed happened at any point between the time that the wine was drawn from the cauldron and the time that it was imbibed, it could always have occurred at the moment that the wine was transferred (if in fact it were transferred) from the bucket-handled vessels of the attendants to the "beakers" in the hands of the courtiers. Either way, however, we may note a situation which still called for some experiment in drinking equipment: for the banqueteers at this particular celebration must have either run the risk of encountering foreign matter in their wine (unless it had been very well sieved before it

was placed in the cauldrons) or they must have had to wait for those in attendance to produce a separate series of utensils with sieves, in order to be sure that their wine would be free of impurities.

12. For references to similar vessels of precious metal in Hittite texts of the 14th–13th century B.C., and for two apparent examples of such Hittite zoomorphic cups, see Muscarella (1974: nos. 123–24).

13. Assyrian influences may also account for the character of certain of the engraved designs (including the depiction of two ram's head beakers in a pottery stand) that distinguish a bronze bowl that was recently recovered from a mid–7th century B.C. tomb at Arjan in Southwest Iran. Compare Majidzadeh 1992: 133–44, fig. 1.

14. D. Stronach et al. Forthcoming. Note also, in the broad context of these comments, both the extensive listing by Calmeyer (1979) of Near Eastern animal-headed vessels; and the more recent survey of Muscarella (1988b: 24–26), which draws direct attention to the corpus of metal animal-headed vessels from Hasanlu IV. Of special interest is the unusually high date (pre-800 B.C.) of the Hasanlu pieces—a circumstance that leads Muscarella to certain quite far-reaching conclusions, namely, to claim that the Assyrians discovered vessels of this kind "as a result of their incursions into Iran," and to assert that the situation provides "an example of a motif that was transmitted from Iran to the West" (Muscarella 1988b: 26). By and large, however, it may be advisable for the present (especially if we give due weight to the absence of any major destruction level within late 9th century B.C. Assyria, not to mention the fact that we still lack any direct evidence for the full variety of vessels that might have been interred with a Neo-Assyrian king or prince) to attribute the seeming precocity of the animal-headed vessels of Hasanlu IV to the accident of excavation.

15. For further observations of significance, see Muscarella 1988a: 185–92, where the view is expressed that the two much-discussed situlae should most probably be left "out of the corpus of Phrygian bronzes."

16. For recent comments on the vigor of the North Syrian metal industry in the early 1st millennium B.C., see Muscarella 1989: 340–41.

17. As far as the true shape of the kind of large cauldron that is to be seen in Fig. 12.4a is concerned, it is possibly worth observing that, while the Assyrian artist was apparently content to imply that the shallow base of each squat vessel was masked by the top bar of its associated rod-tripod, this economy of effort may have been misread by the gifted, and ordinarily irreproachable, Eugène Flandin. In the absence of the original relief (which was lost while it was in transit to Paris), there can of course be no certainty, but it would appear that Flandin was misled into thinking that the deep curve of some kind of U-shaped brace was to be equated with the lower outline of each supported vessel. For the existence of extra bracing bars in rod-tripods from Urartu, compare, for example, the inverted V-shaped bars in a tall bronze stand from Altintepe (Azarpay 1968: pl. 30).

18. In this last respect, it could be significant that the contents of two bronze "cauldrons" from the North West Palace at Nimrud happened to include, in a heterogeneous collection of metalwork that appears to have been stored in them between the two sacks of Nimrud in 614 and 612 B.C. (compare Moorey 1980: 193), a side-spouted wine server (Fig. 12.6b) and a handleless filter bowl (Fig. 12.7b) (Layard 1853: 177, 181).

19. Apart from the fact that vessels of this kind may be descended from an older Hittite form, a Phrygianizing Lydian sieve-spouted (pottery) jug can be said to document the markedly long survival of this shape in Western Anatolia (see *The Bulletin of the Metropolitan Museum of Art*, January 1968, p. 199 and pl. 8).

20. Whether or not the Phrygians used such side-spouted jugs for the consumption of wine is a moot point. For the case that can be made for beer, see Sams 1977: 108–15.

21. Note in particular the presence of an unmistakable duck-head terminal on a bronze ladle of terminal 7th century B.C. date from Carchemish (Woolley 1921: fig. 48).

22. This provisional chronological estimate is based on what could be seen of the large number of outstanding objects from both Tombs 2 and 3, which were very promptly placed on public exhibition following the conclusion of the 1989 season at Nimrud.

23. Compare, for example, a late 8th century B.C. glass bowl with a petal design, which was found at Gordion, but which is presumed to represent an object of "Assyrian manufacture" (Young et al. 1981: 32, 235).

24. The extent to which this and other observations (compare Curtis 1988: 89, n. 9) should perhaps lower the dates that have been ascribed to other bowls with a flat base and heavily protruding gadroons, such as one example from Nimrud which is currently ascribed to the 8th century B.C. (Mallowan 1966: 430, fig. 357), is not an issue that can be given further space here. On the other hand, it may be appropriate to insist, with reference to the new evidence that is now available for the nature of royal plate in Late Assyria (not to mention the well-known testimony in I Kings 10:21, to the effect that "all king Solomon's drinking vessels were of gold"), that the personal drinking bowls of Assurbanipal and his queen would not have been made, as has sometimes been suggested (cf. Hamilton 1966: 4), of silver. Only gold would have sufficed.

25. Apart from the fact that the matching top panels on the legs of Assurbanipal's couch each appear to exhibit a late version of the Syrian "woman at the window" motif (Frankfort 1970: 190), there is the vivid testimony of Amos' warning to the profligates of 8th century B.C. Samaria: "Woe to those who lie upon beds of ivory and stretch themselves upon their couches ... who sing idle songs to the sound of the harp and ... who drink wine in bowls" (Amos 6:4–7). In addition, there is a distinct possibility— perhaps reinforced by the fact that the *kline* makes its initial appearance in Greek art of the 8th century B.C. as "a bier on which a dead body is displayed" (Boardman 1990: 122)—that the feasting-couches of both Greece and the Near East could owe their ultimate origin to the high-legged funerary biers of Egypt.

CHAPTER 13

The Earliest History of Wine and Its Importance in Ancient Egypt

T. G. H. James

1. Introduction

It seems to be a function of philosophers and wise men to encourage moderation in all activities of life. There are some even, the real spoil-sports of the *dolce vita*, who would counsel not just moderation but positive restraint to the point of denial of any level of physical gratification. In Egypt, there has always been a tradition of puritanism which fits well into the strict tenets of Islam in respect of eating and drinking. A quick consideration of the lives led by the early Christian anchorites who swarmed in the Thebaid and in the region just to the west of the Delta—good, potential wine-producing land (Waddell 1936) would soon indicate a general desire on their part to renounce the pleasures of life. How typical was the so-called sage who addressed advice to the vizir Kagemni supposedly, and perhaps actually, in the early 6th Dynasty, about 2300 B.C.?[1]

> When you sit with company
> Shun the food you love;
> Restraint is a brief moment,
> Gluttony is base and is reproved.
> A cup of water quenches thirst,
> A mouthful of herbs strengthens the heart;
> One good thing stands for goodness,
> A little something stands for much.

The last line, in a sense, points to the rather differently intentioned saying: "A little of what you fancy does you good." How can a few words bear such contrary senses? Easily, it would seem, according to the purpose of the speaker and the nature of the audience.

There is plenty of evidence from the New Kingdom in Egypt (see chapters 14 by Lesko and 1 by Grivetti, this volume) that excess in matters of eating and drinking was thought to be reprehensible, and in an ideal society the vice of drunkenness would not be approved. Yet, there are several vignettes included in the banqueting scenes of New Kingdom tombs to show that even in the kind of ideal life pictured in the tomb-chapel of a dead Egyptian official, the occasional guest went beyond the mark.[2] And it may be deduced from at least some of these vignettes that what caused the socially unacceptably behavior was the drinking of wine.

By the time of the New Kingdom, ca. 1550 B.C., it would seem that wine-drinking, although not practised at all levels of society, was far more common than in earlier periods. No doubt, methods of production and distribution had improved sufficiently by the middle of the 2nd millennium to allow greater availability than formerly. It would be very hard to prove such a contention from the evidence from just one site (the Theban Necropolis), much of which is repetitive. The kind of evidence, found in such abundance for the New Kingdom at Thebes, exists only patchily for the Old and Middle Kingdoms; and at these times also there is a bunching of evidence from particular sites, which tends to produce unbalanced pictures. Nevertheless, something can be done even with such an incomplete record.

2. The Early Dynasties

The evidence for wine production from the very start of the historic period—the beginning of the 1st Dynasty in about 3000 B.C.—is incontrovertible, although its interpretation depends much on what is known of later practice. It would also be much more informative if the hieroglyphic script had developed beyond the label stage which is one of its greatest characteristics in the formative period of the early dynasties. In the 18th Dynasty and later (see chapter 14 by Lesko, this volume), it was the practice to mark wine jars with the kinds of information that wine-drinkers down to the present day find useful and instructive: date (vintage), maker (vigneron), and source (château or domaine). It has therefore been assumed that similar information may be included on the inscriptions found stamped on the heavy mud stoppers placed on top of the wine jars deposited in the royal and great-official tombs of the first two dynasties.

Such wine jars have been found in abundance at Abydos and Saqqara, many of them badly damaged, but a few are sufficiently complete to give a good idea of what a jar looked like after it had been filled and stoppered.[3] It was, without stopper, approximately two and a half feet tall, pointed at the base, and sometimes with one or two raised bands just at and below the shoulder of the jar.[4] The mouth with rounded lip was about 6 inches in diameter, and the body of the vessel at its widest point might be about 10 inches in diameter. Some vessels, also possibly for wine, were as much as 15 or 16 inches in diameter. The pottery ware is of the typical reddish-brown color, produced by ordinary Nile alluvial mud when fired; the surface shows no sign of having been coated with any liquid-proof substance (Lucas 1962: 19–20). Such ware has a tendency to porosity, which, on the one hand, could make for cool contents by external evaporation, but, on the other hand, would not bode well for the extended jar-life of the wine inside.

The mouth of the jar was covered with a saucer-shaped pottery lid, and the whole was then sealed by a huge lump of yellowish mud, usually shaped in a conical form, roughly smoothed, and brought down to the shoulder of the vessel. A small vent, kept open probably by the insertion of a hollow reed—not always clearly obvious—allowed the gases of final fermentation to escape. This vent could subsequently be sealed with a little more mud. The whole process of filling and sealing the jars must have been one of carefully judged stages; but, as ever with the technical activities of antiquity, one must always give substantial credit to the specialists, in this case the winemakers. Experience counts for much more than theoretical knowledge, and practical winemakers will surely confirm that at the final point, knowing how the wine is working and what steps should be

Figure 13.1. Cylinder seal impression of King Khasekhemwy, with the name of Memphis and the vine-arbor sign. (Kaplony 1963–64: fig. 310.)

taken in uncommon circumstances, makes all the difference between the production of a good wine, and making something rather ordinary, if not utterly bad.

Almost the final act in the bottling process was the application of what might be called the vineyard's imprimatur. It involved the running of one or two cylinder seals over the mud-cone stopper while the mud was still soft enough to take an impression of the inscription carved on the seal.[5] An essential component of the inscription was the name of the king reigning at the time. To this extent, the contents of the vessel could be dated, for the application of the seal would necessarily follow very soon after the wine was put into the vessel: here, we are talking of hours rather than days. In the 1st Dynasty the inscription might consist solely of the king's name, shown written in a *serekh*—a simplified representation of a palace and its panelled facade, which was topped by the image of the falcon, the god Horus, personification of the living king (compare Figs. 13.2 and 13.4). A second impression, providing rather more information and becoming more common in the 2nd Dynasty, may contain in addition to the royal name, place names often enclosed in ovals representing walled precincts or estates, which are in some cases interpreted as being the places where the wine was produced.[6] More convincing are those seal impressions which contain the vine hieroglyph and recognizable names. For example, one has the name of Memphis, Egypt's first capital city, in its early form "White Walls" (Fig. 13.1). Another names Buto, one of Egypt's former capitals, located in the northern Delta (Kaplony 1963–64: 3: figs. 310–11; see 2:1135). These two seal impressions are dated to the reign of the king Khasekhemwy, last of the 2nd Dynasty, ca. 2650 B.C. The elusive nature of the evidence derived from seal impressions, in general, unfortunately prevents a satisfactory picture to be built up of early wine production, even though it is clear that much wine was made at the time.

It may, however, be possible to crawl a little closer to certainty by approaching the matter more obliquely. A great deal of nonsense has been written about the origins of the vine and of wine in Egypt, much of it based on the fanciful ideas purveyed by classical and post-classical writers, whose authority in other matters of early Egyptian culture are known to be wholly unreliable (Darby et al. 1977: 551–95). The vine does not belong naturally to the native flora of Egypt, and it has been suggested that it may have been introduced into Egypt from Western Asia during predynastic times (see chapter 2 by Zohary, this volume). Grape pips are reported from 4th millennium B.C. contexts at El-Omari, to the east of the Nile and a few miles to the south of Cairo (Renfrew 1973: 127). A recent publication of the site (Debono and Mortensen 1990), however, contains no mention of grapes in the archaeobotanical reports. There is no suggestion that they

 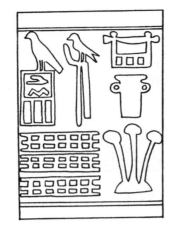

Figure 13.2. Cylinder seal impression of King Den, showing a hieroglyph for a press, probably an oil-press. (Kaplony 1963–64, figs. 238 and 239.)

represent the raw material for winemaking; indeed, such a suggestion would be ludicrous in the circumstances of their discovery. But El-Omari shows, in many aspects of its simple material culture, connections with contemporary Near Eastern cultures (Hayes 1966: 122). If the introduction of the wine to Egypt can be credited to foreigners, possibly traders from the east, then it would not be unexpected to find the earliest vineyards in that part of Egypt first to be entered by Asiatics, namely, the eastern Delta (as reported at Tell Ibrahim [Awad], by O. Thanheiser, personal communication; also see Thanheiser 1991: 41, for Early Dynastic grape pips from Tell el-Fara'in [Buto] in the northwestern Delta).

Some exasperation has been expressed about the inexplicit nature of the hieroglyphic legends found in the impressions of cylinder seals of the early dynasties. In one matter, however, it is more than reasonable to consider individual signs, which are also known from later and better comprehended texts, as clearly identifiable and providing reliable evidence of the existence of particular things at this early time, when they are not otherwise known. A prime example is the hieroglyph which represents a roll of papyrus, tied up and sealed, predating by several centuries the first known written papyrus document. There are two signs found in these early texts, which have strong resonances tor the student interested in wine. But, even for these two, caution needs to be sounded. The first sign occurs on seal impressions dated to the reign of Den (Fig. 13.2), fourth king of the First Dynasty (ca. 2350 B.C.). It shows what has most reasonably been identified as a press (see Fig. 13.3, hieroglyph A) (Kaplony 1963–64: 3: pl. 67, figs. 238–39), and beneath it is a sign showing a wide-mouthed, two-handled vessel (see Fig. 13.3, hieroglyph B). Unfortunately, the best and clearest representations of winepresses, which have so far been found in tomb scenes of the Old Kingdom below, show nothing as well constructed or apparently efficient, as this early sign suggests. The alternative is to take it as an oil-press, an interpretation supported by the nature of the two-handled vessel, of a kind not commonly associated with wine in Egypt at that early time. In fact, no vessels approaching the shape shown have so far been found in excavations. On balance, therefore, it is probably safer to see the sign as being of an oil-press; in time, clinching evidence may turn up.

The second sign is rather more encouraging. In good hieroglyphs of later times, hieroglyph C in Fig. 13.3 is used to determine the word for "grape" and related words (Gardiner 1957: 484, no.

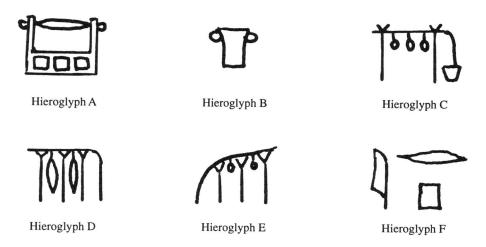

Hieroglyph A Hieroglyph B Hieroglyph C

Hieroglyph D Hieroglyph E Hieroglyph F

Figure 13.3

M.43). It undoubtedly represents a vine growing out of what appears to be a pot or basket, and supported on forked poles. The identification is confirmed by larger and more detailed pictures of vines in tombs of the Old Kingdom. Seals of Khasekhemwy (Fig. 13.1), already mentioned, include hieroglyph D in Fig. 13.3; and others (Fig. 13.4), of the reign of Zoser of the 3rd Dynasty, just a little later in date, show it as hieroglyph E in Fig. 13.3 (Kaplony 1963–64: 3: pl. 82, no. 309; pl. 84, nos. 316–18). The appearance of this sign in these impressions demonstrates, surely without any question, that at least by the last years of the 2nd Dynasty, vines were being cultivated on poles, i.e., as arbors, as they would be for the next two thousand years, if the evidence provided by tomb-scenes can be trusted.

Although the wine jars found in tombs of the early dynasties, up to the 3rd Dynasty, exhibit through their seal umpressions something of date and origin, the information falls far below what is found on the jars of the New Kingdom, dealt with in detail by Lesko (chapter 14, this volume). For the later jars, the details of date, maker and origin are written directly on the vessel; the stoppers themselves will be stamped, but often with only a royal identificatory label. So, from the stopper, you will know that the wine was made and bottled in a particular reign, while from the ink inscription on the jar you learn the regnal year, but not the royal name. Sadly, there is a huge gap in the provision of this kind of useful information from the early Old Kingdom down to the late 18th Dynasty. Material evidence relating to wine scarcely exists for this long period; and since Egyptian archaeology is largely restricted to the evidence from tombs, the implications for the careful study of the continuing tradition of winemaking are serious. The archaeological record, however, reveals some extraordinary facts, not least of which is the extent to which early important burials were serviced with food and drink in a most lavish manner.

It is apparent that when the great tombs of the early dynasties were built, the provisions, which were included in the many magazines that occupied the superstructures, were not seen as token offerings from which the deceased could draw token sustenance in his afterlife. The deposits of wine, in particular, were huge (see Emery 1961: 13, 20), far surpassing, for example, the twenty-six or so jars placed in King Tutankhamun's burial (chapter 14 by Lesko, this volume). Here was a real resource for eternity. In one *mastaba*-tomb at Saqqara, dated to the reign of Djet,

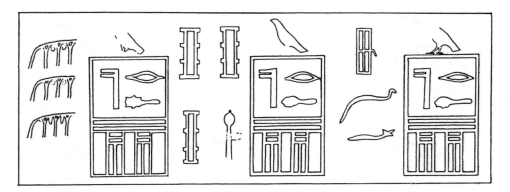

Figure 13.4. Cylinder seal impression of King Zoser, showing the vine-arbor sign and the name of Memphis (Kaplony 1963–64, fig. 317.)

third king of the 1st Dynasty, many hundreds of pottery vessels were found, most, perhaps all, of which could have contained wine.[7] Deposits of such a size are in marked contrast to the modest representation of wine containers in burials of later periods, even when making allowance for the damaged and incomplete nature of most burial equipment. Pottery is among the least desirable of objects for the tomb-robber, and wine jars would have had little attraction if the wine were superannuated, or just evaporated. The absence of jars, therefore, cannot be put down to simple theft. The solution to the problem must lie in the development of the offering inscription or stela, which in its listing and enumeration of the most essential physical requirements of the deceased, did away with the necessity of crowding a burial with huge quantities of food and drink and other obligatory commodities.[8]

The inclusion of stelae was made initially, as it would seem, in the less grand tombs of the early dynasties—those tombs, in fact, whose owners would not have been able to go well-equipped to the afterlife. At the outset, the offering stela was simple, and carried a representation of the dead person seated at a table of offerings piled with symbolic loaves of bread; an inscription, showing little of the precise organization of signs, which was later to be so characteristic of Egyptian monumental texts, might include a title (or two) and the name of the deceased, and a series of ideograms of standard offerings, occasionally accompanied by a few identificatory hieroglyphs with precise consonantal values.[9] Wine is included in the form of a clearly identifiable wine jar, but without clinching hieroglyphs spelling out the word for wine (*irp*). One of the earliest private stelae which displays a well set out offering list was found at Saqqara, and was made for a controller of leather-workers(?) named Imti (Fig. 13.5). It is dated to the late 2nd Dynasty and shows a fine, conically sealed, wine jar beneath the offering table, and includes in the offering-list, in its own compartment, a wine jar with the hieroglyphic sign for "one thousand." Here, then, was Imti guaranteeing for his future life a very adequate provision of wine, which would remain a valid and renewable quantity as long as the stela survived intact. It was certainly intact in 1953, but was subsequently stolen from the Antiquities Service magazine at Saqqara. One may hope that it still survives somewhere, still providing magically posthumous food and drink for Imti, over four and a half millennia after his death.

Figure 13.5. Stela of Imti, with early offering-list. (Smith 1981:49.)

3. The Old Kingdom

A better fate may be contemplated for Wepemnofret, a member of the court of Cheops, builder of the Great Pyramid at Giza, and second king of the 4th Dynasty (about 2530 B.C.). His fine stela is in many ways an enlargement of that of Imti, but it is better provided with text and more elaborate in its design.[10] Here, in the splendid enumeration of offerings, wine occurs, fully written (see hieroglyph F in Fig. 13.3; but with a metathesis of the second and third signs), and determined with a pair of wine jars in what seems to be a wicker frame; as with Imti, 1000 jars is the allotment. The practice of using two wine jars to determine the word for wine becomes almost standard in the hieroglyphic script. The reason has never been satisfactorily explained (Gardiner 1957: 530, no. W21). One may only surmise, frivolously, that for the Egptian wine "connoisseur" "the other half" was just as important as the first drink was for the devoted beer-drinker.

There can be no doubt that in the basic order of priorities, as far as funerary offerings were concerned, beer was in an unassailable position vis-à-vis wine. The standard requirement was for bread, beer, oxen, geese, cloth, and natron. These were the specially selected items that were closely associated with the offering table. But, there was much more that was desirable, and during the Old Kingdom, the list was extended progressively, until it became relatively fixed by the 6th Dynasty. The beginnings of the list can be seen in the stela of Wepemnofret; its extended form, representing a kind of fixed "menu" can be found in the tombs of the great officials of Teti, first king of the 6th Dynasty (about 2323–2291 B.C.), buried at Saqqaar in the neighborhood of the king's pyramid. For example, in the list carved in the burial chamber of the vizir Khentika, five approved wines are listed (James 1953: 64, pl. 36). The first is simply "wine," although elsewhere it is "northern wine," surely a wine from the Delta. The second entry is *"abesh*-cups of wine"; *abesh* has been taken to mean a particular kind of wine, although the word seems to denote a special kind of vessel. The third is *"sunu-*wine" formerly thought to have come from the region of the town Pelusium on the eastern border of the Delta; it is now thought that *sunu* should be identified as the border town of Sile (Cheshire 1985; Meyer 1986: 6: col. 1172). The fourth is *"hamu*-wine" possibly coming from vineyards around Lake Mareotis in the western Delta. The fifth wine, called "of Imet," used to be traced to the region of Buto in the northern Delta; a more correct identification would assign it to Nebesha in the eastern Delta; In the Khentika list, these five wines form part of a series of drinks, for each of which two cups are modestly requested.

These five varieties of wine became more or less standard in later offering lists; they demonstrate the rather haphazard way in which particular items might, for inexplicable reasons, be elevated to canonical status. They occur earlier in the offerings specified in the texts inscribed within the pyramid of Unas, last king of the 5th Dynasty; and even there, the signs of uncertain identification are evident in miswritings.[11] It would not be sensible to rely on this five-wine selection as a guide to the best wines available in the Old Kingdom, any more than on the 1855 classification of the wines of the Médoc as a textbook guide for late twentieth century drinking. The latter may, however, be taken to be the more reliable than the former.

What can be accepted is that wines of different qualities from different sources were drunk by the higher ranks of society in ancient Egypt, and were thought to be suitable constituents among the necessities for a good afterlife. What an individual may have drunk as a matter of course during his life would have been another matter. If it were beer, there was no problem in brewing it on a regular basis domestically, whether the household was small or large.[12] With wine, however, things were different. To make wine, you have to be able to lay your hand on sufficient grapes at the time of the grape-harvest, and in antiquity that would have meant owning your own vineyard and all the necessary equipment for wine production. The inscriptional evidence for the owning of private vineyards and the making of wine is minimal, the only useful early source being the biographical inscription from the tomb of Metjen, an official in charge of many Delta estates, and the owner of substantial lands himself.[13] Metjen, who exercised his official duties during the early 4th Dynasty (about 2550 B.C.), is an excellent example of one whose life and career were firmly based in the Delta. Yet, he was buried at Saqqara. Of his family home and estates, he says "a house of 200 cubits in width and 200 cubits in breadth was built and equipped, planted with good trees; a very large lake was constructed in it; figs and vines were planted ... trees and vines were plentifully planted, and a great deal of wine was made there." He goes on to describe briefly the establishing of a large vineyard within his domaine.

From Metjen's laconic account, it can be seen how vineyards for the production of wine were being established for private purposes in the mid-3rd millennium B.C.; and it must be supposed that the same was happening at least as early as the beginning of the 1st Dynasty, although this conclusion is reached more by implication than by direct evidence. Saqqara, where Metjen's tomb was, held tombs of many of the greatest of Egypt's officials, sited near the pyramids of the kings whom they served, especially for the 5th and 6th Dynasties. It is in some of these tombs that the most informative scenes of early wine-production may be seen. They are found in the complex tomb-chapels, not burial chambers, and they take their place among the many scenes making up the large repertoire of representations of domestic, craft and industrial activities, which were supposedly practiced in the houses, private estates and official domains where the tombs owner lived and carried out his functions. The reality which lay behind what was shown may not have been quite as depicted; for the tomb-scenes were never intended to be precise and comprehensive,

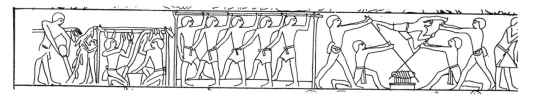

Figure 13.6. Winemaking scenes from the tomb of Ptahhotep. (Davies 1900; pl. 21.)

but only representative. So, the showing of wine-production in a tomb did not necessarily mean that the tomb-owner had owned vineyards and made wine in his lifetime, but only that he expected to enjoy the benefits of wine in his afterlife. The means by which he could insure that this could best happen, were firstly, the inclusion of jars of wine in the burial provision; secondly, the expectation that wine might be offered to his spirit regularly after death by his devoted *ka* (or spirit) servant; thirdly, the entry of wine in his offering-list or menu; and fourthly, illustrating winemaking on the walls of the tomb-chapel, thereby providing for a constant supply of magical vintages for posthumous enjoyment.

For the purpose of studying the ancient methods and techniques of viticulture and wine-production, the tomb-scenes of the Old Kingdom provided excellent general evidence;[14] but it must be kept in mind that the evidence ought not to be pressed too hard to extract the last drop of possible information. The scenes have a magical, though strangely practical purpose, and the artists who prepared them may not be reproducing processes that they have actually witnessed. It is also evident that there was a repertoire of scenes which was drawn on for the decoration of any tomb—perhaps not exactly in the form of a pattern-book—and details were copied from tomb to tomb without necessary regard for precision of detail. Nevertheless, the various sets of vine and wine scenes, studied with a knowledge of Egyptian artistic conventions, and a liberal dose of common sense and skepticism, undoubtedly permit a good general view to be obtained. One further proviso needs mentioning at this point: the scenes on a tomb wall are shown successively, usually in one or two of the parallel registers into which the decorated surface of a wall is divided, with no indications of time intervals. So, picking, treading, pressing, bottling, sealing, etc., follow each other without any note of the many intervening—often the trickiest—stages encountered in careful winemaking. Again, judicious interpretation is called for.

As was noted above, the hieroglyph used to determine words for vine and grapes shows a vine growing out of what seems to be a pot or basket, and supported in arbor-form by forked poles. Vines are shown growing in this fashion in most of the surviving Old Kingdom scenes. The arbors may be represented simply or in some detail, the main stem of the vine rising out of what seems to be some kind of contained area, possibly a specially prepared pit, bounded with a raised rim of stone or plastered mud to allow controlled and concentrated watering to be carried out by hand; such watering from small vessels is shown in some scenes (Fig. 13.6). It is certainly incorrect to think that vines were grown out of pots or baskets; such would not have allowed the satisfactory development of root systems. The ripe grapes, always colored blackish-blue in the early scenes, are picked by men kneeling on one knee beneath the arbor, presumably because arbors were at about that height, perhaps four to five feet. In the tomb of Ty at Saqqara, among badly damaged wine scenes (Wild 1966: pl. 171), are the remains of the picking stage. Here the vine appears to be growing in an upright form, and the men who pick are standing. It has been suggested that a different method of viticulture is being represented, with the new year's vine shoots growing straight from the ground, in the manner of what has been described as the form of culture known to the French as *la vigne basse*.[15] Unfortunately, the suggestion is erroneous. An examination of a careful copy of the scene shows, at the top of the scene, just the end of one forked pole and part of the horizontal pole which would have supported the vine arbor. If the whole scene had been preserved, it would have shown the standard form of vine culture, although certainly in a very splendid version. The standing pickers, are picking from outside the arbor, and therefore do not need to kneel.

In all cases, the bunches of grapes are plucked rather than cut from the vine, and the word used in the legends that accompany the picking in some scenes, suggests "tearing," not cutting.[16] Certainly no form of *sécateur* or scissors was available at this early period, and a well-developed horny thumbnail would have been as much use as anything else. From vineyard to vat, the grapes are carried in baskets and dumped directly into the treading-trough.[17] It is impossible to determine from an inspection of the best preserved scenes of treading, whether the trough was round or rectangular in area, and whether it was made of stone or some other materials. A circular form seems more likely than one with corners, and, on the basis of other domestic structures, it is probable that the trough was made of sun-dried mud brick, well caulked and smoothed with Nile mud, and finished off with a hard layer of gesso-plaster, which when dry would present the white appearance found in tomb reliefs. Stone treading-troughs, if used, might have survived from antiquity, but none has so far been discovered in excavation. Discoveries in the future might well lead to a modification of opinion in this matter. Durability, however, would not have been a prime requirement; if they were made of mud, as suggested here, the construction of new troughs would have taken very little time, and could have been done on an annual basis. The suggestion that troughs were made of wood seems very implausible (Lutz 1933: 53).

Treading is shown to be carried out by teams of men who support themselves in the trough by holding on to a horizontal pole slung across the trough; they give the appearance of standing passengers in a bus or subway train (e.g., Duell 1938: 2: pl. 116; also see Davies 1900: pl. 21). Treading grapes is a slippery business. To insure efficient treading, the stamping of the operators is synchronized by men striking a rhythm with batons or clappers (Duell 1938: 2: pls. 114, 116). Usually there are two men, shown at smaller scale, squatting on the ground, and often placed in a circle as if they were enclosed in a bubble; the circle probably represents a special area, perhaps even a mat. In one case, this sub-scene is labelled with a word which seems to mean "marking time." There is then, at this point in the sequence of activities, one of those moments of uncertainty, noted before. The next stage that is usually shown in the full range of viticultural scenes presents the pressing of the crushed grapes in a primitive press. It must be assumed, however, that other things will have happened in the meanwhile. There is, for example, no sign that the juice already expressed from the grapes, has been drawn off and placed in smaller vessels to continue the fermentation which will probably have started already in the treading trough. In scenes in New Kingdom tombs, the juice is shown pouring out of the trough as the treading proceeds, and being put into jars for final fermentation. The supposition, therefore, is that in the Old Kingdom the juice was left with the remains of the crushed grapes in the vat for some time before being drawn off separately; then, the solid matter could be collected and placed in the press for the extraction of the remaining half-fermented juice.[18] In this way, a red wine would almost certainly have been produced (Lucas 1962: 17–18). Without further and better evidence, certainty cannot be achieved in the matter.

The pressing scene which follows, although absolutely clear in purpose, is almost incomprehensible in detail. In essence, what is shown is a large, elongated, sack full of crushed grapes—a kind of huge jelly-bag, but closed at both ends—which is twisted by a team of men, the juice that is yielded being caught in a wide-mouthed vessel (Duell 1938: pl. 114; Davies 1900: pl. 21). The bag or sack, the prime component in the operation, is not firmly attached to any kind of frame fixed to the ground, but has twisting poles at each end. These poles are turned in opposite directions, and the juice runs out through the texture of the bag, which is probably made of a coarse linen. Normally five men make up the pressing team, two to each pole, and one maintaining tension between the poles. The two pairs of twisters are shown to be exerting great pressure, and it seem impossible to work out from their strained contortions how exactly they are operating. The problem of interpretation certainly lies in the difficulty faced by the artist in showing two men on each pole at different ends, one being in life behind the other, and engaged in an activity outside the common range of movements shown in Egyptian art. It may also be supposed that most of the artists were probably unacquainted with the pressing of wine, and took their inspiration from the work of other artists; in the process of copying, and misunderstanding, awkward positions became impossible ones. The task of the fifth man is even more difficult to explain. His task was to keep the poles as far apart as possible, and he is usually shown as if in mid-air extended at full stretch between the poles, pushing with all his might (Figs. 13.6 and 13.7). In the pressing scene in one 5th Dynasty tomb at Saqqara, he is replaced by a very purposeful baboon, seemingly well-equipped for the acrobatic performance (Moussa and Altenmüller 1971: pls. 8, 12). Occasionally, the team is made up of more than five men;[19] but the intentions is always the same; the more the men, the more the contortions. The scene of pressing is not commonly labelled, but it may be noted here that in one damaged later example of the Middle Kingdom, the word describing the process is precisely that used for launderers "wringing out" linen (Montet 1925: 269; see Newberry 1894a: pls. 24, 31).

After the treading comes the filling of the wine jars and their sealing and storage (Moussa and Alternmuller 1977: pl. 39.16). Again, there are procedures not included; they need to be under-stood, although it is clear that they did not warrant illustration. Nothing dealing with fermentation is shown, and the filling of the jars could represent the decanting of fully fermented or partly fermented wine. As there is good evidence to suggest that when a jar was sealed a vent was left open for the escape of final fermentation gases, it should follow that it was common practice to pour wine into storage jars in the expectation that fermentation would be completed in the jar, or at least that some allowance should be made for the possibility of secondary fermentation. Presumably, the skilled winemaker would have been able to judge by visual, aural or nasal inspection when fermentation was complete. At that point, the vent could be closed, and the wine finally stored. An informative series of scenes in the Saqarra tomb of Akhtihotep, a late 5th Dynasty vizir, illustrates the filling and sealing of wine jars, and it is accompanied by useful labels (Davies 1901: 11, pl. 11; supplemented in Davies 1913: 44, pl. 40). Two scenes deal with the sealing of the jars; one specifies the filling of the jars with wine "for the *prt-ḥrw* offerings"; and one has a man, possibly a winemaker or butler, stating. "May your heart prosper more greatly than the water of your mouth (i.e., possibly 'your palate')." It is significant that the wine, or at least some part of it, is clearly said to be for offering purposes, the *prt-ḥrw* offerings being the standard funerary presentation. The implication of the last label statement seems to be that the drinker (here presumably Akhtihotep) should derive even more spiritual that gustatory pleasure from the wine; the heart was held to be the spiritual core of the body by the Egyptians.

Scarcely anything is known about wine storage in ancient Egypt; a few scenes of apparent storage, mostly in 18th Dynasty tombs at Thebes, show the vessels placed leaning one against the others (see chapter 14 by Lesko, this volume).[20] This procedure was dictated by the form of the vessels which had tapered bases, and it is how they were stored in the magazines of the Early Dynastic tombs.[21] Faced with a storeroom filled with jars stored in this way, the pharaonic butler could only, conveniently, take out those jars nearest the entrance, unless there was a system of small bays or bins. For periods before the New Kingdom, the evidence for storage is negligible, and equally so for the methods of transport and distribution. The Nile would certainly have been

T. G. H. James

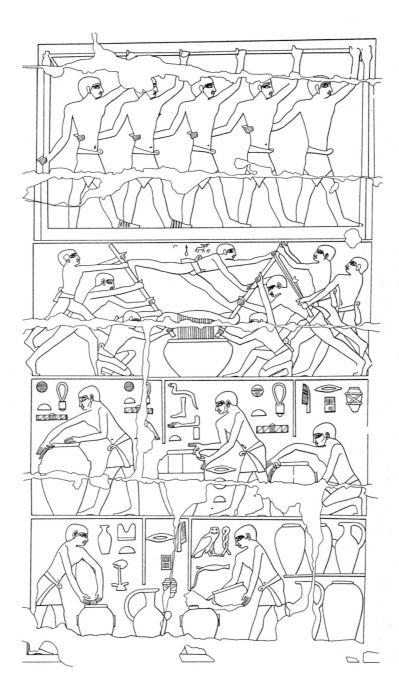

Figure 13.7. Winemaking scenes from the tomb of Niankhkhnum and Khnumhotpe. (Moussa and Altenmüller 1977: fig. 16).

Figure 13.8. Straining and pressing grape juice in the tomb of Baqet. (Newberry 1984: 2: pl. 6.)

Figure 13.9. Winemaking scenes in the tomb of Khety. (Newberry 1894: 2: pl. 16.)

used for initial transport from the Delta vineyards to the residences of the proprietors in Thebes and elsewhere. There is no evidence for a trade in wine, although some exchange must be postulated for the acquisition of wine by those who did not own vineyards or who received wine by some royal of temple distribution.

4. The Middle Kingdom

Knowledge of ancient Egyptian viticulture and wine production, as derived from the informative wine scenes in Old Kingdom tombs, is certainly one-sided and incomplete. The position is not improved as one moves forward to the Middle Kingdom. Now the best evidence, similar in kind to that found for the Old Kingdom in the Saqqara tombs, comes form the tombs in the provincial cemeteries of Middle Egypt. Doubt may be cast on the validity of the evidence as being truly indicative of what went on in the vineyards and *chais* of the feudal lords who operated with substantial local independence until their wings were clipped in the later 12th Dynasty (about 1860 B.C.). There is, however, no reason to doubt the availability of wine at the tables of the great in this part of Egypt, or even the possibility that vines were grown and wine made locally. There is a degree of unoriginality about some scenes of viticulture that suggests the preservation of a pictorial tradition not backed by reality. In the famous tomb of Djehutihotpe at El-Bersha, for example, the damaged winemaking scenes show little change from their Old Kingdom predecessors; they include the extraordinary contortions of the winepressers (Newberry 1894: 1:35, pls. 24, 27, 31). At Meir, a little farther to the south, Middle Kingdom tombs do not contain winemaking scenes, although at least one tomb of the Old Kingdom in this place does contain such (Blackman 1953: pl. 20). In the tomb of Ukhhotpe, son of Ukhhotpe and Mersi, of mid–12th Dynasty date (about 1900 B.C.), there is an unusual scene in which kneeling attendants offer separate parcels of the five canonical offering wines for the spirit of Ukhhotpe (Blackman 1915: 29, pl. 21). The scene is damaged, but it looks as if differently shapes jars are used for each wine; it would be probably a mistake to read too much into what was an attempt by the artist to introduce some meaningless variation into the scene.

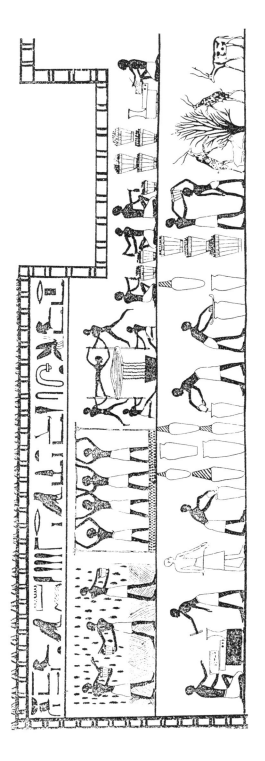

Figure 13.10. Winemaking scenes in the tomb of Khety. (Newberry 1893: 1: pl. 12.)

The most informative Middle Kingdom scenes occur in the fine tomb-chapels at Beni Hasan, north of El-Bersha. Three tombs contain wine scenes, two dated to the late 11th Dynasty (about 2050–2000 B.C.), those of Baqet III (no. 15) and Khety II (no. 17), and one, that of Amenemhet (no. 2), to the early 12th Dynasty (about 1950 B.C.). In general, the stages of wine production depicted are those that have been described for the Old Kingdom, but a few details are new and worth noting. In the Baqet tomb (Fig. 13.8), three scenes survive which apparently belong to winemaking. First, one man is shown stirring the contents of a large jar. Then comes a group of men who hold out a piece of cloth over a jar and pour liquid into the cloth which is evidently acting as a sieve. Can here be shown the stage between treading and pressing, when the juice expressed in the treading is separated from the debris of the crushed grapes? Possibly so, for the next scene show a fixed press with a frame to hold the bag of grape debris; three men engage in twisting the bag, using what seems to be little more than ordinary effort; a fourth man attends to the bag, and the juice is pouring out (dark-colored, and therefore probably grape juice) is caught below. The preliminary scenes of grape-picking and treading, if they were there, have not been preserved. In Khety's tomb (Fig. 13.9), the series of scenes includes picking, treading, pressing, and bottling, all shown very simply and almost as if misunderstood. The treading, for example includes no evident trough. Here, the old form of pressing is shown; but a new detail is that of a scribe who checks off the wine vessels as they are filled. A much more carefully detailed series of scenes in the tomb of Amenemhet (Fig. 13.10) does not unfortunately advance our knowledge substantially. The old, primitive winepress is shown along with picking and treading; scribes note the baskets full of grapes and the filled jars, and it is worth recording that these jars are of different shapes. No texts indicate what the differences may have indicated, but one might hope that they represented various kinds of wine.

Any survey of Egyptian wine production before the New Kingdom runs very thin at this point. It was stated earlier that the patchy nature of the evidence, both chronologically and topographically, prevents a good comprehensive story to be told. The one-sided bias of the evidence also provides the story with too heavy an inclination towards the funerary uses of wine. Nevertheless, there has survived enough reasonable evidence to show that wine was produced and drunk in substanital quantities among the higher ranks of society from at least about 3000 B.C. Periods subsequent to the Middle Kingdom have yielded a wider range of evidence that in fact supports the general thread of the story traced from early times in this study.

Notes

1. Quoted from the translation of "The Instruction addressed to Kagemni" by Lichtheim (1973: 60). The chronological scheme used here for ancient Egypt follows Baines and Malek (1984: 36–37).

2. For example, see the banquet scene in the tomb of Paheri, at El Kab (Naville et al. 1894: 25, pl. 7).

3. A good example is illustrated in Lesko 1977: 10.

4. For Early Dynastic pottery, including wine jars, see Emery 1961: 206.

5. For the technique of sealing, see Emery (1961: 209). The comprehensive work on seals in the early dynasties is Kaplony 1963–64.

6. See, generally, the useful entry by Meyer (Helck and Otto 1986: 6: col. 1169–82; for sources of early wine, col. 1172).

7. See the characteristic distribution of pottery found in tomb no. 3504 at Saqqara, listed in Emery et al. 1954: 68.

8. The development of the offering-list is traced in Barta (1963).

9. A good 2nd Dynasty example can be found in Emery (1961: pl. 32a). Also see Kaplony 1963–64: 3: pls. 138–40, 147.

10. Now in the Lowie Museum, University of California at Berkeley, no. 6.19825; much illustrated, e.g., Smith 1981: 84.

11. Piankoff 1968: 66, though translations on p. 92 need revision. See also Faulkner 1969: 30.

12. On Egyptian brewing generally, see Lucas 1962: 10–16 and Darby et al. 1977: 2:529.

13. The basic text is in Sethe 1932: 4–5. For full discussion of the whole text, see Gödecken 1976.

14. The good early study by Montet (1913) was largely superseded by the same author's later work (1925: 265–273).

15. The photograph of the scene reproduced in Montet (1925: pl. 21) does not show the poles.

16. The word is *w-35h 3*—see Faulkner 1962: 66.

17. The procession of grape-carriers to the treading-trough is clearly shown in Duell 1938: 2: pl. 116.

18. For fermentation with the crushed grapes in the juice, see Montet 1925: 268.

19. Eight men make up the pressing team in Moussa and Altenmüller 1977: pl. 39.16.

20. So in the tomb of Antef at Thebes; see Säve-Söderbergh 1957: 2: pl. 15.

21. A well-stocked magazine is shown in Emery 1961: pl. 20.

CHAPTER 14

Egyptian Wine Production During the New Kingdom

Leonard H. Lesko

1. Introduction

Our documentation of the ancient Egyptians' production, distribution, and consumption of wine is both sporadic and diverse, just as is our knowledge of most other aspects of ancient Egyptian culture. My own interest in the wines of ancient Egypt was excited by the wine jar labels surviving from several sites, other intriguing textual references (both Egyptian and classical), and the detailed artistic representations of winemaking in tomb paintings. But, I am also interested in the wine-related artifacts (mostly from tombs) and the recent excavation reports describing actual ancient wineries. From all these sources it is possible to present a fairly substantial picture of the Egyptians' winemaking techniques and also relate something about their careful attention to the labeling of wine jars, their personal tastes in wines, their moderation in drinking wine, and even a little about their use of wine in medicines and for offerings to their gods. That the jar labels have some historical importance has made an enjoyable project a fairly respectable area of research. A reexamination of these minor records certainly shows that there is still more to be savored from these empty and broken old jars.

Much more information about ancient Egyptian wines comes from the New Kingdom (ca. 1500–1100 B.C.) than from the earlier periods (see chapter 13 by James, this volume). Tomb scenes from the vast Theban necropolis depict almost every aspect of winemaking that we could hope for, from tending the vines, to harvesting the grapes, to crushing them in vats, to pressing the must in sacks, to bottling and storing the wine, even shipping, serving, and drinking it.

2. Tomb Scenes of Viticulture and Viniculture

Theban Tomb (TT) #155 of the early 18th Dynasty belonging to the Royal Herald, Intef, is particularly informative in this respect, with a series of five scenes with accompanying cartoon-like commentary (Figs. 14.1–14.3; Säve-Söderbergh 1957: 17–18 and pls. 14–15). The picking and crushing scenes are known from much more colorful and wonderfully preserved scenes in

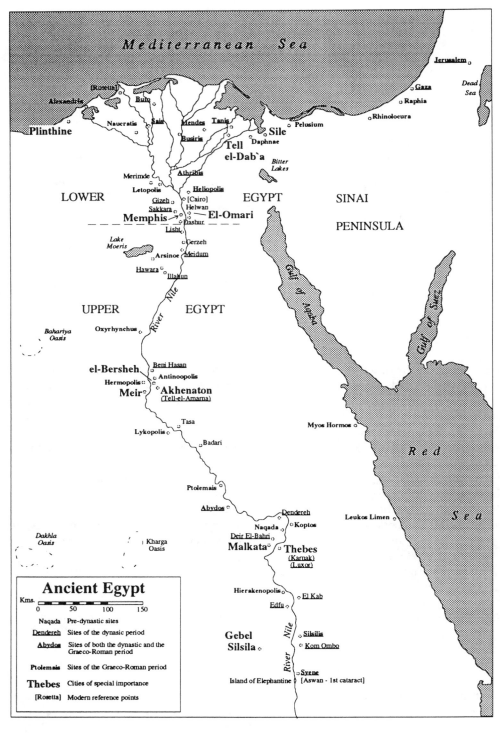

Map 14.1. Egypt: principal sites.

Figure 14.1. Vineyard and grape treading scene from Theban Tomb #155, belonging to the Royal Herald, Intef, early Dynasty 18. (Säve-Söderbergh 1957: pl. 14.)

other tombs, but the dialogue quoted in the texts accompanying these scenes in Intef's tomb, though badly preserved, really brings them alive. In the first scene, of the picking of the grape bunches and putting them in carrying baskets, a paunchy, bearded vintner (who stands holding a whip) is tasting the grapes and certainly commenting on their readiness, though his and the two quotes of his pickers are generally undecipherable. The picker before the vintner says either "Behold ..." or "Take ...," and the vintner responds, "This is indeed (?) wine."

In the second scene (Fig. 14.1), the carriers take the grapes to the crush where four men are holding ropes suspended from above the slippery vat in which they stomp the grapes. The label at the lower left, which probably is intended to follow the long text at the top, says, "What is said [for] the *Ka* (spirit) of the Herald, [Intef]." The label at the same level to the right of the vat is more specific, identifying the text as a "Song to the Lady [Rennutet]," who is the cobra goddess of the harvest depicted in the register above the workman (mostly obliterated) collecting the juice. The crushers sing: "May she (Rennutet) [remain] with us in this work.... May our lord drink it (the wine) as one who is repeatedly favored by his king."

Over the third scene (Fig. 14.2) is a label identifying either the "[Pressing]" of this single scene, or perhaps more likely, (given its size and position in the midst of the whole sequence), the "[Making] of wine by the *ᶜprw* for the Herald Intef." None of these men appears to be Asiatic, though *ᶜprw* are usually associated with a class or tribe of foreigners from the east. The press is a sack of yellow fabric or basketry stretched between two upright poles with workmen twisting its ends in opposite directions. In this case, dark red wine runs from the sack to a white vat. Though the bottling process is not actually depicted here, the jars to the left of the press apparently represent at least two and possibly three stages of bottling. The lowest level of jars are still open, either empty or perhaps with wine undergoing primary fermentation. The center row of jars are sealed completely just like the wine-filled amphorae in the cellar of the last scene (see below). The upper register of three amphorae in ring stands appears different from the bottom register, possibly partially sealed with secondary fermentation locks (compare the amphorae shown in TT #261; see Lesko 1977: 20). Alternatively, this last group of amphorae could be offerings of wine in decorated jars accompanying the grapes on an altar and those in a chest which stand before the image of the goddess Rennutet.

The fourth scene has a serving girl with a long pigtail who presents wine for the approval of the same paunchy, bearded vintner shown in the first scene. This time, however, he is seated and holds a staff instead of a whip. She says, "For your Ka (spirit)! Take what is good from the *Ka* (provisions) of (or "for") the Herald Intef." To which the vintner responds, "How sweet is the wine of the crew! For the *Ka* of the Herald Intef from what Rennutet gives to you (masculine form = Intef)."

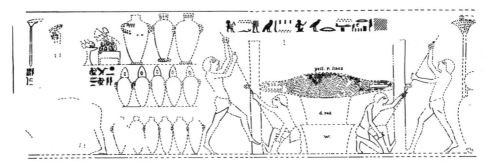

Figure 14.2. Pressing scene, showing stoppered and unstoppered wine jars, from Theban Tomb #155, belonging to the Royal Herald, Intef, early Dynasty 18. (Säve-Söderbergh 1957: pl. 15.)

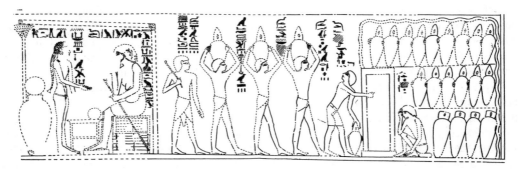

Figure 14.3. Stoppered wine jars being brought to the cellar (right) while vintner is served wine (left), from Theban Tomb #155, belonging to the Royal Herald, Intef, early Dynasty 18. (Säve-Söderbergh 1957: pl. 15.)

The final scene (Fig. 14.3) has an overseer with a small stick or baton supervising four porters who bear sealed amphorae to Intef's cellar. He says, "Move on! We will scorch ourselves." The last porter in front of the overseer remarks that "The amount is burdensome." The third porter says, "Really," in response to the remarks of one or the other of his colleagues. The second porter says about the cellar's watchman, who is holding up everything, that "He is drunk from wine." The first porter, who had set down his jar and is knocking at the door of the cellar, says that "The servant is sleeping," and the awakened watchman claims that "I haven't slept at all."

Although some tomb scenes could represent production at the great royal or temple estates in the Delta, the texts in Intef's tomb indicate that this was not the case here. The Herald Intef was a reasonably highly placed official, but not royalty. The estate, workers, and wines depicted were his, and clearly he and some of his subordinates enjoyed drinking them. He may have offered some wine to his gods or his guests, but the wines made for his use filled a moderate-sized cellar that could have been replenished annually. It is unclear how close to his home the vineyard was located, and we certainly do not know how the wines compared to the finest royal wines. If the royal wines were generally dry, however, as indicated by the rare occurrence of "sweet" on their labels (Lesko 1977: 22 and 27), then the reference to sweetness by Intef's vintner may be a clue that these were not the same.

Clearly, the artist who composed the sequence in Intef's tomb had experienced the various episodes firsthand, and enjoyed conveying the urgency and excitement of the work rather than capturing only an idealized timeless record.

Assuming that all serious wine production took place in the north, the New Kingdom cemetery at Saqqara may eventually provide even better documentation of vintage scenes, though work there cannot progress rapidly enough to satisfy all our wants. There are 23 Memphite tombs with winemaking scenes already known from Giza and Saqqara, mostly of Old Kingdom date (see chapter 13 by James, this volume), with many only partially complete, and the Memphite capital would still have required transport ships for deliveries such as we find pictured on Theban tomb walls (e.g., in TT #261; see Lesko 1977: 28). There are 42 New Kingdom Theban tombs with winemaking scenes (Lerstrup 1992: 61).

A few other well-known scenes of viticulture and enology also deserve mention. The walled-in garden of the temple of Amun from TT #96 (Wilkinson 1883: 1:377; Lutz 1922: 47; and Lesko 1977: 13) was probably not near the Theban temple itself. Rather, this could have been one of the estates of the temple's domain, possibly in the Delta along the Western River. The garden, with its pyloned gates facing the Nile, opens immediately onto a grape arbor which is surrounded by pools, orchards, and magazines. Watering vines and picking grapes are shown very nicely in the 18th Dynasty tomb of Khaemwaset (TT #261), which also shows clearly the sealing of amphorae with clay around a primitive secondary fermentation lock (Lesko 1977: 16 and 20). This tomb also shows the amphorae being unloaded from a colorfully painted sailing vessel. The tomb of Nakht (TT #52) shows five men stomping on grapes in a good-sized vat, while holding on to ropes hanging from an overhead frame (Fig. 14.4; Lesko 1977: 16). Through numerous such tomb scenes, we not only learn something of the grape-picking, winemaking, and storage processes (with variations) of the ancient Egyptians, but also the importance that they placed upon wine production and its consumption.

The problems of what varieties of grapes were used by the Egyptians, and whether true white wines were made in pharaonic times, have still not been resolved. But, different tomb scenes show grapes in many sizes, shapes and colors (ranging from light green to almost black), and juices running from crushing vats and pressing sacks that range in color from light pink to dark red (Lesko 1977: 17–19; and see illustrations from Meir [Blackman 1914–25: 3:30, pl. 24]; Beni Hasan [Newberry 1893–94: 1:12, 26, 29; 2: pls. 4, 13, and 16]; and el-Bersheh [Newberry 1893: pls. 24, 26, and 31]). In classical times, at least, a white wine was being produced in Egypt that was regarded as one of the best wines in the world at that time. Athenaeus, a Greek writer of the 2nd century A.D., described in his tasting notes several Egyptian wines of his day, and since the best pharaonic wines of at least a thousand years earlier came from the same small area in the northwestern Delta, we should consider his careful descriptions. At one point, he cites an authority who said that "the vine was first discovered in Plinthine a city of Egypt" (*The Deipnosophistae* I.34a). This is near the Mediterranean Sea, southwest of Alexandria. Athenaeus (I.33d) described the abundant Mareotic wine from an area directly south of Alexandria as "excellent, white, pleasant, fragrant, easily assimilated, thin, not likely to go to the head, and diuretic." He preferred, however, the Taeniotic wine from the strip of land southwest of Alexandria, near Plinthine. This was somewhat pale, pleasant, aromatic, and mildly astringent, with an oily quality dissolved by the gradual admixture of water (I.33e). There is no evidence for such dilution of wine in our pharaonic material. Though there are references to "blended wines" (*irp sm3*) at Malqata (Hayes 1951: 89; Lesko 1977: 31) and possibly to "mixed wine (*mdg*)" in the instruction of Onkhsheshonqi (see Lichtheim 1980: 3:163), in neither case is there any indication of what was blended. There is also no evidence for the addition of resins or oils either to coat the porous pottery jars or to protect the wines from oxidation.

Figure 14.4. Vintage and fowling scene from Theban Tomb #52, belonging to Nakht, mid-Dynasty 18. (Davies 1917; pl. 26; photograph courtesy of The Metropolitan Museum of Art, New York, Rogers Fund, 1915.)

3. Wine Jar Labels

Although no careful tasting notes survive from Pharaonic times, the wines from the New Kingdom are really best known to us from the wine jar labels on both intact and broken jars from several sites. The typical two-handled wine jar or amphora, a vessel with a rounded or pointed base (see chapters 5 by McGovern and Michel, 15 by Leonard, and 20 by Koehler, this volume), could stand in the sand, on a pottery ring stand, or on a wooden frame. Since such jars were not designed to stand upright by themselves, the shape could have been related to the storage of the wines (partially on their sides with their labels visible). Or, this shape would have been particularly suitable for transport by ship, or useful in serving the wines, or for collecting the dregs, or for resisting the buildup of pressure from within in wines that were not chemically stabilized. At least one jar in Tutankhamon's tomb is known to have burst open after burial (Lucas 1962: 19; Lesko 1977: 21).

Perhaps, the most impressive collection of labeled jars comes from the virtually intact cellar found by Howard Carter in the Annex of Tutankhamon's tomb (Černý 1965: 1–4, 21–24, and pls. 1–5; Lesko 1977: 22–26, 49). Of course, a boy of nineteen was probably not the greatest wine connoisseur of his day. Those who buried him, however, seem to have chosen not only the very finest of everything available, but also provided many personal effects for the boy-king in the

Figure 14.5. Wine jars, stoppered and unstoppered, as found *in situ* in the Annex of Pharaoh Tutankhamon's tomb in the Valley of the Kings, Thebes. (Edwards 1977; p. 226; photograph courtesy of the Egyptian Expedition, The Metropolitan Museum of Art, New York.)

afterlife. Wine would certainly have fallen into one or both of these categories. Among the 5000 treasures crowded into the four small rooms of Tutankhamon's tomb in the Valley of the Kings were 26 wine jars (Fig. 14.5) that were carefully labeled, mostly with stopper sealings. The sealings were still intact when discovered in 1922, but unfortunately the jars contained only the dried sediments of what were probably the greatest wines of a bygone age.

The inscriptions on the 26 wine jars from Tutankhamon's tomb contain better information than many of the labels on today's best bottles (Figs. 14.6–14.7). The "vintage year" was indicated by the regnal year of the king. The location of the vineyard from which the grapes came was noted, and this information provides very early and unexpected evidence of "appellation contrôlée." The ownership or proprietorship of the vineyard was indicated by the seal impressions left on the clay stoppers, and this provided an additional guarantee of quality, especially since the greatest estates or chateaux bore the names of members of the royal family or of the chief temples of Egypt. Finally, the labels on Tutankhamon's wine jars also named the chief winemaker who was responsible for the product.

Figure 14.6. Two Egyptian wine jars, with hieratic inked labels and intact clay stoppers with seal impressions, from Pharaoh Tutankhamon's tomb in the Valley of the Kings, Thebes. Label no. 392 (left) reads: "Year 4. *Šdḥ* of very good quality of the House-of-Aton of the Western River. Chief vintner Khay."; no. 571 (right) reads: "Year 5. Sweet wine of the House-of-Aton from Karet. Chief vintner Ramose." (Photograph courtesy of the Griffith Institute, Ashmolean Museum, Oxford.)

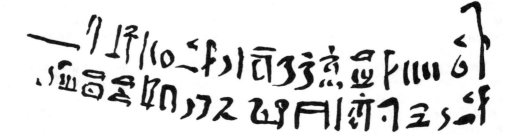

Figure 14.7. Facsimile drawing of a hieratic inked label on a wine jar from Pharaoh Tutankhamon's tomb in the Valley of the Kings, Thebes. The inscription reads: "Year 4. Sweet wine of the House-of-Aton—Life, Prosperity, Health!—of the Western River. Chief vintner Àperershop." (Drawing courtesy of the Griffith Institute, Ashmolean Museum, Oxford.)

Assuming that some of the best wines of Tutankhamon's reign would have been included along with his other great worldly treasures, the wines of his 4th, 5th, and 9th years (1345, 1344, and 1340 B.C., according to the middle chronology) were very likely the best vintages of his short nine-year reign (Lesko 1977: 23). Twenty-three of his jars date to these three years. One jar dated to a year 31 must have had a label from Amenhotep III's reign that was incompletely erased and not relabeled. Other examples show that empty jars were recycled, i.e., sent back to the vineyards for reuse in subsequent years (Hayes 1951: 39). On the other hand, there is also an interesting reference in the Ptolemaic Period instruction of the "prisoner" Onkhsheshonqi, who was denied papyri for his writings and therefore "wrote for his son on the sherds of the jars that were brought in to him containing mixed wine" (Onkhsheshonqi 4, 18; see Lichtheim 1980: 3:163). He obviously did not value these containers, at least not for their intended use. One old jar in Tutankhamon's tomb hardly provides proof of the long-term ageing of wines in ancient Egypt. It would be surprising if wine could have survived for thirty years or so in such porous clay containers. It should be noted, however, that one of Onkhsheshonqi's aphorisms says that "Wine matures as long as one does not open it" (19, 23; see Lichtheim 1980: 3:174).

Most of the vineyards represented in Tutankhamon's cellar were along the Western River, that branch of the Nile which enters the Mediterranean near modern Alexandria. One jar was from the northeastern Delta, an area known for its vineyards already in the Old Kingdom, and one was from the southern oasis of Kharga. Two of the fifteen vintners named on jars from Tutankhamon's tomb had Syrian names, and one of these foreign (or second penetration) immigrants produced the wine in half a dozen of the jars. Àperershop made the wine in jar #1, and Khay produced the wines in jars 4, 5, 14, 15, 16, and 17.

The so-called Syrian spindle flask, with long neck, wide mouth, and single handle, is seen in painted tomb scenes, such as that of the physician Nebamon (TT #17; see Säve-Söderbergh 1957: pl. 23; and Lesko 1977: 9, 26). and also was found in Tutankhamon's tomb and elsewhere. Very likely (and despite their designation as Syrian), the jars of this type from Tutankhamon's tomb and their contents were both Egyptian. These jars had Egyptian seal impressions on their stoppers, though no inked-on labels. The particular scene showing the visit of a Syrian prince to the Egyptian physician, Nebamon, also depicts a Syrian attendant carrying a Syrian spindle flask, so it has been accepted by most as showing an imported product. Even if it were true in this instance, however, this cannot be used to prove that all such jars contained foreign contents (specifically, wines), nor would importation necessarily take anything away from the Egyptian winemaking industry. It could instead indicate the Egyptians' openness, perhaps their interest in comparative tastings, and the fact that doctors have had an interest in wine and the wherewithal to acquire fine imports for several millennia.

Having depictions of Syrian porters carrying Syrian jars and knowing of winemakers with apparently Syrian names would likewise not necessarily make this industry any more foreign than our own Californian wine industry, with so many different ethnic groups attested over the years. Having a Nubian grape-picker depicted in Khaemwaset's tomb and crushers labeled as ⁽prw, who should originally have come from Asia but are represented as Egyptian in Intef's tomb, could be taken to indicate either that captives were given these menial jobs, or that foreign immigrants with winemaking skills found jobs open to them in the social melting-pot that was New Kingdom Egypt. An argument for the former is the statement on the Second Kamose Stele that the Theban ruler would "drink of the wine of [Apophis'] vineyard, which the Asiatics whom I captured press for me" (Habachi 1972: 36, lines 11–12). An argument for the latter is the apparent success of the chief vintner Khay and others, even in higher administrative positions (e.g., Chancellor Bay at the end of the 19th Dynasty). Probably there was some of both, with captives and/or immigrants, or their descendants, able to achieve success in this rich cosmopolitan country.

Concerning the chief vintners represented on Tutankhamon's jars, one aspect that I did not discuss earlier (Lesko 1977: 23) is the large number (eight) identified with a single estate, that of the god Aton. All date to the same year, Tutankhamon's year 5. Five more chief vintners of the same estate are known within a span of five years. Clearly, each of these individuals was responsible for the product he labeled from a vintage that was completed in a relatively short period of time. There was surely not such a great turnover of winemakers in a single vintage or winery, but rather the estate or domain of the Aton must have had extensive land holdings, even along the "Western River" area where eleven of these jars (including six from year 5) originated. Two from this same estate and vintage were actually labeled as coming from different areas, which might in fact have been in the same region. One was located at Tjel in the northeastern Delta and the other was at Karet, also likely in that vicinity (Černý 1965: 4). Since there is no duplication of vintners' names from the Aton estate in this year 5, these jars likely were representative bottlings, perhaps the best from various producers working for the domain, but they were probably not selected by or for Tutankhamon strictly for their quality. Having said this, the year was still likely to have been an exceptional vintage, and these vintners might also have been the best producers. We do not know how many vineyards would have belonged to the temples at this time, but in the later 20th Dynasty, the Great Harris Papyrus (I, 11, 6) referred to Ramses III's gift of 433 vineyards and groves to the Theban temples alone.

Whether or not temple winemakers were generally among the best vintners, it seems that even more credit may be due to the vintner Khay, who produced six of Tutankhamon's wines. Four jars of Khay's wine were likewise from this same year 5, but two were from the preceding year 4 (jars numbered 4 and 5). What is interesting in this case is that the jars of year 5 wines were all from the estate of Tutankhamon, while one of the jars from year 4 contained wine from that same estate, but the other had *šdḥ* (possibly pomegranate wine) from the estate of the Aton. It would appear from this that Khay either oversaw two estates simultaneously in year 4, making *šdḥ* at one and real wine at the other (perhaps at different times during the year), or more likely, he moved from one position to another in Tutankhamon's fourth year. In either event, his skill must have been exceptional, and his move from temple to royal estate should be seen as an obvious promotion. As an example of the status achieved by a vintner, consult the scene of Intef's tomb (above), showing his winemaker presiding over the tasting. Interestingly, the name Khay is foreign, Syrian probably, but there is no way of telling how long he or his family had been in Egypt. Since his name had no special determinatives to indicate that he was a foreigner, he could even have been a native Egyptian who happened to have been given a foreign name, or a descendant of an earlier immigrant. However, since there are several other foreigners represented among the vintners in this collection and since there seems to have been a tradition of their working in this industry, it does seem to point to one immigrant's road to success.

The rather large number of separate vineyards and/ or wineries of the Aton domain that the numerous vintners would imply may also be significant historically, since it is doubtful that the vineyards would all have sprung up on virgin soil following the inception of the Amarna period and its new Aton temples. Surely, they had been either confiscated or acquired by some other means from other estates (perhaps from the vast holdings of the temple of Amon-Re at Karnak), or alternatively, those in charge may have embraced Atonism, changing their allegiance nominally if not actually. In any case the change would probably have resulted in a shift of revenues rather than any major dislocation of personnel or disruption of the economy. Presumably, the name-changing of temple estates would not have been so frequent under ordinary circumstances, and it is probably significant that the estate of the Aton continued to produce wines for Tutankhamon five years after his own name was changed from Tutankhaton to Tutankhamon (Lesko 1977: 26).

Only four jars from the annex of Tutankhamon's tomb were labeled "sweet wine," *irp n̄dm*. Incidentally, this is not to be confused with the *irp bnr* that occurs in the medical texts, and could be either "sweet wine" or "date wine" (Papyrus Ebers 28.9.16–28.10.2; see Von Deines and Westendorf 1959; Lucas 1962: 23). The fact that the sweet wines were so clearly labeled leads me to believe that the vast majority of the wines in this tomb were dry and that the Egyptians' tastes generally ran toward dry wines. Athenaeus' comments (in *The Deipnosophistae*; see above) also seem to support this view, since he made no reference to sweetness but commented on the astringency of the best Egyptian wine. The other beverage named on three of the labels on Tutankhamon's jars was *šdḥ* probably pomegranate wine, and in each case, these had the qualification that the *šdḥ* was of "very good quality." The one jar of wine from the southern oasis also had this qualification, so it is very likely that some such designation was necessary when the guarantee of estate-bottled genuine wine was lacking. We can make a case for the fact that all the wines in these jars were pure, on the basis of labels from the Malqata palace of Amenhotep III that refer to "blended" wines (Hayes 1951: 89).

The 285 wine jar labels found at Malqata on the west bank of the Nile at ancient Thebes were from broken and discarded amphorae, mainly from the last ten years of Amenhotep III's long reign (1403–1366 B.C.). Among other things, these labels have been used to argue for a long co-regency with his son Amenhotep IV, who changed his name to Akhenaton and moved his residence to the site of modern el-Amarna in middle Egypt in his own fifth year (Hayes 1951: 36–37, no. 14). Although such survivals are naturally much more likely to come from the last years before a site is abandoned, the preponderance of labels from years 30, 34 and 37 seem to indicate that the Malqata palace was used almost exclusively for the celebration of Amenhotep III's jubilees in these years. Some wines are even labeled as being for one or the other of his jubilees.

The jar labels from Malqata were sometimes erased and replaced with new labels, occasionally more than once, showing that the jars were generally recycled unless accidentally damaged (Hayes 1951: 39). The fragments were found in ruined magazines attached to the palace, in rubbish heaps, and in a few exceptional cases, in houses. Most are dated with royal years to indicate the vintage. Some are estate-bottled wines of named chief-vintners. There is a "wine of the royal scribe Huy that he made for the royal jubilee" (Hayes 1951: 44, fig. 4, no. 15), and another wine for the jubilee made at the request of the overseer of the treasury (Hayes 1951: 44, fig. 4, no. 16). There is a Memphite wine of a chief steward dated to year 31, not for a festival, but perhaps as a gift to the king (Hayes 1951: 44, fig. 4, no. 17). There are wines of other officials (seal-bearers and royal scribes), and from other places, such as Tjaru in the northeastern Delta; no less than 68 jars were from the "Western River" (Hayes 1951: 85–89). There are wines labeled "genuine," "good," and "very good," and one indicating the quantity—6 *hin* (about 3 liters) (Hayes 1951: 48, fig. 8, no. 86; compare p. 95).

The estates from which the wines for the palace came included Amenhotep III's father's and mother's estates, his wife's, his daughter's, and perhaps six different estates with variations of his own name. It is not surprising that the royal mother lived on and had the continued support of her estate, but interestingly the estate of Thutmose IV (his short-reigned father) produced a wine in year 36 which must have been in Amenhotep III's reign, and another in year 34 made specifically for "his Majesty's" jubilee (Hayes 1951: 45, fig. 5, no. 31). This shows that not all estates would have had their names changed at the death of a king to either that of his successor or another member of his family. The temples of Amon and Re are represented by a relatively much smaller proportion of the estates (only 10 examples together) than that ascribed to these gods and Aton in Tutankhamon's tomb. Of the vintners, one or two represented at Malqata had the same names as Tutankhamon's and may have been the same individuals. For example, Nakht who produced jar no. 10 of Tutankhamon's year 5 could have been the same vintner who produced jar no. 54 for

Amenhotep III at Malqata. Also Pay (Tutankhamon, year 9, Estate of the Aton, jar no. 18) and Pau (Malqata, Estate of Amon, jar no. 66; see Hayes 1951: 102) could have been the same individual. Likewise, one or two of the vintners (Pa and Hati; see Hayes 1951: 102, n. 233) may also be known in labels from el-Amarna (see below).

The jar sealings or impressions made in the clay stoppers found at Malqata are of great variety. None is dated, but many list the region or estate that produced the wine (Hayes 1951: 156–83). Designations of quality are frequent, and the purpose of a special bottling is often given, such as "for the Jubilee" or "for a happy return." Although jar-labeling was common for all sorts of commodities, jar sealing was a practice confined largely to wine.

For the important site of el-Amarna, the city of Pharaoh Akhenaton, who was the son of Amenhotep III and, at the very least, the father-in-law of Tutankhamon, the assemblages of fragmentary jar sealings and labels were studied by Fairman (1951: 143–80; and pls. 81–91). The vast majority of these inscribed objects were found in the central palace area, and the sealings represented estates of the gods Aton, Re-Harakhty, and Ptah, the king, his father, his mother, and his wife. Some had regional designations from Delta locations and elsewhere. The 165 wine jar labels from Amarna came principally from "Western River" estates belonging to the king, his wife, his two parents, four royal daughters, several temples of Aton but also of Amon and Re-Harakhty, a High Priest, and a Chancellor. Other wines consumed at this royal residence were from the eastern Delta, three of the oases, and from Memphis. One fragmentary jar sealing mentioned *Ḥ3rw*, which Fairman (1951: 149 and pl. 83) restored as "[wine of] Syria," but was this seal (in Egyptian hieroglyphs) applied to a wine actually made so far away? If so, it would seem to imply either control over the production at a foreign vineyard or foreign production carefully designated for export to Egypt. It would seem to me more likely that an Egyptian estate would have had Syria in its name either to reflect a family connection or to designate the type of wine being made. Thus, "Wine of Syria" was also represented at Malqata (Hayes 1951: 89), but the example illustrated (Hayes 1951: 47, fig. 7, no. 77) was "of the sealbearer Thutmose."

Two sherds of wine jars with high regnal year dates (28 and 30) were certainly of Amenhotep III, and could possibly have been from reused jars. Otherwise, since wine would not have aged well in these jars and Amenhotep actually ruled for thirty-eight years, these labels would also seem to indicate a long co-regency between Amenhotep III and Akhenaton, just as Fairman (1951: 152–57) suggested. The labels span the years of Akhenaton's occupation of the site (years 5 to 17) rather well, and the lower dates could have been jars moved to the site after its founding or, in some cases, could have been those of Akhenaton's successor, Smenkhkare. One jar even had a year seventeen changed to year one (Fairman 1951: 159). I have pointed out before that the total number of wine labels found at el-Amarna is not very large, and probably reflects the fact that most jars that remained intact must have been returned to the wineries for recycling (Lesko 1977: 29). While it is impossible to say how representative this sampling of labels is, the sealings from the site would not have been saved, even though they would more easily have been crushed under foot.

The storehouses of the Ramesseum (Fig. 14.8), the mortuary temple of Ramses III, remain the best source of wine jar labels for the following 19th Dynasty, again from the west bank of Thebes (Spiegelberg 1923: 25–36). It is also, however, a very uneven selection, since it represented stores for offerings or for the king's afterlife, and was apparently little affected by the king's taste in wine, by his requirements for thirteen jubilee celebrations, or by gifts from relatives or officials. What is interesting is that apparently very little wine was transported to the Theban site after his tenth year and none during his last nine years.

More than three dozen vintners from more than thirty estates are named on the Ramesseum labels. These estates include regional designations from all the Delta branches of the Nile and

Figure 14.8. Storehouses with mudbrick barrel vaulting, Ramesseum, the mortuary temple of Rameses II in western Thebes. (Photograph courtesy of L.H. Lesko.)

other wine-producing areas of the Delta, together with some specified temple and royal estates (no queen's, prince's or princess' estates however). A scribe's practice letter (Papyrus Anastasi IV, 6.10–7.9) provides some information about the size of one small 19th Dynasty estate belonging to and providing wine for the mortuary temple of Sety II (Caminos 1954: 155–56). The scribe reported finding twenty-one persons at the vineyard (seven men, four lads, four old men, and six children), and he apparently took the entire year's produce that he found there to the mortuary temple in Thebes by means of two cattle barges and an escort vessel. This cargo included 1500 jars of wine, 50 jars of *šdḥ* (pomegranate wine), 50 jars of another drink (*p3-wr* "the great one"), and 160 sacks and baskets of pomegranates and grapes.

Though we can hardly believe every claim on royal monuments, and especially not those of Ramses III, the last great pharaoh of Egypt, it is interesting to note his boast addressed to the god Amon in the Great Papyrus Harris (I, 7, 10ff), that he planted vineyards without limit in the oases and in the south, that he multiplied those in the north in the hundreds of thousands, and that he equipped them with vintners, captives of foreign lands. He claimed much more specifically to have presented 59,588 jars of wine to the god (Papyrus Harris I, 15a, 13 and I, 18a, 11), and, although this would be far less than we would expect from hundreds of thousands of vineyards, it is a substantial number indeed for the use of one temple which would have had its own estates supplying for it.

From a 19th Dynasty stela, we have a reference to another interesting wine-related job (Lowie 1979: 50–54). A scribe of the offering table named Neferhotep was also a "royal scribe who is in charge of the vessels in the wine department of the Residence." This not only confirms the existence of palace wine cellars, but also allows us to imagine a wine steward or butler who had charge over jars, the labels of which he could read, and probably over the palace's serving pieces as well.

4. Possible Winemaking Installations

Shortly after I wrote that no grape-crushing vats survived from ancient Egypt (Lesko 1977: 17), it was announced that several intact winemaking installations had been discovered at Marea, about 45 km southwest of Alexandria (el-Fakharani 1983: 175–86). The particular site is much later than the New Kingdom, dating from the 5th or 6th century A.D., but interesting nonetheless because of its location—not far from the great pharaonic vinyards of the western Delta in an area renowned for its wines, according to several classical authors. Apart from the significant location, a large basin with four coats of plaster at the most complete installation, with barely plausible explanations for each of its components, and this was very likely a communal bath. Its location in the middle of town, with drains from the crushing area that could easily become clogged, lacking drainage from the supposed fermentation vat, and with no bottling or storage facility nearby, would all seem to militate against this being a winemaking installation. Further excavation should clarify the situation. If it were a bath, one would expect to find a hypocaustal system beneath either of the surfaces draining into the basin or under the platform on the opposite side of the basin. The millstone in a smaller installation, which is described as a Mareotic winemaking installation, would also seem to preclude that identification; more likely, the platform with holes and drainage beneath it was a typical latrine rather than a stand for amphorae.

The opposite may be true of a context at Tell el-Dabᶜa in the northeastern Delta. There, what was initially described by Bietak as a garden and bath might well have been a vineyard and winemaking installation, as he now argues (Bietak 1985: 267–78). The size of the garden pits, which seemed too small for trees and too large and too widely spaced for most plants, could easily have contained vines. What was interpreted as a plastered stone grape-crushing vat is very small, slightly over a meter long, half a meter wide, and not very deep, but the runoff would have been at a good angle, with nothing to become clogged as at the Marea facilities, and the end of the trough drains in two directions, so that two jars could have been filled with must at the same time. The must could also have been channeled to one or the other spouts so that there would be little interruption to the flow and virtually no loss of the precious liquid. The small size of the vat and its location near the plantings, in a corner of a temple enclosure, would seem to fit a winemaking installation, though one cannot rule out an abattoir. Unfortunately, the only pottery vessel from the site brought into Bietak's argument is an Egyptian-style wine mixing/serving jar of mid-18th Dynasty date (Bietak 1985: 277 and pl. VIII), and no palaeobotanical samples were recovered. The 18th Dynasty jar is actually used to argue for the continued use of the winemaking installation, at least through the middle of the dynasty. The fact that this supposed winemaking installation occurs in a temple of Seth, otherwise not known for producing wine, is probably not significant considering its early New Kingdom date, and the fact that the wines could have been primarily for temple use.

The probable winemaking installation at Tell el Dabᶜa may even provide a link to Asiatic roots through the Hyksos, who worshipped Seth here prior to their expulsion by the Thebans at the start of the 18th Dynasty. As stated above, Kamose, who was involved in this campaign, referred to forcing captive Asiatics to press *their* grapes for him. This installation would thus provide a fixed point for Asiatic involvement in the Egyptian wine industry of the New Kingdom. The common word for "vineyard (*k3mw*)," which is also the basis of the word for "vintner (*k3my*)," first appeared in the Kamose text and has long been considered a loan word (Bietak 1985: 276), though the earlier *k3nw* and *k3ny* are not really so different, and all of them may actually be dialectal variants of the same word (Gardiner 1947: 1:96–97). Since the location of Dab^ca is at or near the site of the very famous 19th Dynasty vineyard at Kaenkeme known from Ramesside jars and texts, this discovery is especially intriguing. For example, in Papyrus Anastasi III, 2, 6, a scribe named Pbes in describing the city Pi-Ramesses, referred to the "mellow wine of Kaenkeme surpassing honey" (Caminos 1954: 74).

5. Wine Use in the New Kingdom

Concerning moderation in the drinking of alcoholic beverages among the ancient Egyptians (see also chapter 1 by Grivetti, this volume), Athenaeus is again the source for the statement that "Among the Egyptians of ancient times, any kind of symposium was conducted with moderation.... They dined while seated using the simplest and most healthful food and only as much as would be sufficient to promote good cheer" (*The Deipnosophistae*, V.191). There are several wisdom texts and scribal practice exercises that urge moderation and aim at discouraging drunkenness. In one of these, the sage, Ani, says: "Don't indulge in drinking beer, lest you utter evil speech and don't know what you're saying. If you fall and hurt your body, none holds out a hand to you; your companions in the drinking stand up, saying: 'Out with the drunk!'" (Ani 4, 6ff; see Lichtheim 1976: 2:137). Indeed the Egyptians knew drunkenness and even represented obvious cases in drawings on papyri and in tomb paintings (Wilkinson 1883: I:392; Lutz 1922: 99; and Lesko 1977: 35), but again on the basis of wine jar labels found at Malqata and el-Amarna, it can be argued that far greater quantities of wine were consumed during jubilee years and during festivals than under ordinary circumstances. A very small number of dated broken wine jars (viz., 165) were recovered from Amarna, which was a capital city for at least twelve years.

Concerning the ancient Egyptians' use of wine in medicine, the surviving prescriptions of the medical texts show that, together with beer and water, wine was one of the most frequently used vehicles by which *materia medica* could be ingested or applied externally (Lesko 1978: 3–4). One section of the Ebers Medical Papyrus (50.21-51.14, prescriptions 284–293) has ten prescriptions for "making the heart accept bread" or to restore one's appetite. Since almost all of these prescriptions contained either wine or beer or both, it seems likely that these alcoholic beverages were more than just the vehicles for the medication, and probably were recognized even then as the principal ingredients of such tonics. Few of us would argue with these prescriptions today, at least regarding wine as an appetite-restorer. The use of most of the other ingredients in these elixirs remains a mystery unless, of course, there was some intention to deceive, as we might expect from more modern purveyors of patent medicines.

A second very frequent use of wine in medical prescriptions, again from Papyrus Ebers, was in driving out the "great weakness," and for this, six of ten prescriptions contained wine (55, 1ff, prescriptions 326–35). Again, the uplifting effect of this mild medication may have been recognized by the Egyptians, though they continued to mix in other ingredients which may or may not have helped. When other *materia medica* were added, they were frequently ground fine and mixed with the wine, but the wine could also be used to wash down whatever else was to be taken. Wine was used in salves, in enemas, and in bandaging. Likewise, the wine lees were used in all three of these ways. For bringing down swelling in the limbs, the lees were to be applied externally. This is according to all but the Berlin Papyrus prescriptions, which recommended plain *irp* "wine" for the purpose, rather than the *t3ht nt irp* or tartrate rich lees (Papyrus Ebers, 33, 13–19, prescriptions

162–63). It seems possible that both the alcohol and the tartrates could have helped to reduce fever and swelling.

6. Conclusion

Although most of the evidence we have concerning the ancient Egyptians' use of wine would point to the fact that it was a luxury item, it was clearly not reserved exclusively for royalty or deities. A King's Messenger under Sety I in charge of a troop of 1,000 men at the quarries of Gebel Silsila recorded the more than adequate provisions for his men and his own *daily* rations, which included both wine and *šdḥ* (Kitchen 1982: 26).

Wine was obviously important to a substantial proportion of the Egyptian population, including those who tended the vines, made the wines, shipped, stored, served, drank, or offered them. The winemakers were apparently respected for their skill regardless of their background, and they probably competed with one another to provide the most satisfying product, especially at the high end of the market. Although their best vintages can no longer be tasted, both their names and their fame survive. The scenes that depict their work are among the most beautiful Egyptian reliefs and paintings that survive, and the wine jar labels that have been recovered are not only useful for reconstructing the chronology and bits of the history of the Egyptians, but also useful in assessing their social history and ultimately our own.

IV

The History and Archaeology of Wine

The Mediterranean

CHAPTER 15

"Canaanite Jars" and the Late Bronze Age Aegeo-Levantine Wine Trade

Albert Leonard Jr.

1. Introduction[1]

Outside the royal palace of Kadmean Thebes, a figure speaks:

> I … am Dionysos, son of the king of gods,…
> I have come a long way. From Lydia and Phrygia,
> The lands of the golden rivers,
> Across the sun-baked steppes of Persia,
> Through the cities of Bactria,
> Smiling Arabia, and all the Anatolian coast,
> Where the salt seas beat on turreted strongholds
> Of Greek and Turk. I have set them all dancing;
> They have learned to worship me
> And know me for what I am:
> A god.
> And now,
> I have come to Greece …
> Euripides, *The Bacchae* lines 14–21 (Curry 1981: 118–19)

Although there has always been some confusion over the details of the true origins of "thrice-born" Dionysos, many have assumed that both he and his cult originated somewhere in the Levant and subsequently spread from east to west throughout the Mediterranean World (Graves 1988: 103–11; Stanislawski 1970, 1975; Hyams 1965; Otto 1965). This concept was vividly depicted by the potter Exekias about the middle of the 6th century B.C. on the interior of a drinking cup (Fig. 15.1) depicting the god reclining in a ship whose mast has sprouted vines and clusters of grapes,

Albert Leonard Jr.

Figure 15.1. The god Dionysos sailing in a ship whose mast has turned into a grapevine. From the interior of a *kylix* (drinking cup) by Exekias, mid-6th century B.C. (Photograph courtesy of Staatliche Antiksammlungen; no. 2044.)

while around the ship cavort a school of dolphins (Richter 1974: 337, fig. 451). This scene recalls an event recorded in the Homeric Hymn to Dionysos (Athanassakis 1976: 56–58, 97–98; cf. also Henrichs 1987: 109–11). While on his way to either Egypt or Cyprus (line 28), Dionysos is threatened by a gang of Tyrsenian pirates. In reaction:

> wonderous deeds unfolded before their eyes
> first through the swift black ship
> sweet and fragrant wine
> formed a gurgling stream and a divine smell
> arose as all the crew watched in mute wonder.
> And next on the topmost sail a vine spread about
> all over, and many grapes were hanging down
> in clusters. Then round the mast dark ivy twined,
> luxuriant with flowers and lovely growing berries.
>   *Hymn to Dionysos* VII:35–41 (Athanassakis 1976: 1)

Perhaps encouraged by such a scene, some scholars believe that the the knowledge of the god would have been impossible without a knowledge of the vine (Stanislawski 1975). They see the spread of viticulture to be a phenomenon contemporary with that of the dissemination of the god (cf. Stanislawski 1973, 1975). Robert Graves (1988: 107, n. 1) states it very simply: "The main clue to Dionysos' mystic history is the spread of the vine cult over Europe, Asia and North Africa."

Be that as it may, Butzer notes that grapes were "widespread and ubiquitous" in the Near East before 3000 B.C. (Butzer 1970: 45; see chapters 9 by Powell and 2 by Zohary, this volume).[2] At the beginnings of the Early Bronze Age at the site of Sitagroi in northern Greece, the change from wild to "domestic" grapes seems to have taken place at roughly the same time (Stratum IV or VA, C. Renfrew 1972: 278 and table 5.1 on 76.). Shortly after that date, the hieroglyphic sign for "winepress" appears in Egypt (Lucas 1989: 16; also see chapter 13 by James, this volume), and records indicate that the First Dynasty pharaohs of Egypt's Old Kingdom were enjoying wine (Egyptian *irp*) produced in their own royal vineyards (I. E. S. Edwards 1964: 20; Stager 1985: 174; Emery 1987: 246). In the contemporary Early Bronze Age cultures of Syria–Palestine, archaeological evidence for the early production of wine is, however, much more difficult to find. Some pioneer excavators interpreted the holes ("cup marks") that they found cut into the bedrock of a site to have been "unquestionably connected with wine presses" (Macalister 1912: I:152–57). However, the small size of these holes (averaging 30–45 cm in both depth and diameter at Lachish-Tufnell 1958: 39) and the lack of an outlet for the juice would argue against their being the pits in which grapes were actually trod. One might posit that these holes had been intended to secure some temporary (wooden?) apparatus connected with wine making, but this would be almost impossible to prove; and, since the holes are cut directly into the bedrock, they are usually impossible to date. We are on "firmer ground" in Palestine at Tell Ta'anach where the remains of an Early Bronze II–III (ca. 2700 B.C.) press were excavated in 1968 (Lapp 1969: 12 and n. 20, fig. 8). It consists of a shallow (ave. depth ca. 20 cm), roughly rectangular (ca. 2 × 3 m) depression from which two circular conduits were cut at an angle through the bedrock so as to flow into a much deeper catchment basin. Based on later, well-documented parallels, the Taànach installation appears to be the earliest treading and catchment arrangement for wine production in the Levant thus far discovered.

In Aegean contexts, clear impressions of vine leaves have been found on the bases of *pithoi* (large storage jars) at Early Bronze Age sites in the Cyclades and Crete (Warren 1972: 239 and note 1, No. 232, fig. 107; J. M. Renfrew 1972: 316 and n. 3; also chapter 16, this volume). More direct evidence for Aegean wine production at this early date, however, comes from Myrtos on Crete (see chapter 18 by Wright, this volume). In addition to the presence of spouted tubs that may have been used in winepressing or olive oil separation (or both), the interiors of some of the *pithoi* in Magazine A were very friable, possibly due to their ancient contents that were posited by the excavator to have been either wine or olives curing in brine (Warren 1972: 48, 147, especially no. P611). Since these vessels often have a small hole near the base, Warren argues that the *pithoi* originally contained wine that was decanted through the hole. In addition, Room 80 produced a *pithos* (no. P605) which still contained grape and grapevine remnants (bits of crushed grape skin, pips, stalks and skins) (Warren 1972: 75, 146; J. M. Renfrew 1972: 316). A spouted bowl in Room 90 also contained the remains of grapes (Warren 1972: 83–84, no. P307; J. M. Renfrew 1972: 316) and may have been part of a winemaking operation specifically intended to provide wine for use in the neighboring Shrine (Room 92). The cultic focus of the shrine was a small terracotta figure of a household goddess clutching a jug to her side (Warren 1972: no. P704, figs. 91–92, pls. 69–70).[3]

In the past, supporters of the theory of a western dispersion of viticulture have also appealed to philology, for *oinos*, the Homeric and Classical Greek word for wine is considered by some to find its ultimate origin in the Hittite word for wine: *wiyanas/wa-a-na-a-s* (Stager 1985: 173; Brown 1969: 147–48; see chapter 11 by Gorny, this volume), a word that is also suspected of being the "root" of the Ugaritic word for wine (*yn* = Hebrew *yayin*) (Selms 1974).[4] In the Aegean, the same ideogram is used for wine in both Linear A and B, and Ventris and Chadwick (1973: 35) think it to have been "borrowed" from the visually similar Egyptian hieroglyph for winepress, a derivation not universally accepted (see chapter 17 by Palmer, this volume). An intermediate form of the word for wine (*wo-no*) appears on some of the early Greek (Linear B) tablets from Knossos and Pylos, and is discussed fully by Palmer in this volume (chapter 17).

Furthermore, the Pylos archive has preserved the personal name *di-wo-nu-so-jo* or "Dionysos" (genitive case, Ventris and Chadwick 1973: 127, 411, 540; Lang 1961: 162; Gérrard-Rousseau 1969: 74–76); and Puhvel (1964) has argued that it is the actual deity which is intended, and not simply a mortal by the same name.

Additional archaeological support for a Bronze Age cult of Dionysos in the Aegean can be found at the site of Ayia Irini on the island of Kea, where a sanctuary that was laid out in the Middle Bronze Age survived, evidently continuously, into the Hellenistic period (Caskey 1981: figs. 1 and 2). Drinking cups are said to have been ubiquitous in many of the phases of the building (Caskey 1981: 130, 132); and a cup offered by Anthippos of Ioulis ca. 500 B.C., inscribed to the god Dionysos, shows that at least by that date the shrine was dedicated to him. In an 8th century B.C. phase of the shrine, the head of a Late Bronze Age female statue had been repositioned in a ring stand to serve as the focus of the cult (Caskey 1981: fig. 6).[5] Surprisingly, the cheeks of the goddess had been scored to suggest a bearded male.

It seems, then, that by the Late Bronze Age (ca. 1550–1150 B.C.), viticulture was well established among the cultures of both the Aegean and the Levant. Whether Dionysos had been a fellow traveler during its journey to Greece cannot be proven, but there is both archaeological and philological support for his worship in the Aegean at that time.

The Late Bronze Age was the first true period of internationalism that the cultures of the eastern Mediterranean had yet experienced (Leonard 1981, 1989; Merrillees 1986; McCaslin 1980: 97–100, table V). It was a time when specialty oils and unguents as well as other products from the Aegean entered an Egypto-Canaanite trading pattern that had existed for centuries. In fact, Aegean pottery (both open table ware and closed containers) has been found at over 140 sites between the Orontes River and the Nile Valley (Hankey and Leonard Forthcoming), a distribution that clearly testifies to the popularity of these vessels and/or their contents in Levantine markets. Colin Renfrew interpreted this distribution of "Mycenaean drinking cups" throughout the Levant as representing a "widespread trade in wine" (C. Renfrew 1972: 290).

The commodities that formed the return trade to Greece, however, are neither as widely dispersed nor as obvious in the archaeological record as their Aegean counterparts in the East. In fact, comparatively few Syro-Palestinian, Cypriote or Egyptian artifacts have been found in the Aegean area (for an inventory of what has been found, Lambrou-Phillipson 1991; Cline 1991; Knapp 1991). Among these, however, the largest category of objects consists of the transport vessel known as the "Canaanite Jar." Because these vessels share a morphological and typological resemblance to the classical amphorae that moved wine from production center to consumer in the Greco-Roman world, many scholars have seen the presence of these Canaanite Jars at sites in the Aegean as certain evidence of a Late Bronze Age maritime wine trade between Greece and ancient Canaan.

The purpose of this paper is to examine the form and function of the Canaanite Jar and—in the light of the finds of the last decade—to review the evidence for its association with the hypothetical Late Bronze Age Aegeo-Canaanite wine trade.

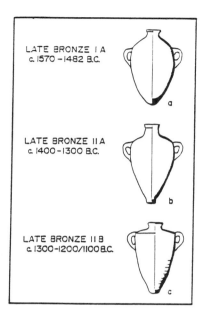

Figure 15.2. A "Canaanite Jar" from Myce-nae. (Demarkopooulou 1988: 250, no. 270.)

Figure 15.3. The morphological and chronological development of the Canaanite Jar through the Late Bronze Age: a) Megiddo Tomb 3028; b) Tell Abu Hawam Stratum V; and c) Megiddo Stratum VIIB. (Chart partially based on Amiran 1969: pl. 43.)

2. The Morphology of the Canaanite Jar

Morphologically, the Canaanite Jar is a simple form averaging ca. 50 cm in height (Figs. 15.2 and 15.3). It consists of an ovoid body that develops a more piriform or triangular profile during the Late Bronze Age (ca. 1500–1150 B.C.), and a highly pointed or stump base for stability on a non-horizontal surface if buttressed one against another or against a vertical support. Two large, vertical loop handles are attached opposite each other below the shoulder, to facilitate manipulation of the vessel. Its neck/mouth is sufficiently narrow for stoppering, and yet wide enough for the easy extraction of its contents (cf. Amiran 1969: 140–41 and pl. 43; Koehler 1986, and also chapter 20, this volume).

This combination of morphological features creates not only a distinctive shape but also results in a vessel of very practical form (structural strength plus ease of handling) (Fig. 15.4). We know from scenes in the New Kingdom Egyptian tombs that the jar can be carried on the shoulder, dragged across the ground, deck or dock, and even carried in a rope sling in much the same way that a handleless related form had been transported for centuries (James 1985: 15 and Wood 1987: 78, upper right, Tomb of Meryet-Amun; James 1985: fig. 11, Tomb of Khaemweset; also see chapters 13 by James and 14 by Lesko, this volume).

When not "in transport," these jars could be leaned either against each other (Fig. 15.5) (Schaeffer 1949: pl. 31; Forbes 1955: 75, fig. 18), or simply against a wall (Lesko 1977: top of 32,

Figure 15.4. Egyptian tomb of Rekhmire (Thebes, mid-Dynasty 18) illustrating the many ways in which the Canaanite Jar could be carried and moved. (Davies 1935: pl. 15; photograph courtesy of the Metropolitan Museum of Art, New York, Rogers Fund, 1930.)

Figure 15.5. Canaanite Jars as found stored in a warehouse at the site of Ras Shamra (Ugarit) on the North Syrian coast. (Schaeffer 1949: p. 31.)

Theban Tomb 155; Stead 1986: fig. 8, Deir el-Medina), reminiscent of the storeroom in Odysseus' palace:

> a great vault where gold and bronze lay piled along with chests of clothes, and fragrant oil. And there were jars of earthenware in rows holding an old wine, mellow, unmixed, and rare; cool stood the jars against the wall, kept for whatever day Odysseus, worn by hardships, might come home.
> *The Odyssey*, Book II:338–43 (Fitzgerald 1983: 29)

On formal or festive occasions, the jars could be placed in a ring stand (Aldred 1972: fig. 47) and, if needed or desired, they could be brightly painted with geometric patterns and floral designs (Hope 1978: 16–21) or even decorated with garlands of actual flowers (Lesko 1977: 38; Wood 1987: 77, upper right).

3. The Origin of the Canaanite Jar and Its Development Through the Middle Bronze Age

In attempting to trace the origin of the Canaanite Jar one can emphasize either the lower portion of the jar with its rounded, later more pointed base, or the upper portion with its opposing sub-shoulder handles and relatively wide mouth/neck. Most scholars consider the lower part of the jar to be the more significant.[6]

Peter Parr (1973), who locates the ultimate genesis of the type in Southern Mesopotamia (1973: 179–80), sees its first arrival in Canaan during the chronological and cultural interface that separated the Early and Middle Bronze Ages in Syria–Palestine, a region where storage jars and transport containers had been traditionally characterized by flat bases. In the Middle Bronze Age, however, a new (at first only slightly) rounded base began to occur on these large forms. The change can be seen at the very beginning of the Middle Bronze Age in the Courtyard Cemetery at Tell el-'Ajjul (Tufnell 1962) sometime after ca. 2000 B.C.[7]

This shift from flat to rounded base was not simply the result of a potter's whim or the passing fancy of some merchant or consumer, because the two types of vessels are structurally quite different. The stress on the junction between base and sidewalls of a flat-based vessel, caused by the sheer weight of the contents, is greatly reduced if not eliminated on vessels with rounder, more pointed bases (Parr 1973: 176–77; Wood 1987: 76). Tufnell saw this morphological change as reflecting the arrival in Palestine of a "wine-drinking instead of a beer-drinking community" at the beginning of the Middle Bronze Age (1958: 220).

Shortly after the appearance of the canonical Canaanite Jar in the markets and storerooms of the eastern Mediterranean, the form was introduced to Egypt. An Egypto-Canaanite trade in olive and resinous oils and/or wine can be documented as early as the beginnings of the Old Kingdom (Stager 1985: 179–80; Emery 1987: 204), and formed part of a trade that may have reached as far west as the island of Crete (see the Tale of Ipu-Wer—Lichtheim 1975: 149–62; Smith 1965: 5, 10; Goedicke 1967: 93; and Ward 1971: 38, n. 150). It is as a container in this established trade network that Egypt may have first received the Canaanite Jar. Whether the introduction was made by land or seaborne commerce is difficult to ascertain, but the distinctive form, with a rounded base and pair of loop handles, is known from the earliest Middle Bronze IIA strata at the site of Tell el-Dab'a in the northeastern part of the Egyptian Delta, which correspond to mid-MB IIA levels at Syro-Palestinian sites (P. E. McGovern, personal communication). This site sits astride trade routes which had connected the two cultures for centuries (Bietak 1986). Previously, large Egyptian jars with pointed bases—including those used to store and transport wine—did not have these handles (Grace 1956: 83 and fig. 1; Parr 1973: 178), and were much more difficult to move from one place to another (cf. fn. 6).

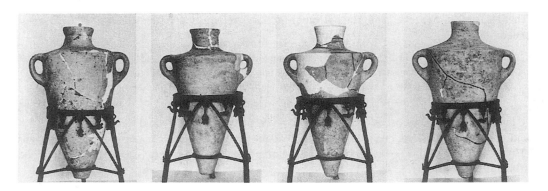

Figure 15.6. Canaanite Jars excavated at the sites of Mycenae and Menidi on the mainland of Greece. (Grace 1956: pl. 10.1-4.)

4. The Canaanite Jar in the Aegean

Phase I: The early history of the study

Whatever we are able to say about the role of the Canaanite Jar in the Aegean is the result of over one hundred years of research by individuals working not only in Greece but also in Egypt and the Levant. This long history of scholarship can be divided into two phases: an earlier period of about a century, ca. 1880–1980, in which progress was slowed by the infancy of the discipline of archaeology as well as by the paucity of examples; and a later period, the last decade, which has been characterized by a major increase in the sample size, and by the increased use of scientific analyses in Mediterranean archaeology.

In 1880, at a time when Heinrich Schliemann was dazzling the archaeological world with the results of his excavations at Troy and Mycenae, and 20 years before Sir Arthur Evans was to begin to unravel the mysteries of the Minoan palace at Knossos, G. Lolling published the results of his excavation of a comparatively small *tholos* ("beehive") tomb at the site of Menidi, northwest of Athens (Lolling 1880; Hope Simpson 1981: 44, Site B10). This richly appointed tomb contained the remains of six individuals who had been interred during the 13th century B.C. (Mycenaean IIIB period). Among the funerary offerings included in the tomb were four large ceramic jars (ca. 50 cm in height (Fig. 15.6) with pointed bases and opposing loop handles on their bodies. These vessels stood out sharply from the rest of the pottery from the tomb because of their distinctive shape, their foreign-looking fabric, and the fact that handles of two of the jars had been incised with characters similar in form to elements of an early Cypriot script (Fig. 15.7) (Tsountas and Manatt 1969: 268; now see Chadwick 1987: 50–56 and Palaima 1989: *passim*). Subsequently, inscribed signs were detected on the handles of the other two jars from this tomb (Åkerström 1975: 1991; Demakopoulou 1988: 250, No. 270). Shortly after the excavation of the Menidi *tholos*, clearing of chamber tombs at Mycenae (Nos. 58 and 59/95?, Tsountas and Manatt 1969: 269) produced three more of these vessels, two of which were also inscribed.

For the archaeologists of the 19th century, the main appeal of these large jars was their inscriptions. Unfortunately, researchers working with these jars labored under the misconception that the signs had been inscribed while the clay was still soft in the potter's atelier. After all, should not the language of the inscription indicate the language of the craftsman or country of origin? Petrie and Pendlebury, both recognizing similarities between these jars and similar vessels made locally in the Nile Valley, thought that the language must have been Egyptian (Pendlebury 1930:

 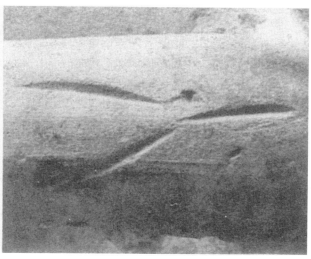

Figure 15.7. Signs, possibly of an early Cypriote script, inscribed on the handles of one of the jars in Fig. 15.6. (Grace 1956: pl. 10-5-6.)

88; Grace 1956: 82 and nn. 6 and 7). But the writing systems of the Bronze Age Aegean were still being identified and isolated at that time. It would be another half-century before one of them, Greek Linear B, would be deciphered.

During the first quarter of the 20th century, two sites in the Argolid, Argos (Chamber Tomb 6, Vollgraff 1904: 376; Deshayes 1953: 69, pl. 21:2), and Asine (Chamber Tomb 2, Åkerström 1975: 185, figs. 1 and 3), were added to the Canaanite Jar distribution map. Both jars were singletons and both came from funerary contexts. By the time of the appearance of Arne Furumark's (1941) landmark study of Mycenaean pottery, therefore, only nine of these distinctive jars had been identified in the archaeological record of the Aegean basin.

Furumark recognized that the jars were not Mycenaean but, for the sake of completeness, he included them in his study under either Form 6/Shape 13B (Pithos with pointed base) or Form 13/Shape 73 (Jar with Vertical Handles on body). He did admit that the two groups could, and probably should, be combined (Furumark 1941: 74–76, 587, 596, and fig. 21: 13a).[8] Furumark's work regularized the study of this jar-type by recognizing it as a distinct class of pottery. But, in the 1940s, most of the discussion about these jars continued to be focused on their inscriptions. As before, the crucial point was whether the signs had been applied to the vessel during the manufacturing process while the clay was still soft (i.e., at the potter's workshop) or after manufacture when the vessel was in use. By the 1940s, however, the suspected point of origin of these jars was slowly moving northward away from the Nile Valley to the region along the Syro-Palestinian coast where previous decades of excavation at sites such as Ras Shamra, Byblos, Megiddo, and Lachish had produced many parallels for them in both form and fabric (for references, see Leonard 1989).

In 1956, Virginia Grace moved the emphasis of discussion away from the inscriptional/philological end of the spectrum and more to the morphological end. Seeing the jars as early manifestations of the "classical" amphora with stamped handle, so often associated with the transportation of wine in later Greek and Roman times, she traced the development of the shape through the 2nd and 1st millennia B.C. Because she saw the homeland of the form among the

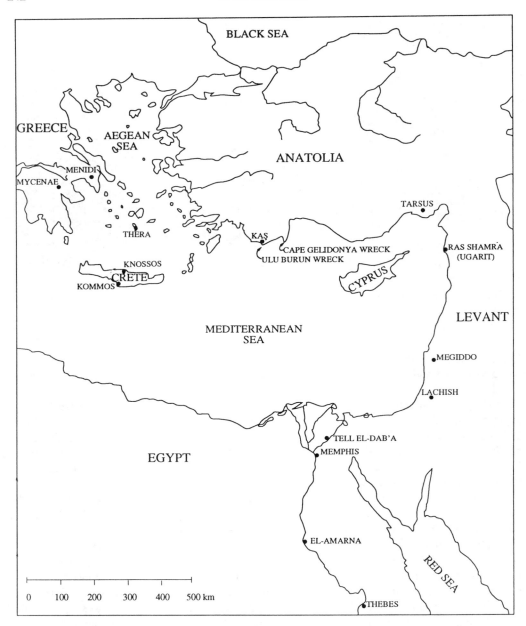

Map 15.1. The Eastern Mediterranean region: principal sites. (Drawing by L. A. Kain.)

countries of the Syro-Palestinian littoral (biblical Canaan), Grace termed the vessel the "Canaanite Jar" (Grace 1956: 80–81, 1961: *passim*; Åkerström 1991; for the geography of Canaan, see Aharoni 1967: 121–73). She (Grace 1956: 88) stressed that most of the inscriptions seemed to her to have been executed after the vessel had been fired, and that Levantine parallels (rather than Egyptian) seemed to be the most appropriate.

By the time that Grace wrote, the corpus of Canaanite Jars from the Aegean area had increased only slightly, still numbering less than a dozen. A single jar with incised handle had been discovered in the well preserved tomb of a wealthy Athenian lady in the heart of what was later to become the classical Agora (Tomb of the Ivory Pyxis, Grace 1956: 101, fig. 5:3, pl. IX.1; Immerwahr 1971: 119, 164, pl. 31.7, 8; Åkerström 1975: 192, no. 11, fig. 6). And, for the first time, three Canaanite Jars were reported from non-funerary (i.e., domestic) contexts at Mycenae: two from the Citadel House and one from the "Causeway Deposit."[9] One of the jars from the Citadel House differed from the others in another respect, because, instead of being inscribed on the handle, it bore a large double-axe or butterfly pattern executed in red "paint" on the body of the vessel (Bennett 1958: 76–77, no. 601; Wace 1955: 178, pl. 208; and see also Åström 1991: 150, from Hala Sultan Tekke).

The 1960s saw the discovery of the Late Bronze Age shipwreck at Cape Gelidonya (Turkey) and the excavation of fragments of seven vessels of related form, which were termed "water jars" by the excavators (cf. J.B. Hennessy and J. du Plat Taylor in Bass 1967: 122–23, fig. 132: P2–P6).

At the close of the decade, Amiran (1969: 140–43) published her classic study of Palestinian pottery. Following Grace's lead, Amiran emphasized the difference between the "Canaanite Jars," which functioned mainly as transport containers, and "decorated jars" which were vessels of similar form but were used primarily as storage containers.

In 1975, Åke Åkerström (1975: 185) clarified our knowledge of the shape of the jar that had been excavated previously at Asine. He presented clear illustrations of a similar vessel from *tholos* tomb 3 at Kato Englianos/Pylos (Åkerström 1975: 185, figs. 2, 4 and 5; Blegen 1973: 94, fig. 174: 4a and 4b), and reported that "fragments of several other Canaanite Jars" had been found in domestic (non-funerary) contexts at the House of the Oil Merchant at Mycenae (Åkerström 1975: 187). At about the same time, the first Canaanite Jar was published from the Cyclades—an early, ovoid variant from a domestic context at Akrotiri on the island of Thera/ Santorini (Room Delta 9, 1, Marinatos 1976: 30 and pl. 49b; Doumas 1983: 119; Barber 1987: 171, 258, n. 9). A few years later, another jar was discovered in a rich Mycenaean chamber tomb at Koukaki in Attica (Cline 1991: 408, no. 287).

Thus, by the end of the 1970s, almost a century after they were first noticed at Menidi, a corpus of less than two dozen Canaanite Jars had been identified in the Aegean (plus seven related vessels from the Cape Gelidonya wreck).

Except for the island of Thera, the distribution of find-spots showed a strong mainland bias. None had yet been found on Crete. In fact, at this stage in the research, if one were to plot a hypothetical commercial route (Map 15.1) from the sources in the Levant to the markets in the Aegean, it would come by Cyprus, past Cape Gelidoniya, across the Aegean (stopping at Thera?), and on to landfall probably in either Attica (Menidi) or the Argolid (Mycenae). This concept, as we shall see, was soon to change.

Furthermore, other than the examples from the houses at Mycenae and Thera, all of the Canaanite Jars known at that time had been found in funerary contexts. Obviously, such large vessels would not have traveled empty. They would have protected and delivered a commodity that, by the very cost of its long journey, would have been extremely attractive in the markets of the Aegean world. For those studying the significance of these imports at that time, it appeared quite reasonable to suggest that they had been filled with some luxurious commodity imported from afar to embellish the afterlife of the upper strata of Aegean society. And what was this presumably very costly, and highly desirable commodity? Although dry goods such as spices (Webster 1959: 66) and grain (Doumas 1983: 119), or liquids such as (olive) oil (Davies and Faulkner 1947; Amiran 1969: 140–43 [or wine]) and beer (Doumas 1983: 119) had been posited, it was wine that was most often thought to have been the contents.

Figure 15.8. An installation interpreted as a winepress from the site of Kato Zakros on the eastern end of the island of Crete. (Platon 1971: opp. p. 30.)

Pendlebury (1930: 88) had been quick to identify the imported "amphorae" in the tombs at Menidi and Mycenae as "wine jars," and Vermeule wrote of "great jars of Canaanite wine" beginning to appear at sites in Greece during the Late Bronze Age (Vermeule 1974: 255, cf. also 258, 267). Harding (1984: 126) saw the presence of these jars in the Aegean as being indicative of the development of "exotic tastes in wine" among the peoples of the Aegean, while Culican (1966: 53) compared the shape of the jars found in Greece to the shape of containers said to be filled with "a light wine made of North Syrian grapes," which formed part of the Canaanite coastal trade with Egypt.[10] Because of wine's "seductive nature," Stanislawski (1975: 428) has suggested that "when contacts are made between wine dispensers and folk who have not known the drink, most of the latter will quickly acquire a taste for it; and a persistent demand—and trade—will begin, even in areas where another alcoholic beverage has been common."

5. Winemaking in the Late Bronze Age Levant

It is from Egypt that we get our clearest indication of how wine was actually made during the Late Bronze Age, and a similar model can most probably be used for winemaking among the contemporary cultures of the Levant and the Aegean. A painting in the Tomb of Khaemweset (Theban Tomb 261, James 1985: 14–15, fig. 11; see chapter 14 by Lesko, this volume) demonstrates almost the complete sequence from the picking and treading of the grapes, through the "bottling" process in Canaanite Jars, to the transportation by ship and the unloading of the finished product. Wine production in Egypt appears to have been a rather peaceful occupation and certainly stands in sharp contrast to the "fist fights and wrestling matches" that accompanied the pressing of grapes on the Shield of Herakles as described by the 8th century B.C. Greek writer Hesiod (*Shield*, lines 290–305, Athanassakis 1983: 137).

Figure 15.9. Satyrs in the act of winemaking, on a Black Figured vase by the Amasis Painter. (Stewart 1987: fig. 10.)

In Crete, spouted tubs that have been identified as footpresses have been found at several Late Bronze Age (i.e., "Late Minoan") sites, including Arkhanes, Gournia, Mallia, Petras, and Kato Zakro (Long 1974: 36 and note 24; Catling 1989: 105; Leonard, personal observation). At first glance, the small diameters of these spouted basins (Fig. 15.8) would seem to argue against their use in grape-pressing, at least as a group activity of the kind shown in Egyptian tombs and in Hesiod's day. These tubs would have been large enough, however, for a single individual to have worked at a time, as do the satyrs on some Black Figured vases by the 6th century B.C. Amasis painter (Fig. 15.9) (Biers 1988: 177–78, fig. 7: 33, from the Antikenmuseum, Basel; and Stewart 1987: 36, fig. 10, from the Wagner Museum, University of Würzburg).

6. The Desirability of Levantine Wine

Although the origins of the Canaanite Jar in Egypt and the Levant can be traced back into the Middle Bronze Age, it is really during the Late Bronze Age, when Canaan was under the direct control of the Egyptian New Kingdom pharaohs (Leonard 1989, Ahituv 1978, Gonen 1984; Several 1972; Weinstein 1981; cf. McGovern 1985: 97–101), that we witness the major *floruit* of the type in Syria–Palestine and hence the widest distribution of its contents.[11] In spite of their own long history of wine production, the quality of the wines of Canaan had for centuries appealed to the palette of the traditionally beer-drinking Egyptian (Stager 1985: 175; Lesko 1977: 14, and chapter 14, this volume; Wilkinson 1988: 53–55; Forbes 1955: II:63–70).[12]

Albert Leonard Jr.

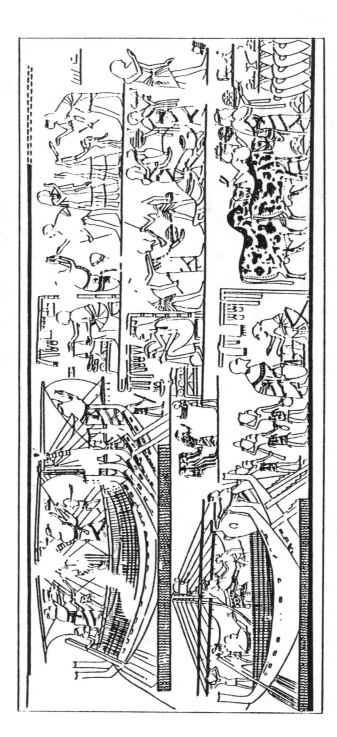

Figure 15.10. Egyptian port scene in the tomb of Kenamun showing Canaanite jars and other commercial goods being unloaded for trade in an active bazaar. (Davies and Faulkner 1947: pl. 8.)

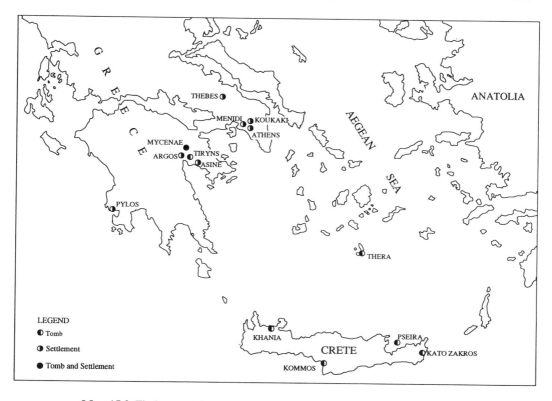

Map 15.2. Findspots of Canaanite Jars in the Aegean. (Drawing by L. A. Kain.)

If such wines could find an honored place on the tables and in the tombs of pharaoh, they would have had a similar appeal to the palettes of the rulers of Mycenae, Pylos, etc. Could not the presence of Canaanite Jars at sites in the Aegean be an extension of this wine trade, perhaps through commercial ventures similar to that shown in the tomb of Kenamun (Davies and Faulkner 1947: 17; Boston Museum of Fine Arts 1982: 16, fig. 3 detail) (Fig. 15.10). Here, we see the arrival of a group of commercial seafarers, led by richly costumed Canaanites who, along with Aegeans(?) in their patterned kilts, unload Canaanite Jars and other recognizable vessels to be traded in a dockside market. This was the most widely held interpretation of Canaanite Jars less than a decade ago.

7. The Canaanite Jar in the Aegean

Phase II: The later history of the study

The second phase of the study of Canaanite Jars consists of the research done in the last ten years. During this time, the *corpus* of known examples in the Aegean increased rapidly as a result of the publication of both earlier finds and new excavations (Map 15.2). During this phase, only one Canaanite Jar from a funerary context was discovered on the mainland of Greece: that from a chamber tomb near Boeotian Thebes (Site 191, actually dug in 1967, Symeonoglou 1985: 52, 289; R. B. Edwards, 1979: 131). Incidentally, this region has been closely associated with the cult of Dionysos and the Near East through both the Kadmos legend (Symeonoglou 1973) and the

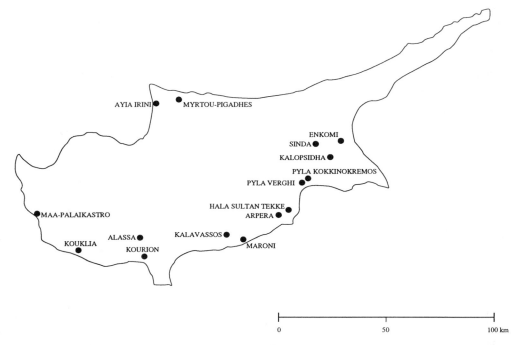

Map 15.3. Findspots of Canaanite Jars in the Cyprus. (Drawing by L. A. Kain.)

famous cache of cylinder seals excavated in the "New Kadmeion" (Demakopoulou and Konsola 1981: 52–53, figs. 11–14; pl. 23; Porada 1965: 173, 1966: 194). Of the remaining recent finds of Canaanite Jars on the Greek mainland, eleven examples were excavated at the site of Tiryns in the Argolid, all of which came from occupational contexts (Kilian 1988; Oliver 1988)! These finds make the Canaanite Jar much less of a "funerary offering for the wealthy" than hitherto had been thought.

The past decade of research has brought to light another surprising and important fact. The "great island" of Crete has now come into its own as a major (if not *the* major) recipient for whatever goods these jars contained. At the site of Kommos on the southern coast of Crete about sixty Canaanite Jars have now been excavated, most of them also coming from domestic or commercial contexts (Shaw 1984: 278–79, 1986: 268–69; Cline 1990: 418–34, nos. 317–73; Vance Watrous, personal communication). The form is now known from the small island of Pseira (Phillip Betancourt, personal communication) in the Gulf of Mirabello to the north of Crete; and from Khania at the southern end of Souda Bay in western Crete (Kilian 1986: 127). Recently, "many Canaanite Jars" have been reported in Neopalatial contexts at Kato Zakros on the eastern end of the island (Catling 1989: 107; French 1990: 73); and a single sherd from such a vessel may have been found at Knossos itself (Cline 1990: 73 and n. 109; personal communication from J.A. MacGilivray). Almost all of these Cretan examples come from non-funerary contexts. Thus, in most instances, the contents of these jars were probably used or consumed by the living and not just hoarded for the glorification of the afterlife. Similarly, on the island of Cyprus, Canaanite Jars tend to be found primarily in domestic contexts and only secondarily in funerary deposits (Map 15.3).[13]

In addition to these newly excavated finds, scientific analyses have been conducted on some of the Canaanite Jars that have been known in Greece for over a century. The most important of these studies is that by Abner Raban (1980),[14] who, in addition to creating a typology of the Canaanite Jars presently known, has supplemented the visual differentiation of fabric types (and hence clay sources) made by the earlier researchers (Pendlebury 1930; Grace 1956; etc.) with instrumental neutron activation analysis (INAA). Clay was tested from ten Canaanite Jars from Argos, Athens, Menidi, Mycenae and Pylos. The results indicated three clay sources, each from the Syro-Palestinian littoral: the coastal area from Philistia to Byblos, the coastal area from Akko to Ugarit, and "South Palestine" (in Jones 1986: 572). This definitely indicates the general area in which the imported jars were made but, unfortunately, the geographical limits of the individual areas are rather amorphous. It is hoped that future testing of a larger sample will allow for more accurate "pinpointing" of the clay sources with less overlapping of source-areas. Recently, tests on Canaanite Jars from sites on Cyprus

Figure 15.11. A diver removing a Canaanite Jar from the Ulu Burun shipwreck. (Bass 1987: 710.)

have been published. A large sample from Maa-Palaikastro has been examined by a combination of petrographic studies and atomic absorption spectroscopy (ASS) (Hadjicosti 1988; Jones and Vaughn 1988); and sherds form Hala Sultan Tekke have been analyzed by secondary ion mass spectrometry (Åström 1988; Fisher 1991a and b). The Brookhaven and MASCA INAA study of Middle Bronze Age amphorae from Syria–Palestine and Tell el-Dab'a includes approximately 300 examples, which are well-defined stratigraphically, chronologically, and by chemical source area, and should provide the basis for future studies (P. E. McGovern, personal communtion).

Finally, this past decade has brought the discovery of the Late Bronze Age (Canaanite?) merchant ship that sank off the Ulu Burun promontory near Kas, on the southern coast of Turkey sometime during the 14th century B.C. Since underwater excavation began in 1984 (Bass 1986, 1987; Bass et al. 1989), well over 100 Canaanite Jars, the best morphological parallels for which can be found in Tombs 58 and 59 at Mycenae (Pulak 1988: 10), have been identified in the wreck (Fig. 15.11). The handle of at least one of these jars was inscribed (Bass 1986: 278). Such a large quantity of jars is certainly impressive, but much more important is the fact that many of them

Figure 15.12. The mouth of a Canaanite Jar and the ancient nodules of *terebinth* with which it had been filled as part of the cargo of the Ulu Burun wreck. (Bass 1987: 709.)

have preserved all or part of their contents. With this material, we are in a much better position to comment on the reason that the Canaanite Jars were traded westward to Aegean shores.

Although one of the jars was found to be full of olive pits (Haldane 1990: 59; Bass 1991: 74), a second was filled with glass beads (KW 8, Bass 1986: 278), and yet another contained orpiment, a yellow arsenic pigment that was associated with glass manufacture in later periods (KW 48, Bass 1986: 278–79; 1991: 74). Almost all of the remaining jars contained a resinous substance (Bass 1986: 277; Pulak 1988: 10). Curt Beck, using infrared spectroscopy, was able to demonstrate that this material was not pine resin (in Bass 1986: 277; see also Pulak 1988: 11), especially not the type of pitch usually associated with the "caulking" of amphorae in the later classical wine trade. In fact, there is no evidence that during the Bronze Age the interiors of these vessels were coated with resin or bitumen to seal the pores of the fabric or to impart a particular flavor to the contents as was done in later classical times (Lucas 1989: 20; Koehler 1986: 50–52, and chapter 20, this volume). Through further study of the plant and seed remains, Haldane was able to identify the leaves and fruit of *Pistacia*, cf. *terebinth* (Pulak 1988: 11 and n. 42). Subsequent testing by Mills and White (1989), using gas-liquid chromatography–mass spectrometry (GLC-MS), supported this identification as *Pistacia atlantica* Desf. (Chian turpentine), which once grew in several areas of the Mediterranean and the Near East (Mills and White 1989: 38; illustrated in Bass 1987: 709; Hepper 1990: 26; Hairfield and Hairfield 1990). This material (Fig. 15.12) has been interpreted as the *ki-ta-no* of the Mycenaean Linear B tablets, a commodity that is recorded in very substantial quantities at the palace at Knossos (Chadwick 1976: 120–21).[15]

8. Non-Viticultural Uses for the Canaanite Jar in Egypt

It was the Ulu Burun wreck and its cargo of Canaanite Jars that called attention to what probably should have been emphasized from the beginning: the Canaanite Jar, as the classical amphora to

Figure 15.13. Water is drawn from the Nile in a *shaduf* made from a broken Canaanite Jar; from the tomb of Ipy. (Manniche 1989: 12.)

which it has been compared so often, would have been used to store and transport not just one, but a variety of commodities.

Returning, with a wider vision, to the richly decorated New Kingdom tombs, one can see that these jars were utilized in many Egyptian industries other than viticulture. For instance, in the Tomb of Vizier Rekhmire they hold some liquid (oil?) used in the preparation of skins in a sandalmakers workshop (Aldred 1972: 66 and fig. 51), and are also used to haul water from a pond to a group of brickmakers (Pritchard 1973: fig. 18). In the Tomb of Nakht, a group of jars stands ready to receive a cache of air-dried waterfowl in a vignette that is iconographically very similar to the famous vineyard scene from the same tomb (Wood 1987: 75).

The hieratic inscriptions painted by Egyptian scribes on the sides of these vessels also reveal a wide range of commodities—in addition to wine—that were once contained, transported, or stored in them. This includes both edibles—ale, beans, beer, curds, fat, fish, fowl, fruit, grain, honey, meat, milk, mutton, and oil—as well as non-edibles—eyepaint, gum, incense, myrrh, purple dye, and unguent (Wood 1987: 76; chapter 5 by McGovern and Michel, this volume). These, however, are just the major categories, and the number of subclassifications of many of the items is often quite large (Hayes 1951; Leahy 1977). For instance, at least ten different varieties of cleaned and dried waterfowl had been packaged in the amphorae found in the Palace of Amenhotep III at Malkata in western Thebes (Hayes 1951: 92–93: Hope 1978: 24–25; also see chapter 14 by Lesko, this volume).

Further obscuring the identification of the commodity (or commodities) traded to the Aegean world in Canaanite Jars is the fact that we are dealing with societies in which the use of these jars in a one-way or one-time capacity would have been unlikely, except under special circumstances (e.g., as burial goods or royal gifts). The production of a Canaanite Jar reflects a substantial investment of time, talent and material and, if intact, they would probably have been cleaned and put back into service in a role that could have been much different than their original function. Lesko (1977: 29) noted the presence of a relatively small number of broken wine jars at el-Amarna, a site that had been occupied for over a decade, and thought that this situation was best explained if empty (but still serviceable) jars had been returned to the production centers for recycling. More direct archaeological evidence for such reuse comes from Amenhotep III's palace at Malkata where "many of the inscribed jar fragments bear, in addition to a relatively fresh label, the faded or partially erased remains of *one or more earlier labels*" (author's emphasis) (Hayes 1951: 39; see also Hope 1978: 8). Organic detritus found inside several of the resin-filled jars from the Ulu Burun wreck has been interpreted as representing a commodity with which the jars had been filled previously (Haldane in Puluk 1988: 11).

Perhaps the clearest evidence for the "ecology-minded" manner with which the ancient Egyptian dealt with the Canaanite Jar is the fact that even when the top of the vessel was completely missing, often due to breakage during the unsealing process (Hope 1978: 8), the bottom of the jar would still be used. One simply connected a rope to the handles and attached the resulting "bucket" to the *shaduf* (Fig. 15.13). With this apparatus, water could be raised from the level of the Nile to that of the garden, in order to irrigate crops that might someday fill more complete vessels of the same shape (see Aldred 1972: 18, fig. 10, Tomb of Ipy; Manniche 1989: 12, Theban Tombs 49 and 217).

9. Summary and Conclusions

This review of the available evidence suggests that the Canaanite Jar during the Late Bronze Age should be considered as a multipurpose container in which a variety of commodities, both edible and inedible, were exchanged among the cultures of the eastern Mediterranean. Certainly, wine could have been one item shipped in Canaanite Jars, but currently the evidence is slim that the vessels were used to transport wine to the Aegean. If one wishes to retain the hypothesis of a wine trade between the Aegean and the Levant that utilized a single, distinctive container, an appeal might be made for the wineskin.[16]

In classical Greece, wine often arrived at the banquet or party in a wineskin and was decanted into a krater (*inter alia*, see Lissarrague 1987: 39, fig. 25 by the Epelios Painter). Once emptied, this left an object that could be inflated to serve as a prop for games of balance and dexterity (Lissarrague 1987: 68–80). A similar event (the *askolia*) took place on the second day of the Festival of Dionysos.

In Homer's time, wine also traveled in wineskins in addition to being transported in pottery containers. Before the walls of Troy, wine is brought onto the battlefield in a goat wineskin (*askos*) to accompany oaths before the proposed contest between Menelaos and Paris (*Iliad* III:245–49, Latimore 1974: 106); and it is in a "goatskin bottle" that Odysseus had transported the sweet dark wine with which he "entertains" the Cyclops Polyphemos (*Odyssey* IX:190–213, Fitzgerald 1963: 150–51). The old priest Maron had stored this "divine drink" in two-handled jars until Odysseus had poured some of it into a goatskin for his long and perilous journey (*Odyssey* IX:203–4). In a similar vein, Aravantinos (1984: 46) has suggested that the wine delivered to the Palace of Nestor at Pylos was brought there in wineskins, and opened and checked in a vestibule (Room 104) before being transferred to the large clay *pithoi* in the Wine Magazine (Room 105) itself (also see chapter 18 by Wright, this volume). One would think that such a manner of conveyance might have had a long pedigree among the cultures of the eastern Mediterranean, but, if so, this thesis is very difficult to prove archaeologically. Skins to hold liquid are depicted in Egyptian tombs (Mekhitarian 1954: 78, Tomb of Nakht; Wilkinson 1988: 35, fig. 39), but unfortunately, they are only associated with the transportation of water. If one posits the existence of a Bronze Age, Aegeo-Canaanite wine trade in which the wine was shipped in skins, the argument is largely *ex silentia*.

For the present, then, the hypothetical Aegeo-Levantine wine trade in Late Bronze Age, referred to in the title of this paper must remain just that—hypothetical. It cannot yet be proven archaeologically. At best, it can only be suggested by the occurrences of similar phenomena in adjacent societies. Perhaps, as the research of the 1980s altered our first interpretation of the Canaanite Jar, future research will provide the knowledge necessary to understand its true role in the trade among the cultures of the ancient Near East. However, in the meantime, those who possess the "eye of faith" will certainly be unable to view the harbor scenes in ancient Egyptian tombs without being reminded of Telamachos' charge to the aged Eurykleia:

> Nurse, get a few two-handled travelling jugs
> filled up with wine ...
> Twelve amphora will do; seal them up tight. (for)
> I sail to sandy Pylos, then to Sparta,
> to see what news there is of father's voyage.
> Homer, *The Odyssey* II: lines 349–59 (Fitzgerald 1963: 29).

Notes

1. For an overview of the Late Bronze Age in Syria–Palestine, see Albright 1965 and Leonard 1989. For the chronology, see Warren and Hankey 1989: 72–118, 137–74; Leonard 1987 and 1989, especially the chart on pp. 6–7. In the text, I have tried to give the minimum number of references for the individual jars. For an extended bibliography for each import, cf. Cline 1991: catalogue nos. 286 (Athens, Agora), 287 (Athens, Koukaki), 288 (Argos), 289 (Asine), 290–93 (Menidi), 294–302 (Mycenae), 303–13 (Tiryns), 314 (Pylos), 315 (Thebes), 316 (Akrotiri/Thera), 317–73 (Kommos), 374–75 (Kato Zakros), 376 (Pseira), 377 (Khania), 378–84 (Kas/Ulu Burun). For the later development of the Canaanite jar (from the 13th through the 4th centuries B.C.), see Sagona 1982. A type collection of the entire series is published in Zener 1978.

2. At this symposium, D. Zohary and J. Green called the participants' attention to the discovery of grape pips in Middle Chalcolithic deposits at Tell esh-Shuneh (North) in Jordan by Reinder Neef of the Biologisch Archeologisch Institut, Groningen, The Netherlands.

3. As published, the goddess is interpreted as the "protectoress of the water supply" (Warren 1972: 266), but might not the tiny jug have contained wine, a supply of which was constantly replenished from a supply "hidden" in the hollow body of the goddess herself? See the profile drawing in Warren 1972: fig. 91, no. P704.

4. Cyrus Gordon would interpret a pair of signs inscribed on a *pithos* from Knossos as the related Northwest Semitic word *ya-ne* (= *yain*, "wine"?) written in the earlier, and as yet undeciphered, Linear A language of Crete (Gordon 1964: 185; 1965: 302), whereas Best (1988: 15–16) believes that *wa*, the syllabic value of the ideogram in both the Linear A and B scripts, reflects a hypothetical Proto-Semitic **wainu*.

5. These finds have generated quite a bit of thought and discussion. Cf., *inter alia*, Rutkowski 1986: 169–72, 175, 198; Burkert 1988: 275–76. Cf. also Warren 1981: 161, 163.

6. A case might be made for the origin of the Canaanite jar in the flat-bottomed, two-handled vases of the Early Bronze Age/Old Kingdom trade (see Smith 1965: figs. 3, 5).

7. Tufnell uses the term "MB I," which is also favored by Kenyon, Parr, and other British archaeologists for the same cultural/chronological period that Albright and American archaeologists refer to as "MB IIA." Cf. Kenyon 1979: 150, n. 4; Parr 1973: 179, note; and the chart in Dever 1978: 149. The absolute dating of the period is currently a matter of debate.

8. Furumark's inclusion in his Shape 13B of two (evidently handleless) variants (1941: 587, FS 13B, Nos. 9,10) from a domestic context at the site of Tsartsane in Macedonia has not had broad acceptance and they are most probably from another, local vessel type—possibly the storage jar or *pithos* (Åkerström 1975: 185, n. 1).

9. Citadel House: Wace 1955: 179, pl. 20B; Åkerström 1975: 191–92 possibly equals Cline 1990: no. 413, from the "South House Annex Storeroom"; and Cline 1990: 413, no. 298. For the relevent position of these two structures, see Wace and Willams 1961: 24–25, plan II. Causeway Deposit: Wardle 1973: 298, no. 194; Cline 1990: 414, no. 302.

10. Both Vermeule (1974: 255) and C. Renfrew (1972: 290) also suggest the existence of a reciprocal trade (west to east) in Greek wines, but not everyone is in agreement (Merrillees and Winter 1972: 126–27).

11. The Egyptians were quick to copy what had been originally an import, and by at least the reign of Thutmosis III in the 15th century B.C. (Wood 1987: 79), the "handled amphora" appears to have been produced locally from several Nile clays and silts (Hope 1978: 66–74). In the Middle Bronze Age, Nile alluvial clays were used for Canaanite jars as early as MB IIA at Tell el-Dab'a (P. E. McGovern, personal communication). On the whole, the Egyptian version exhibits a more slender profile than its Canaanite counterpart (Wood 1987), but it too demonstrates a morphological development from an oval (earlier) profile to a severely pointed (later) form the Egyptian New Kingdom (cf. Wood 1987: 80–81, sidebar, with Amiran 1969: fig. 43; cf. also Hope 1987: 9, 49; and Rose 1984). This parallel development should not be surprising since the two cultures were in constant contact throughout the period. Because of this similarity in form, however, it is often very difficult, in the absence of direct visual examination or petrographical analysis of the fabric (Hope 1978: 66–69; 75–79), to separate the locally produced from the imported jar. This difficulty is compounded when one is dealing with tomb paintings made by an ancient Egyptian artist, who may not have been conscious of the subtleties of detail assumed (and demanded) by modern archaeologists.

12. The scale of Canaanite production had also not gone unnoticed. New Kingdom Pharaoh Thutmose III's impression of the Canaanite region of Djahi as a place where wines "flow like rivers" (Temple of Karnak, Goor and Nurock 1968: 20), simply echoes the earlier, Middle Kingdom description of the Canaanite "Land of Yaa" as a place where wine was "even more plentiful than water" (*Story of Sinuhe*, Breasted 1988 I:238, no. 496).

13. The information used to compile Map 15.3 was obtained from the following sources: Åkerström 1975; Åstrom 1972 and 1977; Catling 1962 and 1968; Daniels 1941; Hadjisavvas 1986; Jones 1986; Karageorghis and Demas 1984; Kilian 1986; Megaw 1953; and Merrillees 1974.

14. This study in Hebrew has not been available to me while preparing this article. I have had to use secondary sources which reference the original, such as Jones 1986, Kilian 1986, and Cline 1990.

15. At present, the use(s) of Chian turpentine in the Late Bronze Age is uncertain (cf. Haldane 1990, for the use in the classical period). Turpentine has been recognized archaeologically in some Egyptian funerary contexts, but these burials are all later (the 26th Dynasty of the 7th–6th centuries B.C.) than the period with which we are presently concerned. When found in these Egyptian funerary contexts, the Chian turpentine is closely associated with the sarcophagus, and hence the body of the deceased. It does not seem to be included in the tomb simply as an offering or as part of the provisions for the afterlife.

16. On the subject of wineskins, see now Immerwahr 1992, which appeared after this paper was presented.

CHAPTER 16

Palaeoethnobotanical Finds of *Vitis* from Greece

Jane M. Renfrew

---

1. Introduction

The cultivated grape, *Vitis vinifera* L., is closely related to an aggregate of the wild and feral vine forms which are distributed in the Mediterranean area and northwards into areas of relatively mild climate in central Europe and Western Asia (see Map 16.1). These wild and feral forms belong to the subspecies (ssp.) *sylvestris* (C. C. Gmelin) Berger within *Vitis vinifera*, and are considered to be the stock from which the cultivated grape vine was derived.

The *sylvestris* vines are primarily perennial woody climbers with coiled tendrils, and are thought to be native to the woodlands south and west of the Caspian Sea and extending along the southern shores of the Black Sea and westwards to northern Greece and the southern Balkans. They are also found in Italy, France, Spain, North Africa, and in the Rhine and Danube Valleys of Central Europe.

There are some problems in establishing the exact distribution of the truly wild *sylvestris* forms, since spontaneous crossing between wild plants and cultivars occurs repeatedly where vineyards are established close to natural stands of the *sylvestris* forms, and the F1 hybrids are fully fertile like the wild form (see chapters 3 by Olmo and 2 by Zohary, this volume). So the modern distribution of *sylvestris* may reflect truly wild forms growing in primary habitats, escapes from cultivation, and hybrids between ssp. *sylvestris* and ssp. *vinifera* propagated by self-sown seed (Zohary and Hopf 1988: 136). Unfortunately, it is not possible to distinguish between their seeds.

In Greece, *sylvestris* has been growing at least since the Pleistocene. Today, it is found widely distributed, especially in the north in Thrace, eastern and western Macedonia, Epirus, Thessaly, Euboea, and in the Peloponnese (Map 16.2). It occurs in open mixed woodland, on alluvial and poor dry soils, but prefers those soils that are relatively damp. It clambers to great heights (30 m or more) over mature trees of the following species: *Cercis siliquastrum*, *Laurus nobilis*, *Arbutus unedo* and *Arbutus andrachne*, *Olea oleaster*, *Platanus orientalis*, *Quercus coccifera*, *Pistacia*

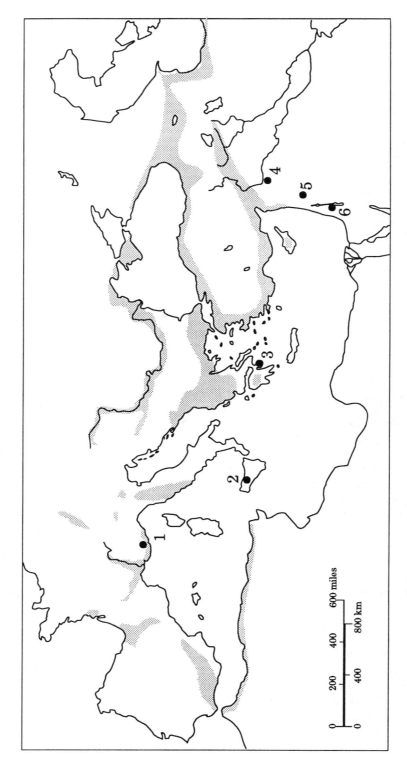

Map 16.1. Mediterranean region: distribution (shadowed) of modern wild grape, *Vitis vinifera* subsp. *sylvestris*. Late Paleolithic–Mesolithic (12th–9th millennium B.C.) finds of wild grape pips are at numbered sites as follows: 1 = Terra Amata, 2 = Grotta del'Uzzo, 3 = Franchthi Cave, 4 = Tell Abu Hureyra, 5 = Tell Aswad, 6 = Jericho.

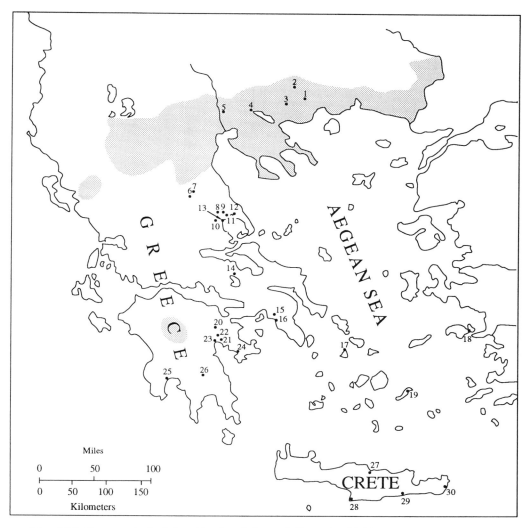

Map 16.2. Greece: principal sites. Numbered sites as follows: 1 = Dikili Tash, East Macedonia; 2 = Sitagroi, East Macedonia; 3 = Dimitra, East Macedonia; 4 = Assiros, West Macedonia; 5 = Kastanas, West Macedonia; 6 = Agrissa, Thessaly; 7 = Arapi, Thessaly; 8 = Sesklo, Thessaly; 9 = Dimini, Thessaly; 10 = Nea Nikomedeia, Thessaly; 11 = Pefkakia, Thessaly; 12 = Iolkos, Thessaly; 13 = Demetrias, Thessaly; 14 = Orchomenos, Boeotia; 15 = Athens, Attica; 16 = Aghios Kosmas, Attica; 17 = Chalandriani, Syros; 18 = Samos, Eastern Aegean; 19 = Markiani, Amorgos; 20 = Mycenae, Argolid; 21 = Synoro, Argolid; 22 = Tiryns, Argolid; 23 = Lerna, Argolid; 24 = Franchthi, Argolid; 25 = Nichoria, Messenia; 26 = Menelaion, Sparta; 27 = Knossos, Crete; 28 = Phaistos, Crete; 29 = Myrtos, Crete; 30 = Kato Zakro, Crete.

terebinthus, Clematis vitalba, Ulmus campestris, Cornus mas and *Cornus sanguinea, Corylus avellana, Rubus* sp., *Fagus silvatica, Pyrus amygdaliformis, Rosa* sp. and *Castanea sativa* (Logothetis 1962: 33). It can grow at heights up to 400 m above sea level, occasionally as high as 800 m. It requires a temperature of at least 16°C in the warmest summer month.

Wild grapes are dioecious, and their populations contain roughly equal proportions of male and female forms; fruit-setting is dependent on cross-pollination. This contrasts with domesticated forms which are self-fertile, with flowers containing both pistils and anthers, and the fruit-setting without the need for cross-pollination. In the wild *sylvestris* plants, the sex is controlled by a single gene. The female forms are homogametic and carry the homozygotic recessive genotype Su^mSu^m, which prevents the growth of anthers. The male forms have a Su^fSu^m genotype. The change to hermaphrodism under domestication was attained by a shift to the Su^+ allele, which dominates over Su^m and brings about the development of both anthers and pistils in the flowers. Cultivated clones may be of two types: either they are still heterozygous and show the Su^+Su^m constitution, or they have the Su^+Su^+ genotype. Although the domesticated forms produce self-fertile fruits, they are in fact propagated by vegetative means, by cuttings or grafting (see Zohary and Hopf 1988: 139).

A study of *Vitis vinifera* ssp. *sylvestris* in Greece (Logothetis 1962) identified a number of different forms: male, female, and hermaphrodite (the latter probably originating from escapes from cultivation). All have small spherical fruits with thick dark skins, small cordiform pips with short stalks/beaks, and small chalazas in the center of the dorsal side. He identified six male forms on the basis of the morphology of their leaves, the key characteristics being overall shape, indentations on the margins, hairiness of the lower surface, and prominence of the veins. He also distinguished three female forms.

In all these groups, the bunches of grapes were found to fall into two types:

> Type B1: Bunch of grapes 12–14 cm long and very lax, spherical fruits, blue-black in color, with a diameter of 7–8 mm. Thick hard skins, pulp lacking in juice, acidic. 1 or 2 pips, 5–5.5 mm long and 4–4.5 mm broad, with a short beak and circular chalaza in the center of the dorsal side with a well-defined raphus.

> Type B2: Cylindrical bunches of grapes 13–16 cm long, small spheroid fruits, blue-black in color, with a diameter of 8–9 mm. Thick skins, mostly not very juicy. 1–3 pips, 5.5–6 mm in length and 4 mm in breadth, with short stalk sometimes thin, sometimes thick. Chalaza in the centre of the dorsal side, raphus well-formed.

In the Chalcidice area of northern Greece and also in the region of Mount Olympus, Logothetis (1962: 38) discovered hermaphrodite forms of *sylvestris* which he considers to be escapes from cultivation. Their pips show distinctive ovoid chalazas, and they have relatively long stalks.

It is estimated that, at present, there are about 10,000 cultivars which are all thought to be derived from the simple wild species *Vitis vinfera* ssp. *sylvestris* of the Near East (Olmo 1976: 295; and chapter 3, this volume). These cultivars were put into three main groups by Negrul (1938):

1. The small berried wine grapes of Western Europe = *occidentalis* form.
2. The large oval-berried table grapes = *orientalis* form.
3. Intermediate types from Asia Minor and Eastern Europe.

Cultivated grape vines are propagated vegetatively by rooting twigs in autumn/winter when they are dormant, or by grafting. Almost all cultivated forms of *Vitis vinifera* ssp. *vinifera* have hermaphrodite flowers and are self-pollinating. The thousands of distinct clones thus produced in the Old World exhibit a wide variety of characteristics in habit, climate and soil requirements, in the shape, colour, sweetness and juiciness of their fruits, and in the numbers of pips they contain. As the grapevine is a perennial climber, it needs to be pruned annually to keep it down to a manageable size and to promote its fruitfulness. Usually vines start to produce fruits three years after planting. The fruit is a berry which is rich in sugar (15–20%), almost equally divided between dextrose and levulose. It also contains tartaric and malic acids. Grapes provide fresh fruit, dried raisins, sultanas and currants (according to the type of cultivar), wine, vinegar, grape juice, as well as a light salad oil that is obtained from crushing the pips. The leaves are also used in cooking, being pickled and stuffed. In the past, they were used by potters as mats on which to stand their damp clay wares to dry in the air before being fired in an oven or kiln (see below). The leaves also have astringent properties and are used to stop haemorrhages. Among its many other uses, however, the fermentation of grape juice to wine, which was easily stored, transported and traded, was a most significant factor in the rise of early civilizations in the Aegean area in the Bronze Age.

2. The Problem of Distinguishing Between Wild and Cultivated Grapes in the Archaeological Record

Modern *sylvestris* grapes are usually rather small and acid-tasting, although they can be quite successfully made into wine. Their pips are more or less globular in shape, with short stalks or beaks—less than 1 mm long—that are constricted where they join the globular part of the pip. On the ventral surface, the two grooves which flank the ventral "bridge" usually diverge from it at the top of the stem, making a V shape with it. By contrast, the pips of the cultivated *vinifera* forms are usually longer than those of the wild types, with longer stalks (at least more than 1 mm), and chalazal scars on the dorsal side which are usually larger and more ovoid than in the wild form (diameter usually 1.5–2 mm), and grooves on the ventral side which run more or less parallel to the ventral bridge.

Stummer (1911: 286) sought to quantify these differences in the form of grape pip, using a breadth/length (B/L) index (calculated as $100 \times$ B/L). In his wide-ranging study of wild and domesticated vines from Austria, he observed that this index for *sylvestris* pips ranged 54–82 {with a peak around 64}, whereas this index for *vinifera* pips ranged from 44 to 75 {with a peak around 55}. A similar study of vines at thirteen locations in the Danube valley (Schiemann 1953: 320) yielded somewhat different ranges for B/L indices—specifically, 64–83 for *sylvestris*, 54–70 for *vinifera*—but confirmed Stummer's two conclusions, that (1) because of the large overlap in the ranges of these indices, statistically significant results would only achievable when a large number of pips was available from a single source; and (2) as a corollary, when only a few pips occur, the problem of separating wild and cultivated forms becomes very complex unless they have indices at the extremes of each range, i.e., between 44 and 54 (*vinifera*); or between 75 and 83 (*sylvestris*).

An additional complication is the fact that the dimensions of pips can be altered by carbonization. Logothetis (1970: 28) conducted experiments which yielded the following results for changes in pip length:

	Fresh	Carbonized, 300°C	Carbonized, 400°C
Modern cultivated grapes	7.06 mm	6.08 mm	5.66 mm
Modern wild grapes	5.38 mm	4.66 mm	4.40 mm

Similarly, a recent study of charred *cultivated* grape pips (Smith and Jones 1990) showed that all of them, whether fresh or dry before charring, decreased in size. At higher temperatures of carbonization (about 450°C), length decreased more than breadth and breadth decreased more than thickness. Thus, the pips became more rounded with charring—several instances of B/L indices of more than 80 were recorded—and so moved closer to wild pips in their form. Those authors suggest that the length of the stalk of the pip may be a more reliable parameter than the B/L index for distinguishing wild and cultivated forms.

It should also be noted that not all ancient pips are carbonized; for example, those from Dimitra (Renfrew, unpublished) include several which, by mineralization, were preserved in their original dimensions, more or less. Another factor bearing on the size and shape of the pips is whether the fruits were ripe or unripe when picked (see below).

Sometimes, in association with the archaeological finds of grape pips, there are fragments of fruit stalks (pedicels), which frequently break off from the main stem of a bunch of domestic grapes when the fruit is picked. In the wild *sylvestris* forms, the stems are stout and robust, and do not break when the grapes are pulled from the bunch. Pedicels that are unattached to the grapes, taken together with other features, point to the presence of cultivated grapes.

Apart from pips and pedicels, there is another source of evidence of viticulture that should be considered here—leaf impressions, on the bases of ancient pottery. At Menelaion, near Sparta, such impressions were also found on a clay sealing of a jar (see *Annual of the British School of Archaeology in Athens* 16 [1925]: 9–10). To the writer's knowledge, no information has been published as to whether these impressions are of wild or cultivated vine leaves. Because most of the examples belong to the Bronze Age, it has been *assumed* that the leaves come from cultivated grapes, which would have been easily available for these purposes. One might also assume that grape leaves were being used for culinary purposes, as they are in Greece today.

3. Discussion of the Prehistoric Remains of Grapes in Greece

Grape pips, stalks, and skins have been recovered from a number of archaeological excavations of prehistoric and classical period sites in Greece (see Appendix). They are found as a result of painstaking examination of archaeological deposits for botanical remains especially of cultivated plants used in the diet or contributing to the basic economy of the site and past community being studied. Usually the finds of grape remains form a very small proportion of the total botanical material recovered, the bulk of which are usually the annual crops—chiefly cereals and pulses. Recovery of this sort of material is done by water flotation or wet sieving of large quantities of soil samples. The finds of impressions of leaves or pips are much less common, but they are revealed by a detailed examination of handmade pottery.

a. The Neolithic finds

The earliest finds of grapes in Greece come from the late Palaeolithic/Mesolithic levels in the Franchthi Cave, Argolid, dating to about 11000 B.C. A single grape pip from these levels may indicate that *Vitis vinifera* ssp. *sylvestris* was collected to supplement the diet of the hunter/gatherers who camped in the cave overlooking the seashore.

Remains of grapes are known from three early Neolithic locations (Argissa, Achilleion, and Sesklo), dating to the period 6400–5300 B.C. Again, all appear to have been wild *sylvestris* forms. The pip from Achilleion, with a length of 3.5 mm and a breadth of 3.7 mm, has the squat rounded form that is characteristic of *sylvestris* (Renfrew 1989: 309).

The Middle Neolithic period in Greece (5300–4300 B.C.) also yielded remains of *Vitis vinifera* ssp. *sylvestris*, at two sites: Sesklo in Thessaly, and Sitagroi in East Macedonia. The pips from levels belonging to phases I and II at Sitagroi, have the following measurements:

Sitagroi I–II	Average	Size range
Length (8 pips)	4.5 mm	4.0–4.9 mm
Length of stalk (7 pips)	0.6 mm	0.3–1.0 mm
Diameter of chalaza	1.2 mm	1.0–1.5 mm
B/L index	82	65–92

These pips are the earliest in a sequence of finds from Sitagroi that show the importance of the collection of wild grapes from the middle Neolithic until the Early Bronze Age in eastern Macedonia (Renfrew 1971: 73). By the end of the sequence (i.e., during Sitagroi IV and V: see below) there is some evidence for the emergence of cultivated vines (as evidenced by elongated, larger pips on longer stalks; and by finds of friut pedicel stems, etc.). The argument is stengthened by similar finds from contemporary levels at Dikili Tash and Dimitra (see data tables below) in the same region of Greece.

For the succeeding Late Neolithic period (4300–2800 B.C.), there is a mass of detailed evidence. This period was one in which there seems to have been a greater concentration on the collection and use of fruits of all sorts—almonds, pears, figs, and acorns, as well as grapes (Renfrew 1973b: 147). Grape pips have been found on eight sites of this period: Franchthi Cave in the Argolid; Arapi, Dimini, Sesklo, and Pefkakia (all in Thessaly); and Dimitra, Dikili Tash, and Sitagroi III (all in East Macedonia). The best documented are those in East Macedonia.

At Dimitra, grape pips occurred in 35 out of the 48 samples of seeds from the Late Neolithic levels. All the finds contain pips of a elongated/piriform shape which may be regarded as domesticated, whereas there are pips in 12 samples that, with their short stalks and more globular form, have *sylvestris* characteristics.

Most of the pips are preserved by carbonization, but mineralized pips do occur, often in the same samples as the carbonized ones. Some of the carbonized seeds are very small (typically less than 3 mm long), although otherwise characteristic in appearance. These small pips do not appear to be immature, so it was probably the exposure to extreme heat that caused such dramatic shrinkage. They must have been carbonized under different conditions than the bulk of the charred pips which retained a more normal size. Some of the mineralized pips are mere skeletons; others are extremely well preserved, plump-looking, and with very good surface definition. They are all of a pale colour, some being quite white in appearance.

All the pips of the wild type are preserved by carbonization, whereas those of the cultivated type are both carbonized and mineralized. The following measurements were obtained from these pips:

Dimitra (124 pips)	Average	Size range
Carbonized, cultivated form (86 pips)		
Length	5.5 mm	4.0–6.5 mm
Breadth	3.2 mm	2.5–4.0 mm
Length of stalk	1.23 mm	1.0–2.0 mm
Diameter. of chalaza	1.3 mm	1.0–2.0 mm
B/L index	57	42–80
Wild form (18 pips)		
Length	4.2 mm	3.0–5.0 mm
Breadth	3.2 mm	2.0–4.0 mm
Length of stalk	0.9 mm	0.5–1.0 mm
Diameter of chalaza	1.2 mm	1.0–1.5 mm
B/L index	76	57–100
Mineralized pips (cultivated form) (20 pips)		
Length	5.6 mm	4.0–6.5 mm
Breadth	3.1 mm	2.5–3.5 mm
Diameter of chalaza	1.3 mm	1.0–1.5 mm
B/L index	56	46–70

A contrasting picture emerges at Sitagroi, which lies in the next plain to the east of Dimitra in East Macedonia and was occupied simultaneously (as Sitagroi III). Here, it appears that all the grape pips recovered from these levels belonged to the *sylvestris* type:

Sitagroi III (11 pips)	Average	Size range
Length	4.5 mm	4.0–5.0 mm
Length of stalk	0.7 mm	0.5–1.0 mm
Diameter of chalaza	1.2 mm	1.0–1.5 mm
B/L index	81	66–90

These measurements match closely with those for the wild pip forms from Dimitra.

Across the plain of Drama to the southeast of Sitagroi and close to Philippi is the site of Dikili Tash. Grape pips have been found here in levels contemporary with Sitagroi III and IV. Logothetis (1970: 36) in his study of these pips found that they fell into two types—a larger form and a smaller one, with the following measurements:

Dikili Tash	Type A	Type B
Average length (and range)	4.6 (4.0–5.0 mm)	5.4 (5.1–6.0 mm)
Average breadth (and range)	3.7 (3.1–4.2 mm)	3.8 (3.0–4.2 mm)
Average length of stalk	0.6 (0.2–1.0 mm)	0.8 (0.6–1.0 mm)
Average B/L index	80	70

Fruit stalks were associated with some of these finds.

The first indications of grape domestication in Greece occur in Sitagroi IV contexts (ca 2400 B.C.). Eleven pips show distinct differences from those in the preceeding phases at this site. They are longer and have longer stalks and larger chalazal scars.

Sitagroi IV (11 pips)	Average	Size range
Length	5.3 mm	4.0–6.0 mm
Length of stalk	1.0 mm	0.5–1.5 mm
Diameter of chalaza	1.8 mm	1.0–2.0 mm
B/L index	71	50–93

The short berry stalks that are most often found in cultivated grapes today appear here for the first time.

These Late Neolithic finds from Northern Greece can be compared with those from the Franchthi Cave in the Argolid. The following measurements, according to J. M. Hansen, place them firmly in the *sylvestris* range:

Franchthi Cave	Average	Size range
Length	3.8 mm	3.3–4.4 mm
Breadth	3.4 mm	3.2–3.7 mm
Length of stalk	0.8 mm	0.3–1.4 mm
Diameter of chalaza	1.1 mm	0.9–1.8 mm
B/L index	89	

Thus, it appears that grapes most likely came into cultivation in the East Macedonian area sometime during the Late Neolithic. While there was some concentration on cultivated forms at the same sites, wild grapes continued to be exploited, just as they were in Thessaly and the Argolid at that time.

b. Bronze Age and later finds of grapes in Greece

Finds of grape seeds dating to the Early Bronze Age come from eleven widespread locations in Greece: from Sitagroi and Kastanas in the north, through Thessaly (Argissa) to Attica (Aghios Kosmas), the Peloponnese (Lerna, Tiryns, and Synoro) and, for the first time, on Crete (Phaistos and Myrtos) and in the Cyclades (Chalandriani on Syros, and Markiani on Amorgos). The finds are not only of grape pips but also of fruit stalks and skins (Myrtos) and of vine leaves (Synoro, Myrtos, Chalandriani, and Markiani).

The early finds from Crete are especially interesting. At the Early Minoan settlement of Myrtos, on the southern coast of Crete, two deposits were found that contained remains of grapes. The first contained just carbonized grape pips; the second and larger find was of pips, loose stalks, and empty grapeskins, from inside a pithos. In both deposits, the pips were notably small and give the appearance of coming from unripe fruit. But there were some pips of larger size and more rounded appearance that appear to have come from fully ripened grapes. In the first deposit, there were four pips with the following dimensions:

Length of pip: 4.0, 4.2, 4.0, and 5.0 mm.

Breadth of pip: 3.0, 3.2, 2.5, and 3.0 mm.

Length of stalk: 0.5, 0.7, 0.5, 1.0 mm, respectively.

The average B/L index for this deposit (4 pips) is 68, with individual indices ranging 60–75.

The average B/L index for the second deposit (68 pips) is again 68, with individual indices ranging between 67 and 80. But the largest pips in both deposits have a length of 5.0 mm, that in the second deposit being somewhat broader (3.5 mm).

The B/L index averages and ranges here suggest overlapping size distributions for wild and domesticated plants during the Early Bronze Age on Crete. Possibly, the wild form occurs at the extreme limit of the Myrtos measurements. But, it must be remembered that the Myrtos pips seem to be immature, and that an increase in length and breadth on maturity would possibly place them well inside the index for the cultivated form. The suspicion that we have instances of the cultivated grape here is substantiated by the presence of so many grape stalks in the second deposit. Since Logothetis (1962) does not refer to any wild vines growing in Crete today, possibly even in Minoan times they were only found truly wild on the mainland.

The find of empty grape skins associated with grape pips and stalks in the pithos is suggestive of winemaking (see chapter 10 by Zettler and Miller, this volume). The pressed skins of grapes are used in the early stages of fermenting grape juice, because the wine yeast *Saccharomyces ellipsoideus* is naturally present in the "bloom" on the grape skin. Red and white wines are distinguished by the presence or absence of anthocyanin pigments in the grape skins (see chapters 6 by Singleton, 7 by Formenti, and 5 by McGovern and Michel, this volume), and can be produced from the same red grape depending upon whether or not the skins are present during the early stages of fermentation (Baker 1965: 121).

The final evidence for the presence of vines at Myrtos in Early Minoan times is the vine leaf impression on the base of a pottery vessel. The use of vine leaves as mats for drying pottery seems to have been a widespread practice in the Early Bronze Age Aegean (cf. finds from Syros, Amorgos, and Naxos). The find of grape pips in a pithos from House I at Aghios Kosmas in Attica (Early Bronze Age) is similar to the Myrtos find (Mylonas 1959: 39).

The pips from Early Bronze Age site of Phaistos, on Crete, also appear to be small (Logothetis 1970: 42). The five measured pips vary in length between 3 and 5 mm (average 4.4 mm) and in breadth between 2.4 and 3 mm (average 2.9 mm), with the pip stalks being between 0.5 and 1.00 mm long.

In the Argolid, the finds of both carbonized grape pips and impressions of pips in Early Helladic pottery at Lerna have provided an excellent group of material, and it is clear that both wild and cultivated forms are present. The majority of the pips (61%) fall in the overlap zone of the *sylvestris/vinifera* B/L indices, while 10% of the samples are clearly in the cultivated B/L index range, 24% in the normal *sylvestris* range, and 5% have an extreme B/L index (83 and 100). The four impressions of pips in pottery (recording the size of the pip when waterlogged in the damp clay before firing) had dimensions of 6.6 × 4.4 mm, 6.4 × 3.8 mm, 6.2 × 2.8 mm, and 6.8 × 4.8 mm, making them all comparable to cultivated form.

At the Early Bronze site of Synoro, Willerding (1973) has identified a leaf impression on the base of a vessel as that of *Vitis,* according to careful comparisons with the broadly similar leaves of *Acer pseudoplatanus*, *Acer platanoides*, *Platanus* sp., *Populus alba*, and *Vitis vinifera*. Similar vine leaf impressions are the only evidence so far for the cultivation of the grape in the Cyclades. Unpublished impressions have been found on the bases of Early Cycladic cups and bowls at Chalandriani, in Syros (Fitzwilliam Museum, Cambridge) and at Markiani, in Amorgos, during the recent excavations. Vine leaf impressions on the bases of Early Cycladic pots are also illustrated by Zervos on pottery from Naxos.

In northern Greece, the trend begun at the end of the Neolithic period continues with large finds of grape pips from Kastanas, in western Macedonia, which display the characteristics of the cultivated grape, but with an admixture of *sylvestris* types also present. In the Early Bronze Age contexts at Sitagroi (Sitagroi V) only two pips have been found:

Sitagroi V (2 pips)	Average	Size range
Length	5.0 mm	4.5–5.5 mm
Length of stalk	0.8 mm	0.5–1.0 mm
Diameter of chalaza	1.7 mm measured for only one pip	
B/L index	75	73–78

The Middle Bronze Age is represented by a number of finds of pip impressions. From Knossos in Crete, one large pip had been impressed into a Middle Minoan II/III hemispherical cup. It measured about 8 mm long by 3.7 mm broad, and was "bottle-like" in shape with a distinct stalk. The finds of two impressions on a Middle Helladic bowl from the Athenian Agora are also of a good size (6.0 × 5.0 mm and 6.7 × 4.8 mm), and must unquestionably belong to cultivated grapes. So too must the pip from Middle Helladic site of Orchomenos, identified by Wittmack in 1907.

At the Middle Bronze site of Nichoria, eleven grape pips were found, with B/L indices ranging between 56 and 66, with the exception of one of 80. Again, a mixture of types is evident, but the cultivated form probably predominates. The pips range between 4.1 and 5.3 mm in length (average 4.9 mm) and 2.8–3.5 mm in breadth (average 3.1 mm). The charcoal of grape wood was also found at this site.

The carbonized grape pip from a Late Bronze Age context at Kato Zakro, measuring 4.7 × 6.5 (with a stalk length of 2.1 mm), clearly is also cultivated. These dimensions are much larger than those obtained for the Mycenean grapes at Iolkos, in Thessaly, that measured as follows:

Iolkos (12 pips)	Average	Size range
Length	5.2 mm	4.8–6.0 mm
Breadth	3.3 mm	3.0–3.7 mm
Thickness	2.5 mm	2.0–3.1 mm
B/L index	64	62–66

Could it be that different cultivars were already developing, adapted to different conditions? At Kastanas in the Late Bronze Age, cultivated grapes also appear to have been much larger than those which occur in the succeeding period, and indeed than those of the Early Bronze Age.

Three groups of grape pips from Tiryns, of Later Mycenean date, show the following range of dimensions (Kroll 1982, 1984):

Tiryns (44 pips)	Average	Size range
Group a (23 pips)		
Length	4.9 mm	3.8–6.0 mm
Breadth	3.3 mm	2.7–4.2 mm
Thickness	2.8 mm	2.2–3.6 mm
B/L index	67	60–85
Group b (10 pips)		
Length	5.2 mm	4.3–6.0 mm
Breadth	3.1 mm	2.9–3.4 mm
Thickness	2.9 mm	2.6–3.4 mm
B/L index	60	57–67
Group c (11 pips)		
Length	5.3 mm	4.8–6.0 mm
Breadth	3.3 mm	2.7–4.0 mm
Thickness	2.8 mm	2.2–3.8 mm
B/L index	62	56–67

The only find of more or less complete carbonized fruits for the Iron Age comes from an Early Geometric Grave in the Athenian Agora (Hopf 1971: 268). The fruits have an average diameter of 10.7 mm (range, 8.0–15.0 mm), and may originally have contained three or four pips in their complete form.

4. Conclusions

Clearly, the early exploitation of wild grapes, which began in the late Palaeolithic and continued well after farming was first established in Greece shortly before 6000 B.C., led to cultivation of the vine as one of the first fruit crops. This process involved controlling growth by severe pruning and controlling reproduction by vegetative methods—cutting and grafting—rather than sexually. Beginning in the Late Neolithic period and for sometime thereafter, both cultivated and wild grapes are found together. Backcrossing between wild and cultivated forms probably occurred, and no doubt there was also selection of different types for different purposes, such as raisins, currants and dessert grapes, and different types of wine and vinegar.

Winemaking was the most significant development—indications of which occur in Early Minoan Myrtos and Early Helladic Aghios Kosmas—because it then became possible to make, from quite modest raw materials, a luxury item which stored well and could be extensively traded in pottery vessels. This development held the key to the growth of prosperity in Greece and the rise of early civilizations in the Bronze Age Aegean, and is underlined by the appearance in the archaeological record of exotic drinking vessels, made from precious materials.

In studying the palaeoethnobotanical aspects of the domestication of grapes and winemaking, we have to contend with how well the pips, stalks, skins, whole fruits, and leaves have been preserved. Each part of the plant has its own characteristic properties of degradation, not to mention differences that arise from the state of ripeness of the botanical material and the accidental means by which it came to be preserved. The physical remains of the grapes from ancient Aegean civilization give us some hints as to how they were being cultivated and used, but leave a great many questions still unanswered.

Appendix: Catalogue of Palaeoethnobotanical Finds of Grapes in Greece

Palaeolithic/Mesolithic
> Franchthi Cave, Argolid   Hansen 1978

Early Neolithic
> Argissa, Thessaly   Kroll 1981, 1983
> Achilleion, Thessaly   Renfrew 1989
> Sesklo, Thessaly   Kroll 1981, 1983

Middle Neolithic
> Sitagroi, East Macedonia   Renfrew 1971, 1973
> Sesklo, Thessaly   Kroll 1981, 1983; Renfrew 1979

Late Neolithic
> Arapi, Thessaly   Kroll 1981, 1983
> Dimitra, East Macedonia   Renfrew, Forthcoming
> Dikili Tash, East Macedonia   Logothetis 1970; Renfrew 1971
> Dimini, Thessaly   Kroll 1979
> Franchthi, Argolid   Hansen 1978
> Sitagroi, East Macedonia   Renfrew 1971, 1973
> Sesklo, Thessaly   Kroll 1981, 1983
> Pefkakia, Thessaly   Kroll 1981, 1983

Early Bronze Age
> Argissa, Thessaly   Kroll 1981, 1983
> Chalandriani,Syros[1]   Renfrew 1969
> Phaistos, Crete   Logothetis 1970
> Kastanas, West Macedonia   Kroll 1983
> Lerna, Argolid   Hopf 1962; Logothetis 1970
> Markiani, Amorgos[1]   Renfrew, Unpublished
> Myrtos, Crete[1]   Renfrew 1972
> Synoro, Argolid[1]   Witterding 1973
> Sitagroi, East Macdonia   Renfrew 1971, 1973
> Tiryns, Argolid   Kroll 1982, 1984
> Aghios Kosmas, Attica   Mylonas 1959

Middle Bronze Age

Argissa, Thessaly	Kroll 1981, 1983
Assiros, West Macedonia	Jones 1979
Athens, Attica	Hopf 1971
Knossos, Cretea	Åström and Hjelmqvist 1971
Lerna, Argolid	Hopf 1962
Nichoria, Messenia	Shay and Shay 1978
Pefkakia, Thessaly	Kroll 1981, 1983
Orchomenos, Boeotia	Bulle 1907

Late Bronze Age

Assiros, West Macedonia	Jones 1979
Dimitra, East Macedonia	Renfrew, Forthcoming
Iolkos, Thessaly	Renfrew 1966
Kastanas, West Macedonia	Kroll 1983
Kato Zachro, Crete	Logothetis 1970
Knossos, Crete	Åström and Hjelmqvist 1971; Jones 1984
Mycenae, Argolid	Hehn 1911
Tiryns, Argolid	Kroll 1982
Menelaion, Sparta[1]	Vickery 1936

Iron Age

Assiros, West Macedonia	Jones 1979
Athens, Attica	Hopf 1971
Kastanas, West Macedonia	Kroll 1983
Demetrias, Thessaly	Kroll 1981, 1983
Samos, Eastern Aegean	Kucan 1991

Note

1. Includes vine leaf impressions.

CHAPTER 17

Wine and Viticulture in the Linear A and B Texts of the Bronze Age Aegean

Ruth Palmer

---

1. Introduction

In classical Greek culture, wine was important as an aristocratic drink, an offering to the gods, and as a valuable trade commodity, one which required special techniques and labor requirements for growing and production. Much of the information we possess about wine in the Classical period comes from literary sources, genre scenes of drinking and wine-making on vases, and transport amphorae (see chapter 20 by Koehler, this volume). For the Greek prehistoric period, the evidence is scantier—sets of wine serving and drinking vessels from graves, storerooms full of goblets at the Palace of Nestor in Pylos, and the rare fresco showing drinking point to the ceremonial aspect of wine in Bronze Age Aegean society (see chapter 18 by Wright, this volume). The main source of information about the production and distribution of wine comes from the Minoan and Mycenaean administrative records, written in the Linear A and B scripts. But this information about wine is not presented in a clear, formal manner as in the later classical treatises on vines and wine; rather, wine is just one of many commodities recorded by the palaces in a purely administrative manner. Therefore, it is necessary first to understand the nature of the Linear A and B writing systems, and the types of information recorded, before analyzing the contexts in which wine appears. Although a relatively small number of texts have been preserved, contexts indicate that the Bronze Age Aegean civilizations held a view of wine similar to that of classical Greece.

The Linear A and B texts found in the palaces and regional centers of Crete and Mainland Greece differ greatly in quantity, time span, and range of subjects from the corpora of texts found in the Near East and Egypt. These Aegean texts are all temporary records originally inscribed on unfired clay, meant to be discarded once their information was no longer relevant or when it was transferred onto other materials such as papyrus or parchment. All the tablets, sealings, and roundels now extant were preserved by the fires that destroyed the palaces. Consequently, these records refer only to the short period, at most a few months, immediately before the various destructions. The texts therefore do not show how the palaces managed resources from year to year.

The Aegean archives are small by Near Eastern standards. The number of Linear B tablets is large enough, and their formats are sufficiently repetitive to have presented Ventris with sufficient material to decipher the script and to identify the language as Greek (*Docs.* 14–22).[1] The largest group of tablets found, the Linear B archives at Knossos, numbers some 3300 texts; there are about 1100 tablets from Pylos on the Greek mainland, and Mycenae has produced 73 (Bartonek 1983: 16). By the early 1990s, ca. 320 Linear A tablets had been found, many extremely fragmentary.[2] The largest Linear A archive, from the Cretan regional center of Haghia Triadha, contains 147 tablets. All the other palace sites in Crete and most of the regional centers have produced tablets, but in much smaller numbers (see *GORILA* 5, for quantities and types of texts). Linear A has not been deciphered precisely because such a small number of texts have been preserved, and because their short, simple formats do not provide enough examples of the words and phrases to analyze the language systematically, as Ventris did for Linear B. The Linear B syllabograms, ideograms, and bookkeeping formats undoubtedly developed from Linear A, but the attempt to apply the phonetic value of the Linear B signs to the corresponding Linear A forms merely demonstrates that the language of Linear A is not Greek.

The Minoan writing systems developed in conjunction with the early palaces in Crete in the Middle Minoan I/II period (ca. 1900–1800 B.C.), but no earlier than 1900 B.C (Olivier 1989: 40–43). In fact, the organization of resources needed to build and maintain the palace system would have required complex record-keeping methods (Cadogan 1980: 33–34; Branigan 1969: 20–22). The origin of the script is obscure. Some of the signs in the Cretan Hieroglyphic script, which developed before the Linear A script (Olivier 1989: 40; Palmer 1994: 31), were thought to resemble signs from the Near Eastern or Egyptian scripts, and the evidence of imports in Crete in this period shows contact with these regions; nevertheless, it is unlikely that the Hieroglyphic or Linear A scripts were directly derived from any known Eastern writing system (*Docs.* 29). The increasing craft specialization and differential control of wealth developing in the later Early Minoan period culminated in the development of the palaces themselves as central places for collection, storage, and distribution of goods (Branigan 1988; Cadogan 1980: 28). The earliest Hieroglyphic and Linear A texts on clay bars, roundels, and tablets, which were found at Protopalatial Phaistos and Knossos, are all economic texts, recording the flow of agricultural products into and out of the palaces and regional centers (*Docs.* 30–31).

The Linear A and Hieroglyphic scripts use ideograms to represent commodities, and syllabic signs to spell out other words phonetically, such as place and personal names. The same form may appear both as a syllabogram and as an ideogram, in which case the syllabic value of the sign probably serves as an abbreviation for the name of the item represented by the ideogram (Chadwick 1989: 30). The Linear A format however distinguishes quite clearly between a sign used as an ideogram and one used as a syllabogram (*Docs.* 24). When ideograms and syllabograms appear in conjunction, the syllabogram appears to alter or further define some aspect of the commodity that the ideogram represents (*Docs.* 34–35). The syllabograms added to the ideogram probably represent abbreviations of descriptive words. Ligatures to the wine ideogram, for instance, might show type, quality, color, or person or place of origin for the wine.

The similarities in format between the Linear A and B tablets, and the heavy use of ideograms and number signs in both scripts concerning products, livestock, men and women, show that these clay tablets dealt only with the economic administration of the Minoan and Mycenaean centers in which they were found. The preserved texts contain no examples of literature, law codes, private court cases or contracts, foreign affairs or domestic policy beyond the day-to-day management of palace resources. The tablets present enough varied information that we can gain a complex picture of the concerns of the palace administrators, and of the relationship between the bureaucracy and the peoples of the kingdoms. The tablets range in complexity from detailed series recording several different aspects of production controlled directly by the palace, such as wool production and the textile industry, to assessment and collection of taxes in agricultural produce from the countryside, to the occasional tablet listing payment for labor or imported materials. The goods collected by the palaces could have been used as raw materials in palace industries, such as perfumed oil production (e.g., items listed on PY Un 267, discussed below) or could have been items consumed directly by the work force, such as wheat, barley, and figs. None of the tablets which give details of palace-controlled industries, however, are concerned with the actual production of staple crops. Instead, assessment tablets show that these staples were levied and collected from the countryside. Palace officials recorded the areas of each holding and the type and amounts of crops found there; from this information, the amount of produce to be paid in taxes was calculated.

How does wine fit into this pattern of palace production versus collection of goods? Is wine production one of the industries closely monitored and administered directly by the palaces, like the textile industry, or does the palace assume that a supply sufficient for its needs can be drawn from non-palatial sources, as is the case with grain? The contexts in which wine appears both in the texts and in the archaeological record show how both the Linear A and B palace administrations handled wine as a commodity. To this end, a number of questions help delineate the use of wine by the palaces:

1. How and where were vines grown?

2. Was wine available everywhere, or was it produced in only a few places?

3. Did the palace carefully oversee all aspects of wine production, or simply collect as much as it needed at any given time?

4. What was the relative value of wine compared to other commodities handled by the palace? Was it a luxury product, or a major export?

5. Who collected and distributed wine, and according to what criteria?

Not only the information in the tablets, but also comparative data gathered from Greek and Roman agricultural writers, modern anthropological studies, and analysis of the seed evidence for domestication of grapes in Greece, have helped to reveal the picture of wine in Mycenaean Greece. Furthermore, the ways in which the palaces handled wine can offer clues as to how the Mycenaean people in general viewed wine.

2. Background to Wine Production in Greece

The seed evidence shows that vines had been cultivated in Greece for at least 1500 years before the beginning of the Mycenaean period in 1600 B.C. (see chapter 16 by Renfrew, this volume; Hansen 1988: 47–48, table 1; Sarpaki 1992: 64–66, tables 1–3), and production of both wine and raisins from wild grapes almost certainly preceded cultivation. By the Early Bronze Age, ca. 2500 B.C., vines and olives were grown alongside wheat and barley, in Crete and Mainland Greece (Renfrew 1972: 282–84). The earliest physical evidence for wine was found at Myrtos: Fournou Korifi in Crete, dating to the Early Minoan II period, ca. 2170 B.C., where a pithos held crushed grape skins and seeds in its base (Warren 1972: 75, 315–16). The Early Helladic III site of Aghios

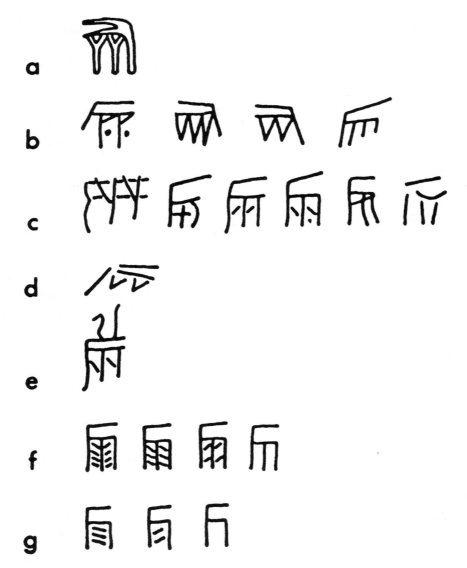

Figure 17.1. Wine ideograms: a) Egyptian hieroglyphic sign *irp*; b) Cretan hieroglyphic sign 116—Sundwall's orientation; c–d) Linear A forms of AB 131; e) AB 131 + 60—form found at both Zakros and Kea; f) Linear B forms of AB 131; and g) Linear B forms of AB 131b. (After Neumann 1977.)

Kosmas in Attica (ca. 2100 B.C.) produced a pithos with a spout in its base, which contained grape pips (Mylonas 1959: 39–40, 161). Eleven sites in Crete dating from Early Minoan II at Myrtos (ca. 2170 B.C.) to Late Minoan IIIB at Kommos (ca. 1300–1200 B.C.) have wine pressing installations which consist of plastered pressing floors, or more commonly of shallow terracotta vats with base spouts, set on platforms above receptacles (Palmer 1994: 18–22, 24, table 1.1; also see chapter 15 by Leonard, this volume). The vats are large enough for only one person to tread at a time, and seem geared toward small-scale, household production rather than large-scale manufacture of wine.

Vines, olives, and wheat grow best on the same type of land, and although the crops for all three do not ripen at the same time, to a certain extent they compete for labor. Vines require skilled heavy labor in the early spring, when trenches are dug around the base of each vine to aerate the soil and allow moisture to reach the roots, and again some months later when the trenches are refilled. If this work is not done, the yield diminishes greatly. The harvest period in late summer does call for a larger work force than grain or olives require, because grapes ripen within a short period and must be picked immediately (Forbes 1982: 240, 259–62; Aschenbrenner 1972: 55–56). A self-sufficient farmer probably aimed to produce enough grain and olives to meet his needs for the coming year, before he could afford to raise vines in any quantity. The corollary here is that any farmer with enough land and labor probably would have planted vines, or traded surplus food to get wine. The archaeological and archaeobotanical evidence, as well as the classical and modern parallels for viticulture, show that vines and wine have been part of traditional agricultural economy in both Grece and Crete since the Early Bronze Age.

3. The Wine Ideogram

The history of the wine ideogram in the Aegean scripts shows that wine was one of the agricultural products collected by the earliest palaces. The Cretan Hieroglyphic form of the wine ideogram, sign 116, occurs on sealstones, and on clay texts from Knossos, Phaistos, and Mallia; the ideogram in its later standard form, AB 131, occurs in both Linear A and B texts (Fig. 17.1). The Linear A ideogram is found on seven sites on Crete (Knossos, Phaistos, Pyrgos near Myrtos, Haghia Triada, Zakros, Archanes, and Khania) and one site in the Cyclades (Kea); the Linear B ideogram is found at Knossos on Crete, and at Pylos and Mycenae on Mainland Greece (Palmer 1994: 28–34, and pl. I). The Linear A and Cretan Hieroglyphic texts range in date from ca. 1800 to 1450 B.C., and the Linear B date from ca. 1375 to 1200 B.C. The Linear A wine ideogram appears on both tablets and pottery vases, presumably to identify their contents, while the Linear B ideogram occurs only on tablets and sealings. The ideogram is found earliest on texts from Middle Minoan II Phaistos, dating to ca. 1800 B.C., in the Protopalatial period. In the Phaistos texts, the ideogram appears in two forms: the Cretan Hieroglyphic form appears on PH 9b and Wc 43, and PH 25 shows a form ancestral to the canonical Linear A and B ideogram (*GORILA 5*: XLIV; see Fig. 17.1b,c). The two forms are definitely related, although the orientation of the Hieroglyphic sign is often quite different from AB 131. In fact, Sir Arthur Evans originally interpreted this sign as "ship" (Evans 1909: 225; compare Figs. 17.1b and 17.2). The Finnish scholar Sundwall who followed Evans' belief that the Minoan scripts copied Near Eastern forms (Evans 1909: *passim*), originally connected the ideogram with a variant of the Egyptian wine ideogram *irp* representing a vine propped on two forked sticks (Sundwall 1944: 10–12, fig. 17; *Docs.* 35; Neumann 1977: 125). This ideogram (Fig. 17.1a) has been found primarily in First Dynasty tombs, and was superseded swiftly by the canonical Egyptian wine ideogram, which represents jars of wine on a rack (chapter 13 by James, this volume). None of the other correlations between Aegean signs and supposed Egyptian prototypes are accepted today. In the past thirty years, Aegean scholars have shown that the forms of the scripts developed within the Aegean and were not copied from any Near Eastern script (Olivier 1989: 41). Furthermore, the form and orientation of the Cretan Hieroglyphic sign, which probably predates the Linear A version, does not match the Egyptian sign, whose period of use antedates both Minoan scripts by some hundreds of years. If the Aegean sign represents a vine stock supported by two stakes (the most common way of training vines), the ideogram may have developed independently in Crete (Neumann 1977: 125). By analyzing the contexts in which the

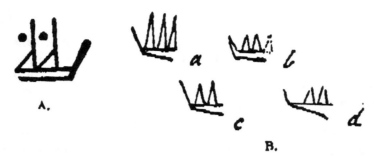

Figure 17.2. Cretan Hieroglyphic sign 116 as originally published by Evans (1909: 225). The first three signs (A and B.a. c) are the same as in Figure 17.1b, although rotated 180°.

ideogram appeared, Bennett showed that AB 131 was wine not because of its form, but because the ideogram was always accompanied by the signs for liquid measure, the subunits S, V and Z (Bennett 1950: 212–19; for the estimated values of these subunits, see *Docs.* 393–94).

The wine ideogram is one of the ideograms created to record basic commodities, during the early development of the scripts. The other recognizable ideograms found in these early texts all represent agricultural staples such as grains, olives, olive oil, wine and figs (*Docs.* 35), which formed the foundation of the palatial redistributive system according to the Linear B texts. The wine ideogram occurs frequently on texts from the Minoan centers of Haghia Triada, Phaistos, and Zakros, in long lists recording collection or distribution of wine alone, and in company with other basic commodities. Wine clearly is an item that the Minoan centers wished to acquire and control. The site of Zakros in East Crete provides extensive evidence for local wine production; in the Late Minoan I period alone (1550–1450 B.C.), six substantial townhouses near the palace, and a large villa in the countryside nearby, contained elaborate pressing floors and vat installations (Palmer 1994: 24, table 1.1). One compound version of the wine ideogram found only on Crete at Zakros also appeared incised on a local jug from Kea in the Cyclades (Bikaki 1984: 22, 32, pl. 25; see Fig. 17.1e); this shows that not only was the wine ideogram known outside of Crete in the Late Minoan I period by 1500 B.C., but it probably was also transmitted through trade in wine. The region of Zakros may have been a major exporter of wine.

Although we do now know the language of Linear A, it is possible to compare the formats of the Linear A tablets to the deciphered Linear B lists. Tablets listing the wine ideogram repeatedly in connection with single words or short entries probably record place names or people from whom wine is collected, or to whom wine is disbursed. The Linear A wine ideogram is often accompanied by ligatures or adjuncts; the added symbols qualify or further define the wine ideogram, perhaps describing in abbreviations the type, origin, quality, or color of the wine. The largest archive of Linear A tablets comes from the secondary center of Haghia Triadha. This center may have served as a local production and collection site for the nearby Palace of Phaistos, and so would focus more upon agricultural commodities than palace industries or imported goods.

On most of the Linear A and B tablets dealing with wine, the commodity is represented by standard wine ideogram AB 131. Both scripts also share the same major variant of the ideogram, AB 131b (see Fig. 17.1g). This abbreviated form looks like a wine ideogram which has been cut in half lengthwise. The meaning of 131b must be connected with wine, yet be fundamentally different from it. Two possibilities exist: that the sign represents either must (*Docs.* 226) or vinegar. PY Un 267,[3] which records ingredients for perfume-making, lists both wine (AB 131) and AB 131b in lines 7 and 8 (Shelmerdine 1985: 17–19):

PY Un 267
.1 o-do-ke, a-ko-so-ta
.2 tu-we-ta, a-re-pa-zo-o
.3 tu-we-a, a-re-pa-te [[,ze-so-me]]
.4 ze-so-me-no [[ko]]
.5 ko-ri-a$_2$-da-na AROM 6
.6 ku-pa-ro$_2$ AROM 6 *157 16
.7 *KAPO* 2 T 5 VIN (*131) 20 *ME* 2
.8 LANA 2 VIN (**131b**) 2

AB 131b would be used in perfume-making either for its aromatic or acidic qualities. It seems more likely that this form of the wine ideogram represents vinegar rather than must, because must is available only once a year for a short time at the grape harvest, while vinegar can be found all year round (Palmer 1994: 88–91).

4. Linear B Vocabulary of Wine and Vines

On three Linear B texts, a word pertaining to wine modifies or replaces the ideogram. In each case, the word appears only once. On PY Vn 20, the Greek word for wine, *wo-no* [οἶνος] appears on line 2, instead of the wine ideogram (*Docs.* 348, 512; Palmer 1965: 369). *Wo-no* is the sole subject of the tablet, which records large amounts of this commodity sent to nine different regional centers (see below, §5):

PY Vn 20
.1 o-a$_2$, e-pi-de-da-to
.2 pa-ra-we-wo, wo-no
.3 pi-*82-de 50
.4 me-ta-pa-de 50
.5 pe-to-no-de 100
.6 pa-ki-ja-na-de 35
.7 a-pu$_2$-de 35
.8 a-ke-re-wa-de 30
.9 e-ra-to-de 50
.10 ka-ra-do-ro-de 40
.11 ri-jo-de 20
.12 vacat

The word *me-ri-ti-jo* accompanies the wine ideogram on the inscribed nodule PY Wr 1360. The clay nodules each bearing a single seal impression acted as proof that the seal holder had delivered wine to the palace (see §7 below).

PY Wr 1360 (*CMS I*, no. 363)
.a VIN
.b me-ri-ti-
.c -jo

Me-ri-ti-jo has been interpreted as an adjective, *melitios*, which might refer to wine flavored with honey, μέλι. Honey was a common flavoring for classical wines. However, the word could also be a personal or place name referring to the origin of the wine (*Docs.* 560; Palmer 1965: 379).

The third word, *de-re-u-ko*, on the fragmentary tablet KN Uc 160 definitely refers to wine:

KN Uc 160

sup. mut.
.1] vest. [
.2] Z 3 [[ ]]
.3]V 1 Z 1 VIN (*131b) S 1 V 3 Z 2
.4] V 5 Z 3 de-re-u-ko VIN (*131) S 4
.5]V 5 Z 2 CYP 1[

Kn Uc 160 is a collection or inventory tablet listing at least two kinds of wine or wine product (*131b and *de-re-u-ko*), and on the last line, the commodity *cyperus* which is often used in perfume making. *De-re-u-ko* is a variant of the later Greek word γλεῦκος, which is a technical term for either "must" or "sweet wine made from fermented free run must" (Stanley 1982: 578). The second meaning is more likely the correct one, since the tablets may have been written a few months before the grape harvest (Chadwick 1976: 188–90), and unfermented must is only available for a short while at harvest. For this same reason, AB 131b, which appears in line 3 of this tablet, cannot be must.

Other Linear B texts contain words referring to vines and orchards, using the Greek base φυτ– ("plant"), which denotes in particular trees and vines, as opposed to grains (*Dictionnaire* 1233– 34). No specific occupational title exists for vine-growers. The terms *pu-ta*, *pe-pu₂-te-me-no*, *pu-te-re*, and *pu-te-ri-ja* refer to orchards and orchard growers in general. The Mycenaeans apparently raised different types of fruit trees together; Homer's descriptions of the orchards belonging to Alcinoos and Laertes (*Odyssey* 9.108, 24.246–247) also reflect this practice of mixed horticulture. However, the appearance of the word *wo-na-si* ("vineyards") in KN Gv 863 (see below) suggests that some farmers specialized in growing vines.

Only two tablets list vines: PY Er 880 and KN Gv 863 (both texts also record fig trees). The format of these two tablets show that the palace administrations were interested in the number and types of trees grown in these orchards, as well as the size of the holdings:

PY Er 880

.1]ke-ra₂[   ]ti-me-no, e-ke
.2 sa-ra-pe-do[*pe-]pu₂-te-me-no*
.3 to-so [ ]GRA 30[ ]
.4 to-so-de, [   ]to, pe-ma GRA 42[
.5 to-sa, we-je[-we]1100[
.6 to-sa-de, su-za[ ]1000[
.7 vacat
.8 ku-su-to-ro-qa, to-so, pe-ma 94

KN Gv 863

.1]qa-ra, / jo-e-ke-to-qo, wo-na-si, si[
.2]we-je-we *174 420 su ARB 104[

Both tablets use the word *we-je-we* (υἱῆϜες) to describe the vines on these estates; this rare Greek word refers to vines trained to climb other trees and produce long shoots (*Dictionnaire* 1153). This technique was common in Italy in the Classical period. PY Er 880 lists how many vines and figs are planted on two large holdings (lines 3 and 4); the alternating entries in this tablet (*to-sa...to-sa-de*) suggest that the vines and the figs were grown in separate plots. KN Gv 863 uses the word *wo-na-si* ("vineyards"), the dative plural form of οἰνάδες (*Docs.* 273), to describe the plants listed in the tablet. Since in this tablet both the climbing vines and the fig trees (here abbreviated *su*) are listed on the same line, the fig trees must belong in these vineyards. In KN Gv 863, the *we-je-we* are listed with fig trees in a 4 to 1 ratio, implying that in this vineyard, four vines were trained up each fig tree. The supporting tree, however, would have to be pruned heavily, to allow the sun to reach the ripening grapes, and if this tree were itself a fruit tree, its estimated yield must have been lower than other, unburdened fruit trees. The format of Gv 863 thus reflects the method of training the vines, and presumably a reduced yield from the fruit trees as a result of the vines growing upon them (Hiller 1984: 174). Such a practice—growing vines on fruit trees—reveals an intensive use of orchard land.

5. Assessment, Distribution, and Collection of Wine

Both PY Er 880 and KN Gv 863, discussed above, list estates not directly worked by the palace administrations. The presence of assessment tablets for wine, as for other agricultural staples, indicates that the palaces did not engage directly in such production, but sent out officials to monitor the potential and actual yield of orchard land.

Wine appears in two formats in the Linear B tablets, either as the only commodity listed on the tablets (three times at Pylos and twice at Knossos), but more frequently on texts which also list other commodities (six times at Pylos, thirteen times at Knossos). The two tablets from Knossos recording wine alone are so fragmentary that it is impossible to tell if they are distribution or collection records. The three tablets from Pylos recording wine alone are all distribution records, but use quite different formats. The palaces distributed goods either regularly, as rations, in which case they formed an important part of the livelihood of the person receiving them, or infrequently, as a gift or offering on special occasions. The types and amounts of goods distributed as rations were related to the rank of the recipient.

PY Vn 20 (above, §4) records a large amount of wine sent by the palace to nine towns of the Nearer Province, probably on the occasion of a festival rather than for rations. The total amount, 410 units (11,808 l; one liquid unit = 28.8 l: *Docs.* 394) is divided up in multiples of 5 (Shelmerdine 1973: 275). The quantity which each town received did not directly correspond to the number of people in the town, or their need for wine, but rather was based proportionally on the total amount that the palace was willing to supply. Each town did not receive the same amount; instead, the wine was divided proportionally among the towns according to the assessed value of each town in relation to the rest. The first line of PY Vn 20 contains the word *e-pi-de-da-to*; this word is derived from the verb δατέομαι ("divide, portion," *Dictionnaire* 254). *E-pi-de-da-to* is a past participle meaning "distributed"; in Vn 20, it describes the wine already sent out to the nine towns. The palace also distributed wine, food, and other goods directly to individuals or groups, according to their specific needs or rank, as in PY Gn 720 and 428; Gn 720 records large amounts of wine sent to two individuals in two different places, and Gn 428 lists wine disbursed to important religious officials.

PY Gn 720
.1 da-ka-ja-pi, pi-ke-te-i VIN 10
.2 i-ka-sa-ja, ru-ki-jo VIN 9
.3-8 vacant

PY Gn 428
.1] vacat [
.2]-jo, [
.3 ka-ra-te-mi-de VIN 1 S 2 [
.4 tu-ra-te-u-si VIN S 1
.5 o-ro-ke-we VIN S 1 i-do-me-ni-jo, S 1
.6 ki-jo-ne-u-si S 1
.7-8 vacant

Tablets recording distributions of wine are rare. Wine is not listed on ration tablets for slave workers or lower level religious personnel. Rather the palace administration reserved wine for special occasions such as festivals, or for people of high rank. This distribution pattern by the palaces reflects the relative scarcity of wine compared to grains, figs, and olives in the traditional farming system. Only successful farmers could spare land and labor for grapevines, and access to large amounts of wine was a mark of status. But although not every farmer would have produced wine, enough would have done so that wine was widely available throughout the Mycenaean kingdoms. The palaces would have used the same methods to acquire wine as were used to collecting staple crops. Products vital to the running of the palace system, or commodities for which a surplus was desired, such as wheat, barley, oil or flax, would have been assessed directly from each producer, and collected according to estimated yield. PY Er 880 and KN Gv 863 (above, §3) demonstrate how the palace administrations counted the vines on estates. The fragmentary tablet KN Gm 840 shows wine collected from four different people or areas:

KN Gm 840
    .1]ni-jo, / a-pu-da-se-we
    .2]1 VIN 168
    .3] VIN 100
    .4]25 VIN 75[
    .5]to [(~)]125 VIN 155

The four totals are irregular, and reflect the actual amount of wine produced, rather than a round figure set by the palace and then subdivided. The first line of this tablet lists an official called the *a-pu-da-se-we* who collects the wine. This form is a dative singular noun, also derived from the verb δατέομαι ("divide, portion"), and means "someone who portions" (*Docs.* 533). Other derivatives and compounds of this verb also appear on assessment, collection, and distribution tablets recording other commodities. This vocabulary of portioning shows that the palace officials saw their work in terms of establishing amounts, and that they viewed the different methods of assessment and distribution not as separate and distinct, but as interrelated systems which could be tailored according to need. No special apportioning system was devised for wine; instead it was assessed, collected, and distributed in the same manner as the other agricultural staples.

6. Wine in Mixed Commodity Texts

Most of the texts recording wine at both Pylos and Knossos list it along with other commodities. At Pylos, these texts are varied in format and content. They list wine as a perfume ingredient, as a trade item, and, most frequently, as one of many luxury foods provided by the palace at religious festivals. At Knossos, wine appears with other commodities in two contexts, primarily in the Fs series as part of proportionally determined meals for gods, but also in a few collection and inventory tablets (see KN Uc 160, §4 above).

PY Un 267 lists 20 units of wine (576 l) and 2 units of AB 131b (57.6 l), along with other ingredients for perfume-making. This tablet presents a rare use of wine in an industrial context. Wine is also one of many items transferred from one official to another within the bureaucracy, and forms part of the offerings of food and clothing collected and sent to sanctuaries for festivals. Wine appears most often with livestock intended for sacrifice (usually sheep and goats, but once a bull), grain and figs, but it also occurs with offerings of honey, cheese, clothing, wool, and perfumed oil.

The tablet PY Un 718, which describes items collected for Poseidon, best shows the types of commodities which appear with wine in these texts:

PY Un 718

.1 sa-ra-pe-da, po-se-da-o-ni, do-so-mo
.2 o-wi-de-ta-i, do-so-mo, to-so, e-ke-ra$_2$-wo
.3 do-se, GRA 4 VIN 3 BOS^m 1
.4 tu-ro$_2$, *TURO$_2$* 10 ko-wo, *153 1
.5 me-ri-to, V 3
.6 vacat
.7 o-da-a$_2$, da-mo, GRA 2 VIN 2
.8 OVIS^m 2 *TURO$_2$* 5 a-re-ro *AREPA* V 2 *153 1
.9 to-so-de, ra-wa-ke-ta, do-se
.10 OVIS^m 2 me-re-u-ro, FAR T 6
.11 VIN S 2 o-da-a$_2$, wo-ro-ki-jo-ne-jo, ka-ma
.12 GRA T 6 VIN S 1 *TURO$_2$* 5 me-ri[
.13   -to V 1

Four individual or group donors, *E-ke-ra$_2$-wo*, the *da-mo*, the *ra-wa-ke-ta* and the *wo-ro-ki-jo-ne-jo ka-ma*, give several items to Poseidon, but whether these serve as offerings, rent, or taxes is not clear (Killen 1985: 245). Some of the quantities are quite large. All of the donations include wine. *E-ke-ra$_2$-wo* gives the most offerings, including the largest amount of wine, 3 units (86.4 l), and a bull. The *da-mo*, the community as a whole, provides 2 units of wine (57.6 l), and fewer other types of offerings. The *ra-wa-ke-ta*, an important palace official, gives S2, 2 subunits of wine (19.2 l; one subunit = 1/3 unit or 9.6 l). The last donor, the *wo-ro-ki-jo-ne-jo ka-ma*, a religious consortium, gives S1, one subunit (9.6 l) (*Docs.* 282–83). Apart from the perfumed oil donated by the *da-mo* in line 8, which is a manufactured item rather than a direct agricultural product, all the commodities on this tablet were most likely produced on the lands of the donors. Wine is the only item that every donor provides, which implies that each estate had vines, or enough resources to trade for wine. This supports the assumption that wine was readily available throughout the kingdom of Pylos. But how often would the average Mycenaean have drunk wine? Wine is not part of the ration or handout given to lower-level personnel.

The other items recorded on the mixed commodity tablets provide a clue concerning the relative value of wine. The commodity most frequently listed with wine is meat in the form of live animals, and meat is not a staple food for the lowest classes. Meat animals appear only on tablets listing trade goods, inventory, or offerings. The other items listed—cheese, honey, and wine—can be considered staples, only if a landholder could produce them himself, and in quantity. In both ancient and modern Greece, until approximately 30 years ago, the ordinary countryman ate meat only at festivals or private feast days, such as name days and weddings. The poorer people, who had no access to meat and milk products on a regular basis, would get this type of food at least several times a year at such events. Evidence from several shrines in Late Bronze Age Greece and Crete shows that food and drink were consumed as part of the religious ritual. The goods listed in PY Un 718 and in at least seven other tablets recording similar goods sent to sanctuaries are reminiscent of the types of foods provided at the great public sacrifices in the Classical period (Parke 1977: 17–18; Palmer 1994: 101–13). In all other tablets recording commodities for festivals, the palace provided the food. Conspicuous consumption of expensive commodities at religious ceremonies heightened the prestige of the palace, and created a bond of obligation between the deities honored and the palace. Un 718 may indicate a special obligation for designated landholders to provide food, drink and gifts at a major festival of Poseidon. Since wine appears along with meat and honey in offerings and as a trade good (see §8), this supports the idea that wine is a "luxury" food, locally produced, and available to all on special occasions, but not regularly consumed by the common people.

The Fs series of tablets from Knossos record offerings of different foods given in small and fixed proportional amounts (*Docs.* 308). The six commodities offered are grain, figs, wheat flour, olive oil, wine, and honey, in quantities that suggest that they represent typical meals for an upper-class person over a 10-day period (Palmer 1994: 125–34). KN Fs 19 illustrates the format and standard amounts listed in the Fs tablets:

KN Fs 19
.1 e-ti-wa, HORD T 1 *NI* V 3
.2 FAR V 1 OLE Z 2 VIN V 1
v. *ME+RI* Z 1

These tablets list no meat or milk products; perhaps at Knossos they were not acceptable to the gods, or perhaps even in an elite diet, meat was not eaten frequently. Of the six foods listed, the grain and the figs, which are staples in the diet of palace workers, make up 75% of the total volume of offerings, and 80% of the caloric value. The remainder of the offerings consists of "luxury" foods—oil, honey, wheat flour, and wine. These foods would have been used to flavor the grain, or as side dishes, would have provided diversity of taste and much needed vitamins and fats (Palmer 1994: 131–32). Olive oil, too, was not a staple, but a luxury in the eyes of the palace administration. The palace of Knossos also sent out periodic offerings consisting wholly of honey, or olive oil (*Docs.* 303–10). One important tablet (PY Tn 316) records gold and silver drinking vessels given to gods in a single ceremony. Wine therefore was a status symbol which the higher classes and the gods regularly enjoyed, but which the common people probably tasted rarely. The tablets do not indicate exactly what role wine played in ritual, but Wright (chapter 18, this volume) has analyzed the implements used in public and private drinking ceremonies.

7. The Wine Magazine

The evidence of the tablets has shown that wine was valued as a luxury at Pylos and Knossos, but that the palace administration did not consider it necessary to control actual production. Instead, palace officials throughout the kingdoms collected wine along with other commodities, first estimating production quotas by assessing the number and type of the vines grown on each holding, and then distributing wine according to how much was required where and by whom. But what evidence exists about who produced and delivered the wine, and where was it stored? The sealings from the Wine Magazine at Pylos provide evidence for the requisition and delivery of wine to the palaces. The sealings are in the form of small three-sided nodules of clay with a string in the center, and a single seal impression in one side (Palmer 1994: 147). These sealings were attached to the items delivered to the palace, and indicated that the sealholder had fulfilled his responsibility to the palace.

The building called Wine Magazine at the Palace of Nestor at Pylos is a two-roomed outbuilding to the northeast of the central palace complex. The main room, Room 105, held three rows of storage jars with pointed bases set into the floor; 25 vessels were found, with room for 10 more. A quantity of coarse-ware cooking vessels, large lids, and a "souvlaki grill" were found in the northern half of the room, presumably where they had fallen from shelves. Along the southern and eastern walls of Room 105, clustered in three groups, 35 clay nodules bearing seal impressions came to light near the level of the shoulders and necks of the jars; apparently, they too had fallen from above when the building burned (Palmer 1994: 156). In the outer room, 14 more impressed clay nodules were excavated in the doorway of Room 104 near floor level. Four of the nodules found in the main Room 105 were inscribed with the wine ideogram to show what commodity had been delivered; on two of these nodules, a word which most likely described the source of the wine

Table 17.1

Sealing Sets and Nodule Forms from the Wine Magazine

Neatly made nodules	Sloppily made nodules	Total
2 singletons	31 singletons	33
1 set of two nodules	3 sets of two nodules	8
None	1 set of three nodules	3
1 set of five nodules	None	5
Total: 9	Total: 40	49

accompanied the ideogram (*P of N I*: fig. 303, nos. 26, 28–30; also see text of PY Wr 1360, §4 above). Carl Blegen, the excavator of the palace at Pylos, called the building the Wine Magazine, because the combination of storage jars and inscribed sealings suggested to him that wine was stored there (*P of N I*: 342–48).

Forty-nine recognizable sealings were discovered in the Wine Magazine. Thirty-three of the nodules bear impressions of unique seal types found nowhere else at Pylos. These singleton nodules then represent deliveries from 33 different sealholders. In a few instances, the same seal impressed two or more nodules, creating sets of nodules. These sets indicate multiple shipments from an individual sealholder. The largest set consists of five nodules with the same seal type, three of which are inscribed with the wine ideogram. Other sets are made up of three and two nodules, impressed by the same seal (see Table 17.1). There are six sets of sealings in all, comprising a total of 16 nodules representing deliveries from six different sealholders. Thus the number of individual sealholders represented by the 49 nodules in the Wine Magazine is 39.

Further information concerning the sealholders and their deliveries can be deduced from the findspots and forms of the nodules. The nodules were found in four different deposits, one lying inside the outer doorway in Room 104, and the other three behind the storage jars along the wall in Room 105 (Palmer 1994: 147, 151–56). These deposits probably represent four different deliveries. The nodules from the three earlier deliveries had been hung or stored above the storage jars, while the nodules from the latest delivery were set by the doorway to the building, where they had been collected as the goods came in. The nodules themselves differ greatly in quality. Nine were neatly made, with clay pinched around fine thin strings; this type includes the set of five, three of which were inscribed; a set of two, including the remaining inscribed sealing; and two singleton sealings. These nine sealings were impressed by a total of 4 seals. The other 40 nodules were sloppily made, and consequently had broken open during the destruction; their cross-sections reveal a wide variety of string impressions. These 40 sealings were impressed by 35 seals, and include one set of three impressions, three sets of two impressions, and 31 singletons (Table 17.1). The overall pattern shows a distinction between neatly made inscribed nodules that occur in sets and sloppily formed nodules, the majority representing only one example of each seal type.

One of the sealing deposits in Room 105 consists of seven of the nine neatly made uniform nodules. The seal impressions from these seven nodules belong to the set of five (three of which are inscribed) and two singletons. The other two neatly made nodules (one of which bears the fourth inscribed wine ideogram) form a set of two, and were found in another deposit along with five badly made nodules, two of which did not even have stringholes. The other two deposits contained only sloppily made nodules, formed in different ways (Palmer 1994: 150–51). Thirty-one out of 40 of the sloppily made nodules were impressed by seal types that occur only once, while seven of the nine neatly made nodules (three of them inscribed) belong to sets, and all but two of the nine were found in the same deposit (Palmer 1994: 150–51).

Who holds the seals? Bureaucrats? None of these seal types were used to impress nodules found elsewhere in the palace. The set of five with the three inscribed sealings and the set of two which includes the remaining inscribed example could represent the work of an official such as the *a-pu-da-se-we* on KN Gm 840, who collected wine. On the other hand, the other uninscribed nodules probably represent individual landholders who delivered goods to the palace, either in single or multiple consignments. They would have impressed a nodule of wet clay with their seals and left it with the official in charge, to show that they had paid their taxes. These landholders probably came from an area near to the palace; the farmers who made wine in the districts farther from the palace would have delivered their taxes in kind to the district capitals (Palmer 1994: 163–64). Therefore, these sealings provide independent evidence that the palace collected and stored wine drawn from individual landholders in the countryside. The amount collected would depend upon the amount produced, or more likely, upon the estimated production based on the number of vines each farmer possessed.

Using the measurements recorded for several of the excavated pithoi (*DHF I* 131–38), the total capacity for the 25 pithoi in the magazine can be approximately estimated to be between 4500 to 6200 l (Palmer 1994: 168–69). Even if all the pithoi held wine, which is by no means certain, the 20 units of wine (576 l) mentioned in PY Un 267 as one of the ingredients for perfumed oil, would have used up 10% of the amount stored there. The wine listed in the inventory tablet PY Ua 17, amounting to a little over 1371 l, would account for between 25% and 33% of the estimated capacity of the pithoi. PY Ua 17 also records a large number of animals, under the care of the same official responsible for the inventoried commodities, but probably not kept in the same place as the wine:

PY Ua 17
    .1]1 T 1 VIN 47 S 1 V 5
    .2]7 OVIS^f 7 WE 17 CAP^m 31 SUS^f 20
    17 *lat. inf*]14 [
    17 v.]30[ ]T 7 [ ] T 4 V 2

The total volume of wine listed in all the Pylos tablets, around 16,000 l, is almost three times the total capacity of the pithoi available in the Wine Magazine (Palmer 1994: 196). The extant Pylos tablets represent about five months worth of palace records; clearly, the amount of wine which the palace administration handled was many times greater than the capacity of this single storeroom. The records show that wine was constantly disbursed, and the four clusters of impressed nodules in the storeroom probably represented four separate deliveries to the Magazine. Moreover, the inventory records indicate that the Wine Magazine was only one of many such storerooms set up near the palace, and throughout the Kingdom.

8. Evidence for the Mycenaean Wine Trade

The Linear B clay texts are all temporary records which refer only to transactions within each kingdom. Texts recording external trade probably were kept on papyrus or parchment. (For discussion of the types of information about trade in the Linear B records, see Killen 1985: 262–70 and Palaima 1991: 273–310). Several Linear B texts do record internal trade, where the palace exchanged goods for needed material. But such references are understandably rare, because the palaces normally used other methods (taxation, various kinds of long-term work contracts) to get the resources they needed (Palmer 1994: 92–94). One of these trade texts, PY An 35, records a transaction on lines 5 and 6 where wine is part of the price for the mineral alum:

PY An 35
>.1 to-ko-do-mo, de-me-o-te
>.2 pu-ro VIR 2 me-te-to-de VIR 3
>.3 sa-ma-ra-de VIR 3 re-u-ko-to-ro VIR 4
>.4 vacat
>.5 a-ta-ro, tu-ru-pte-ri-ja, o-no
>.6 LANA 2 CAP^f 4 *146 3 VIN 10 *NI* 4

This tablet records 10 units of wine (288 l) as part of the price paid by the palace for *tu-ru-pte-ri-ja*, the imported mineral alum; the rest of the price consists of wool, goats, some sort of garment, and figs. These are all items locally produced outside the palace, and collected by the administration as taxes. Alum is not found in Messenia; the closest good source known from this period is the Cyclades (Baumbach 1987: 53). The palace, however, would need large quantities of alum for building, leatherworking, and cloth dyeing (Shelmerdine 1985: 136–37). The palace did not import alum itself, but instead relied on middlemen, whom they paid in surplus goods from the palace stores. Special products made by palace workers, such as perfumed oil or high quality cloth, are notably absent from the price paid for the alum. This evidence, scanty as it is, combined with the fact that the Mycenaean bureaucracy did not direct wine production, but merely assessed and collected a portion of the farmers' production, suggests that the Mycenaean palaces of Pylos and Knossos did not specialize in exporting wine in the same way that they managed the trade in palace-produced cloth or perfumed oil. But given the fact that the palace collected large quantities of wine as taxes, any surplus not consumed or distributed within the kingdom could have been traded abroad. The palaces probably provided the bulk of the wine shipped from the Aegean, but by no means held a monopoly on the wine trade. Individual vine growers, or traders such as *a-ta-ro* in PY An 35, could have dealt in wine, only on a much smaller scale. The Linear A evidence also shows movement of both wine and the wine ideogram in the Aegean, perhaps due to palace trade as well as small entrepreneurs.

9. Conclusions

The many contexts in which wine appears in the Linear B tablets allows a survey of the different ways in which the palaces collected and distributed this product. The assessment tablets for vines and fruit trees show that vines were often grown with fig trees, and that the palace assessors noted method of cultivation as well as number of vines, in order to estimate yield more accurately. The palaces were not directly involved in the production of wine, but collected the fermented product from local farmers.

The seed evidence from Greek sites dating back to the Neolithic period shows that vines had been cultivated at least a thousand years before the Mycenaean kingdoms formed, and that by this late period, vine-growing was widespread throughout Greece and Crete. The appearance of the wine ideogram in the earliest Linear A texts in Crete shows that wine was a desirable commodity collected and monitored by the Minoan bureaucracies from the Protopalatial period, after ca. 1800 B.C. The similarities in format between the Linear B tablets listing wine and the undeciphered Linear A tablets which also record that commodity suggest that both Minoan and Mycenaean palace administrations treated wine as a common but relatively valuable agricultural product. The evidence from the Wine Magazine at Pylos on the Mainland shows that numerous landholders brought in wine in periodic consignments. A set proportion of the vintage would be collected from each producer, which would then be distributed directly according to individual need, or in special circumstances, sent out to the towns or sanctuaries.

The wine collected by the palace had a variety of uses: for immediate consumption as part of upper class ritual and diet, as the palace rooms full of *kylikes* suggest (e.g., the 600 *kylikes* in Room 9 of the palace at Pylos; *P of N I*: 102); for perfume manufacture; for trade; or as a gift to gods, to be consumed at festivals. The relative value of wine is demonstrated by the types of commodities listed and distributed with it, such as meat, cheese and honey, which were frequently given to gods and high-ranking individuals. The ordinary Mycenaeans who did not raise their own vines, probably drank wine only on special occasions, such as at public festivals or private celebrations. This pattern of wine use in Late Bronze Age Greece is ancestral to the traditional use of wine in the Classical period. The evidence shows that Greece is heir to a tradition of wine-making and enjoyment reaching back at least 5000 years.

Notes

1. The texts dealing with Linear A and B tablets are cited according to the following abbreviations:

    CMS I: A. Sakellariou, *Corpus der minoischen und mykenischen Siegel*, Vol. 1: *Die minoischen und mykenischen Siegel des Nationalmuseum in Athen*, Berlin, 1964.

    CMS I Supplement: J. A. Sakellarakis, *Corpus der minoischen und mykenischen Siegel*, Vol. I supplementum: *Athenisches Nationalmuseum*, Berlin, 1982.

    DHF I: D. H. French, Unpublished excavation notebook, Palace of Nestor excavations, 1958.

    Dictionnaire: P. Chantraine, *Dictionnaire étymologique de la langue grecque*, Vols. 1–4, Paris, 1968–80.

    Docs.: M. Ventris and J. Chadwick, *Documents in Mycenaean Greek*, 2nd ed., Cambridge, 1973.

    GORILA 5: L. Godart and J.-P. Olivier, *Recueil des inscriptions in Linéaire A*, Paris, 1985.

    KT 5: J. T. Killen, and J.-P. Olivier, *The Knossos Tablets*, 5th ed., Minos Supplement 11, Salamanca, 1989.

    PTT I: E. L. Bennett Jr. and J.-P. Olivier, *The Pylos Tablets Transcribed*, Vol. 1: *Texts and Notes*, Incunabula Graeca 51, Rome, 1976.

    P of N I: C. W. Blegen and M. Rawson, *The Palace of Nestor in Western Messenia*, Vol 1: *The Buildings and Their Contents*, Princeton, 1966.

2. The definitive edition of the Linear A texts published in 1985, *GORILA*, lists 318 published tablets (*GORILA 5*: 126). In the next ten years, a few more tablets and fragments were found at various sites in Crete and the Aegean islands—see Olivier 1992: 445–47 for a brief enumeration of these texts.

3. The method of labelling the Linear B texts reflects the site where the tablet was found, the subject of the tablet, and its accession number. Therefore, for PY Un 267, PY shows that it was found at Pylos, Un shows that it records more than one kind of item, and 267 is its inventory number within the whole group of tablets from Pylos. The tablets from Knossos are preceded by the abbreviation KN. The syllabic signs are transliterated as consonant + vowel, or single vowel groups, separated by hyphens

(e.g. the transliterated word *o-do-ke* from line 1, PY Un 267 in Linear B is written with three signs only). The ideograms in Linear B are either schematized drawings of items (in some cases, almost completely abstract symbols) or abbreviations for the Linear B words. For instance, the ideogram for honey on PY Un 718 is a combination of the two syllabic signs making up the word *me-ri* ("honey"). If the ideogram is a schematized or an abstract drawing, it is transliterated with a Latin abbreviation. The sign for wine (see Fig. 17.1 for actual shape) therefore is transliterated as VIN, the abbreviation of Latin VINUM. For a more complete explanation, see Hooker 1980: 35–44.

CHAPTER 18

Empty Cups and Empty Jugs: The Social Role of Wine in Minoan and Mycenaean Societies

James C. Wright

1. Introduction

Preserved texts and archaeological remains of winemaking installations document clearly enough the production of wine in Minoan and Mycenaean society. How wine was used is less clear, although Mycenaean texts record its use in a variety of ways.[1] Because of the important role that wine plays in social institutions and in the formation of complex societies (Dietler 1990), this is an important theme to pursue. The best evidence for studying this problem is found in pictorial and artifactual material illustrative of the consumption of wine. Because of the notorious ambiguity of such evidence in pre- and proto-historic societies, special attention has to be given to the study of its archaeological context. This perspective will be highlighted in this chapter, which will examine the evidence from the Minoan and Mycenaean periods.[2] For the period of the first palaces on Crete, this investigation cannot succeed because of the poverty of representations. In such instances where vessels are displayed, such as in association with activities of the "genii," other activities, such as lustration, are more plausibly argued (Weingarten 1991). With the advent of the Neopalatial period, a much broader scheme of artistic representation develops, but unfortunately, there is no scene preserved that shows vessels being used for drinking, a group of vessels that could be identified as a wine service, or recognizable attributes of grapes—all of which are common in classical Greece. Only two artifacts illustrate grapes, viz., painted vessels from Thera (Fig. 18.1; see also Marinatos 1970: pl. 56, 1; Marinatos 1974: pl. 79).[3]

James C. Wright

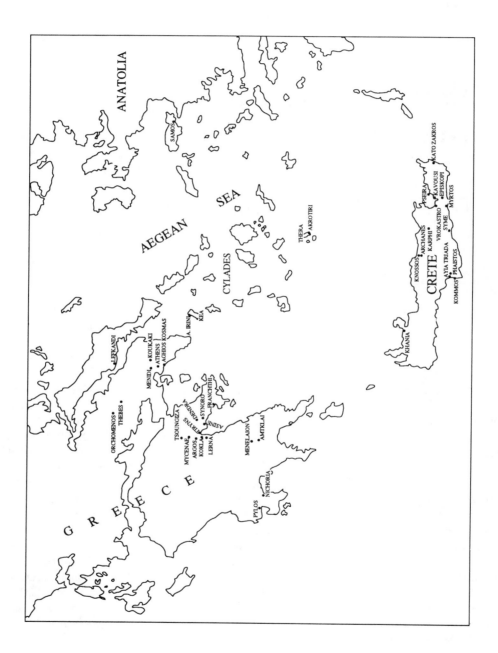

Map 18.1. Sites of Minoan and Mycenaean wine production.

Figure 18.1. Jugs painted with clusters of grapes from Thera: (left) below handle on body; and (right) on body. (Marinatos 1970: pl. 56$_1$, and 1974: pl. 79; permission requested.)

2. Neopalatial Crete

Robert Koehl has argued that the Chieftain's Cup from Ayia Triada represents a scene of part of a coming of age ritual for young men, and suggests that the cup, which is a form of Minoan chalice, was a token of this rite (Fig. 18.2; Koehl 1986: 99–110). Koehl pointed to the sanctuary at Syme as providing confirmatory evidence that such rituals took place. Aside from difficulties that may exist in his use of much later evidence as a way of fleshing out his hypothesis, he is right to suggest this assocation. The presence of hundreds of pottery chalices and numerous ones of stone in the Neopalatial remains at Syme suggests that an important ceremony associated with drinking took place there (Fig. 18.3). This issue has already been examined in a study by A. Lebessi and P. Muhly (1987: 102–13), who have argued that at the sanctuary in the Geometric and Archaic period a male rite of passage into adulthood took place. The question of what kind of rituals occurred during the Neopalatial period, when the sanctuary reached an acme of development, is still unanswered, though the authors (Lebessi and Muhly 1990: 333–36) have recently demonstrated that it consisted of open-air activity within a large enclosure and that there is a high degree of continuity in the cult after the end of the Neopalatial era.

Because the chalice was so commonly used at Syme, it is important to pursue its use in Neopalatial Crete as a way of delving more deeply into this problem. Burkert (1985: 36) has emphasized that the ambiguity of the evidence does not allow a distinction to be made between feasting and burnt offerings in Minoan religion. Lebessi and Muhly (1990: 324–27) argue that the faunal evidence, which consists of unburnt bones, indicates that feasting, rather than burnt sacrifices, was the central activity, and contend that the "the presence of cups and jugs of various types demonstrates that liquids were also brought and consumed during the feasting" (1990: 327).

Figure 18.2. Stone Chieftain's Cup from Ayia Triada. (Marinatos and Hirmer 1973: pl. 100; reproduced by permission of Hirmer Verlag, München.)

Figure 18.3. Pottery chalice from Syme. (Lebessi and Muhly 1990: fig. 11a; reproduced by permission of P. Muhly.)

Nonetheless, they believe that the chalices were reserved for offerings to the divinities. The question to be pursued here is whether wine was the liquid used in these vessels, both the common ones for worshippers and the special ones purported to be for deities.

The chalice was a common shape among Minoan stone vases, as Warren's catalogue illustrates (1969: 36–37; *s.v.* "cups" and "tankards"), yet it is relatively unknown as a pottery form, especially from contemporaneous domestic deposits.[4] Elegant stone chalices ar e found in the Treasure Room Deposit at Kato Zakros (Fig. 18.4; Platon 1971: 133–48, illustrations on pp. 6, 14, 65, 137–42, 144). This context is clearly very special because of its location, because the other objects found there were so ornate and made of precious materials, and because among them was the tripartite peak sanctuary shrine rhyton (Shaw 1978). Thus, there is little room for debate about interpreting these chalices as having been stored for use in ceremonies by leading authorities or priests of the palace. The context is perhaps best compared to that of the so-called Temple Repositories at Knossos, discovered by Sir Arthur Evans (1921: 463–85, 495–23, 557–61), and containing, among many figurines and other items of undoubtedly sacred use, two elegant, small faience cups and a small silver jug (compare Fig. 18.7). These cups are not the same shape as the Zakros chalices, though they are generally similar to those examples from Ayia Triada and Syme just cited, and must have been used in ceremony carried out in the cult area.[5]

3. The Greek Mainland and Thera

Not much more can be inferred from the archaeological evidence of Neopalatial Crete. Turning abroad, however, the pottery and marble chalices of the Zakros type should be noted at Akrotiri,

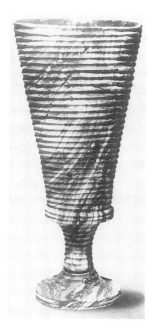
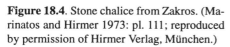

Figure 18.4. Stone chalice from Zakros. (Marinatos and Hirmer 1973: pl. 111; reproduced by permission of Hirmer Verlag, München.)

Figure 18.5. Stone chalice from Thera. (Marinatos 1972: pl. 67; permission requested.)

Thera (Fig. 18.5; Marinatos 1972: 31, pls. 67–68; Warren 1979: 93, pl. 15), while ones made of gypsum showed up in Graves IV and V of Grave Circle A at Mycenae (Fig. 18.6; Karo 1930–33: 118, no. 600; 148, no. 854). Their appearance in these tombs is not accidental. Of the wealthy graves at Mycenae, IV and V contained the lion's share of riches. This can be illustrated by observing that of a total of 112 gold and silver vessels known from Mainland contexts dating between Middle Helladic III and Late Helladic I, 49% derive from these two tombs alone! What is perhaps more significant is the fact that many items compare with those from special deposits, such as the Treasure Room at Zakros and the Temple Repositories at Knossos. For example, in Grave A of Circle B were a faience cup and silver jug, very much the same as those from the Temple Repositories (Fig. 18.7).[6] In such a circumstance, it seems impossible to think that such goods were available in an open market for anyone to purchase. More likely is the conclusion that somehow the occupants of these graves had access to these items in the palaces themselves. One might argue that they represent booty, but, despite their gross over-representation in Graves IV and V, similar objects of wealth occur in many graves between Middle Helladic III and Late Helladic II, and thus are not easily accounted for by proposing Mycenaean aggression against Crete. The most likely explanation is that these items represent traffic between emerging elite or chiefly groups at Mainland centers and those ruling the Minoan palaces. This is familiar in the model of ceremonial or prestige exchange, as derived from ethnographic studies (Mauss 1967; Friedman and Rowlands 1977; Dalton 1977: 204–10; Dietler 1990: 378).

How this mechanism worked in the Aegean is a major unsolved problem, especially to explain the nature of the relationship of the Mainlanders to the Minoans.[7] The most likely solution, I

Figure 18.7. Silver jug and faience cup from
Mycenae. (Mylonas 1972: pl. 16a.)

Figure 18.6. Stone chalice from Mycenae.
(Karo 193–31: pl. 138.)

believe, is that the Mainlanders provided professional military service for the Minoans.[8] As mercenaries, the Mycenaeans would have helped subdue piracy in the islands (and hence have been painted in the north frieze of the miniature fresco of the West House at Akrotiri: see Immerwahr 1977). They may also have been employed around Knossos and, perhaps, in some of the other palaces, to help police the grounds or territory. In the process, they may have become welcome in the courts of the palace officials, and were eventually adopted by court society and initiated into Minoan ceremony and ritual.

The mercenary role of the Mycenaeans in the Minoan culture is an old idea, but not as far-fetched as it may seem. In one of the frescoes from the Palace of Minos which dates to the period of Mycenaean domination, there is a clear record of Mycenaean and Minoan ceremonial use of drinking vessels. The painting is known as the "Campstool Fresco," because it preserves fragments which illustrate men seated on folding stools. Two of the fragments show men holding up vessels in their hands (Fig. 18.8). These are well enough preserved to identify a Mycenaean goblet in one hand and the stem of a Minoan chalice in another (Evans 1935: 379–96; Immerwahr 1990: 95; Cameron 1964: 51–52). Thus, by at least LH IIIA, if not earlier, the Mycenaeans had developed an interest in polite drinking and in doing it with Minoans, probably to honor each other. Here then, we have the first unequivocal evidence of individuals using the chalice (and the goblet). Given the abundance of evidence that Palmer (chapter 17, this volume) has adduced for wine production and recording in Neopalatial Crete, it is difficult to imagine that the men in the "Campstool Fresco" were drinking anything but wine, and equally difficult to think that the chalice used here was not used in the same manner as the special ones found at Syme or those from Zakros.

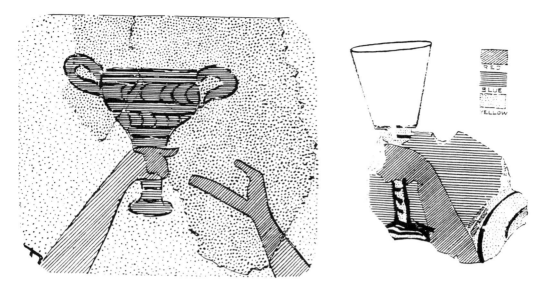

Figure 18.8. Fragments of the "Campstool Fresco" from Knossos. (Evans 1935: figs. 324–35.)

4. Sociopolitical Complexity and Wine

Such a pattern of usage suggests one of the ways that societies can learn from one another. M. Dietler (1990) has recently pursued this topic, arguing that the acquisition of both the knowledge of wine and the etiquette that goes with it is an important element in the development of sociopolitical complexity. In a society unaccustomed to drinking wine, access to it and to the customs of its proper consumption set the possessor of this commodity and knowledge apart from his colleagues and underlings. Dietler's study of prestige exchange among the Celts, in which elites acquire wine from the Etruscans and Greeks, is an excellent example of how this process occurs. The process stimulates competitive ceremonies of drinking and feasting among different chiefs, a widely recognized activity in chiefdom level societies (Dietler 1990: 384–85, *passim*; Murray 1983: 197).

Certainly, this intriguing model deserves exploration with respect to the question of the emergence of Mycenaean chiefdoms during the period Middle Helladic III–Late Helladic II. Particular similarities deserve special attention. For example, one problem that Dietler investigates, which had not adequately been addressed by other scholars, is why the wine paraphernalia are found concentrated in a few wealthy tombs. Dietler's position is that the possession of wine and the vessels associated with its consumption were marks of an emerging chief and were not shared with others by "redistribution." Rather, they were retained as high status markers (see 1990: 386, on the distinction between hieratic and hierarchic organization; pp. 356–57, on redistribution). This explanation also would fit with the extreme wealth of Graves IV and V at Mycenae, among others like them. Additionally, it is remarkable that the introduction of the vine into Celtic Europe was not immediate (Dietler 1990: 382–83). In part, there was probably no strong desire to do so, since, as Dietler stresses, the process itself of acquiring wine and its paraphernalia from abroad was of importance as a way of demonstrating the special powers of the chiefs who could obtain it.

Figure 18.9. Pottery assemblage from Tsoungiza. (Nemea Valley Archaeological Project archives, photograph by T. Dabney.)

On the Mainland of Greece in earlier periods, it cannot, however, be argued that the grapevine was unknown. Archaeobotanical evidence for grape is documented in deposits from the Early and Middle Bronze Ages (chapter 16 by Renfrew, this volume), and it is not unreasonable to think that wine may already have been produced in these periods. In fact, ceremonies involving wine drinking may be native elements of the Indo-European speaking inhabitants of Middle and Late Helladic Greece.

Linguistic evidence from the Indo-European root words, *kheo*, *leibo*, and *spendo*, are all associated with liquid offerings, whether to the dead, to deities, or to seal oaths or pacts, and wine is a natural candidate for such use.[9] None of these terms require the use of wine, but they do require vessels for holding and pouring, and in Classical Greek the wine jug *par excellence* is named the *oinochoe*.

Such vessels are the natural archaeological correlates of such behavior, and among graves of the late Middle Helladic and early Late Helladic periods, they are frequently found in different burial grounds, as shown in Table 18.1. What is of interest here is the combination of vessels for pouring and drinking. Some vessel forms, namely the goblet *kantharos*, and various native cup forms, occur together frequently in archaeological deposits, but not always. A contemporary floor deposit from a house at Tsoungiza well illustrates this grouping of pottery types (Fig. 18.9). Aside from the coarse ware vessels, there are two jugs, two *kantharoi*, a goblet, and a ladle (Wright 1982; Rutter 1989). At Mycenae in the graves of Circle B, these vessels are normal among adult graves, particularly those of males (Table 18.2).

The main difference between the contents of the grave circles in Table 18.2 and the burials represented in Table 18.1 is in the increased frequency of the goblet and foreign-made and foreign-influenced forms in the grave circles, together with the introduction of metal weapons and vessels. These data show a consistency in the forms of vessels deposited with burials from the end of the Middle Helladic through Late Helladic I, a period marked by the transition in the social organization of Mycenaean society with increased acquisition of highly valued foreign-made items. One aspect of the rise in interest in burial goods is the shift of attention from pottery vessels to vessels of precious metal. The consistency of this development may very possibly reflect an

Figure 18.10. Golden Cup of Nestor from Mycenae. (Karo 1930–31: pl. 210; reproduced by permission of Hirmer Verlag, München.)

Figure 18.11. Silver goblet with *niello* from Mycenae. (Marinatos and Hirmer 1973: pl. 208; reproduced by permission of Hirmer Verlag, München.)

amplification of traditions which were already a part of indigenous behavior; thus, foreign objects are introduced alongside prestigious items of local origin. Accompanying these objects must be a change in behavior that explains their presence. The role of drinking in early Celtic society, as described by Dietler (1990: 375–80, 382–90) is especially relevant, since it includes adoption of "foreign drinking customs," and offers a model of how the evidence from Neopalatial Crete, the new wealthy Mainland graves, and the older Middle Helladic burial traditions are linked into a process of interdependent change. The prestige enhancement that accompanies the introduction of foreign but not altogether new ceremonies of drinking, and the social distance expressed by the luxurious vessels used in the ceremonies are fundamental aspects of the emergence of chiefly groups at developing Mainland centers. Hybrid vessels incorporate all these elements and document the syncretistic nature of early Mycenaean social and political ideology. Examples are the "Nestor's Cup" from Grave IV at Mycenae (Fig. 18.10). It is a hybrid form of a Vapheio cup, a chalice stem, and *kantharos* handles (Karo 1930–33: 100, no. 412; Davis 1979: 183–86). Likewise, the pedestalled goblet from Grave IV is Minoan in execution but Mycenaean in form (Fig. 18.11: Karo 1930–33: 94, no. 390; Davis 1979: 211).

5. Ceremonial Uses of Wine Vessels

Although this argument has so far focused on the prestige value that can be recognized in the use of certain special vessels, a second, equally important and not exclusive distinction has been implicit, namely recognizing the actual ceremonies in which these vessels were used. The "Campstool Fresco" appears to represent an activity focused on drinking, a kind of proto-historic *symposion*, and in this context the prestige function of special vessels would be emphasized. At

Table 18.1

Pottery Groups from Selected Cemeteries in the Corinthia and Argolid

Site and grave	Cup form				Kantharos form		Jar form		Jug form	
	Goblet	Paneled	Vapheio	Semi-globular	Normal	Shallow hemispherical	Spherical bridge-spouted	1-handled	Spouted jar/jug	Cut-away spout
ASINE (Dietz 1980)										
Grave 1971-3	28,29 30,31 32,33	26	36	40	34,38		35	41		25,27 37
CORINTH (Blegen et al. 1964)										
Grave 1				1-2						1-1 1-3
2				2-3				2-2		2-1
3										3-5
5				5-4		5-3			5-1	5-2
6										6-1
7				7-1						
8				8-1	8-2					8-3
9						9-2		9-1		
10			10-1							
11				11-3						11-1
13				13-2					13-1	

PROSYMNA (Blegen 1937)

Grave					
I					
III	9,10		*3,5*		
IV	55		*54*	4	53
XIII	584		*581,585*		
XVI			*587*	586	
XVII			*521*	522	
XVIII			*581*	579,580; 582,583	
XIX		*565,588*	*589*	566,567; 568,590	
XX head		*577,578*		591	
XX legs		*571,572; 574,592*		576; 569,570; 573,575	
XXI Group C			*558*		559
XXVI				697	698
XXXVIII				743	
XXXI			*1201*	1200	1202

Italics = loop-handle.

Table 18.2

Selected Vessel Groups from Grave Circle B
(according to the order of Graziadio [1988])

Burial	Sex	Weapons	Vessel type				
			Goblet	Cup form	Kantharos	Jar form	Jug form
Zeta	M	Y	2	1 vapheio	1		1 spouted jug 1 cut-away spout
Eta	M	Y	1	1 semi-globular	2	1 one-handled m-p	1 cut-away spout
Iota early	U			1 vapheio	1		1 cut-away spout
Iota late	M	Y	4			1 one-handled m-p	
Lambda 2	M			1 loop-handled			1 cut-away spout
Xi early	U(adolescent?)		3		1	1 one-handled m-p	1 spherical bridge-spouted
Rho	U		2	1 teacup	1		
Beta	M	Y	4				
Epsilon fill	U		(1)	1 panelled			
Lambda fill	U		4	1 vapheio			
Lambda inside	M	Y	4	2 panelled 1 semi-globular		1 one-handled m-p	
Nu roof	U		4	1 Au vapheio 1 AE jug			
Ypsilon	F	N	6				

Context	Sex		No.		No.		No.	
Gamma fill								
MYC 58	F	N	3	1 AE cup 1 Au vapheio 4 panelled 2 vapheio 2 loop-handled 3 semi-globular	1	1 one-handled m-p	1	1 cut-away spout
Delta fill	U		2	1 Ag vapheio		1 one-handled m-p		
Alpha*	M	Y	1		2	1 piriform		1 cut-away spout
Epsilon inside later	U							1 AE jug spout
Nu later	M			1 Au vapheio 1 AE 'phiale'				
PI	U		3					3 various types
Mu early	U		2	1 teacup 1 loop-handled 2 semi-globular		3 various types		
Gamma central	M	Y		1 semi-globular 1 Au vapheio				
southern	M	N			3	1 squat LH I type		
Delta								
MYC 61	M	Y						
MYC 60	F?	Y		1 AE 'phiale'				

*25 vases were excavated, but only 8 were published. Key: F = female, M = male, U = unidentified, Y = yes, N = no, AE = bronze, Ag = silver, Au = gold, m-p = matt-painted.

Figure 18.12. Silver vessels from Dendra. (Persson 1942: fig. 99; photograph courtesy of the Swedish Institute at Athens.)

the same time, such an activity would naturally include the use of vessels that marked the attainment of status, such as a cup received as a part of an initiation into manhood as suggested by Koehl (1986). But, the evidence from the Mainland examined thus far comes nearly exclusively from tombs, and it is important not to confuse ceremonies carried on in life with those of the funeral, even if they are closely related. In this regard, it should be observed that grave goods accompanying the dead, especially those grouped close at hand around the deceased, may best be understood (at least in Mycenaean burials) as belonging to the dead, while those items set apart from the deceased (either outside the tomb or not directly associated with the corpse) may, in some cases, relate to mortuary ceremonies. Actual proof of these distinctions is lacking and relies, for now, on common sense more than scientific demonstration, but it is worth observing that the high status vessels discussed so far tend to occur in close juxtaposition to the dead. This will continue to be the case for similar material found in later Mycenaean mortuary contexts.

As Mycenaean pottery forms begin to evolve into the mature forms of Late Helladic II and III, some of the indigenous and foreign-inspired shapes lose their meaning. The Panelled Cup disappears after Late Helladic I. The Vapheio cup undergoes a metamorphosis into a mug. From the Middle Bronze Age tradition of the *kantharos* and goblet emerges the Mycenaean goblet and *kylix*.[10] From the Middle Helladic and Minoan cut-away jugs emerge Mycenaean jug forms. But it is not clear from the archaeological contexts of the pottery, especially that deposited in tombs, whether the vessels carried a specific meaning. No study to date has documented the production of services, that is, pottery made to be used together, such as table settings or wine services.[11] The finds from tombs are notoriously difficult to sort out according to individual burials, because of extended periods of use and multiple burials in chamber tombs.

Metal versions of the pottery vessels, however, point to a service set. For example, the group of silver vessels from Tomb 10 (shaft II) at Dendra (Fig. 18.12) includes a large goblet, two *kylikes*, a small dipper and a shallow wide-rimmed bowl. From the same context comes a nearly identical group in pottery (Persson 1942: 87–88, figs. 99, 103; pp. 135–37, fig. 117; see also tomb 11, p. 98, fig. 109: nos. 5–9). The discovery in other tombs of these shapes made as pottery, but covered in tin to give the appearance of silver, reinforces the interpretation of these as special status vessels.[12]

The prestige attached to these vessels is likely related to the use of real silver and gold ones by the ruling elite, particularly in ceremonies. The appearance of these vessel shapes as ideograms in Linear B is noteworthy (see chapter 17 by Palmer, this volume), especially those forms that are

Figure 18.13. Ideograms in Linear B.

known to have been made of gold and silver and used in ceremonies. In this connection, the famous religious tablet from Pylos, Tn 316, is the best evidence. It refers to three forms of vessels that are given to deities and heroes and used in ceremonies at their shrines (Chadwick 1973: 284–89; Gérard-Rousseau 1968: *passim*; Palmer 1963: 261–68). The vessels are golden bowls (possibly conical cups or bowls: ideogram 213[vas]; see Vandenabeele and Olivier 1979: 183–85), golden goblets (ideogram 215[vas]; seeVandenabeele and Olivier 1979: 210–12), and golden chalices (ideogram 216[vas]; Vandenabeele and Olivier 1979: 212–16), all illustrated in Figure 18.13.[13] Mentioned together with these gifts on Tn 316 are a shrine of Poseidon, a shrine of a dove (?) goddess, deities named *ipemedea* (Iphimedeia), *diwija* (Diwija, for the female counterpart of Zeus), *emaa* (Hermes), *diwe* (Diwe, for Zeus), *era* (Hera), *dirimija* (Drimios), a priest (?) of Zeus, *potnia* (Potnia), *manasa* (Mnasa or Manasa), *posidaeja* (Poseideia), *tiriseroe* (the Thrice-hero?), and *dopota* (the Despotis—"lord of the house"?).

Of these names, that of *manasa* is particularly tantalizing since it appears to be a non-Greek name. It has been suggested that it may be a Minoan deity (Gérard-Rousseau 1968: 137). More intriguing, however, is the appearance of the goblet and the chalice as ideograms, which strengthens the interpretation offered here of ceremonial drinking as shown in the "Campstool Fresco" from Knossos.

One cannot ignore the similarity of this assemblage of vessels in tablet Tn 316 from the Bronze Age palace at Pylos to the scene in the Odyssey where Telemachos arrives at Nestor's Pylos in search of his father. Accompanied by Athena, who is in disguise, he approaches the palace where he finds Nestor and his sons celebrating a feast of Poseidon. Telemachos and his companion are invited by Peisistratos, son of Nestor, to sit down with them, and he

> gave them portions of the vitals and poured wine for them in a golden cup, and spoke [...] "my guest, make your prayer now to the lord Poseidon, for his is the festival you have come to on your arrival; but when you have poured to him and prayed, according to custom, then give this man also a cup of the sweet wine, so that he too can pour, for I think he also will make his prayer to the immortals. All men need the gods. But this one is a younger man than you, and of the same age as I am. This is why I am first giving you the golden goblet." (Lattimore 1967: 3:40–50)

Later, when they have returned to the palace after the feast they retired within and

> took their places in order on chairs and along the benches, and as they came in the old man mixed the wine bowl for them with wine sweet to drink which the housekeeper had opened in its eleventh year

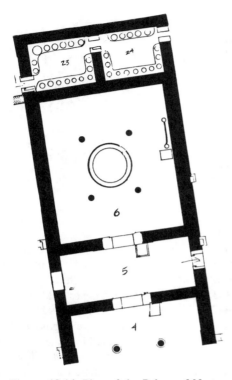

Figure 18.14. Plan of the Palace of Nestor. (Blegen and Rawson 1966: 1: foldout; copyright © 1966 PUP; reproduced by permission of Princeton University Press and the University of Cincinnati.)

Figure 18.15. Miniature *kylike* from the Palace of Nestor. (Blegen and Rawson 1966: fig. 359; copyright © 1966 PUP; reproduced by permission of Princeton University Press and the University of Cincinnati.)

and loosed the sealing upon it. The old man mixed the wine in the bowl and prayed much, pouring a libation out to Athene daughter of Zeus of the Aegis. (Lattimore 1967: 3:389–394)

The scene could have taken place in a number of areas of the palace, though the central room with its great hearth seems the most likely (Fig. 18.14). Here also is located the throne. Next to it are two basins, formed in the plaster floor and connected by a channel, that are thought to have received libations (Blegen and Rawson 1966: 88; Hägg 1990: 178).[14] This idea is strengthened by the observation that a few miniature *kylikes* were found scattered on the floor of the *megaron* (Fig. 18.15). These vessels are not common in the palace area, showing up otherwise only in Room 7 of the Archives and in the pottery storerooms 18–20, 24, and 60 (Blegen and Rawson 1966: 366). It seems reasonable to reconstruct a scene where a small portion of liquid, probably wine, is poured off to honor a deity, to appease the gods, or to seal an oath or pact.

Furthermore, fragmentary evidence from the Pylos frescoes provides additional support for a drinking ceremony. The fresco fragments from the *megaron* at Pylos preserve scenes showing a bull being led, and of individuals seated on stools facing each other across a table (Fig. 18.16) (Lang 1969: 80–81, pls. 125, 126, fragments 44aH6, 44bH6). A recent restudy of the frescoes suggests that the fragments represent a comprehensive pictorial program associated with sacrifice (McCallum 1987: 260; Hägg 1985: 216).[15] The innermost scene is located in the *megaron* where, along with the familiar lyre-player and hoopoe-like bird flying towards the throne, are the fragments of seated figures. Unfortunately, the upper portions of these figures are missing, but the basic features of the "Campstool Fresco" are present: campstool and robed persons seated on them. Given the derivative nature of much of Mycenaean fresco painting, it seems likely to see in the "Campstool Fresco" a prototype of the Pylos painting (Lang 1969: 81).

This discussion, then, returns to its point of departure and demonstrates the coherence of the use, special meaning, and representation of vessels in Mycenaean society. There is, in conse-

Figure 18.16. Reconstructed drawing of procession and sacrifice fresco from the Palace of Nestor. (Lang 1969: pl. 119; copyright © 1966 PUP; reproduced by permission of Princeton University Press and the University of Cincinnati.)

quence, little doubt that the juxtaposition of the Minoan chalice and the Mycenaean goblet/*kylix* in the fresco is a representation of the ceremonial importance of drinking among Mycenaean noblemen, and that in all likelihood the liquid consumed was wine.

6. Other Aspects of Wine and Wine-Drinking

Drinking may also have taken place at a more mundane, but equally important, level. Again, the tablets are silent on this matter, but the spatial organization of the palace at Pylos gives some hint of this activity. We need first recognize that the two room suite which constitutes the Archives at Pylos (rooms 7–8; Palaima and Wright 1985) is an architectural feature found in association with entrances (Fig. 18.14: Rooms 7–8, 9–10, 39–40). As Blegen suggested, it may be a kind of reception suite in the palace (Blegen and Rawson 1966: 102–3; Säflund 1980: 237–46). In Room 9 he found five or six hundred *kylikes* smashed on the floor, while in the outer room (10) were two storage jars, which he thought had held wine, and in the adjacent corner, a stucco bench. Surely, it is worth restating Blegen's notion that ceremonial drinking occurred in this room, and that the activity had something to do with conducting business in the palace.

One feature of wine-drinking, however, is missing from our discussion. Nestor is said to have mixed the wine in the bowl, but the Mycenaean version of this practice has not been identified. This custom could be understood as an anachronistic reference to the Greek etiquette of wine consumption, where the krater was used to mix the strong wine with water. It was considered barbaric to drink wine undiluted; only Dionysos and the other gods did so, because they could better bear the effects of intoxication. Yet, the krater is a Mycenaean form. The shape is known from the late Middle Helladic and Late Helladic I era (Davis 1979: 241–47). It continues through Late Helladic II (Catling 1977: 31; Rutter and Rutter 1976: 56, cat. no. 887), and takes its standard form during Late Helladic IIIA (Fig. 18.17). Interestingly, the krater is not well known in Mainland contexts (Furumark 1941: 586; Mountjoy 1986: 61); it is best represented in Cyprus where it was a popular shape, especially for carrying pictorial scenes, and it was frequently deposited in graves (Vermeule and Karageorghis 1982: 2). The relative scarcity of kraters in tombs on the Mainland of Greece may be because of its high cost; at any rate, its role in Mycenaean mortuary ceremony is unknown.

Figure 18.17. Krater. (Mountjoy 1986: fig. 70; published with permission of P. Mountjoy.)

There is no certain evidence that the krater was used for mixing wine, though a very few of the pictorial examples have depictions that suggest the special use of the vessel type. An important fragment from Enkomi, in the British Museum, shows what might be interpreted as a service of vessels: rhyton, ladle or one-handled cup, goblet or krater, jug and chalice (Fig. 18.18; see also Vermeule and Karageorghis 1982: cat. no. III.21). A small fragment from Lefkandi on Euboia shows a two-handled bowl or cup between two large legs, apparently with a human standing behind (Vermeule and Karageorghis 1982: cat. no. XI.66).

The meaning of these scenes on kraters is ambiguous. They are no doubt vestiges of standard compositions of Aegean fresco painting, lost to us except in the fragments recovered at sites dating variously from the 16th through the 13th centuries B.C. (Vermeule and Karageorghis 1982: 1; Morris 1989: 521–22). But, the full meaning of these scenes is largely disconnected from the complex cultural matrix that produced them. We must exercise extraordinary caution when interpreting them, because what appears to us as a thread of evidence may actually be multiple and unconnected strands of a richer tapestry than we can perceive. The late record of pictorial painting makes this clear. For example, a scene on a fragmentary krater from Tiryns suggests both the themes of ceremonial dining and respects paid to the deceased (Fig. 18.19). The krater depicts an enthroned person holding up a goblet, and before her or him chariots are departing. Kilian (1980) has argued that the person is a female deity and the chariots are participating in funeral games. He compares this scene to the rare but clearer representations found on terra cotta sarcophagi. One of the latter, of Late Minoan III B date from Episkopi, Ierapetras, Crete, depicts an individual raising a *kylix*/goblet (Kanta 1979: 150, fig. 63), while another example from Tanagra in Boeotia shows two people on one side of the sarcophagus, one individual with hands raised in a gesture of

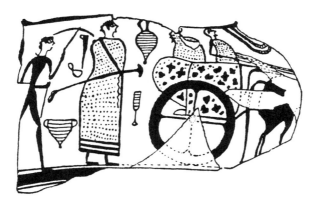

Figure 18.18. Krater fragment from Enkomi. (Furumark 1941: fig. 75.)

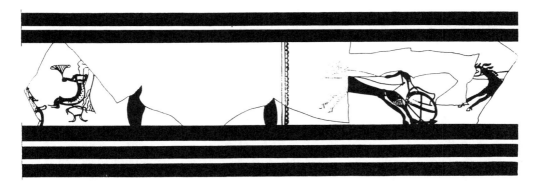

Figure 18.19. Reconstructed roll-out of scene on krater from Tiryns. (Kilian 1980: fig. 2.)

mourning, the other with a *kylix*/goblet raised in a probable gesture of respect. Are these scenes related? Does the scene on the Tanagra sarcophagus depict humans mourning the dead? Does the upheld goblet link it to the chariot race scene, where Kilian recognizes a divinity? Or are these part of separate iconographic traditions painted by perhaps untrustworthy artisans of the 13th century B.C., who are at best tertiary recipients of an ancient tradition?

Kilian (1980) also cites an important, much overlooked piece of evidence that almost certainly elevates the act of raising a cup to the religious sphere. A fragment of a Mycenaean pottery figure from Amyklai outside Sparta (Demakopoulou 1982: 54–56; Buchholz and Karageorghis 1971: cat. no. 1249) preserves a hand grasping the stem of a cup, presumably a *kylix*/goblet. Since these figures are normally associated with cult structures within the citadels (French 1985: 277–79), this example seems especially secure evidence of the religious importance of ceremonial drinking. But, the meaning is again ambiguous, since it is not clear how the iconography of deities relates to the actions of humans, and the omnipresent shadow of Minoan iconography and practice can easily lead to prejudgments of Mycenaean intent. Thus the well-known scene from the Tiryns Ring (Fig. 18.20), with its enthroned deity receiving a group of "genii" (Sakellariou 1964:

Figure 18.20. Tiryns Ring. (Marinatos and Hirmer 1973; pl. 229; reproduced by permission of Hirmer Verlag GmbH, München.)

201–03, cat. no. 179), is definitely related to the terra cotta figures. The "genii" appear, however, to be part of an altogether different tradition having to do with lustration rather than with drinking (Weingarten 1991; Baurain 1985, 1986; Stürmer 1985: 120–21; Gill 1964). The iconographic picture is fragmentary and suggests that multiple meanings and even different traditions are at work, especially during the latter part of the Mycenaean palace period (13th century B.C.). The threads of evidence are worn and frayed and only patches of cloth remain to verify meaning from one area to another. Certainly, one must differentiate the evidence that shows the role of ceremonial drinking among elite members of the society from these scenes. As Dietler (1990) has demonstrated, it is an important persistent tradition among many societies, and is one that itself has a rich variety of cultural meaning.

It is significant that Crete provides examples of the latest of these illustrations, because there the evidence of some continuity from the Late Bronze Age into the Iron Age is best preserved. Of special interest is the existence of shrines and residences at Karphi, Vrokastro and Kavousi-Vronda (Pendlebury and Money-Coutts 1937–38; Mazarakis Ainian 1988: 106) where arrangements of benches and hearths and discoveries of animal bones and drinking vessels suggest the continuation of rituals of feasting and drinking. Beyond this point, the evidence falls off and loses coherence, with Crete remaining distinct from the islands and the mainland. Many of the usual forms of vessels disappear in the ensuing sub-Mycenaean and Protogeometric periods, and the architectural evidence is notoriously slender (Mazarakis Ainian 1988). During the Geometric and early Archaic periods, when the stirrings of a nascent new Greek society begin, we can detect the revival of shapes and representation that again take up the theme of drinking. With the emergence of the *polis* between the late 8th and early 6th centuries B.C., feasting and wine drinking are fully adopted in the *symposion as a ritual of polite male society (Murray 1983, 1990)*.

7. Conclusions

In this chapter, the tradition of ritual drinking during the Minoan and Mycenaean periods in Greece has been argued to have been associated probably originally with ceremonies of initiation and to have been a sign of the genteel, courtly behavior of the aristocrat. Although incontrovertible linkage of this activity with wine consumption is not demonstrable, wine remains the best candidate as the alcoholic beverage of choice of these groups. Its production involves an investment in labor and time that only the wealthy could afford and, as Palmer (chapter 17, this volume) has shown, the Mycenaean texts document clearly how wine production was linked to the palatial system of agricultural production. The clearer record of wine production and the iconography and paraphernalia of drinking-ceremonies from the Mycenaean era excellently document the multiple roles played by intoxicants and the etiquette which goes with their consumption. The probable use of wine in Mycenaean society seems to foreshadow its widespread adoption in historic Greek society, and it seems most likely that the intervening "dark age" between these eras of early Greek societies was one marked by a continuity in usage.

Acknowledgments

I am grateful to the organizers of this conference for the invitation to participate, because the challenge to think about this problem has been exceptionally fruitful. I have been helped by numerous colleagues who have made suggestions for pursuing this research, offered comments on earlier drafts of this article, provided useful bibliography, and shared their own thinking on these matters. In alphabetical order, they are Mary K. Dabney, Keith Dickey, Giampaolo Graziadio, Richard Hamilton, Robert Koehl, Nanno Marinatos, Thomas G. Palaima, Ruth Palmer, and Jeremy B. Rutter. Naturally, they are in no way responsible for my "intoxicated" views. I dedicate this study to the memory of Edmund Bucynski. This manuscript was submitted for publication in July 1992, and the author had no subsequent opportunity to update it.

Notes

1. Palmer (1989: 82–126; also see her chapter 17, this volume) discusses the different contexts of wine in the tablets. She classifies the use of wine into four categories: internal supplies, and possible commercial transactions, in religious activities, among general lists of commodities. I thank Tom Palaima for refocusing my attention to this part of her work.

2. Minoan periods are designated by pottery phases as Middle Minoan I, II, III and Late Minoan I, II, III. Mycenaean periods are similarly defined, i.e. Middle Helladic, Late Helladic I, II, III. "Middle" and "Late" refer in general to Middle and Late Bronze Age. Middle Minoan I and II comprise the period of the first palaces (roughly 2000–1700/1650 B.C.) and Middle Minoan III through Late Minoan Ib span the period of the second palaces (roughly 1700/1650–1480/1425 B.C.). Late Helladic I and IIA are coterminous with Late Minoan I, as is Late Helladic IIB with Late Minoan II. In conventional chronology Late Helladic II dates roughly from ca. 1500 to 1440/1390 B.C., Late Helladic IIIA from ca. 1390 to 1330, and Late Helladic IIIB from ca. 1330 to 1185 B.C. (Warren and Hankey 1989: 169).

3. Fig. 18.1a is an ewer with pendant grapes on the vessel body, and Fig. 18.1b is a jug with pendant grapes beneath the handle. The Minoans could paint accurate depictions of flora when they wished to (Rackham 1978: 756; Möbius 1933: 1–39, esp. p. 30 and fig. 20). Compare Cameron 1968: 1–31, esp. fig. 5b, identified as the common mallow (*Malva sylvetris* L.). See also Morgan 1988: 17–32. Rackham (1978) and Cerceau (1985: 181–184) point out that, in details, the Theran artists made mistakes that confuse precise botanical identification.

4. The shape is unknown during the Protopalatial period (Middle Minoan I–II) and earlier, when the only shapes comparable are the cylindrical handleless cups, the egg-cup or conical based handleless cup, and the conical stemmed handleless cup (Walberg 1976: 17–18). The only pottery version from a domestic context and contemporaneous with the stone ones is from Akrotiri on Thera (Marinatos 1972: 31, pl. 61b). Another example was found by Fouquè in 1867 (Renaudin 1922: 123, 146, cat. no. 1). Later pottery versions are largely confined to the Eastern Mediterranean (Karageorghis 1957), though one is known from *tholos* tomb III at Pylos (Blegen et al. 1973: 93–94). It is also represented in pottery painting (see Figs. 18.8 and 18.18).

5. We should probably be careful not to adhere too closely to our own typological distinctions. The cups and chalices at Syme compare to a range of stone cups illustrated in Warren 1969.

6. Vessels from the Temple Repositories (Evans 1921: 495–523, fig. 377; for a faience jug like the silver one at Mycenae see fig. 346, p. 495). From Mycenae, Grave Circle B: cat. nos. A 240, A 325 in Mylonas 1973: 27, 31; pl. 16. From Circle A, there is also a similar gold jug from Grave III: Karo 1930–33: pl. 103, cat. no. 74.

7. O. Dickinson (1977: 55, 108) rightly posited a "special relationship" between Mycenae and Knossos but based it on control by Mycenae of trade with the Balkans and Europe, a view challenged A. Harding (1984: 280).

8. The subject has generated an enormous literature. One summary and critical discussion with bibliography, is that of J. Hooker 1976: 45–54; see also Vermeule 1964: 109–10. I hope to expand upon this subject in a future paper.

9. Hägg 1990: 177–78; Burkert 1985: 35–36; Benveniste 1973, but see his analysis of libation, pp. 470–80, where the Greek *spendo* is linked in its two meanings: "to make a liquid offering" and "to conclude a pact," the former of which consecrated the latter. With *leibo*, we have a word that was used by Homer to designate the pouring of wine and which Benveniste argues was used specifically to designate an action that appeased the gods and warded off their wrath. Lastly, the word *kheo* also means "to pour," and gives its name to a special vessel that the Greeks used for wine, the *choe*. This word was used in the religious sense to pour offerings to the dead, and is derived from the Indo-European verb **g'heu*, which Benveniste states, "is one of the best established items in the Indo-European vocabulary," with offshoot verbs in several other Indo-European languages that carry this meaning of making an offering.

10. The origin of the Mycenaean goblet is an excellent example of the complexity of interaction that occurs during the Late Helladic I phase. The specific origin of the goblet (FS 254) is the deep semi-globular cup (FS 211: Mountjoy 1986: 34), but, as Blegen (1921: 41, 48, 54–57) observed, the goblet owes much to Middle Bronze Age "Minyan Ware." The nature of Late Helladic I pottery has been clarified by recent studies that emphasize its relation to the the Minyan tradition (Dickinson 1974: 111–14; Rutter and Rutter 1976: 13–14; Davis 1979).

11. Jeremy Rutter urged me to document sets of pottery used in Mycenaean contexts, and I have not found clear evidence supporting their presence, especially in the best contexts, namely burials. Both P. Pelagatti (1961–62) and A. MacGillivray (1987) have discussed the evidence for sets of pottery vessel types made in Protopalatial Cretan workshops. I mention below a late illustration of a possible set of Mycenaean pottery: a rhyton, goblet/krater, jug, chalice, which can perhaps be best compared to the assemblage on a seal from Naxos (Kardara 1977: 6. pl. 6; Pini 1975: cat. no. 608). The question that needs to be pursued is whether this assemblage is specific to ritual activity or also includes ceremonial feasting and drinking.

12. Silver goblets from Kokla (Demakopoulou 1990); tinned vessels from Tomb III in the Athenian Agora (Immerwahr 1971: 127–28 and pp. 171–76).

13. In addition to these vessels are numerous others, among which is the Vapheio cup (218[vas]), also in gold (Vandenabeele and Olivier 1979: 200–5).

14. These are stucco hollows in the floor and not made from stone as stated by Burkert 1985: 36.

15. McCallum's argument is in part based on the idea that the paintings in the palaces were highly formalized scenes—a point well made by Hägg (1985: 209–17), Cameron (1987: 320–28) and Morgan (1985: 15–19).

CHAPTER 19

The Beginnings of
Grape Cultivation and
Wine Production in
Phoenician/Punic
North Africa

Joseph A. Greene

---

1. A Phoenician Introduction of the Grape?

There is no ecological reason why the vine could not have been established very early in North Africa, long before the arrival of the Phoenicians. The Maghreb lies well within the primitive range of wild grape (see chapter 2 by Zohary, this volume) and the climate along the Mediterranean seaboards of modern Morocco, Algeria and especially Tunisia is quite hospitable to cultivated vines (Map 19.1). North Africa in many ways resembled the Phoenicians' homeland in coastal Lebanon, where the typical Mediterranean triad of cereals, olive and grape had already been established for millennia. North Africa, in short, was environmentally pre-adapted to viticulture, needing only human agents to introduce cultivated vine into a pristine landscape.

This environmental pre-adaptation was a fortunate circumstance for the founders of Carthage, for they brought with them from their homeland not only their religion, their language and their legendary commercial acumen, but also their well-cultivated taste for wine. Southern coastal Syria, Lebanon and Palestine had been a grape-growing and wine-exporting region since the late 4th millennium B.C. In the Early Bronze Age, Byblos was a center for the export of wine and other luxury products to the elites of Old Kingdom Egypt (see chapter 13 by James, this volume). In the Middle and Late Bronze Ages, many commodities, including wine, were shipped from Canaan to all parts of the eastern Mediterranean and Aegean in so-called "Canaanite Jars" (see chapter 15 by Leonard, this volume). In the early Iron Age, wine, fine textiles and carved ivory headed a list of precious goods distributed from the cities of coastal Phoenicia to points throughout the Near East

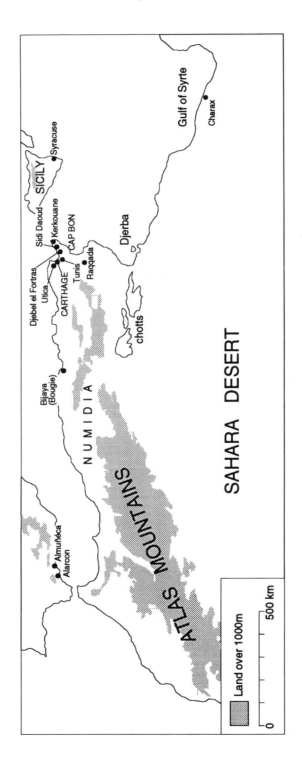

Map 19.1. Finds of wild grape along the Mediterranean seaboard.

and Mediterranean world (Harden 1971: ch. 12; Gras et al. 1989: ch. 4). Such precedents suggest that it was indeed the Phoenicians who introduced domesticated grape to North Africa.

The evidence that the Phoenicians were responsible for introduction of domesticated vine to North Africa is, however, largely negative. North African Neolithic sites of the 2nd millennium B.C. and earlier have so far yielded only traces of wild *Vitis* (Santa 1958–59). Stephen Gsell's assessment of the literary evidence and such archaeobotanical data available early in this century led him to suppose that classical authors who mentioned indigenous North Africa vines must have been referring to *Vitis silvestris* and that the Phoenicians introduced *Vitis vinifera* to the region (Gsell 1913: 166, n. 4). Since Gsell wrote, specific archaeological, archaeobotanical and analytical evidence for grape cultivation and wine consumption before the period of Phoenician contact have still not been found. This lack of evidence of course may be more apparent than real and future discoveries may push back the date of the introduction of vine to North Africa.

For the present, the absence of contrary evidence supports the assumption that North Africa was a land without cultivated vines when the Phoenicians founded Carthage. The accumulated archaeological evidence suggests a date for that foundation sometime in the mid-to-late 8th century B.C. (Niemeyer 1989: 23; see also Harden 1927, 1937; Cintas 1970; Stager 1982). The literary sources support a somewhat earlier date (814 B.C.) than does the archaeological evidence, though the texts could reflect memories of a prior "contact period" that left only ephemeral material traces (Bunnens 1979: 368–74; see Niemeyer 1989). A far earlier and also legendary date of 1110 (or 1101) B.C. given for Utica, a site just to the north of Carthage along the coast, has so far not been corroborated by stratified remains (Cintas 1951, 1954; Bunnens 1979: 367–68). If the Phoenicians did in fact introduce *Vitis vinifera* into North Africa, then they did so probably no earlier than the 8th century B.C.

2. The Present State of Evidence for the Phoenician/Punic Period

While archaeology has firmly fixed the date of earliest settlement at Carthage in the 8th century B.C., the earliest excavated evidence for *Vitis vinifera* there goes back only to the 4th century B.C. Waterlogged sediments in the Late Punic commercial port (ca. 350–146 B.C.) yielded seeds and pollen grains of domesticated grape (van Zeist and Bottema 1982). Charred grape seeds were also preserved in the burned debris of palatial homes on the Byrsa, the citadel of Carthage destroyed by the Romans in 146 B.C. (Van Der Veen and van Zeist 1982; see also Stager 1977; Hurst and Stager 1978). These data attest only to the presence of domesticated grapes, most likely consumed as raisins or as fresh fruit. They do not necessarily prove that grapes were made into wine and drunk by the Carthaginians.

Literary testimonia, likewise dated from the mid-4th to the mid-2nd centuries B.C., provide direct evidence for vine cultivation and wine consumption in Late Punic North Africa. In Plato's final dialogue, the *Laws* (composed ca. 350 B.C.), his protagonist, Clinias the Athenian, cites with evident approval a contemporary Carthaginian prohibition against consumption of wine by certain classes of society at certain times: soldiers on active duty, incumbent city magistrates and judges, ships' pilots, married couples intent upon procreation, all citizens during daytime hours, and all slaves, male or female, at anytime (*Laws* 674 A—Bury 1926). It is unclear whether the law existed in precisely the form Plato stated or whether he somehow garbled its actual text (see Picard and Picard 1958: 150–51). In any case, this supposed public regulation of sobriety does not answer questions about local production of wine at Carthage, since Carthaginians intent upon breaking the law (if it did exist) might have as easily gotten drunk on imported wine as on domestic vintage. Other texts, however, do mention specifically the cultivation of vines in the vicinity of the city.

In 310 B.C. the Sicilian Greek army led by Agathocles the tyrant of Syracuse landed on Cap Bon opposite Carthage and advanced through a flourishing agricultural hinterland.

> Agathocles led the army against a place called Megalopolis. The intervening countryside through which it was necessary for them to march was divided into gardens and plantations of every kind, through which many streams of water were led by channels, irrigating every part. There were also country houses one after another, constructed in luxurious fashion and covered with stucco, which gave evidence of the wealth of the people who possessed them.... Part of the land was planted in vines and part yielded olives and was also thickly planted with other varieties of fruit-bearing trees.... On each side herds of cattle and flocks of sheep pastured on the plain, and the neighboring meadows were filled with horses.
>   Diodorus Siculus 20.8.3-4—Oldfather 1933–67

At the time of Agathocles' invasion, the peninsula apparently served as a market garden for urban Carthage, providing the city with meat, oil and, very likely, wine. Punic settlement is confirmed archaeologically on Cap Bon from at least the 6th century B.C. and the peninsula may have formed an early agricultural hinterland for Carthage. Punic settlements have been excavated on Cap Bon at Kerkouane (Morel 1969; Fantar 1984, 1985, 1986) and recorded in surface remains at Ain Takerdouch, Ainet Tarfa, Djebel el Fortras and several other sites on the peninsula (Aquarao et al. 1973; Barreca and Fantar 1983). None of the archaeological data so far collected from these sites give evidence for viticulture in the Punic period. The writings of Mago the Carthaginian agronomist, however, do discuss Punic viticulture and in a manner that permits the integration of textual, archaeological and ecological data on the topic.

3. Mago the Carthaginian on Viticulture

Mago composed in twenty-eight books a wide-ranging treatise on agriculture in his native North Africa. Its precise title is not recorded and its full contents are not known, since no copy of the original Punic text has survived. Ironically, after the destruction of Carthage in 146 B.C. and the dispersal of the city's library to Rome's Numidian allies, the Roman senate decreed that Mago's treatise be translated from Punic into Latin (Pliny, *Natural History* 18.22—Rackham et al. 1949–62; Gsell 1920: 403). While that translation does not survive either, portions of Mago's text are preserved as excerpts quoted in the writings of later Roman authors on agriculture, including Varro (1st century B.C.) and Columella and Pliny (1st century A.D.).

Scattered through these later works are thirty-one fragments of Mago's original text (Mahaffy 1890: 30). These vary greatly in length and completeness, making it often difficult to disentangle Mago's actual words from later interpretations and accretions. The most readily identifiable passages treat a range of topics: stock-raising, tree-cultivation, beekeeping, and even the philosophy of rural land ownership. Significant for the present discussion are Mago's remarks on viticulture.

On this topic, Mago offered detailed instructions for the planting and pruning of vines. He recommends that vines be located on north-facing slopes. This, he claims, will make them more productive though perhaps the quality of their grapes may suffer as a consequence. In quoting this passage, Columella agrees with Mago that vines cultivated in "the hot provinces" (namely, Numidia [modern Algeria and Tunisia] and Egypt) "will be exposed more properly to the north alone" (3.12.5-6). As to the trenching vines for planting, Mago observes that the holes in which vine stocks are placed be left only partially filled and gradually levelled up over two year's time following the initial planting. Columella, citing this procedure, concedes that it may be good advice for drier Africa, but advises against it for wetter Italy, cautioning that the accumulation of rain water in the half-filled planting holes can "kill the plant before they have time to gain strength" (5.5.4-6). In both instances, Mago's instructions clearly reflect the conditions imposed on viticulture by the North African environment.

Those parts of North Africa most favorable to grape cultivation lie within the Mediterranean climatic zone. This stretches along the northern coastline of Africa from Morocco to Tunisia following the arc of the Atlas Mountains. These mountains are the region's principal relief feature and strongly influence the distribution of rainfall there (Birot and Dresch 1953: 391–419; Despois and Raynal 1967: 9–18). Oriented southwest to northeast, the mountains lie directly across the paths of rains swept inland from the Mediterranean by winter storms. As a consequence, the north-facing slopes capture much of the available moisture, leaving the southern slopes in a rain shadow (Great Britain, Admiralty 1945: 81–82; Despois and Raynal 1967: 243). The effects of this rain shadow is enhanced by increased solar heating on south-facing slopes and their direct exposure to the desiccating winds blowing north from the Sahara. As a result, these southern slopes tend to lose readily what little moisture they do receive (Bortoli et al. 1969: 17–19). Mago understood this and advised accordingly those of his readers who wished to grow grapes.

Columella also copies in full Mago's recipe for raisin wine (*passum*), prefacing it with his personal testimony as to the wine's excellence.

> Mago gives the following instructions for making the best raisin-wine, as I myself have also made it. Gather the early grapes when they are quite ripe, rejecting the berries which are mouldy or damaged. Fix in the ground forks or stakes four feet apart for supporting reeds and yoke them together with poles, then put the reeds on top of them and spread out the grapes in the sun, covering them at night so that dew may not fall on them. Then when they have dried, pluck the berries and throw them into a barrel or wine-jar and add the best possible must thereto so that the grapes are submerged. When they have absorbed the must and are saturated with it, on the sixth day put them in the wine-press and remove the raisin-wine. Next tread the wine-skins, adding very fresh must, made from other grapes which you have dried for three days in the sun; then mix together and put the whole kneaded mass under the press and immediately put this raisin-wine of the second pressing in sealed vessels so that it may not become too rough; then twenty or thirty days later, when it has finished fermenting, strain it into other vessels and plaster down the lids immediately and cover them with skins.
>   Columella 12.39.1-2—Hooper 1934

Mago's work cannot be dated precisely, so meager is the textual evidence; but he probably wrote during the period of expanding rural settlement around Carthage in the 3rd and early 2nd centuries B.C (Greene and Kehoe 1991). From the founding of Carthage until ca. 400 B.C. there were relatively few rural sites on the mainland west of the city. Only in the final two centuries of Carthage's existence, during the era of the Punic Wars, did numerous settlements spring up on the mainland west of Carthage (Greene forthcoming: ch. 4). Some of these were perhaps the country estates of wealthy Carthaginian city dwellers whom Mago admonished in his introduction. Results of archaeological survey in vicinity of the city do not bear out the literary accounts which claim that the Carthaginians sought to possess the North African hinterland from the 5th century B.C. (e.g., Warmington 1969: ch. 3; cf. Gsell 1913: 464–65). On the contrary, the weight of the literary evidence accords much better with a 3rd/2nd century dating for Carthage's "imperial" advance into Africa (Whittaker 1978a). Results of excavations on Cap Bon demonstrate Punic settlement on the peninsula began there earlier, in the 6th century B.C., and there, perhaps, is to be sought the archaeological background for an early dating of Carthage's African hinterland offered by some of the ancient literary sources. Despite the relative lateness of Phoenician/Punic settlement in the African hinterland, the archaeobotanical evidence from Carthage, together with the literary sources, offer strong circumstantial evidence for viticulture and wine production in North Africa prior to the 4th century B.C.

4. Viticulture and Social Complexity in North Africa

The introduction of vine in North Africa by the Phoenicians, whenever exactly it occurred, involved more than merely the introduction of a new cultigen. It was part of a process of cultural change that altered irrevocably the social, political and economic landscape of the Maghreb. Before the Phoenicians, there were no complex societies in the Maghreb, only relatively simple agrarian and pastoral communities effectively isolated from the Mediterranean world. There is no evidence that the region underwent a "horticultural revolution" similar to that in the Near East more than two millennia before (Zohary and Spiegel-Roy 1975). Prior to the period of Phoenician contact, North Africa was only just emerging from the Neolithic. At 1000 B.C., agriculture in North Africa was not far advanced; its native peoples were still subsistence cultivators and herders (Roubet 1979; Camps 1982). While knowledge of the domesticated grape and of the relatively simple techniques of fermentation are sufficient to permit winemaking to satisfy subsistence wants, successful production above levels of household consumption carries heavier prerequisites: a fund of accumulated capital, an existing external demand, and a network of exchange to service that demand.

Would-be commercial vintners must accumulate significant capital before the first vine is even planted. Capital is required to pay for the fixed assets that form the bases of production: land for vineyards, vine stocks for planting, production tools like treading basins and fermentation vats, a ready supply of empty vessels to be filled with new wine, and storerooms to hold the vintage once produced. Return on investment is not immediate. At the outset, vines must be tended for some years before they bear a harvestable crop; and grapes, once harvested, crushed and fermented, must be aged months or years into wine. Therefore it takes time and money to make viticulture pay, two things which subsistence farmers who must depend upon a regular annual harvest to make their livelihood rarely have in abundance. Added to this are the attendant risks of poor yields or unfavorable markets which can quickly deplete assets so painstakingly built up. Subsistence cultivators find these risks, along with the heavy initial capital outlays required, strong disincentives to experiment with large scale viticulture.

Successful large scale viticulture also requires external demand for the product, wine, and a network for its distribution, a means getting it from producers to consumers. While subsistence producers can tap into preexisting networks by increasing or diversifying production in order to satisfy external demand, they cannot, of themselves, create such demand or sustain such networks. Like wealth and time, this prerequisite is beyond the means of subsistence producers.

In all these regards the Phoenicians were better equipped than the native peoples of North Africa, for the newcomers brought with them not only the domesticated vine and the technical expertise to make wine, but also the economic prerequisites of investment capital and established connections with long-distance exchange networks. As specialists in maritime exchange, they had extensive previous trading experience, and wine was only one of many commodities that they traded. Moreover, the fact that the Phoenicians could undertake settlement abroad from their homeland demonstrates the availability of investment capital (Greene 1990).

The technical problem of the transplantation of domesticated vines from the Near East to North Africa was apparently easily solved. Vine-cuttings may be carried long distances over periods lasting some months if the cuttings are kept moist and cool during shipment, just as the first vines were brought from the Old World to the New in the late 15th and 16th centuries A.D. (Hobhouse 1991). At the longest, the voyage from Tyre to Carthage might have taken four weeks, and much less under favorable conditions (Casson 1971: ch. 12). If, as seems likely, the first vines were brought to Egypt by sea from the Levant perhaps as early as the Old Kingdom (see chapter 13 by James, this volume) and certainly by the New Kingdom (Lesko, chapter 14, this volume), then the

Phoenicians, or rather their 3rd millennium ancestors, already had experience with long-distance horticultural transplantation by sea.

Admittedly, this is speculative, since the early period of Phoenician contact period in North Africa is still poorly documented archaeologically. There are as yet only meager material traces of the indigenous cultures the Phoenicians encountered in North Africa early in the 1st millennium B.C. (Camps 1960, 1961, 1964; Cintas 1961; Camps-Faber 1966; Niemeyer 1989, 1991; Greene forthcoming: ch. 1). There is even less evidence for native social organization (Gsell 1913: 240–69; Whittaker 1978b). The legendary sources for the foundation of Carthage speak of a native "king" (*basileius* in the Greek texts, though this term may be either misleading or irrelevant), who controlled territory around Carthage and effectively limited, the ability of the newcomers to possess land (Bunnens 1979: 174–86, 368–74). We are so far unable to specify in archaeological terms the details of early interaction between Phoenicians and native North Africans (but see Niemeyer 1991). We cannot, for instance, yet know if the Phoenicians found the North African natives to be as thirsty for wine as the Greeks found the Gauls of southern France (Deitler 1990).

Broadly speaking, though, it is assured that the arrival of the Phoenicians in North Africa drew the region and its native peoples gradually but inexorably into the ancient Mediterranean system of complex urban societies and maritime economies. If the advent of horticulture generally (and viticulture particularly) is an outgrowth of the emergence of complex societies, as it is in the Near East of the late 4th and early 3rd millennium B.C. (Stager 1985; see, however, Runnels and Hansen 1986, for contrary evidence from the 3rd millennium B.C. Aegean), then this may explain in part the belated beginnings of vine cultivation and wine production in North Africa. The difference in this case is that social complexity in North Africa, like the cultivated vine, was an exogenous introduction, not an indigenous development.

5. Prospects for Future Research

Though the existing data for grape cultivation and wine production in North Africa are tantalizing, speculation without further evidence is far from satisfactory. Aside from the obvious need to collect more archaeobotanical samples from sites dating earlier than the 4th century B.C. (both those of the Phoenician contact period and of the late North African Late Neolithic), there are several other kinds of data whose collection would greatly enhance our understanding of viticulture and winemaking in Phoenician and Punic North Africa.

The most glaring lacuna is the complete lack of any analytical proof that Phoenician or Punic pottery ever contained wine. Certain types of ceramic vessels characteristic of Phoenician sites in the west Mediterranean may have been associated with wine-drinking. Proto-Corinthian kotylai, an important index fossil for 8th- and 7th-century B.C. west Phoenician sites, were used as drinking cups, perhaps for wine (Fig. 19.1a–b). Phoenician red-slipped juglets with single handles and pinched spouts look like nothing so much as wine carafes (Figs. 19.2 and 19.3). Traces of wine in such vessels, if they could be found, could indicate that early Phoenician seafarers and settlers brought with them from home their own wine and wine-drinking paraphernalia. More conclusive of North African viticulture would be traces of wine found in Phoenician and Punic vessels, especially storage or transport amphorae, actually manufactured in the west. The Carthaginians are reported to have exchanged wine (presumably domestic vintages decanted in locally made amphorae) for *silphium*, a medicinal herb, at Charax on the Gulf of Syrte (Strabo, *Geography* 17.3.20—Jones 1917–35). While Carthaginian amphorae have been much studied and are reasonably well understood as to their typology, chronology and geographic distribution (e.g., Cintas 1950; Wolff 1986; see also references cited by Gras et al. 1989: 94, n. 22), so far no examples ever

Figure 19.1a. Black-painted Early Proto-Corintyian *kotyle* from Tomb 19 at Almuñécar, ca. 720–690 B.C. (After Pellicer Catalán 1962: fig. 35.1.)

Figure 19.1b. Black-painted Middle Proto-Corinthian kotyle from Tomb A.195 (ca. 690–650 B.C.) on the Byrsa (citadel) at Carthage. (After Lancel 1982: fig. 450.)

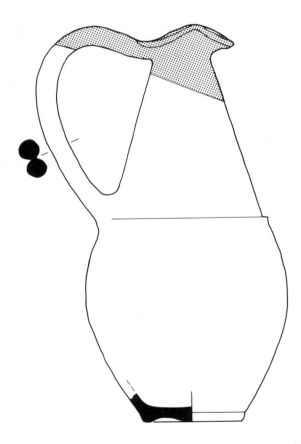

Figure 19.2. Juglet with red-slipped trefoil mouth from Tomb A.183 (ca. 675–650 B.C.) on the Byrsa at Carthage. (After Lancel 1982: fig. 490.)

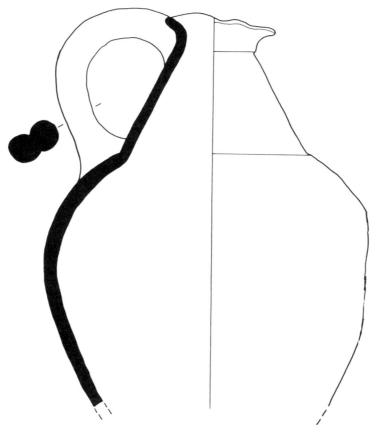

Figure 19.3. Juglet in coarse ware with trefoil mouth from Alarcón, Spain. (After Maass-Lindemann 1988: fig. 2b.)

have been analyzed for evidence that they may have once held wine. Such analytical data are not unobtainable, but so far remain uncollected.

The body of evidence for olive cultivation and oil production in Roman North Africa suggests other lines of enquiry. Numerous rural sites discovered by archaeological survey in southern Tunisia and western Libya preserve substantial surface remains of oil presses dating from the 1st to the 6th centuries A.D. (Mattingly 1988; Hitchner and Mattingly 1991). African amphorae occur in Italy from the Imperial period onward (Carandini 1983). In one significant instance, sherds of transport amphorae originating in Africa excavated in a 5th century A.D. context at Rome (Whitehouse 1981) were found to contain the residues of fatty acids (lipids), demonstrating conclusively that these jars carried African olive oil to Italy (Rothschild-Boros 1981). Explicit textual references mention large surpluses of African oil available for export from southern Tunisia as early as the 1st century B.C. (Caesar, *African War* 97.3—Way 1955), suggesting that such surpluses were already being produced in the Punic period. Similar sorts of data, archaeological, analytical and textual, as have been assembled here in preliminary fashion, could be collected for the production and exchange of North African wine in the Phoenician and Punic periods.

Ruined oil presses visible today at archaeological sites in southern Tunisia testify to ancient oil production in the region. Likewise, grape cultivation and wine production ought also to have left archaeological traces in the grape-growing regions of North Africa. The Phoenicians, if they did in fact introduce the grape into North Africa, will have brought with them the technology for turning grapes into wine. Some aspects of that technology should have left archaeologically detectable remains. Rock cuttings found throughout the limestone hill county on both side of the Jordan Rift Valley are usually called "winepresses," though technically it may be more correct to term them "treading basins" (Fig. 19.4). Their association with wine production has always been assumed, and though the available evidence is not necessarily conclusive, it is strongly presumptive (see, e.g., Åhlstrom 1978). The limestone hill country of northern Tunisia and eastern Algeria, the prime grape-growing region of North Africa, appears to lack such installations. Their absence, however, may only be apparent. Very little archaeological survey has been conducted in the viticultural heartland of Punic North Africa and the presses (or treading basins) that may exist there have not yet been discovered. In addition and perhaps more importantly, a thorough program of archaeological survey will recover evidence for rural settlement connected with early grape cultivation and wine production in North Africa. As with the examination of ceramic vessels for traces of ancient contents and the detection of archaeobotanical remains of *Vitis* in early occupational levels, such evidence will not be found unless and until we search for it.

6. Of the Vine, There Is No End

Once begun, the practice of fermenting grapes and drinking wine never really disappeared from North Africa. Evidence for later practices is mostly historical and ethnographic, but nonetheless they demonstrate strong connections with antiquity. The Arab invasions of the late 7th century A.D. and the accompanying Islamic prohibition against alcoholic drink did not bring an immediate halt to viticulture in the Maghreb, though the attendant civil insecurity, depopulation and economic dislocation must have affected production and distribution (See Greene forthcoming: ch. 6). Grape seeds are absent in the single post-Byzantine deposit from which archaeobotanical material was collected on the Byrsa at Carthage, but this is a very small and perhaps unrepresentative sample and can be dated only broadly to the "medieval period" (Van Der Veen and van Zeist 1982). The perdurance of Jewish and Christian communities in the Maghreb in the centuries after A.D. 700 makes likely the continuation of wine production and wine-drinking in the Islamic North Africa (Julien 1975: 277–79). References by Arab historians attest to the persistence of grape growing and wine production well into the medieval period (Despois 1961: 229; Lequément 1980: 192–93). In 9th-century Raqqada (Tunisia), Ibrahim the Aghlabid sanctioned the sale of *nebid*, a fermented concoction of dates, honey and raisins, which from its ingredients seems to have been a medieval version of Mago's *passum* (al-Bikrī cited by Lequément 1980: 192). In 1118, the Muslim divine, Ibn Tumart, founder of the reforming Almohad movement, fulminated against his co-religionists whom he found still trafficking in wine at Bougie in Algeria (Le Tourneau 1969: 50–51). Grapevines are depicted Jan Vermayen's tapestry "The Battle in the Ruins of Carthage," one of twelve woven panels recording Charles V's expedition to Tunis in 1535 (Bauer 1976: fig. 11 and pl. 2). While the rendering of the vines is probably accurate (Vermayen accompanied Charles V on the campaign as official artist), it is impossible to determine whether these are wine or table grapes. Down to modern times the Jewish inhabitants of Djerba, an island just off the southeastern coast of Tunisia, continued to grow grapes, dividing their vineyards equally between table varieties and wine grapes (Brulard 1885).

Elsewhere in Tunisia by the 19th century, grape production had declined dramatically. The French who ousted the Ottomans from Tunisia and established the Regency of Tunis in 1881

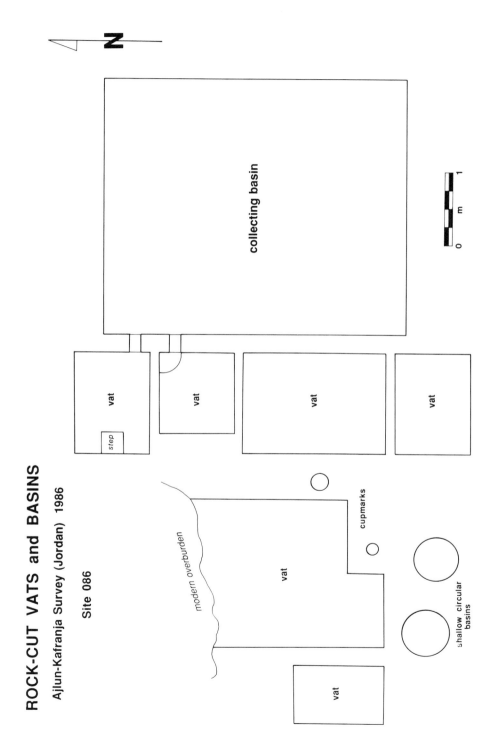

Figure 19.4. "Treading basin" complex from Site 086 in the Ajlun-Kafranja Valley, Jordan. The outlines of the cuttings were visible at the surface, but the vats were filled with modern overburden so that their respective depths could not be determined. (Greene 1986.)

discovered only about 1000 hectare of vineyards in the vicinity of Tunis and Cap Bon. Most of these vines were table varieties, not wine grapes. In the late 19th and early 20th century, French agricultural colonists reintroduced viticulture to Tunisia, along with European wine grapes, modern techniques of vine cultivation and western habits of wine consumption. The settlers established vineyards on the light, well-watered soils of the footslopes in the maritime plains. Farther inland, they found conditions were too damp or too cold, while to the south, the landscape was too hot and dry and too exposed to scirocco winds from the Sahara (Nuttonson 1961: 587). The colonial viticulturalists might have taken advice from Mago the Carthaginian, who had written about precisely these problems some twenty-two centuries before.

CHAPTER 20

Wine Amphoras in Ancient Greek Trade

Carolyn G. Koehler

1. Introduction

Transport amphoras were as much a part of the Mediterranean landscape in antiquity as they are for today's archaeologists, unobtrusive but omnipresent.[1] Their enormous numbers offer solid evidence of the traffic in wine, probably their commonest cargo, which formed a large component of international trade in the Greco-Roman period. In addition, they bear indirect witness to the importance of wine for the consumer as well as for those engaged in its production, shipping, and retail sale. The study of transport amphoras is reaching a point at which a considerable amount of data can be analyzed to answer questions about trade and production and to shape some new inquiries about wine in the ancient world. This chapter focuses on wine amphoras made in Greek-speaking regions of the classical world (although the evidence bearing upon the jars ranges more broadly than that in both space and time), and attempts to suggest the scope of current investigations.[2]

Since Mycenaean times in Greece, amphora has been the generic term, occurring on Linear B tablets with an identifying ideogram, for a vessel with narrow neck and two handles.[3] Amphoras produced for transport and storage share this name with their more elegant cousins, painted table amphoras which have a flat base. Large jars with pointed bottoms, usually undecorated and made of coarser clay, were well suited for carrying liquids and such dry goods as could be poured in and out of them, but they are best known as containers for wine.[4] Their excellent design proved its practicality over three millennia, from the Middle Bronze Age almost to the modern era. While the rounded shape distributed the weight of the contents evenly all around the walls of the jar, the pointed toe actually served as a third handle to help in emptying the vessel. A broad base would have made the jar unwieldy and added significantly to its weight.

Although wine was sometimes exported in small amphoras holding about ten liters or even less, larger jars are commoner. The Hellenistic amphoras of the island of Rhodes generally held about 26 l (the size also of the Roman capacity unit amphora). A jar weighing 10 kg or so empty that contained about 25 l of wine would be a good load for one person; some very large specimens that

Figure 20.1. Amphoras from the debris of the destruction of Athens by the Romans in 86 B.C. From left: Rhodian (SS 8602), Knidian (SS 7918, Chian (P 19120) and Roman (SS 7319). Scale 1:10. (Grace 1979: fig. 36; photograph courtesy of the American School of Classical Studies at Athens.)

would weigh 60 to 70 kg filled will have needed two people to carry them.[5] When transport amphoras had to be stored upright, they were stabilized in an earthen floor or sandy bank or set into stands of pottery, wood, or wicker (Koehler 1986: 61–62, figs. 13–18).

2. Identification and Dating

The pointed shape seems first to have occurred to some early–2nd millennium B.C. Canaanite specialist in container design (Grace 1956: 82–83). Semitic peoples in the Delta region first copied the Canaanite shape in clay from the Nile (personal communication, P.E. McGovern); Egyptian potters eventually modified it to the distinctive local form pictured in New Kingdom wall paintings (see chapters 14 by Lesko and 15 by Leonard, this volume).[6] As trade became a vital part of the Greek enterprise early in the Archaic period (8th and 7th centuries B.C.), the Greeks developed their own version of the transport amphora, which generally had taller neck and handles than eastern models, and a pronounced toe (Figs. 20.1 and 20.2). They may have gotten their inspiration from jars brought from the Levant by the Phoenicians, or perhaps from their own traders who journeyed to Egypt and such entrepôts as Al Mina. At least one Greek series, however, grew out of an indigenous class of vessels. Corinthian Type A amphoras evolved in the late 8th century B.C. from the large, globular storage jars common at Corinth from the Middle Geometric period (first half of the 8th century B.C.) onwards, and retained for centuries some of their techniques of manufacture and characteristics of style (Koehler 1981: 451; Vandiver and Koehler 1986: 179–92).

Figure 20.2. Left, Lesbian amphoras of the early and late 5th century B.C. (P 24875, P 11018); right, Thasian of the 4th and 3rd centuries B.C. (P 675, SS 8932). The left jar of each pair was designed for a smaller capacity, the Lesbian example reducing the standard body shape equally in all dimensions, the Thasian drawing in the lower body. Scale 1:10. (Grace 1979; fig. 52; photograph courtesy of the American School of Classical Studies at Athens.)

Different city-states in the Greek world produced their own distinctive shapes, so that presumably a jar from a particular city would have been recognizable in the marketplace. A number of these amphora classes can be identified and dated today by archaeologists, in large measure thanks to the pioneering work of Virginia R. Grace. Based at the Agora Excavations of the American School of Classical Studies at Athens, she has in the course of half a century amassed archives on Greek amphoras found throughout the Mediterranean and in museums around the world. These archives are the largest existing collection of information on Greek amphoras and provide indispensable source material for an analysis of the jars and their significance.

Stylistic details (e.g., shape of rim and toe, arch of handles) and fabric link amphoras in a class, which can then be related to a place of origin by various kinds of evidence. Occasionally, the stamps impressed on the handle while the clay was still slightly soft attest the manufacturing site: Thasian and Knidian jars are often so labelled, Koan and Parian sometimes so. For other classes, the clay and/or temper of the jars has been analyzed and matched with local mineral deposits, as in the case of Corinthian Type A jars (Whitbread 1986: 339–43, 389–91), or with the fabric of wares of known provenance (compare Jones 1986: 706–23). Coin devices have proven useful in identifying amphora series such as that from Chios, whose coinage portrays the distinctive profile of its jars (Grace 1979: fig. 51). Stamps on Rhodian vessels often include the head of the sun god Halios with radiate crown or the characteristic Rhodian rose, both of which were also frequently struck on coins of Rhodes.[7] Jars have also been attributed to Mende because the most familiar emblem on that city's coinage, Dionysos reclining on a donkey, appears on its amphora handles.[8]

The stamps on the handles are particularly important for establishing the chronology of a class of amphoras. For instance, wine jars from Rhodes usually had a stamp on the top of each handle, recording in one the name of the priest of Halios, the eponymous magistrate who gave his name to the year. The other stamp shows the name of the person who made the jar, or who possibly was in charge of the factory or his agent. Often in one stamp or the other also appeared the month in which the jar was made. By grouping together the magistrates whose names appear on jars by the same fabricant, and by examining all the archaeological contexts in which stamps have been found, Virginia Grace has been able to date the magistrates' years and the fabricants' spans very closely during the 3rd, 2nd, and early 1st centuries B.C. For this reason, stamped Rhodian handles (and those belonging to other well-dated classes such as Knidian) are especially helpful to excavators.[9]

Not all series of jars are stamped, however, nor are Rhodian and others stamped throughout the period of their production. In such instances, the shape of the amphora can often provide a date for the excavator, though generally in less precise terms than do stamps, because the profiles of jars within a series evolved gradually over time. Thus, the unmistakable, tall, vertical handles with angular tops on 3rd- and 2nd-century Rhodian jars gave way in stages to slant-sided ones in the 1st century B.C. (see Fig. 20.1, left), and finally to an equally distinctive bowed shape with a horned top on Rhodian jars from the 1st century A.C. (Grace 1979: fig. 62). The body steadily grows longer and narrower as well, in keeping with the general trend for Greek amphoras in the classical (5th and 4th centuries B.C.) and Hellenistic (3rd to 1st centuries B.C.) periods.

A number of series of jars have been identified and dated by these several means, although refinements continue to be made. There remain still many unattributed jars and groups, and chronologies that as yet can be only roughly sketched. Work continues at the Stamped Amphora Handle Department at the Athenian Agora, as newly discovered material pours in, along with requests for information from excavators and other scholars studying the classical world. The nature of these data and their sheer mass demanded computerization, and in 1986 a project (called AMPHORAS) was begun to enter the material in Virginia Grace's archives into an electronic data base. Many of the figures below depend upon its General Amphora File (GAF), which by now contains over 75,000 records of a projected total of up to 150,000 on individual jar fragments, and upon the several related data bases (Study Files) through which the chronology of particular classes is worked out.[10]

3. Contents

Until recently the evidence for the contents of the amphoras of the various states has come from written sources: inventories and receipts, lawcourt speeches, nonfiction prose works by authors such as Pausanias and Pseudo-Aristotle, and literature such as the poetry of Sappho and Aristophanes. The first generally and the others sometimes name jars by their cities, while in other cases, a combination of less specific sources on wine export may support an inference that the characteristic trade containers of a place were for wine. Thus, wine has been nominated as the chief export in amphoras from a number of Greek cities, including Chios, Kerkyra, Knidos, Kos, Lesbos, Mende, Paros, Rhodes, Sinope (and other sites in the region of the Black Sea), and Thasos (Map 20.1).[11] Although residues of the contents of Greek transport amphoras have all too rarely been preserved, analysis and identification of organic remains in excavated pottery is becoming increasingly common and may eventually verify whether other amphora classes held wine.[12]

In using amphoras as tracers for ancient trade in wine, the assumption made is that (in their initial shipping at least) jars from one city normally would have held a single kind of produce. We are unaware of instances in the written sources that would suggest jars of a particular city or region were being used for the bulk export of different products. Indeed, the rationale behind creating distinctive state types of vessels should be commodity advertising, exemplified by Cassander's commissioning the sculptor Lysippos to design a special *keramon* in which to export Mendean wine from the nearby city of Cassandreia founded by him in 316 B.C. (Athenaeus, *The Deipnoso-*

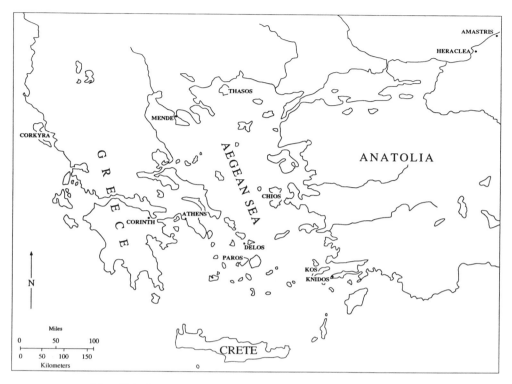

Map 20.1. Centers of the ancient wine trade during the classical period.

phistae 11.784). Reuse of amphoras was frequent, but probably secondary in importance and tending to be local.[13] It can also be assumed that amphoras travelled because of their contents, although conceivably they might have been shipped empty on occasion.[14]

With these qualifications, some of the textual evidence may be cited for certain amphora classes that were used to transport wine. Knidian and Koan *keramia* of wine turn up in the temple accounts of Delos and in papyri that tallied ships' cargoes at Alexandria.[15] Such records also mention Chian jars transporting the celebrated vintages of Chios. Rhodes contributed 10,000 *keramia* of its wine in response to an embassy from Sinope when it was under siege by Mithridates in ca. 220 B.C. (Polybius 4.56). Aristophanes mentions the wine of Thasos in "little Thasian jars," a wine shipped not only to Athens but throughout the eastern Mediterranean (*Ecclesiazusae* 1118; cf. *Lysistrata* 193–205).

Mendean jars are linked with wine because that city was also known as a major producer for export; the appearance of Dionysos in its coins and amphora stamps is significant in this regard. Demosthenes' speech against Artemon and Apollodoros furnishes more tangible evidence. It includes a loan contract, purportedly read aloud in court, which specified that the pair were to ship 3000 amphoras of Mendean wine with the money they were borrowing; instead, they put on board only 400 jars (Demosthenes 35.10–13).[16]

Amphoras from Lesbos likely carried the well-attested wine of Mytilene (Clinkenbeard 1982: 254, 256). Strabo (17.1.33 [C 808]) mentions the shipload of wine brought by Sappho's brother Charaxos from Lesbos to Naukratis, and Athenaeus (1.28) quotes the comic poet Alexis as saying that all Naukratites could import Lesbian wine free of duty.[17] The large numbers of amphoras manufactured at sites around the Black Sea, such as Sinope, Heraclea Pontica, and Amastris on the southern shores and Chersonesos in the Crimea, also testify to a healthy local wine production,[18] and evidence for a mutual trade in wine between these cities and a number of Aegean states is documented by finds of imported jars in both.

4. Wine in the Jar

Archaeological evidence, direct and indirect, gives many details about ways in which amphoras were handled and stored, but how the physical characteristics of these containers and their handling might have affected the wine they so often carried remains somewhat speculative. There exists some evidence in ancient writers, mostly of the Roman period, such as Pliny the Elder, whose 37-volume *Natural History* [hereafter *NH*] is essentially an encyclopedia of the classical world. Dating also to the 1st century A.C. is Columella's *De Re Rustica*, a detailed treatise by a successful farmer-landowner written to promote practical methods by which Italian agriculture might be improved (see chapter 19 by Greene, this volume). These and other sources which mention ancient wine and winemaking and selling are sometimes inconsistent and occasionally irreconcilable.[19] Enologists and archaeological chemists may be able to determine which ones are factual and to suggest, for example, what factors affected the flavor and other qualities of wine during storage and transport.

Perhaps the most significant question is the way in which the flavor of the wine might have been altered by the container itself. A shipper had to line the interior of unglazed jars to keep the contents from seeping out through their porous walls (Koehler 1986: 50–52; Mills and White 1989). Most commonly used for coating wine amphoras was pine pitch, prepared by heating the exuded resin or resinous wood (Beck and Borromeo 1991: 51). Such a lining would have been soluble in the alcohol, so that resinated wines probably began as a natural, and accidental, result of the requirements of packaging for shipping and storage.[20] Since Pliny follows his recommendation to use Bruttian pitch for coating wine vessels with an enumeration of the flavors of pitch from other regions, he implies that it would have made a difference in the taste of the wine (*NH* 14.25.127–28).

Pliny also discusses the use of pitch for preserving both wine and must (*NH* 14.24.120) and from Columella we get the precise amount to be added to wine as a preservative (*De Re Rustica* 12.22.2–3). Sometimes the resulting flavor was not appreciated; in the same reference, Columella prescribes a further addition of roasted salt so that it will be impossible to detect the pitch.[21] Often, however, pitch or resin (and occasionally both) was purposely used to enliven a wine, enhance its bouquet, or mask some disagreeable quality (*NH* 14.24–25.120,124,125; Plutarch, *Moralia* 5.676.b–c). Raw resin has indeed been found in ancient vessels, apparently the residue from lumps thrown in to flavor the wine in much the same way that modern Greek winemakers achieve resinated wines today.[22]

Of course, jars had to be securely closed for shipment, but amphoras of the Greek period have rarely been found with stoppers or closures in place. Fifteen of the 52 Greco-Italic jars of the early 3rd century B.C. that were raised from a shipwrecked cargo near Lipari, however, had cork stoppers intact, sitting flush with the rim and anchored with pitch.[23] Pottery disks have been excavated at various sites and could have been so used, presumably fixed in the same manner. Jars may often have been sealed with organic materials that would not have been preserved (even under water), such as the wad of plant material placed in the mouth and covered over with clay which is documented for the Mycenaean period (Koehler 1986: 53 and n. 22). A method might be devised

Figure 20.3. Amphora stopper from the Athenian Agora (P 20977), profile. (Koehler 1986; fig. 4; photograph courtesy of the Agora Excavations of the American School of Classical Studies.)

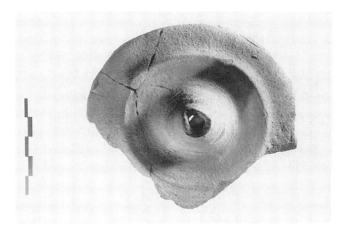

Figure 20.4. Amphora stopper from the Athenian Agora (P 20796), upper face. (Koehler 1986: fig. 3; photograph courtesy of the Agora Excavations of the American School of Classical Studies.)

for testing how well such a closure for a vessel filled with wine would have stood up over time and travel.

There are several stoppers of a special kind from the Agora Excavations in Athens which are probably of Hellenistic date, and were not apt to have been used in shipping (Figs. 20.3 and 20.4).[24] Their diameters approximate the inner dimension of the neck on common types of Greek amphoras of the period; the central "spindle" which acts as a sort of handle is pierced and could have permitted the passage of some air into the jar or allowed gases to escape. Perhaps wine was fermented in jars so stoppered. Papyri from Egypt say that *keramia* were made there for the vineyards and that wine was stored in them on producing estates—presumably during fermentation.[25]

The transport amphora was clearly designed to adapt to all means of conveyance, from a strong human shoulder (on which it was carried horizontally, or occasionally upright) to a boat.[26] On the ship that went down off Cyprus near Kyrenia at the end of the 4th century B.C., laden with about 375 jars, the amphoras had been stowed nearly vertically in the hold. The bottom layer leaned toward the slope of the hull, and into the interstices between the necks of those jars were set the toes of an upper row. Dunnage of branches or other cushioning material around the vessels will have protected and stabilized them.[27] But no matter how secure the amphoras were, the long trek by sea will have been rough on the wine inside, particularly on such delicate vintages as those of Thasos and Chios, which are known from amphora finds to have travelled extensively. Pliny (*NH* 14.22.118) comments that the effect of a sea voyage, for wines that can withstand it, is to double their previous maturity.

There is some evidence that wine might have been shipped in various concentrations. It was the custom for Greeks and Romans to dilute even ordinary wine with water to about half- or quarter-strength (Athenaeus, *The Deipnosophistae* 10.426), but vintages are known that were diluted with 20 parts of water to one of wine (Pliny, *NH* 14.5.54, citing Homer, *Odyssey* 9.209–10). Perhaps more concentrated wines, and the syrupy *syraeum* and *defrutum*, made by boiling down must to one-third or one-half of its original volume, respectively (*NH* 14.11.80–81), would have survived transport more readily.

Amphoras were stored on land—presumably often with their contents intact—sometimes in a more or less upright position, sometimes upside-down on their mouths, and sometimes horizontally (Koehler 1986: 62, 66). It cannot be determined archaeologically what was the most common position. A related question concerns the optimum level to which an amphora should be filled for storing and shipping wine.[28] Pliny cautions that jars should never be completely filled (*NH* 14.27.133–35); elsewhere he says that the finest wines of Campania should be set out in jars open to sun, moon, rain and wind (*NH* 14.27.136). Both the characteristics of the wine and the climate had to be taken into consideration in determining the best means of storage (*NH* 14.27.133–35). Reuse of containers, a practice which was well-known but whose frequency is currently unquantifiable, could also have affected longevity of the contents.[29] Pliny deals with this eventuality too: it is better to put wine into containers that previously contained vinegar, rather than sweet wine or mead (*NH* 14.25.128).

Wines, of course, varied enormously in their age at maturation and their longevity thereafter.[30] Ancient references to different vintages abound, but poetry offers some quite specific details, of which a handful may be mentioned here. As early as Homer, wine was recognized as "old" (*Odyssey* 2.340); Nestor had the seal broached on wine that was ten years old in his luxurious palace (*Odyssey* 3.391). Theocritus (7.147) and Horace (*Odes* 1.9.7) refer to four-year-old wines, while Martial (8.45) promises to honor a friend with an especially fine wine that had been kept for a century. Indeed, Pliny (*NH* 14.6.55) records Opimian wine that lasted 200 years, admittedly no longer potable but used to flavor other wines. Such choice wines had been transferred from the very large containers in which they were originally kept, to age further in amphoras,[31] as, for instance, Horace's sealed bottles hung to mature above a smokey fire the year Tullus was consul (*Odes* 3.8.10). Some inscriptions painted on Roman amphoras actually give two dates, i.e., that of the vintage and that when the wine was put into the jar (Tchernia 1986: 30).

5. Greek Trade in Wine

With the proper recording, identification, and dating of amphoras in large numbers, reliable statistics about commerce can be gained. This is most important because of the dearth of written testimonia on trade in ancient Greece. We are still some way from a complete synthesis of these data into a general picture of the ancient wine trade, but even in their current state, the figures reveal telling details of segments of the market. In the Agora of Athens, for instance, Virginia Grace has used stamped amphora handles to date key deposits, and has thereby documented the Athenian importation of various wines at specific times. Those figures can in turn be compared with those on imports at other sites, such as Alexandria and Corinth.

Slicing the data another way, the geographical, as well as the chronological, distribution can be plotted for several series of amphoras, notably thus far the Knidian and the Corinthian (Koehler 1979a and 1979b).[32] When all individual pieces are on the computer, and when the major class studies have been finished, we shall gain a multidimensional network of exchanges marked by amphora remains. Eventually, it will be possible to assess the relative volumes of export of wine for various cities and regions.

Local patterns of trade vary from site to site. Figures for Hellenistic Athens, for instance, show that the city imported much more Knidian wine than Rhodian on the whole. At Athens, by far the greatest mass of amphora material has been excavated in the Agora, its ancient marketplace and civic center. A count of the stamped amphora handles in the collection made in 1960 totalled 19,267, a figure which is still useful today, since only about 400 stamped amphoras and handles have been found since then (Grace 1985: 7). Of that number, 62% (12,002) are Knidian and 23% (4,432) are Rhodian.

There are several difficulties in translating such counts into volumes. Firstly, jars from various states were of different mean sizes; for example, Knidian amphoras held on average 30 l, while Rhodian had a capacity of 25 l. Secondly, classes differed widely in the proportion of jars stamped.[33]

Even in the Knidian and Rhodian series, which were nearly all stamped in the periods under discussion, a small number of unstamped jars are not included in the totals. Furthermore, the system of stamping has to be taken into account for each class. Because Knidian jars were usually impressed on each handle with the same stamp, the total number of handles is divided by two to get a very rough approximation of the number of jars; for Rhodian amphoras, counting either all fabricant stamps or else all eponym stamps will arrive at an estimate for actual jars.

Finally, numbers of handles retrieved may be skewed because it has been the practice at some excavations to leave duplicate examples uncatalogued. Even with all these factors taken into consideration, however, it is clear that more Knidian wine than Rhodian was imported by Athens.

In contrast, the great Ptolemaic port of Alexandria (which today holds the largest collection of stamped amphora handles in the world) took in for its Greek population vastly greater quantities of Rhodian than Knidian wine. A count made by Virginia Grace in 1967 of the approximately 18,000 datable Rhodian handles stamped with fabricants' names in the Benaki Collection in Alexandria forms the basis for Fig. 20.5, a graphic representation of the average number of these stamps per year for each of her Periods from the late 3rd to early 1st centuries B.C.[34] Initially, wine was imported from Rhodes at a significant but modest level in the latter part of the 3rd century. That rate doubled for the first half of the 2nd century B.C. and then in the second half (Period V) it leapt up, trebling itself, before dropping somewhat after 108 B.C.

Knidian imports at Alexandria mirror the Rhodian pattern, roughly speaking, but on a much smaller scale (Fig. 20.6). The 2,924 datable Knidian stamped handles in the Benaki Collection, representing about 1500 jars, chronicle a steady rise in Knidian wine imports that peaks in Period V and then falls off at the end of the 2nd century B.C. Alexandria is unusual in increasing its Knidian imports in Period V, when Athenians and other mainland Greeks appear to have drunk less Knidian wine than before.

Perhaps political or economic difficulties in Athens account for the difference, since there does not seem to have been that much less Knidian available (Fig. 20.7). Certainly afterwards in Period

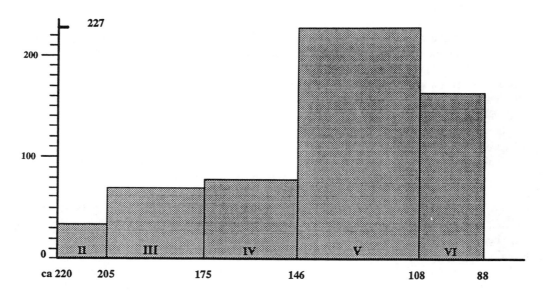

Figure 20.5. Rhodian imports into Alexandria (Benaki Collection): 17,435 Rhodian stamped amphora handles (SAH) by period (based on figures in Grace 1985: 42–43). These numbers are of fabricant stamps and give an approximate number of imported jars that have been preserved and dated, an average of 227 per year.

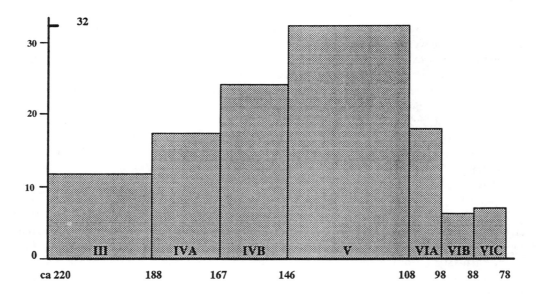

Figure 20.6. Knidian imports into Alexandria (Benaki Collection): 2899 Knidian stamped amphora handles (SAH) by period, an average of 32 per year. The number of actual jars represented would be approximately half of the numbers given here.

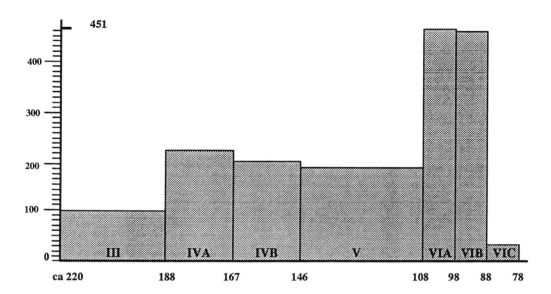

Figure 20.7. Knidian exports: 29,051 stamped amphora handles (SAH) by period according to current figures in the AMPHORAS database, which include most, but not all, Knidian handles, and are therefore to be regarded as preliminary. The number of actual jars represented would be approximately half that of the stamped amphora handles, which average 451 per year.

VI, total Knidian exports rise sharply, as do Knidian imports at Athens—but this jump contrasts with the strong decrease in Knidian imports at Alexandria in Period VI. Alexandria's higher importation of Knidian wine in Period V seems to be a local phenomenon, providing an important detail about the economy of that capital city.

Amphoras tell us not only about the wine bottled, shipped and stored in them and about the fluctuating patterns of trade in wine, but also about the economic significance of wine to the individual states which produced it in quantity for sale abroad. On Thasos, work by scholars of the French School at Athens, particularly in the past 15 years, has advanced our understanding of an especially important wine-producing center in the classical and early Hellenistic periods. Several discoveries demonstrate the state's interest in its wine industry. Official decrees of the 5th century B.C. controlled the terms under which wine was to be sold with reference to certain containers, prevented the sale of grapes before a certain time, and also specified that Thasian ships could not import foreign wine to the mainland opposite the island (Daux 1926: 213–26; Salviat 1986: 147–50).

The stamps on the handles of Thasian amphoras may also show state involvement, since they indicate both fabricant and city magistrate; it is possible that they reflect a regulation of the size of the containers.[35] Recent excavations and surveys on Thasos have uncovered a number of amphora manufacturing sites with kilns, rich fills of stamped fragments, and wasters that allow us to associate particular stamps and kilns. Further details are coming to light about the situation of these widely scattered potters' workshops, their connection with estate vineyards, and their fabricants.[36] All these remains, however fragmentary and imperfectly understood, yield glimpses of the internal organization, both public and private, which underlay large-scale wine production on Thasos.

Although the usefulness of the evidence offered by transport amphoras for various aspects of the Greek wine trade and its place in the ancient economy may be clear, much work remains to be done as this study comes into its own. Some of the directions in which research is now moving have been suggested above. Analysis proceeds apace on the chronological and geographical definition of exports and imports of many states, increasingly with the help of computerized databases. Methods of physicochemical analysis and other scientific techniques can help determine the contents and the place of manufacture of wine jars where these essential facts are unknown. With further controlled excavation and detailed recording of material from sites of production and trade, it should eventually prove possible to understand more of the internal workings of the commerce in wine. Finally, the traces that wine left by means of its containers in the archaeological record may help us fit its importance as a commodity within the socioeconomic structure as well as the historical context of individual city-states.

Acknowledgments

I owe Philippa M. Wallace Matheson, co-director of the AMPHORAS project, particular thanks not only for a number of references used here and for discussions of various points but also for producing the graphs on Knidian and Rhodian stamped amphora handles from the Benaki Collection in Alexandria and on total Knidian exports (Figs. 20.5–20.7). Since our database (see below) is in intermediate stages of creation, this meant considerable labor. The numbers reported here will inevitably change, and must be regarded as preliminary results used to demonstrate current working hypotheses. I am also very grateful to Malcolm B. Wallace for his comments on this paper in draft and for numerous references.

Notes

1. Dates are B.C. unless otherwise identified. A.C. (After Christ) is used for the current era when a particular year cannot be specified.

2. See Grace 1979: *passim*, for a general introduction to amphoras in the Greco-Roman world. For Roman amphoras, see Peacock and Williams 1986; Patterson 1982; and Callender 1965.

3. See Grace 1979: fig. 19, with accompanying text. Such jars, labelled with the abbreviation A for *amphiphoreus*, were said on the tablets to contain honey. There is no conclusive evidence from the Late Bronze Age, either archaeological or written, for the actual vessels being associated with wine. The common Mycenaean shipping container was the stirrup jar, and if wine travelled long distances, that is likely what was used. I thank R. Palmer for this summary introduction to the complexities of containers on the Linear B tablets and for a reference to Vandenabeele and Olivier 1979: 259–67.

4. Examples of commodities shipped in transport amphoras (besides wine, discussed below) include oil, olives, pickled or dried fish, fruits, honey, and nuts. For a list of some thirty items evidenced as contents, see Callender 1965: 37–41.

5. For jars of 11 l and 38 l capacity, see Koehler and Wallace 1987: 49–57; for Hellenistic Rhodian jars of 25–27 l weighing 14–15.75 kg empty, see Matheson and Wallace 1982.

6. Grace 1956: 82–87, New Kingdom paintings in figs. 2–4. P. E. McGovern has kindly related to me the evidence from his recent neutron activation analyses of amphora fabrics in collaboration with G. Harbottle, which demonstrate that the Canaanites had connections with Egyptians in the Delta early in the Middle Bronze Age and that Canaanite jars were made of Nile alluvial clay even at that early date.

7. See Kraay 1976: 3–4 and fig. 12, for the punning Rhodian coin type of the *rhodos* (translated as "rose," although the flower looks more like that of the pomegranate).

8. Grace 1949: 178, 186, under no. 1, and pl. 20:1. For a correction on the date of the deposit, see Corbett 1949: 337, under no. 106.

9. An introduction to the Rhodian class is given in Grace and Savvatianou-Pétropoulakou 1970: 289–302. Rhodian period dates, however, have been revised since then (see Grace 1974 and 1985: 7–13, 42). Period I now seems to have begun in the last quarter or last decade of the 4th century B.C.

10. For a more detailed description of the AMPHORAS project, see Koehler and Matheson 1993. Abstracts of relevant papers delivered at the 87th and 92nd General Meetings of the Archaeological Institute of America appear in the *American Journal of Archaeology* 90 (1986): 224 and 95 (1991): 336.

11. See n. 4 above, for contents other than wine. For names of wines labelled on the jars themselves, see Callender 1965: 37–38 and *Corpus Inscriptionum Latinarum* 15.4529–4654.

12. The number of amphoras suitable for testing from shipwrecks of the classical and Hellenistic periods is rather limited, and the soil and climate in Greece are not conducive to the preservation of organic remains in land excavations. Newly excavated pottery is often washed in a dilute solution of hydrochloric acid to remove lime deposits and so aid in the identification and mending of vessels. Archaeologists should examine pottery closely for any trace of residues before cleaning and reserve at least a representative sample of all pottery that is untreated and can be tested for organic material in the future. For recent analyses, see Biers and McGovern 1991.

13. See n. 29, below.

14. Egyptian vintners, for instance, might have wanted jars of Greek shapes, since they are known to have produced different kinds of wine, including Knidian and Chian (in addition to native wine) from vine cuttings imported in the 29th to 34th years of Ptolemy Philadelphus' reign, i.e., 256–51 B.C. (Rostovtzeff 1967: 95). Local imitations—honest or otherwise—of foreign containers are also known. For example, Rhodian potters seem at one point to have made jars of the recognized Knidian shape, using Rhodian clay (Grace and Savvatianou-Pétropoulakou 1970: 319–20, with n. 1, p. 320). Amphoras from central Italy and Roman Spain whose shapes are classified as Dressel 2–4 (see Fig. 7.3, this volume) sometimes imitate very closely the Koan shape; for an introduction to this complex typology, see Patterson 1982: 149–50 and references. Without entering into burdensomely detailed discussion of such copies, it can be noted here that the existence of imitations reinforces the notion of associating a given shape with specific contents.

15. A number of the ancient testimonia mentioned in this and the following paragraph appear in Grace 1947: 444–45 and 1949: 175–76. For a full presentation of ancient texts on Thasian wine, see Salviat 1986: 147–73.

16. For information on Athenian maritime trade which we gain from court speeches by Demosthenes and other orators, see Casson 1979 and Millett 1983.

17. Specific reference to a Lesbian amphora appears in Athenaeus' quotation of an epigram by Hedylus in which the courtesan Kallistion, "who could hold her own in the drinking contest with men," dedicates a *lesbion* (i.e., a jar from Lesbos, as Virginia Grace believes) to Aphrodite (*The Deipnosophistae* 11.486; the translation is that of Gulick 1963: 159). A similar usage may be seen in a passage from the Aristotelian corpus, *On Marvellous Things Heard*, 103 (not by Aristotle, though perhaps contemporary with him), which mentions Corcyraean amphoras brought up by merchants from the Adriatic to a common marketplace on a mountain in northern Greece, who join others from the Black Sea bringing Lesbian, Chian, and Thasian [amphoras or goods]).

18. See Monakhov 1984: 109–28, especially p. 125 with nn. 107–10, on viticulture and amphora manufacture in Chersonesos. I am grateful to P. M. W. Matheson for the reference, and to both her and O. Bakich for translating this article from the Russian.

19. Further references on amphoras and other equipment used in making and storing wine are found in White 1975: 112–48, *passim*; on sources ancient and modern, White 1970a; on arboriculture, White 1970b: 229–46.

20. Not all archaeological chemists agree that pine pitch would have been soluble in wine, e.g., Shackley (1982). André 1958: 143 (on Pliny, *NH* 14.25.124) states that raw resin would have been soluble and pitch not, and notes that the distinction seems to be borne out by the view of the ancients that the effects of wine treated with resin were harmful but of that flavored with pitch, less so (Pliny, *NH* 23.24.46–47). Pliny also says, however, that wine is healthiest if nothing has been added to the must, and that it is better if the vessels have not been pitched (*NH* 23.24.45)—implying that the pitch does react with the wine. It would be illuminating to have tests carried out that measured the rate at which a pitch lining of (hypothetically) 1–2 mm thickness dissolves in wine, and if so, how much time is required for a resinous taste to develop.

21. In fact, Columella says that salt should be added to every vintage, to prevent a moldy taste. He and Pliny regard the practice of using salt or seawater as a preservative for wine as usual. V. L. Singleton (personal communication), however, does not think that either salt or pitch would have much to do with preservation at levels tolerable for drinking. Both would modify the taste, so as to cover up spoilage, particularly vinegar spoilage. Furthermore, he adds, salt would tend to minimize consumption and therefore drunkenness.

22. I am indebted to C. Beck of the Amber Research Laboratory, Vassar College, for sharing with me his evidence for the deliberate creation of resinated wine in antiquity and for references. A publication of the analysis in his laboratory of the raw resin, used as flavoring, from a 5th-century B.C. bronze situla, found at Spina, is now in preparation for *Studi Etruschi*.

23. Frey et al. 1978: 288–89 with fig. 12A,B; Koehler 1986: 52–53 with nn. 19 and 20. For discussion and illustration of other methods of closing amphoras, see Koehler 1986: 52–56 and figs. 1–4.

24. Koehler 1986: 54 and fig. 4. In an unpublished paper read at the 1986 General Meeting of the Archaeological Institute of America (abstract in *American Journal of Archaeology* 91 [1987]: 275), S. Wolff identifies these stoppers as Punic, probably Carthaginian, and cites others from excavations at Carthage, viz., Ferron and Pinard, 1960–61: nos. 431–34, pp. 148–49, pl. 74. I thank S. Wolff for sharing with me a copy of his paper. Other pierced stoppers, from South Stoa wells at Corinth, are published in Broneer 1947: 240, pl. 58:10.

25. Rostovtzeff 1922: 160, 181.

26. For discussion and illustration of these and other ways in which amphoras could be carried and transported, see Koehler 1986: 56–60 and figs. 7–11.

27. For stowage and dunnage, see Wallinga 1964. I thank M. Katzev, whose publication of the Kyrenia ship is in preparation, for information on the material from his excavation; see also Katzev 1978, and Katzev and Katzev 1974.

28. It would be especially helpful to metrologists attempting to determine whether amphoras of a given city had a standard capacity at a particular time to know how far up the neck to take their volumetric measures; for this we have no direct evidence. On amphora capacities in general, see Matheson and Wallace 1982, and Wallace 1986. A paper on the methods used, "Measuring Amphora Capacities" is in preparation by B. L. Johnson, C. G. Koehler, P. M. W. Matheson and M. B. Wallace.

29. Wine amphoras were resold on occasion; see Amyx 1958: 174–78; Kent 1953: 128. In Egypt, the government systematically collected wine jars for storing water along the desert highway to Syria (Herodotus 3.6–7). Van Doorninck Jr. (1989: 252–53) reports wine in Byzantine amphoras which earlier may have held olives.

30. For the periods of maturation for a long list of western wines, see Athenaeus, *The Deipnosophistae* I.25f–27c (cited in Tchernia 1986: 30). Pliny says that all wines made abroad are thought to require seven years to reach a medium age (*NH* 14.10.70). A Greek inscription, however, records that a

Macedonian garrison bought wine fresh and tested it, and threw the remainder out after five years (*Inscriptiones Graecae* 12, Supplement 644 [Chalkis]).

31. Gow 1952: 167 (on 7.147; note also his comment on the pitch used to seal the lid or stopper).

32. A volume by the present author, Corinthian A and B Transport Amphoras, is in final preparation. Corinth may have produced two series of jars from the Archaic to the Hellenistic periods. Analysis of the fabric of Type A jars has verified that identification (see above). Type B jars, found in large proportion at Corinth, have been linked both with that city and with the Corinthian colony of Corcyra (see the reference to Pseudo-Aristotle in n. 17 above); analyses have attributed Corinthian B jars to one or the other site (Jones 1986: 712–20). At least some of them were manufactured in Corcyra, as recent excavations of kilns on Corfu have shown. (I thank K. Preka of the Greek Archaeological Service for permission to mention her finds.) The ancient contents have not been determined for either class, although the pitch lining suggests that Type B amphoras may have held wine.

33. A manuscript publishing Knidian stamp types is nearing completion; its authors are V. R. Grace, C. G. Koehler, P. M. W. Matheson, and M. Savvatianou-Pétropoulakou. Empereur 1982: 226–29. For more recent figures on the percentages of stamped Thasian fragments to unstamped ones, see Garlan 1986: 230–39. Garlan 1983: 28–32 discusses some of these and other considerations relevant to quantitative studies of amphoras and their usefulness for historians.

34. Period II in Virginia Grace's Rhodian chronology, ca. 240 to ca. 205 B.C. (see n. 9 above), has been truncated here to accord with the beginning of Period III in her Knidian chronology. Names in Knidian stamps begin in the last quarter of the 3rd century, permitting their close dating and so furnishing comparison with the Rhodian series. For information on the Knidian series in general, see Grace and Savvatianou-Pétropoulakou 1970: 317–24. The Knidian chronology laid out there starts only early in the 2nd century. See Grace 1985: 13–18, especially for stamps dating before about 183 B.C., and for general sharpening of the chronology, including a working list of Knidian eponym names individually annotated with period dates (pp. 31–35).

35. Studies have been undertaken to sort out the capacities of amphoras in the Thasian series (as in others) to test this hypothesis, but are not yet finished; see n. 28 above. Garlan (1983: 32–34) suggests that Thasian jars were stamped as part of some administrative control for purposes, perhaps fiscal, internal to the island.

36. For a brief introduction to Thasian amphoras, see Garlan 1988. The comprehensive publication of Thasian jars and their stamps is Bon and Bon in collaboration with Grace 1957. Recent discoveries are presented in *Bulletin de Correspondance Hellénique*. Supplement 13; in that volume, the early (pre-340 B.C.) Thasian stamps are discussed by Garlan (1986), and the later stamps by Debidour (1986). On the kiln sites, see there also (*inter alia*) Picon and Garlan (1986).

Bibliography

Abu al-Soof, B.
  1985   *Uruk Pottery*. Baghdad: State Organization of Antiquities and Heritage.

Acquaro, E.; Bartolini, P.; Ciasca, A; and Fantar, M.
  1973   *Prospezione archeologia al Capo Bono, I*. Collezione di Studi Fenici 2. Rome: Consiglio Nazionale delle Ricerche.

Adams, R. McC.
  1981   *Heartland of Cities*. Chicago: University of Chicago.

Adams, W. Y.
  1977   *Nubia: Corridor to Africa*. Princeton: Princeton University.

Addeo, F.; Barlotti, L.; Boffa, G.; Di Luccia, A.; Malorni, A.; and Piccioli, G.
  1979   Constituenti acidi di una oleoresina di conifere rinvenuta in anfore vinarie durante gli scavi archeologici di Oplonti. *Annali della Facolta di Scienze Agrarie della degli Studi Napoli, Portici* 13: 144–48.

Aharoni, Y.
  1967   *The Land of the Bible: A Historical Geography*. Trans. A. F. Rainey. Philadelphia: Westiminster.

A-32h ituv, S.
  1978   Economic Factors in the Egyptian Conquest of Canaan. *Israel Exploration Journal* 28: 93–105.

Åhlström, G.
  1978   Wine Presses and Cup-Marks of the Jenin-Megiddo Survey. *Bulletin of the American Schools of Oriental Research* 231: 19–49.

Åkerström, A.
  1975   More Canaanite Jars from Greece. *Opuscula Atheniensia* 11: 185–92.

Akurgal, E.
  1968   *The Art of Greece: Its Origins in the Mediterranean and the Near East.* New York: Crown.

Albenda, P.
  1974   Grapevines in Ashurbanipal's Garden. *Bulletin of the American Schools of Oriental Research* 215: 5–17.
  1976   Landscape Bas-Reliefs in the *Bit-Hilani* of Ashurbanipal. *Bulletin of the American Schools of Oriental Research* 224: 49–72.
  1977   Landscape Bas-Reliefs in the *Bit-Hilani* of Ashurbanipal. *Bulletin of the American Schools of Oriental Research* 225: 29–48.

Albright, W. F.
  1965   The Role of the Canaanites in the History of Civilization. Pp. 438–87 in *The Bible and the Ancient Near East*, ed. G. E. Wright. New York: Doubleday.

Alden, J.
  1982   Trade and Politics in Proto-Elamite Iran. *Current Anthropology* 23: 613–28.

Aldred, C.
  1972   *Tutankhamun's Egypt.* New York: C. Scribner's.

Algaze, G.
  1986   Habuba on the Tigris: Archaic Nineveh Reconsidered. *Journal of Near Eastern Studies* 45: 125–37.
  1989   The Uruk Expansion: Cross-Cultural Exchange in Early Mesopotamian Civilization. *Current Anthropology* 30: 571–608.
  1990   *Town and Country in Southeastern Anatolia.* Vol. 2: *Stratigraphic Sequence at Kurban Höyük.* Oriental Institute Publications, vol. 110. Chicago: Oriental Institute.
  1993   *The Uruk World System: The Dynamics of Expansion of Early Mesopotamian Civilization.* Chicago: University of Chicago Press.

Algaze, G.; Breuninger, R.; Lightfoot, C.; and Rosenberg, M.
  1991   The Tigris–Euphrates Archaeological Reconnaissance Project: A Preliminary Report on the 1989–1990 Seasons. *Anatolica* 17: 175–240.

Algaze, G.; Goldberg, P.; Honça, D.; Matney, T.; Mısşr, A.; Miller, A.; Schlee, D.; and Sommers, L.
  1995   Titriş Höyük, A Small EBA Urban Center in Southeastern Anatolia: The 1994 Season. *Anatolica* 21.

Alkım, U. B.; Alkım, H.; and Biligi, Ö.
  1988   *Ikiztepe I.* Türk Tarih Kurumu Yayınları, ser. 5, no. 39. Ankara: Türk Tarih Kurumu Başımevi.

Allen, H. W.
  1961   *A History of Wine: Great Vintage Wines from the Homeric Age to the Present Day.* London: Faber and Faber.

Alp, S.
  1967   Die Libationsgefässe "Schnabelkanne" und "Armformiges Gerät" und ihre hethitischen Bezeichnungen. *Belleten* 31: 531 ff.
  1968   *Zylinder- und Stempelsiegel aus Karahöyük bei Konya,* ser. 6, no. 31. Ankara: Türk Tarih Kurumu Yayınları.

Amerine, M. A.
    1954   Composition of Wines: I. Organic Constituents. *Advances in Food Research* 5: 353–510.
    1974   Wine Making. Pp. 875–84 in *The New Encyclopedia Britannica*, Macropædia, vol. 19. Chicago: Encyclopedia Britannica.

Amiet, P.
    1972   *Glyptique Susienne*. Mémoires de la Délégation Archéologique Française en Iran 43. Paris: P. Geuthner.
    1985   La période IV de Tépé Sialk reconsidérée. Pp. 293–312 in *De l'Indus aux Balkans: Recueil à la mémoire de Jean Deshayes*, eds. J.-L. Hout, M. Yon, and Y. Calvet. Paris: Éditions Recherche sur les Civilisations.
    1986   *L'âge des échanges inter-iraniens, 3000–1700 avant J.-C.* Paris: Éditions de la Réunion des musées nationaux.

Amiran, R.
    1969   *Ancient Pottery of the Holy Land, from Its Beginnings in the Neolithic Period to the End of the Iron Age*. Jerusalem: Massada.

Ampolo, C.
    1980   Le condizioni materiali della produzione agricoltura e paesaggio agrario, *Dialoghi di Archeologia* (La Formazione della Città nel Lazio) n.s. 1: 15–46.

Amyx, D. A.
    1958   The Attic Stelai: Part III. *Hesperia* 27: 163–307.

Anderson, E. N.
    1980   "Heating" and "Cooling" Foods in Hong Kong and Taiwan. *Social Science Information* 19: 237–68.

Andre, J.
    1958   Pline d'Ancien, Histoire Naturelle, Livre XIV. Collection des universités de France [Bude]. Paris: Société d'edition "Les Belles Lettres."

Aragon, H.
    1916   *La vigne dans l'antiquité*. Toulouse: Edouard.

Arano, L. C.
    1976   *The Medieval Health Handbook: Tacuinum Sanitatis*. New York: Braziller.

Aravantinos, V. L.
    1984   The Use of Sealings in the Administration of Mycenaean Palaces. Pp. 41–48 in *Pylos Comes Alive: Industry and Administration in a Mycenaean Palace*, eds. G. Palaima and C. Shelmerdine. New York: Fordham University.

Aschenbrenner, S.
    1972   A Contemporary Community. Pp. 47–53 in *Minnesota Messenia Expedition*, eds. W. McDonald and G. Rapp. Minneapolis: University Of Minnesota.

Ash, H. B.
    1941   *Lucius Junius Moderatus Columella, On Agriculture*. Vol. 1. London: W. Heinemann.

Ash, H. B.; Foster, E. S.; and Heffner, E. H., trans.
    1941-65   Columella, *On Agriculture*. 3 vols. Cambridge: Harvard University.

Asher-Greve, J. M., and Stern, W. B.
    1983   A New Analytical Method and Its Application to Cylinder Seals. *Iraq* 45: 57–162.

Åström, P.
   1972   *The Late Bronze Age, Architecture and Pottery. The Swedish Cyprus Expedition.* Vol.
           4, pt. 1C. Lund: Swedish Cyprus Expedition.
   1991   Canaanite Jars from Hala Sultan Tekke. Pp. 149–51 in *Bronze Age Trade in the
           Mediterranean,* ed. N. H. Gale. Jonesered: P. Åström.

Åström, P., and Hjelmqvist, H.
   1971   Grain Impressions from Cyprus and Crete. *Opuscula Athenensia* 10: 9–14.

Åström, P.; Hult, G.; and Strandberg Olofsson, M.
   1977   *Hala Sultan Tekke 3, Excavations 1972.* Studies in Mediterranean Archaeology 45.3.
           Göteborg: P. Åström.

Athanaeus
   1927   *The Deipnosophists.* The Loeb Classical Library. 10 vols. Trans. C. B. Gulik. New
           York: Putnam.

Athanassakis, A. N.
   1976   *The Homeric Hymns.* Baltimore: Johns Hopkins.
   1983   Hesiod: *Theogony, Works and Days, Shield.* Baltimore: Johns Hopkins University.

Azarpay, G.
   1968   *Urartian Art and Artifacts: A Chronological Study.* Berkeley: University of California.

Badler, V. R.
   1988   The Uruk Period Pottery Development of Godin VI–V and Nippur Inanna XXI–XV.
           Abstracts of 35th Rencontre Assyriologique Internationale.
   1989   Social Structure Changes Suggested by Artifact Assemblages of Godin V and VI.
           Paléorient 15: 277–78.
   n.d.   Godin V and the Chronology of the Late Uruk Period. Ph.D. dissertation, Department
           of Near Eastern Studies, University of Toronto. In preparation.

Badler, V. R.; McGovern, P. E.; and Michel R. H.
   1990   Drink and Be Merry!: Infrared Spectroscopy and Ancient Near Eastern Wine. Pp.
           25–36 in *Organic Contents of Ancient Vessels, Materials Analysis and Archaeological
           Investigation,* eds. W. R. Biers and P. E. McGovern. MASCA Research Papers in
           Science and Archaeology 7. Philadelphia: MASCA, The University Museum of Ar-
           chaeology and Anthropology.

Baines, J., and Malek, J.
   1984   *Atlas of Ancient Egypt.* Oxford: Phaidon.

Baker, H. G.
   1965   *Plants and Civilisation.* Belmont, CA: Wadsworth Publishing.

Ball, W.
   1990   The Tell al-Hawa Project: The Second and Third Seasons of Excavations at Tell
           al-Hawa. *Mediterranean Archaeology* 3: 75–92.

Ballard, P.
   1981   *Wine in Everyday Cooking: Cooking with Wine for Family and Friends.* San Francisco:
           Wine Appreciation Guild.

Barber, R. L. N.
   1987   *The Cyclades in the Bronze Age.* Iowa City: University of Iowa.

Barlow, J. A.; Bolger, D. L.; and Kling, B., eds.
1991   *Cypriot Ceramics: Reading the Prehistoric Past*. University Museum Symposium Series 2, University Museum Monograph 74. Philadelphia: A. G. Levantis Foundation and University Museum.

Barnett, R. D.
n.d.   *Assyrian Palace Reliefs*. London: Batchworth.

Barnett, R. D., and Falkner, M.
1962   *The Sculptures of ... Tiglath-Pileser III*. London: Trustees of the British Museum.

Barreca, F., and Fantar, M.
1983   *Prospezione archeologia al Capo Bono, II*. Collezione di Studi Fenici 14. Rome: Consiglio Nazionale delle Ricerche.

Barry, E.
1775   *Observations, Historical, Critical, and Medical, on the Wines of the Ancients*. London: T. Cadell.

Barta, W.
1963   *Die altägyptische Opferliste von der Frühzeit bis zur griechisch–römischen Epoche*. Berlin: B. Hessling.

Bartonek, A.
1983   The Linear B Texts and their Quantitative Evaluation. Pp. 15–27 in *Res Mycenaeae*. Akten des VII. Internationalen mykenologischens Colloquiums 1981, eds. A. Heubeck and G. Neumann. Göttingen: Vandenhoeck and Ruprecht.

Bass, G. F.
1966   *Archaeology Under Water*. London: Penguin.
1967   Cape Gelidonya: A Bronze Age Shipwreck. *Transactions of the American Philosophical Society*, New Series 57. Philadelphia: American Philosophical Society.
1986   A Bronze Age Shipwreck at Ulu Burun (Kaş): 1984 Campaign. *American Journal of Archaeology* 90: 269–96.
1987   Oldest Known Shipwreck Reveals Bronze Age Splendors. *National Geographic* 172: 693–733.
1991   Evidence of Trade from Bronze Age Shipwrecks. Pp. 69–82 in *Bronze Age Trade in the Mediterranean*, ed. N. H. Gale. Jonesered: P. Åström.

Bass, G. F.; Pulak, C.; Collon, D.; and Weinstein, J.
1989   The Bronze Age Shipwreck at Ulu Burun: 1986 Campaign. *American Journal of Archaeology* 93: 1–29.

Bauer, R.
1976   *Historische Schlachten auf Tapisserien aus dem Besitz des Kunsthistorichen Museum Wien*. Vienna: Amt der Burgenländregierung, Kulturabteilung.

Baumbach, L.
1987   Mycenaean *tu-ru-pte-ri-ja* and Herodotus II.180. Pp. 49–54 in *Tractata Mycenaea*. Proceedings of the Eighth International Colloquium on Mycenaean Studies 1985, eds. P. Ilievski and L. Crepejac. Skopje: Macedonian Academy of Sciences and Arts.

Baurain, C.
    1985   Pour une autre interprétation des génie minoens. Pp. 95–118 in *L'iconographie mi-noénne. Bulletin Correspondance Hellénique*, suppl. 11, ed. O. Picard. Paris: École française d'Athènes.
    1986   Les génies à carapace. *Archeologia* 211: 39–44.

Baus, H. M.
    1973   *How to Wine Your Way to Good Health*. New York: Mason and Lipscomb.

Beal, R.
    1983   Studies in Hittite History. *Journal of Cuneiform Studies* 35: 115–26.
    1986   The Organization of the Hittite Military. Unpublished Ph.D. dissertation, University of Chicago.

Beale, T. W.
    1973   Early Trade in Highland Iran: A View From a Source Area. *World Archaeology* 5: 133–48.

Bechtel, J. H.
    1893   *Temperance Selections, Comprising Choice Readings and Recitations in Prose and Verse from the Ablest Speakers and Writers in England and America*. Freeport: Books for Libraries; reprinted 1970.

Beck, C. W., and Borromeo, C.
    1990   Ancient Pine Pitch: Technological Perspectives from a Hellenistic Wreck. Pp. 51–58 in *Organic Contents of Ancient Vessels: Materials Analysis and Archeological Investiga-tion*, eds. W. R. Biers and P. E. McGovern. MASCA Research Papers in Science and Archaeology 7. Philadelphia: MASCA, The University Museum of Archaeology and Anthropology.

Beck, C. W.; Fellows, C. A.; and MacKennan, E.
    1974   Nuclear Magnetic Resonance Spectrophotometry in Archaeology. Pp. 226–35 in *Ar-chaeological Chemistry*, ed. C. W. Beck. Advances in Chemistry Series, no. 138. Washington, DC: American Chemical Society.

Becker, W.
    1979   Production and Consumption of Wine: Facts, Opinions, Tendencies. Pp. 157–86 in *Fermented Food Beverages in Nutrition*, eds. C. F. Gastineau, W. J. Darby, and T. B. Turner. New York: Academic.

Beckman, G.
    1983   *Hittite Birth Rituals*. Studien zu den Boğazköy Texten 29. Wiesbaden: O. Har-rassowitz.

Behm-Blancke, M. R.; Roh, M. R.; Karg, N.; Masch, L.; Parsche, F.; Weiner, K. L.; v. Wickede, A.; and Wiedermayer, G.
    1984   Hassek Höyük: Vorläufiger Bericht über die Grabungen in den Jahren 1981–1983. *Istanbuler Mitteilungen* 34: 31–150.

Benjamin, G. A. H.; Darling, E. J.; and Sales, B.
    1990   The Prevalence of Depression, Alcohol Abuse, and Cocaine Abuse among United States Lawyers. *International Journal of Law and Psychiatry* 13: 233–46.

Bennett, E. L., Jr.
    1950   Fractional Quantities in Minoan Bookkeeping. *American Journal of Archaeology* 54: 204–22.

1958   The Mycenaean Tablets II. Pp. 76–77 in *Transactions of the American Philological Society*, New Series 48. 1, ed. E. L. Bennett, Jr. Philadelphia: American Philological Society.

Bennett, E. L., Jr., and Olivier, J.-P.
1973   *The Pylos Tablets Transcribed*. Vol. 1: *Texts and Notes*. Incunabula Graeca 51. Roma: Ateneo.

Benveniste, E.
1973   *Indo-European Language and Society*. Coral Gables, FL: University of Miami.

Bernier, O., trans.
1978   *Dali: The Wines of Gala*. New York: Abrams.

Best, J.
1988   The Oldest Scripts in Crete: Derivation, Development, Decipherment. Pp. 1–29 in *Ancient Scripts from Crete and Cyprus* by J. Best and F. Woudhuizen. Leiden: E. J. Brill.

Beyer, D.
1985   Scellements de portes du palais de Mari. *M.A.R.I.* 4: 375–84.

Biers, W. R.
1988   *The Archaeology of Greece: An Introduction*. Ithaca, NY: Cornell University.

Bietak, M.
1985   Ein altägyptischer Weingarten in einem Tempelbezirk (Tell el-Dabᶜa 1. März bis 10. Jun: 1985). *Anzeiger der philosophisch-historischen Klasse der Österreichischen Akademie der Wissenschaften*, 122: 267–78.
1986   *Avaris and Piramesse: Archaeological Exploration in the Eastern Nile Delta*. Mortimer Wheeler Archaeological Lecture 1979. 2nd ed. Oxford: Oxford University.

Bikaki, A. H.
1984   *Ayia Irini: The Potters' Marks*. Keos, vol. 4. Mainz on Rhine: P. von Zabern.

Billiard, R.
1913   *La Vigne dans l'antiquité*. Lyon.

Birot, M.
1960   Le miel et le vin. Pp. 270–73 in *Textes administratifs de la salle 5 du palais*, ed. M. Birot. Archives Royales de Mari, vol. 9. Paris: Imprimerie Nationale.

Birot, P., and Dresch, J.
1953   *Le Mediterranée et le Moyen-Orient*. Paris: Universitaires de France.

Bissell, P.; Ewart, A.; and Sangtippawan, W.
1989   Loading Concentrations for Tartaric and Malic Acid for Single Column HPLC Organic Acid Analysis. *American Journal of Enology and Viticulture* 40: 316–19.

Blackman, A. M.
1914–25 *The Rock Tombs of Meir*. 4 vols. London: Egypt Exploration Fund.
1915   *The Rock Tombs of Meir*. Vol. 3. London: Egypt Exploration Fund.
1953   *The Rock Tombs of Meir*. Vol. 5. London: Egypt Exploration Fund.

Blackman, A. M., trans.
1966   *Adolf Erman's The Ancient Egyptians: A Sourcebook of Their Writings*. New York: Harper and Row; Torchbook.

Blegen, C.
   1921   *Korakou*. New York: American School of Classical Studies.
   1937   *Prosymna*. Cambridge: Cambridge University.

Blegen, C.; Palmer, H.; and Young, R.
   1964   *Corinth. The North Cemetery*. Vol. 13. Princeton: American School of Classical
           Studies.

Blegen, C., and Rawson, M.
   1966   *The Palace of Nestor in Western Messenia*. Vol. 1: *The Buildings and Their Contents*.
           Princeton: Princeton University.

Blegen, C.; Rawson, M.; Taylour, W.; and Donovan, W.
   1973   *The Palace of Nestor at Pylos in Western Messenia*. Vol. 3: *Acropolis and Lower Town;
           Tholoi, Grave Circle and Chamber Tombs; Discoveries outside the Citadel*. Princeton:
           Princeton University.

Bleibtreu, E.
   1980   *Die Flora der neuassyrischen Reliefs: Eine Untersuchung zu den Orthostatenreliefs
           des 9.–7. Jahrhunderts v. Chr*. Wiener Zeitschrift für Kunde des Morgenlandes, special
           vol. 1. Vienna: Institut für Orientalistik.

Bleichsteiner, R.
   1951–52 Zeremonielle Trinksitten und Raumordnung bei den turko-mongolischen Nomaden.
           Archiv für Völkerkunde 6/7: 181–208.

Boardman, J.
   1974   *Athenian Black Figure Vases*. London: Thames and Hudson.
   1990   *Symposion* Furniture. Pp. 122–31 in *Sympotica: A Symposium on the Symposion*, ed.
           O. Murray. Oxford: Clarendon.

Boehmer, M. R.
   1983   *Die Relief keramik von Boğazköy: Grabungskampagnen 1906–1912, 1931–1939,
           1952–1978*. Boğazköy-Ḫattuša 13. Berlin: Gebr. Mann.

Bon, A., and A.-M. (in collaboration with V. R. Grace)
   1957   *Les timbres amphoriques de Thasos*. Etudes thasiennes 4. Paris: École française
           d'Athènes.

Borger, R.
   1956   *Die Inschriften Asarhaddons, Königs von Assyrien*. Archiv für Orientforschung, suppl.
           9. Graz: E. Weidner.

Bortoli, L.; Gounot, M.; and Jacquinet, J.-C., eds.
   1969   *Climatologie et bioclimatologie de la Tunisie septentrionale*. Annales de l'institut de la
           recherche agricole de Tunisie, vol. 42, no. 1. Tunis: Imprimerie Officielle.

Boston Museum of Fine Arts
   1982   *Egypt's Golden Age*. Catalogue of the Exhibition, The Art of Living in the New
           Kingdom 1558–1085 B.C. Boston: Museum of Fine Arts.

Botta, P. E., and Flandin, E.
   1849   *Monument de Ninive*, 5 vols. Paris: Imprimerie Nationale.

Bottema, S.
   1984   The composition of modern charred seed assemblages. *Review of Paleobotany and
           Palynology* (van Zeist Festschrift) 73: 207–12.

Bottéro, J.
1958   Breuvages. Pp. 268–69 in *Textes économiques et administratifs* by J. Bottéro. Archives Royales de Mari 7. Paris: Imprimerie Nationale.

Boubals, D.; Cordonnier, R.; and Pistre, R.
1962   Etude du mode de transmission héréditaire du caractore "diglucosides anthocyaniques" des baies dans le genre *Vitis. Progrès Agricole et Viticole*, pp. 187–92.

Bouquet, A.
1982   Origine et evolution de l'encépagement français à travers les siècles. *Progrès Agricole et Viticole.* 99: 110–20.

Boyer, G.
1958   *Textes juridiques.* Archives Royales de Mari 8. Paris: Imprimerie Nationale.

Branigan, K.
1969   The Earliest Minoan Scripts: The Prepalatial Background. *Kadmos* 8: 1–22.
1988   *Prepalatial: The Foundations of Palatial Crete.* 2nd ed. Amsterdam: A. M. Hakkert.

Breasted, W.
1988   *Ancient Records of Egypt: Historical Documents from the Earliest Times to the Persian Conquest.* Vols. 1–5. London: Histories and Mysteries of Man.

Brentjes, B.
1982   Holozän-Geologie und Archaeologie: Gedanken und Fragen zur Korrelation der Resultate zweier Wissenschaften. Pp. 453–84 in *Paleoclimates, Paleoenvironments, and Human Communities in the Eastern Mediterranean Region in Later Prehistory.* British Archaeological Reports, International Series 33. Oxford: British Archaeological Reports.
1988   Die dunklen Jahrhunderte der frühen Eisenzeit und die Kulturgeschichte mittelasien. *Hallesche Beiträge zur Orientwissenschaft* 12: 5–24.

Brock, A. J., trans.
1928   *On the Natural Faculties.* New York: Putnam.
1929a,b   (a) On Habits, and (b) On Simple Drugs. Pp. 181–91 and 191–95 in *Greek Medicine, Being Extracts Illustrative of Medical Writers From Hippocrates to Galen.* London: Dent.

Broneer, O.
1947   Investigations at Corinth, 1946–1947. *Hesperia* 16: 233–47.

Bronner, J. P.
1857   *Die wilden Trauben des Rheintals.* Heidelberg.

Brothwell, D., and Brothwell, P.
1969   *Food in Antiquity: A Survey of the Diet of Early Peoples.* London: Thames and Hudson.

Broughton, T. R. S.
1938   Roman Asia Minor. Pp. 499–918 in *An Economic Survey of Ancient Rome*, vol. 4, ed. T. Frank.

Brown, J. P.
1969   The Mediterranean Vocabulary of the Vine. *Vetus Testamentum* 19: 146–70.

Brunt, P. A.
1971   *Italian Manpower, 225 B.C.–A.D. 14.* Oxford: Oxford University.

Buchholz, H.-G., and Karageorghis, V.
1971   *Altagäis und Altkypros.* Tübingen: Wasmuth.

Buhler, G.
    1896   *The Sacred Books of the East*. Vol. 2, pt. 1: *Apastamba and Gautama*, ed. F. M. Muller. Oxford: Clarendon.

Bulard, A.
    1885   *Monographie de L'Ile de Dierba*. Besançon: Ch. Delagrange.

Bulle, H.
    1907   *Orchomenos I*. Munich: no publisher.

Bunnens, G.
    1979   *L'expansion phénicienne en Méditerranée: Essai d'interpretation fondé sur une ana-lyse des traditions littéraires*. Brussels: Institut historique Belge de Rome.
    1989   Emar on the Euphrates in the 13th Century B.C. *Abr-Nahrain* 27: 23–36.

Burde, C.
    1974   *Hethitische medizinische Texte*. Studien zu den Boğazköy Texten 19. Wiesbaden: O. Harrossowitz.

Burke, M. L.
    1964   Lettres de Numušda-naḫrâi et trois autres correspondants à Idiniatum. Pp. 81–101 in *Textes divers*, eds. G. Dossin et al. Archives Royales de Mari 13. Paris: Ministère des Affaires Étranger/P. Geuthner.

Burkert, W.
    1985   *Greek Religion*. Cambridge: Harvard University.
    1988   Final Discussion. Pp. 274–76 in *Early Greek Cult Practice*, eds. R. Hägg, N. Marina-tos, and G. C. Nordquist. Stockholm: P. Åström.

Bury, R. G., trans.
    1926   Plato, *The Laws*. 2 vols. Cambridge: Harvard University.

Butzer, K. W.
    1970   Physical Conditions in Eastern Europe, Western Asia and Egypt before the Period of Agricultural and Urban Settlement. Pp. 35–69 in *The Cambridge Ancient History*, vol. 1, pt. 1. 3rd ed., rev. London: Cambridge University.

Cadogan, G.
    1980   *Palaces of Minoan Crete*. New York: Barrie and Jenkins.

Caldwell, J. R.
    1967   *Investigations at Tal-i-Iblis*. Illinois State Museum Preliminary Reports 9. Springfield: Illinois State Museum.

California Wine Advisory Board
    1978   *Gourmet Wine Cooking, The Easy Way*. San Francisco: Wine Appreciation Guild.

Callender, M. H.
    1965   *Roman Amphorae*. London: Oxford University.

Calmeyer, P.
    1979   Zum Tongefäss in Form eines Gazellenkopfes. Pp. 195–201 in *Bastam*, vol. 1: *Aus-grabungen in den urartäischen Anlagen 1972–1975* by W. Kleiss. Berlin: D. Reimer.

Cameron, M.
    1964   An Addition to "La Parisienne." *Kretika Chronika* 18: 38–53.
    1968   Unpublished Paintings from the House of the Frescoes. *Annual of the British School of Athens* 63: 1–31.

1987   The Palatial Thematic System in the Knossos Murals. Pp. 320–28 in *The Function of the Minoan Palaces*, eds. R. Hägg and N. Marinatos. Stockholm: Swedish Institute at Athens.

Caminos, R. A.
1954   *The Late Egyptian Miscellanies*. Brown Egyptological Studies 1. London: Oxford University.

Campbell, A. F.
1964–65 Homer and Ugaritic Literature. *Abr-Nahrain* 5: 29–56.

Camps, G.
1960   *Aux origines de la Berbérie: Massinissa ou les débuts de l'histoire*. Libyca Archéologie-Épigraphie 8.

1961   *Aux origines de la Berbérie: Rites et monuments funéraires*. Paris: Arts et Métiers Graphiques.

1964   *Corpus des poteries modelées retiées des monuments funéraries protohistoriques de l'Afrique du Nord*. Paris: Arts et Métiers Graphiques.

1982   Beginnings of Pastoralism and Cultivation in North West Africa and the Sahara: Origins of the Berbers. Pp. 548–623 in *Cambridge History of Africa I*. Cambridge: Cambridge University.

Camps-Faber, H.
1966   *Matière et art mobilier dans la préhistoire Nord-Africaine et Saharienne*. Paris: Arts et Métiers Graphiques.

Carandini, A.
1983   Pottery and the African Economy. Pp. 145–62 in *Trade in the Ancient Economy*, eds. P. D. A. Garnsey, K. Hopkins, and C. R. Whittaker. Berkeley: University of California.

Carbonneau, A.
1983a   Stérilité male et femelle dans le genre *Vitis*. *Agronomie* 3: 635–44.
1983b   Stérilité male et femelle dans le genre *Vitis*. II. Conséquences en génétéque et sélection. *Agronomie* 3: 645–49.

Caskey, M. E.
1981   Ayia Irini, Kea: The Terracotta Statues and the Cult in the Temple. Pp. 127–35 in *Sanctuaries and Cults in the Aegean Bronze Age*, eds. R. Hägg and N. Marinatos. Proceedings of the First International Symposium at the Swedish Institute in Athens, 12–13 May, 1980. Stockholm: P. Åström.

Casson, L.
1971   *Ships and Seamanship in the Ancient World*. Princeton: Princeton University.
1979   Traders and Trading. *Expedition* 21: 25–32.
1989   *The Periplus Maris Erythraei, Text with Introduction, Translation, and Commentary*. Princeton: Princeton University.

Catling, H. W.
1962   Patterns of Settlement in Bronze Age Cyprus. *Opuscula Atheniensia* 4: 129–69.
1988   Unpublished Finds from Cyprus: (1) Graffiti in the Late Cypriot Linear Script. Pp. 325–27 in *Report of the Department of Antiquities of Cyprus*, pt. 1. Nicosia: Department of Antiquities.
1989   Archaeology in Greece. Pp. 3–116 in *Archaeological Reports for 1988–1989*, no. 35. London: British School at Athens.

Cerceau, I.
  1985   Les représentation végétales dans l'art égéen: problèmes d'identifications. Pp. 181–84 in *L'iconographie minoénne. Bulletin Correspondance Hellénique*, suppl. 11, ed. O. Picard. Paris: École française d'Athènes.

Černý, J.
  1965   *Hieratic Inscriptions from the Tomb of Tut^cankhamun*. Tut^cankhamun's Tomb Series 2. Oxford: Griffith Institute.

Chadwick, J.
  1976   *The Mycenaean World*. Cambridge: Cambridge University.
  1987   *Linear B and Related Scripts*. Berkeley: University of California.

Chadwick, J.; Mann, W. N.; Lonie, I. M.; and Withington, E. T.
  1978a–c *Hippocratic Writings*: (a) *Aphorisms*; (b) *Regimen for Health*; (c) *Regimen in Acute Disease*. Harmondsworth: Penguin.

Chantrain, P.
  1968–80 *Dictionnaire étymologique de la langue grecque*, 4 vols. Paris: Klincksäeck.

Charles, M. P.
  1987   Onions, Cucumbers and the Date Palm. *Bulletin on Sumerian Agriculture* 3: 1–21.

Chase, E.
  1960   *The Pleasures of Cooking with Wine*. Englewood Cliffs: Prentice-Hall.

Cheshire, W.
  1985   Remarks on the Names of Pelusium. *Göttinger Miszellen* 84: 19ff.

Christian Economic and Social Research Foundation
  1976   *Alcohol and Crime*. Occasional paper C.2. London: Christian Economic and Social Research Foundation.

Christoffel, K.
  1957   *Durch die Zeiten strömt der Wein: Die wunderbare Historie des Weines*. Hamburg: Cram, de Gruyter.

CILOP (Centre International de Liaison des Organismes de Propagandes en Faveur des Produits de la Vigne)
  1983   *Vin et Civilisations*. Turin: Dalmasso.

Çınaroğlu, A.
  1990–91 Kastamonu Kökenli Bir Grup Hitit Gümüş(?) Eseri. *Müze* 4: 53–61.

Cintas, P.
  1950   *Céramique punique*. Paris: Klincksieck.
  1951   Deux campaigns des fouilles à Utique. *Karthago* 2: 5–79.
  1954   Nouvelles recherches à Utique. *Karthago* 5: 89–154, 294–308.
  1961   *Elements d'étude pour une protohistoire de la Tunisie*. Paris: Universitaires de France.
  1970–76 *Manuel d'archéologie punique*. 2 vols. Paris: A. and J. Picard.

Civil, M.
  1964   A Hymn to the Beer Goddess and a Drinking Song. Pp. 67–89 in *Studies Presented to A. Leo Oppenheim*, eds. R. D. Briggs and J. A. Brinkman. Chicago: Oriental Institute.

Clark, J. A., and Goldblith, S. A.
  1975   Processing of Foods in Ancient Rome. *Food Technology* 29: 30–32.

Clement, P. A., and Hoffleit, H. B., trans.
  1969   Table-Talk (*Quaestiones Convivales*). In *Plutarch's Moralia*, vol. 8. London: W. Heinemann.

Cline, E.
  1991   Orientalia in the Late Bronze Age Aegean. Unpublished Ph.D. dissertation, University of Pennsylvania.

Clinkenbeard, B. G.
  1982   Lesbian Wine and Storage Amphoras. *Hesperia* 51: 248–67.

Collon, D.
  1987   *First Impressions: Cylinder Seals in the Ancient Near East.* Chicago: University of Chicago.

Columella
  1941   *On Agriculture and Trees.* The Loeb Classical Library, vol. 3, bk. 12, trans. E. S. Forster and E. Hiffner. Cambridge: Harvard University.

Condamin, J., and Formenti, F.
  1976   Recherche de traces d'huile d'olive et de vin dans les amphores antiques. *Figlina* 1: 143–58.
  1978   Détection du contenu d'amphores antique (huile, vin): Etude méthodologique. *Revue d'Archéométrie* 2: 43–58.

Condamin, J.; Formenti, F.; Metais, M. O.; Michel, M.; and Blond, P.
  1976   The Application of Gas Chromatography to the Tracing of Oil in Ancient Amphorae. *Archaeometry* 18: 195–201.

Corbett, P. E.
  1949   Attic Pottery of the Athenian Agora. *Hesperia* 18: 298–351.

Cornelssen, and Albath, W.
  1984   *Doktor Bacchus: Wein und Gesundheit: Erkenntnisse und Ratschläge.* Stuttgart: Seewald.

Coşkun, Y.
  1979   *Boğazköy Metinlerinde Geçen Bazı seçme Kap Isimleri.* Ankara Üniversitesi Dil ve Tarih Fakultes, Yayınları 285. Ankara: Ankara Üniversitesi.

Costantini, L.
  1977   Le Piante. Pp. 159–71 in *La città bruciata del deserto salato.* Venice: Erizzo Editrice.

Costantini, L., and Costantini-Biasini, L.
  1985   Agriculture in Baluchistan between the 7th and the 3rd Millennium B.C. *Newsletter of Baluchistan Studies* 2: 16–30.

Crawford, H. E. W.
  1973   Mesopotamia's Invisible Exports in the Third Millennium. *World Archaeology* 5: 232–41.

Culican, W.
  1966   *The Ancient Levant: The First Merchant Venturers in History and Commerce.* London: Thames and Hudson.

Curry, N.
  1981   *Euripides: The Trojan Women, Helen, the Bacchae.* Cambridge: Cambridge University.

Curtis, J. E.
   1988   Assyria as a Bronzeworking Centre in the Late Assyrian Period. Pp. 83–96 in *Bronze-Working Centres of Western Asia*, ed. J. E. Curtis. London: Kegan Paul International in association with the British Museum.

Curtis, J. E., and Green, A. R.
   1986   Preliminary Report on Excavations at Khirbet Khatuniyeh, 1985. Pp. 73–77 in *Researches on the Antiquities of Saddam Dam Basin Salvage and Other Researches*. Baghdad.

Dalley, S.
   1984   *Mari and Karana: Two Old Babylonian Cities*. Ch. 4: Food and Drink. London: Longman.

Dalley, S., and Postgate, J. N.
   1984   *The Tablets from Fort Shalmaneser*. Cuneiform Texts from Nimrud 3. London: British School of Archaeology in Iraq.

Dalley, S.; Walker, C. B. F.; and Hawkins, J. D.
   1976   *The Old Babylonian Tablets from Tell al-Rimah*. London: British School of Archaeology in Iraq.

Dalton, G.
   1977   Aboriginal Economies in Stateless Societies. Pp. 191–212 in *Exchange Systems in Prehistory*, eds. T. K. Earle and J. E. Ericson. New York: Academic.

Daniels, J.
   1941   Prolegomena to the Cypro-Minoan Script. *American Journal of Archaeology* 45: 249–82.

Darby, W. J.
   1979   The Nutrient Contributions of Fermented Beverages. In *Fermented Food Beverages in Nutrition*, eds. C. F. Gastineau, W. J. Darby, and T. B. Turner. New York: Academic.
   1981   Wine and Medical Wisdom through the Ages. Pp. 125–147 in *Wine, Health and Society: A Symposium*. San Francisco: GRT Book.

Darby, W. J.; Ghalioungui, P.; and Grivetti, L.
   1977   *Food: The Gift of Osiris*. 2 vols. Vol. 2, esp. pp. 551–618. London: Academic.

Dash, V. B., and Kashyap, V. L.
   1987   *Diagnosis and Treatment of Disease in Arurveda*. New Delhi: Concept.

Daux, G.
   1926   Nouvelles inscriptions de Thasos (1921–1924). *Bulletin de Correspondance Hellénique* 50: 211–49.

Davies, N. de G.
   1900   *The Mastaba of Ptahhetep and Akhethetep*. Vol. 1. London: Egypt Exploration Fund.
   1901   *The Mastaba of Ptahhetep and Akhethetep*. Vol. 2. London: Egypt Exploration Fund.
   1913   *Five Theban Tombs*. London: Egypt Exploration Fund.
   1930   *The Tomb of Ken-Amun at Thebes*. Vol. 2. New York: Metropolitan Museum of Art.

Davies, N. de G., and Faulkner, R. O.
   1947   A Syrian Trading Venture to Egypt. *Journal of Egyptian Archaeology* 33: 40–46.

Davies, P. H.
1967 *Vitis L.* Pp. 521–22 in *The Flora of Turkey and the East Aegean Islands*, eds. P. H. Davis, J. Cullen, and M. J. E. Coode. Edinburgh: Edinburgh University.

Davis, E.
1979 *The Vapheio Cups and Aegean Gold and Silver*. New York: Garland.

Debidour, M.
1986 En classant les timbres thasiens. Pp. 311–34 in *Bulletin de Correspondance Hellénique*, suppl. 13: *Recherches sur les amphores grecques*, eds. J.-Y. Empereur and Y. Garlan. Paris: École française d'Athènes.

Debono, F., and Mortensen, B.
1990 *El Omari*. Archäologische Veröffentlichungen 82. Mainz: P. von Zabern.

Dechandol, H.; Feuillet, P.-P.; and Odiot, Th.
1983 Le grand complexe viticol du Molard. *Histoire-Archéologie-Dossiers* 78: 56–57.

de Genouillac, H.
1934 *Fouilles de Tello*. Vol. 1. Paris: P. Geuthner.

Deimel, A.
1925 Die altšumerische Baumwirtschaft. *Orientalia* 16: 1–87.

de Jesus, P. S.
1980 *The Development of Prehistoric Mining and Metallurgy in Anatolia*. British Archaeological Reports, International Series 74. Oxford: British Archaeological Reports.

De Lattin, G.
1939 Über den Ursprung und die Verbreitung der Reben. *Der Züchter* 11: 217–25.

Deller, K.
1985 SAG.DU UR. MAḪ, Löwenkopfsitula, Löwenkopfbecher. *Baghdader Mitteilungen* 16: 327–46.

del Monte, G. F., and Tischler, J.
1978 *Répertoire géographique des textes cunéiformes*. Vol. 6: *Die Orts- und Gewässernamen der hethitischen Texte*. Wiesbaden: D. L. Reichert.

De Luca, J. A.
1979 The Wine Industry and Changing Attitudes of Americans: An Overview. Pp. 187–94 in *Fermented Food Beverages in Nutrition*, eds. C. F. Gastineau, W. J. Darby, and T. B. Turner. New York: Academic.

Demakopoulou, E.
1982 *To Mykenaiko Iero sto Amyklaio kai i YE IIIC Periodou sti Lakonia*. Athens: privately published.

Demakopoulou, K., ed.
1988 *The Mycenaean World: Five Centuries of Early Greek Culture, 1600–1100 B.C.* Athens: National Hellenic Committee.

Demakopoulou, K., and Konsola, D.
1981 *Archaeological Museum of Thebes*. Athens: General Direction of Antiquities and Restoration.

Demirji, M. S., ed.
  1987   *Researches on the Antiquities of the Saddam Dam Basin Salvage and Other Researches.* Baghdad: State Organization of Antiquities and Heritage.

Denton, K., and Krebs, B.
  1990   From the Scene of the Crime: The Effect of Alcohol and Social Context on Moral Judgment. *Journal of Personality and Social Psychology* 59: 242–48.

Desbat, A., and Picon, M.
  1989   Ateliers lyonnais: succursales de potiers italiens et imitation d'amphores. *Le courrier du CNRS* 73: 49–51.

Deshayes, J.
  1953   Les Vases mycéniens de la Deiras (Argos). *Bulletin de Correspondance Hellénique* 77: 59–89.

Despois, J.
  1961   Development of Land Use in North Africa, with Reference to Spain. Pp. 219–37 in *A History of Land Use in Arid Regions*, ed. L. D. Stamp. UNESCO Arid Zone Research, no. 17. Paris: UNESCO.

Despois, J., and Raynal, R.
  1967   *Géographie de l'Afrique du nord-ouest.* Paris: Payot.

de St. Denis, E.
  1943   *Falx vinitoria. Revue Archéologigue* 41: 163–76.

Dever, W. G.
  1987   The Middle Bronze Age: The Zenith of the Urban Canaanite Era. *Biblical Archaeologist* 50: 148–77.

Dewdney, J. C.
  1971   *Turkey: An Introductory Geography.* New York: Praeger.

Dickinson, O.
  1977   *The Origins of Mycenaean Civilisation.* Studies in Mediterranean Archaeology 49. Göteborg: P. Åström.

Dietler, M.
  1990   Driven by Drink: The Role of Drinking in the Political Economy and the Case of Early Iron Age France. *Journal of Anthropological Archaeology* 9: 358–72.

Dietrich, M., and Loretz, O.
  1969   Die soziale Struktur von Alalakh und Ugarit (V): Die Weingarten Gebietes von Alalakh im 15. Jahrhundert. *Ugarit-Forschungen* 1: 37–64.

Dietz, S.
  1980   Asine II. *Results of the Excavations East of the Acropolis, 1970–1974*, fasc. 2: *The Middle Helladic Cemetery, The Middle Helladic and Early Mycenaean Deposits.* Stockholm: Swedish Institute at Athens.

Dossin, G.
  1978   *Correspondence féminine.* Archives Royales de Mari 10. Paris: Librairie Orientaliste P. Geuthner.

Doumas, C.
  1983   *Thera: Pompeii of the Ancient Aegean, Excavations at Akrotiri 1967–1969.* London: Thames and Hudson.

Duell
1938   *The Mastaba of Mereruka*. Vol. 2. Chicago: University of Chicago.

Dunham, S.
1989   Metal Animal Headed Cups at Mari. Pp. 213–20 in *To the Euphrates and Beyond: Archaeological Studies in Honour of Maurits N. van Loon*, eds. O. M. C. Haex, H. H. Curvers, and P. M. M. G. Akkermans. Rotterdam: A. A. Balkema.

du Plat Taylor, J.
1957   *Myrtou-Pigadhes: A Late Bronze Age Sanctuary in Cyprus*. Oxford: Ashmolean Museum.

Durand, J.-M.
1983   Textes concernant le vin. Pp. 104–19 in *Textes administratifs des salles 134 et 160 du palais de Mari*. Archives Royales de Mari 21. Paris: Librairie Orientaliste P. Geuthner.

Dyson, R. H., Jr.
1987   The Relative and Absolute Chronology of Hissar II and the Proto-Elamite Horizon of Northern Iran. Pp. 647–78 in *Chronologies in the Near East*, eds. O. Aurenche, J. Evin, and F. Hours. British Archaeological Reports. International Series 379. Oxford: British Archaeological Reports.

Ebeling, E.
1927   *Keilschrifttexte aus Assur juristischen Inhalts*. Leipzig: O. Zeller.

Eddy, R.
1887   *Alcohol in History: An Account of Intemperance in All Ages*. New York: National Temperance Society.

Edwards, I. E. S.
1964   The Early Dynastic Period in Egypt. Pp. 3–74 in *The Cambridge Ancient History*. 2nd rev. ed. London: Cambridge University.

Edwards, R. B.
1979   *Kadmos the Phoenician: A Study in Greek Legends and the Mycenaean Age*. Amsterdam: Adolf M. Hakkert.

Eegriwe, E.
1933   Reaktionen und Reagenzien zum Nachweis organischer Verbindungen II. *Zeitschrift für Analytische Chemie* 95: 323–27.

Ehelof, H.
1933   Heth. *milit* = "Honig." *Orientalistische Literaturzeitung* 33: 2–7.

Eichmann, R.
1986   Die Steingeräte aus dem "Riemchengebäude" in Uruk-Warka. *Baghdader Mitteilungen* 17: 97–130.

el-Fakharani, F.
1983   Recent Excavations at Marea in Egypt. Pp. 175–86 in *Das Römisch-Byzantinische Ägypten: Akten des internationalen Symposions 26–30 September 1978 in Trier*. Aegyptiaca Treverensia 2, ed. E. Winter. Mainz: P. von Zabern.

Ellis, R.
1882   *The Wine Question in the Light of the New Dispensation*. New York: private publication.

Emerson, E. R.
  1908   *Beverages, Past and Present*. New York: G. P. Putnam's Sons.

Emery, W. B.
  1961   *Archaic Egypt*. Harmondsworth: Penguin; reprint ed., 1987.

Emery, W. B.; James T. G. H.; Klasens, A.; Anderson, R.; and Burney, C. A.
  1954   *Great Tombs of the First Dynasty*. Vol. 2. London: Egypt Exploration Society.

Empereur, J.-Y.
  1982   Les anses d'amphores timbres et les amphores: Aspects quantitatifs. *Bulletin de Corre-spondance Hellénique*. 106: 219–33.

Englund, R. K., and Grégoire, J.-P.
  1991   *The Proto-Cuneiform Texts from Jemdet Nasr*. Berlin: Gebr. Mann.

Enjalbert, H. and B.
  1987   *History of Wine and the Vine*. Paris: Éditions Bardi.

Ergenzinger, P.J., Frey, W.; and Kühne, H.
  1988   The reconstruction of environment, irrigation, and development of settlement in the Habur of NE Syria. *Environmental Archaeology*, pp. 109–28

Erinç, S.
  1950   Climatic Types and the Variation of Moisure Regimes in Turkey. *Geographical Review*, pp. 224–35.
  1978   Changes in the Physical Environment of Turkey Since the Last Glacial. Pp. 87–110 in *The Environmental History of the Near and Middle East*, ed. W. C. Brice. London: Academic.

Esin, U.
  1982   Die kulturellen Beziehungen zwischen Ostanatolien und Mesopotamien sowie Syrien anhand einiger Grabung und Oberflachfunde aus dem oberen Euphrattal im 4. Jt. v. Chr. Pp. 13–22 in *Mesopotamien und Seine Nachbarn*, eds. H.-J. Nissen and J. Renger. Berlin: D. Reimer.

Evans, A.
  1909   *Scripta Minoa I*. Oxford: Oxford University.
  1921   *The Palace of Minos at Knossos*. Vol. 1. London: Macmillan.
  1935   *The Palace of Minos at Knossos*. Vol. 4, pt. 2. London: Macmillan.

Evans, J.
  1990   Come Back King Alfred, All is Forgiven. Pp. 7–9 in *Organic Contents of Ancient Vessels: Materials Analysis and Archaeological Investigation*, eds. W. R. Biers and P. E. McGovern. MASCA Research Papers in Science and Archaeology 7. Philadelphia: MASCA, The University Museum of Archaeology and Anthropology.

Evins, M. A.
  1989   The Late Chalcolithic/Uruk Period in the Karababa Basin, Southeastern Turkey. In "Out of the Heartland: The Evolution of Complexity in Peripheral Mesopotamia During the Uruk Period, Workshop Summary," ed. M. Rothman. *Paléorient* 15: 270–71.

Eylaud, J.-M.
  1960   *Vin et santé: Vertus hygièniques et thérapeutiques du vin.* Soissons: La Diffusion Nouvelle du Livre.

Fairman, H. W.
  1951   The Inscriptions. In *The City of Akhenaten.* Part 3: *Central City and the Official Quarters* by J. D. S. Pendlebury. 2 vols. Egypt Exploration Society, mem. 44. London: Egypt Exploration Society.

Fales, F. M., and Postgate, J. N.
  1992   *Imperial Administration Records.* Part I: *Palace and Temple Administration.* States Archives of Assyria VII. Helsinki.

Fantar, M.
  1984   *Kerkouane: Cité punique du cap Bon (Tunisie), I.* Tunis: Institut national d'archéologie et d'art.
  1985   *Kerkouane: Cité punique du cap Bon (Tunisie), II.* Tunis: Institut national d'archéologie et d'art.
  1986   *Kerkouane: Cité punique du cap Bon (Tunisie), III.* Tunis: Institut national d'archéologie et d'art.

Farkaš, J.
  1988   *Technology and Biochemistry of Wine.* 2 vols. New York: Gordon and Breach.

Faulkner, R. O.
  1962   *Concise Dictionary of Middle Egyptian.* Oxford: Griffith Institute.
  1969   *The Ancient Egyptian Pyramid Texts.* Oxford: Oxford University.

Feigl, F.; Anger, V.; and Oesper, R. E.
  1966   *Spot Tests in Organic Analysis.* 7th ed. New York: Elsevier.

Ferron, J., and Pinard, M.
  1960–1 *Les fouilles de Byrsa* (suite). Cahiers de Byrsa 9. Paris: Librairie orientaliste P. Geuthner.

Finet, A.
  1964   Lettres de Iawi-Ilâ. Pp. 137–56 in *Textes divers*, eds. G. Dossin et al. Archives Royales de Mari 13. Paris: Ministère des Affaires Étranger/P. Geuthner.
  1969   L'Euphrate, route commerciale de la Mesopotamie. *Annales Archéologiques Arabes Syriennes* 19: 37–48.
  1974–77 Le vin à Mari. *Archiv für Orientforschung* 25: 122–31.
  1985   Le Port d'Emar sur l'Euphrate, entre le royaume de Mari et le pays de Canaan. Pp. 27–38 in *The Land of Israel: Crossroads of Civilization.* Orientalia Lovaniensia Analecta 19. Leuven: Peeters.

Finkbeiner, U.
  1987   Uruk-Warka, 1983–1984. *Archiv für Orientforschung* 34: 140–44.

Fiorani, E., and Fedecostante, R.
  1981   *Vini Medicinali.* Milan: Erboristeria Domani-Libri.

Fischer, F.
  1963   *Die Hethitische Keramik von Boğazköy.* Berlin: Gebr. Mann.

Fischer, P. M.
  1991a   Canaanite Pottery from Hala Sultan Tekke: An Analysis with Secondary Ion Mass
          Spectrometry. Pp. 152–61 in *Bronze Age Trade in the Mediterranean*, ed. N. H. Gale.
          Jonesered: P. Åström.
  1991b   Canaanite Pottery from Hala Sultan Tekke: Traditional Classification and Micro Col-
          our Analysis (MCA). Pp. 73–80 in *Cypriot Ceramics: Reading the Prehistoric Past*,
          eds. J. A. Barlow, D. L. Bolger, and B. Kling. University Museum Symposium Series
          2, University Museum Monograph 74. Philadelphia: A. G. Levantis Foundation and
          University of Pennsylvania Museum.

Fisher, W. B.
  1978   *The Middle East: A Physical, Social, and Regional Geography.* 7th ed. London:
          Methuen.

Fitzgerald, R.
  1963   *The Odyssey of Homer.* Garden City, NY: Anchor.

Follieri, M., and Coccolini, G. B. L.
  1983   Palaeoethnobotanical Study of the VI A and VI B Periods of Arslantepe (Malatya,
          Turkey): Preliminary Report. *Origini, Preistoria e Protoistoria delle Civittà Antiche*
          12: 599–617.

Forbes, H.
  1982   Strategies and Soils: Technology, Production and Environment in the Peninsula of
          Methana, Greece. Unpublished Ph.D. dissertation, University of Pennsylvania.

Forbes, R. J.
  1955   *Studies in Ancient Technology*, 9 vols. Leiden: E. J. Brill.
  1965   *Studies in Ancient Technology.* Vol. 3. 2nd ed. Leiden: E. J. Brill.

Formenti, F.; Hesnard, A.; and Tchernia, A.
  1978   Une amphore "Lamboglia 2" contenant du vin dans l'épave de la Madrague de Giens.
          Archaeonautica 2: 95–100.

Frankena, R.
  1966   *Briefe aus dem British Museum.* Altbabylonische Briefe in Umschrift und
          Übersetzung, vol. 2. Leiden: E. J. Brill.
  1974   *Briefe aus dem Berliner Museum.* Altbabylonische Briefe in Umschrift und
          Übersetzung, vol. 6. Leiden: E. J. Brill.

Frankfort, H.
  1970   *The Art and Architecture of the Ancient Orient.* Harmondsworth: Penguin.

French, D. H.
  1972   Excavations at Can Hasan III 1969–1970. Pp. 181–90 in *Papers in Economic Prehis-
          tory*, ed. E. S. Higgs. Cambridge: Cambridge University.

French, E. B.
  1985   The Figures and Figurines. Pp. 209–80 in *The Archaeology Cult: The Sanctuary at
          Phylakopi*, by C. Renfrew, suppl. vol. 18. London: British School of Archaeology.
  1990   Archaeology in Greece 1989–90. Pp. 3–82 in *Archaeological Reports for 1989–1990.*
          London: British School at Athens.

Frey, D.; Hentschel, F. D.; and Keith, D. H.
1978   Deepwater Archaeology: The Capistello Wreck Excavation, Lipari, Aeolian Islands. *International Journal of Nautical Archaeology and Underwater Exploration* 7: 279–300.

Friedman, J., and Rowlands, M.
1977   Notes Towards an Epigenetic Model of the Evolution of "Civilisation." Pp. 201–76 in *The Evolution of Social Systems*, eds. J. Friedman and M. Rowlands. London: Duckworth.

Friedrich, J.
1952   *Hethitische Wörterbuch.* Heidelberg: C. Winter.
1959   *Die hethitische Gesetze.* Documenta et Monumenta Orientis Antiqui 7. Leiden: E. J. Brill.

Furumark, A.
1941   *The Chronology of Mycenaean Pottery.* Stockholm: Kungl. Vitterhets Historie och Antikvitets Akademian.
1972   *Mycenaean Pottery.* Vol. 1: *Analysis and Classification.* Stockholm: Swedish Institute at Athens.

Gale, N. H., ed.
1991   *Bronze Age Trade in the Mediterranean.* Papers Presented at the Conference held at Rewley House, Oxford, in December 1989. Jonesered: P. Åström.

Gallagher, D. A. and I. J., trans.
1966   *Saint Augustine: The Catholic and Manichaean Ways of Life.* Washington, DC: The Catholic University of America.

Gardiner, A. H.
1947   *Ancient Egyptian Onomastica.* London: Oxford University.
1957   *Egyptian Grammar.* 3rd ed. Oxford: Oxford University.

Garlan, Y.
1983   Greek Amphorae and Trade. Pp. 27–35 in *Trade in the Ancient Economy*, eds. P. Garnsey, K. Hopkins, and C. R. Whittaker. Berkeley: University of California.
1986   Quelques nouveaux ateliers amphoriques à Thasos. Pp. 201–76 in *Bulletin de Correspondance Hellénique*, suppl. 13: *Recherches sur les amphores grecques*, eds. J.-Y. Empereur and Y. Garlan. Paris: École française d'Athènes.
1988   Vin et amphores de Thasos. *Sites et monuments* 5. Athens: École française d'Athènes.

Gastineau, C. F.; Darby, W. J.; and Turner, T. B., eds.
1979   *Fermented Food Beverages in Nutrition.* New York: Academic.

Gates, M.-H.
1988   Dialogues between Ancient Near Eastern Texts and the Archaeological Record: Test Cases from Bronze Age Syria. *Bulletin of the American Schools of Oriental Research* 270: 63–91.

Gelb, I. J.
1982   Terms for Slaves in Ancient Mesopotamia. Pp. 81–98 in *Societies and Languages of the Ancient Near East: Studies in Honor of I. M. Diakonoff.* Warminster, Eng.: Aris and Phillips.

George, A. R.
1990   Royal Tombs at Nimrud. *Minerva* 1: 29–31.

Gérard-Rousseau, M.
    1968   *Les mentions religieuses dans les tablettes myceniennes.* Incunabula Graeca 29. Rome: Edizioni dell'Ateneo.

Gerhardt, K. O.; Searles, S.; and Biers, W. R.
    1990   Corinthian Figure Vases: Extraction Studies and Gas Chromotagraphy–Mass Spectrometry of Organic Remains. Pp. 41–50 in *Organic Contents of Ancient Vessels: Materials Analysis and Archaeological Investigation*, eds. W. R. Biers and P. E. McGovern. MASCA Research Papers in Science and Archaeology 7. Philadelphia: MASCA, The University Museum of Archaeology and Anthropology.

Germer, R.
    1985   *Flora des pharaonisches Ägypten.* Mainz: P. von Zabern.

Gianfrotta, P. G., and Pomey, P.
    1981   *Archeologia subacquea.* Milan: A. Mondadori.

Gill, M.
    1964   The Minoan Genius. *Athenische Mitteilungen* 79: 1–21.

Godart, L., and Olivier, J.-P.
    1985   *Recueil des inscriptions en Linéaire A.* Etudes Crétoises, vol. 21, 5. Paris: P. Geuthner.

Godeckin, K. B.
    1976   *Eine Betrachtung der Inschriften des Meten im Rahmen der sozialen und rechtlichen Stellung von Privatleuten im ägyptichen Alten Reich.* Wiesbaden: O. Harrassowitz.

Godley, A. D.
    1920   *Herodotus with an English Translation.* Vol. 1. London: W. Heinemann; reprinted with corrections, 1960.

Goedicke, H.
    1967   Admonitions 3, 6–10. *Journal of the American Research Center in Egypt* 6: 93–95.

Goetze [Götze], A.
    1940   *Kizzuwatna and the Problem of Hittite Geography.* Yale Oriental Series Researches 22. New Haven: Yale University.
    1969a   Laws from Mesopotamia and Asia Minor: The Hittite Laws. Pp. 188–97 in *Ancient Near Eastern Texts Relating to the Old Testament*, ed. J. B. Pritchard, 3rd ed., with supplement. Princeton: Princeton University.
    1969b   *Die Annalen des Muršukuš.* Darmstadt: Wissenschaftliche Buchgesellschaft.

Goldy, R. G.; Ballinger, W. E.; and Maness, E. P.
    1986   Fruit Anthocyanin Content of Some *Euvitis-Vitis rotundifolia* Hybrids. *Journal of the American Society of Horticultural Science* 111: 955–60.

Gonen, R.
    1984   Urban Canaan in the Late Bronze Age. *Bulletin of the American Schools of Oriental Research* 253: 61–73.

Goor, A., and Nuruck, M.
    1968   *The Fruits of the Holy Land.* Jerusalem: Israel University.

Gordon, C.
    1964   Notes on Linear A. Pp. 183–86 in *Mycenaean Studies*, ed. E. L. Bennett, Jr. Proceedings of the Third Colloquium for Mycenaean Studies held at "Wingspread," 4–8 September 1961. Madison, WI: University of Wisconsin.

1965   *The Common Background of Greek and Hebrew Civilizations*. New York: W. W. Norton.

Gorny, R.
1989   Environment, Archaeology and History in Hittite Anatolia. *Biblical Archaeologist* 52: 78–96.
1990   Alişar Höyük in the Second Millennium B.C. Unpublished Ph.D. dissertation, University of Chicago.

Gow, A. S. F., ed.
1952   *Theocritus*. Vol. 2. Cambridge: Cambridge University.

Grace, V. R.
1947   Wine Jars (Illustrated). *The Classical Journal* 42: 443–52.
1949   Standard Pottery Containers of the Ancient Greek World. Pp. 175–89 in *Commemorative Studies in Honor of Theodore Leslie Shear*. *Hesperia*, suppl. 8. Princeton: The American School of Classical Studies at Athens.
1956   The Canaanite Jar. Pp. 80–109 in *The Aegean and the Near East: Studies Presented to Hetty Goldman*, ed. S. S. Weinberg. Locust Valley, NY: J. J. Augustin.
1961   *Amphoras and the Ancient Wine Trade*. Picture Book 6, Excavations of the Athenian Agora. Princeton: American School of Classical Studies at Athens.
1974   Revisions in Hellenistic Chronology. *Athenische Mitteilungen* 89: 193–200.
1979   *Amphoras and the Ancient Wine Trade*. Rev. ed. Picture Book 6, Excavations of the Athenian Agora. Princeton: American School of Classical Studies at Athens.
1985   The Middle Stoa Dated by Amphora Stamps. *Hesperia* 54: 1–54.

Grace, V. R., and Savvatianou-Pétropoulakou, M.
1970   *L'îlot de la Maison des Comediens*. Explorations archéologiques de Delos 27. Paris: École française d'Athènes.

Gras, M.; Rouillard, P.; and Texidor, J.
1989   *L'Univers Phénicien*. Paris: Arthaud.

Graves, R.
1988   *The Greek Myths I*. London: Penguin.

Graziadio, G.
1988   The Chronology of the Graves at Circle B at Mycenae: A New Hypothesis. *American Journal of Archaeology* 92: 343–72.

Great Britain, Admiralty, Naval Intelligence Division
1945   *Tunisia*. London: HM Stationery Office.

Green, M. V.
1980   Animal Husbandry at Uruk in the Archaic Period. *Journal of Near Eastern Studies* 39: 1–35.

Green, M. W.
1989   Early Cuneiform. Pp. 43–57 in *The Origins of Writing*, ed. W. M. Senner. Lincoln, NB: University of Nebraska.

Green, M. W., and Nissen, H. J.
1987   *Zeichenliste der Archäischen Texte aus Uruk*. Archäische Texte aus Uruk, vol. 2. Berlin: Gebr. Mann.

Greene, J. A.
1986   Ajlun-Kafranja Archaeological Survey 1986, Preliminary Report. On file at the Department of Antiquities of Jordan Registration Center, Amman, Jordan.
1990   Phoenician "Colonization" and Settlement at Carthage. Paper presented at Carthage Re-Explored: A Symposium, March 30–April 1, Cincinnati Art Museum.
Forth.   *Ager and ᶜArosot: Rural Settlement and Agrarian History in the Carthaginian Countryside*. Redditch: Caradoc.

Greene, J. A., and Kehoe, D. P.
1991   Mago the Carthaginian on Agriculture: Archaeology and the Ancient Sources. Paper presented at the Troisième Congrés International des Etudes phéniciennes et puniques, November 11–16, Tunis.

Grivetti, L. E.
1978   Comments. *Current Anthropology* 18: 298–99.
1981   Cultural Nutrition: Anthropological and Geographical Themes. *Annual Review of Nutrition* 1: 47–68.
1991a–c Nutrition Past—Nutrition Today: Prescientific Origins of Nutrition and Dietetics. Part 1: Legacy of India; Part 2: Legacy of the Mediterranean; Part 3: Legacy of China. *Nutrition Today* 26(1): 13–24; (4): 18–29; (6): 6–17.

Gruner, O. C., trans.
1930   *Ibn Sina's A Treatise on the Canon of Medicine of Avicenna*. London: Luzac.

Gsell, S.
1913   *Histoire ancienne de l'Afrique du Nord*. Vol. 1: *Les conditions du dévelopment historique; Les temps primitif, la colonisation phénicienne et l'empire de Carthage*. Paris: Hachette.
1920   *Histoire ancienne de l'Afrique du Nord*. Vol. 3: *Histoire militaire de Carthage*. Paris: Hachette.

Gulick, C. B., trans.
1927–41 *Athenaeus, The Deipnosophists*. 7 vols. New York: Putnam.
1963   *Athenaeus, The Deipnosophists*. Loeb Classical Library. Cambridge: Harvard University.

Güterbock, H. G.
1968   Oil Plants in Hittite Antolia. *Journal of the American Oriental Society* 88: 66–71.
1989   Marginal Notes on Recent Hittitological Publications. *Journal of Near Eastern Studies* 48: 307–9.

Güterbock, H. G., and Hoffner, H. A.
1990a   (:)lim(m)a. P. 62 in *The Chicago Hittite Dictionary*, vol. 3: L-N. Chicago: Oriental Institute.
1990b   (ᴳᴵˢ)maḫla–. Pp. 112–13 *The Chicago Hittite Dictionary*, vol. 3: L-N. Chicago: Oriental Institute.
1990c   *marnuwa-, marnuwant-*. Pp. 193–95 in *The Chicago Hittite Dictionary*, vol. 3: L-N. Chicago: Oriental Institute.
1990d   *milit-*. Pp. 250–52 in *The Chicago Hittite Dictionary*, vol. 3: L-N. Chicago: Oriental Institute.
1990e   *muri-, murin-, muriyan-*. P. 333 in *The Chicago Hittite Dictionary*, vol. 3: L-N. Chicago: Oriental Institute.

1990f   *nink-, nik-*. Pp. 443–45 in *The Chicago Hittite Dictionary*, vol. 3: L-N. Chicago: Oriental Institute.

Gwatkin, W. E.
1930   Cappadocia as a Roman Procuratorial Province. *University of Missouri Studies* 4: 1–66.

Haas, V.
1988   Magie in Hethitische Gärten. Pp. 121–42 in *Documentum Asiae Minoris Antiquae*. Festschrift für H. Otten zum 75. Geburstag. Wiesbaden: O. Harrassowitz.

Habachi, L.
1972   *The Second Stele of Kamose*. Abhandlungen des Deutschen Archäologischen Instituts, Kairo, Ägyptologische Reihe 8. Gluckstadt: J. J. Augustin.

Hadjicosti, M.
1988   Canaanite Jars from Maa-Palaikastro. Pp. 340–85 in *Excavations at Maa-Palaikastro 1979–1986* by V. Karageorghis amd M. Demas. Nicosia: Department of Antiquities.

Hadjisavvas, S.
1986   Alassa: A New Late Cypriote Site. Pp. 62–67 in *Report of the Department of Antiquities of Cyprus*. Cyprus: Department of Antiquities.

Haelbeck, H.
1959   Archaeology and Agricultural Botany. Pp. 44–59 in *Institute of Archaeology, Annual Report 9*. London: University of London.
1960   The Paleobotany of the Near East and Europe. Pp. 99–118 in *Prehistoric Investigations in Iraqi Kurdistan*. Studies in Ancient Oriental Civilizations, no. 3, eds. R. J. Braidwood and B. Howe. Chicago: University of Chicago.
1961   Late Bronze Age and Byzantine Crops at Beycesultan in Anatolia. *Anatolian Studies* 11: 77–97.

Haevernick, Th. E.
1963   Beiträge zur Geschichte des antiken Glases: X. Römischer Wein. *Jahresband des Römische–Germanische Zentralmuseum* 10: 118–22.
1967   Römischer Wein? *Acta Archaeologica* 19: 15–23.

Hägg, R.
1985   Pictorial Programmes in Minoan Palaces and Villas. Pp. 209–17 in *L'iconographie minoénne. Bulletin Correspondance Hellénique*, suppl. 11, ed. O Picard. Paris: École française d'Athènes.
1990   The Role of Livarions in Mycenaean Ceremony and Cult. In *Celebrations of Death and Divinity in the Bronze Age Argolid*, eds. R. Hägg and G. Nordquist. Stockholm: Swedish Institute at Athens.

Hahn, E.
1976   *The Cooking of China*. New York: Time–Life.

Hairfield, H. H. and E. M.
1990   Identification of a Late Bronze Age Resin. *Analytical Chemistry* 62: 41–45.

Haldane, C. W.
1990   Shipwrecked Plant Remains. *Biblical Archaeologist* 53(1): 55–60.

Haller, A.
  1954   *Die Gräber und Grüfte von Assur.* Wissenschaftliche Veröffentlichungen der Deut-
         scher Orient-Gesellschaft 65. Berlin: Deutsches Orient-Gesellschaft.

Hamilton, R. W.
  1966   A Silver Bowl in the Ashmolean Museum. *Iraq* 28: 1–17.

Hammond, S. M., and Carr, J. G.
  1976   The Antimicrobial Activity of SO_2 — With Particular Reference to Fermented and
         Non-Fermented Fruit Juices. *Society for Applied Bacteriology Symposium Series* 5:
         89–110.

Hankerson, F. P.
  1947   *The Cooperage Handbook.* Brooklyn: Chemical.

Hankey, V., and Leonard, A., Jr.
  Forth. *Egypt and the Levant: Aegean Imports in the 2nd Millennium B.C. Tübinger Atlas des
         Vorderen Orients,* Sonderforschungbericht 19. Tübingen: University of Tübingen.

Hansen, D. P.
  1980–83 Lagaš. Pp. 426–30 in *Reallexikon der Assyriologie und Vorderasiatischen Archäologie,*
         vol. 6, eds. D. O. Edzard et al. Berlin: W. de Gruyter.

Hansen, J. M.
  1978   The Earliest Seed Remains in Greece: Palaeolithic through Neolithic at the Franchthi
         Cave. *Berichte der Deutschen Gesellschaft* 91: 39–46.
  1988   Agriculture in the Prehistoric Aegean: Data Versus Speculations. *American Journal of
         Archaeology* 92: 39–52.
  1992   *The Palaeoethnobotany of the Franchthi Cave.* Bloomington, IN: Indiana University.

Haran, M.
  1958   The Bas-Reliefs on the Sarcophagus of Ahiram, King of Byblos. *Israel Exploration
         Journal* 8: 15–25.

Harden, D. B.
  1927   Punic Urns from the Precinct of Tanit at Carthage. *American Journal of Archaeology*
         31: 297–310.
  1937   The Pottery from the Precinct of Tanit at Salammbô, Carthage. *Iraq* 4: 59–89.
  1971   *The Phoenicians.* Revised ed. New York: Penguin.

Harding, A. F.
  1984   *The Mycenaeans and Europe.* London: Academic.

Hawkins, D.
  1982   The Neo-Hittite States in Syria and Anatolia. Pp. 372–441 in *Cambridge Ancient
         History,* vol. 3, pt. 1, eds. J. Boardman I. E. S. Edwards, N. G. L. Hammond, and E.
         Sollberger. Cambridge: Cambridge University.

Hawkins, J. D.
  1986   Royal Statements of Ideal Prices: Assyrian, Babylonian, and Hittite. Pp. 93–102 in
         *Ancient Anatolia, Aspects of Change and Cultural Development: Essays in Honor of
         Machteld J. Mellink,* eds. J. V. Canby, E. Porada, B. Ridgeway, and T. Stech. Madison:
         University of Wisconsin.

Hawkins, J. D.; Morpurgo-Davies, A.; and Neumann, G.
   1974   *Hittite Hieroglyphics and Luwian: New Evidence for the Connection.* Göttingen: Vandenhoeck and Ruprecht.

Hayes, W. C.
   1951   Inscriptions from the Palace of Amenhotep III. *Journal of Near Eastern Studies* 10: 35–56, 82–111, 157–83, and 231–42.
   1966   *Most Ancient Egypt.* Chicago: University of Chicago.

Hehn, V.
   1911   *Kulturpflanzen und Haustiere I.* no place: no publisher.

Heinrich, E.
   1936   *Kleinfunde aus den archäischen Tempelschichten in Uruk.* Leipzig: O. Harrassowitz.
   1937   Die Grabung im Planquadrat K XVII. *Vorläufiger Bericht über die von der Deutschen Forschungsgemeinschaft in Uruk-Warka unternommenen Ausgrabungen* 8: 27–55.
   1938   Grabungen im Gebiet des Anu-Antum-Tempels. *Vorläufiger Bericht über die von der Deutschen Forschungsgemeinschaft in Uruk-Warka unternommenen Ausgrabungen* 9: 9–30.
   1982   *Die Tempel und Heiligtümer in Alten Mesopotamien.* Berlin: W. de Gruyter.
   1984   *Dis Paläste im alten Mesopotamien.* Berlin: W. de Gruyter.

Helbaek, H.
   1948   Les empreintes de céréales. Pp. 205–07 in *Hama: Fouilles et recherches de la Foundation Carlsberg 1931–1938*, vol. 2, pt. 3: *Les Cimitières à crémation* by P. J. Riis. Nationalmuseets Skrifter, Større Beretninger, vol. 1. Copenhagen: National Museum.
   1966   What Farming Produced at Cypriote Kalopsidha. Pp. 115–26 in *Excavations at Kalopsida and Ayios Iakovos in Cyprus*, by P. Åström. Studies in Mediterranean Archaeology 2. Lund: P. Åström.

Helck, W., and Otto, E., eds.
   1986   *Lexikon der Ägyptologie.* Vol. 6. Wiesbaden: O. Harrassowitz.

Held, S.
   1984   *Wein als Gesundbrunnen: Ein Kompendium über die Naturheilkräfte des Weines.* Ronsberg: Epikur.

Heltzer, M.
   1985   The Late Bronze Age Service System and Its Decline. Pp. 7–18 in *The Land of Israel: Crossroads of Civilization.* Orientalia Lovaniensia Analecta 19. Leuven: Peeters.

Henrichs, A.
   1987   Myth Visualized: Dionysos and His Circle in Sixth-Century Attic Vase-Painting. Pp. 92–124 in *Papers on the Amasis Painter and His World*, eds. J. Walsh and M. True. Malibu, CA: J. P. Getty Museum.

Henrickson, E. F., and McDonald, M. M. A.
   1983   Ceramic Form and Function: An Ethnographic Search and an Archaeological Application. *American Anthropologist* 85: 640–43.

Hepper, F. N.
   1990   *Pharaoh's Flowers: The Botanical Treasures of Tutankhamun.* London: H. M. S. O.

Hermann, G.
   1968   Lapis Lazuli: The Early Phases of its Trade. *Iraq* 30: 21–57.

Herodotus
  1922   *Herodotus.* The Loeb Classical Library, vol. 3, bks. I–II, trans. A. D. Godley. London: St. Edwardsburg; 1990 reprint.

Hesnard, A.
  1977   Notes sur un atelier d'amphores Dr. 1 et Dr. 2–4 près de Terracine. *Mefra (Mélanges de l'École française de Rome: Antiquité)* 89: 157–68.

Hesnard, A., et al.
  1988   L'épave romaine du Grand Ribaud D (Hyères, Var). *Archaeonautica* 8.

Hide, C. M.
  1990   Archaeobotanical Remains from Tell es-Sweyhat, Northwest Syria. MASCA Ethnobotanical Report 7, unpublished ms. on file, Museum Applied Science Center for Archaeology, University Museum, University of Pennsylvania.

Hiller, S.
  1984   Fruchtbaumkulturen auf Kreta und in Pylos. Pp. 171–201 in *Res Mycenaeae*. Akten des VII. Internationalen mykenologischen Colloquiums 1981, eds. A. Heubeck and G. Neumann. Göttingen: Vandenhoeck and Ruprecht.

Hillman, G.
  1975   The Plant Remains from Tell Abu Hureyra: A Preliminary Report. Appendix in The Excavations of Tell Abu Hureyra in Syria: A Preliminary Report by A. M. T. Moore. *Proceedings of the Prehistoric Society* 41: 70–73.

Hitchner, R. B., and Mattingly, D. J.
  1991   The Fruits of Empire: The Production of Olive Oil in Roman Africa. *National Geographic Research and Exploration* 7: 36–55.

Hobhouse, H.
  1991   New World, Vineyard to the Old. In *Seeds of Change: A Quincentennial Commemoration*, eds. H. J. Viola and C. Margolis. Washington, DC: Smithsonian Institution.

Hoffner, H.
  1963   The Laws of the Hittites. Unpublished Ph.D. dissertation, Brandeis University.
  1967   An English–Hittite Glossary. *Revue hittite et asianique* 80: 17–18.
  1968   A Hittite Text in Epic Style about Merchants. *Journal of Cuneiform Studies* 22: 34–45.
  1974a   *Alimenta Hethaeorum: Food Production in Hittite Asia Minor.* American Oriental Series, vol. 55. New Haven: American Oriental Society.
  1974b   The ARZANA House. *Anatolian Studies Presented to Hans Gustav Güterbock on the Occasion of His 65th Birthday*, eds. K. Bittel, Ph. H. J. ten Cate, and E. Reiner. Istanbul: Nederlands Historisch-Archaeologisch Instituut in Het Nabije Oosten.
  1990   *Hittite Myths.* Atlanta: Scholars.

Holmes, Y. L.
  1975   Foreign Trade of Cyprus during the Late Bronze Age. Pp. 97–109 in *The Archaeology of Cyprus*. Park Ridge, NJ: Noyes.

Homer
  1961   *The Iliad.* Trans. R. Lattimore. Chicago: University of Chicago.

Hooker, J. T.
  1976   *Mycenaean Greece.* London: Routledge and Kegan Paul.
  1980   *Linear B: An Introduction.* Bristol: Bristol Classical.

Hooper, W. D., and Ash, H. B., trans.
1934 *Varro, On Agriculture.* Cambridge: Harvard University.

Hope, C.
1977 *Jar Sealings and Amphorae of the 18th Dynasty: A Technological Study.* Excavations at Malkata and the Birket Habu 1971–1974, vol. 5. Warminster, Eng.: Aris and Phillips.
1978 *Malkata and the Birket Habu: Jar Sealings and Amphorae.* Warminster, Eng.: Aris and Phillips.
1987 *Egyptian Pottery.* Aylesburg, Eng.: Shire Egyptology.

Hope Simpson, R.
1981 *Mycenaean Greece.* Park Ridge, NJ: Noyes.

Hopf, M.
1961 Pflanzenfunde aus Lerna/Argolis. *Der Züchter* 31: 239–47.
1962 Nutzplanzen vom Lernschen Golf. *Jahrbuch der Römisch-Germanishes Zentralmuseums* 9: 1–19.
1971 Plant Remains from the Athenian Agora: Neolithic to Byzantine. Pp. 267–69 in *The Neolithic and Bronze Ages* by S. A. Immerwahr. The Athenian Agora 13. Princeton: American School of Classical Studies.
1978 Plant Remains. Pp. 64–82 in *Early Arad I: The Chalcolithic Settlement and Early City* by R. Amiran, U. Paran, Y. Shiloh, R. Brown, Y. Tsafrir, and A. Ben-Tor. Jerusalem: Israel Exploration Society.
1983 Jericho Plant Remains. Pp. 576–621 in *Excavations at Jericho*, vol. 5: *The Pottery Phases of the Tell and Other Finds*, eds. K. M. Kenyon and T. A. Holland. London: British School of Archaeology in Jerusalem.
1992 Plant Remains from Boğazköy, Turkey. *Review of Paleobotany and Palynology* (van Zeist Festschrift) 73: 99–104.

Horne, L. C.
1988 The Spacial Organization of Rural Settlement in Khar O Tauran, Iran: An Ethnoarchaeological Case Study. Unpublished Ph.D. dissertation, University of Pennsylvania.

Hornung, E.
1990 *The Valley of the Kings: Horizons of Eternity.* New York: Timken.

Houwink ten Cate, Ph. H. J.
1983 The History of Warfare According to the Hittite Sources: The Annals of Ḫattušili I. *Anatolica* 10: 91–109.

Hulsewe, A. F. P.
1979 *China in Central Asia: The Early Stage, 125 B.C.–A.D. 23.* Leiden: E. J. Brill.

Hurst, H. R., and Stager, L. E.
1978 A Metropolitan Landscape: The Late Punic Port at Carthage. *World Archaeology* 9: 334–46.

Hyams, E.
1965 *Dionysus: A Social History of the Wine Vine.* London: Thames and Hudson.

Immerwahr, H. R.
1992 New Wine in Ancient Wineskins: The Evidence from Attic Vases. *Hesperia* 61: 121–32.

Immerwahr, S. A.
    1971   *Excavations in the Athenian Agora*. Vol. 13: *The Neolithic and Bronze Ages*. Princeton: American School of Classical Studies.
    1977   Mycenaeans at Thera: Some Reflections on the Paintings from the West House. Pp. 173–91 in *Greece and the Eastern Mediterranean in Ancient History and Prehistory*, ed. H. H. Kinzl. New York: W. de Gruyter.
    1990   *Aegean Painting*. College Park, PA: Pennsylvania State University.

James, T. G. H.
    1953   *The Mastaba of Khentika called Ikhekhi*. London: Egypt Exploration Society.
    1985   *Egyptian Painting and Drawing in the British Museum*. London: British Museum.

Joffe, A. H.
    Forth.   Alcohol and Early Complexity in Ancient Western Asia. In *Drinking in the Past: Perspectives on Alcohol and Its Social Roles in Ancient Societies*, ed. M. Dietler. Cambridge: The University Press.

John, C. H. W.
    1901   *An Assyrian Doomsday Book or Liber Censualis of the District around Ḥarran; in the Seventh Century B.C.* Assyriologische Bibliothek, vol. 17. Leipzig: J. C. Hinrichs.

Johnson, H.
    1989   *Vintage: The Story of Wine*. New York: Simon and Schuster.

Jones, G.
    1979   An Analysis of the Plant Remains of Assiros Toumba. Unpublished Masters of Philosophy thesis, University of Cambridge.

Jones, H. L., trans.
    1917–35 Strabo, *Geography*. 8 vols. Cambridge: Harvard University.

Jones, R. E.
    1986   *Greek and Cypriot Pottery: A Review of Scientific Studies*. Fitch Laboratory Occasional Paper 1. Athens: British School at Athens.

Jones, R. E., and Vaughan, S. J.
    1988   A Study of Some Canaanite Jar Fragments from Maa-Palaikastro by Petrographic and Chemical Analysis. Pp. 386–98 in *Excavations at Maa-Palaikastro 1979–1986* by V. Karageorghis and M. Demas. Nicosia: Department of Antiquities.

Julien, C.-A.
    1975   *Histoire de l'Afrique du nord*. Paris: Payot.

Kammenhuber, A.
    1958   Die hethitische Geschichtsschreibung. *Saeculum* 9: 136–55.

Kane, J. P.
    1981   Alcoholic Beverages and High Density Lipoproteins. Pp. 29–38 in *Wine, Health and Society: A Symposium*. San Francisco: GRT Book.

Kanta, A.
    1979   *The Late Minoan III Period in Crete*. Studies in Mediterranean Archaeology 58. Göteborg: P. Åström.

Kaplony, P.
    1963–64 *Die Inschriften der ägyptischen Frühzeit*. 3 vols. and suppl. Wiesbaden: O. Harrassowitz.

Karageorghis, V.
  1957   A Mycenaean Chalice and a Vase Painter. *Annual of the British School at Athens* 52: 38–41.

Karageorghis, V., and Demas, M.
  1984   *Pyla-Kokkinokremos: A Late 13th Century B.C. Fortified Settlement in Cyprus.* Nicosia: Department of Antiquities.
  1988   *Excavations at Maa-Palaikastro 1979–1986.* Nicosia: Department of Antiquities.
  1991   *The Coroplastic Art of Ancient Cyprus.* 2 vols. Nicosia: A. G. Leventis Foundation

Kardara, C.
  1967   *Aplomata Naxou.* Athens: Archaeological Society.

Karo, G.
  1930–33 Die Schachtgräber von Mykenai. Munich: F. Bruckmann.

Kassis, H. E.
  1983   *A Concordance of the Qur'an.* Berkeley: University of California.

Katz, S. H., and Voigt, M. M.
  1986   Bread and Beer: The Early Use of Cereals in the Human Diet. *Expedition* 28: 23–34.

Katzev, M. L.
  1978   Cyprus Underwater Archaeological Search, 1969. Pp. 289–305 in *National Geographic Society Research Reports: 1969 Projects.* Washington, DC: National Geographic Society.

Katzev, S. W. and M. L.
  1974   The Last Harbor for the Oldest Ship. *National Geographic* 146: 618–25.

Keller, M.
  1859   The Grapes and Wine of Los Angeles. Report of the Commissioner of Patents for the year 1858, Washington, DC.

Kelly-Buccellati, M.
  1974   The Early Trans-Caucasian Culture: Geographical and Chronological Interaction. Unpublished Ph.D. dissertation, University of Chicago.

Kent, J. H.
  1953   Stamped Amphora Handles from the Delian Temple Estates. Pp. 127–34 in *Studies Presented to David Moore Robinson*, vol. 2, eds. G. E. Mylonas and D. Raymond. St. Louis: Washington University.

Kenyon, K. M.
  1979   *Archaeology in the Holy Land.* 4th ed. London: E. Benn.

Kepinsky, C., and Lebeau, O.
  1985   Une fortresse sur l'Euphrate. *Archéologia* 205: 46–55.

Kerr, N. S.
  1881   *Wines, Scriptural and Ecclesiastical.* London: National Temperance Publication Depot.

al-Khalesi, Y. M.
  1978   *The Court of Palms: A Functional Interpretation of the Mari Palace.* Malibu, CA: Undena.

Kilian, K.
  1980   Zur Darstellung eines Wagenrennens aus Spätmykenisher Zeit. *Athenischer Mitteilungen* 86: 21–31.
  1986   Mycenaeans Up to Date: Trends and Changes in Recent Research. Pp. 115–52 in *Problems in Greek Prehistory: Papers Presented at the Centenary Conference of the British School of Archaeology at Athens, Manchester, April 1986*, eds. E. French and K. Wardle. Bristol: Bristol Classical.
  1988   Ausgrabungen in Tiryns, 1982/1983, Bericht zu den Grabungen. Pp. 105–51 in *Archäologischer Anzeiger*. Berlin: de Gruyter.

Killen, J. T.
  1985   The Linear B Tablets and the Mycenaean Economy. Pp. 241–305 in *Linear B: A 1984 Survey*, eds. A. Morpurgo Davies and Y. Duhoux. *Bibliothèque des Cahiers de l'Institut de Linguistique de Louvain* 26. Louvain: Peeters.

Killen, J. T., and Olivier, J.-P.
  1989   *The Knossos Tablets.* 5th ed. "Minos," suppl. 11. Salmanaca: Ediciones Universidad de Salamanca.

King, L. W., and Thompson, R. C.
  1966   *Cuneiform Texts from Babylonian Tablets in the British Museum.* Vol. 21. London: The Trustees of the British Museum.

Kinnier Wilson, J. V.
  1966   Leprosy in Ancient Mesopotamia. *Revue d'Assyriologie* 60: 47–58.
  1972   *The Nimrud Wine Lists: A Study of Men and Administration at the Assyrian Capital in the Eighth Century B.C.* Cuneiform Texts from Nimrud 1. London: British School of Archaeology in Iraq.

Kitchen, K. A.
  1982   *Pharaoh Triumphant: The Life and Times of Ramesses II, King of Egypt.* Warminster, Eng.: Aris and Phillips.

Klatsky, A. L.
  1979   Effects of Alcohol on the Nervous System. Pp. 317–40 in *Fermented Food Beverages in Nutrition*, eds. C. F. Gastineau, W. J. Darby, and T. B. Turner. New York: Academic.

Klengel, H.
  1974   Hungerjahre in Ḫatti. *Altorientalische Forschungen* 1: 165–74.
  1979   Handel und Kaufleute in hethitisch Reich. *Altorientalische Forschungen* 6: 69–80.
  1986   The Economy of the Hittite Household (É). *Oikumene* 5: 23–31.

Klengel-Brandt, E.
  1992   Gefäss in Formes eines Widderkopfes. P. 188 in *Das Vorderasiatische Museum, Staatliche Museen zu Berlin* by L. Jakob-Rust, E. Klengel-Brandt, J. Marzahn, and R.-B. Wartke. Mainz: P. von Zabern.

Kliewe, H.
  1981   *Wein und Gesundheit: Eine medizinisches Weinbrevier.* Munich: Droemersche, T. Knaur.

Knapp, A. B.
  1991   Spice, Drugs, Grain and Grog: Organic Goods in Bronze Age East Mediterranean Trade. Pp. 69–82 in *Bronze Age Trade in the Mediterranean*, ed. N. H. Gale. Jonesered: P. Åström.

Knudsen, A. K.
1961   A Study of the Relationship between Phrygian Metalwork and Pottery in the 8th and 7th Centuries B.C. Ann Arbor: University Microfilms.

Koehl, R.
1986   A Minoan Ritual of Initiation? *Journal of Hellenic Studies* 106: 99–110.

Koehler, C. G.
1979a   Corinthian A and B Transport Amphoras. Unpublished Ph.D. dissertation, Princeton University.
1979b   Transport Amphoras as Evidence for Trade. *Archaeological News* 8: 54–61.
1981   Corinthian Developments in the Study of Trade in the Fifth Century. *Hesperia* 50: 449–58.
1986   Handling of Greek Transport Amphoras. Pp. 49–67 in *Bulletin de Correspondance Hellénique*, suppl. 13: *Recherches sur les amphores grecques*, eds. J.-Y. Empereur and Y. Garlan. Paris: École française d'Athènes.
In prep.   *Corinthian A, A' and B Transport Amphoras.*

Koehler, C. G., and Matheson, P. M. W.
1993   AMPHORAS: Computer-Assisted Study of Ancient Wine Jars. Pp. 88–107 in *Accessing Antiquity: The Computerization of Classical Studies*, ed. Jon Solomon. Tucson: The University of Arizona Press.

Koehler, C. G., and Wallace, M. B.
1987   Appendix: The Transport Amphoras: Description and Capacities. Pp. 49–57 in The Hellenistic Shipwreck at Serce Limani, Turkey: Preliminary Report by C. Pulak and R. F. Townsend. *American Journal of Archaeology* 91: 31–57.

Kohl, P. L.
1989   Comments on Guillermo Algaze, "The Uruk Expansion: Cross-Cultural Exchange in Early Mesopotamian Civilization." *Current Anthropology* 30 (5): 593–94.

Köhnlechner, M.
1978   *Heilkräfte des Weines: Ein medizinisches Weinbrevier.* Munich: Droemersche, T. Knaur.

König, M.
1989   Ein Fund römerzeitlicher Traubenkerne in Piesport/Mosel. *Dissertationes Botanicae* 133: 107–16. Berlin: J. Cramer.

Košay, H., and Akok, M.
1966   *Alaca Höyük Kazısı 1940–1948: Deki Çalıšma ve Keşiflere Ait İlk Rapor.* Türk Tarih Kurumu Yayınları 5, no. 6. Ankara: Türk Tarih Kurumu.
1973   *Alaca Höyük Kazısı 1963–1967: Çalıšmalari ve Keşiflere Ait İlk Rapor.* Türk Tarih Kurumu Yayınları 5, no. 28. Ankara: Türk Tarih Kurumu.

Kottek, S. S.
1989   "Do Not Drink Wine or Strong Drink": Alcohol and Responsibility in Ancient Jewish Sources. *Medicine and Law* 8: 255–59.

Köymen, M. A.
1982   Selçuklar Zamanında Beslenme Sistemi. Pp. 41–43 in *Türk Mutfağı Sempozyumu Bildirileri*. Ankara: Ankara Üniversitesi.

Kraay, C. M.
1976   *Archaic and Classical Greek Coins*. London: Methuen.

Kroll, H. J.
1979   Kulturpflanzen aus Dimini. Pp. 173–89 in *Festschrift Maria Hoft, Archaeophysika* 8, ed. U. Korbe Grohne. Cologne: Rheinland.
1981   Thessalische Kulturpflanzen. *Zeitschrift für Archaeologie* 15: 97–103.
1982   Kulturpflanzen aus Tiryns. *Archäologischer Anzeiger*, pp. 467–85.
1983   *Die Pflanzenfunde*. Ch. 1 in *Kastanas: Ausgrabungen in einem Siedlungshügel der Bronze- und Eisenzeit Makedoniens 1975–1979*. Prähistorische Archäologie in Südosteuropa, vol. 2. Berlin: V. Spiess.
1984   Zum Ackerbau gegen Ende der Mykenischen Epoche in der Argolis. *Archäologischer Anzeiger*, pp. 211–22.
1991   Südosteuropa. Pp. 161–77 in *Progress in Old World Palaeoethnobotany*, eds. W. van Zeist, K. Wasylikowa, and K.-E. Behre. Rotterdam: A. A. Balkema.

Kühne, H.
1976   *Die Keramik vom Tell Chuera und Ihre Beziehnungen zu Funden aus Syrien–Palästina, Der Türkei und dem Iraq*. Berlin: Gebr. Mann.

Kupper, J.-R.
1982   Les prix à Mari. *Orientalia Lovaniensia Analecta* 13: 115–21.

Kučan, D.
1991   Eine Methode zur Fixierung fossiler unverkohlter Pflanzenreste. Pp. 15–38 in *New Light on Early Farming: Recent Developments in Palaeoethnobotany*, ed. J. Renfrew. Edinburgh: Edinburgh University.

Lafont, B.
1988   La correspondence de Ṣidqum-Lanasi. Ch. 2 (pp. 509–41) in *Archives épistolaires de Mari I/2*, eds. D. Charpin et al. Archives Royales de Mari 26. Paris: Éditions Recherche sur les Civilisations.
1991   Une homme d'affaire à karkemiš. Pp. 275–86 in *Mélanges P. Garelli*. Paris: Éditions Recherche sur les Civilisations.

Lamb, H. H.
        Climate: Present Past and Future. Vol. 2: *Climatic History and the Future*. London: Methuen.

Lamberg-Karlovsky, C. C., and Tosi, M.
1973   Shahr-i Sokhta and Tepe Yahya: Tracks on the Earliest History of the Iranian Plateau. *East and West* 23: 29–58.

Lambert-Gocs, M.
1990   *The Wines of Greece*. London: Faber and Faber.

Lambrou-Phillipson, C.
1990   *Hellenorientalia: The Near Eastern Presence in the Bronze Age Aegean, ca. 3000–1100 B.C.* Göteborg: P. Åström.

Lamikanra, O.
1989   Anthocyanins of *Vitis rotundifolia* Hybrid Grapes. *Food Chemistry* 33: 225–37.

Lancel, S.
1982   *Byrsa II, Rapports préliminaires sur les fouilles 1977–1978: Niveau et vestiges puniques*. Collection de l'École française de Rome, no. 41. Rome: École française de Rome.

Landsberger, B., and Gurney, O. R.
1958   Practical Vocabulary of Assur. *Archiv für Orientforschung* 18: 328–41.

Lang, M. L.
1961   The Palace of Nestor Excavations of 1960, Part II. *American Journal of Archaeology* 65: 158–63.
1969   *The Palace of Nestor at Pylos in Western Messenia*. Vol. 2: *The Frescoes*. Princeton: Princeton University.

Langdon, S.
1912   *Die neubabylonischen Königsinschriften*. Vorderasiatische Bibliothek, vol. 4. Leipzig: J. C. Hinrichs.

Lapp, P.
1969   The 1968 Excavations at Tell Ta'annek. *Bulletin of the American Schools of Oriental Research* 195: 2–49.

Larsen, M. T.
1987   Commercial Networks in the Ancient Near East. Pp. 47–56 in *Centre and Periphery in the Ancient World*, eds. M. Rowlands, M. T. Larsen, and K. Kristiansen. Cambridge: Cambridge University.

Lattimore, R. A.
1967   *The Odyssey of Homer*. New York: Harper and Row.
1974   *The Iliad*. Chicago: University of Chicago.

Laubenheimer, F.
1989   Les amphores gauloises sous l'empire: recherches nouvelles sur leur production et leur chronologie. Pp. 105–38 in *Amphores romaines et histoire économique: Dix ans de recherche*. Collection de l'École française de Rome 114. Rome: École française de Rome.
1990   *Le temps des amphores en gaule: vins, huiles et sauces*. Paris: Errance.
1991   Les vides sanitaires et les amphores de la porte dorée à Fréjus (Var). *Gallia* 48: 229–65.

Lauer, B.
1967   The Grape-vine. Pp. 220–45 in *Sino-Iranica: Chinese Contributions to the History of Civilization in Ancient Iran, with Special Reference to the History of Cultivated Plants and Products*. New York: Krause Reprint.

Lauer, J. P.; Laurent-Täckholm, V.; and Åberg, E.
1950   Les plantes découvertes dans les souterrains de l'enceinte du roi Zoser à Saqqarah (IIIe dyn.). *Bulletin d'Institut d'Egypte* 32: 121–49.

Lavie, P.
1970   Contribution a l'étude caryosystematique des *Vitacies*. Unpublished thesis, Université Montpellier, Faculté des Sciences.

Layard, A. H.
1853   *Discoveries in the Ruins of Nineveh and Babylon*. London: J. Murray.

Leahy, M. A.
1977   *Excavations at Malkata and the Birket Habu, 1971–1974: The Inscriptions*. Warminster, Eng.: Aris and Phillips.

Leal, M. da S.
1944   *O Vinho na terapeutica e na dietética*. Lisbon: C. Carregal.

Lebessi, A., and Muhly, P.
  1987   The Sanctuary of Hermes and Aphrodite at Syme, Crete. *National Geographic Research* 3: 102–13.
  1990   Aspects of Minoan Cult, Sacred Enclosures: The Evidence from the Syme Sanctuary (Crete). *Archäologischer Anzeiger* 105: 315–36.

Le Brun, A.
  1971   Recherches stratigraphiques à l'Acropole de Suse, 1969–1971. *Cahiers de la Délégation Archéologique Française en Iran* 1: 163–216.
  1978   Le niveau 17B de l'Acropole de Suse. *Cahiers de la Délégation Archéologique Française en Iran* 9: 57–154.

Lee, F. A.
  1951   Fruits and Nuts. Pp. 1348–1561 in *Chemistry and Technology of Foods and Food Products*, ed. M. B. Jacobs. New York: Interscience.

Leemans, W. F.
  1960   *Foreign Trade in the Old Babylonian Period as Revealed by Texts from Southern Mesopotamia.* Leiden: E. J. Brill.

Lees, F. R.
  1970   *The Temperance Bible—Commentary, Giving at One View, Version, Criticism, and Exposition, in Regard to All Passages of Holy Writ Bearing on "Wine" and "Strong Drink."* New York: Sheldon.

Legrain, L.
  1937   *Business Documents of the Third Dynasty of Ur.* Ur Excavation Texts, vol. 3. London: Trustees of the British Museum and of the University Museum, University of Pennsylvania.

Lenzen, H.
  1958   Liste der Funde aus dem Riemchengebäude. *Vorläufiger Bericht über die von der Deutschen Archäologischen Institut und der Deutschen Orient-Gesellschaft aus Mitteln der Deutschen Forschungsgemeinschaft in Uruk-Warka unternommenen Ausgrabungen* 14: 30–35.

Leonard, A., Jr.
  1981   Considerations of Morphological Variation in the Mycenaean Pottery from the Southeastern Mediterranean. *Bulletin of the American Schools of Oriental Research* 241: 87–101.
  1987   Some Problems Inherent in Mycenaean/Syro-Palestinian Synchronisms. *Problems in Greek Prehistory: Papers Presented at the Centenary Conference of the British School of Archaeology at Athens*, eds. E. B. French and K. A. Wardle. Bedminster, Eng.: Bristol Classical.
  1989   Archaeological Sources for the History of Palestine: The Late Bronze Age. *Biblical Archaeologist* 52: 4–39.

Lequément, R.
  1980   Le vin africaine a l'époque impérial. *Antiquités africaines* 16: 185–93.

Lerstrup, A.
  1992   The Making of Wine in Egypt. *Göttinger Miszellen* 129: 61–82.

Lesko, L. H.
  1977   *King Tut's Wine Cellar.* Berkeley: B. C. Scribe.

1978   The Wine Wisdom of King Tutankhamon. *Bulletin of the Society of Medical Friends of Wine* 20: 3–4.

Le Tourneau, R.
1969   *The Almohad Movement in North Africa in the Twelfth and Thirteenth Centuries.* Princeton: Princeton University.

Levadoux, L.
1946   Etude de la fleur et de la sexualité chez la vigne. *Annales de l'École Nationale d'Agriculture de Montpellier* 27: 1–89.
1954   Les Lambrusques. *Bulletin Societe de Horticulture et d'Arboriculture des Bouches-du-Rhone (Marseilles)* 10: 12–15; 11: 9–12.
1956   Les populations sauvages et cultivées de *Vitis vinifera* L. *Annales de la'Amélioration des Plantes* 1: 59–118.

Lewis, B.
1971   *Everyday Life in Ottoman Turkey.* London: Dorset.

Lichtheim, M.
1973   *Ancient Egyptian Literature I.* Berkeley: University of California.
1976   *Ancient Egyptian Literature II: The New Kingdom.* Berkeley: University of California.
1980   *Ancient Egyptian Literature III: The Late Period.* Berkeley: University of California.

Lion, B.
1992   Vignes au Royaume de Mari. Pp. 107–13 in *Florilegium Marianum: Recueil d'études en l'honneur de Michel Fleury.* Paris: E. de Boccard.

Lisitsina, G. N.
1984   The Caucasus: A Centre for Ancient Farming in Eurasia. Pp. 285–92 in *Plants and Ancient Man: Studies in Palaeoethnobotany*, eds. W. van Zeist and W. A. Casparie. Rotterdam/Boston: A. A. Balkema.

Lissarrague, F.
1990   *The Aesthetics of the Greek Banquet: Images of Wine and Ritual.* Trans. A. Szegedy-Maszak. Princeton, NJ: Princeton University.

Lloyd, S., and Safar, F.
1943   Tell Uqair, Excavations by the Iraq Goverment Directorate of Antiquities in 1940 and 1941. *Journal of Near Eastern Studies* 2: 131–58.

Loeschcke, S.
1933   *Denkmäler von Weinbau aus der Zeit der Römer-Herrschaft an Mosel, Saar und Ruwer.* Trier: Römische Abteilung der Deutschen Weinbaumuseums.

Logothetis, B. C.
1962   *Les vignes sauvages* (Vitis vinifera *L ssp* sylvestri *Gmel*) *en taut que matériel primitif viticole en Grèce.* Thessaloniki: Thessaloniki University.
1970   *The Development of the Vine and Viticulture in Greece Based on Archaeological Findings in the Area* [Greek, with English Summary]. Thessalonika: Aristoteleion Panepistimion.

Lolling, H. G.
1880   *Das Kuppelgrab bei Menidi.* Athens.

Long, C. R.
    1974   *The Ayia Triadha Sarcophagus: A Study of Late Minoan and Mycenaean Funerary Practices and Beliefs.* Studies in Mediterranean Archaeology 41. Göteborg: P. Åström.

Lowie, D. A.
    1979   A Nineteenth Dynasty Stela in the Louvre. Pp. 50–54 in *Orbis Aegyptiorum Speculum: Glimpses of Ancient Egypt: Studies in Honour of H. W. Fairman,* eds. J. Ruffle et al. Warminster, Eng.: Aris and Phillips.

Lucas, A.
    1924   Use of Chemistry in Archaeology. *Cairo Science Journal* 12: 144–45; *Chemical Abstracts* 18: 3496.
    1962   *Ancient Egyptian Materials and Industries.* 4th ed., rev. and enlarged by J. R. Harris. London: E. Arnold.

Lucia, S. P.
    1963   *A History of Wine as Therapy.* Philadelphia: Lippincott.
    1969   Wine and Tranquility. In *Wine and Health: Proceedings of the First International Symposium on Wine and Health.* Menlo Park, CA: Pacific Coast.

Luckenbill, D. D.
    1924   *The Annals of Sennacherib.* Oriental Institute Publications, vol. 2. Chicago: University of Chicago.
    1926   *Ancient Records of Assyria and Babylonia.* Vol. 1: *Historical Records of Assyria from Earliest Times to Sargon.* Chicago: University of Chicago.
    1927   *Ancient Records of Assyria and Babylonia.* Vol. 2: *Historical Records of Assyria from Sargon to the End.* Chicago: University of Chicago.

Lutz, H. F.
    1922   *Viticulture and Brewing in the Ancient Orient.* Leipzig: J. C. Hinrichs.

Maass-Lindemann, G.
    1988   Alarcón: Vorbericht über die Funde aus der Grabungskampagne 1984. *Madrider Breiträger* 14: 189–97.

Macalister, R. A. S.
    1912   *The Excavation of Gezer: 1902–5 and 1907–9.* 3 vols. London: J. Murray for Palestine Exploration Fund.

MacGillivray, J.
    1987   Pottery Workshops and the Old Palaces in Crete. Pp. 273–78 in *The Function of the Minoan Palaces,* eds. R. Hägg and N. Marinatos. Stockholm: Swedish Institute at Athens.

Magie, D.
    1950   *Roman Rule in Asia Minor to the End of the Third Century After Christ.* Princeton: Princeton University; reprinted 1975, Salem: Ayer.

Mahaffy, J. P.
    1890   The Work of Mago on Agriculture. *Hermathena* 7: 29–35.

Majidzadeh, Y.
    1979   An Early Prehistoric Coppersmith Workshop at Tepe Gabristan. *Archäologische Mitteilungen aus Iran, Ergänzungsband* 6: 82–92.
    1992   The Arjan Bowl. *Iran* 30: 131–44.

Mallowan, M. E. L.
  1966   *Nimrud and Its Remains*. 3 vols. London: Collins.
  1972   Forward. Pp. i–xv in *The Nirmrud Wine Lists* by J. V. Kinnier Wilson. London: British School of Archaeology.

Mallowan, M. E. L., and Davies, L. G.
  1970   *Ivories in Assyrian Style*. London: British School of Archaeology in Iraq.

Manniche, L.
  1989   *An Ancient Egyptian Herbal*. Austin: University of Texas.

Marcé, R. M.; Calull, M.; Borrull, F.; and Ruis, F. X.
  1990   Determination of Major Carboxylic Acids in Wine by an Optimized HPLC Method with Linear Gradient Elution. *American Journal of Enology and Viticulture* 41: 289–94.

Margueron, J. Cl.
  1982   *Recherches sur les palais mésopotamiens de l'age du bronze*. Paris: Librairie Orientaliste P. Geuthner.
  1992   Le bois dans l'architecture: Premier essai pour une estimation des besoins dans le bassin mésopotamien. *Bulletin on Sumerian Agriculture* 6: 79–96.

Margueron, J.; Pierre-Muller, B.; and Renisio, M.
  1990   Les appartments royaux du premier étage dans le palais de Zimri-lim. *M.A.R.I.* 6: 433–51.

Marinatos, S.
  1970   *Excavations at Thera III*. Athens: Archaeological Society.
  1972   *Excavations at Thera V (1971 Season)*. Athens: Archaeological Society.
  1974   *Excavations at Thera VI*. Athens: Archaeological Society.
  1976   *Excavations at Thera VII: 1973 Season*. Athens: Athens Archaeological Society.

Marschner, R. F., and Wright, H. T.
  1978   Asphalts from Middle Eastern Archaeological Sites. Pp. 150–71 in *Archaeological Chemistry II*, ed. G. F. Carter. Washington, DC: American Chemical Association.

Martin, A. C.; Zim, H. S.; and Nelson, A. L.
  1961   *American Wildlife and Plants*. New York: Dover.

Matheson, P. M. W., and Wallace, M. B.
  1982   Some Rhodian Amphora Capacities. *Hesperia* 51: 292–320.

Mattingly, D. J.
  1988   Oil for Export?: A Comparison of Libyan, Spanish, and Tunisian Olive Oil Production in the Roman Empire. *Journal of Roman Archaeology* 1: 33–56.

Maury, E. A.
  1976   *Wine is the Best Medicine*. Kansas City: S. Andrews and McMeel.

Mauss, M.
  1967   *The Gift: Forms and Functions of Exchange in Primitive Societies*. Trans. I. Cunnison. New York: W. W. Norton.

Mazarakis Ainian, A.
  1988   Early Greek Temples: Their Origin and Function. Pp. 105–09 in *Early Greek Cult Practices*, eds. R. Hägg, N. Marinatos, and G. Nordquist. Stockholm: Swedish Institute at Athens.

McCallum, L.
    1987   Frescoes from the Throne Room at Pylos: A New Interpretation. *American Journal of Archaeology* 91: 296.

McCaslin, D.
    1980   *Stone Anchors in Antiquity: Coastal Settlements and Maritime Trade Routes in the Eastern Mediterranean ca. 1600–1050 B.C.* Studies in Mediterranean Archaeology 61. Göteborg: P. Åström.

McConnell, C. and M.
    1987   *The Mediterranean Diet: Wine, Pasta, Olive Oil, and a Long, Healthy Life.* New York: W. W. Norton.

McCreery, D. W.
    1981   Flotation of the Bab edh-Dhra and Numeira Plant Remains. Pp. 165–69 in *The Southeastern Dead Sea Plain Expedition: An Interim Report of the 1977 Season*, eds. W. E. Rast and R. T. Schaub. Annual of the American Schools of Oriental Research, vol. 46, ed. J. A. Callaway. Cambridge, MA: American Schools of Oriental Research.

McDonald, J. T.
    1981   Wine and Human Nutrition. Pp. 107–18 in *Wine, Health and Society: A Symposium.* San Francisco: GRT Book.

McDouall, R.
    1968   *Cooking with Wine.* London: Penguin.

McGovern, P. E.
    1985   *Late Bronze Palestinian Pendants: Innovation in a Cosmopolitan Age.* Journal for the Society of Old Testament/American Schools of Oriental Research monograph 1. Sheffield, Eng.: Sheffield Academic.

McGovern, P. E., and Michel, R. H.
    1990a   Royal Purple Dye: Its Identification by Complementary Physicochemical Techniques. Pp. 69–76 in *Organic Contents of Ancient Vessels: Materials Analysis and Archaeological Investigation*, eds. W. R. Biers and P. E. McGovern. MASCA Research Papers in Science and Archaeology 7. Philadelphia: MASCA, The University Museum of Archaeology and Anthropology.
    1990b   Royal Purple Dye: The Chemical Reconstruction of the Ancient Mediteranean Industry. *Accounts of Chemical Research* 23: 152–58.

McMahon, G.
    1991   *The Hittite State Cult of the Tutelary Deities.* Assyriological Studies, no. 25. Chicago: Oriental Institute.

Meek, T. J.
    1935   *Old Akkadian, Sumerian, and Cappadocian Texts from Nuzi.* Excavations at Nuzi, vol. 3. Cambridge: Harvard University.

Megaw, A. H. S.
    1953   Archaeology in Cyprus. *Journal of Hellenic Studies* 73: 133–37.

Mekhitarian, A.
    1954   *Egyptian Painting.* Trans. S. Gilbert. Geneva: Éditions d'Art A. Skira.

Mellink, M.
  1986   The Early Bronze Age in West Anatolia: Aegean and Asiatic Correlations. Pp. 139–52 in *The End of the Early Bronze Age in the Aegean*. Leiden: E. J. Brill.

Meriggi, P.
  1967   *Manuale di eteo geroglifico*. P. 117 in *Parte II: Testi — Iᵃ Serie. I Testi neo-etei piu o meno completi*. Incunabula Graeca 15. Rome: Edizioni dell'Ateneo.

Merrillees, R. S.
  1974   *Trade and Transcendence in the Bronze Age Levant*. Studies in Mediterranean Archae-ology 39. Göteborg: Studies in Mediterranean Archaeology.
  1986   Political Conditions in the Eastern Mediterranean during the Late Bronze Age. *Biblical Archaeologist* 49: 42–50.

Merrillees, R. S., and Winter, J.
  1972   Bronze Age Trade between The Aegean and Egypt: Minoan and Mycenaean Pottery from Egypt in the Brooklyn Museum. Pp. 101–35 in *Miscellanea Wilbouriana* 1. New York: Brooklyn Museum.

Michel, R. H.; McGovern, P. E.; and Badler, V. R.
  1992   The Chemical Confirmation of Beer from Proto-Historic Mesopotamia. *Nature* 360: 24.
  1993   The First Wine and Beer: Chemical Detection of Ancient Fermented Beverages. *Analytical Chemistry* 65: 408A–413A.

Miki, S.
  1956   Seed Remains of *Vitaceae* in Japan. *J. Inst. Polytech.* (Osaka City University Series D) 7: 247–71.

Miller, J. M., and Hayes, J. H.
  1986   *A History of Ancient Israel and Judah*. Philadelphia: Westminster.

Miller, N. F.
  1982   Economy and Environment of Malyan: A Third Millennium B.C. Urban Center in Southern Iran. Unpublished Ph.D. dissertation, The University of Michigan.
  1986   Vegetation and Land Use. In "The Chicago Euphrates Archaeological Research Project 1980–1984: An Interim Report." G. Algaze et al. *Anatolica* 13: 37–148.
  1990   Godin Tepe, Iran: Plant Remains from Period V, the Late Fourth Millenium B.C. MASCA Ethnobotanical Report 6, unpublished ms. on file, Museum Applied Science Center for Archaeology, University Museum, University of Pennsylvania.
  1991   The Near East. Pp. 133–60 in *Progress in Old World Palaeoethnobotany*, eds. W. van Zeist, K. Wasylikowa, and K.-E. Behre. Rotterdam: A. A. Balkema.

Millett, P.
  1983   Maritime Loans and the Structure of Credit in Fourth-Century Athens. Pp. 36–52 in *Trade in the Ancient Economy*, eds. P. Garnsey, K. Hopkins, and C. R. Whittaker. Berkeley: University of California.

Mills, J., and White, R.
  1989   The Identity of the Resins from the Late Bronze Age Shipwreck at Ulu Burun (Kaş). *Archaeometry* 31: 37–44.

Mitchell, S.
  1993   *Anatolia: Land, Men, and Gods in Asia Minor*. Vol. 1: *Anatolia and the Impact of Roman Rule*. Oxford: Clarendon.

Möbius, M.
    1933   Pflanzenbilder der minoischen Kunst in botanischer Betrachtung. *Jahrbuch des Deutschen Archäologischen Instituts* 48: 5–39.

Monakhov, S. Iu.
    1984   La production amphorique dans la Chersonese hellénistique. *Vestnik drevnej istorii* 1: 109–28.

Mongrain, S., and Standing, L.
    1989   Impairment of Cognition, Risk-Taking, and Self-Perception by Alcohol. *Perceptual and Motor Skills* 69: 199–210.

Montet, P.
    1913   La fabrication du vin dans les tombeaux antérieurs au Nouvel Empire. *Recueil de Travaux* 35: 117–24.
    1925   *Scènes de la vie privée dans les tombeaux égyptiens de l'Ancien Empire.* Strasbourg: University of Strasbourg.

Moorey, P. R. S.
    1980   Metal Wine Sets in the Ancient Near East. *Iranica Antiqua* 15: 181–97.

Morel, J.-P.
    1969   Kerkouane, Ville punique du cap Bon: Remarques archéologique et historiques. Mélanges de l'École française de Rome. *Archéologie* 81: 473–518.

Morgan, L.
    1985   Idea, idiom and iconography. Pp. 15–19 in *L'iconographie minoénne, Bulletin Correspondance Hellénique,* suppl. 11, ed. O. Picard. Paris: École française d'Athènes.
    1988   *The Miniature Paintings from Thera.* Cambridge: Cambridge University.

Morris, S.
    1989   The Miniature Frescoes from Thera and the Origins of Greek Poetry. *American Journal of Archaeology* 93: 511–35.

Mountjoy, P.
    1983   The Ephyraean Goblet Reviewed. *Annual of the British School at Athens* 78: 265–71.
    1986   *Mycenaean Decorated Pottery.* Studies in Mediterranean Archaeology 73. Göteborg: P. Åström.

Moussa, A. M., and Altenmüller, H.
    1971   *The Tomb of Nefer and Ka-hay.* Archäologische Veröffentlichungen 5. Mainz: P. von Zabern.
    1977   *Das Grab des Nianchchnum und Chnumhotep.* Mainz: P. von Zabern.

Müller-Karpe, A.
    1988   *Hethitische Töpferei der Oberstadt von Hattuša: Beiträger zur Kenntnis spät-grossreichzeitlicher Keramik und Töpferbetriebe.* Marburg: Hitzeroth.

Murray, O.
    1983   The Symposium as Social Organisation. Pp. 195–99 in *The Greek Renaissance of the Eighth Century B.C.: Tradition and Innovation,* ed. R. Hägg. Stockholm: Swedish Institute at Athens.

Murray, O., ed.
    1990   *Sympotica: A Symposium on the Symposion.* Oxford: Oxford University.

Muscarella, O. W.

1974   *Ancient Art: The Norbert Schimmel Collection*. Mainz: P. von Zabern.

1988a   The Background to the Phrygian Bronze Industry. Pp. 177–92 in *Bronze-Working Centres of Western Asia*, ed. J. E. Curtis. London: Kegan Paul International in association with the British Museum.

1988b   *Bronze and Iron: Ancient Near Eastern Artifacts in The Metropolitan Museum of Art*. New York: Metropolitan Museum of Art.

1989   King Midas of Phrygia and the Greeks. Pp. 333–44 in *Anatolia and the Ancient Near East: Studies in Honor of Tahsin Özgüç*, eds. K. Emre, B. Hrouda, M. Mellink, N. Özgüç. Ankara: Türk Tarih Kurumu Başımevi.

Mylonas, G.

1959   *Aghios Kosmas: An Early Bronze Age Settlement and Cemetery of Attica*. Princeton: Princeton University.

1973   *Ho Taphikos Kyklos B ton Mykenon*. Athens: Archaeological Society.

Nagy, S.; Attaway, J. A.; and Rhodes, M. E.

1988   *Adulteration of Fruit Juice Beverages*. New York: M. Dekker.

Narimanov, I. G.

1987   *Kultura drevneyshego zemledelchesko-skoto-vodcheskogo nasleniya Azerbayshana (epokha eneolita VI–IV tys. do n.e.)* [Early Agricultural and Pastoralist Societies of Azerbaijan: The Eneolithic of the 6th to 4th Millennia B.C.]. Baku: ELM.

Naville, E.

1894   *Ahnas el Medineh*. London: Egypt Exploration Fund.

Negi, S. S., and Olmo, H. P.

1966   Sex Conversion in a Male *Vitis vinifera* L. by a Kinid. *Science* 152: 1624–25.

1971a   Induction of Sex Conversion in Male *Vitis*. *Vitis* 10: 1–19.

1971b   Conversion and Determination of Sex in *Vitis vinifera* L. (*silvestris*). *Vitis* 9:265–79.

1973   Certain Embryological and Biochemical Aspects of Cytokinin SD8339 in Converting Sex of a Male *Vitis vinifera sylvestris*. *American Journal of Botany* 59: 851–57.

Negrul, A. M.

1938   Evolution of cultivated forms of grapes. *Comptes rendues Academy of Science U. S. S. R.* 18: 585–88.

1946   Proles of Cultivated Grapevines and Their Classification. Pp. 133–216 in *Ampelography: U.S.S.R.*, vol. 1. Moscow.

1960   Nuove indagini sull'origine delle varietà centro-asiatiche della vite. *Atti. Acad. Ital. Vite e Vino* 12: 113.

Negrul, A. M.; Ivanov, I. K.; Katerov, K. I.; and Dontchev, A. A.

1965   *Wild* vinifera *of Bulgaria*. Moscow.

Nesbitt, M.

1993a   Ancient Crop Husbandry at Kamn-Kalehöyük: 1991 Archaeobotanical Report. *Bulletin of the Middle East Culture Center in Japan* 7: 103–25.

1993b   The Archaeobotany of Turkey: A Review. Pp. 329–50 in *Proceedings of the 5th Optima Meeting, Istanbul, 8–15 September 1986*. Ankara: British Institute of Archaeology.

Neumann, G.

1977   Das Zeichen *VINUM* in den ägäischen Schriften. *Kadmos* 16: 124–30.

Neve, P.
1987   Hattusha, Haupt und Kultstadt der Hethiter: Ergebnisse der Ausgrabungen in der
        Oberstadt. *Hethitica* 8: 297–318.

Newberry, P. E.
1893   *Beni Hasan* I. London: Egypt Exploration Fund.
1893–94 *Beni Hasan*. 2 vols. London: Egypt Exploration Fund.
1894a   *El Bersheh*. Vol. 1. *The Tomb of Tehutihetep*. London: Egypt Exploration Fund.
1894b   *Beni Hasan*. Vol. 2. London: Egypt Exploration Fund.

Niemeyer, H. G.
1989   Das frühe Karthago und die phönizische Expansion im Mittelmeerraum: Als öffen-
        tlicher Vortrag der Joachim Jungius-Gesellschaft der Wissenschaften gehalten am 31
        Mai 1988 in Hamburg. Göttingen: Vanderhoeck and Ruprecht.
1991   Phéniciens et puniques au centre et dans l'ouest méditerranéen: Bilan et récentes
        découvertes. Paper presented at the Troisième Congrés International des Etudes phé-
        niciennes et puniques, November 11–16, Tunis.

Nissen, H.-J.
1970   Grabung in den Planquadraten K/L XII in Uruk-Warka. *Baghdader Mitteilungen* 5:
        101–92.
1976   Zur Frage der Arbeitsorganisation in Babylonien während der Spät-uruk-Zeit. Pp. 5–14
        in *Wirtschaft und Gesellschaft in Alten Vorderasien*, eds. J. Harmatta and G.
        Komaróczy. Budapest: Akadémiai Kiadó.
1985   The Emergence of Writing in the Ancient Near East. *Interdisciplinary Science Reviews*
        10: 349–61.
1986a   The Archaic Texts from Uruk. *World Archaeology* 17: 317–34.
1986b   The Development of Writing and of Glyptic Art. Pp. 316–31 in *Ǧamdat Nasr—Period
        or Regional Style?* eds. U. Finkbeiner and W. Röllig. Wiesbaden: Reichert.

Nuttonson, M. Y.
1961   *An Introduction to North Africa and a Survey of the Physical Environment of Morocco,
        Algeria and Tunisia*. 2 vols. Washington, DC: American Institute for Crop Ecology.

Nyrop, R. F. et al.
1973   *Area Handbook for the Republic of Turkey*. 2nd ed. Washington, DC: U.S. Government
        Printing Office.

Oakes, H.
1954   *The Soils of Turkey*. Ankara: FAO.

Oates, J.
1959   Late Assyrian Pottery from Fort Shalmaneser. *Iraq* 21: 130–46.
1985   Tell Brak: Uruk Pottery from the 1984 Season. *Iraq* 47: 175–86.
1986   Tell Brak: The Uruk/Early Dynastic Sequence. Pp. 245–73 in *Ǧamdat Nasr: Period or
        Regional Style?*, eds. U. Finkbeiner and W. Röllig. Weisbaden: Ludwig Reichert.

Oldfather, C. H., trans.
1933–76 *Diodorus of Sicily, Books of History*. Cambridge: Harvard University.

Olivier, J.-P.
1988   Tirynthian Graffiti: Ausgrabungen in Tiryns 1982/1983. *Archäologischer Anzeiger* 103: 253–68.
1989   The Possible Methods in Deciphering the Pictographic Cretan Script. Pp. 39–50 in *Problems in Decipherment*, eds. Y. Duhoux, T. G. Palaima, and J. Bennet. *Bibliothèque des Cahiers de l'Institut de Linguistique de Louvain* 49. Louvain: Peeters.
1992   Rapport sur les textes en hiéroglyphique crétois, en linéaire A et en linéire B. Pp. 443–56 in *Mykenaïka. Actes du IXe colloque internationale sur les textes mycéniens et égéenes (1990)*, ed. J. P. Olivier. BCH supplément 25. Paris.

Olmo, H. P.
1976   Grapes *Vitis, Muscadinia (Vitaceae)*. Pp. 294–98 in *Evolution of Crop Plants*, ed. N. W. Simmonds. London: Longman Gray.
1978   Genetic Problems and General Methodology of Breeding. Pp. 3–10 in Proceedings of the Second International Symposium on Grapevine on Genetics and Breeding. Paris: INRA.

Olmo, H. P., and Koyama, A.
1980   Natural Hybridization of Indigenous *Vitis californica* and *V. girdiana* with Cultivated *vinifera* in California. Pp. 31–41 in *Proceedings of the Third International Symposium of Grape Breeding*, University of California, Davis.

Oppenheim, A. L., et al.
1956a   *The Assyrian Dictionary*. Vol. G. Chicago: The Oriental Institute.
1956b   *The Assyrian Dictionary*. Vol. Ḫ. Chicago: The Oriental Institute.
1958   *The Assyrian Dictionary*. Vol. E. Chicago: Oriental Institute.
1959   *The Assyrian Dictionary*. Vol. D. Chicago: The Oriental Institute.
1960   *The Assyrian Dictionary*. Vol. I/J. Chicago: The Oriental Institute.
1971   *The Assyrian Dictionary*. Vol. K. Chicago: The Oriental Institute.
1973   *The Assyrian Dictionary*. Vol. L. Chicago: The Oriental Institute.

Orthmann, W.
1984   Keramik aus den ältesten Schichten von Büyükkale Grabungen bis 1979. Pp. 9–62 in *Boğazköy VI*. Berlin: Gebr. Mann.

Otten, H.
1958   *Hethitische Totenrituale*. Veröffentlichungen des Instituts für Orientforschung der Deutschen Akademie der Wissenschaften (Berlin) 37. Berlin: Akademie.
1988   *Die Bronzetafel aus Boğazköy: Ein Staatsverträg Tuthalijas IV*. Wiesbaden: O. Harrassowitz.
1989   *Die 1986 in Boğazköy gefundene Bronzetafel: Zwei Vorträge*. Innsbruck: Institut für Sprachwissenschaft der Universität Innsbruck.

Otto, W. F.
1965   *Dionysus: Myth and Cult*. Trans. R. B. Palmer. Bloomington, IN: Indiana University.

Özdogan, M.
1977   *Lower Euphrates Basin Survey, 1977*. Istanbul: Middle Eastern Technical University.

Özgüç, N.
1950   Tiergestaltige Gefässe die in Kültepe im Jahre 1948–49 gefunden wurden. Pp. 218–25 in *Der Zweite Bericht über die Ausgrabungen in Kültepe 1949*. Türk Tarih Kurumu Yayınları 5, no. 10. Ankara: Türk Tarih Kurumu.

Özgüç, T.
1988a *Inandı: An Important Cult Center in the Old Hittite Period*. Türk Tarih Kurumu Yayınları 5, no. 43. Ankara: Türk Tarih Kurumu.
1988b *Kültepe-Kaniš II: New Researches at the Trading Center of the Ancient Near East*. Türk Tarih Kurumu Yayınları 5, no. 41. Ankara: Türk Tarih Kurumu.

Özgüç, T. and N.
1950 *Ausgrabungen in Kültepe 1949*. Türk Tarih Kurumu Yayınları 5, no. 10. Ankara: Türk Tarih Kurumu.

Palaima, T. G.
1989 Cypro-Minoan Scripts: Problems of Historical Context. Pp. 121–87 in *Problems of Decipherment*, eds. Y. Duhoux, T. G. Palaima, and J. Bennet. Louvain-La-Neuve: Peeters.
1991 Maritime Matters in the Linear B Tablets. Pp. 273–310 in *Thalassa. L'Egée prehistorique et la Mer*, eds. R. Laffineur and L. Basch. *Aegaeum* 7 (Liège).

Palaima, T. G., and Wright, J.
1985 Ins and Outs of the Archives Rooms at Pylos: Form and Function in a Mycenaean Palace. *American Journal of Archaeology* 89: 251–62.

Palmer, L. R.
1965 *The Interpretation of Mycenaean Greek Texts*. 2nd ed. Oxford: Oxford University.

Palmer, R.
1990 Wine in the Mycenaean Palace Economy. Ph.D. dissertation, University of Cincinnati. Ann Arbor: University Microfilms.
1994 Wine in the Mycenaean Palace Economy. *Aegaeum* 10 (Liège).

Palmieri, A.
1973 Scavi nell'area sud-occidentale di Arslantepe. *Origini* 7.
1989 Storage and Distribution at Arslantepe-Malatya in the Late Uruk Period. Pp. 419–29 in *Anatolia and the Ancient Near East: Studies in Honor of Tahsin Özgüç*, eds. K. Emre, M. Mellink, B. Hrouda, and N. Özgüç. Ankara: Türk Tarih Kurumu Başımevi.

Pan, Y. J.
1965 Chinas Weinindustrie. *Weinberg und Keller* 12: 25–27.

Para, M.-H., and Riviere, H.
1982 Notre histoire dans le fond des amphores: Détermination des acides amines et des acides phénoliques en chromatographie liquide haute performance. Dissertation, Institut de Chimie et Physique Industrielles de Lyons.

Pariser, E. R.
1975 Foods in Ancient Egypt and Classical Greece. *Food Technology* 29: 23, 26–27.

Parke, H. W.
1977 *Festivals of the Athenians*. London: Thames and Hudson.

Parpola, S.
1970 *Letters from Assyrian Scholars to the Kings Esarhaddon and Assurbanibal*. Part 1: *Texts*. Alter Orient und Altes Testament 5/1. Neukirchen-Vluyn: Butzon und Bercker Kevelaer.
1979 *Neo-Assyrian Letters from the Kuyunjik Collection*, Cuneiform Texts from Babylonian Tablets in the British Museum 53. London: The Trustees of the British Museum.

Parr, P.
 1973   The Origin of the Canaanite Jar. Pp. 173–81 in *Archaeological Theory and Practice: Studies Presented to W. F. Grimes*, ed. D. E. Strong. London: Seminar.

Parrot, A.
 1958   *Le Palais: Architecture*. Paris: Librairie Orientaliste P. Geuthner.
 1959   *Le Palais: Documents et monuments*. Paris: Librairie Orientaliste P. Geuthner.

Parry, J. W.
 1969   *Spices*. Vol. 1. New York: Chemical.

Patterson, J.
 1982   Survey Article "Salvation from the Sea": Amphorae and Trade in the Roman West. *Journal of Roman Studies* 72: 146–57.

Peacock, D. P. S., and Williams, D. F.
 1986   *Amphorae and the Roman Economy: An Introductory Guide*. London: Longman.

Pecchioli Daddi, F.
 1982   *Mestieri, professioni e dignità nell'Anatolia ittita*. Incunabula Graeca 79. Rome: Edizione dell'Ateneo.

Pelagatti, P.
 1961–62 Osservazioni sui ceramisti del I° palazzo di Festòs. *Kretika Chronika* 15/16: 99–111.

Pellicer Catalán, M.
 1962   Excavations en la nécropolis púnica, "Laurita" del Cerro de San Cristóbal (Almuñécar, Granada). *Excavaciones Arqueologicas en España* 17. Madrid: Servicio nacional de excavaciones arqueologicas.

Pendlebury, H.; Pendlebury, J.; and Money-Coutts, M.
 1937–38 Excavations in the Plain of Lasithi, III: Karphi, a City of Refuge of the Early Iron Age in Crete. *Annual of the British School at Athens* 38: 57–145.

Pendlebury, J. D. S.
 1930   Egypt and the Aegean in the Late Bronze Age. *Journal of Egyptian Archaeology* 16: 75–92.

Pennington, J. A. T.
 1989   *Bowes and Church's Food Values of Portions Commonly Used*. New York: Harper and Row.

Perevolotsky, A.
 1981   Orchard Agriculture in the High Mountain Regions of Southern Sinai. *Human Ecology* 9: 331–57.

Persson, A.
 1942   *New Tombs at Dendra near Midea*. London: H. Milford.

Peterson, M. S.
 1975   Food Logistics in Historical Perspective. *Food Technology* 29: 34–36.

Pettinato, G.
 1972   Il commercio con l'estero della Mesopotamia meridionale nel 3.millennio av. Cr. alla luce delle fonti letterarie e lessicali sumeriche. *Mesopotamia* 7: 43–166.

Piankoff, A. trans.
 1968   *The Pyramid of Unas*. Princeton: Princeton University.

Picard, G. C. and C.
    1958   *La Vie quotidienne à Carthage au temps d'Hannibal, IIIe siècle avant Jésus-Christ.*
            Paris: Hachette.

Picon, M., and Garlan, Y.
    1986   Recherches sur l'implantation des ateliers amphoriques à Thasos et analyse de la pâte
            des amphores thasiennes. Pp. 287–309 in *Bulletin de Correspondance Hellénique*,
            suppl. 13: *Recherches sur les amphores grecques*, eds. J.-Y. Empereur and Y. Garlan.
            Paris: École française d'Athènes.

Pini, I.
    1975   *Corpus der Minoischen und Mykenischen Siegal.* Vol. 5, pt. 2: *Kleinere griechische
            Sammlungen.* Berlin: Gebr. Mann.

Place, V.
    1867   *Ninive et l'Assyrie.* Vol. 1. Paris: Imprimerie Nationale.

Platon, N.
    1971   *Zakros: The Discovery of a Lost Palace of Ancient Crete.* New York: C. Scribner's.

Pliny the Elder
    1945   *Natural History.* The Loeb Classical Library. 10 vols., bks. 1–27. Trans. H. Rackham.
            Cambridge: Harvard University.

Porada, E.
    1965   Cylinder Seals from Thebes: A Preliminary Report. *American Journal of Archaeology*
            69: 173.
    1966   Further Notes on the Cylinders from Thebes. *American Journal of Archaeology* 70:
            194.
    1990   More Seals of the Time of the Sukkalmah. *Revue d'Assyriologie* 84: 171–80.

Postgate, J. N.
    1974   *Taxation and Conscription in the Assyrian Empire.* Studia Pohl, Series Maior 3. Rome:
            Biblical Institute.
    1987   Notes on Fruit in the Cuneiform Sources. *Bulletin on Sumerian Agriculture* 3: 115–44.

Postgate, J. N., and Powell, M. A.
    1988   Irrigation and Cultivation in Mesopotamia I. *Bulletin on Sumerian Agriculture* 4.
    1990   Irrigation and Cultivation in Mesopotamia II. *Bulletin on Sumerian Agriculture* 5.

Potter, P., trans.
    1980   *Hippocrates.* Vols. 5 and 6. Cambridge: Harvard University.

Powell, M. A.
    1972   Sumerian Area Measures and the Alleged Decimal Substratum. *Zeitschrift für Assyri-
            ologie* 62: 165–222.
    1977   Sumerian Area Measures and the Alleged Decimal Substratum. *Zeitschrift für Assyri-
            ologie* 72: 165–221.
    1984   On the Absolute Value of Assyrian *qa* and *emar. Iraq* 46: 57–61.
    1987a   The Tree Section of ur_5(=HAR)-ra = hubullu. *Bulletin on Sumerian Agriculture* 3:
            145–51.
    1987b   Classical Sources and the Problem of the Apricot. *Bulletin on Sumerian Agriculture* 3:
            153–56.
    1988   Evidence for Agriculture and Waterworks in Babylonian Mathematical Texts. *Bulletin
            on Sumerian Agriculture* 4: 161–72.

1989–90 Masse und Gewichte. Pp. 457–517 in *Reallexikon der Assyriologie und Vorderasiatis- chen Archäologie*, vol. 7, eds. D. O. Edzard et al. Berlin: W. de Gruyter.

1990 Identification and Interpretation of Long Term Price Fluctuations in Babylonia: More on the History of Money in Mesopotamia. *Altorientalische Forschungen* 17: 76–99.

1991 Epistemology and Sumerian Agriculture: The Strange Case of Sesame and Linseed. Pp. 155–64 in *Ancient Near Eastern Studies in Honor of Miguel Civil on the Occasion of His Sixty-Fifth Birthday. Aula Orientalis 9.*

Forth. Metron Ariston: Measure as a Tool for Studying Beer in Ancient Mesopotamia. *Bere e bevande nel Vicino Oriente antico*, ed. L. Milano. Rome.

Pritchard, J. B.
1964 *Winery, Defenses, and Soundings at Gibeon.* Museum monograph 26. Philadelphia: University Museum.

1973 *The Ancient Near East: An Anthology of Texts and Pictures.* Vol. 1. Princeton: Princeton University.

Psaras, P. G., and Zambartas, A. M.
1981 The Wines in Cyprus: History, Culture, Technology and Economics. Pp. 242–56 in *Quality of Foods and Beverages: Chemistry and Technology*, eds. G. Charalambous and G. Inglett. Proceedings of a Symposium of the 2nd International Flavor Conference, vol. 1. New York: Academic.

Puhvel, J.
1964 Eleuther and Oinoatis: Dionysiac Data from Mycenaean Greece. Pp. 161–70 in *Mycenaean Studies*, ed. E. Bennett. Madison: University of Wisconsin.

1984a *eku-, aku-.* Pp. 261–68 in *Hittite Etymological Dictionary*, vol. 2. Amsterdam: Mouton.

1984b *im(m)iya-, imme(y)a-.* Pp. 363–65 in *Hittite Etymological Dictionary*, vol. 2. Amsterdam: Mouton.

Pulak, C.
1988 The Bronze Age Shipwreck at Ulu Burun, Turkey: 1985 Campaign. *American Journal of Archaeology* 92: 1–35.

Raban, A.
1980 The Commercial Jar in the Ancient Near East: Its Evidence for Interconnections amongst the Biblical Lands [Hebrew]. Unpublished Ph.D. dissertation, Hebrew University, Jerusalem.

Rackham, H., trans.
1945 *Pliny, Natural History in Ten Volumes.* Vol. 4. London: W. Heinemann; revised and reprinted 1968.

Rackham, H.; Jones, W. H. S.; and Eichholtz, D. E., trans.
1949–62 *Pliny, Natural History.* 10 vols. Cambridge: Harvard University.

Rackham, O.
1978 The Flora and Vegetation of Thera and Crete before and after the Great Eruption. Pp. 755–64 in *Thera and the Aegean World*, vol. 1, ed. C. Doumas. London: Thera and the Aegean World.

Rapp, A., and Mandery, H.
1986 Wine Aroma. *Experientia* 42: 873–84.

Rapp, A., and Markowetz, A.
1990 Wine Analysis with Nuclear Magnetic Resonance. *Weinwirtschaft Technik* 4: 14–18.

Reade, J.
  1983   *Assyrian Sculpture*. London: The British Museum.

Reiner, E.
  1971a   *karānu*. Pp. 202–06 in *The Assyrian Dictionary of the Oriental Institute of the University of Chicago* by A. L. Oppenheim et al. Vol. 8: K. Chicago: Oriental Institute.
  1971b   *kurunnu*. Pp. 579–81 in *The Assyrian Dictionary of the Oriental Institute of the University of Chicago* by A. L. Oppenheim et al. Vol. 8: K. Chicago: Oriental Institute.

Reiner, E., et al.
  1980   *The Assyrian Dictionary*. Vol. N, part II. Chicago: The Oriental Institute.
  1982   *The Assyrian Dictionary*. Vol. Q. Chicago: The Oriental Institute.

Renaudin, L.
  1922   Vases Préhelléniques de Théra. *Bulletin Correspondance Hellénique* 46: 113–59.

Renfrew, C.
  1972   *The Emergence of Civilization: The Cyclades and the Aegean in the Third Millennium B.C.* London: Methuen.

Renfrew, J. M.
  1966   A Report on Recent Finds of Carbonized Cereals and Seeds from Prehistoric Thessaly. *Thessalika* 5: 21–36.
  1969   Palaeoethnobotany and the Neolithic Cultures of Greece and Bulgaria. Unpublished Ph.D. thesis, Cambridge University.
  1971   Recent Finds of *Vitis* from Neolithic Contexts in S.E. Europe. *Acta Museorum Agriculturae Praguae*. Prague: no publisher.
  1972   The Plant Remains. Pp. 315–17, Appendix V in *Myrtos: An Early Bronze Age Settlement in Crete* by P. M. Warren, suppl. vol. 7. Athens: British School of Archaeology. Oxford: Alden.
  1973a   The Plant Remains. Pp. 315–18, Appendix 5 in *Myrtos: An Early Bronze Age Settlement in Crete* by P. M. Warren, suppl. vol. 7. Athens: British School of Archaeology.
  1973b   Agriculture. Pp. 147–64 in *Neolithic Greece*, ed. D. Theochares. Athens: National Bank of Greece.
  1973c   *Palaeoethnobotany: The Prehistoric Food Plants of the Near East and Europe*. London: Columbia University.
  1987   Fruits from Ancient Iraq: The Palaeoethnobotanical Evidence. *Bulletin on Sumerian Agriculture* 3: 157–61.

Ribéreau-Gayon, P.
  1959   *Recherches sur les anthocyanes des végétaux: Application au genre* Vitis. Paris: Librarie Générale de l'Enseignement.

Ricci, C.
  1924   *La cultara della vite e la fabricazione del vino nell'Egitto Greco-Romano*. Milan: Aegyptus.

Richter, G. M. A.
  1974   *A Handbook of Greek Art*. New York: Phaidon.

Rivera Núñez, D., and Walker, M. J.
  1989   A Review of Palaeobotanical Findings of Early *Vitis* in the Mediterranean and of the Origins of Cultivated Grape-Vines, with Special Reference to New Pointers to Prehistoric Exploitation in Western Mediterranean. *Review of Palaeobotany and Palynology* 61: 205–37.

Roaf, M.
   1990   *Cultural Atlas of Mesopotamia and the Near East.* New York: Facts on File.

Roaf, M., and Killick, R.
   1987   A Mysterious Affair of Styles: The Ninevite 5 Pottery of Northern Mesopotamia. *Iraq* 49: 199–230.

Röllig, W.
   1964   Erzwägungen zu neuen Stelen König Nabonids. *Zeitschrift für Assyriologie und vorderasiatische Archäologie* 56: 218–60.

Root, W.
   1980   *Food: An Authoritative and Visual History and Dictionary of the Foods of the World.* New York: Simon and Schuster.

Rose, P.
   1984   The Pottery Distribution Analysis. Pp. 133–53 in *Amarna Reports I* by B. J. Kemp. London: Egypt Exploration Society.

Rosner, F.
   1978   *Julius Preuss' Biblical and Talmud Medicine.* New York: Sanhedren.

Rosner, F., and Muntner, S., trans.
   1970–71   *The Medical Aphorisms of Moses Maimonides.* 2 vols. New York: Bloch.

Rostovtzeff, M. I.
   1922   *A Large Estate in Egypt in the Third Century B.C.: A Study in Economic History.* University of Wisconsin Studies in the Social Sciences and History 6. Madison, WI: University of Wisconsin; reprint ed., 1967. Studia Historica 52, Rome: "L'Erma" di Bretschneider.

Rothschild-Boros, M.
   1981   The Determination of Amphora Contents. Pp. 74–89 in *Archaeology and Italian Society: Prehistoric, Roman and Medieval Studies.* British Archaeological Reports. International Series 102, eds. G. Barker and R. Hodges. Oxford: British Archaeological Reports.

Röttlander, R. C. A.
   1990   Lipid Analysis in the Identification of Vessel Contents. Pp. 37–40 in *Organic Contents of Ancient Vessels: Materials Analysis and Archaeological Investigation*, eds. W. R. Biers and P. E. McGovern. MASCA Research Papers in Science and Archaeology 7. Philadelphia: MASCA, The University Museum of Archaeology and Anthropology.

Roubet, C.
   1979   *Économie pastorale préagricole en Algérie orientale: Le Neolithic de tradition capsienne.* Paris: Centre national de la recherche scientifique.

Rowton, R.
   1967   The Woodlands of Ancient Western Asia. *Journal of Near Eastern Studies* 26: 261–77.

Rutkowski, B.
   1986   *The Cult Places of the Aegean.* New Haven: Yale University.

Rutter, J.
   1989   A Ceramic Definition of Late Helladic I from Tsoungiza. *Hydra* 6: 1–9.
   1990   Middle Helladic Pottery Groups from Tsoungiza. *Hesperia* 59: 375–458.

Rutter, J. and S.
   1976   *The Transition to Mycenaean.* Monumenta Archaeologica 4. Los Angeles: Institute of
           Archaeology, UCLA.

Safar, F.; Lloyd, S.; and Mustafa M. A.
   1981   *Eridu.* Baghdad: State Organization of Antiquities and Heritage.

Säflund, G.
   1980   Sacrificial Banquets in the Palace of Nestor. *Opuscula Atheniensia* 13: 237–46.

Saggs, H. W. F.
   1962   *The Greatness that Was Babylon.* New York: Hawthorn Books.

Sagona, A.
   1982   Levantine Storage Jars of the 13th to 4th Century B.C. *Opuscula Athenensia* 14:
           73–110.
   1984   *The Caucasian Region in the Early Bronze Age.* British Archaeological Reports.
           International Series 214. Oxford: British Archaeological Reports.

Sakellarakis, J. A.
   1982   *Corpus der minoischen und mykenischen Siegel.* Vol. 1 suppl. *Athen Nationalmuseum.*
           Berlin: Gebr. Mann.

Sakellariou, A.
   1964   *Corpus der minoischen und mykenischen Siegel.* Vol. 1: *Die minoischen und mykenis-
           chen Siegel des Nationalmuseum in Athen.* Berlin: Gebr. Mann.

Salonen, A.
   1939   *Die Wasserfahrzeuge in Babylonien.* Studia Orientalia 8/4. Helsinki: Societas Orien-
           talis Fennica.

Salviat, F.
   1986   Le vin de Thasos: Amphores, vin et sources écrites. Pp. 145–96 in *Bulletin de Corre-
           spondance Hellénique*, suppl. 13: *Recherches sur les amphores grecques*, eds. J.-Y.
           Empereur and Y. Garlan. Paris: École française d'Athènes.

Sams, G. K.
   1977   Beer in the City of Midas. *Archaeology* 30: 108–15.

Santa, S.
   1958–59 Essai de reconstruction de paysages végétaux quaternaires d'Afrique du Nord. *Libyca
           Archéologie-Épigraphie* 6/7: 37–77.

Sarpaki
   1992   The Paleoethnobotanical Approach. The Mediterranean Triad, or Is It a Quartet? Pp.
           61–76 in *Agriculture in Ancient Greece.* Stockholm: Swedish Institute at Athens.

Sarvis, S.
   1973   *American Wines and Wine Cooking.* Des Moines, IA: Creative Home Library.

Säve-Söderbergh, T.
   1957   *Four Eighteenth Dynasty Tombs.* Private Tombs at Thebes 1. Oxford: Griffith Institute.

Savulesai, T.
   1958   *The Flora of the Republic of Romania*, vol. 6. Bucharest.

Schaeffer, C. F.-A.
   1949   *Ugaritica II.* Mission de Ras Shamra, vol. 5. Paris: P. Geuthner.

Schiemann, E.
1953   *Vitis* in Neolithicum der Mark Brandenberg. *Der Züchter* 23: 318–26.

Schmandt-Besserat, D.
1992   *Before Writing*. Austin: University of Texas.

Schneider, J.
1977   Was There a Pre-Capitalist World-System? *Peasant Studies* 6: 20–29.

Schumann, F.
1974   Untersuchungen an Wildreben in Deutschland. *Vitis* 13: 128–205.

Scienza, A.; Prutti, A.; Conca, E.; and Romano, F.
1986   Diffusione e caratteristiche "della" *Vitis vinifera silvestris*, Gmelin in Italia. Suppl. 12, Edagricole, Bologna. *Vignevini* 13: 86–95.

Seigneur, M.; Bonnet, J.; Dorian, B.; and Benchimol, D.
1990   Effect of the Consumption of Alcohol, White Wine, and Red Wine on Platelet Function and Serum Lipids. *Journal of Applied Cardiology* 5: 215–22.

Seltman, C.
1957   *Wine in the Ancient World*. London: Routledge and Kegan Paul.

Sethe, K.
1932   *Urkunden des Alten Reiches*. Leipsig: J. C. Hinrichs.

Several, M.
1972   Reconsidering the Egyptian Empire during the Amarna Period. *Palestine Exploration Quarterly* 104: 123–33.

Shackley, M.
1982   Gas Chromatographic Identification of a Resinous Deposit from a 6th Century Storage Jar and Its Possible Identification. *Journal of Archaeological Science* 9: 305–6.

Sharma, P., trans.
1981   *Caraka-Samhita*. Vol. 1: *Sutrasthana to Indriyastthana*. Delhi: Chaukambha Orientalia.

Shaw, J. W.
1978   Evidence for the Minoan Tripartite Shrine. *American Journal of Archaeology* 82: 429–48.
1984   Excavations at Kommos (Crete) during 1982–1983. *Hesperia* 53: 251–87.
1986   Excavations at Kommos (Crete) during 1984–1986. *Hesperia* 55: 219–69.

Shay, J. M. and C. T.
1978   Modern Vegetation and Fossil Plant Remains. In *Excavations at Nichoria in Southwest Greece*, eds. G. Rapp and S. E. Aschenbrenner. Minneapolis: University of Minnesota.

Shelmerdine, C. W.
1973   The Pylos Ma Tablets Reconsidered. *American Journal of Archaeology* 77: 261–75.
1985   *The Perfume Industry of Mycenaean Pylos*. Göteborg: Paul Åströms.

Sherrat, A.
1987   Cups that Cheered. Pp. 81–114 in *Bell Beakers of the Western Mediterranean*, eds. W. H. Waldren and R. C. Kennard. Oxford: British Archaeological Reports.

Siegelová, J.
1971 *Appu Märchen und Hedamma Mythus.* Studien zu den Boğazköy Texten 14. Wiesbaden: O. Harrassowitz.

Simoons, F. J.
1991 *Food in China: A Cultural and Historical Inquiry.* Boston: CRC.

Simpson, K.
1988 *Qraya Modular Reports.* Vol. 1: *Early Soundings.* Malibu, CA: Undena.

Singer, I.
1983 *The Hittite KI.LAM Festival.* Studien zu den Boğazköy Texten 27. Wiesbaden: O. Harrassowitz.

Sjöberg, Å. W., in collaboration with H. Behrens et al.
1984 *The Sumerian Dictionary of the University Museum of the University of Pennsylvania,* in collaboration with H. Behrens, B. L. Eichler, M. W. Green, E. Leichty, and D. Loding. Philadelphia: Babylonian Section of the University Museum.

Smith, C. A.
1976 Exchange Systems and the Spatial Distribution of Elites: The Organization of Stratification in Agrarian Societies. Pp. 309–74 in *Regional Analysis,* vol. 2, ed. C. A. Smith. New York: Academic.

Smith, H., and Jones, G.
1990 Experiments on the Effects of Charring on Cultivated Grape Seeds. *Journal of Archaeological Science* 17: 317–27.

Smith, W. S.
1965 *Interconnections in the Ancient Near East: A Study of the Relationships Between the Arts of Egypt, the Aegean, and Western Asia.* New Haven: Yale University.
1981 *Art and Architecture of Ancient Egypt.* Rev. ed. by W. K. Simpson. Harmondsworth: Penguin.

Snell, D.C.
1982 *Ledgers and Prices: Early Mesopotamian Merchant Accounts.* Yale Near Eastern Researches 8. New Haven: Yale University.

Soderstrom, C. A.; Birschbach, J. M.; and Dischinger, P. C.
1990 Injured Drivers and Alcohol Use: Culpability, Convictions, and Pre-Crash and Post-Crash Driving History. *Journal of Trauma* 30: 1208–14.

Sommer, F.
1932 *Die Ahhijava-Urkunden.* Munich: Bayerische Akademie der Wissenschaft.

Soyer, A.
1977 *The Pantropheon or a History of Food and Its Preparation in Ancient Times.* London: Paddington; reprint of 1853 ed.

Spencer, W. G., trans.
1935–38 *Celsus' De medicina.* 3 vols. Cambridge: Harvard University.

Spiegelberg, W.
1923 Bemerkungen zu den hieratischen Amphoreninschriften des Ramesseums. *Zeitschrift für ägyptische Sprache und Altertumskunde* 58: 25–36.

Spiegel-Roy, P.
    1986   Domestication of Fruit Trees. Pp. 201–11 in *The Origin and Domestication of Cultivated Plants*, ed. C. Barigozzi. New York: Elsevier.

Stager, L.
    1977   Carthage, 1977: The Punic and Roman Harbors. *Archaeology* 30: 198–200.
    1982   Carthage: A View from the Tophet. Pp. 155–66 in *Phönizier im Westen: Die Beiträge des Internationalen Symposiums über "Die phönizische Expansion im westlichen Mittelmeeraum" in Köln, 24–27 April, 1979*, ed. H. G. Niemeyer. Madrider Beiträge, vol. 8. Mainz: P. von Zabern.
    1985   The Firstfruits of Civilization. Pp. 172–88 in *Palestine in the Bronze and Iron Ages: Papers in Honour of Olga Tufnell*, ed. J. N. Tubb. London: Institute of Archaeology.

Stanislawski, D.
    1970   *Landscapes of Bacchus: The Vine in Portugal*. Austin: University of Texas.
    1973   Dark Age Contributions to the Mediterranean Way of Life. *Annals of the Association of American Geographers* 63: 397–410.
    1975   Dionysus Westward: Early Religion and the Economic Geography of Wine. *The Geographic Review* 65: 427–44.

Stanley, P. V.
    1982   KN Uc 160 and Mycenaean Wines. *American Journal of Archaeology* 86: 577–78.

STE (Subcommittee on the Tenth Edition of the RDAs, Food and Nutritional Board, National Regulatory Commission)
    1989   *Recommended Dietary Allowances*. Washington, DC: National Academy.

Stead, M.
    1986   *Egyptian Life*. London: British Museum.

Steiner, G.
    1966   Getränke B. Nach hethitischen Texten. Pp. 306–08 in *Reallexikon der Assyriologie und Vorderasiatischen Archäologie*, vol. 3, eds. E. Ebeling and B. Meissner. Berlin: W. de Gruyter.

Stern, E.
    1982   *Material Culture of the Land of the Bible in the Persian Period, 538–332 B.C.* Warminster, Eng.: Aris and Phillips.

Stewart, A. F.
    1987   Narrative, Genre, and Realism in the Work of the Amasis Painter. Pp. 29–42 in *Papers on the Amasis Painter and His World*, eds. J. Walsh and M. True. Malibu, CA: J. P. Getty Museum.

Stewart, R. B.
    1976   Palaeoethnobotanical Report: Çayönü 1972. *Economic Botany* 30: 219–25.

Stol, M.
    1976–80   Kanal(ization). Pp. 355–65 in *Reallexikon der Assyriologie und Vorderasiatischen Archäologie*, vol. 5, ed. D. O. Edzard. Berlin: W. de Gruyter.
    1980–83   Leder(industrie). Pp. 527–43 in *Reallexikon der Assyriologie und Vorderasiatischen Archäologie*, vol. 6, eds. D. O. Edzard et al. Berlin: W. de Gruyter.

Strabo
    1927   *The Geography*. Trans. H. L. Jones. The Loeb Classical Library, vol. 5. New York: Putnam.

Striem, M. J.; Spiegel-Roy, P.; et al.
1990   Genomic DNA Fingerprinting of *Vitis vinifera* by the Use of Multi-Loci Probes. *Vitis*
        29: 223–27.

Strommeneger, E.
1964   *5000 Years of the Art of Mesopotamia.* New York: H. N. Abrams.
1980   *Habuba Kabira: Eine Stadt vor 5000 Jahren.* Mainz: P. von Zabern.

Stronach, D.
1991   The Garden as a Political Statement: Case Studies from the Near East in the First
        Millennium B.C. *Bulletin of the Asia Institute* 4: 171–80.

Stronach, D.; Lumsden, S.; and Bedal, L.-A.
Forth. *Excavations at Ninevah: 1987–1990.* Vol. 1.

Stummer, A.
1911   Zur Urgeschichte der Rebe und des Weinbaues. *Mitteilungen der Anthropologischen
        Gesellschaft in Wien* 61: 283–96.

Stürmer, V.
1985   Schnabelkannen: Eine Studie zur darstellenden Kunst in der minoisch-mykenischen
        Kulter. Pp. 119–34 in *L'iconographie Minoénne, Bulletin Correspondance Hellénique*,
        suppl. 11, ed. O. Picard. Paris: École française d'Athènes.

Sundwall, J.
1944   Uber Schilf- und Baumkult in den Hagia Triada Urkunden. *Acta Academiae Aboensis,
        Hum.* vol. 14, no. 10: 1–15.

Sürenhagen, D.
1986   The Dry Farming Belt: The Uruk Period and Subsequent Developments. Pp. 7–43 in
        *The Origins of Cities in Dry-Farming Syria and Mesopotamia in the Third Millennium
        B.C.* ed. H. Weiss. Guilford, CT: Four Quarters.

Symeonoglou, S.
1973   *Kadmeia I: Mycenaean Finds from Thebes, Greece.* Göteborg: P. Åström.
1985   *The Topography of Thebes from the Bronze Age to Modern Times.* Princeton: Princeton
        University.

Taeschner, F.
1960   Anadolu. Pp. 461–80 in *Encyclopaedia of Islam*, vol. 2, eds. H. A. R. Gibb, J. H.
        Kramers, R. Lévi-Provençal, and J. Schacht. Leiden: E. J. Brill.

Talon, P.
1985   Le Vin. Pp. 212–16 and nos. 64–81 in *Textes administratifs des salles "Y et Z" du
        palais de Mari* by P. Talon. Archives Royales de Mari 24. Paris: Éditions Recherche sur
        les Civilisations.

Tannahill, R.
1988   *Food in History.* London: Penguin.

Tarter, R. E., and van Thiel, D. H.
1985   *Alcohol and the Brain: Chronic Effects.* New York: Plenum Medical.

Tchernia, A.
1986   *Le vin de l'Italie romaine: Essai d'histoire économique d'après les amphores.* Rome:
        École française de Rome. Pp. 285–92.

Temir, A.
1974   Turkey. Pp. 782–791 in *The New Encyclopedia Britannica*, Macropædia. Vol. 19. Chicago: Encyclopedia Britannica.

Thanheiser, U.
1991   Untersuchungen zur Landwirtschaft der vor- und frühdynastischen Zeit in Tell-el-Fara'in–Buto. *Ägypten und Levante* 2: 39–45.

Thiebault, S.
1989   A Note on the Ancient Vegetation of Baluchistan Based on Charcoal Analysis of the Latest Periods from Mehrgarh, Pakistan. Pp. 186–88 in *South Asian Archaeology 1985: Papers from the Eighth International Conference of the Association of South Asian Archaeologists in Western Europe.*

Thompson, M., and Olmo, H. P.
1963   Cytohistological Studies of Cytochimeric and Tetraploid Grapes. *American Journal of Botany* 50: 901–6.

Thompson, M.; Brenner, D.; and Anwar, R.
1989   *Biogeographic Survey and Collection of Temperate Fruit and Nut Genetic Resources in Northern Pakistan.* Islamabad, Pakistan: Ministry of Agriculture.

Thureau-Dangin, F.
1912   Une relation de la huitième campaigne de Sargon. Musée du Louvre, Textes Cunéiformes III. Paris: P. Geuthner.
1925   *Les Cylindres de Goudéa.* Musée du Louvre, Textes cunéiformes, vol. 8. Paris: P. Geuthner.

Tiffney, B. H., and Barghoorn, E. S.
1976   Fruits and Seeds of the Brandon Lignite: I. *Vitaceae. Review of Paleobotany and Palynology* 22: 169–91.

Tobler, A. J.
1950   *Excavations at Tepe Gawra.* Vol. 2. Philadelphia: University of Pennsylvania.

Townsend, C. C., and Guest, E., eds.
1980   *Flora of Iraq.* Vol. 4, pt. 1. Baghdad: Ministry of Agriculture and Agrarian Reform, Republic of Iraq.

Trescases, G.
1980   Production et travail du liège. *Revue Française d'Oenologie* 77: 34–44.

Tsountas, C., and Manatt, J. I.
1969   *The Mycenaean Age: A Study of the Monuments and Culture of Pre-Homeric Greece.* Chicago: Argonaut; reprint of 1897 ed.

Tufnell, O.
1958   *Lachish IV (Tell ed Duweir): The Bronze Age.* London: Oxford University.
1962   The Courtyard Cemetery at Tell el-ᶜAjjul. *Bulletin of the Institute of Archaeology, London* 3: 1–37.

Turnball, G. H.
1950   *Fruit of the Vine: As Seen by Many Witnesses of All Times.* Baltimore: Lord Baltimore.

Tylor, J. J., and Griffith, F. L.
1894   *The Tomb of Paheri at El Kab.* London: Egypt Exploration Fund.

Ulrich, R.
   1979   Organic Acids. Pp. 89–118, in *Biochemistry of Fruits and Their Products*, ed. A. C.
            Hulme. Vol. 1. New York: Academic.

Ünal, A.
   1977   Naturalkatastrophen in Anatolien in 2. Jahrtausend v. Chr. *Belleten* 41: 447–72.

Unwin, T.
   1991   *Wine and the Vine: An Historical Geography of Viticulture and the Wine Trade.*
            London: Routledge.

Vaiman, A. A.
   1976   Über die Protosumerische Schrift. Pp. 15–27 in *Wirtschaft und Gesellschaft in Alten
            Vorderasien*, eds. J. Harmatta and G. Komaróczy. Budapest: Akadémiai Kiadó.

Vámbéry, A.
   1879   *Primitive Cultur des turk-tatarischen Volkes.* Leipzig: F. A. Brockhaus.

Vandenabeele, F., and Olivier, J.-P.
   1979   *Les idéogrammes archéologiques du Linéar B.* Etudes crétoises 24. Paris: École
            française d'Athènes.

van den Hout, Th. P. J.
   1990   Masse und Gewichte: Bei den Hethitern. Pp. 517–27 in *Reallexikon der Assyriologie
            und Vorderasiatischen Archäologie*, vol. 7, ed. D. O. Edzard et al. Berlin: W. de
            Gruyter.

Van Der Veen, M., and van Zeist, W.
   1982   Analyses Paleobotaniques. P. 389 in *Byrsa II, Rapports préliminaires sur les fouilles
            1977–1978: Niveau et vestiges puniques*, ed. S. Lancel. Collection de l'École française
            de Rome, no. 41. Rome: École française de Rome.

Vandiver, P. B., and Koehler, C. G.
   1986   The Structure, Processing, Properties and Style of Corinthian Transport Amphoras. Pp.
            173–215 in *The Technology and Style of Ceramics*, ed. W. D. Kingery. Ceramics and
            Civilization, vol. 2. Columbus, OH: American Ceramics Society.

van Driel, G., and van Driel-Murray, C.
   1979   Jebel Aruda, 1977–78. *Akkadica* 12: 2–8.
   1983   Jebel Aruda, the 1982 Season of Excavations. *Akkadica* 33: 1–26.

Van Doorninck, F. H. Jr.
   1989   The Cargo Amphoras on the 7th Century Yassi Ada and 11th Century Serce Limani
            Shipwrecks: Two Examples of a Reuse of Byzantine Amphoras as Transport Jars. Pp.
            247–57 in *Bulletin de Correspondance Hellénique*, suppl. 18: *Recherches sur la
            Ceramique Byzantine*, eds. V. Deroche and J.-M. Speiser. Athens: École française
            d'Athènes.

van Selms, A.
   1974   The Etymology of *Yayin*, "Wine". *Journal of Northwest Semitic Languages* 3: 76–84.

van Zeist, W.
   1988   Paleobotanical Remains from Ikiztepe. Pp. 256–60 in *Ikiztepe I* by U. B. Alkım, H.
            Alkım, and Ö. Bilgi. Türk Tarih Kurumu Yayınları, ser. 5, no. 39. Ankara: Türk Tarih
            Kurumu Başımevi.

1991   Economic Aspects. Pp. 109–30 in *Progress in Old World Palaeoethnobotany*, eds. W. van Zeist, K. Wasylikowa, and K.-E. Behre. Rotterdam: A. A. Balkema.

van Zeist, W., and Bakker-Heeres, J. A. H.
1979   Some Economic and Ecological Aspects of the Plant Husbandry of Tell Aswad. *Paléorient* 5: 161–69.
1982   Archaeobotanical Studies in the Levant: 1. Neolithic Sites in the Damascus Basin: Aswad, Ghoraife, Ramad. *Palaeohistoria* 24: 165–256.

van Zeist, W., and Bottema, S.
1982   Palaeobotanical Studies of Carthage. *Bulletin de Centre d'étude et documentation archéologique de la conservation de Carthage* 5: 18–22.

van Zeist, W.; Wasylikowa, K.; and Behre, K.-E., eds.
1991   *Progress in Old World Palaeoethnobotany*. Rotterdam: A. A. Balkema.

Vavilov, N. I.
1926   Studies on the Origin of Cultivated Plants. *Bulletin of Applied Botany*. 16: 1–248.
1931   The Role of Central Asia in the Origin of Cultivated Plants. *Bulletin of Applied Botany* 26.

Ventris, M., and Chadwick, J.
1973   *Documents in Mycenaean Greek*. 2nd ed. Cambridge: Cambridge University.

Vermeule, E.
1964   *Greece in the Bronze Age*. Chicago: University of Chicago.

Vermeule, E., and Karageorghis, V.
1982   *Mycenaean Pictorial Vase Painting*. Cambridge: Harvard University.

Vickers, M.
1986   Silver, Copper, and Ceramics in Ancient Athens. Pp. 137–51 in *Pots and Pans: Proceedings of the Colloquium on Precious Metals and Ceramics in the Islamic, Chinese, and Greco-Roman Worlds*. Oxford: Ashmolean Museum.

Vickery, K. P.
1936   *Food in Early Greece*. University of Illinois Studies in the Social Sciences, vol. 20, no. 3. Urbana: University of Illinois.

Vingilis, E.; Blefgen, H.; Colbourne, D.; and Culver, P.
1990   The Adjudication of Alcohol-Related Criminal Driving Cases in Ontario: A Survey of Crown Attorneys. *Canadian Journal of Criminology* 32: 639–49.

Vollgraff, W.
1904   Fouilles d'Argos. *Bulletin de Correspondance Hellénique* 28: 364–99.

Von Deines, H., and Westendorf, W.
1959   *Wörterbuch der ägyptischen Drogennamen*. Grundriss der Medizin der Alten Ägypter 6. Berlin: Akademie.

von der Osten, H. H.
1937   *The Alishar Hüyük Seasons of 1930–1932*. Pt. II. Chicago: University of Chicago.

von Soden, W.
1959–81*Akkadisches Handwörterbuch*. Wiesbaden: O. Harrassowitz.

Von Staden, H.
   1989   *Herophilus: The Art of Medicine in Early Alexandria.* Cambridge: Cambridge University.

Wace, A. J. B.
   1955   Mycenae 1939–1954, Part I: Preliminary Report on the Excavations of 1954. *Annual of the British School at Athens* 50: 175–89.

Wace, H., and Williams, C.
   1961   *Mycenae Guide.* Meriden, CT: Meriden Gravure for the British School at Athens.

Waddell, H.
   1936   *The Desert Fathers.* London: Constable.

Waetzoldt, H.
   1972   *Untersuchungen zur neusumerischen Textilindustrie.* Rome: Centro per le Antichità e la Storia dell'Arte del Vicino Oriente.

Walberg, G.
   1976   *Kameres: A Study of the Character of Palatial Middle Minoan Pottery.* Uppsala Studies in Ancient Mediterranean and Near Eastern Civilisation 8. Uppsala: University of Uppsala.

Walker, C. B. F.
   1976   Miscellaneous Texts from the Palace Area. Ch. 4 in *The Old Babylonian Tablets from Tell al Rimah* by S. Dalley et al. London: British School of Archaeology in Iraq.

Wallace, M. B.
   1986   Progress in Measuring Amphora Capacities. Pp. 87–94 in *Bulletin de Correspondance Hellénique*, suppl. 13: *Recherches sur les amphores grecques*, eds. J.-Y. Empereur and Y. Garlan. Paris: École française d'Athènes.

Wallinga, H. T.
   1964   Nautika I: The Unit of Capacity for Ancient Ships. *Mnemosyne* 17: 28–36.

Ward, W. A.
   1971   *Egypt and the East Mediterranean World 2200–1900 B.C.* Beirut: American University of Beirut.

Wardle, K. A.
   1973   A Group of Late Helladic IIIB2 Pottery from Mycenae. *Annual of the British School at Athens* 68: 297–348.

Warmington, B. H.
   1969   *Carthage.* London: R. Hale.

Warren, P.
   1969   *Minoan Stone Vases.* Cambridge: Cambridge University.
   1972   *Myrtos: An Early Bronze Age Settlement in Crete.* British School of Archaeology, suppl. vol. 7. London: Thames and Hudson.
   1979   The Stone Vessels from Akrotiri, Thera. *Archaiologikis Ephemeris tis Archaiologikis Etaireias* 82–113.
   1981   Minoan Crete and Ecstatic Religion: Preliminary Observations on the 1979 Excavations at Knosos. Pp. 155–67 in *Sanctuaries and Cults in the Aegean Bronze Age*, eds. R. Hägg and N. Marinatos. Proceedings of the First International Symposium at the Swedish Institute in Athens, 12–13 May, 1980. Stockholm: P. Åström.

Warren, P., and Hankey, V.
1989   *Aegean Bronze Age Chronology*. Bristol: Bristol Classical.

Wasylikowa, K.; Cârciumaru, M.; Hajnalová, E.; Hartyányi, B. P.;
Pashkevich, G. A.; and Yanushevich, Z. V.
1991   East-Central Europe. Pp. 239–67 in *Progress in Old World Palaeoethnobotany*, eds. W. van Zeist, K. Wasylikowa, and K.-E. Behre. Rotterdam: A. A. Balkema.

Watkin, D. M.
1979   Role of Alcohol Beverages in Gerontology. Pp. 225–42 in *Fermented Food Beverages in Nutrition*, eds. C. F. Gastineau, W. J. Darby, and T. B. Turner. New York: Academic.

Way, A. G., trans.
1955   Julius Caesar, *Alexandrine, African, and Spanish Wars*. Cambridge: Harvard University.

Webster, T. B. L.
1959   *From Mycenae to Homer*. New York: Praeger.

Weingarten, J.
1991   *The Transformation of Egyptian Taweret into the Minoan Genius: A Study in Cultural Transmission in the Middle Bronze Age*. Studies in Mediterranean Archaeology 88. Göteborg: P. Åström.

Weinstein, J.
1981   The Egyptian Empire in Palestine: A Reassessment. *Bulletin of the American Schools of Oriental Research* 241: 1–28.

Weiss, H.
1990   Tell Leilan 1989: New Data for Mid–Third Millennium Urbanization and State Formation. *Mitteilungen der Deutschen Orient-Gesellschaft* 122: 193–218.

Weiss, H., and Young, T. C., Jr.
1975   The Merchants of Susa; Godin V and Plateau–Lowland Relations in the Late Fourth Millennium B.C. *Iran* 13: 1–17.

Wenzel, H.
1937   *Die Steppe als Lebensraum: Forschungen in Inneranatolien*. Vol. 2. Kiel.

Werch, C. E.
1990   Perception of Intoxication and Blood Alcohol Concentration of Drinkers in Social Settings. *International Journal of the Addictions* 25: 253–62.

Whitbread, I. K.
1986   The application of ceramic petrology to the study of ancient Greek transport amphorae, with special reference to Corinthian amphora production. Unpublished Ph.D. dissertation, University of Southampton.

White, K. D.
1967   *Agricultural Implements of the Roman World*. Cambridge: Cambridge University.
1970a   *A Bibliography of Roman Agriculture*. Bibliographies in Agricultural History 1. Reading, Eng.: University of Reading.
1970b   *Roman Farming*. Ithaca, NY: Cornell University.
1975   *Farm Equipment of the Roman World*. Cambridge: Cambridge University.
1977   *Country Life in Classical Times*. Ithaca, NY: Cornell University.

Whitehouse, D.
    1981   The Schola Praeconum and the Food Supply of Rome in the Fifth Century A.D. Pp.
            191–95 in *Archaeology and Italian Society: Prehistoric, Roman and Medieval Studies*.
            British Archaeological Reports. International Series 102, eds. G. Barker and R.
            Hodges. Oxford: British Archaeological Reports.

Whittaker, C. R.
    1978a   Carthaginian Imperialism in the Fifth and Fourth Centuries. Pp. 59–90 in *Imperialism
            in the Ancient World*, eds. P. D. A. Garnsey and C. R. Whittaker. New York: Cambridge
            University.
    1978b   Land and Labor in North Africa. *Klio* 60: 331–62.

Wieczorek, W. F.; Welte, J. W.; and Abel, E. L.
    1990   Alcohol, Drugs and Murder: A Study of Convicted Homicide Offenders. *Journal of
            Criminal Justice* 18: 217–27.

Wild, H.
    1966   *Le Tombeau de Ti*. Cairo: Institut Française.

Wilkinson, J. G.
    1883   *The Manners and Customs of the Ancient Egyptians*. 3 vols. Boston: S. E. Cassino.
    1988   *A Popular Account of the Ancient Egyptians*. New York: Crescent; reprint of 1854 ed.

Wilkinson, T. J.
    1990   *Town and Country in Southeastern Anatolia*. Oriental Institute Publications 109.
            Chicago: Oriental Institute.

Willerding, U.
    1973   Bronzezeitliche Pflanzenreste aus Iria and Synoro. Pp. 221–40 in *Tiryns: Forschungen
            und Berichte*, vol. 6. Athens: Deutsches Archäologisches Institut Athens.

Wine Advisory Board
    1975   *Uses of Wine in Medical Practice: A Summary*. San Francisco: Wine Advisory Board.

Winter, I. J.
    1983   The Program of the Throneroom of Assurnasipal II. Pp. 15–31 in *Essays on Near
            Eastern Art and Archaeology in Honor of Charles Kyrle Wilkinson*, eds. P. O. Harper
            and H. Pittman. New York: Metropolitan Museum of Art.
    1986   The King and the Cup: Iconography of the Royal Presentation Scene on Ur III Seals.
            Pp. 253–68 in *Insight through Images: Studies in Honor of Edith Porada*, ed. M.
            Kelly-Buccellati. Malibu, CA: Undena.

Wiseman, D. J.
    1952   A New Stela of Assur-nasir-pal II. *Iraq* 14: 24–44.
    1983   Mesopotamian Gardens. *Anatolian Studies* 33: 137–44.

Wolff, S. R.
    1986   Maritime Trade at Punic Carthage. Unpublished Ph.D. dissertation, University of
            Chicago.

Wood, B.
    1987   Egyptian Amphorae of the New Kingdom and Ramesside Periods. *Biblical Archaeolo-
            gist* 50: 75–83.

Woolley, C. L.
    1921   *Carchemish*. Vol. 2. London: The Trustees of the British Museum.

1934   *The Royal Cemetery*. Ur excavations, vol. 2. London: British Museum and The University Museum.

Wright, J.
1982   Excavations at Tsoungiza (Archaia Nemea) 1981. *Hesperia* 51: 375–92.

Wulff, H.
1966   *The Traditional Crafts of Persia: Their Development, Technology, and Influences on Eastern and Western Civilizations*. Cambridge: MIT.

Xenophon
1932   *Anabasis*. Trans. C. L. Brownson. The Loeb Classical Library, vol. 4, bk. 8. Cambridge: Harvard University.

Yakar, J.
1986   Imıkuşağı. Pp. 183–99 in *Kazi Sonuclari Toplantisis I*, vol. 7, pt. 1. Ankara: Dept of Antiquities.

Yener, A.K.
1983   The Production, Exchange, and Utilization of Silver and Lead Metals in Anatolia. *Anatolica* 10: 1–15.

Young, R. S.
1958   The Gordion Campaign of 1957, Preliminary Report. *American Journal of Archaeology* 62: 139–54.
1960   The Gordion Campaign of 1959, Preliminary Report. *American Journal of Archaeology* 64: 227–43.

Young, R. S.; Devries, K.; Kohler, E. L.; McClellan, J. F.; Mellink, M. J.; and Sams, G. K.
1981   *Three Great Early Tumuli*. Philadelphia: University of Pennsylvania, University Museum.

Young, T. C., Jr.
1969   *Excavations at Godin Tepe: First Progress Report*. Toronto: Royal Ontario Museum.
1986   Godin Tepe Period VI/V and Central Western Iran at the End of the Fourth Millennium. Pp. 212–28 in *Ğamdat Nasr—Period or Regional Style?*, eds. U. Finkbeiner and W. Röllig. Wiesbaden: Reichert.

Younger, W.
1966   *Gods, Men, and Wine*. London: The Wine and Food Society.

Zaccagnini, C.
1979   *The Rural Landscape of the Land of Arrapḫe*. Roma: Istituto di Studi del Vicino Oriente.

Zagarell, A.
1986   Trade, Women, Class, and Society in Ancient Western Asia. *Current Anthropology* 27: 415–30.

Zapriagaeva, V. I.
1964   *Wild Growing Fruits in Tadzhikistan* [Russian, with English summary]. Moscow: Nauka.

Zemer, A.
1978   *Storage Jars in Ancient Sea Trade*. Haifa: National Maritime Museum Foundation.

Zhang, F.; Luo, F.; and Gu, D.
  1990   Studies on Germplasm Resources of Wild Grape Species (*Vitis* spp.) in China. Pp. 50–57 in Proceedings of the 5th International Symposium on Grape Breeding, Sept. 12–16, 1989, St. Martin, Pfalz, Germany. Special issue of *Vitis*.

Zohary, D., and Hoff, M.
  1988   *Domestication of Plants in the Old World: The Origin and Spread of Cultivated Plants in West Asia, Europe, and the Nile Valley*. Oxford: Clarendon.
  1993   *Domestication of Plants in the Old World: The Origin and Spread of Cultivated Plants in West Asia, Europe, and the Nile Valley*. 2nd ed. Oxford: Oxford University.

Zohary, D., and Spiegel-Roy, P.
  1975   Beginning of Fruit Growing in the Old World. *Science* 187: 319–27.

Zugla, M., and Kiss, A.
  1987   Alkaline Degradation of Parent Chromonoid Compounds (Chromone, Flavone, Isoflavone). *Acta Chimica Hungarica* 124: 485–89.

Zukovskij, P. M.
  1962   *Cultivated Plants and Their Wild Relatives*. Trans. P. S. Hudson. Farnham, Eng.: Commonwealth Agricultural Bureau.

INDEX